D0706855

A Bibliography
of Geographic Thought

A Bibliography
of Geographic Thought

Compiled by
Catherine L. Brown
and
James O. Wheeler

Bibliographies and Indexes in Geography, Number 1

Greenwood Press
New York • Westport, Connecticut • London

Library of Congress Cataloging-in-Publication Data

A Bibliography of geographic thought.

 (Bibliographies and indexes in geography,
ISSN 1044-8349 ; no. 1)
 Includes bibliographical references.
 ISBN 0-313-26899-1 (lib. bdg. : alk. paper)
 1. Geography—Philosophy—bibliography. I. Brown,
Catherine L., 1948- . II. Wheeler, James O.
III. Series.
Z6001.B5814   1989   [G70]   016.91   89-25958

British Library Cataloging in Publication Data is available.

Library of Congress Catalog Card Number: 89-25958
ISBN: 0-313-26899-1
ISSN: 1044-8349

First published in 1989

Greenwood Press, Inc.
88 Post Road West, Westport, Connecticut 06881

Printed in the United States of America

∞™

The paper used in this book complies with the
Permanent Paper Standard issued by the National
Information Standards Organization (Z39.48-1984).

10 9 8 7 6 5 4 3 2 1

To
C. C. and Wu Ti

Contents

Preface   ix

A Bibliography of Geographic Thought

Books   1

Biographical   33

Geography and Other Disciplines   95

Geography in Various Countries   111

Geographic Techniques and Models   167

Philosophy in Geography   189

The Profession of Geography   273

Subdisciplines in Geography   335

Applied Geography   411

Educational Geography   423

Author Index   469

Subject Index   509

Biographical Index   515

Preface

In October of 1973 James O. Wheeler published a
33-page <u>Bibliography on Geographic Thought, Philosophy
and Methodology, 1950-1973</u> (Geography Curriculum Project,
School of Education, University of Georgia, Athens,
Georgia). That bibliography was started in 1970 while
the compiler was teaching an undergraduate course on the
history of geography at Michigan State University. In
February of 1975, the bibliography was revised and
extended to 42 pages. A revision (third edition) in July
of 1978 fattened the bibliography to 63 pages. In May of
1983 James O. Wheeler published a 98-page <u>Bibliography on
Geographic Thought</u> (Department of Geography, University
of Georgia, Aids to Geographic Research Series, No. 5).

A Whitney-Carnegie Award through the American Library
Association enabled this most recent and greatly expanded
project to be completed. Though most of this compilation
was done at the University of Georgia, libraries at UCLA
and San Diego State University were also used.

<u>A Bibliography on Geographic Thought</u> is intended as a
comprehensive listing of books and articles in English on
the history, philosophy, and methodology of geography --
a definitive bibliography on the history of what
geographers have thought about geography and other
geographers. Book citations are listed alphabetically by
the author's last name, and the periodical articles are
grouped into nine categories, also listed alphabetically
by the author's last name.

Compiling the nearly 6,000 citations to periodical
articles and the nearly 600 books has been a delightful
task that has taken the compilers through many a
well-worn volume -- and many a dusty volume -- of
geographic lore. We often thought of Sir Philip Sidney
as we worked:

> Oft turning others' leaves to see if
> thence would flow some fresh and
> fruitful showers upon my sunburnt
> brain.

Ecclesiastes (III, 9) asked, "What gain has the worker for his toil?" Our gain has been the task itself, the pleasures of reviewing the rich literature of geography and of trying to make it more accessible to all those interested in the history of geography and geographic thought, now and in the future. We agree with William Faulkner, despite his sloppy sentence splice, that "The past is never dead, it is not even past."

The compilers wish to thank Ms. Audrey Hawkins and Ms. Dorothy Osborn for typing this bibliography through its several iterations. We also wish to thank the many people who have assisted in a variety of ways with this bibliography over the years. Dr. Marion J. Rice, former Director of the Geography Curriculum Project and Professor Emeritus of Social Science Education at the University of Georgia, is thanked for his encouragement and help in the 1970s when this bibliography was young. We also thank Professor Thomas Baucom, Jacksonville State University, Jacksonville, Alabama, and Ms. Maureen Hanink, University of Connecticut, Storrs, Connecticut, for their assistance in earlier revisions of this bibliography. All errors and omissions are the responsibility of the compilers. Please call them to our attention.

Catherine L. Brown   James O. Wheeler
Oceanside, CA   Athens, GA

A Bibliography
of Geographic Thought

Books

A-1. Abler, Ronald et al. 1975. <u>Human Geography in a Shrinking World</u>. North Scituate, MA: Duxbury Press.

A-2. Abler, Ronald, Adams, John S., and Gould, Peter. 1971. <u>Spatial Organization: Geographer's View of the World</u>: Englewood Cliffs, NJ: Prentice-Hall.

A-3. Ackerman, Edward A. 1958. <u>Geography as a Fundamental Research Discipline</u>. Chicago: University of Chicago Press.

A-4. Ackerman, Edward A. 1965. <u>The Science of Geography</u>. Washington, DC: Report of the <u>ad hoc</u> Committee on Geography, National Academy of Sciences - National Research Council.

A-5. Adams, Percy G. 1983. <u>Travel Literature and the Evolution of the Novel</u>. Lexington, KY: The University Press of Kentucky.

A-6. Ahmad, N. 1947. <u>Muslim Contributions to Geography</u>. Lahore: Muhammud Ashraf.

A-7. Alavi, S. M. Ziauddin. 1966. <u>Geography in the Middle Ages</u>. Delhi: Sterling Publishers.

A-8. Altengarten, James S. and Molyneaux, Gary A. 1976. <u>The History, Philosophy, and Methodology of Geography: A Bibliography Selected for Education and Research</u>. Monticello, IL: Council of Planning Librarians, Exchange Bibliography 957.

A-9. Amadeo, Douglas and Golledge, Reginald G. 1975. <u>An Introduction to Scientific Reasoning in Geography</u>. New York: Wiley.

A-10.   Anonymous. 1977. Certaine Brief and Necessarie
        Rules of Geographie. London: Walter J. Johnson
        [reprint of 1573 ed.].

A-11.   Anuchin, V. A. 1960. Theoretical Problems of
        Geography. Columbus, OH: Ohio State University
        Press, 1977, translation of Teoreticheskie
        Problemy Geografii (Fuchs, R. J. and Demko, G.
        J., eds.).

A-12.   Appleton, Jay. 1978. The Experience of
        Landscape. New York: Wiley.

A-13.   Babcock, W. H. 1922. Legendary Islands of the
        Atlantic, A Study in Medieval Geography. New
        York: American Geographical Society, Research
        Series No. 8.

A-14.   Bacon, P., ed. 1970. Focus on Geography: Key
        Concepts and Teaching Strategies. Washington,
        DC: National Council of the Social Studies.

A-15.   Bagrow, L. and Skelton, R. A. 1964. History of
        Cartography. Cambridge: Harvard University
        Press.

A-16.   Bagrow, Leo and Castner, Henry W., ed. 1975. A
        History of the Cartography of Russia up to 1800.
        Wolfe Island, Ontario: The Walker Press.

A-17.   Baker, Alan R. H. and Billings, Mark, eds.
        1982. Period and Place: Research Methods in
        Historical Geography. Cambridge: Cambridge
        University Press.

A-18.   Baker, Alan R. H. and Gregory, Derek, eds.
        1984. Explanations in Historical Geography:
        Interpretive Essays. Cambridge: Cambridge
        University Press.

A-19.   Baker, J. N. L. 1963. The History of
        Geography. New York: Barnes & Noble.

A-20.   Balchin, W., ed. 1972. Geography: An Outline
        for the Intending Student. London: Routledge
        and Kegan Paul.

A-21.   Bale, J., Graves, N. and Walford, R., eds.
        1973. Perspectives in Geographical Education.
        Edinburgh: Oliver and Boyd.

A-22.   Ball, J., Steinbrink, J. and Stoltman, J. 1971.
        The Social Sciences and Geographic Education: A
        Reader. New York: Wiley.

A-23.   Barnes, A. E. 1925. History and Prospects of
        the Social Sciences. New York: Alfred A. Knopf.

A-24. Barrows, H. H. 1962. <u>Lectures of the Historical</u>
       <u>Geography of the U.S.</u>, <u>as Given in 1933</u>. ed. W.
       A. Koelsch, Chicago: University of Chicago
       Press.

A-25. Bartlett, R. A. 1962. <u>Great Surveys of the</u>
       <u>American West</u>. Norman, OK: University of
       Oklahoma Press.

A-26. Beaujeu-Garnier, J. 1976. <u>Methods and</u>
       <u>Perspectives in Geography</u>. London, New York:
       Longmans, translated by J. Bray.

A-27. Beazly, C. R. 1895. <u>Prince Henry the</u>
       <u>Navigator</u>. New York: G. P. Putman's Sons.

A-28. Beazly, C. R. 1967 and 1968. <u>The Dawn of Modern</u>
       <u>Geography</u>. Vols. 1, 2, & 3. New York: reprinted
       by Ben Franklin.

A-29. Beck, H., 1959 and 1961. <u>Alexander von</u>
       <u>Humboldt</u>. Vols. I and II, Wiesbaden.

A-30. Beckman, Martin. 1968. <u>Location Theory</u>. New
       York: Random House.

A-31. Bennet, R. J., ed. 1981. <u>European Progress in</u>
       <u>Spatial Analysis</u>. London: Pion.

A-32. Berdoulay, V. 1974. <u>The Emergence of the French</u>
       <u>School of Geography</u>. Ph.D. Dissertation,
       University of California, Berkeley.

A-33. Berg, L. L. 1946. <u>One Hundred Years of the</u>
       <u>All</u>-<u>Union Geographical Society (1845-1945)</u>.
       Moscow: Academy of Science of the USSR.

A-34. Berry, Brian J. L., ed. 1978. <u>The Nature of</u>
       <u>Change in Geographical Ideas</u>. DeKalb: Northern
       Illinois University Press.

A-35. Berry, Brian J. L., ed. 1979. <u>Perspectives in</u>
       <u>Geography 3</u>: <u>The Nature of Change in</u>
       <u>Geographical Ideas</u>. DeKalb: Northern Illinois
       University Press.

A-36. Berry, Brian J. L. and Pred, Allen, eds. 1962.
       <u>Central Place Studies</u>: <u>A Bibliography of Theory</u>
       <u>and Applications</u>. Philadelphia: Regional
       Science Research Institute [Bib. Ser. No. 1].

A-37. Berry, Brian J. L. and Horton, Frank E. 1970.
       <u>Geographic Perspectives on Urban Systems</u>.
       Englewood Cliffs, NJ: Prentice-Hall.

A-38. Berry, Brian J. L. and Marble, Duane, eds.
       1968. <u>Spatial Analysis</u>: <u>A Reader in Statistical</u>
       <u>Geography</u>. Englewood Cliffs, NJ: Prentice-Hall.

A-39.   Billinge, Mark, Gregory, Derek and Martin, Ron,
         eds. 1984. Recollections of a Revolution:
         Geography as Spatial Science. London:
         Macmillan.

A-40.   Blackemore, M. J. and Harley, J. B. 1980.
         Concepts in the History of Cartography, a Review
         and a Perspective. Toronto: University of
         Toronto Press [Cartographica, 17:4, monograph
         26].

A-41.   Bladen, Wilford H. and Karan, Pradyvmna P., eds.
         1983. The Evolution of Geographic Thought in
         America: A Kentucky Root. Dubuque:
         Kendall/Hunt.

A-42.   Blouet, B. W. 1975. Sir Halford Mackinder
         1861-1947: Some New Perspectives. School of
         Geography Research Paper 13, Oxford: University
         of Oxford.

A-43.   Blouet, Brian W. 1981. The Origins of Academic
         Geography in the United States. Hamden, CT:
         Archon Books.

A-44.   Blouet, Brian. 1987. Halford Mackinder: A
         Biography. College Station: Texas A & M
         University Press.

A-45.   Board, C., et al., eds. 1969, 1970, 1971, 1972,
         1973, 1974. Progress in Geography. Vols. 1, 2,
         3, 4, 5 & 6. London: St. Martin's Press.

A-46.   Boardman, David. 1983. Graphicacy and Geography
         Teaching. London: Methuen.

A-47.   Boardman, P. 1978. The Worlds of Patrick
         Geddes: Biologist, Town Planner, Re-educator,
         Peace Warrior. London: Routledge and Kegan
         Paul.

A-48.   Boardman, S. J., ed. 1983. Revolution in the
         Earth Sciences. Dubuque, IA: Kendall/Hunt.

A-49.   Boggs, S. Whittemore. 1940. International
         Boundaries: A Study of Boundary Functions and
         Problems. New York: Columbia University Press.

A-50.   Botting, Douglas. 1973. Humboldt and the
         Cosmos. London: Michael Joseph.

A-51.   Bowen, Margarita. 1981. Empiricism and
         Geographical Thought from Francis Bacon to
         Alexander von Humboldt. Cambridge: Cambridge
         University Press.

A-52.   Bowman, I. 1921. The New World Problems in
         Political Geography. New York: World Book Co.

A-53.   Bowman, Isaiah. 1934. Geography in Relation to
        the Social Sciences. New York: Charles
        Scribner's Sons.

A-54.   Brewer, J. G. 1978. The Literature of
        Geography: A Guide to Its Organization and Use.
        Hamden, CT: Shoe String Press.

A-55.   Brigham, A. P. 1903. Geographic Influences in
        American History. Boston: Ginn & Co.

A-56.   Broek, J. O. M. 1965. Geography: Its Scope and
        Spirit. Columbus, OH: Merrill.

A-57.   Brown, E. 1931. The Approach to Geography.
        London: Christophers.

A-58.   Brown, E. H. 1980. Geography Yesterday and
        Tomorrow. Oxford: Oxford University Press for
        the Royal Geographical Society.

A-59.   Brown, L. A. 1949. The Story of Maps. Boston:
        Little, Brown, and Co.

A-60.   Brown, L. A. 1960. Map Making: The Art That
        Became a Science. Boston: Little, Brown and Co.

A-61.   Brown, Lawrence A. 1981. Innovation Diffusion:
        A New Perspective. New York: Methuen.

A-62.   Brown, T. N. L. 1971. The History of the
        Manchester Geographical Society, 1884-1950.
        Manchester: University Press.

A-63.   Browne, Janet. 1983. The Secular Ark: Studies
        in the History of Biogeography. New Haven, CT:
        Yale University Press.

A-64.   Browning, C. E. 1970. A Bibliography of
        Dissertations in Geography, 1901-1969. Chapel
        Hill, NC: University of North Carolina,
        Department of Geography, Studies in Geography No.
        1.

A-65.   Brunhes, Jean. 1952. Human Geography. London:
        G. G. Harrap [abridged ed., 1910, trans. by E.
        F. Row].

A-66.   Bunbury, E. H. 1883. A History of Ancient
        Geography Among the Greeks and Romans from the
        Earliest Ages Till the Fall of the Roman Empire.
        2 Vols., London: John Murray.

A-67.   Bunbury, E. H. 1959. A History of Ancient
        Geography. London (reprinted in New York): John
        Murray.

A-68.   Bunge, William. 1966. Theoretical Geography.
        Lund, Sweden: Gleerups.

A-69.   Bunge, William Wheeler, Jr. 1960. Theoretical
        Geography. Ph.D. dissertation. Seattle:
        University of Washington.

A-70.   Buranelli, V. 1964. Josiah Royce. New York.

A-71.   Burgess, Jacqueline and Gold, John R., eds.
        1985. Geography, the Media and Popular Culture.
        London: Croom Helm.

A-72.   Burnett, A. D. and Taylor, P. J., eds. 1981.
        Political Studies from Spatial
        Perspectives--Anglo-American Essays on Political
        Geography, New York: Wiley.

A-73.   Buttimer, A. 1971. Society and Milieu in the
        French Geographic Tradition. Chicago: Rand
        McNally, Association of American Geographers.

A-74.   Buttimer, Anne. 1974. Values in Geography.
        Washington, D.C.: Association of American
        Geographers. Commission on College Geography
        Resource Paper, No. 24.

A-75.   Buttimer, Anne. 1983. The Practice of
        Geography. New York: Longman.

A-76.   Buttimer, Mary Annette. 1964. Some Contemporary
        Interpretation and Historical Precedents of
        Social Geography: With Particular Emphasis on
        the French Contributions to the Field. Ph.D.
        dissertation, Seattle: University of Washington.

A-77.   Butzer, Karl W. 1982. Archaeology as Human
        Ecology. Methods and Theory for a Contextual
        Approach. New York: Cambridge University Press.

A-78.   Cain, Stanley. 1944. Foundations of Plant
        Geography. New York: Harper Brothers.

A-79.   Cambis, Mario. 1979. Planning Theory and
        Philosophy. New York: Tavistock Publications.

A-80.   Cantor, L. M. 1960. "Halford Mackinder: His
        Contribution to Geography and Education,"
        Unpublished MA Thesis. University of London.

A-81.   Carlstein, T., Parkes, D. and Thrift, N., eds.
        1978. Timing Space and Spacing Time. 3 Vols.
        New York: Wiley.

A-82.   Carpenter, Nathanael. 1977. Geography
        Delineated Forth in Two Books. London: Walter
        J. Johnston (reprint of 1625 ed.).

A-83. Chamberlain, T. C., et al. 1892. Report of the
       Geography Conference to the Committee of Ten of
       the N.E.A. Washington, D.C.: U.S. Bureau of
       Education; part of the Report of the Committee on
       Secondary School Studies (Bulletin 205), Gov't
       Printing Office.

A-84. Chapman, G. P. 1977. Human and Environmental
       Systems: A Geographer's Appraisal. New York:
       Academic Press.

A-85. Chappell, J. 1968. Huntington and His Critics:
       The Influence of Climate on Civilization. Ph.D.
       dissertation. Manhattan: University of Kansas.

A-86. Chatterjee, S. P. 1964/68. Fifty Years of
       Science in India: Progress of Geography.
       Calcutta: Indian Science Congress Association.

A-87. Chatterjee, S. P. 1968. Progress of Geography
       in India. Calcutta: 21st International
       Geographical Congress.

A-88. Cherry, G. E. 1974. The Evolution of British
       Town Planning in the United Kingdom During the
       20th Century and of the Royal Town Planning
       Institute, 1914-74, New York: Wiley.

A-89. Chisholm, Michael. 1966. Geography and
       Economics. New York: Praeger.

A-90. Chisholm, Michael. 1975. Human Geography:
       Evolution or Revolution? Baltimore: Penguin
       Books.

A-91. Chisholm, Michael, Frey, Allan E., and Haggett,
       Peter, eds. 1971. Regional Forecasting.
       London: Archon Books.

A-92. Chorley, R. J., Dunn, A. J., and Beckinsale, R.
       P. 1964. A History of the Study of Landforms,
       or the Development of Geomorphology:
       Geomorphology Before Davis. London: Methuen.

A-93. Chorley, Richard J., ed. 1973. Directions in
       Geography. London: Methuen.

A-94. Chorley, Richard J. and Haggett, Peter, eds.
       1967. Frontiers in Geographical Teaching.
       London: Methuen.

A-95. Chorley, Richard J. and Haggett, Peter, eds.
       1967. Models in Geography. London: Methuen.

A-96. Chuanjun, Wu, Nailiang, Wang, Chao, Lin, and
       Songqiao, Zhao, eds. 1984. Geography in China.
       Beijing: Science Press.

A-97.   Clark, Gordon L. and Dear, Michael. 1978. The
         Future of Radical Geography. Cambridge: Harvard
         University, Department of City and Regional
         Planning.

A-98.   Clark, Rose B., ed. 1934. Geography in the
         Schools of Europe. New York: Scribner's Sons.

A-99.   Clarke, J. I., ed. 1984. Geography and
         Population. London: Pergamon.

A-100.   Cliff, A. D. and Ord, J. K. 1973. Spatial
         Autocorrelation. London: Pion Limited.

A-101.   Coates, D. R. and Vitek, J. D. 1980. Thresholds
         in Geomorphology. Stroudsburg, PA: George Allen
         & Unwin, 498 pp.

A-102.   Coffey, William J. 1981. Geography: Toward a
         General Spatial Systems Approach. New York:
         Methuen.

A-103.   Cohen, Saul B., ed. 1967. Problems and Trends
         in American Geography. New York: Basic Books.

A-104.   Cole, J. P. and King, C. A. M. 1969.
         Quantitative Geography. New York: Wiley.

A-105.   Colter, C. 1966. The Astronomical and
         Mathematical Foundations of Geography. New
         York: American Elsevier Publishing Co.

A-106.   Cooke, R. U. and Johnson, J. H. 1969. Trends in
         Geography: An Introductory Survey. London:
         Permagon Press.

A-107.   Corna-Pellegrini, Giacomo and Brusa, Carlo, eds.
         1980. Italian Geography, 1960-1980. Varese:
         Ask Edizioni.

A-108.   Costa, J. E. and Fleisher, P. J., eds. 1984.
         Developments and Applications of Geomorphology.
         New York: Springer-Verlag.

A-109.   Cottler, Joseph and Jaffe, Haym. 1937.
         Mapmakers. Boston: Little, Brown and Co.

A-110.   Coves, E., ed. 1965. History of the Expedition
         Under Lewis and Clark. Republished in 3 vols.
         from 1893. New York: Dover.

A-111.   Crane, A. O., ed. 1944. The New Geography.
         London: Todd Publishing Co., Ltd.

A-112.   Cressey, G. B. 1934. China's Geographic
         Foundations. New York: McGraw-Hill.

A-113.   Crone, G. R. 1950. Maps and Their Makers, An
          Introduction to the History of Cartography. New
          York: Capricorn Books.

A-114.   Crone, G. R. 1962. Maps and Their Makers. New
          York: Capricorn Books.

A-115.   Crone, G. R. 1964. Background to Geography.
          London: Museum Press.

A-116.   Crone, G. R. 1970. Modern Geographers: An
          Outline of Progress Since A.D. 1800. London:
          Royal Geographical Society.

A-117.   Darby, H. C., ed. 1936. A Historical Geography
          of England Before A.D. 1800. Cambridge:
          Cambridge University Press.

A-118.   Darby, H. C. 1973. A New Historical Geography
          of England. London: Cambridge University Press.

A-119.   Darrah, W. C. 1951. Powell of the Colorado.
          Princeton, NJ: Princeton University Press.

A-120.   Daupaquier, J., ed. 1983. Malthus Past and
          Present. London: Academic Press.

A-121.   David, M. E. 1937. Professor David: The Life
          of Sir Edgeworth David. London: Edward Arnold.

A-122.   Davies, G. L. H. 1969. The Earth in Decay. A
          History of British Geomorphology, 1578-1878.
          London: MacDonald and Co.

A-123.   Davies, G. L. H. 1984. Irish Geography: The
          G.S.I. 1934-1984. Dublin: Geographical Society
          of Ireland, Supplement to Irish Geography, 17.

A-124.   Davies, Wayne K. E., ed. 1972. The Conceptual
          Revolution in Geography. Totowa, NJ: Rowman and
          Littlefield.

A-125.   Davis, W. M. 1954. Geographical Essays. New
          York: Dover Publications.

A-126.   Deacon, Richard. 1968. John Dee: Scientist,
          Geographer, Astrologer and Secret Agent to
          Elizabeth I. London: Muller.

A-127.   Debenham, Frank. 1950. The Use of Geography.
          London: English Universities Press.

A-128.   Debord, J. 1977. The Society of the Spectacle.
          Detroit: Red and Black.

A-129.   De Jong, G. 1962. Chorological Differentiation
          as the Fundamental Principle of Geography.
          Netherlands: Groningen.

A-130.   Dendrinos, D. S. and Mullally, D. S. 1985.
         Urban Evolution: Studies in the Mathematical
         Ecology of Cities. Oxford: Oxford University
         Press.

A-131.   Denis, J., ed. 1964. Geography in Belgium.
         Namur: National Committee of Geography.

A-132.   Deselincourt, A. 1962. The World of Herodotus.
         Boston: Little, Brown, and Co.

A-133.   Deskins, Donald R., Jr. et al. 1977.
         Geographic Humanism, Analysis, and Social
         Action: Proceedings of Symposia Celebrating a
         Half Century of Geography at Michigan. Ann
         Arbor: Department of Geography, University of
         Michigan.

A-134.   de Terra, H. 1955. The Life and Times of
         Alexander von Humboldt. New York: Alfred A.
         Knopf.

A-135.   Dickinson, Robert E. 1947. City, Region and
         Regionalism: A Geographical Contribution to
         Human Ecology. London: Kegan Paul, Trench,
         Trubner & Co., Ltd.

A-136.   Dickinson, Robert E. 1960. Some Problems of
         Human Geography; An Inaugural Lecture. Leeds:
         Leeds University Press.

A-137.   Dickinson, Robert E. 1969. The Makers of Modern
         Geography. New York: Praeger.

A-138.   Dickinson, Robert E. 1971. Regional Ecology: A
         Study of Man's Environment. New York: Wiley.

A-139.   Dickinson, Robert E. 1976. Regional Concept:
         The Anglo-American Leaders. London: Routledge
         and Kegan Paul.

A-140.   Dickinson, Robert E. and Howarth, O. J. R.
         1933. The Making of Geography. Oxford:
         Clarendon Press.

A-141.   Dicks, D. 1960. The Geographical Fragments of
         Hipparchus. London: University of London,
         Athlone Press.

A-142.   Diller, Aubrey. 1952. The Tradition of the
         Minor Greek Geographers. New York: American
         Philological Association.

A-143.   Dunbar, G. S. 1978. Elisée Reclus, Historian of
         Nature. Hamden, Archon Books.

A-144.   Dunbar, Gary S., ed. 1983. The History of
         Geography: Translations of Some French and
         German Essays. Malibu, CA: Undena Pub.

A-145.   Dunbar, Gary S. 1985. History of Modern
         Geography: An Annotated Bibliography of Selected
         Works. London: Garland.

A-146.   Duncan, Otis D., Cuzzort, Roy P. and Duncan,
         Beverly. 1961. Statistical Geography: Problems
         in Analyzing Areal Data. Free Press: New York.

A-147.   Durrenberger, R. W. 1971. Geographical Research
         and Writing. New York: Thomas Y. Crowell Co.

A-148.   East, W. G. 1938. The Geography Behind
         History. London: Nelson.

A-149.   Edington, J. M. and Edington, M. A. 1986.
         Ecology, Recreation and Tourism. Cambridge:
         Cambridge University Press.

A-150.   Eliot Hurst, Michael E. 1978. Human and
         Inhuman Geography: An Autocritique - A Journey
         Through the Corridors of Positivism and the
         Collective Discovery of an Altogether Different
         Harmony. Armidale, N.S.W.: Geography
         Department, University of England.

A-151.   Elliot, Sir Henry Miles. 1956. Early Arab
         Geographers. Calcutta: Susil Gupta.

A-152.   Embleton, C., Brunsden, D. and Jones, D. K. C.,
         eds. 1978. Geomorphology: Present Problems and
         Future Prospects. Oxford: Oxford University
         Press.

A-153.   Evans, Ifor M. and Lawrence, Heather. 1979.
         Christopher Saxon: Elizabethan Map-Maker.
         Amsterdam: Holland Press (Cartographica Series,
         Vol. 6).

A-154.   Eyles, John, ed. 1986. Social Geography in
         International Perspective. London: Croom Helm.

A-155.   Eyles, John. 1988. Research in Human
         Geography. London: Blackwell.

A-156.   Eyles, John and Woods, K. J. 1983. The Social
         Geography of Medicine and Health. New York: St.
         Martin's Press.

A-157.   Fagles, R. and Steiner, G., eds. 1962. Homer.
         Englewood Cliffs, NJ: Prentice-Hall.

A-158.   Faris, John T. 1925. Real Stories of the
         Geography Maker. Boston: Ginn.

A-159.   Firth, C. H.   1918.   The Oxford School of
         Geography.   Oxford: B. H. Blackwell.

A-160.   Fischer, E., et al.   1969.   A Question of Place,
         The Development of Geographic Thought.
         Arlington, VA: Beatty.

A-161.   Flowerdew, Robin, ed.   1982.   Institutions and
         Geographical Patterns. New York: St. Martin's
         Press.

A-162.   Frazier, John, ed.   1982.   Applied Geography:
         Selected Perspectives. Englewood Cliffs, NJ:
         Prentice-Hall, Inc.

A-163.   Freeman, Donald B.   1979.   The Geography of
         Development and Modernization: A Survey of
         Present Trends and Future Prospects.   Toronto:
         Department of Geography, York University.

A-164.   Freeman, T. W.   1981.   A History of Modern
         British Geography. London: Longman.

A-165.   Freeman, T. W.   1962.   A Hundred Years of
         Geography.   Chicago: Aldine Publishing Co.

A-166.   Freeman, T. W.   1967.   The Geographer's Craft.
         London: Methuen.

A-167.   Freeman, T. W.   1971.   The Writing of Geography.
         Manchester: Manchester University Press.

A-168.   Friis, H. R., ed. 1967.   The Pacific Basin, A
         History of its Geographical Exploration.   New
         York: American Geographical Society, Special
         Publications No. 38.

A-169.   Fuson, R. H.   1969.   A Geography of Geography.
         Dubuque, IA: W. C. Brown Co.

A-170.   Gaile, Gary and Willmont, Cort J., eds.   1984.
         Spatial Statistics and Models.   Boston: D.
         Reidel Publishing Company.

A-171.   Gale, S. and Olsson, G., eds.   1979.   Philosophy
         and Theory in Geography. Boston: D. Reidel
         Publishing Company.

A-172.   Garrison, William L. and Marble, Duane F., eds.
         1967. Quantitative Geography: Economic and
         Cultural Topics, Part I.   Evanston: Studies in
         Geography No. 13, Department of Geography,
         Northwestern University.

A-173. Garrison, William L. and Marble, Duane F., eds.
        1967. _Quantitative Geography_: _Physical and
        Cartographic Topics_, _Part II_. Evanston: Studies
        in Geography No. 14, Department of Geography,
        Northwestern University.

A-174. Gatrell, Anthony C. 1983. _Distance and Space_:
        A Geographical Perspective. Oxford: Oxford
        University Press.

A-175. Gerasimov, I. P., ed. 1978. _Geographical
        Education_, _Geographical Literature_, _and
        Dissemination of Geographical Knowledge_.
        London: Pergamon.

A-176. Gilbert, E. W. 1955. _Geography as a Human
        Study_. Oxford: Clarendon Press.

A-177. Gilbert, Edmund W. 1972. _British Pioneers in
        Geography_. New York: Barnes and Noble.

A-178. Glacken, C. J. 1967. _Traces on the Rhodian
        Shore_, _Nature and Culture in Western Thought from
        Ancient Times to the End of the Eighteenth Cen-
        tury_. Berkeley: University of California Press.

A-179. Glover, T. 1969. _Herodotus_. Freeport, NY:
        Books for Libraries Press.

A-180. Goddard, Stephen, ed. 1983. _A Guide to
        Information Sources in the Geographical
        Sciences_. London: Croom Helm.

A-181. Gold, John R. and Burgess, Jacquelin, eds.
        1982. _Valued Environments_. London: George Allen
        and Unwin, Ltd.

A-182. Golledge, Reginald G. and Rayner, John N. 1982.
        Proximity and Preference, _Problems in the
        Multidimensional Analysis of Large Data Sets_.
        Minneapolis: University of Minnesota Press.

A-183. Golledge, Reginald G., Couclelis, Helen, and
        Gould, Peter, eds. 1988. _A Ground for Common
        Search_.

A-184. Gopsill, G. H. 1956. _The Teaching of
        Geography_. New York: Macmillan and Company.

A-185. Gore, Charles. 1984. _Regions in Question_:
        Space, Development, Theory and Regional Policy.
        New York: Methuen.

A-186. Gottmann, Jean. 1973. _The Significance of
        Territory_. Charlottesville: University of
        Virginia Press.

A-187.   Goudie, Andrew, ed. 1981. _Geomorphological_
          Techniques. London: George Allen and Unwin.

A-188.   Gould, Peter. 1985. _The Geographer at Work_.
          London: Methuen, Inc.

A-189.   Gould, Peter and Olsson, Gunnar, eds. 1982. _A_
          Search for Common Ground. London: Pion Limited.

A-190.   Gregory, D. J., 1978. _Ideology, Science and_
          Human Geography. London: Hutchinson.

A-191.   Gregory, D. and Urry, J., eds. 1985. _Social_
          Relations and Spatial Structures. London:
          MacMillan.

A-192.   Gregory, K. J. 1985. _The Nature of Physical_
          Geography. London: Edward Arnold.

A-193.   Gregory, S. 1971. _Statistical Methods and the_
          Geographer. New York: Longmans, 1963, revised.

A-194.   Griffen, P. 1952. _Richard Elwood Dodge - His_
          Life and Contributions to Geography. Ph.D.
          dissertation. New York: Columbia Teacher's
          College.

A-195.   Griffith, Daniel A. 1983. _Evolving Geographical_
          Structures. Netherlands: Kluwer Academic.

A-196.   Grosvenor, Gilbert. 1952. _The National_
          Geographic Society: _Its Magazine_. Washington,
          DC: National Geographic Society.

A-197.   Guelke, Leonard T. 1982. _Historical_
          Understanding in Geography: _An Idealist_
          Approach. Cambridge: Cambridge University
          Press.

A-198.   Guelke, Leonard, ed. 1986. _Geography and_
          Humanistic Knowledge. Ontario: Department of
          Geography, University of Waterloo.

A-199.   Guyot, A. 1849. _The Earth and Man_: _Lectures on_
          Comparative Physical Geography in Its Relation to
          the History of Mankind. Boston: Gould and
          Lincoln.

A-200.   Guyot, A. 1873. _Physical Geography_. New York:
          Scribner Armstrong and Co.

A-201.   Gwynn, Stephen. 1932. _The Life of Mary_
          Kingsley. London: Macmillan Company, Ltd.

A-202.   Habibur-Ratiman, Mohammad. 1945. _Geography and_
          Geographers; _A Critical Analysis of the History_
          of Geography and Geographical Discoveries.
          Allahabad: Urdu Publishing House.

A-203. Haggett, Peter. 1966. <u>Locational</u> <u>Analysis</u> <u>in</u>
        <u>Human</u> <u>Geography</u>. New York: St. Martin's Press.

A-204. Haggett, Peter. 1972. <u>Geography</u>: <u>A</u> <u>Modern</u>
        <u>Synthesis</u>. New York: Harper and Row.

A-205. Haggett, Peter and Chorley, Richard J. 1970.
        <u>Network</u> <u>Analysis</u> <u>in</u> <u>Geography</u>. New York: St.
        Martin's Press.

A-206. Hakluyt, R. 1965. <u>Hakluyt's</u> <u>Voyages</u>. (ed. I.
        R. Blacker), New York: Viking Press.

A-207. Hale, J. R. 1966. <u>Age</u> <u>of</u> <u>Exploration</u>. New
        York: Time, Inc.

A-208. Hall, D. H. 1976. <u>History</u> <u>of</u> <u>the</u> <u>Earth</u> <u>Sciences</u>
        <u>During</u> <u>the</u> <u>Scientific</u> <u>and</u> <u>Industrial</u> <u>Revolutions</u>
        <u>with</u> <u>Special</u> <u>Emphasis</u> <u>on</u> <u>the</u> <u>Physical</u>
        <u>Geosciences</u>. Amsterdam: Elsevier Scientific
        Pub. Co.

A-209. Hall, R. B. and Noh, T. 1970. <u>Japanese</u>
        <u>Geography</u>: <u>A</u> <u>Guide</u> <u>to</u> <u>Japanese</u> <u>Reference</u> <u>and</u>
        <u>Research</u> <u>Materials</u>. Ann Arbor, MI: University
        of Michigan Press.

A-210. Hallam, A. 1973. <u>A</u> <u>Revolution</u> <u>in</u> <u>the</u> <u>Earth</u>
        <u>Sciences</u> <u>from</u> <u>Continental</u> <u>Drift</u> <u>to</u> <u>Plate</u>
        <u>Tectonics</u>. Oxford: Oxford University Press.

A-211. Halliwell, Jaems O. 1842. <u>The</u> <u>Private</u> <u>Diary</u> <u>of</u>
        <u>Dr</u>. <u>John</u> <u>Dee</u>. London: J. B. Nichols and Son.

A-212. Hanson, E. P., ed. 1967. <u>South</u> <u>from</u> <u>the</u> <u>Spanish</u>
        <u>Main</u>. New York: Delacorte Press.

A-213. Harris, Chauncy D. 1962. <u>Soviet</u> <u>Geography</u>:
        <u>Accomplishments</u> <u>and</u> <u>Tasks</u>. New York: American
        Geographical Society, Occasional Publication No.
        1.

A-214. Hart, J. F. 1966. <u>Geographic</u> <u>Manpower</u>: <u>A</u>
        <u>Report</u> <u>on</u> <u>Manpower</u> <u>in</u> <u>American</u> <u>Geography</u>.
        Washington: Assn. of American Geographers,
        Commission on College Geography, Pub. No. 3.

A-215. Hartshorne, R. 1939. <u>The</u> <u>Nature</u> <u>of</u> <u>Geography</u>, <u>A</u>
        <u>Critical</u> <u>Survey</u> <u>of</u> <u>Current</u> <u>Thought</u> <u>in</u> <u>the</u> <u>Light</u>
        <u>of</u> <u>the</u> <u>Past</u>. Lancaster, PA: Association of
        American Geographers.

A-216. Hartshorne, R. 1959. <u>Perspective</u> <u>on</u> <u>the</u> <u>Nature</u>
        <u>of</u> <u>Geography</u>. Chicago: Rand McNally.

A-217. Harvey, David. 1969. <u>Explanation</u> <u>in</u> <u>Geography</u>.
        New York: St. Martin's Press.

A-218.   Harvey, David. 1982. The Limits to Capital.
         Chicago: University of Chicago Press.

A-219.   Harvey, Milton E. and Holly, Brian P., eds.,
         1981. Themes in Geographic Thought. New York:
         St. Martin's Press.

A-220.   Hauser, Philip M. and Duncan, Otis Dudley, eds.
         1959. The Study of Population: An Inventory and
         Appraisal. Chicago: University of Chicago
         Press.

A-221.   Hawley, Amos. 1950. Human Ecology - A Theory of
         Community Structure. New York: Ronald Press.

A-222.   Hillyer, V. M. 1929. A Child's Geography of the
         World. New York: The Century Co.

A-223.   Holt-Jensen, A. 1981. Geography: Its History
         and Concepts--A Student's Guide. Totowa, NJ:
         Barnes and Noble.

A-224.   Hooson, D. 1984. Continuity and Change in
         Soviet Geographical Thought, Chicago: University
         of Chicago--Department of Geography.

A-225.   House, J. W. 1975. The Geographer in a
         Turbulent Age. Inaugural Lecture. University of
         Oxford, 21 October 1975. Oxford: Clarendon
         Press.

A-226.   Huntington, Ellsworth. 1940. Principles of
         Human Geography. New York: Wiley [5th ed.,
         largely rewritten].

A-227.   Ibn-Batuta. 1958. The Travels of Ibn-Batuta,
         A.D. 1325-1354. Trans. by Detremery and B. R.
         Sanguinetti. Cambridge: Cambridge University
         Press.

A-228.   Isard, W. 1956. Location and Space Economy.
         Cambridge, MA: M.I.T. Press.

A-229.   Isard, Walter. 1960. Methods of Regional
         Analysis: An Introduction to Regional Science.
         Cambridge, MA: M.I.T. Press.

A-230.   Jakle, John A. 1982. The American Small Town:
         Twentieth Century Place Images. Hamden, CT:
         Shoe String Press.

A-231.   Jackson, Peter and Smith, Susan J. 1981. Social
         Interaction and Ethnic Segregation. London:
         Academic Press.

A-232.   Jackson, Peter and Smith, Susan J. 1984.
         Exploring Social Geography. London: George Allen
         and Unwin.

A-233. James, Preston Everett. 1959. New Viewpoints in
        Geography. Washington, DC: National Council for
        the Social Studies.

A-234. James, Preston E. and Martin, Geoffrey J. 1966.
        A Geography of Man. Waltham, MA: Ginn.

A-235. James, Preston E. and Jones, C. F., eds. 1954.
        American Geography: Inventory and Prospect.
        Syracuse: Syracuse University Press

A-236. James, Preston E. and Martin, Geoffrey J. 1980.
        All Possible Worlds: A History of Geographical
        Ideas. New York: Odyssey Press.

A-237. James, Preston E. and Martin, G. J. 1978. The
        AAG: The First Seventy- Five Years. Washington,
        DC: Association of American Geographers.

A-238. Johnson, D. W. 1921. Battlefields of the World
        War Western and Southern Fronts: A Study in
        Military Geography. New York: American
        Geographical Society, Research Series, No. 3.

A-239. Johnson, H. 1963. Carta Marina: World
        Geography in Strassburg, 1525. Minneapolis:
        University of Minnesota Press.

A-240. Johnston, D. F., ed. 1981. Measurement of
        Subjective Phenomena. Washington, DC: U.S.
        Bureau of the Census, CDS-80-3.

A-241. Johnston, R. J. 1979. Anglo-American Human
        Geography Since 1945. Geography and Geographers.
        London: Edward Arnold.

A-242. Johnston, R. J. 1981. The Dictionary of Human
        Geography. London: Basil Blackwell.

A-243. Johnston, R. J., ed. 1985. The Future of
        Geography. London: Methuen.

A-244. Johnston, R. J. 1985. On Human Geography.
        London: Basil Blackwell.

A-245. Johnston, R. J., ed. 1986. Philosophy and Human
        Geography: An Introduction to Contemporary
        Approaches. London: Edward Arnold, 2nd ed.

A-246. Johnston, R. J. 1987. Geography and
        Geographers. London: Edward Arnold.

A-247. Johnston, R. J. and Claval, P., eds. 1984.
        Geography Since the Second World War. London:
        Croom Helm.

A-248. Jones, H., trans. 1932. The Geography of Strabo
        [8 volumes] Cambridge: Harvard University Press.

A-249.   Kasperson, Roger E. and Minghi, Julian V., eds.
         1969. The Structure of Political Geography.
         Chicago: Aldine Press.

A-250.   Kay, G. 1970. The Geographer's Task. Inaugural
         Lecture, University College of Rhodesia,
         Salisbury.

A-251.   Keane, J. 1899. The Evolution of Geography.
         London: Edward Stanford.

A-252.   Kellner, L. 1963. Alexander von Humboldt.
         London: Oxford University Press.

A-253.   Keltie, John Scott. 1921. The Position of
         Geography in British Universities. American
         Geographical Society Research Series, No. 4.

A-254.   Keltie, J. Scott and Howarth, O. J. R. 1913.
         History of Geography. New York: Putnam's.

A-255.   Keltie, Scott. 1890. Applied Geography: A
         Preliminary Sketch. London: G. Philip & Son,
         Ltd.

A-256.   Kent, Ashley, ed. 1985. Perspectives on a
         Changing Geography. Sheffield: The Geographical
         Association.

A-257.   Kimble, George H. T. 1938. Geography in the
         Middle Agess. London: Methuen.

A-258.   King, Leslie J. 1969. Statistical Analysis in
         Geography. Englewood Cliffs, NJ: Prentice-Hall.

A-259.   King, Russell. 1985. Geographical Futures.
         Sheffield: Geographical Association.

A-260.   Kish, George A. 1978. A Source Book in
         Geography. Cambridge: Harvard University
         Press.

A-261.   Kish, George. ed. 1978. Bibliography of
         International Geographical Congresses,
         1871-1976. Boston: G. K. Hall & Co.

A-262.   Kivchi, Shinzo (ed.) 1966. Geography in Japan.
         Tokyo: University of Tokyo Press.

A-263.   Knadler, G. 1958. Isaiah Bowman, Background to
         His Contribution in Thought. Ph.D.
         dissertation. Bloomington: Indiana University.

A-264.   Koelsch, W. A. 1976. Lectures on the Historical
         Geography of the U.S. As Given in 1933. by
         Harlan H. Barrow. New York: Oxford University
         Press.

A-265. Kravath, Fred. F. 1987. Christopher Columbus,
        Cosmographer: A History of Meteorology, Geodesy,
        Geography and Exploration from Antiquity to the
        Columbian Era. Rancho Cordova, CA: Landmark
        Enterprises.

A-266. Kurath, H. 1949. A Word Geography of the
        Eastern United States. Ann Arbor, MI: University
        of Michigan Press.

A-267. LaGory, Mark and Pipkin, John. 1981. Urban
        Social Space. Belmont, CA: Wadsworth Publishing
        Company.

A-268. Lanegran, David A. and Palm, Risa, eds. 1978.
        An Invitation to Geography. New York:
        McGraw-Hill Book Co.,2nd ed.,

A-269. Langnas, I. A. 1959. Dictionary of
        Discoveries. New York: Philosophical Library,
        Inc.

A-270. Learmonth, Andrew. 1978. Patterns of Disease
        and Hunger: A Study in Medical Geography.
        London: David and Charles.

A-271. Lee, W. T. 1922. The Face of the Earth as Seen
        From the Air: A Study in the Application of
        Airplane Photography to Geography. New York:
        American Geographical Society.

A-272. Leighly, J., ed. 1963. Land and Life, A
        Selection from the Writings of Carl Ortwin
        Sauer. Berkeley, CA: University of California
        Press.

A-273. Ley, D. 1980. Geography Without Man: A
        Humanistic Critique. Oxford: University of
        Oxford, School of Geography, Research Paper, Vol.
        24.

A-274. Ley, David and Samuels, Marwyn, eds. 1978.
        Humanistic Geography: Prospects and Problems,
        Chicago: Maaroufa Press.

A-275. Livingstone, David N. 1987. Nathaniel Southgate
        Shaler and the Culture of American Science.
        Tuscaloosa: University of Alabama Press.

A-276. Lowenthal, D. 1958. George Perkins Marsh:
        Versatile Vermonter. New York: Columbia
        University Press.

A-277. Lowenthal, D. and Bowden, M. J., eds. 1976.
        Geographics of the Mind: Essays in Historical
        Geography in Honor of John Kirtland Wright. New
        York: Oxford University Press.

A-278.   Lowenthal, David. 1985. The Past Is a Foreign
         Country. Cambridge: Cambridge University Press.

A-279.   Lowenthal, David and Binney, Marcus, eds. 1981.
         Our Past Before Us: Why Do We Save It? London:
         Maurice Temple Smith, Ltd.

A-280.   Lutwack, Leonard. 1984. The Role of Place in
         Literature. Syracuse: Syracuse University Press.

A-281.   Lynam, Edward. 1945. British Maps and
         Map-Makers. London: William Collins.

A-282.   MacKaye, Benton. 1928. The New Exploration: A
         Philosophy of Regional Planning. New York:
         Harcourt, Brace and Company.

A-283.   Makkreel, R. 1975. Silthey, A Philosopher of
         the Human Studies. Princeton: Yale University
         Press.

A-284.   Mallory, William and Simpson-Housley, Paul, eds.
         1987. Geography and Literature: A Meeting of
         the Disciplines. Syracuse: Syracuse University
         Press.

A-285.   Manson, Gary and Ridd, Merrill K. 1977. New
         Perspectives on Geographic Education: Putting
         Theory Into Practice. New York: Kendall-Hunt.

A-286.   Markham, A. H. 1917. The Life of Sir Clements
         R. Markham, KCB, FRS. London: J. Murray.

A-287.   Markham, Sir Clements Robert. 1895. Major James
         Rennell and the Rise of Modern English
         Geography. London: Cassell and Company,
         Limited.

A-288.   Marsh, A. 1964. Landscape in the Thought of See
         Shih. Ph.D. dissertation. Seattle: University
         of Washington.

A-289.   Marsh, G. P. 1864. Man and Nature, or Physical
         Geography as Modified by Human Action. New
         York: Charles Scribner (Republished, David
         Lowenthal, ed., Cambridge, MA: Harvard
         University Press, 1965).

A-290.   Martin, Geoffrey J. 1968. Mark Jefferson:
         Geographer. Ypsilanti: Eastern Michigan
         University.

A-291.   Martin, Geoffrey J. 1973. Ellsworth
         Huntington: His Life and Thought. Hamden, CT:
         Anchor Books.

A-292.   Martin, Geoffrey J. 1980. The Life and Thought
         of Isaiah Bowman. Hamden, CT: Shoe String Press.

A-293.   Massey, Doreen. 1984. Spatial Divisions of
         Labor: Social Structures and the Geography of
         Production. London: Macmillan.

A-294.   May, J. A. 1970. Kant's Concept of Geography
         and Its Relation to Recent Geographic Thought.
         Toronto: University of Toronto Press.

A-295.   Mayer, Harold M. and Kohn, Clyde F., eds. 1959.
         Reading in Urban Geography. Chicago: University
         of Chicago Press.

A-296.   McBoyle, G., Mitchell, B. and Zylack, S. 1982.
         Job Opportunities for Geography Graduates.
         Waterloo, Ont.: University of Waterloo
         Department of Geography Publication Series No.
         OP10.

A-297.   McConnell, Harold and Yassen, David, eds. 1971.
         Perspectives in Geography I: Models of Spatial
         Variation. Dekalb, IL: Northern Illinois
         University Press.

A-298.   McDermott, Philip and Taylor, Michael. 1982.
         Industrial Organization and Location. Cambridge
         Geographical Studies 16. New York: Cambridge
         University Press.

A-299.   McGee, E. R. 1915. Life of W. J. McGee.
         Farley, IA: N.P.

A-300.   McKay, Ian A. 1986. Geography: An Introduction
         to Concept and Method. New York: Kendall-Hunt.

A-301.   Meinig, D. W., ed. 1971. On Geography:
         Selected Writings of Preston James. Syracuse:
         Syracuse University Press.

A-302.   Mercer, D. and Powell, J. 1972. Phenomenology
         and Other Nonpositivist Approaches in Geography.
         Publication No. 1. Monash, Australia: Monash
         University Publications.

A-303.   Miernyk, William H. 1982. Regional Analysis and
         Regional Policy. Cambridge, MA: Oelgeschlager,
         Gunn and Hain, Publishers, Inc.

A-304.   Mikesell, Marvin W., ed. 1973. Geographers
         Abroad: Essays on the Problems and Prospects of
         Research in Foreign Areas. Chicago: University
         of Chicago, Research Paper No. 152.

A-305.   Mill, Hugh Robert. 1945. Life Interests of a
         Geographer, 1861-1944: An Experiment in
         Autobiography. East Grinstead, Sussex:
         Privately Issued.

A-306.   Miller, M. 1976. Kropotkin. Chicago, IL:
         University of Chicago Press.

A-307.   Minshull, Roger. 1967. Regional Geography:
         Theory and Practice. Chicago: Aldine.

A-308.   Minshull, Roger. 1970. The Changing Nature of
         Geography. London: Hutchinson.

A-309.   Mirsky, J., ed. 1964. The Great Chinese
         Travelers. New York: Pantheon Books.

A-310.   Misra, R. P., ed. 1983. Contributions to Indian
         Geography: Vol. 1, Concepts and Approaches.
         Columbia, MO: South Asia Books.

A-311.   Mitchell, Bruce and Draper, Dianne. 1982.
         Relevance and Ethics in Geography. London:
         Longman.

A-312.   Mitzman, A. 1970. The Iron Cage: An Historical
         Interpretation of Max Weber. New York: Knopf.

A-313.   Monkhouse, F. J., ed. 1970 A Dictionary of
         Geography. Chicago: Aldine Publishing Co.

A-314.   Monroe, Elizabeth. 1973. Philby of Arabia.
         London: Faber and Faber.

A-315.   Mood, Fulmer. 1944. The English Geographers and
         the Anglo-American Frontier in the Seventeenth
         Century. Berkeley: University of California
         Press.

A-316.   Morison, S. E. 1942. Admiral of the Ocean Sea,
         A Life of Christopher Columbus. New York:
         Little, Brown.

A-317.   Morison, S. E., trans. and ed. 1963. Journals
         and Other Documents on the Life and Voyages of
         Christopher Columbus. Heritage Press: New York.

A-318.   Mossman, Jennifer, ed. 1986. Encyclopedia of
         Geographic Information Sources. Detroit: Gale.

A-319.   Murphey, Rhodes. 1961. The Scope of Geography.
         Chicago: Rand McNally.

A-320.   National Academy of Sciences (National Research
         Council, Earth Science Division). 1965. The
         Science of Geography. Washington, DC: National
         Academy of Science.

A-321.   Natoli, S. J. and Bond, A. R. 1985. Geography
         in Internationalizing the Undergraduate
         Curriculum, Washington, DC: Association of
         American Geographers, Resource Publication in
         Geography.

A-322. Neft, David S. 1966. Statistical Analysis of
        Areal Distributions. Philadelphia: Regional
        Science Research Institute.

A-323. Newman, O. 1972. Defensible Space. New York:
        Macmillan.

A-324. Norton, William. 1984. Historical Analysis in
        Geography. London: Longman Group Limited.

A-325. Norwine, Jim and Anderson, Thomas D. 1980.
        Geography as Human Ecology? Lanham, MD:
        University Press of America.

A-326. Nozawa, H., ed. 1986. Cosmology, Epistemology
        and the History of Geography. Kyushu University,
        Institute of Geography, Japanese Contributions to
        the History of Geographical Thought.

A-327. Oliver, Roland. 1957. Sir Harry Johnston and
        the Scramble for Africa. London: Chatto and
        Windus.

A-328. Onokerhoraye, A. G. 1984. Introduction to the
        History of Geographic Thought, Vol. II. Benin:
        Ideh Education Publications.

A-329. O'Sullivan, Patrick. 1986. Geopolitics.
        London: Croom Helm.

A-330. van Paassen, C. 1957. The Classical Tradition
        of Geography. Groningen: J. B. Walters.

A-331. Pacione, Michael. 1987. Social Geography:
        Progress and Prospect. Beckenham: Croom Helm.

A-332. Parker, Geoffrey. 1985. Western Geopolitical
        Thought in the Twentieth Century. London: Croom
        Helm.

A-333. Parker, W. H. 1982. Mackinder: Geography as an
        Aid to Statecraft. New York: Clarendon Press.

A-334. Parks, G. B. 1928. Richard Hakluyt and the
        English Voyages. New York: American Geographical
        Society, Special Publication, No. 10.

A-335. Parks, G. 1961. Richard Hakluyt and the English
        Voyages. New York: Unger.

A-336. Paterson, John L. 1984. David Harvey's
        Geography. Totowa, NJ: Barnes and Noble.

A-337. Peattie, Roderick. 1936. Mountain Geography: A
        Critique and Field Study. Cambridge, MA:
        Harvard University Press.

A-338.   Peattie, Roderick. 1940. Geography in Human
         Destiny. New York: George W. Stewart.

A-339.   Peattie, Roderick. 1941. The Incurable
         Romantic. New York: Macmillan Company.

A-340.   Peet, J. R. 1978. Radical Geography:
         Alternative Viewpoints on Contemporary Social
         Issues. New York: Methuen and Co. Ltd.

A-341.   Penrose, B. 1952. Travel and Discovery in the
         Rennaissance, 1420- 1620. Cambridge, MA:
         Harvard University Press.

A-342.   Pfeifer, Gottfried. 1938. Regional Geography in
         the United States Since the War: A Review of
         Trends in Theory and Method. New York: American
         Geographical Society.

A-343.   Pickles, John. 1985. Phenomenology, Science and
         Geography: Spatiality and the Human Sciences.
         Cambridge: Cambridge University Press.

A-344.   Pinkerton, J. 1802. Modern Geography ...
         Digested on a New Plan. London: T. Cadell.

A-345.   Pipkin, John S. et al., 1983. Remaking the
         City: Social Science Perspectives on Urban
         Design. Albany: State University of New York
         Press.

A-346.   Pitty, A. F., ed. 1985. Themes in
         Geomorphology. London: Croom Helm.

A-347.   Platt, Robert S. 1959. Field Study in American
         Geography. Chicago: University of Chicago
         Research Paper, No. 61.

A-348.   Pocock, D. C. D., ed. 1981. Humanistic
         Geography and Literature. London: Croom Helm.

A-349.   Polo, M. 1930. The Travels of Marco Polo.
         Revised from Marsden's translation, edited and
         with an introduction by Manuel Komroff. New
         York: Liverright.

A-350.   Porritt, Jonathan. 1985. Seeing Green: The
         Politics of Ecology Explained. Oxford:
         Blackwell.

A-351.   Quainig, Massimo. 1982. Geography and Marxism.
         Oxford: Blackwell.

A-352.   Quill, H. 1930. John Harrison, The Man Who
         Found Longitude. London: Pall Mall.

A-353.   Rahman, Shah M. H.   1945.   Geography and
          Geographers: A Critical   Analysis of the History
          of Geographers and Geographical Discoveries.
          Allahabad, India: Urdu Publishing House.

A-354.   Ratzel, Friedrich.   1896-98.   History of
          Mankind.   2 Vols.   London: Macmillan Co.

A-355.   Relph, E.   1976.   Place and Placelessness.
          London: Pion.

A-356.   Relph, Edward.   1981.   Rational Landscapes and
          Humanistic Geography. London: Croom Helm.

A-357.   Rigdon, V.   1934.   The Contributions of William
          Morris Davis to Geography in America.   Ph.D.
          dissertation, University of Nebraska.

A-358.   Robinson, A.   1947.   Foundations of Cartographic
          Methodology.   Ph.D. dissertation.   Ohio State
          University.

A-359.   Rolfe, W. D. Ian, ed.   1983.   Geological Howlers,
          Boners and Bloomers. Boston: Allen and Unwin.

A-360.   Rondinelli, Dennis.   1983.   Development Projects
          as Policy Experiments: An Adaptive Approach to
          Development Administration.   London: Methuen.

A-361.   Rose, Harold M., ed.   1972.   Perspectives in
          Geography 2:   Geography of The Ghetto,
          Perceptions, Problems and Alternatives.   DeKalb:
          Northern Illinois University Press.

A-362.   Rowley, V. M.   1964.   J. Russell Smith:
          Geographer, Educator and Conservationist.
          Philadelphia: University of Pennsylvania Press.

A-363.   Rowley, Virginia Marie.   1961.   J. Russell
          Smith: Geographer, Educator and
          Conservationist.   Ph.D. dissertation, Columbia
          University.

A-364.   Ryan, Bruce.   1983. Seventy-five Years of
          Geography at the University of Cincinnati.
          Cincinnati: University of Cincinnati.

A-365.   Sack, R. D.   1980.   Conceptions of Space in
          Social Thought.   A Geographic Perspective.
          Minneapolis: University of Minnesota Press.

A-366.   Samuels, M.S.   1971.   Science and Geography: An
          Existential Appraisal. Ph.D. Dissertation,
          University of Washington, Seattle.

A-367.   Saushkin, Yu. G.   1980.   Economic Geography:
          Theory and Methods.   Moscow: Progress
          Publishers.

A-368.   Schmenner, Roger W.   1982.   Making Business
         Location Decisions. Englewood Cliffs: Prentice
         Hall.

A-369.   Schroder, Franz.   1919.   Foundations of Geography
         in the Twentieth Century.   Oxford: Clarendon
         Press.

A-370.   Semple, E. C.   1911.   Influences of Geographic
         Environment, on the Basis of Ratzel's System of
         Anthropo-Geography.   New York: Henry Holt.

A-371.   Seymour, W. A.   ed.   1980.   A History of the
         Ordinance Society. Folkestone: Dawson.

A-372.   Shafer, R. J., ed.   1969.   A Guide to Historical
         Method.   Homewood, IL: Dorsey Press.

A-373.   Shairp, J. C., Tait, P. G. and Adams-Reilly, A.
         1973.   Life and Letters of James David Forbes, F.
         R. S.   London: R. Clay, Sons, and Taylor.

A-374.   Shaler, N. S.   1905.   Man and the Earth.   New
         York: Duffield.

A-375.   Shirley, Rodney W.   1984.   The Mapping of the
         World.   Early Printed World Maps, 1472-1700.
         London: Holland Press.

A-376.   Showket, Ibrahim.   1954.   Arab Geography Till the
         End of the Tenth Century.   Ph.D. dissertation.
         Worcester, MA: Clark University.

A-377.   Siddall, William Richard.   1959.   Idiographic and
         Nomothetic Geography: The Application of Some
         Ideas in the Philosophy of History and Science to
         Geographic Methodology.   Ph.D. dissertation.
         Seattle: University of Washington.

A-378.   Simon, W.   1963.   European Positivism in the
         Nineteenth Century.   Cornell: Cornell University
         Press.

A-379.   Skelton, R. A., ed.   1964.   History of
         Cartography.   Cambridge, MA: Harvard University
         Press.

A-380.   Skelton, R. A.   1972.   Maps, A Historical Survey
         of Their Study and Collecting.   Chicago:
         University of Chicago Press.

A-381.   Smith, D. M.   1977.   Human Geography: A Welfare
         Approach.   London: Edward Arnold.

A-382.   Smith, J. Russell.   1928.   Geography and Our Need
         of It.   Chicago: American Libraries Association.

A-383.   Spilhaus, Margaret Whiting. 1935. The
          Background of Geography. London: G. G. Harrap
          and Co., Ltd.

A-384.   Stamp, L. Dudley and Wooldridge, S. W., eds.
          1951. London Essays in Geography. Cambridge:
          Harvard University Press.

A-385.   Steel, Robert W. 1984. The Institute of British
          Geographers: The First Fifty Years. London:
          Institute of British Geographers.

A-386.   Steel, Robert W., ed. 1987. British Geography,
          1918-1945. Cambridge: Cambridge University
          Press.

A-387.   Stern, E. and Meir, A., eds. 1984. Geography
          Research Forum: Vols. 2-6, 1980-1983. Oxford:
          Clio Distribution Transaction Books.

A-388.   Stern, Eliahe and Krackover, Shaul, eds. 1987.
          Geography Research Forum. Vol. 8. New
          Brunswick, NJ: Transaction Books.

A-389.   Stoddart, D. R., ed. 1981. Geography, Ideology
          and Social Concern. Oxford: Basil Blackwell.

A-390.   Stoddart, D. R. 1986. On Geography and Its
          History. Oxford: Basil Blackwell.

A-391.   Stout, Cyril L. 1937. Trends of Methods,
          Contents, and Beliefs in Geography Textbooks,
          1784-1895. Ph.D. dissertation. Nashville:
          George Peabody College for Teachers.

A-392.   Strabo. 1917. The Geography of Strabo. Trans.
          H. L. Jones. New York: G. P. Putnam's Sons.

A-393.   Sugden, David. 1982. Arctic and Antarctic: A
          Modern Geographical Synthesis. Totowa, NJ:
          Barnes and Noble Books.

A-394.   Sundaram, K. V., ed. 1985. Geography and
          Planning, Essays in Honour of V.L.S. Prakasa
          Rao. New Delhi: Concept Publishing Company.

A-395.   Sykes, P. 1961. A History of Exploration from
          the Earliest Times to the Present Day. New
          York: Harper Bros.

A-396.   Szymanski, Richard and Agnew, John. 1981. Order
          and Skepticism: Human Geography and the
          Dialectic of Science. Washington, DC:
          Association of American Geographers [Resource
          Publications in Geography].

A-397.   Taaffe, Edward J., et al. 1970. Geography.
          Englewood Cliffs, NJ: Prentice Hall.

A-398.   Tanabe, H., ed. 1982. Applied Aspects of
          Geography - Aspects Appliques de Geographie.
          [Proceedings of the Symposium on Applied
          Geography at Yokohama, 1980) Tokyo: n. p.

A-399.   Taylor, D. R. F., ed. 1983. Progress in
          Contemporary Cartography, Vol. 2: Graphic
          Communciation and Design in Contemporary
          Cartography. New York: John Wiley.

A-400.   Taylor, E. G. R. 1930. Tudor Geography,
          1485-1593. London: Methuen.

A-401.   Taylor, E. G. R. 1934. Late Tudor and Early
          Stuart Geography, 1583- 1650. London: Methuen.

A-402.   Taylor, E. G. R. 1957. The Haven-Finding Art:
          A History of Navigation from Odysseus to Captain
          Cook. New York: Abeland Schuman.

A-403.   Taylor, Griffith. 1951. Geography in the
          Twentieth Century. New York: Philosophical
          Library.

A-404.   Taylor, Griffith. 1960. Geographers and
          World-Peace. Seaforth, Australia: The Author.

A-405.   Taylor, J. A., ed. 1984. Themes in
          Biogeography. London: Croom Helm.

A-406.   Taylor, Thomas Griffith. 1979. The Griffith
          Taylor Collection: Diaries and Letters of a
          Geographer in Antarctica. Armindale, N.S.W.:
          Geography Department, University of New England.

A-407.   Teitz, Michael Bernard. 1964. Regional Theory
          and Regional Models. Ph.D. dissertation.
          University of Pennsylvania.

A-408.   Theakstone, W. H. and Harrison, C. 1970. The
          Analysis of Geographical Data. London:
          Heinemann Educational Books

A-409.   Thomas, William L., ed. 1956. Man's Role in
          Changing the Face of the Earth. Chicago:
          University of Chicago Press

A-410.   Tidswell, W. V. and Barker, S. M. 1971. Quanti-
          tative Methods: An Approach to Socio-Economic
          Geography. London: University Tutorial Press.

A-411.   Tinkler, Keith J. 1985. A Short History of
          Geomorphology. Totowa, NJ: Barnes and Noble
          Books.

A-412.   Tooley, R. V. 1949. Maps and Map-Makers. New
          York: Crown.

A-413.   Tooley, Ronald Vere. 1949. Tooley's Dictionary
          of MapMakers. New York: Alan R. Liss, Inc.

A-414.   Torayah, A. Sharaf. 1948. A Short History of
          Geographical Discovery. London: Harrap and Co.

A-415.   Tozer, H. F. 1935. A History of Ancient
          Geography. Cambridge: Cambridge University
          Press, 2nd ed.

A-416.   Tozer, H. F. 1964. A History of Ancient
          Geography. Cambridge: Cambridge University
          Press. reprinted New York: Biblo and Tannen.

A-417.   Tripathi, Maya Prasad. 1969. Development of
          Geographic Knowledge in Ancient India.
          Varanasi: Bharatya Vidya Prakashan.

A-418.   Tuan, Yi-Fu. 1977. Space and Place: The
          Perspective of Experience. Minneapolis:
          University of Minnesota Press.

A-419.   Tuan, Yi-Fu. 1982. Segmented Worlds and Self:
          Group Life and Individual Consciousness.
          Minneapolis: University of Minnesota Press.

A-420.   Tufte, Edward R. 1983. The Visual Display of
          Quantitative Information. Cheshire, CT: Graphics
          Press.

A-421.   Ulaby, Fawwa, Moore, Richard K. and Fund, Adrian
          K. 1981. Microwave Remote Sensing: Active and
          Passive. Volume 1: Microwave Remote Sensing
          Fundamentals and Radiometry. Reading, MA:
          Addison-Wesley Publishing Company.

A-422.   Ullman, E. L. 1980. Geography as Spatial
          Interaction. ed. R. R. Boyce. Seattle:
          University of Washington Press.

A-423.   Van Cleef, Eugene. 1937. Trade Centers and
          Trade Routes. New York: D. Appleton-Century
          Company.

A-424.   Van Cleef, Eugene. 1946. Getting Into Foreign
          Trade. New York: The Ronald Press.

A-425.   Varenius, B. 1733. A Compleat System of General
          Geography. London: Stephen Austen.

A-426.   Wanklyn, H. 1961. Friedrich Ratzel, A
          Biographical Memoir and Bibliography. Cambridge,
          England: Cambridge University Press.

A-427.   Wann, T., ed. 1964. Behaviorism and
          Phenomenology. Chicago. University of Chicago
          Press.

A-428.   Warman, Henry J.   1954.   Geography - Backgrounds,
         Techniques and Prospects.   Worcester: Clark
         University Press.

A-429.   Warnes, Anthony.   1982.   Geographical
         Perspectives on the Elderly. New York: John
         Wiley and Sons, Inc.

A-430.   Warntz, William.   1964.   Geography Now and Then.
         New York: American Geographical Society, Research
         Series No. 25.

A-431.   Warntz, William and Wolfe, Peter.   1971.
         Breakthroughs in Geography.   New York: New
         American Library.

A-432.   Webber, M. J.   1984.   Explanation, Prediction and
         Planning: The Lowry Model.   London: Pion.

A-433.   Weichhart, Peter.   1975.   Geographie in Umbruch:
         Ein Methodologischer Beitrag zur Neukonzeption
         der Komplexen Geographie.   Vienna: Franz
         Deuticke, 1975 [reviewed by Homer Aschaman,
         Geographical Survey, Vol. 6, No. 4, pp. 32-34].

A-434.   Whittlesey, Derwent.   1939.   The Earth and the
         State: A Study of Political Geography.   New
         York: Henry Hold and Company, Inc.

A-435.   Wilford, John Noble.   1981.   The Mapmakers.
         London: Junction Books.

A-436.   Wilkinson, Clennel.   1929.   William Dampier.
         London: John Lane, The Bodley Head [The Golden
         Head Series].

A-437.   Williams, F. L.   1963.   Matthew Fontaine Maury,
         Scientist of the Sea.   New Brunswick, NJ:
         Rutgers University Press.

A-438.   Wilson, Alan G.   1981.   Geography and the
         Environment.   New York: John Wiley and Sons.

A-439.   Wilson, H. E.   1985.   Down to Earth: One Hundred
         and Fifty Years of The British Geological
         Survey.   Edinburgh: Scottish Academic Press.

A-440.   Women and Geography Study Group of the IBG.
         1984.   Geography and Gender. London: Hutchinson.

A-441.   Wood, E.   1927.   The Development of the Modern
         Concept of Geography. Ph.D. Dissertation,
         University of Wisconsin, Madison.

A-442.   Wood, J. David.   1982.   Rethinking Geographical
         Inquiry.   (Geographical Monographs, 11) Toronto:
         York University, Department of Geography.

A-443. Woodcock, G. and Auakumovic, I. 1950. The
        Anarchist Prince: A Biographical Study of Peter
        Kropotkin. London: T. V. Boardman.

A-444. Wooldridge, S. W. and East, W. G. 1966. The
        Spirit and Purpose of Geography. London and New
        York: Hutchinson's University Library.

A-445. Wright, John K. 1966. Human Nature in
        Geography. Cambridge, MA: Harvard University
        Press.

A-446. Wright, John Kirtland. 1925. The Geographical
        Lore of the Time of the Crusades: A Study in the
        History of Medieval Science and Tradition. New
        York: American Geographical Society [Research
        Series No. 15].

A-447. Wright, John Kirtland. 1952. Geography in the
        Making: The American Geographical Society,
        1951-1951. New York: American Geographical
        Society.

A-448. Wright, John Kirtland and Platt, Elizabeth T.
        1947. Aid to Geographical Research. New York:
        American Geographical Society, 2nd ed.

A-449. Wrigley, N. and Bennett, R. J., eds. 1982.
        Quantitative Geography: A British View. Boston:
        Routledge and Kegan Paul.

A-450. Yeates, Maurice H. 1968. An Introduction to
        Quantitative Analysis in Economic Geography.
        Englewood Cliffs, NJ: Prentice-Hall.

A-451. Yeates, Maurice H. 1974. An Introduction to
        Quantitative Analysis in Human Geography.
        Englewood Cliffs, NJ: Prentice-Hall.

A-452. Zelinsky, W. et al., eds. 1970. Geography and
        a Crowding World. New York: Oxford University
        Press.

A-453. Ziauddin, S. M. 1965. Arab Geography in the
        Ninth and Tenth Centuries. Aligarh: Aligarh
        Muslim University, Department of Geography.

Biographical

B-1.   Abbe, C. Jr. 1905. "Ferdinand von Richthofen as a Teacher," Journal of Geography, Vol. 4, pp. 415-416.

B-2.   Ackerman, Edward A. 1967. "Gilbert Hovey Grosvenor, 1875-1966," Annals of the Association of American Geographers, Vol. 57, p. 197.

B-3.   Adams, Charles C. and Fuller, George D. 1940. "A Memoir of Henry Chandler Cowles," Annals of the Association of American Geographers, Vol. 30, pp. 39-43.

B-4.   Aiken, Charles S. 1975. "Expréssions of Agrarianism in American Geography: The Cases of Isaiah Bowman, J. Russell Smith, and O. E. Baker," Professional Geographer, Vol. 27, pp. 19-29.

B-5.   Aiken, Charles S. 1983. "Merle Charles Prunty, Jr., 1917-1982," Southeastern Geographer, Vol. 23, pp. 1-9.

B-6.   Alexander, Lewis M. 1958. "Samuel Whittemore Boggs: An Appreciation," Annals of the Association of American Geographers, Vol. 48, pp. 237-243.

B-7.   Alexandrovskaya, Olga Andreyevna. 1980. "Andrey Nikolaevich Krasnov, 1862-1914," Geographers: Biobibliographical Studies, Vol. 4, pp. 77-86.

B-8.   Alexandrovskaya, Olga Andreyevna. 1982. "Mikhail Vasilyevich Lomonosov, 1711-1765," Geographers: Biobibliographical Studies, Vol. 6, pp. 65-70.

B-9.   Alexandrovskaya, Olga Andreyevna. 1982. "Vasili Nikitich Tatishcher, 1686-1750," Geographers: Biobibliographical Studies, Vol. 6, pp. 129-132.

B-10. Alexandrovskaya, Olga Andreyevna. 1983. "Pyotr Alexeivich Kropotkin, 1842-1921," Geographers: Biobibliographical Studies, Vol. 7, pp. 57-62.

B-11. Allan, Douglas A. 1960. "John George Bartholomew: A Centenary," Scottish Geographical Magazine, Vol. 76, pp. 85-88.

B-12. Allan, D. A. and Crone, G. R. 1962. "John Bartholomew - Obituary," Scottish Geographical Magazine, Vol. 78, pp. 114-116.

B-13. Alston, A. H. G. 1948. "Henry Walter Bates: A Centenary," Geographical Journal, Vol. 112, pp. 1-4.

B-14. Anderson, E. W. 1975. "Bebe: Pioneer British Geographer," Area, Vol. 7, pp. 223-224.

B-15. Anderson, J. H. 1983. "Thomas Aisken Larcom, 1801-1879," Geographers: Biobibliographical Studies, Vol. 7, pp. 71-74.

B-16. Anderson, James R. 1973. "Arch G. Gerlach (1911-1972)," Geographical Review, Vol. 63, pp. 577-578.

B-17. Anderson, Jeremy. 1986. "Otis Willard Freeman: A Preliminary Bibliography," Yearbook, Association of Pacific Coast Geographers, Vol. 47, pp. 105-114.

B-18. Andrews, Howard F. 1986. "The Early Life of Paul Vidal de la Blanche and the Makings of Modern Geography," Transactions - Institute of British Geographers, Vol. 11, pp. 174-182.

B-19. Andrews, Howard F. 1987. "Paul Vidal de la Blanche and the Concours de'agregation of 1866," Canadian Geographer, Vol. 31, pp. 12-20.

B-20. Anonymous. 1859. "Humboldt Commemoration," Journal of the American Geographical and Statistical Society, Vol. 1, pp. 225-246.

B-21. Anonymous. 1884. "Samuel Weels Williams, LL.D.," Journal of the American Geographical Society of New York, Vol. 16, pp. 186-193.

B-22. Anonymous. 1895. "M. Elisee Reclus and the Geographie Universille," Scottish Geographical Magazine, Vol. 11, pp. 248-251.

B-23.   Anonymous. 1904. "Bishop, Isabella," Scottish
         Geographical Magazine, Vol. 20, pp. 595-597.

B-24.   Anonymous. 1904. "Eli Sowerbutts," Journal of
         the Manchester Geographical Society, Vol. 20,
         pp. 181-182.

B-25.   Anonymous. 1906. "Baron Ferdinand von
         Richthofen: Obituary," Bulletin of the
         Geographical Society of Philadelphia, Vol. 4, pp.
         60-61.

B-26.   Anonymous. 1906. "Nathaniel Southgate Shaler:
         Obituary," Bulletin of the Geographical Society
         of Philadelphia, Vol. 4, No. 4, pp. 51-53.

B-27.   Anonymous. 1907. "Obituary: Angelo Heilprin,"
         Bulletin of the Geographical Society of
         Philadelphia, Vol. 5, No. 4, pp. 67-68.

B-28.   Anonymous. 1908. "Addresses Delivered at the
         Meeting Held in Honor of the Memory of Professor
         Angelo Heilprin," Bulletin of the Geographical
         Society of Philadelphia, Vol. 6, pp. 1-30.

B-29.   Anonymous. 1915. "James Geikie, LL.D., D.C.L.,
         F.R.S., 1839-1915. An Appreciation," Scottish
         Geographical Magazine, Vol. 31, pp. 202-205.

B-30.   Anonymous. 1915. "Obituary: A. J. Herbertson,
         Professor of Geography in The University of
         Oxford," Scottish Geographical Magazine, Vol. 31,
         pp. 486-490.

B-31.   Anonymous. 1916. "Death of Sir Clements
         Markham," Geographical Journal, Vol. 47, pp.
         161-177.

B-32.   Anonymous. 1918. "Obituary: Professor Paul
         Vidal de la Blanche," Scottish Geographical
         Magazine, Vol. 34, pp. 266-267.

B-33.   Anonymous. 1919. "James Geikie: His Life and
         Works," Scottish Geographical Magazine, Vol. 34,
         pp. 68-69.

B-34.   Anonymous. 1930. "An Appreciation of the
         Contributions to Earth Science of Albert Perry
         Brigham," Annals of the Association of American
         Geographers, Vol. 20, entire issue No. 2, pp.
         51-104.

B-35.   Anonymous. 1930. "Bibliography of Albert Perry
         Brigham," Annals of the Association of American
         Geographers, Vol. 20, pp. 99-104.

B-36.   Anonymous. 1930. "Obituary: Dr. George G. Chisholm," _Scottish Geographical Magazine_, Vol. 46, pp. 101-104.

B-37.   Anonymous. 1932. "Obituary: Professor J. W. Gregory," _Scottish Geographical Magazine_, Vol. 48, pp. 226-228.

B-38.   Anonymous. 1954. "A Selected Bibliography on Careers in Geography," _Professional Geographer_, Vol. 6, No. 3, pp. 29-35.

B-39.   Anonymous. 1955. "Obituary Notice of Dr. S. L. Hora," _National Geographical Journal of India_, Vol. 1, pp. 123-124.

B-40.   Anonymous. 1964. "Griffith Taylor," _Australian Geographical Studies_, Vol. 2, pp. 1-9.

B-41.   Anonymous. 1965. "Editorial: A. J. Herbertson, 1865-1915," _Scottish Geographical Magazine_, Vol. 81, pp. 143-147.

B-42.   Anonymous. 1965. "Editorial: Geography and the Changing Scottish Scene," _Scottish Geographical Magazine_, Vol. 81, pp. 75-77.

B-43.   Anonymous. 1970. "Obituary: H. J. Fleure, D.Sc., LL.D., M.A., F.S.A., F.R.S.," _Transactions - Institute of British Geographers_, No. 49, pp. 201-210.

B-44.   Anonymous. 1972. "Obituary: David Leslie Linton," _Transactions - Institute of British Geographers_, Vol. 55, pp. 171-178.

B-45.   Anonymous. 1977. "Directory of Soviet Geographers [some biographical information]," _Soviet Geography: Review and Translation_, Vol. 18, pp. 433-556.

B-46.   Anonymous. 1982. "Obituary: Dora K. Smee," _Transactions - Institute of British Geographers_, Vol. 8, pp. 120-121.

B-47.   Anonymous. 1983. "Obituary: Kenneth Charles Edwards," _Transactions - Institute of British Geographers_, Vol. 7, pp. 250-251.

B-48.   Anonymous. 1983. "Obituary: R. Ogilvie Buchanan," _Transactions - Institute of British Geographers_, Vol. 8, pp. 112-114.

B-49.   Anonymous. 1983. "Obituary: Robert E. Dickinson," _Transactions - Institute of British Geographers_, Vol. 8, pp. 122-124.

B-50.   Anonymous. 1984. "Obituary: Charles Alfred
        Fisher," Transactions - Institute of British
        Geographers, Vol. 9, pp. 252-254.

B-51.   Anonymous. 1984. "Obituary: Emrys G. Bowen,"
        Transactions - Institute of British Geographers,
        Vol. 9, pp. 374-380.

B-52.   Anonymous. 1984. "Obituary: Frank Henry Winn
        Green," Transactions - Institute of British
        Geographers, Vol. 9, pp. 124-127.

B-53.   Anonymous. 1984. "Obituary: Harry Cyric Knapp
        Henderson," Transactions - Institute of British
        Geographers, Vol. 9, pp. 255-256.

B-54.   Anonymous. 1984. "Obituary: John William
        House," Transactions - Institute of British
        Geographers, Vol. 9, pp. 381-384.

B-55.   Anonymous. 1985. "Obituary: Arthur Eltringham
        Smailes," Transactions - Institute of British
        Geographers, Vol. 10, pp. 120-122.

B-56.   Anonymous. 1985. "Obituary: Robin H. Best,"
        Transactions - Institute of British Geographers,
        Vol. 10, pp. 123-126.

B-57.   Anonymous. 1985. "Obituary: Stanley Henry
        Geaner," Transactions - Institute of British
        Geographers, Vol. 10, pp. 504-506.

B-58.   Anonymous. 1986. "Donald Grant Moir,
        1902-1906," Scottish Geographical Magazine, Vol.
        102, pp. 130-133.

B-59.   Anonymous. 1986. "Obituary: Professor Ronald
        F. Peel," Transactions - Institute of British
        Geographers, Vol. 11, pp. 370-373.

B-60.   Anstey, Robert L. 1958. "Arnold Guyot, Teacher
        of Geography," Journal of Geography, Vol. 57, pp.
        441-447.

B-61.   Armstrong, Patrick. 1985. "Charles Darwin,
        1809-1882," Geographers: Biobibliographical
        Studies, Vol. 9, pp. 37-46.

B-62.   Atwood, Wallace W. 1932. "Ellen Churchill
        Semple," Journal of Geography, Vol. 31, p. 267.

B-63.   Auble, P. 1978. "Some Comments on William
        Applebaum: His Work and Its Impact," Ohio
        Geographers: Recent Research Themes, Vol. 6, pp.
        77-84.

B-64.   Aujac, Germaine. 1978. "Eratosthenes c. 275 -
         c. 195 B. C.," <u>Geographers</u>: <u>Biobibliographical</u>
         <u>Studies</u>, Vol. 2, pp. 39-44.

B-65.   Aurousseau, M. 1964. "Obituary: T. Griffith
         Taylor," <u>Australian Geographer</u>, Vol. 9, pp.
         131-133.

B-66.   Babicz, Jozef. 1977. "Eugeniusz Romer,
         1871-1954," <u>Geographers</u>: <u>Biobibliographical</u>
         <u>Studies</u>, Vol. 1, pp. 89-96.

B-67.   Babicz, Jozef, Buttner, Manfred and Nobis,
         Herbert M. 1982.   "Nicholas Copernicus,
         1472-1543," <u>Geographers</u>: <u>Biobibliographical</u>
         <u>Studies</u>, Vol. 6, pp. 23-30.

B-68.   Babicz, Jozef, Slabczynski, Waclaw and Vallance,
         Thomas G. 1978. "Pawel Edmund Strzelecki,
         1797-1873," <u>Geographers</u>: <u>Biobibliographical</u>
         <u>Studies</u>, Vol. 2, pp. 113-118.

B-69.   Badcock, Blair. 1987. "Review Article Through
         the Tail of Harvey's Comet," <u>Australian</u>
         <u>Geographical Studies</u>, Vol. 25, pp. 98-104.

B-70.   Bahrin, Tunki Sham. 1973. "Obituary: Robert
         Ho," <u>Transactions</u> - <u>Institute</u> <u>of</u> <u>British</u>
         <u>Geographers</u>, No. 59, pp. 155-157.

B-71.   Baker, Alan R. W. 1974. "In Pursuit of Wilbur
         Zelinsky and Other Historical Geographers,"
         <u>Historical</u> <u>Geography</u> <u>Newsletter</u>, Vol. 4, pp.
         17-19.

B-72.   Baker, J. 1948. "Mary Somerville and Geography
         in England," <u>Geographical</u> <u>Journal</u>, Vol. 111, pp.
         207-222.

B-73.   Baker, J. 1955.   "The Geography of Bernard
         Varenius," <u>Transactions</u> - <u>Institute</u> <u>of</u> <u>British</u>
         <u>Geographers</u>, Vol. 21, pp. 51-60.

B-74.   Baker, J. N. L. 1948. "Mary Somerville and
         Geography in England," <u>Geographical</u> <u>Journal</u>, Vol.
         111, pp. 207-222.

B-75.   Baker, J. N. L. 1955. "The Geography of Bernard
         Varenius," <u>Transactions</u> - <u>Institute</u> <u>of</u> <u>British</u>
         <u>Geographers</u>, Vol. 21, pp. 51-60.

B-76.   Baker, J. N. L. 1958. "A Practical Geographer:
         Review," <u>Geographical</u> <u>Journal</u>, Vol. 124, pp.
         236-238.

B-77.   Baker, O. E. 1933. "Memoir of Albert Perry
        Brigham," Annals of the Association of American
        Geographers, Vol. 23, pp. 27-32.

B-78.   Baker, S. J. K. 1984. "John Harold Wellington,
        1892-1981," Geographers: Biobibliographical
        Studies, Vol. 8, pp. 135-140.

B-79.   Balchin, W. G. V. 1984. "Sidney William
        Wooldridge, 1900-1963," Geographers:
        Biobibliographical Studies, Vol. 8, pp. 141-150.

B-80.   Barbour, George B. 1958. "John Lyon Rich,
        1884-1956," Annals of the Association of American
        Geographers, Vol. 48, pp. 174-177.

B-81.   Barnes, Carleton P. 1949. "W. Elmer Ekblow,
        1882-1949," Annals of the Association of American
        Geographers, Vol. 39, pp. 294-295.

B-82.   Barnes, Carleton P. 1960. "Hugh Hammond
        Bennett, 1881-1960," Annals of the Association of
        American Geographers, Vol. 50, pp. 506-507.

B-83.   Barr, Brenton M. 1984. "J. Lewis Robinson and
        Canadian Regional Geography: An Acknowledgment,"
        B.C. Geographical Series, No. 37, pp. 19-26.

B-84.   Bartholomew, J. G. 1912. "Mrs. Livingstone
        Bruce and the Scottish Geographical Society,"
        Scottish Geographical Magazine, Vol. 28, pp.
        312-314.

B-85.   Bartholomew, John, Linton, David L. and a
        Student. 1954. "Alan Grant Ogilvie," Scottish
        Geographical Magazine, Vol. 70, pp. 1-5.

B-86.   Barton, Thomas Frank. 1965. "Publications of
        Leaders in Geographic Education: Katherine
        Thomas Whittemore," Journal of Geography, Vol.
        64, pp. 211-213.

B-87.   Batchelet, Clarence E. 1958. "Malcolm Jarvis
        Proudfoot, 1907-1955," Annals of the Association
        of American Geographers, Vol. 48, pp. 172-173.

B-88.   Baulig, Henri. 1950. "William Morris Davis:
        Master of Method," Annals of the Association of
        American Geographers, Vol. 40, pp. 188-195.

B-89.   Beck, H. 1968. "Alexander von Humboldt," in
        International Encyclopedia of the Social
        Sciences, D. Sills, ed., New York: Macmillan and
        the Free Press, Vol. 6, pp. 545-546.

B-90.   Beckinsale, Robert P. 1976. "The International
        Influence of William Morris Davis," Geographical
        Review, Vol. 66, pp. 448-466.

B-91.   Beckinsale, Robert P. and Chorley, Richard J.
        1981.   "William Morris Davis, 1850-1934,"
        Geographers: Biobibliographical Studies, Vol. 5,
        pp. 27-34.

B-92.   Bederman, Sanford H. 1984.   "Oscar MacCarthy,
        1815-1894," Geographers: Biobibliographical
        Studies, Vol. 8, pp. 57-60.

B-93.   Berdoulay, Vincent. 1977.   "Louis-Auguste Himly,
        1823-1906," Geographers: Biobibliographical
        Studies, Vol. 1, pp. 43-48.

B-94.   Berdoulay, Vincent and Chapman, R. Louis. 1987.
        "Le Possibilisme de Harold Innis," Canadian
        Geographer, Vol. 33, pp. 2-11.

B-95.   Bergsten, Karl-Erik. 1984.   "Hans Hugold von
        Schwerin, 1853-1912," Geographers:
        Biobibliographical Studies, Vol. 8, pp. 81-86.

B-96.   Bergsten, Karl-Erik. 1984.   "Helge Nelson,
        1882-1966," Geographers: Biobibliographical
        Studies, Vol. 8, pp. 69-76.

B-97.   Berman, Mildred. 1974.   "Sex Discrimination and
        Geography: The Case of Ellen Churchill Semple,"
        Professional Geographer, Vol. 26, pp. 8-11.

B-98.   Berman, Mildred. 1980.   "Millicent Todd
        Bingham: Human Geographer and Literary Scholar,"
        Professional Geographer, Vol. 32, pp. 199-204.

B-99.   Berry, Brian J. L. and Harris, Chauncy D. 1970.
        "Walter Christaller: An Appreciation,"
        Geographical Review, Vol. 60, pp. 116-119.

B-100. Beyer, Rudiger. 1984.   "Ewald Banse, 1883-1953,"
        Geographers: Biobibliographical Studies, Vol. 8,
        pp. 1-6.

B-101. Bird, James H. 1975.   "Methodological
        Implications for Geography from the Philosophy of
        K. R. Popper," Scottish Geographical Magazine,
        Vol. 91, pp. 153-163.

B-102. Bird, James H. 1985.   "Geography in Three
        Worlds: How Popper's System Can Help Elucidate
        Dichotomies and Changes in the Discipline,"
        Professional Geographer, Vol. 37, pp. 403-409.

B-103. Birkenhauer, J. A. C. 1986.   "Johann Gottfried
        Hender, 1744-1803," Geographers:
        Biobibliographical Studies, Vol. 10, pp. 77-84.

B-104. Bisson, Jean. 1981. "Robert Capot-Rey,
        1897-1977," Geographers: Biobibliographical
        Studies, Vol. 5, pp. 13-20.

B-105.   Black, Lloyd D. 1948. "Troll's Critique of
          Geographical Science in Germany from 1933 to
          1945," Annals of the Association of American
          Geographers, Vol. 38, pp. 72-73.

B-106.   Black, Richard B. 1957. "Richard Evelyn Byrd,"
          Geographical Review, Vol. 47, pp. 579-581.

B-107.   Block, R. H. 1980. "Frederick Jackson Turner
          and American Geography," Annals of the
          Association of American Geographers, Vol. 70, pp.
          31-42.

B-108.   Block, Robert H. 1984. "Henry Garrett,
          1846-1914," Geographers: Biobibliographical
          Studies, Vol. 8, pp. 45-50.

B-109.   Blouet, B. W. 1976. "Sir Halford Mackinder as
          British High Commissioner to South Russia,
          1919-1920," Geographical Journal, Vol. 142, pp.
          228-236.

B-110.   Blouet, Brian W. 1987. "Political Geographers
          of the Past V: The Political Career of Sir
          Halford Mackinder." Political Geography
          Quarterly, Vol. 6, pp. 355-368.

B-111.   Blunden, J. R. 1983. "Andrew Learnmonth and the
          Evaluation of Medical Geography," in Geographical
          Aspects of Health, N. D. McGlashan & J. R.
          Blunden, eds., (Academic Press), pp. 15-32.

B-112.   Bollinger, Clyde J. 1946. "Memorial to Samuel
          Weidman," Annals of the Association of American
          Geographers, Vol. 36, pp. 148-150.

B-113.   Bosse, D. 1986. "From Maps to the Macabre:
          Ambrose Bierce as Topographer." Bulletin -
          Special Libraries Association, Geography & Map
          Division, Vol. 144, pp. 2-15.   ·

B-114.   Bowden, Marty N. J. 1970. "John Kirtland
          Wright, 1891-1969," Annals of the Association of
          American Geographers, Vol. 60, pp. 394-403.

B-115.   Bowen, E. G. 1970. "Herbert John Fleure,"
          Geographical Review, Vol. 60, pp. 443-445.

B-116.   Bowen, Emrys George. 1970. "Herbert John Fleure
          and Western European Geography in the Twentieth
          Century," Geographische Zeitschrift, Vol. 58, pp.
          28-35.

B-117.   Bowen, M. J. 1970. "Mind and Nature: The
          Physical Geography of Alexander Von Humboldt,"
          Scottish Geographical Magazine, Vol. 86, pp.
          222-233.

B-118.   Bowman, Isaiah. 1934. "William Morris Davis,"
         Geographical Review, Vol. 24, pp. 177-181.

B-119.   Bowman, Isaiah. 1940. "John Huston Finley,
         1863-1940," Geographical Review, Vol. 30, pp.
         353-357.

B-120.   Bowman, Isaiah. 1950. "Mark Jefferson,"
         Geographical Review, Vol. 40, pp. 134-137.

B-121.   Boyce, Roland R. 1985. "Edward Louis Ullman,
         1912-1976," Geographers: Biobibliographical
         Studies, Vol. 9, pp. 129-136.

B-122.   Bridges, R. C. 1976. "W. D. Cooley, The RGS and
         African Geography in the Nineteenth Century:
         Part 1," Geographical Journal, Vol. 142, pp.
         27-47.

B-123.   Bridges, R. C. 1976. "W. D. Cooley, The RGS and
         African Geography in the Nineteenth Century:
         Part 2," Geographical Journal, Vol. 142, pp.
         274-286.

B-124.   Brigham, Albert Perry. 1913. "Memoir of Ralph
         Stockman Tarr," Annals of the Association of
         American Geographers, Vol. 3, pp. 93-98.

B-125.   Brigham, Albert Perry. 1920. "Memoir of
         Frederick Valentine Emerson," Annals of the
         Association of American Geographers, Vol. 10, pp.
         149-152.

B-126.   Brigham, Albert Perry. 1929. "An Appreciation
         of William Morris Davis," Annals of the
         Association of American Geographers, Vol. 19, pp.
         61-62.

B-127.   Broc, Numa. 1977. "Franz Schrader, 1844-1924,"
         Geographers: Biobibliographical Studies, Vol. 1,
         pp. 97-104.

B-128.   Broc, Numa. 1978. "Eugene Cortambert,
         1805-1881," Geographers: Biobibliographical
         Studies, Vol. 2, pp. 21-26.

B-129.   Broc, Numa. 1982. "Ludovic Drapeyron,
         1839-1901," Geographers: Biobibliographical
         Studies, Vol. 6, pp. 35-38.

B-130.   Brock, E. J. and Twidace, C. R. 1984. "J. T.
         Judson's Contributions to Geomorphological
         Thought," Australian Journal of Earth Sciences,
         Vol. 31, pp. 107-121.

B-131.   Broek, Jan O. M. 1952. "Leo Heinrich Waibel:
         An Appreciation," Geographical Review, Vol. 42,
         pp. 287-292.

B-132.   Brooks, C. F. 1931. "Robert DeCourcy Ward, 1867-1931," Harvard Alumni Bulletin, Vol. 34, pp. 236-238.

B-133.   Brooks, C. F. 1932. "Biographical Notes on Robert DeCourcy Ward," Bulletin - American Meteorological Association, Vol. 13, pp. 87-90.

B-134.   Brooks, Charles F. 1932. "Robert DeCourcy Ward, Climatologist," Annals of the Association of American Geographers, Vol. 22, pp. 33-43.

B-135.   Brown, Ralph H. 1941. "The American Geographies of Jedidiah Morse," Annals of the Association of American Geographers, Vol. 31, pp. 145-218.

B-136.   Brown, Robert M. 1930. "[Albert Perry Brigham] Educator," Annals of the Association of American Geographers, Vol. 20, pp. 91-98.

B-137.   Brown, S. E. 1978. "Guy-Harold Smith, 1895-1976," Annals of the Association of American Geographers, Vol. 68, pp. 115-118.

B-138.   Brown, S. Earl. 1985. "Eugene Van Cleef, 1887-1973," Geographers: Biobibliographical Studies, Vol. 9, pp. 137-144.

B-139.   Browne, W. R. 1975. "Frank Alfred Craft: 1906-1973," Australian Geographer, Vol. 13, pp. 1-3.

B-140.   B, R. N. R. with I. B. and A. G. O. 1950. "Hugh Robert Mill," Scottish Geographical Magazine, Vol. 66, pp. 1-2.

B-141.   Bruce, William S. 1913. "The Late Captain Robert Falcon Scott...," Journal of Geography, Vol. 29, pp. 148-153.

B-142.   Bruman, Herny. 1976. "In Memory of Carl Sauer," Historical Geography Newsletter, Vol. 6, pp. 5-6.

B-143.   Bryan, Kirk. 1930. "[Albert Perry Brigham] Physiographer," Annals of the Association of American Geographers, Vol. 20, pp. 71-72.

B-144.   Bryan, Kirk. 1935. "William Morris Davis - Leader in Geomorphology and Geography," Annals of the Association of American Geographers, Vol. 25, pp. 23-31.

B-145.   Bryant, Henry G. 1908. "Professor Heilprin, Traveler and Explorer," Bulletin of the Geographical Society of Philadelphia, Vol. 6, pp. 3-6.

B-146.   Bucher, Walter. 1946. "Memorial to Nevin M.
          Fenneman," Proceedings, Geological Society of
          America, for 1945, pp. 215-228.

B-147.   Bunge, William. 1979. "Fred K. Schaefer and the
          Science of Geography," Annals of the Association
          of American Geographers, Vol. 69, pp. 128-132.

B-148.   Bunkse, E. V. 1981. "Humboldt and an Aesthetic
          Tradition in Geography," Geographical Review,
          Vol. 71, pp. 127-140.

B-149.   Burgy, J. Herbert. 1947. "George Henry Primmer,
          1889-1946," Annals of the Association of American
          Geographers, Vol. 37, pp. 120-121.

B-150.   Burrill, Meredith. 1949. "Philip Sidney Smith,
          1877-1949," Annals of the Association of American
          Geographers, Vol. 39, p. 293.

B-151.   Burrill, Meredith F. 1974. "Arch Clive Gerlach,
          1911-1972," Annals of the Association of
          American Geographers, Vol. 64, pp. 293-296.

B-152.   Bushong, Allen D. 1975. "Women As Geographers:
          Some Thoughts of Ellen Churchill Semple,"
          Southeastern Geographer, Vol. 15, pp. 102-109.

B-153.   Bushong, Allen D. 1984. "Ellen Churchill
          Semple, 1863-1932," Geographers:
          Biobibliographical Studies, Vol. 8, pp. 87-94.

B-154.   Bushong, Allen D. 1987. "Unpublished Sources in
          Biographical Research: Ellen Churchill Semple,"
          Canadian Geographer, Vol. 31, pp. 79-81.

B-155.   Buttner, Manfred. 1978. "Bartholomaus
          Keckermann, 1572-1609," Geographers:
          Biobibliographical Studies, Vol. 2, pp. 73-80.

B-156.   Buttner, Manfred. 1979. "Philipp Melanchthon,
          1497-1560," Geographers: Biobibliographical
          Studies, Vol. 3, pp. 93-98.

B-157.   Buttner, Manfred. 1986. "Kant and the Modern
          Religious Geography: The Debate of Micro- and
          Macro-Geography," Geographica Religionum, Vol. 2,
          pp. not known.

B-158.   Buttner, Manfred and Burmeister, Karl H. 1979.
          "Sebastian Munster, 1488-1552," Geographers:
          Biobibliographical Studies, Vol. 3, pp. 99-106.

B-159.   Buttner, Manfred and Burmeister, Karl H. 1980.
          "George Joachim Rheticus, 1514-1574,"
          Geographers: Biobibliographical Studies, Vol. 4,
          pp. 121-126.

B-160.   Buttner, Manfred and Hoheisel, Karl. 1980.
          "Immanuel Kant, 1724-1804," Geographers:
          Biobibliographical Studies, Vol. 4, pp. 55-68.

B-161.   Buttner, Manfred and Jakel, Reinhard. 1982.
          "Anton Friedrick Busching, 1724-1793,"
          Geographers: Biobibliographical Studies, Vol. 6,
          pp. 7-16.

B-162.   Butzer, Karl W. 1976. "Carl Troll: 1899-1975,"
          Geographical Review, Vol. 66, pp. 234-236.

B-163.   Bywater, Vincent. 1983. "Pierre Teilhard de
          Chardin, 1881-1955," Geographers: Biobiblio-
          graphical Studies, Vol. 7, pp. 129-134.

B-164.   Calef, Wesley. 1982. "Charles Carlyle Colby,
          1884-1965," Geographers: Biobibliographical
          Studies, Vol. 6, pp. 17-22.

B-165.   Campbell, Eila M. J. 1973. "Obituary: A. E. F.
          Moodie," Transactions - Institute of British
          Geographers, Vol. 59, pp. 159-161.

B-166.   Campbell, Tony. 1987. "Obituary: Ronald Vere
          Tooley (1898-1986)," Imagio Mundi, Vol. 39, pp.
          80-81.

B-167.   Carol, Hans. 1970. "Walter Christaller: A
          Personal Memoir," Canadian Geographer, Vol. 14,
          pp. 67-69.

B-168.   Carre, F. 1978. "Camille Vallaux, 1870-1945,"
          Geographers: Biobibliographical Studies, Vol. 2,
          pp. 119-126.

B-169.   Carter, George F. 1948. "Clark Wissler,
          1870-1947," Annals of the Association of American
          Geographers, Vol. 38, pp. 145-146.

B-170.   Carter, George F. 1950. "Isaiah Bowman,
          1878-1950," Annals of the Association of American
          Geographers, Vol. 40, pp. 335-350.

B-171.   Casada, James A. 1974. "James A. Grant and the
          Royal Geographical Society," Geographical
          Journal, Vol. 140, pp. 245-253.

B-172.   Casada, James A. 1977. "Sir Harry H. Johnston
          as a Geographer," Geographical Journal, Vol.
          143, pp. 393-406.

B-173.   Chao, Lin and Wong, En-Yong. 1984. "Dr. Chu
          Ko-Chen and the Department of Geography at Peking
          University," Acta Geographica Sinici, Vol. 39,
          pp. 17-19 [English Summary].

B-174.   Chapman, S. 1941. "Edmond Halley as Physical
          Geographer," Occasional Notes, Royal Astronomical
          Society, No. 9, N. P.

B-175.   Chappell, J. 1971. "Harlan Barrows and
          Environmentalism," Annals of the Association of
          American Geographers, Vol. 61, pp. 198-201.

B-176.   Chernyayeva, F. A. 1974. "I. A. Strelbitsky -
          The Foremost Russian Cartographer of the 19th
          Century," Canadian Geographer, Vol. 11, pp.
          99-106.

B-177.   Chester, C. M. 1904. "Some Early Geographers of
          the United States," Proceedings - Eighth
          International Geographical Congress, pp. 913-929.

B-178.   Chetwoode, Field-Marshal Sir Philip. 1939.
          "Address at the Annual General Meeting,"
          Geographical Journal, Vol. 94, pp. 185-192.

B-179.   Chetwoode, Field-Marshal Sir Philip. 1940.
          "Address at the Annual General Meeting,"
          Geographical Journal, Vol. 96, pp. 81-85.

B-180.   Chetwoode, Field-Marshal Sir Philip. 1941.
          "Address at the Annual General Meeting,"
          Geographical Journal, Vol. 98, pp. 1-5.

B-181.   Chisholm, George G. 1912. "Miss Semple on the
          Influences of Geographical Environment,"
          Geographical Journal, Vol. 39, pp. 31-37.

B-182.   Cho, George C. H. 1977. "Robert Ho, 1921-1972,"
          Geographers: Biobibliographical Studies, Vol. 1,
          pp. 49-54.

B-183.   Chow, C. 1979. "The Critiques on the Mo Tzu's
          Geographic Thought," Geographical Research, Vol.
          5, pp. 1-9.

B-184.   Church, R. J. Harrison. 1967. "Obituary:
          Professor Sir Dudley Stamp," Horizon, Vol. 16,
          pp. 2-4.

B-185.   Church, R. J. Harrison. 1981. "Hilda Ormsby,
          1877-1973," Geographers: Biobibliographical
          Studies, Vol. 5, pp. 95-98.

B-186.   Churchill, William. 1915. "Memoir of William W.
          Rockhill," Annals of the Association of American
          Geographers, Vol. 5, pp. 131-134.

B-187.   Clark, Andrew H. 1954. "Titus Smith, Junior,
          and the Geography of Nova Scotia in 1801 and
          1802," Annals of the Association of American
          Geographers, Vol. 44, pp. 291-314.

B-188.   Colby, Charles C.   1929.   "Memorial of Charles
          Redway Dryer," Annals of the Association of
          American Geographers, Vol. 19, pp. 62-64.

B-189.   Colby, Charles C.   1933.   "Memoir of Ellen
          Churchill Semple," Annals of the Association of
          American Geographers, Vol. 23, pp. 229-240.

B-190.   Colby, Charles C.   1960.   "Dr. Vernor C. Finch,
          1883-1959," Journal of Geography, Vol. 59, p.
          239.

B-191.   Colby, Charles C.   1960.   "Willington Downing
          Jones, 1886-1957," Annals of the Association of
          American Geographers, Vol. 50, pp. 51-54.

B-192.   Colby, Charles C. and White, Gilbert F.   1961.
          "Harlan H. Barrows, 1877-1960," Annals of the
          Association of American Geographers, Vol. 51, pp.
          395-400.

B-193.   Comeaux, Malcolm C.   1976.   "Lauren Chester
          Post," California Geographer, Vol. 16, pp. 85-86.

B-194.   Comeaux, Malcolm C.   1979.   "Jonas Wenger Hoover,
          1889-1979," Geographical Bulletin, Vol. 18, pp.
          6-11.

B-195.   Cook, K. L.   1969.   "William Morris Davis -- An
          Assessment of His Contribution to Geomorphology,"
          Horizon, Vol. 18, pp. 69-73.

B-196.   Coppens, Linda Miles.   1985.   "Ralph Hall Brown,
          1898-1948," Geographers: Biobibliographical
          Studies, Vol. 9, pp. 15-20.

B-197.   Corley, Nara T.   1973.   "Geographical
          Literature," Encyclopedia of Library and
          Information Science, Vol. 9 (New York: Marcel
          Dekker), pp. 266-282.

B-198.   Cotet, Petre.   1979.   "Alexandre
          Dimitresco-Aldem, 1880-1917," Geographers:
          Biobibliographical Studies, Vol. 13, pp. 35-38.

B-199.   Coughlan, R.   1945.   "Isaiah Bowman, World's
          Leading Political Geographer Now Has a New Set of
          Boundary Worries," Life, Vol. 19, pp. 118-120,
          Oct. 22.

B-200.   Council, The.   1950.   "The Resolution," [on Dr.
          Bowman's Death] Geographical Review, Vol. 40, pp.
          175-176.

B-201.   Cressey, George B.   1949.   "Wallace W. Atwood,"
          Annals of the Association of American
          Geographers, Vol. 39, pp. 296-306.

B-202.   Crisler, Robert M. 1950. "Lewis F. Thomas, 1887-1950," _Annals of the Association of American Geographers_, Vol. 40, pp. 351-353.

B-203.   Crone, G. 1962. "Jewels of Antiquity: The Work of the Hakluyt Society," _Geographical Journal_, Vol. 128, pp. 321-324.

B-204.   Crone, G. R. 1937. "Geography," in _The March of Science: A First Quinquennial Review, 1931-1935_, pp. 24-37.

B-205.   Crone, G. R. 1959. "A Founder of Modern Geography," _Geographical Journal_, Vol. 125, pp. 405-406.

B-206.   Cross, W. K. 1967. "John Leland the Geographical Antiquary, and Others of His Like and Kind," _Canadian Geographer_, Vol. 11, pp. 172-179.

B-207.   Cullum, General George W. 1887. "Biographical Sketch of Dr. Isaac L. Hayes," _Journal of the American Geographical Society of New York_, Vol. 13, pp. 110-124.

B-208.   Cumberland, K. B. 1975. "George Jobberns," _New Zealand Journal of Geography_, Vol. 31, pp. 1-5.

B-209.   Cunningham, Frank F. 1977. "Lyell and Uniformitarianism," _Canadian Geographer_, Vol. 21, pp. 164-174.

B-210.   Cunningham, Frank F. 1983. "James David Forbes, 1809-1868," _Geographers: Biobibliographical Studies_, Vol. 7, pp. 31-38.

B-211.   Dainelli, Giotto. 1933. "The Geographical Work of H. R. H., The Late Duke of Abruzzi," _Geographical Journal_, Vol. 82, pp. 1-16.

B-212.   Darton, N. H. 1913. "Memoir of W. J. McGee," _Annals of the Association of American Geographers_, Vol. 3, pp. 103-110.

B-213.   Darton, N. H. 1917. "Memoir of Henry Gannett," _Annals of the Association of American Geographers_, Vol. 7, pp. 68-70.

B-214.   Darwin, Sir Charles. 1960. "Darwin as a Traveller," _Geographical Journal_, Vol. 126, pp. 129-139.

B-215.   Das Gupta, S. P. 1976. "Field Techniques in Social Science, An Appraisal of N. K. Bose as a Field Scientist," _Geographical Review of India_, Vol. 38, pp. 102-108.

B-216.   Davies, Gordon L. Herries. 1985. "James Hutton
          and the Study of Landforms," _Progress in
          Physical Geography_, Vol. 9, pp. 382-390.

B-217.   Davis, William Harper. 1932. "Edward Drinker
          Cope as a Geographer," _Bulletin of the Virginia
          Geographical Society_, Vol. 30, pp. 157-162.

B-218.   Davis, W. M. 1907. "Heltner's Conception of
          Geography," _Journal of Geography_, Vol. 6, pp.
          49-53.

B-219.   Davis, W. M. 1932. "The Life of Robert DeCourcy
          Ward," _Annals of the Association of American
          Geographers_, Vol. 22, pp. 29-32.

B-220.   Davis, William Morris. 1921. "Memoir of
          Frederick Putnam Gullinee," _Annals of the
          Association of American Geographers_, Vol. 11, pp.
          112-116.

B-221.   Dean, W. G. 1962. "VilhJalmur Stefansson, 3
          November 1879-26 August 1962," _Canadian
          Geographer_, Vol. 6, pp. 93-95.

B-222.   Dean, William G. 1969. "In Memoriam: Frederick
          B. Watts," _Canadian Geographer_, Vol. 13, pp.
          1-2.

B-223.   DeBres, Karen. 1986. "Political Geographers of
          the Past IV: George Renner and the Great Map
          Scandal," _Political Geography Quarterly_, Vol. 5,
          pp. 385-394.

B-224.   Demko, George J. and Fuchs, Roland J. 1984.
          "Yulian Glebovich Saushkin (1911-1982), A
          Remembrance," _Soviet Geography_, Vol. 25, pp.
          61-62.

B-225.   Denis, J. 1986. "Marguerite Alice Lefevre,
          1894-1967," _Geographers: Biobibliographical
          Studies_, Vol. 10, pp. 105-110.

B-226.   Derruau, Max. 1979. "Philippe Arbos,
          1882-1956," _Geographers: Biobibliographical
          Studies_, Vol. 3, pp. 7-12.

B-227.   deSouza, Anthony R. 1983. "Talks With
          Teachers: Elizabeth Eiselen," _Journal of
          Geography_, Vol. 82, pp. 265-270.

B-228.   deSouza, Anthony R. 1983. "Talks With
          Teachers: John Fraser Hart," _Journal of
          Geography_, Vol. 82, pp. 54-58.

B-229.   deSouza, Anthony R. 1984. "Talks With
          Teachers: Clyde F. Kohn," _Journal of Geography_,
          Vol. 83, pp. 159-164.

B-230. deSouza, Anthony R. 1985. "Talks With
        Teachers: Richard L. Morrill," Journal of
        Geography, Vol. 84, pp. 158-160.

B-231. De Vorsey, Louis Jr. 1970. "William Gerard De
        Brahm: Eccentric Genius of Southeastern
        Geography," Southeastern Geographer, Vol. 10, pp.
        21-29.

B-232. De Vorsey, Louis, Jr. 1986. "William Gerard De
        Brahm, 1718-1779," Geographers: Biobibliographi-
        cal Studies, Vol. 10, pp. 41-48.

B-233. Dodge, Richard Elwood. 1906. "Editorial:
        Nathaniel Southgate Shaler," Journal of
        Geography, Vol. 5, pp. 326-327.

B-234. Dodge, Richard Elwood. 1930. "Albert Perry
        Brigham," Annals of the Association of American
        Geographers, Vol. 20, pp. 55-62.

B-235. Dodge, Stanley D. 1948. "Ralph Hall Brown,
        1898-1948," Annals of the Association of American
        Geographers, Vol. 38, pp. 305-309.

B-236. Downes, Alan. 1971. "The Bibliographic
        Dinosaurs of Georgian Geography (1714-1830),"
        Geographical Journal, Vol. 137, pp. 379-387.

B-237. Downes, Alan. 1977. "James Rennell, 1742-1830,"
        Geographers: Biobibliographical Studies, Vol. 1,
        pp. 83-88.

B-238. Dugdale, G. S. 1967. "The Motto of the Royal
        Geographical Society and William Richard
        Hamilton," Geographical Journal, Vol. 133, pp.
        51-53.

B-239. Dukie, Dusan. 1981. "Paule Vujevie, 1881-1966,"
        Geographers: Biobibliographical Studies, Vol. 15,
        pp. 129-132.

B-240. Dunbar, G. S. 1974. "Elisee Reclus and the
        Great Globe," Scottish Geographical Magazine,
        Vol. 90, pp. 57-66.

B-241. Dunbar, G. S. 1981. "Lorin Blodget, 1823-1901,"
        Geographers: Biobibliographical Studies, Vol. 5,
        pp. 9-12.

B-242. Dunbar, Gary. 1979. "Elisee Reclus, Geographer
        and Anarchist," Antipode, Vol. 10, pp. 16-21.

B-243. Dunbar, Gary S. 1978. "George Davidson,
        1825-1911," Geographers: Biobibliographical
        Studies, Vol. 2, pp. 33-38.

B-244.   Dunbar, Gary S.   1985.   "Harold Innis and
          Canadian Geography," Canadian Geographer, Vol.
          29, pp. 159-163.

B-245.   Dury, G. H.   1970.   "Inventory and Prospect:
          Griffith Taylor's Department and Geographical
          Education in New South Wales During the 1950's
          and 1960's, Australian Geographer, Vol. 11, pp.
          221-241.

B-246.   East, W. Gordon.   1956.   "An Eighteenth-Century
          Geographer: William Guthrie of Brechin,"
          Scottish Geographical Magazine, Vol. 72, pp.
          32-37.

B-247.   Emery, F. V.   1958.   "The Geography of Robert
          Gordon, 1580-1661 and Sir Robert Sibbald,
          1641-1772," Scottish Geographical Magazine, Vol.
          74, pp. 3-12.

B-248.   Emery, F. V.   1984.   "Geography and Imperialism:
          The Role of Sir Bartle Frere," Geographical
          Journal, Vol. 150, pp. 342-350.

B-249.   Entrikin, J. N.   1977.   "Geography's Spatial
          Perspective and the Philosophy of Ernst
          Cassiver," Canadian Geographer, Vol. 21, pp.
          209-222.

B-250.   Entrikin, J. N.   1980.   "Robert Park's Human
          Ecology and Human Geography," Annals of the
          Association of American Geographers, Vol. 70, pp.
          43-58.

B-251.   Entrikin, J. Nicholas.   1981.   "Archival
          Research: Carl O. Sauer and Chorology,"
          Canadian Geographer, Vol. 31, pp. 77-78.

B-252.   Entrikin, J. Nicholas.   1984.   "Carl O. Sauer,
          Philosopher in Spite of Himself," Geographical
          Review, Vol. 74, pp. 387-408.

B-253.   Esakov, Vasily Alexeyevich 1978.   "Dmitry
          Nikolaevich Anuchin, 1843- 1923," Geographers:
          Biobibliographical Studies, Vol. 2, pp. 1-8.

B-254.   Esakov, Vasily Alexeyevich.   1980.   "Vasily
          Vasilyevich Dokuchaer, 1846- 1903," Geographers:
          Biobibliographical Studies, Vol. 4, pp. 33-42.

B-255.   Eyre, J. D.   1978.   "Edward Ullman: A Career
          Profile," Department of Geography, University of
          North Carolina, Studies of Geography, Vol. 11,
          pp. 1-15.

B-256.   Fairchild, Wilma B.   1948.   "Explorers: The Men
          and Their Motives," Annals of the Association of
          American Geographers, Vol. 38, pp. 74.

B-257.   Fairchild, Wilma B. 1966. "Adventures in
          Longevity: Fifty Years of the Geographical
          Review," Geographical Review, Vol. 56, pp. 1-11.

B-258.   Fairchild, Wilma B. 1976. "Gladys Mary
          Wrigley: 1885-1975, Geographical Review, Vol.
          66, pp. 331-333.

B-259.   Fairchild, Wilma B. 1976. "Jacques M. May
          (1896-1975)," Geographical Review, Vol. 66, pp.
          236-237.

B-260.   Fairchild, Wilma Belden. 1948. "Explorers: Men
          and Machines," Geographical Review, Vol. 38, pp.
          414-415.

B-261.   Fedosseyev, I. A. 1978. "Alexander Ivanovitch
          Voyeikov, 1842-1916," Geographers:
          Biobibliographical Studies, Vol. 2, pp. 135-142.

B-262.   Fedosseyev, I. A. 1979. "Alexy Andreyevich
          Tillo, 1839-1900," Geographers:
          Biobibliographical Studies, Vol. 3, pp. 155-160.

B-263.   Felland, Nordis. 1972. "Ena L. Yonge,
          1895-1971," Geographical Review, Vol. 62, pp.
          414-417.

B-264.   Felland, Nordis. 1974. "Raye Roberts Platt
          (1891-1973)," Geographical Review, Vol. 64, pp.
          296-297.

B-265.   Ferrell, Edith H. 1981. "Arnold Henry Guyot,
          1807-1884," Geographers: Biobibliographical
          Studies, Vol. 5, pp. 63-72.

B-266.   Fischer, C., Mercier, C. and Raffestin, C.
          1986. "William Rosier, 1856-1924," Geographers:
          Biobibliographical Studies, Vol. 10, pp. 149-154.

B-267.   Fletcher, C. R. L. 1928. "David George
          Hogarth," Geographical Journal, Vol. 71, pp.
          321-345.

B-268.   Fogelberg, Paul. 1968. "The Scientific
          Production of Helmer Smeds," Acta Geographica
          Sinica, Vol. 20, pp. 5-14.

B-269.   Forbes, S. V. 1949. "Col. R. J. Gordon's
          Contribution To Case Geography," South African
          Geographical Journal, Vol. 31, pp. 3-35.

B-270.   Fraser, J. Keith. 1983. "Presidential Address:
          The Road Less Travelled: Reflections on a Career
          in Geography," Canadian Geographer, Vol. 27, pp.
          395-312.

B-271.   Freeman, T. W.   1977.   "The Geography of
         Geographers," Professional Geographer, Vol. 29,
         pp. 218-220.

B-272.   Freeman, T. W.   1977.   "Hugh Robert Mill,
         1861-1950," Geographers: Biobibliographical
         Studies, Vol. 1, pp. 73-78.

B-273.   Freeman, T. W.   1979.   "Edmund William Gilbert,
         1900-1973," Geographers: Biobibliographical
         Studies, Vol. 3, pp. 63-72.

B-274.   Freeman, T. W.   1981.   "Percy Maude Roxby,
         1880-1947," Geographers: Biobibliographical
         Studies, Vol. 5, pp. 109-116.

B-275.   Freeman, T. W.   1982.   "Charles Bungay Fawcett,
         1883-1952," Geographers: Biobibliographical
         Studies, Vol. 6, pp. 39-46.

B-276.   Freeman, T. W.   1983.   "Introduction [on
         Geographers]," Geographers: Biobibliographical
         Studies, Vol. 7, pp. 2-24.

B-277.   Freeman, T. W.   1984.   "Robert Neal Rudmose
         Brown, 1929-1957," Geographers: Biobiblio-
         graphical Studies, Vol. 8, pp. 7-16.

B-278.   Freestone, R.   1981.   "Marcel Aurousseau and the
         True Tint of Geography," Australian Geographer,
         Vol. 15, pp. 1-7.

B-279.   French, R. A.   1963.   "V. A. Obruchev: The
         Centenary of a Great Geographer," Geographical
         Journal, Vol. 129, pp. 494-498.

B-280.   Friis, Herman R.   1953.   "W. L. G. Joerg
         1885-1953," Annals of the Association of American
         Geographers, Vol. 43, pp. 255-283.

B-281.   Fuller, G. D.   1939.   "Henry Chandler Cowles,"
         Science, Vol. 40, pp. 363-364.

B-282.   Fussell, Tim and Walker, John.   1983. "Interview
         With Professor M. Wise," Horizon, Vol. 31, pp.
         51-53.

B-283.   Gabler, Robert E.   1982.   "In Memoriam, Herbert
         Henry Gross (1905-1981)," Journal of Geography,
         Vol. 81, pp. 78-79.

B-284.   Gade, Daniel W.   1970.   "The Contributions of O.
         F. Cook to Cultural Geography," Professional
         Geographer, Vol. 22, pp. 206-209.

B-285.   Gage, Maxwell.   1978.   "Charles Andrew Cotton,
         1885-1970," Geographers: Biobibliographical
         Studies, Vol. 2, pp. 27-32.

B-286. Gallagher, James W. 1970. "Reminiscences,"
        [Arthur W. Watterson] Geographical Bulletin, Vol.
        1, pp. 55-58.

B-287. Gartner, Rainer. 1985. "Wilhelm Volz,
        1870-1958," Geographers: Biobibliographical
        Studies, Vol. 9, pp. 145-150.

B-288. Geddes, A. 1936. "Lewis," Scottish Geographical
        Magazine, Vol. 52, pp. 217-231, 300-313.

B-289. Geddes, Patrick. 1905. "A Great Geographer:
        Elisee Reclus, 1830-1905," Scottish Geographical
        Magazine, Vol. 21, pp. 490-496, 548-550.

B-290. Gelfand, Lawrence. 1954. "Ellen Churchill
        Semple: Her Geographical Approach to American
        History," Journal of Geography, Vol. 53, pp.
        30-41.

B-291. Genthe, Martha Krug. 1904. "School Geography in
        the United States," Education, Vol. 25, pp.
        135-141.

B-292. Gerasimov, I. P. 1967. "Salvador Massip [on his
        75th Birthday]," Soviet Geography: Review and
        Translation, Vol. 8, pp. 44-46.

B-293. Giblin, Beatrice. 1979. "Elisee Reclus,
        1830-1905," Geographers: Biobibliographical
        Studies, Vol. 3, pp. 125-132.

B-294. Gilbert, A. H. 1919. "Pierre Davity: His
        Geography and Its Use by Milton," Geographical
        Review, Vol. 7, pp. 322-338.

B-295. Gilbert, E. 1951. "The Seven Lamps of
        Geography: An Appreciation of Sir Halford
        Mackinder," Geography, Vol. 36, pp. 21-40.

B-296. Gilbert, E. W. 1947. "The Rt. Hon. Sir Halford
        J. Mackinder, P.C., 1861-1947," Geographical
        Journal, Vol. 110, pp. 94-100.

B-297. Gilbert, E. W. 1961. "The Right Honourable Sir
        Halford J. Mackinder, P.C., 1861-1947,"
        Geographical Journal, Vol. 127, pp. 27-29.

B-298. Gilbert, E. W. 1965. "Andrew John Herbertson,
        1865-1915," Geographical Journal, Vol. 131, pp.
        516-519.

B-299. Gilbert, Edmund W. and W. H. Parker. 1969. "H.
        J. Mackinder's Democratic Ideals and Reality
        after Fifty Years," Geographical Journal, Vol.
        135, pp. 228-230.

B-300.   Gladkov, N. A.   1963.   "The Defense of V. A.
          Anuchin's Doctoral   Dissertation," Soviet
          Geography: Review and Translation, Vol. 4, No.
          8, pp. 34-45.

B-301.   Gold, John R., Haigh, Martin J. and Warwick, G.
          T.   1983.   "David Leslie Linton, 1906-1971,"
          Geographers: Biobibliographical Studies, Vol. 7,
          pp. 75-84.

B-302.   Gold, John R. and Shepherd, Ifan D. H.   1983.
          "An Interview With Ron Johnston," Journal of
          Geography in Higher Education, Vol. 7, pp.
          109-124.

B-303.   Goldberger, Joseph.   1986.   "Eduard Richter,
          1847-1905," Geographers: Biobibliographical
          Studies, Vol. 10, pp. 143-148.

B-304.   Gottmann, Jean.   1944.   "Vauban and Modern
          Geography," Geographical Review, Vol. 34, pp.
          120-128.

B-305.   Goudie, A.   1972.   "Vaughan Cornish: Geographer,
          With a Bibliography of His Published Works,"
          Transactions - Institute of British Geographers,
          No. 55, pp. 1-16.

B-306.   Goudie, A. S.   1978.   "Colonel Julian Jackson and
          His Contribution to Geography," Geographical
          Journal, Vol. 144, pp. 264-270.

B-307.   Goudie, A. S.   1980.   "George Nathaniel
          Curzon--Superior Geographer," Geographical
          Journal, Vol. 146, pp. 203-209.

B-308.   Goudie, Andrew S.   1986.   "William John McGee,
          1853-1912," Geographers: Biobibliographical
          Studies, Vol. 10, pp. 111-116.

B-309.   Gourou, Pierre, 1977.   "Jacques Weulersse,
          1905-1946," Geographers: Biobibliographical
          Studies, Vol. 1, pp. 107-112.

B-310.   Gowing, D.   1984.   "The World of Malthus,"
          Geographical Magazine, Vol. 56, pp. 203-204.

B-311.   Grano, Olavi.   1979.   "Johannes Gabriel Grano,
          1882-1956," Geographers: Biobibliographical
          Studies, Vol. 3, pp. 73-84.

B-312.   Greene, Frank B.   1908.   "With Professor Heilprin
          in the Rocky Mountains," Bulletin of the
          Geographical Society of Philadelphia, Vol. 6, pp.
          20-24.

B-313.   Gregory, J. W.   1913.   "Livingstone as an
          Explorer: An Appreciation," Scottish
          Geographical Magazine, Vol. 29, pp. 225-242.

B-314.   Gregory, P.   1984.   "Space, Time, and Politics in
          Social Theory: An   Interview with Anthony
          Gidden," Environnment and Planning D: Society
          and Space, Vol. 2, pp. 123-132.

B-315.   Grigg, David B.   1977.   "Ernst Georg Ravenstein,
          1834-1913,"   Geographers: Biobibliographical
          Studies, Vol. 1, pp. 79-82.

B-316.   Grimm, Frank M.   1973.   "The Content of Ratzel's
          Politische Geographie," Professional Geographer,
          Vol. 25, pp. 271-277.

B-317.   Grotewald, Andreas.   1959.   "Von Thunen in
          Retrospect,"   Economic Geography, Vol. 35, pp.
          346-355.

B-318.   Gueffroy, Edna M.   1953.   "Harry Owen Lathrop,
          1887-1951," Annals of the Association of American
          Geographers, Vol. 43, pp. 12-13.

B-319.   Guerlack, H.   1968.   "Copernicus and Aristotle's
          Cosmos," Journal of the History of Ideas, Vol.
          29, pp. 109-113.

B-320.   Gugiuman, Ion.   1982.   "Mahai David, 1886-1954,"
          Geographers: Biobibliographical Studies, Vol. 6,
          pp. 31-34.

B-321.   Guilcher, A.   1986.   "Francis P. Shepard
          (1897-1985), Pere de la Geomorphologie Marine,"
          [father of marine geomorphology] Annals de
          Geographie, No. 527, pp. 87-98 [English Summary].

B-322.   Gulley, J. L. M.   1961.   "The Practice of
          Historical Geography, A Study in the Writings of
          Professor Roger Dion," Tijdschrift voor
          Economische en Sociale Geografie, Vol. 52, pp.
          169-183.

B-323.   Gulois, Bob.   1976.   "Ideology and the Idea of
          Nature: The Case of Peter Kropotkin," Antipode,
          Vol. 8, pp. 1-16.

B-324.   Gutierre de MacGregor, Maria Teresa.   1983.
          "Jorge Leonides Tamayo, 1912-1978," Geographers:
          Biobibliographical Studies, Vol. 7, pp. 125-128.

B-325.   Haas, William H. and Ward, Harold.   1933.
          "Memoir of J. Paul Goode," Annals of the
          Association of American Geographers, Vol. 23, pp.
          241-246.

B-326.   Hall, Arthur R.   1955.   "Mackinder and the Course
          of Events," Annals of the Association of American
          Geographers, Vol. 45, pp. 109-126.

B-327.   Hall, Elial F.   1878.   "Gerard Mercator: His
          Life and Works," Journal of the American
          Geographical Society of New York, Vol. 10, pp.
          163-196.

B-328.   Hall, Robert Burnett.   1953.   "William Herbert
          Hobbs, 1864-1953," Annals of the Association of
          American Geographers, Vol. 43, pp. 284-288.

B-329.   Hance, William A.   1973.   "Wilma Belden
          Fairchild," Geographical Review, Vol. 63, pp.
          2-5.

B-330.   Hanley, W. S.   1980.   "Griffith Taylor's
          Antarctic Achievements: A Geographical
          Foundation," Australian Geographer, Vol. 18, pp.
          22-36.

B-331.   Hard, A.   1927.   "Friendly Impressions; Dr. Helen
          Strong Who Made Geography Her Career," Women
          Citizen, Vol. 12, N.S., pp. 12-13.

B-332.   Harley, J. B.   1978.   "William Roy and the
          Ordinance Survey," Chartered Surveyor, Vol. 110,
          pp. 163-169.

B-333.   Harney, David.   1983.   "Owen Lattimore -- A
          Memoire," Antipode, Vol. 15, pp. 3-11.

B-334.   Harper, Roland M.   1916.   "The Geographical Work
          of Dr. E. W. Hilgard," Geographical Review, Vol.
          1, pp. 368-370.

B-335.   Harris, Chauncy D.   1963.   "Alice Foster,
          1872-1962," Journal of Geography, Vol. 62, p. 77.

B-336.   Harris, Chauncy D.   1964.   "Robert Swanton Platt
          (1891-1964)," Geographical Review, Vol. 54, pp.
          444-445.

B-337.   Harris, Chauncy D.   1966.   "Charles C. Colby,
          1884-1965," Annals of the Association of American
          Geographers, Vol. 56, pp. 378-382.

B-338.   Harris, Chauncy D.   1968.   "Stephen Sargent
          Visher, 1887-1967," Journal of Geography, Vol.
          67, pp. 378-379.

B-339.   Harris, Chauncy D.   1987.   "Theodore Shabad:
          1922-1987," Soviet Geography: Review and
          Translation, Vol. 28, pp. 376-385.

B-340.   Harris, R. Cole. 1976. "Andrew Hill Clark,
          1911-1975," Journal of Historical Geography, Vol.
          2, pp. 1-2.

B-341.   Hartshorne, Richard. 1958. "The Concept of
          Geography as a Science of Space, from Kant and
          Humboldt to Hettner," Annals of the Association
          of American Geographers, Vol. 48, pp. 97-108.

B-342.   Hartshorne, Richard. 1961. "Verner Clifford
          Finch, 1883-1959," Annals of the Association of
          American Geographers, Vol. 51, pp. 339-342.

B-343.   Hartshorne, Richard. 1964. "Robert S. Platt,
          1891-1964," Annals of the Association of American
          Geographers, Vol. 54, pp. 630-637.

B-344.   Hartshorne, Richard. 1979. "Notes Toward a
          Bibliography of The Nature of Geography," Annals
          of the Association of American Geographers, Vol.
          69, pp. 63-76.

B-345.   Harvard College, Class of 1889. 1939. "Robert
          De Courcy Ward," Fiftieth Anniversary Report, pp.
          395-400.

B-346.   Hawley, Arthur J. 1968. "Environmental
          Perception: Nature and Ellen Churchill Semple,"
          Southeastern Geographer, Vol. 8, pp. 54-59.

B-347.   Hegen, Edmund E. 1959. "Moses, Prophet -- and
          Geographer," Memorandum Folio of the Southeastern
          Association of American Geographers, Vol. 11, pp.
          74-77.

B-348.   Henderson, H. 1978. "The Legacy of E. F.
          Schumacher," Environment, Vol. 20, pp. 30-36.

B-349.   Henry, Alfred Judson. 1917. "Memoir of
          Cleveland Abbe," Annals of the Association of
          American Geographers, Vol. 7, pp. 61-67.

B-350.   Herman, Theodore. 1965. "George Bacock Cressey,
          1896-1963," Annals of the Association of American
          Geographers, Vol. 55, pp. 360-364.

B-351.   Herndon, G. Melvin. 1985. "William Tatham:
          Early Virginia Surveyor, Geographer and
          Cartographer," Virginia Geographer, Vol. 17,
          Fall/Winter, pp. 27-41.

B-352.   Herrmann, Anne Marie. 1980. "Ludwig von Hohnel,
          1857-1942," Geographers: Biobibliographical
          Studies, Vol. 4, pp. 43-48.

B-353.   Heske, Henning. 1987. "Karl Haushofer: His
          Role in German Geopolitics and Nazi Politics."
          Political Geography Quarterly, Vol. 6, pp.
          135-144.

B-354.   Hewes, Leslie. 1983. "Carl Sauer: A Personal
          View," Journal of Geography, Vol. 82, pp.
          140-147.

B-355.   Hobbs, William Herbert. 1920. "Memoir of Robert
          Edwin Peary," Annals of the Association of
          American Geographers, Vol. 10, pp. 93-108.

B-356.   Hoheisel, Karl. 1981. Henricus Glareanus,
          1488-1563," Geographers: Biobibliographical
          Studies, Vol. 5, pp. 49-54.

B-357.   Hoheisel, Karl. 1981. "Johannes Stoffler,
          1452-1531," Geographers: Biobibliographical
          Studies, Vol. 5, pp. 123-128.

B-358.   Hoheisel, Karl. 1982. "Gregor Reisch, c.
          1470-1525," Geographers: Biobibliographical
          Studies, Vol. 6, pp. 99-104.

B-359.   Hoheisel, Karl. 1984. "Peter Apianus, 1495 or
          1501-1552," Geographers: Biobibliographical
          Studies, Vol. 6, pp. 1-6.

B-360.   Holmes, David H. 1972. "Paul Wheatley: An
          Assessment," Bloomsbury Geographer, Vol. 5, pp.
          15-27.

B-361.   Holmes, K. L. 1979. "Francis Drake's Course in
          the North Pacific, 1579," Geographical Bulletin,
          Vol. 17, pp. 5-41.

B-362.   Holtgrieve, D. 1974. "Frederick Jackson Turner
          as a Regionalist," Professional Geographer, Vol.
          26, pp. 159-165.

B-363.   Honeybone, R. C. 1984. "James Fairgrieve,
          1870-1953," Geographers: Biobibliographical
          Studies, Vol. 8, pp. 27-34.

B-364.   Hooson, David. 1983. "National Cultures and
          Academic Geography in an Urbanizing Age," in The
          Expanding City: Essays in Honour of Professor
          Jean Gottmann, John Patten, ed. (London:
          Academic Press), pp. 157-178.

B-365.   Hotles, Karlheinz, Hotles, Ruth and Scholler,
          Peter. 1983. "Walter Christaller, 1893-1969,"
          Geographers: Biobibliographical Studies, Vol. 7,
          pp. 11-16.

B-366.   Hotles, Ruth. 1983. "Walter Christaller,"
          Annals of the Association of American

B-367.   Hoyle, B. S.   1965.   "Clement Gillman,
          1882-1946: Biographical Notes on a Pioneer East
          African Geographer," East African Geographial
          Review, No. 3, pp. 1-16.

B-368.   Hoyle, B. S.   1977.   "Clement Gillman,
          1882-1946," Geographers: Biobibliographical
          Studies, Vol. 1, pp. 35-42.

B-369.   Hoyle, B. S.   1986.   "Gillman of Tanganyika,
          1882-1946: Pioneer Geographer," Geographical
          Journal, Vol. 152, pp. 354-366.

B-370.   Hsieh, Chiao-Min.   1958.   "Hsia-Ke Hsu--Pioneer
          of Modern Geography in China," Annals of the
          Association of American Geographers, Vol. 48, pp.
          73-82.

B-371.   Hudson, Brian J.   1982.   "The Geographical
          Imagination of Arnold Bennett," Transactions -
          Institute of British Geographers, Vol. 7, pp.
          365-379.

B-372.   Humphries, W. J.   1937.   "Robert De Courcy Ward,"
          Science, Vol. 75, pp. 183-184.

B-373.   Hunt, Gary.   1983.   "Interview with Professor J.
          C. Pugh," Horizon, Vol. 31, pp. 51-59.

B-374.   Huntington, Archer M.   1950.   "Isaiah Bowman:
          Yale," Geographical Review, Vol. 40, p. 173.

B-375.   Huntington, Ellsworth.   1912.   "William Morris
          Davis, Geographer," Bulletin of the Geographical
          Society of Philadelphia, Vol. 10, pp. 26-36.

B-376.   Huntington, Ellsworth.   1917.   "The Geographical
          Work of Dr. M. A. Veeder," Geographical Review,
          Vol. 3, pp. 188-211, 303-316.

B-377.   Huntington, Ellsworth.   1921.   "Memoir of Sumner
          Webster Cushing," Annals of the Association of
          American Geographers, Vol. 11, pp. 109-111.

B-378.   Hyde, R.   "John Ogilby's Eleventh Hour," Map
          Collector, Vol. 11, pp. 2-8.

B-379.   Ilie, I. D.   1975.   "Constantin Bratescu
          (1882-1945)," Geoforum, Vol. 6, pp. 78.

B-380.   Inglis, Harry R. G.   1918.   "John Adair: An
          Early Map-Maker and His Work," Scottish
          Geographical Magazine, Vol. 34, pp. 60-66.

B-381.   Isachenko, A. G.   1977.   "Berg's
          Landscape-Geographic Ideas, Their Origins and
          Their Significance," Soviet Geography: Review
          and Translation, Vol. 18, pp. 13-18.

B-382.   Jaatinen, Stig.   1985.   "Johan Evert Rosberg,
          1864-1932," Geographers: Biobibliographical
          Studies, Vol. 9, pp. 101-108.

B-383.   Jackson, S. P.   1981.   "Obituary: Professor John
          Wellington," South African Geographical Journal,
          Vol. 63, pp. 1-2.

B-384.   Jacobsen, N. Kings.   1986.   "Niels Nielsen,
          1893-1981," Geographers: Biobibliographical
          Studies, Vol. 10, pp. 117-124.

B-385.   Jain, Devendra.   1970.   "Syed Muzaffer Ali,"
          Deccan Geographer, Vol. 8, pp. 169-171.

B-386.   Jakel, Rimhard.   1981.   "Johann Michael Franz,
          1700-1761," Geographers: Biobibliographical
          Studies, Vol. 5, pp. 41-48.

B-387.   James, Preston E.   1977.   "Grove Karl Gilbert,
          1843-1918," Geographers: Biobibliographical
          Studies, Vol. 1, pp. 25-34.

B-388.   James, Preston E.   1978.   "Albert Perry Brigham,
          1855-1932," Geographers: Biobibliographical
          Studies, Vol. 2, pp. 13-20.

B-389.   James, Preston E.   1979.   "John Wesley Powell
          United States," Geographical Review, Vol. 67, pp.
          446-461.

B-390.   James, Preston E. and Ehrenberg, Ralph.   1975.
          "The Original Members of the Association of
          American Geographers," Professional Geographer,
          Vol. 27, pp. 327-335.

B-391.   Janke, James.   1984.   "Geography in University
          Cooperative Extension," Professional Geographer,
          Vol. 36, pp. 240-241.

B-392.   J.A.S.   1952.   "Obituary: Margaret Swamson
          Anderson," Geographical Journal, Vol. 118, p.
          517.

B-393.   Jay, L. J.   1979.   "Andrew John Herbertson,
          1865-1915," Geographers: Biobibliographical
          Studies, Vol. 3, pp. 85-92.

B-394.   Jay, L. J.   1986.   "John Scott Keltie,
          1840-1927," Geographers: Biobibliographical
          Studies, Vol. 10, pp. 93-98.

B-395.   Joerg, W. L. G.   1931.   "Memoir of Cyrus
          Cornelius Adams," Annals of the Association of
          American Geographers, Vol. 21, pp. 171-178.

B-396.   Joerg, W. L. G.   1936.   "Memoir of Leon Dominican,"
         Annals of the Association of American Geographers,
         Vol. 26, pp. 197-198.

B-397.   Johnson, D.   1934.   "William Morris Davis," Science,
         Vol. 79, May 18, pp. 445-449.

B-398.   Johnston, R. J.   1986.   "Review Essay: J. L.
         Paterson, David Harvey's Geography," Antipode, Vol.
         18, pp. 96-109.

B-399.   Johnston, Sir Harry.   1913.   "David Livingstone: A
         Review of His Work As Explorer and Man of Science,"
         Scottish Geographical Magazine, Vol. 29, pp.
         281-304.

B-400.   Johnston, Sir Harry H.   1913.   "Livingstone As an
         Explorer," Geographical Journal, Vol. 41, pp.
         423-446.

B-401.   Johnston, W. B.   1981.   "George Jobberns,
         1895-1974," Geographers: Biobibliographical Studies,
         Vol. 5, pp. 73-76.

B-402.   Jong, W. W. de.   1974.   "Seventy Years H.J.K.,"
         [Hendrik Jacob Kevning] Tidjschrift voor Economische
         in Sociale Geografie, Vol. 65, pp. 65-70.

B-403.   Karan, P. P.   1985.   "Geographers As Consultants on
         U.N. Projects," Professional Geographer, Vol. 37,
         pp. 470-474.

B-404.   Karpov, L. N., et al.   1983.   "N. N. Baranskiy and
         the Geography of Foreign Countries," Soviet
         Geography: Review and Translation, Vol. 24, pp.
         423-429.

B-405.   Kasai, Yamata.   1975.   "Von Richtofen and Modern
         Geography--System and Unity of the Geographic
         Sciences," Science Reports of the Tohoku University,
         Seventh Series (Geography), Vol. 25, pp. 95-103.

B-406.   Kearns, Gerry.   1985.   "Halford John Mackinder,
         1861-1947," Geographers: Biobibliographical Studies,
         Vol. 9, pp. 71-86.

B-407.   Kemp, Harold S.   1940.   "Mussolini -- Geographer,"
         Annals of the Association of American Geographers,
         Vol. 30, pp. 61-62.

B-408.   Kersten, Earl W.   1983.   "Sauer and Geographic
         Influences," Yearbook, Association of Pacific Coast
         Geographers, Vol. 44, pp. 47-74.

B-409.   Kiewietdejonge, I.C.J.   1984.   "Budel's
         Geomorphology," Progress in Physical Geography, Vol.
         8, pp. 218-248.

B-410.   Kimble, G. H.   1933.   "Some Notes on Mediaeval
          Cartography with Special Reference to M. Behaim's
          Globe," Scottish Geographical Magazine, Vol. 33,
          pp. 91-98.

B-411.   Kimble, George H. T.   1952.   "The Uses of
          Geography," Geographical Review, Vol. 42, pp.
          507-509.

B-412.   Kimble, George H. T.   1967.   "Laurence Dudley
          Stamp," Geographical Review, Vol. 57, pp.
          246-249.

B-413.   Kindle, Edward M.   1936.   "Memoir of Reginald
          Walter Brock," Annals of the Association of
          American Geographers, Vol. 26, pp. 194-196.

B-414.   King, Cuchlaine A.M.   1980.   "William Vaughan
          Lewis, 1907-1961," Geography: Biobibliographical
          Studies, Vol. 4, pp. 113-120.

B-415.   Kish, George.   1968.   "Adolf Drik Nordenskiold
          (1832-1901):   Polar Explorer and Historian of
          Cartography," Geographical Journal, Vol. 134, pp.
          487-505.

B-416.   Kitts, D. B.   1980.   "Analogies in G. K.
          Gilbert's Philosophy of Science," Geological
          Society of America, Special Paper, Vol. 183, pp.
          143-148.

B-417.   Knadler, G.   1968.   "Isaiah Bowman," in
          International Encyclopedia of the Social
          Sciences, D. Sills, ed.   New York: Macmillan and
          The Free Press, pp. 137-138, Vol. 2.

B-418.   Koelsch, William A.   1969.   "The Historical
          Geography of Harlan H. Barrows," Annals of the
          Association of American Geographers, Vol. 59, pp.
          632-651.

B-419.   Koelsch, William A.   1979.   "Nathaniel Southgate
          Shaler, 1841-1906," Geographers:
          Biobibliographical Studies, Vol. 3, pp. 133-140.

B-420.   Koelsch, William A.   1979.   "Wallace Atwood's
          Great Geographical Institute," Annals of the
          Association of American Geographers, Vol. 70, pp.
          567-582.

B-421.   Koelsch, William A.   1982.   "In Memoriam, Henry
          John Warman (1907-1982)," Journal of Geography,
          Vol. 81, pp. 159-160.

B-422.   Koelsch, W. A.   1983.   "Robert DeCourcy Ward, 1867-1931," Geographers: Biobibliographical Studies, Vol. 7, pp. 145-150.

B-423.   Kolb, Albert.   1983.   "Ferdinand Freiherr von Richthofen, 1833-1905," Geographers: Biobibliographical Studies, Vol. 7, pp. 109-116.

B-424.   Kollmorgen, Walter M.   1979.   "Kollmorgen as a Bureaucrat," Annals of the Association of American Geographers, Vol. 69, pp. 77-88.

B-425.   Kondracki, Jerzy.   1981.   "Stanislaw Lencewicz, 1899-1944," Geographers: Biobibliographical Studies, Vol. 5, pp. 77-82.

B-426.   Konovalenko, V. G.   1963.   "About S. V. Kalesnik's Article on 'Monism' and 'Dualism' in Soviet Geography," Soviet Geography: Review and Translation, Vol. 4, No. 10, pp. 20-34.

B-427.   Kramer, F.   1967.   "Edvard Hahn and the End of the Three Stages of Man," Geographical Review, Vol. 57, pp. 73-89.

B-428.   Kramer, Fritz L.   1959.   "A Note on Carl Ritter, 1779-1859," Geographical Review, Vol. 49, pp. 406-409.

B-429.   Kriesel, Karl Marcus.   1968.   "Montesquieu: Possibilistic Political Geographer," Annals of the Association of American Geographers, Vol. 58, pp. 557-574.

B-430.   Krolzik, Udo O. F.   1981.   "Johann Albert Fabricius, 1668-1736," Geographers: Biobibliographical Studies, Vol. 5, pp. 35-40.

B-431.   Krout, Igor V.   1983.   "Vladimir Ivanovich Vernadsky, 1863-1945," Geographers: Biobibliographical Studies, Vol. 7, pp. 135-144.

B-432.   Kuklinski, A.   1987.   "Torsten Hägerstrand, Laudatio," GeoJournal, Vol. 14, pp. 503-510.

B-433.   Kunze, Donald.   1983.   "Giambattista Vico as a Philosopher of Place: Comments on a Recent Article," Transactions - Institute of British Geographers, Vol. 8, pp. 237-248.

B-434.   Lagarde, Lucie.   1982.   "Louis Vivien de Saint-Martin, 1802-1896," Geographers: Biobibliographical Studies, Vol. 6, pp. 133-138.

B-435.   Lagarde, Lucie.   1985.   "Philippe Bruche, 1700-1773," Geographers: Biobiliographical Studies, Vol. 9, pp. 21-28.

B-436.   Lamey, Robert.   1978.   "Albertus Magnus,"
         Bloomsburg Geographer, Vol. 8, pp. 28-36.

B-437.   Lane, Bernard.   1970.   "Geography and Manning in
         the Republic of Ireland," Geographical Viewpoint,
         Vol. 2, pp. 117-124.

B-438.   Lattimore, O.   1978.   "Douglas Carruthers and
         Geographical Contrasts in Central Asia,"
         Geographical Journal, Vol. 144, pp. 208-217.

B-439.   Lawton, R.   1985.   "Wilfred Smith, 1903-1955,"
         Geographers: Biobibliographical Studies, Vol. 9,
         pp. 121-128.

B-440.   Lazar, Margarete.   1985.   "Philipp Pavlitschke,
         1854-1899," Geographers: Biobibliographical
         Studies, Vol. 9, pp. 95-100.

B-441.   Learmonth, Andrew T. A.   1978.   "Arthur Geddes,
         1895-1968," Geographers: Biobibliographical
         Studies, Vol. 2, pp. 45-52.

B-442.   Le Boutillier, Theodore.   1908.   "Professor
         Heilprin: The Man," Bulletin of the Geographical
         Society of Philadelphia, Vol. 6, pp. 25-30.

B-443.   Leighly, John.   1964.   "Charles Warren
         Thorthwaite, 1899-1963," Annals of the
         Association of American Geographers, Vol. 54, pp.
         615-621.

B-444.   Leighly, John.   1976.   "Carl Ortwin Sauer,
         1889-1975," Annals of the Association of American
         Geographers, Vol. 66, pp. 337-348.

B-445.   Leighly, John.   1976.   "Carl Ortwin Sauer,
         1889-1975," Historical Geography Newsletter, Vol.
         6, pp. 3-4.

B-446.   Leighly, John.   1977.   "Matthew Fontaine Maury,
         1806-1873," Geographers: Biobibliographical
         Studies, Vol. 1, pp. 59-64.

B-447.   Leighly, John.   1978.   "Carl Ortwin Sauer,
         1889-1975," Geographers: Biobibliographical
         Studies, Vol. 2, pp. 99-108.

B-448.   Leighly, John.   1978.   "Scholar and Colleague:
         Homage to Carl Sauer," Yearbook, Association of
         Pacific Coast Geographers, Vol. 40, pp. 117-134.

B-449.   Leighly, John.   1979.   "Drifting into Geography
         in the Twenties," Annals of the Association of
         American Geographers, Vol. 69, pp. 4-8.

B-450.   Leighly, John.   1987.   "Ecology as Metaphor:
         Carl Sauer and Human Ecology," Professional
         Geographer, Vol. 39, pp. 405-412.

B-451.   Leszczycki, Stanislaw.   1982.   "Jerzy Smolenski,
         1881-1940," Geographers: Biobibliographical
         Studies, Vol. 6, pp. 123-128.

B-452.   Leszczycki, Stanislaw.   1985.   "Ludomir Slepowran
         Sawick, 1884-1928," Geographers: Biobiblio-
         graphical Studies, Vol. 9, pp. 113-120.

B-453.   Lewis, Robert A.   1962.   "Lester Earl Klimm,
         1902-1960," Annals of the Association of American
         Geographers, Vol. 52, pp. 115-117.

B-454.   Libbey, William E.   1884.   "The Life and
         Scientific Work of Arnold Guyot," Journal of the
         American Geographical Society of New York, Vol.
         16, pp. 194-221.

B-455.   Libby, William.   1908.   "Address," [re: Angela
         Heilprin] Bulletin of the Geographical Society
         of Philadelphia, Vol. 6, pp. 19-20.

B-456.   Light, Richard U.   1950.   "George Herbert Tinley
         Kimbley - John Kirtland Wright - Gladys Mary
         Wrigley," Geographical Review, Vol. 40, pp. 1-6.

B-457.   Limbird, Arthur.   1987.   "From Where Do We Come,
         To Where Do We Go?" Operational Geographer, No.
         12, p. 5.

B-458.   Linke, Max.   1981.   "Carl Ritter, 1779-1859,"
         Geographers: Biobibliographical Studies, Vol. 5,
         pp. 99-108.

B-459.   Linton, David L.   1957.   "Robert Neal Rudmose
         Brown: Obituary," Scottish Geographical
         Magazine, Vol. 73, p. 123.

B-460.   Little, C.   1960.   "Prince Henry the Navigator,"
         Canadian Geographical Journal, Vol. 61, pp.
         219-225.

B-461.   Livingstone, D. N.   1984.   "Science and Society:
         Nathaniel S. Shaler and Racial Ideology,"
         Transactions - Institute of British Geographers,
         Vol. 9, pp. 181-210.

B-462.   Livingstone, David N.   1980.   "Nature and Man in
         America: Nathaniel Southgate Shaler and the
         Conservation of Natural Resources," Transactions
         - Institute of British Geographers, Vol. 5, pp.
         369-382.

B-463.   Livingstone, David N., and Harrison, Richard T.
         1981.   "Immanuel Kant, Subjectivism, and Human
         Geography: A Preliminary Investigation,"
         Transactions - Institute of British Geographers,
         Vol. 6, pp. 359-374.

B-464.   Lobeck, Armia K.   1944.   "Douglas Johnson,"
         Annals of the Association of American
         Geographers, Vol. 34, pp. 216-222.

B-465.   Longstaff, T. G.   1934.   "Douglas Freshfield,
         1845-1934," Geographical Journal, Vol. 83, pp.
         257-263.

B-466.   Lowenthal, D.   1953.   "George Perkins Marsh and
         the American Geographical Tradition,"
         Geographical Review, Vol. 43, pp. 207-213.

B-467.   Lowenthal, David.   1960.   "George Perkins Marsh
         on the Nature and Purpose of Geography,"
         Geographical Journal, Vol. 126, pp. 413-417.

B-468.   Lowenthal, David.   1969.   "Ephraim Ketchall: A
         Forgotten Pioneer of Modern Geography,"
         Professional Geographer, Vol. 21, pp. 5-7.

B-469.   Lowenthal, David.   1969.   "John Kirtland Wright,
         1891-1969," Geographical Review, Vol. 59, pp.
         598-604.

B-470.   MacGregor, D. R.   1975.   "Catherine Park
         Snodgrass," Scottish Geographical Magazine, Vol.
         91, pp. 128-129.

B-471.   MacLean, Kenneth.   1975.   "George G. Chisholm:
         His Influence on University and School
         Geography," Scottish Geographical Magazine, Vol.
         91, pp. 70-78.

B-472.   Mag, J. A.   1982.   "The Geographical
         Interpretation of Ptolemy in the Renaissance,"
         Tijdschrift voor Economische en Sociale
         Geografie, Vol. 73, pp. 350-361.

B-473.   Manheim, Frank J.   1937.   "George Stillman
         Hillard - An Early American Apostle of Human
         Geography," Bulletin of the Geographical Society
         of Philadelphia, Vol. 35, pp. 1-7.

B-474.   Mardin, O.   1981.   "Piri Reis: Turkish Admiral
         and Cartographer," Map Collector, Vol. 16, pp.
         16-21.

B-475.   Marion, Donald.   1985.   "Wang Yung, 1899-1956,"
         Geographers: Biobibliographical Studies, Vol. 9,
         pp. 151-154.

B-476.   Markov, K. K.   1977.   "Recollections About L. S.
          Berg," Soviet Geography: Review and Translation,
          Vol. 18, pp. 19-22.

B-477.   Marschner, F. J.   1963.   "Carleton P. Barnes,
          1903-1962," Annals of the Association of
          American Geographers, Vol. 53, pp. 233-234.

B-478.   Marsden, W. E.   1979.   "Archibald Geikie,
          1835-1924," Geographers: Biobibliographical
          Studies, Vol. 3, pp. 39-52.

B-479.   Marsden, W. E.   1979.   "James Geikie, 1839-1915,"
          Geographers: Biobibliographical Studies, Vol. 3,
          pp. 53-62.

B-480.   Marshall, A.   1980.   "Griffith Taylor's
          Correlative Science," Australian Geographical
          Studies, Vol. 18, pp. 184-193.

B-481.   Marshall-Cornwall, James.   1965.   "Three
          Soldier-Geographers," Geographical Journal, Vol.
          131, pp. 357-365.

B-482.   Marshall-Cornwall, J.   1978.   "An Early
          Scandinavian Traveller," Geographical Journal,
          Vol. 144, pp. 250-255.

B-483.   Marti-Henneberg, Jordi.   1985.   "Emilio Huguet
          del Villar, 1871-1951," Geographers:
          Biobibliographical Studies, Vol. 9, pp. 55-60.

B-484.   Marti-Henneberg, Jordi and Radeff, Anne.   1986.
          "Henri-Francois Pittier, 1837-1950,"
          Geographers: Biobibliographical Studies, Vol.
          10, pp. 135-142.

B-485.   Martin, A. I.   1980.   "A Study of Edward's Map of
          Angus, 1678,"   Scottish Geographical Magazine,
          Vol. 96, pp. 39-45.

B-486.   Martin, Geoffrey J.   1972.   "Robert Lemogne
          Barrett, 1871-1969; Last of the Founding Members
          of the Association of American Geographers,"
          Professional Geographer, Vol. 24, pp. 29-31.

B-487.   Martin, Geoffrey J.   1977.   "Isaiah Bowman,
          1878-1950," Geographers: Biobibliographical
          Studies, Vol. 1, pp. 9-18.

B-488.   Martin, Geoffrey J.   1984.   "John Paul Goode,
          1862-1932," Geographers: Biobibliographical
          Studies, Vol. 8, pp. 51-56.

B-489.   Martin, Geoffrey J.   1987.   "On Whittlesey,
          Bowman and Harvard," Annals of the Association of
          American Geographers, Vol. 78, pp. 152-158.

B-490.   Martin, Geoffrey J.   1988.   "Preston E. James,
           1899-1986," Annals of the Association of American
           Geographers, Vol. 78, pp. 164-175.

B-491.   Martin, Gunter.   1984.   "Wilhelm Sievers,
           1860-1921," Geographers: Biobibliographical
           Studies, Vol. 8, pp. 107-110.

B-492.   Martin, Lawrence.   1912.   "Memoir of Christopher
           Webber Hall," Annals of the Association of
           American Geographers, Vol. 2, pp. 101-104.

B-493.   Martin, Lawrence.   1930.   "[Albert Perry Brigham]
           Populizer of Geography and Geology in the United
           States," Annals of the Association of American
           Geographers, Vol. 20, pp. 82-85.

B-494.   Martin, Lawrence.   1950.   "Davis: Investigator,
           Teacher, and Leader in Geomorphology," Annals of
           the Association of American Geographers, Vol. 40,
           pp. 172-180.

B-495.   Mathewson, Kent.   1987.   "Humane Ecologist: Carl
           Sauer As Metaphor?" Professional Geographer, Vol.
           39, pp. 412-413.

B-496.   Matley, Ian M.   1986.   "John Die, 1527-1608,"
           Geographers: Biobibliographical Studies, Vol.
           10, pp. 49-56.

B-497.   Matznetter, Josef.   1983.   "Johann Solch,
           1883-1951," Geographers: Biobibliographical
           Studies, Vol. 7, pp. 117-124.

B-498.   Maury, Mytton.   1874.   "On Martin Behaim's Globe
           and His Influence on Geographical Science,"
           Journal of the American Geographical and
           Statistical Society, Vol. 4, pp. 432-452.

B-499.   McCorkle, B.   1984.   "From Duodecimo to Doughty
           Folio -- The Geographic Dinosaurs of the
           Eighteenth Century," Bulletin -- Special
           Libraries Association, Geography and Map
           Division, Vol. 136, pp. 2-10.

B-500.   McIntire, William G.   1973.   "Richard Joel
           Russell (1895-1971)," Geographical Review, Vol.
           63, pp. 276-279.

B-501.   McIntyre, L.   1985.   "Humboldt's Way," National
           Geographic, Vol. 168, pp. 318-351.

B-502.   McKinney, William M.   1968.   "Carey, Spender and
           Modern Geography," Professional Geographer, Vol.
           20, pp. 103-106.

B-503.   McManis, Douglas R.   1976.   "Andrew Hill Clark,
         1911-1975," Historical Geography Newsletter, Vol.
         6, pp. 13-20.

B-504.   McNee, Robert B.   1968.   "The Education of a
         Geographer: 1962-1967," Journal of Geography,
         Vol. 67, pp. 70-75.

B-505.   Mead, W. R.   1979.   "Zachris Topelius,
         1818-1898," Geographers: Biobibliographical
         Studies, Vol. 3, pp. 161-164.

B-506.   Meinig, Donald W.   1955.   "Isaac Stevens:
         Practical Geographer of the Early Northwest,"
         Geographical Review, Vol. 45, pp. 542-558.

B-507.   Mensching, H. G.   1984.   "Julius Budel and His
         Concept of Climatic Geomorphology--Retrospect and
         Appreciation," Erdkunde, Vol. 38, pp. 157-166
         [English Summary].

B-508.   Meyen, Emil.   1983.   "Albrecht Penck, 1858-1945,"
         Geographers: Biobibliographical Studies, Vol. 7,
         pp. 101-108.

B-509.   Meyer, William B.   1986.   "Henry Charles Carey,
         1793-1879," Geographers: Biobibliographical
         Studies, Vol. 10, pp. 25-28.

B-510.   Meynen, Emil.   1980.   "Alfred Kirchhoff,
         1838-1907," Geographers: Biobibliographical
         Studies, Vol. 4, pp. 69-76.

B-511.   Middleton, Dorothy.   1977.   "George Adam Smith,
         1856-1942," Geographers: Biobibliographical
         Studies, Vol. 1, pp. 105-106.

B-512.   Mihailescu, Vinfila.   1977.   "Simion Mehedinti,
         1868-1962," Geographers: Biobibliographical
         Studies, Vol. 1, pp. 65-72.

B-513.   Mikesell, M.   1968.   "Friedrich Ratzel," in
         International Encyclopedia of the Social
         Sciences, D. Sills, ed., New York: Macmillan and
         the Free Press, pp. 327-329, Vol. 13.

B-514.   Mikos, M. J.   1984.   "Joachim Lelewel: Polish
         Scholar and Map Collector." Map Collector, Vol.
         26, pp. 20-24.

B-515.   Mill, Hugh Robert.   1943.   "Major Leonard
         Darwin," Geographical Journal, Vol. 101, pp.
         172-177.

B-516.   Miller, David H.   1988.   "John Leighly,
         1895-1986," Annals of the Association of American
         Geographers, Vol. 78, pp. 347-357.

B-517.   Miller, O. M.   1969.   "Charles Baker Hitchcock,
         1906-1969," Geographical Review, Vol. 59, pp.
         605-609.

B-518.   Miller, Ronald.   1971.   "Mungo Park, 1771-1971,"
         Scottish Geographical Magazine, Vol. 87, pp.
         159-165.

B-519.   Milne, Kathleen.   1979.   "Geoffrey Milne,
         1898-1942," Geographers: Biobibliographical
         Studies, Vol. 2, pp. 89-92.

B-520.   Minamoto, Shokyu.   1984.   "Shigetaka Shiga,
         1863-1927," Geographers: Biobibliographical
         Studies, Vol. 8, pp. 95-106.

B-521.   Minamoto, Shokyu.   1985.   "A Study of J. M. D.
         Meikle-John's A New Geography on the Comparative
         Method -- One Aspect of The History of Geography
         in the Meij Period," Geographical Review of
         Japan, Vol. 58B, pp. 195-207.

B-522.   Misra, Hariskesh Narain.   1971.   "Ram Narain
         Misra," Deccan Geographer, Vol. 9, pp. 127-129.

B-523.   Monbeig, P.   1968.   "Paul Vidal de la Blanche,"
         in International Encyclopedia of the Social
         Sciences, D. Sills, ed.   New York: Macmillan and
         The Free Press, pp. 316-318, Vol. 16.

B-524.   Morrill, Richard J.   1976.   "Edward Ullman
         (1912-1976)," Regional Science Association
         Papers, Vol. 37, pp. 5-6.

B-525.   Morrill, R. L.   1978.   "Geography as Spatial
         Interaction," Department of Geography, University
         of North Carolina, Studies in Geography, Vol. 11,
         pp. 16-29.

B-526.   Morrison, A. J.   1922.   "John G. De Brahm," South
         Atlantic Quarterly, Vol. 1, pp. 252-258.

B-527.   Mowat, Charles L.   1942.   "That Old Being, De
         Brahm," Florida Historical Quarterly, Vol. 20,
         pp. 323-345.

B-528.   Mukerjee, Sudershan.   1972.   "Bimla Churn Law,
         1891-1969," Deccan Geographer, Vol. 10, pp.
         97-101.

B-529.   Murzayev, E. M.   1977.   "The Career of J. S.
         Berg," Soviet Geography: Review and Translation,
         Vol. 13, pp. 4-12.

B-530.   Murzayev, E. M.   1981.   "Jev Semenovich Berg,
         1876-1950," Geographers: Biobibliographical
         Studies, Vol. 5, pp. 1-8.

B-531.   Myklebost, Hallstein. 1986. "Fridtjov Eide
          Isachsen, 1906-1979," Geographers:
          Biobibliographical Studies, Vol. 10, pp. 85-92.

B-532.   Nardy, Jean-Pierre. 1978. "Emile Levasseur,
          1828-1911," Geographers: Biobibliographical
          Studies, Vol. 2, pp. 81-88.

B-533.   Nedelco, Eugen. 1982. "Nicolai Orghidan,
          1881-1967," Geographers: Biobibliographical
          Studies, Vol. 6, pp. 77-80.

B-534.   Newcomb, Robert M. 1976. "Carl O. Sauer,
          Teacher," Historical Geography Newsletter, Vol.
          6, pp. 21-30.

B-535.   Newman, R. P. 1983. "Lattimore and His
          Enemies," Antipode, Vol. 15, pp. 12-26.

B-536.   Nicod, Jean. 1977. "Jules Blanche, 1893-1970,"
          Geographers: Biobibliographical Studies, Vol. 1,
          pp. 1-8.

B-537.   Nimigeanu, George. 1980. "Constantin Bratescu,
          1882-1945," Geographers: Biobibliographical
          Studies, Vol. 4, pp. 19-24.

B-538.   Nolan, Edward J. 1908. "Professor Heilprin's
          Scientific Work," Bulletin of the Geographical
          Society of Philadelphia, Vol. 6, pp. 7-12.

B-539.   Noltze, Richard H. 1976. "Sarah Kerr Myers:
          Director of the American Geographical Society,"
          Geographical Review, Vol. 66, pp. 380-382.

B-540.   Nunn, G. E. 1935. "Iniago Mundi and Columbus,"
          American History Review, Vol. 40, pp. 646-661.

B-541.   Nunn, Patrick. 1981. "Palissy, de'Maillet and
          Voltaire: Some Incipient Ideas in the Philosophy
          of Geomorphology," Bloomsburg Geographer, Vol.
          10, pp. 17-21.

B-542.   Ogilvie, A. G. 1950. "Isaiah Bowman: An
          Appreciation," Geographical Journal, Vol. 116,
          pp. 226-230.

B-543.   Olwig, Kenneth. 1980. "Historical Geography and
          the Society/Nature 'Problematic': The
          Perspective of J. F. Schoun, G. P. Marsh and E.
          Reclus," Journal of Historical Geography, Vol. 6,
          pp. 29-46.

B-544.   Olwig, Kenneth. 1983. "Commentary on
          Sonnenfeld's Egocentric Perspectives on
          Geographical Orientation," Annals of the
          Association of American Geographers, Vol. 73, pp.
          151.

B-545.   Ormeling, F. J.   1975.   "Obituary: Profile of
          the Geographer Jan Broek," Tijdschrift voor
          Economische en Sociale Geografie, Vol. 66, pp.
          3-5.

B-546.   Ormeling, F. J. Sr.   1978.   "Professor K. A.
          Salichtchev/Honorary Fellow of the ICA," Canadian
          Cartographer, Vol. 15, pp. 100-104.

B-547.   Oughton, Marguerita.   1978.   "Mary Somerville,
          1780-1872," Geographers: Biobibliographical
          Studies, Vol. 2, pp. 109-112.

B-548.   Paasi, A.   1984.   "Connection Between J. G.
          Granos' Geographical Thinking and Behavioural and
          Humanistic Geography," Fennia, Vol. 162, pp.
          21-31.

B-549.   Page, John L.   1952.   "William Oscar Blanchard,
          1886-1952," Annals of the Association of American
          Geographers, Vol. 42, pp. 324-326.

B-550.   Pansa, Gerhard.   1986.   "Ernst Emil Kurt Hassert,
          1868-1947," Geographers: Biobibliographical
          Studies, Vol. 10, pp. 69-76.

B-551.   Papy, Louis.   1983.   "Cavailles, Arque and
          Revert: Three Geographers of Bordeaux,"
          Geographers: Biobibliographical Studies, Vol. 7,
          pp. 5-10.

B-552.   Papy, Louis.   1983.   "Pierre Camena L'Almeida,
          1865-1943," Geographers: Biobibliographical
          Studies, Vol. 7, pp. 1-4.

B-553.   Parker, Ian.   1988.   "Harold Innis as a Canadian
          Geographer," Canadian Geographer, Vol. 32, pp.
          63-69.

B-554.   Parsons, James J.   1976.   "Carl Ortwin Sauer:
          1889-1975," Geographical Review, Vol. 66, pp.
          83-89.

B-555.   Parsons, James J.   1979.   "The Later Sauer
          Years," Annals of the Association of American
          Geographers, Vol. 69, pp. 9-15.

B-556.   Pastoureau, Mireille.   1979.   "Antoine d'Abbadie,
          1810-1897," Geographers: Biobibliographical
          Studies, Vol. 3, pp. 29-34.

B-557.   Patrick, Austin L.   1961.   "Hugh Hammond
          Bennett," Geographical Review, Vol. 51, pp.
          121-124.

B-558.   Pattison, William D.   1960.   "Harold W.
          Fairbanks, California Geography," Journal of
          Geography, Vol. 59, pp. 351-357.

B-559.   Pattison, William P. 1982. "Rollin D. Salisbury
         1858-1922," Geographers: Biobibliographical
         Studies, Vol. 6, pp. 105-114.

B-560.   Patton, Donald J. 1974. "Edward A. Ackerman
         (1911-1973)," Geographical Review, Vol. 64, pp.
         150-153.

B-561.   Pearcy, G. Etzel. 1958. "George Renner,
         1900-1955," Annals of the Association of American
         Geographers, Vol. 48, pp. 244-249.

B-562.   Pederson, Leland R. 1984. "Robert Eric
         Dickinson, 1905-1981," Geographers:
         Biobibliographical Studies, Vol. 8, pp. 17-26.

B-563.   Peel, R. F. 1973. "Obituary: Oliver Dennis
         Kendall," Transactions - Institute of British
         Geographers, No. 58, pp. 137-138.

B-564.   Peet, Richard. 1985. "Introduction to the
         Thought of Karl Wittfogel," Antipode, Vol. 17,
         pp. 3-20.

B-565.   Peterman, William A. 1975. "Geography,
         Environment, and the Philosophy of Alfred North
         Whitehead," Journal of Geography, Vol. 74, pp.
         531-538.

B-566.   Peucker, Thomas K. 1968. "Johann Georg Kohl, A
         Theoretical Geographer of the 19th Century,"
         Professional Geographer, Vol. 20, pp. 247-251.

B-567.   Pfeifer, Gottfried. 1982. "Leo Heinrich Waibel,
         1888-1951," Geographers: Biobibliographical
         Studies, Vol. 6, pp. 139-148.

B-568.   Phillips, Mary Viola. 1965. "Zoe Agnes
         Thralls," Journal of Geography, Vol. 64, p. 299.

B-569.   Pitte, Jean-Robert. 1986. "Obituary: Fernand
         Brandel, 1902-1985," Journal of Historical
         Geography, Vol. 12, pp. 307-308.

B-570.   Platt, Robert S. 1957. "A Note on Rollin D.
         Salisbury," Annals of the Association of American
         Geographers, Vol. 47, p. 276.

B-571.   Pleva, Edward G. 1985. "Norman T. Nicholson
         1920-1984," Canadian Geographer, Vol. 29, pp.
         98-99.

B-572.   Plewe, E. 1969. "Carl Ritter," in International
         Encyclopedia of the Social Sciences, D. Sills,
         ed. New York: Macmillan and The Free Press, pp.
         517-520, Vol. 13.

B-573. Plewe, Ernst.   1982.   "Alfred Hettner,
        1859-1941," Geographers: Biobibliographical
        Studies, Vol. 6, pp. 55-64.

B-574. Popovici, I.   1975.   "Simon Mehedinti
        (1868-1962)," Geoforum, Vol. 6, pp. 76-77.

B-575. Popp, N.   1975.   "George Valsan (1895-1935),"
        Geoforum, Vol. 6, pp. 77.

B-576. Popp, Nicolae.   1978.   "George Valsan,
        1885-1935," Geographers: Biobibliographical
        Studies, Vol. 2, pp. 127-134.

B-577. Porter, Philip W.   1987.   "Ecology as Metaphor:
        Sauer and Human Ecology," Professional
        Geographer, Vol. 39, p. 414.

B-578. Porter, R. S.   1978.   "George Hoggart Toulmin and
        James Hutton: A Fresh Look," Bulletin,
        Geological Society of American, Vol. 89, pp.
        1256-1258.

B-579. Potter, S. R.   1983.   "Peter Alexeivich
        Kropotkin, 1842-1921," Geographers:
        Biobibliographical Studies, Vol. 7, pp. 63-70.

B-580. Powell, J. M.   1978.   "The Bowman, Huntington and
        Taylor Correspondence, 1928," Australian
        Geographer, Vol. 14, pp. 123-125.

B-581. Powell, J. M.   1979.   "Thomas Griffith Taylor,
        1880-1963," Geographers: Biobibliographical
        Studies, Vol. 3, 141-153.

B-582. Powell, J. M.   1981.   "The Cyclist on the Ice:
        Griffith Taylor as Explorer," [Barr Memorial
        Lecture, 1979] Proceedings, Royal Geographical
        Society of Australasia, (S.A.), pp. 1-28.

B-583. Powell, J. M.   1981.   "Ferdinand Jakob Heinrich
        van Mueller, 1825-1896," Geographers:
        Biobibliographical Studies, Vol. 5, pp. 89-94.

B-584. Powell, J. M.   1981.   "Thomas Livingstone
        Mitchell, 1792-1855," Geographers:
        Biobibliographical Studies, Vol. 5, pp. 83-88.

B-585. Powell, J. M.   1982.   "Archibald Grenfell Price,
        1892-1977," Geographers: Biobibliographical
        Studies, Vol. 6, pp. 87-92.

B-586. Powell, J. M.   1983.   "George Woodroofe Goyder,
        1826-1898," Geographers: Biobibliographical
        Studies, Vol. 7, pp. 47-50.

B-587.   Powell, J. M.   1983.   "James Macdonald Holmes, 1896-1966," Geographers: Biobibliographical Studies, Vol. 7, pp. 51-55.

B-588.   Powell, J. M.   1983.   "Les Pionniers de la Geographie Austrahennie," [Pioneers of Australian Geography] Espace Geographique, Vol. 12, pp. 279-289.

B-589.   Powell, J. M.   1984.   "John Forrest, 1847-1918 and Alexander Forrest, 1849-1901," Geographers: Biobiblio- graphical Studies, Vol. 8, pp. 39-44.

B-590.   Powell, J. M.   1984.   "Obituary -- Marcel Aurousseau, 1891-1983," Australian Geographical Studies, Vol. 22, pp. 319-320.

B-591.   Pred, Allan.   1977.   "The Choreography of Existence: Comments on Hagerstrand's Time-Geography and Its Usefulness," Economic Geography, Vol. 53, pp. 207-221.

B-592.   Proctor, Nigel.   1986.   "The Pioneers of Geography: A New and Currently Relevant Perspective," Transactions - Institute of British Geographers, Vol. 11, pp. 75-85.

B-593.   Prudden, Hugh.   1984.   "J. H. B. Peel: A Literary Geographer," Geography, Vol. 69, pp. 339-341.

B-594.   Pruitt, Evelyn L.   1961.   "Homor Leroy Shantz, 1876-1958," Annals of the Association of American Geographers, Vol. 51, pp. 392-394.

B-595.   Putnam, D. F.   1963.   "Griffith Taylor, 1880-1963," Canadian Geographer, Vol. 7, pp. 197-200.

B-596.   Rahman, Fareeha.   1968.   "Arthur Geddes, 1897-1968," Pakistan Geographical Review, Vol. 23, pp. 114-115.

B-597.   Raisz, Erwin.   1947.   "James Warren Bagley, 1881-1847," Annals of the Association of American Geographers, Vol. 37, pp. 122.

B-598.   Rakhilin, V. K.   1983.   "Alexander Nikolayevich Formozor, 1899-1973," Geographers: Biobibliographical Studies, Vol. 7, pp. 39-46.

B-599.   Ramchandran, P. S.   1962.   "Sir Patrick Geddes' Contribution to Regional Planning," Bombay Geographical Magazine, Vol. 10, pp. 71-79.

B-600.   Raup, Hugh M.   1950.   "Merritt Lyndon Fernald, 1874-1950," Annals of the Association of American Geographers, Vol. 40, pp. 354-355.

B-601.   Raup, Hugh M.   1959.   "Charles C. Adams, 1873-1955, Annals of the Association of American Geographers, Vol. 49, pp. 164-167.

B-602.   Raup, H. F.   1977.   "A Wreath of Words [for Myrta Lisle McClellan]," Professional Geographer, Vol. 29, pp. 305-306.

B-603.   Ravenhill, W.   1978.   "John Adams, His Map of England, Its Projection and His 'Index Villaris' of 1680," Geographical Journal, Vol. 144, pp. 424-437.

B-604.   Redmond, Roland L.   1947.   "Richard Upjohn Light: President of the American Geographical Society," Geographical Review, Vol. 37, pp. 175-176.

B-605.   Rees, Ronald.   1976.   "John Constable and the Art of Geography," Geographical Review, Vol. 66, pp. 59-72.

B-606.   Rees, Ronald.   1982.   "Constable, Turner and Views of Nature in the Nineteenth Century," Geographical Review, Vol. 72, pp. 253-269.

B-607.   Rich, John L.   1945.   "Memorial to Nevin M. Fenneman," Annals of the Association of American Geographers, Vol. 35, pp. 181-189.

B-608.   Rigdon, Vera E.   1935.   "Physiographic Nonmenclature à la William Morris   Davis," Annals of the Association of American Geographers, Vol. 25, pp. 52-53.

B-609.   Rikkinen, Kalevi.   1985.   "Ragnar Hult, 1857-1899," Geographers: Biobibliographical Studies, Vol. 9, pp. 61-70.

B-610.   Ristow, Walter W.   1968.   "Simeon De Witt: Pioneer American Cartographer: Canadian Cartographer, Vol. 5, pp. 90-107.

B-611.   Ritchie, Capt. G. S.   1964.   "Sir John Barrow," Geographical Journal, Vol.   130, pp. 350-354.

B-612.   Rizvi, S. Q. A.   1958.   "A Survey of Urban Geography," Geographer, Vol. 10, pp. 26-42.

B-613.   Robinson, Arthur H.   1970.   "Erwin Josephus Raisz, 1893-1968," Annals of the Association of American Geographers, Vol. 60, pp. 189-193.

B-614.   Robinson, Guy and Parten, John.   1980.   "Edmund
         W. Gilbert and the Development of Historical
         Geography, with a Bibliography of His Work,"
         Journal of Historical Geography, Vol. 6, pp.
         409-420.

B-615.   Rodgers, A.   1984.   "The Contributions of Chauncy
         Harris to Geographical Studies of the Soviet
         Union: An Appreciation," Research Paper -
         University of Chicago, Department of Geography,
         No. 211, pp. 1-9.

B-616.   Rogers, Garry F. and Robertson, John M.   1986.
         "Henry Chandler Cowles,   1869-1939,"
         Geographers: Biobibliographical Studies, Vol.
         10, pp. 29-34.

B-617.   Romanova, Maria Mikhailovna.   1982.   "Aleksei
         Petrovich Pavlov, 1854-1929," Geographers:
         Biobibliographical Studies, Vol. 6, pp. 81-86.

B-618.   Rose, John Kerr. 1964.   "Griffith Taylor,
         1880-1963," Annals of the Association of American
         Geographers, Vol. 54, pp. 622-629.

B-619.   Rose, John Kerr.   1971.   "Stephen Sargent Visher,
         1887-1967," Annals of the Association of American
         Geographers, Vol. 61, pp. 394-406.

B-620.   Rosenkranz, Erhard.   1981.   "Heinrich
         Schmitthenner, 1887-1957," Geographers:
         Biobibliographical Studies, Vol. 5, pp. 117-122.

B-621.   Rudra, K.   1981.   "Identification of the Ancient
         Mouths of the Ganga as Described by Ptolemy,"
         Geographical Review of India, Vol. 43, pp.
         97-104.

B-622.   Ruiz-Gomez, Manuel Molla.   1986.   "Juan Dantin
         Cereceda, 1881-1943," Geographers:
         Biobibliographical Studies, Vol. 10, pp. 35-40.

B-623.   Rumble, Heber Eliot.   1943.   "Morse's School
         Geographies: An Eighteenth- Century Science
         Textbook Series Used at the Junior-High-School
         Level," Journal of Geography, Vol. 42, pp.
         174-180.

B-624.   Russell, Joseph A.   1958.   "Sidman Parmelee
         Poole, 1893-1955," Annals of the Association of
         American Geographers, Vol. 48, pp. 168-171.

B-625.   Russell, Joseph A.   1961.   "Lester E. Klimm,"
         Geographical Review, Vol. 51, pp. 424-426.

B-626.   Ryabchiicov, A. M. and Sdasyuk, G. V. 1963.
          "Professor Nikocai Nifocayevich Baransky,"
          Geographical Review of India, Vol. 25, pp.
          270-271.

B-627.   Ryan, Bruce. 1986. "Nevin Melancthon Fenneman,
          1865-1945," Geographers: Biobibliographical
          Studies, Vol. 10, pp. 57-68.

B-628.   Rzepa, Zbigniew. 1980. "Joachin Lelewel,
          1786-1861," Geographers: Biobibliographical
          Studies, Vol. 4, pp. 103-112.

B-629.   Salome, A. I. 1973. "Obituary: Professor Dr.
          William Van Rogen [sic] 1900-1973," Tijdschrift
          voor Economische en Sociale Geografie, Vol. 64,
          pp. 135-136.

B-630.   Sanderson, M. 1974. "Mary Somerville: Her Work
          in Physical Geography," Geographical Review, Vol.
          64, pp. 410-420.

B-631.   Sanderson, Marie. 1982. "Presidential Address:
          Griffith Taylor: A Geographer to Remember,"
          Canadian Geographer, Vol. 26, pp. 293-299.

B-632.   Sanguin, Andre-Louis. 1985. "Political
          Geographers of the Past II: Andre Siegfried, an
          Unconventional French Political Geographer,"
          Political Geography Quarterly, Vol. 4, pp. 79-84.

B-633.   Sargent, R. H. 1942. "Memoir of Colonel Claude
          Hall Birdseye," Annals of the Association of
          American Geographers, Vol. 32, pp. 309-315.

B-634.   Sarkar, R. M. 1976. "Nirman Kumar Bose: The
          Field Scientist," Geographical Review of India,
          Vol. 38, pp. 95-98.

B-635.   Sauer, Carl O. 1929. "Memorial of Ruliff S.
          Holway," Annals of the Association of American
          Geographers, Vol. 19, pp. 64-65.

B-636.   Sauer, Carl O. 1969. "David I. Blumenstock,
          1913-1963," Yearbook, Association of Pacific
          Coast Geographers, Vol. 30, pp. 9-12.

B-637.   Sauer, Carl O. 1971. "The Formative Years of
          Ratzel in the United States," Annals of the
          Association of American Geographers, Vol. 61, pp.
          245-254.

B-638.   Sauer, Carl. O. 1976. "Casual Remarks,"
          Historical Geography Newsletter, Vol. 6, pp.
          70-76.

B-639.   Saushkin, Yu. G.   1977.   "Excerpts From Letters
         by Berg on Theoretical Problems in Geography,"
         Soviet Geography: Review and Translation, Vol.
         18, pp. 23-32.

B-640.   Saushkin, Yu G.   1963.   "V. A. Anuchin's Doctoral
         Dissertation Defense," Soviet Geography: Review
         and Translation, Vol. 4, No. 1, pp. 53-59.

B-641.   Saushkin, Yu. G. and Smirnov, A. M.   1971.   "The
         Role of Lenin's Ideas in the Development of
         Theoretical Geography," Soviet Geography: Review
         and Translation, Vol. 12, pp. 559-569.

B-642.   Saushkin, Yu. G. et al.   1969.   "Boris Lnzarevich
         Gurevich (1904-1968)," Soviet Geography: Review
         and Translation, Vol. 10, pp. 353-354.

B-643.   Savors, Ann.   1962.   "Sir James Clark Ross,
         1800-62," Geographical Journal, Vol. 128, pp.
         325-328.

B-644.   Scarfe, Neville E.   1954.   "James Fairgrieve,
         1870-1953," Journal of Geography, Vol. 53, pp.
         84-86.

B-645.   Scarfe, Wolfgang.   1986.   "Max Eckert's
         Kartenwissen--Schaft-The Turning Point in German
         Cartography," Imago Mundi, Vol. 38, pp. 61-66.

B-646.   Schoen, Meera Guka.   1976.   "Research and Field
         Methods of Nirmal Kumar Bose," Geographical
         Review of India, Vol. 38, pp. 99-101.

B-647.   Scholten, Arnhild.   1980.   "Al-Muqaddasi, c.
         945-c.988," Geographers: Biobibliographical
         Studies, Vol. 4, pp. 1-6.

B-648.   Schroder, Karl Heinz.   1982.   "Robert Gradmann,
         1865-1950," Geographers: Biobibliographical
         Studies, Vol. 6, pp. 47-54.

B-649.   Schulz, J.   1978.   "Jacopo de Barbari's View of
         Venice: Map Making City Views and Moralized
         Geography Before the Year 1500," Art Bulletin,
         Vol. 60, pp. 427-474.

B-650.   Schwarz, Gabriele.   1986.   "Joseph Franz Maria
         Partsch, 1851-1925," Geographers: Biobiblio-
         graphical Studies, Vol. 10, pp. 125-134.

B-651.   Sevrin, Robert.   1985.   "Political Geography
         Around the World IV, Research Themes in
         Political Geography -- a French Perspective,"
         Political Geography Quarterly, Vol. 4, pp. 67-78.

B-652.   Shabad, Theodore. 1986. "Nikolay Nikolayevich
          Baranskiy, 1881-1963," Geographers: Biobiblio-
          graphical Studies, Vol. 10, pp. 1-16.

B-653.   Shafti, M. 1966. "Obituary - Professor Sir L.
          Dudley Stamp (1898-1966)," Geographer, Vol. 13,
          pp. 112-113.

B-654.   Shalowitz, A. 1959. "Mercator -- Map Maker
          Extraordinaire," Surveying and Mapping, Vol. 29,
          pp. 691-694.

B-655.   Shantz, Homer Leroy. 1936. "A Memoir of Curtis
          Fletcher Market," Annals of the Association of
          American Geographers, Vol. 26, pp. 113-124.

B-656.   Sheail, G. M. 1985. "The Papers of Professor
          Gordon Manley, Weather, Vol. 40, pp. 22-23.

B-657.   Sherwood, Morgan. 1977. "Alfred Hulse Brooks,
          1871-1924," Geographers: Biobibliographical
          Studies, Vol. 1, pp. 19-24.

B-658.   Shibanov, F. A. 1971. "Some Aspects of the
          Cartography of the Pre- Petrine Period (16th-17th
          Centuries) and the Role of S. Yu. Remezov in the
          History of Russian Cartography," Canadian
          Cartographer, Vol. 8, pp. 84-89.

B-659.   Shibanov, F. A. 1973. "The Essence and Content
          of the History of Cartography and the Results of
          Fifty Years of Work by Soviet Scholars," Canadian
          Cartographer, Vol. 10, pp. 21-25.

B-660.   Singh, D. N. 1972. "Ram Lochan Singh," Deccan
          Geographer, Vol. 10, pp. 102-104.

B-661.   Singh, Rann P. B. 1986. "Obituary: Preston
          James (1899-1986), John Barger Leightly
          (1895-1986)," National Geographical Journal of
          India, Vol. 32, pp. 275-277.

B-662.   Sinnhuber, K. 1959. "Alexander von Humboldt,
          1769-1859," Scottish Geographical Magazine, Vol.
          75, pp. 89-101.

B-663.   Sinnhuber, K. 1959. "Carl Ritter, 1779-1859,"
          Scottish Geographical Magazine, Vol. 75, pp.
          153-163.

B-664.   Sitwell, O. F. G. 1972. "John Pinkerton: An
          Armchair Geographer of the Early Nineteenth
          Century," Geographical Journal, Vol. 138, pp.
          470-479.

B-665.   Slabczynski, Waclaw. 1980. "Jan Stanislaw
          Kubarg, 1846-1896," Geographers:
          Biobibliographical Studies, Vol. 4, pp. 87-90.

B-666.   Smail, J. C.   1967.   "Douglas Alexander Allan:
          An Appreciation," Scottish Geographical Magazine,
          Vol. 83, pp. 197-198.

B-667.   Smith, Charles H.   1984.   "Alfred Russel Wallace,
          1823-1913," Geographers: Biobibliographical
          Studies, Vol. 8, pp. 125-134.

B-668.   Smith, Ernestine L.   1976.   "Marguerite Elizabeth
          Uttley, 1892-1976," Journal of Geography, Vol.
          75, p. 383.

B-669.   Smith, Gregory.   1976.   "Nonmember Geographers:
          Bernard De Voto and His Biographer, Wallace
          Stegner," Professional Geographer, Vol. 28, pp.
          147-150.

B-670.   Smith, Guy-Harold.   1948.   "Guy Woolard Conrey,
          1887-1948," Annals of the Association of American
          Geographers, Vol. 38, pp. 227-228.

B-671.   Smith, Guy-Harold.   1957.   "Roderick Peattie,
          1891-1955," Annals of the Association of American
          Geographers, Vol. 47, pp. 97-99.

B-672.   Smith, Guy-Harold.   1959.   "Armin Kohl Lobeck,
          Geomorphologist and Landscape Artist,
          1886-1958," Annals of the Association of American
          Geographers, Vol. 49, pp. 83-87.

B-673.   Smith, J. R.   1942.   "Mackinder: 1942," New
          Republic, Vol. 107, pp. 322- 323, Sept. 14.

B-674.   Smith, Neil.   1984.   "Political Geographers of
          the Past. Isaiah Bowman: Political Geography
          and Geopolitics," Political Geography Quarterly,
          Vol. 3, pp. 69-76.

B-675.   Smith, Neil.   1986.   "Bowman's New World and the
          Council on Foreign Relations," Geographical
          Review, Vol. 76, pp. 438-460.

B-676.   Smith, Philip S.   1925.   "Alfred Hulse Brooks."
          Annals of the Association of American
          Geographers, Vol. 15, pp. 159-161.

B-677.   Smith, Philip S.   1930.   "[Albert Perry Brigham]
          Geologist," Annals of the Association of American
          Geographers, Vol. 20, pp. 63-70.

B-678.   Smith, T. Russell.   1916.   "Ellsworth Huntington,
          Geographer," Bulletin of the Geographical Society
          of Philadelphia, Vol. 14, pp. 21-24.

B-679.   Solot, Michael.   1986.   "Carl Sauer and Cultural
          Evolution," Annals of the Association of American
          Geographers, Vol. 76, pp. 508-520.

B-680.   Spate, O. H. K.   1952.   "Toynbee and Huntington:
           A Study in Determinism," _Geographical Journal_,
           Vol. 120, pp. 406-428.

B-681.   Spate, O. H. K.   1953.   "The Compass of
           Geography," an Inaugural lecture given at the
           Australian National University, Canberry, 8
           September 1953, 29 pp.

B-682.   Spate, O. H. K.   1956.   "Modern Geography and Its
           Meaning for India," _National Geographical Journal
           of India_, Vol. 2, pp. 175-185.

B-683.   Spate, O. H. K.   1957.   "Region is a Term of
           Art," _Orbis_, Vol. 1, pp. 343-351.

B-684.   Spate, O. H. K.   1960.   "Lord Kelvin Rides
           Again," _Economic Geography_, Vol. 36, (facing) p.
           95.

B-685.   Spate, O. H. K.   1972. "Journeyman Taylor: Some
           Aspects of His Work (The Griffith Taylor Memorial
           Lecture, 1971)," _Australian Geographer_, Vol. 12,
           pp. 115-122.

B-686.   Spate, O. H. K.   1974.   "Ellsworth Huntington: A
           Geographical Giant: Review," _Geographical
           Journal_, Vol. 140, pp. 117-119.

B-687.   Spate, O. H. K. and Spate, A. P.   1985.   "Joseph
           Newell Jennings, 1916-1984," _Australian
           Geographical Studies_, Vol. 23, pp. 325-337.

B-688.   Specklin, Robert.   1979.   "Jacques Ancel,
           1882-1943," _Geographers: Biobibliographical
           Studies_, Vol. 3, pp. 1-6.

B-689.   Spencer, Joseph E.   1975.   "Carl Sauer: Memories
           About a Teacher," _California Geographer_, Vol. 15,
           pp. 83-86.

B-690.   Speth, William W.   1973.   "Julian H. Steward
           (1902-1972)," _Geographical Review_, Vol. 63, pp.
           117-119.

B-691.   Speth, William W.   1975.   "Friedrich Ratzel and
           the Shaping of American Anthropology,"
           _Proceedings of the Twenty-Second International
           Geographical Congress_, Vol. 7, pp. 230-233.

B-692.   Speth, William W.   1983.   "Clark Wissler,
           1870-1947," _Geographers: Biobibliographical
           Studies_, Vol. 7, pp. 151-154.

B-693.   Stablein, G.   1983.   "Alfred Wegner, from
           Research in Greenland to Plate Tectonics,"
           GeoJournal, Vol. 7, pp. 361-368.

B-694.   Stamp, L. Dudley.   1964.   "Sidney William
         Wooldridge (1900-1963)," Geographical Review,
         Vol. 54, pp. 129-131.

B-695.   Stanislawski, Dan.   1975.   "Carl Ortwin Sauer,
         1889-1975," Journal of Geography, Vol. 74, pp.
         549-554.

B-696.   Starkey, Otis P.   1966.   "John Ewing Orchard,
         1893-1963," Annals of the Association of American
         Geographers, Vol. 56, pp. 569-572.

B-697.   Starkey, Otis P.   1967.   "Joseph Russell Smith,
         1874-1966," Annals of the Association of American
         Geographers, Vol. 57, pp. 198-202.

B-698.   Steers, J. A.   1973.   "William Morris Davis:
         Review," Geographical Journal, Vol. 139, pp.
         524-528.

B-699.   Steers, J. A.   1982.   "A. R. Hinks and the Royal
         Geographical Society," Geographical Journal, Vol.
         148, pp. 1-7.

B-700.   Stephens, Nicholas.   1974.   "Obituary: Dr.
         Anthony Farrington: B.E., D.Sc., Sc.D.,
         1893-1973," Transactions - Institute of British
         Geographers, No. 62, pp. 154-158.

B-701.   Stevenson, W. Iain.   1978.   "Patrick Geddes,
         1854-1932," Geographers: Biobibliographical
         Studies, Vol. 2, pp. 53-68.

B-702.   Stoddart, D. R.   1966.   "Darwin's Impact on
         Geography," Annals of the Association of American
         Geographers, Vol. 56, pp. 683-698.

B-703.   Stoddart, D. R.   1975.   "'That Victorian
         Science': Huxley's Physiography and Its Impact
         on Geography," Transactions - Institute of
         British Geographers, Vol. 66, pp. 17-40.

B-704.   Stoddart, D. R.   1981.   "Humane Geographer: The
         Enigma of Elisée Reclus," Progress in Human
         Geography, Vol. 5, pp. 119-123.

B-705.   Stoddart, D. R.   1983.   "Biogeography: Darwin
         Devalued or Darwin Revalued," Progress in
         Physical Geography, Vol. 7, pp. 256-264.

B-706.   Stoddart, D. R.   1988.   "Obituary: James Alfred
         Steers," Transactions - Institute of British
         Geographers, Vol. 13, pp. 109-115.

B-707.   Storrie, M. C.   1969.   "William Bald, F.R.S.E.,
         C. 1789-1857:   Surveyor, Cartographer and Civil
         Engineer," Transactions - Institute of British
         Geographers, No. 47, pp. 205-232.

B-708.   Sullivan, Walter. 1963. "Vilhjalmur Stefansson,
          1879-1962," Geographical Review, Vol. 53, pp.
          287-291.

B-709.   Surface, George Thomas. 1909. "Thomas
          Jefferson: A Pioneer Student of American
          Geography," Bulletin of the American Geographical
          Society, Vol. 41, pp. 743-750.

B-710.   Sutton, Keith. 1979. "Augustin Bernard,
          1865-1947," Geographers: Biobibliographical
          Studies, Vol. 3, pp. 19-28.

B-711.   Tamsma, R. 1985. "In Memoriam: Professor Dr.
          H. J. Keuning," Tijdschrift voor Economische en
          Sociale Geografie, Vol. 76, p. 321.

B-712.   Taylor, E. 1963. "Richard Hakluyt and England's
          Sea Story," Geographical Magazine, Vol. 35, pp.
          694-703.

B-713.   Taylor, E. G. R. 1928. "Master John Dee: A
          Cambridge Geographer," Proceedings, Twelfth
          International Congress, pp. 439-443.

B-714.   Taylor, E. G. R. 1928. "William Bourne: A
          Chapter in Tudor Geography," Geographical
          Journal, Vol. 72, pp. 329-342.

B-715.   Taylor, E. G. R. 1929. "Roger Barlon: A New
          Chapter In Early Tudor Geography," Geographical
          Journal, Vol. 74, pp. 157-170.

B-716.   Taylor, E. G. R. 1931. "Compendium
          Cosmographiae: A Text-Book of Columbus,"
          Scottish Geographical Magazine, Vol. 47, pp.
          214-219.

B-717.   Taylor, E. G. R. 1962. "Geriard Mercator: A.D.
          1512-94," Geographical Journal, Vol. 128, pp.
          201-203.

B-718.   Teller, James T. 1983. "Jean de Charpentier,
          1786-1855," Geographers: Biobibliographical
          Studies, Vol. 7, pp. 17-22.

B-719.   Temple, Paul. 1977. "Obituary: Professor Harry
          Thorpe O.B.E., M.A., M. Litt., Ph.D., F.S.A.,
          1913-1977," Transactions - Institute of British
          Geographers, Vol. 2, pp. 255-256.

B-720.   Thoman, Richard S. 1979. "Robert Swanton Platt,
          1891-1964," Geographers: Biobibliographical
          Studies, Vol. 3, pp. 107-116.

B-721.   Thomas, Colin. 1985. "Anton Melik, 1890-1966,"
          Geographers: Biobibliographical Studies, Vol. 5,
          pp. 87-94.

B-722.   Thomas, Colin. 1986. "Emrys George Bowen,
          1900-1983," Geographers: Biobibliographical
          Studies, Vol. 10, pp. 17-24.

B-723.   Thomas, David. 1976. "[Emrys George Bowen: An
          Appreciation]," Cambria, Vol. 3, pp. 169-171.

B-724.   Thovez, Jean-Pierre. 1983. "Jacques M. May,
          1896-1975," Geographers: Biobibliographical
          Studies, Vol. 7, pp. 85-88.

B-725.   Thrower, Norman. 1964. "Geomorphology in
          Strabo's Geography," California Geographer, Vol.
          5, pp. 11-15.

B-726.   Thrower, Norman. 1969. "Edmond Halley as a
          Thematic Geo-Cartographer," Annals of the
          Association of American Geographers, Vol. 59, pp.
          652-676.

B-727.   Tiggesbaumker, Gunter. 1983. "Erich von
          Drygalski, 1865-1949," Geographers:
          Biobibliographical Studies, Vol. 7, pp. 23-30.

B-728.   Tilley, Philip D. 1980. "Hermann Lautensach,
          1886-1971," Geographers: Biobibliographical
          Studies, Vol. 4, pp. 91-102.

B-729.   Tilley, Philip D. 1984. "Carl Troll,
          1899-1975," Geographers: Biobibliographical
          Studies, Vol. 8, pp. 111-124.

B-730.   Tiwari, R. N. 1971. "Ram Nath Dubey
          (1896-1960)," Deccan Geographer, Vol. 9, pp.
          124-126.

B-731.   Tomkins, G. A. 1972. "Griffith Taylor and the
          Beginnings of Academic Geography in Canada,"
          Proceedings of the Twenty Second International
          Geographical Congress, pp. 939-941.

B-732.   Trindell, Roger T. 1969. "Franz Boas and
          American Geography," Professional Geographer,
          Vol. 21, pp. 328-331.

B-733.   Tsujita, Usao. 1977. "Naomasa Yamasaki,
          1870-1928," Geographers: Biobibliographical
          Studies, Vol. 1, pp. 113-118.

B-734.   Tsujita, Usao. 1982. "Takuji Ogawa, 1870-1941,"
          Geographers: Biobibliographical Studies, Vol. 6,
          pp. 71-76.

B-735.   Turner, B. C. III. 1987. "Comment on Leightly,"
          [regarding Sauer] Professional Geographer, Vol.
          39, pp. 415-416.

B-736.   Turnock, D. 1987. "Urban Geography and Urban
          Development in Romaina: The Contribution of
          Viotila Mihailescu," GeoJournal, Vol. 14, pp.
          181-202.

B-737.   Turnock, David. 1984. "Viotila Mihailescu,
          1890-1978," Geographers: Biobibliographical
          Studies, Vol. 8, pp. 61-68.

B-738.   Tweedie, Alan. 1984. "Obituary: K. W.
          Robinson," Australian Geographical Studies, Vol.
          22, pp. 156-157.

B-739.   Tyrrell, J. B. 1911. "David Thompson, a Great
          Geographer," Geographical Journal, Vol. 37, pp.
          49-59.

B-740.   Ulrich, J. 1986. "Johann Gottfried Otto
          Krummel, 1854-1912," Geographers:
          Biobibliographical Studies, Vol. 10, pp. 99-104.

B-741.   Unstead, J. F. 1949. "H. J. Mackinder and the
          New Geography," Geographical Journal, Vol. 113,
          pp. 47-58.

B-742.   Vallaux, C. 1934. "Paul Marie Vidal de la
          Blanche," in Encyclopedia of the Social Sciences,
          E. Seligman and A. Johnson, eds. New York:
          Macmillan, pp. 251-252, Vol. 15.

B-743.   Van Cleef, Eugene. 1970. "My Reminiscences
          Concerned with American Geography," Geographical
          Bulletin, Vol. 1, pp. 7-13.

B-744.   Van Royen, William. 1968. "Nels August
          Bengston, 1879-1963," Annals of the Association
          of American Geographers, Vol. 58, pp. 601-605.

B-745.   Van Valkenburg, S. 1959. "Charles F. Brooks,
          1891-1958," Annals of the Association of American
          Geographers, Vol. 49, pp. 461-465.

B-746.   Vasovic, Milorad. 1980. "Jovan Cvijic,
          1865-1927," Geographers: Biobibliographical
          Studies, Vol. 4, pp. 25-32.

B-747.   Vaughn, J. E. 1985. "William Hughes,
          1818-1876," Geographers: Biobibliographical
          Studies, Vol. 9, pp. 47-54.

B-748.   Visher, S. S. 1944. "Memoir of Arthur Keith,"
          Annals of the Association of American
          Geographers, Vol. 34, pp. 132-134.

B-749.   Visher, S. S. 1948. "Francois Emile Matthes,
          1874-1948," Annals of the Association of American
          Geographers, Vol. 38, pp. 301-304.

B-750.   Visher, S. S. 1948. "Memoir of Ellsworth
          Huntington, 1876-1947," Annals of the Association
          of American Geographers, Vol. 38, pp. 38-50.

B-751.   Visher, S. S. 1948. "Nelson H. Darton,
          1865-1948," Annals of the Association of American
          Geographers, Vol. 38, pp. 226.

B-752.   Visher, S. S. 1949. "Bailey Willis, 1857-1949,"
          Annals of the Association of American
          Geographers, Vol. 39, pp. 291-292.

B-753.   Visher, S. S. 1949. "Mark Jefferson,
          1863-1949," Annals of the Association of
          American Geographers, Vol. 39, pp. 307-312.

B-754.   Visher, Stephen S. 1950. "The Presidents and
          Vice Presidents of the AAG (1904-1948): Where
          They Received Their College and Graduate
          Training," Professional Geographer, Vol. 2, pp.
          41-46.

B-755.   Visher, S. S. 1952. "Herbert Ernest Gregory,
          1869-1952," Annals of the Association of American
          Geographers, Vol. 42, pp. 322-325.

B-756.   Visher, S. S. 1952. "Richard Elwood Dodge,
          1868-1952," Annals of the Association of American
          Geographers, Vol. 42, pp. 318-321.

B-757.   Visher, Stephen S. 1953. "Rollin D. Salisbury
          and Geography," Annals of the Association of
          American Geographers, Vol. 43, pp. 4-11.

B-758.   Visher, S. S. 1958. "Joseph Burton Kincer,
          1874-1954," Annals of the Association of American
          Geographers, Vol. 48, pp. 166-167.

B-759.   Visher, Stephen S. 1965. "Notable Contributors
          to American Geography," Professional Geographer,
          Vol. 17, No. 3, pp. 25-29.

B-760.   Visher, Stephen S. 1966. "Notable Contributors
          to American Geography, II," Professional
          Geographer, Vol. 18, pp. 227-229.

B-761.   Visher, S. S. and Hu, Charles Y. 1950. "Oliver
          Edwin Baker, 1883-1949," Annals of the
          Association of American Geographers, Vol. 40, pp.
          328-334.

B-762.   Von Engeln, O. D. 1912. "Emil Von Sydon and the
          Development of German School Cartography,"
          Bulletin of the American Geographical Society,
          Vol. 44, pp. 846-848.

B-763.   Von Engeln, O. D.   1912.   "Ralph Stockmann Tarr,"
         Bulletin of the American Geographical Society,
         Vol. 44, pp. 283-285.

B-764.   Von Engeln, O. D.   1940.   "Symposium: Walther
         Penck's Contribution to Geomorphology," Annals
         of the Association of American Geographers, Vol.
         30, pp. 219-236.

B-765.   Waites, Bryan.   1980.   "William Scoresby,
         1789-1857," Geographers: Biobibliographical
         Studies, Vol. 4, pp. 139-148.

B-766.   Waites, Bryan.   1985.   "Vaughan Cornish,
         1862-1948," Geographers: Biobibliographical
         Studies, Vol. 9, pp. 29-36.

B-767.   Wake, William H.   1968.   "John William Keith,
         March 22, 1914-August 9, 1967," California
         Geographer, Vol. 9, pp. 61-64.

B-768.   Walker, H. Jesse.   1980.   "Richard Joel Russell,
         1895-1971," Geographers: Biobibliographical
         Studies, Vol. 4, pp. 127-138.

B-769.   Wallis, Helen.   1973.   "Obituary: Raleigh Ashlin
         Skelton," Transactions - Institute of British
         Geographers, No. 58, pp. 139-148.

B-770.   Wallis, Helen.   1981.   "Obituary: Coolie Verner
         (1917-1979)," Imago Mundi, Vol. 33, pp. 99-102.

B-771.   Walters, Raymond.   1945.   "Nevin M. Fenneman,"
         Science, Vol. 102, pp. 142-143.

B-772.   Walton, K.   1966.   "Andrew C. O'Deel: An
         Appreciation," Scottish Geographical Magazine,
         Vol. 82, pp. 198-201.

B-773.   Ward, David.   1977.   "Andrew Hill Clark,
         1911-1975," Annals of the Association of American
         Geographers, Vol. 67, pp. 145-148.

B-774.   Ward, R. Gerard.   1960.   "Captain Alexander
         Maconochie, R.N., K.H., 1787-1860," Geographical
         Journal, Vol. 126, pp. 459-468.

B-775.   Ward, R. Gerard.   1985.   "On Cooke's Second Law,"
         Area, Vol. 17, pp. 322-324.

B-776.   Ward, Robert DeC.   1909.   "Geography at Harvard
         University," Journal of Geography, Vol. 7, pp.
         105-108.

B-777.   Ward, Robert DeCourcy.   1913.   "Memoir of Albert
         Lawrence Rotch," Annals of the Association of
         American Geographers, Vol. 3, pp. 99-102.

B-778.   Warkentin, John.   1987.   "Obituary/George Tatham,
          1907-1987," _Canadian Geographer_, Vol. 31, pp.
          381.

B-779.   Warman, Henry J.   1977.   "Samuel Van Valkenburg,
          1890-1976," _Annals of the Association of American
          Geographers_, Vol. 67, pp. 273-277.

B-780.   Watson, J. Wreford.   1968.   "Arthur Geddes: An
          Appreciation," _Scottish Geographical Magazine_,
          Vol. 84, pp. 127-128.

B-781.   Watson, J. Wreford.   1976.   "Land Use and Adam
          Smith: A Bicentennial Note," _Scottish
          Geographical Magazine_, Vol. 92, pp. 127-134.

B-782.   Weaver, D. C.   1981.   "Henry Mayhew--A Neglected
          Pioneer of Urban and Social Geography," _Ecumene_,
          Vol. 13, pp. 28-34.

B-783.   Whatman, Norman H.   1975.   "George Jobberns: A
          Tribute on Behalf of Early Students," _New Zealand
          Journal of Geography_, Vol. 59, pp. 31-32.

B-784.   Wheeler, Keith.   1978.   "Geoffrey Edward
          Hutchings, 1900-1964," _Geographers:
          Biobibliographical Studies_, Vol. 2, pp. 67-72.

B-785.   Whitaker, J. Russell.   1940.   "Memoir of Almon
          Ernest Parkins," _Annals of the Association of
          American Geographers_, Vol. 31, pp. 46-50.

B-786.   Whitbeck, R. H.   1930.   "[Albert Perry Brigham]
          Human Geographer," _Annals of the Association of
          American Geographers_, Vol. 20, pp. 73-81.

B-787.   White, Gilbert F.   1974.   "Edward A. Ackerman,
          1911-1973," _Annals of the Association of American
          Geographers_, Vol. 64, pp. 297-309.

B-788.   Whittlesey, Derwent.   1951.   "Kirk Bryan,
          1888-1950," _Annals of the Association of American
          Geographers_, Vol. 41, pp. 88-94.

B-789.   Wilcock, A. A.   1974.   "The English Strabo: The
          Geographical Publications of John Pinkerton,"
          Geographical Journal, Vol. 139, pp. 116-119.

B-790.   Wilcock, A. A.   1977.   "Fritz Loewe, 1895-1974,"
          Australian Geographer, Vol. 13, pp. 306-310.

B-791.   Wilcock, Arthur A.   1975.   "The Geographer Before
          1800," _Area_, Vol. 7, pp. 45-46.

B-792.   Wileman, D.   1973.   "Karl Baer and the
          Development of Russian Geography," _Geographical
          Journal_, Vol. 139, pp. 116-119.

B-793.   Williams, Donovan. 1968. "Clements Robert
          Markham and the Geographical Department of the
          India Office, 1867-77," Geographical Journal,
          Vol. 134, pp. 343-352.

B-794.   Williams, Frank E. 1930. "[Albert Perry
          Brigham] Geographer-Envoy from America to
          Europe," Annals of the Association of American
          Geographers, Vol. 20, pp. 86-90.

B-795.   Williams, Frank E. 1933. "Memoir of Henry Grier
          Bryant," Annals of the Association of American
          Geographers, Vol. 23, pp. 247-250.

B-796.   Williams, Frank E. 1940. "Memoir of Ray Hughes
          Whitbeck: Geographer, Teacher, and Man," Annals
          of the Association of American Geographers, Vol.
          30, pp. 210-218.

B-797.   Williams, Frank E. 1956. "Lawrence Martin,
          1880-1955," Annals of the Association of American
          Geographers, Vol. 46, pp. 357-364.

B-798.   Williams, M. 1978. "George Woodroofe Goyder: A
          Practical Geographer," Proceedings, Royal
          Geographic Society of Australasia, Vol. 79, pp.
          1-21.

B-799.   Williams, Michael. 1983. "'The Apple of My
          Eye': Carl Sauer and Historical Geography,"
          Journal of Historical Geography, Vol. 9, pp.
          1-28.

B-800.   Williams, Michael. 1987. "Sauer and Man's Role
          in Changing the Face of the Earth," Geographical
          Review, Vol. 77, pp. 218-231.

B-801.   Winsberg, M. D. 1981. "James Richard Anderson,
          1919-1980," Southeastern Geographer, Vol. 21, pp.
          1-9.

B-802.   Wise, M. J. 1975. "A University Teacher of
          Geography," Transactions - Institute of British
          Geographers, Vol. 66, pp. 1-16.

B-803.   Wise, M. J. 1983. "Three Foudner Members of the
          I.B.G.: T. Ogilvie Buchanan, Sir Dudley Stamp,
          S. W. Wooldridge. A Personal Tribute,"
          Transactions - Institute of British Geographers,
          Vol. 8, pp. 41-54.

B-804.   Wise, M. J. 1986. "The Scott Keltie Report,
          1885, and the Teaching of Geography in Great
          Britain," Geographical Journal, Vol. 152, pp.
          367-382.

B-805.   Wise, Michael J.   1980.   "Llewellyn Rodwell
          Jones, 1881-1947," Geographers: Biobiblio-
          graphical Studies, Vol. 4, pp. 49-54.

B-806.   Winston, Victor H.   1987.   "Ted Shabad: A
          Eulogy," Soviet Geography: Review and
          Translation, Vol. 28, pp. 373-375.

B-807.   Wolf, Laurence G.   1970.   "John Wesley Coulter,
          1893-1967," Annals of the Association of American
          Geographers, Vol. 60, pp. 185-188.

B-808.   Wood, Walter A. and Washburn, A. Lincoln.   1973.
          "Louise Arner Boyd (1887-1972)," Geographical
          Review, Vol. 63, pp. 229-282.

B-809.   Wright, John K.   1944.   "Douglas Johnson,
          1878-1944," Geographical Review, Vol. 34, pp.
          317-318.

B-810.   Wright, John K.   1961.   "Daniel Coit Gilman,
          Geographer and Historian," Geographical Review,
          Vol. 51, pp. 381-399.

B-811.   Wright, John K.   1962.   "Miss Semple's Influences
          of the Geographic Environment, Notes Toward a
          Bibliography," Geographical Review, Vol. 52, pp.
          346-361.

B-812.   Wrigley, Gladys M.   1950.   "Hugh Robert Mill: An
          Appreciation," Geographical Review, Vol. 40, pp.
          657-660.

B-813.   Wrigley, Gladys M.   1951.   "Isaiah Bowman,"
          Geographical Review, Vol. 41, pp. 7-65.

B-814.   Yacher, Leon.   1982.   "Erwin Josephus Raisz,
          1893-1968," Geographers: Biobibliographical
          Studies, Vol. 6, pp. 93-98.

B-815.   Yugai, R. L.   1983.   "Ivan Vasylievitch
          Mushketov, 1850-1902," Geographers:
          Biobibliographical Studies, Vol. 7, pp. 89-92.

B-816.   Yugai, R. L.   1984.   "Alexei Pavlovich Fedchenko,
          1844-1873," Geographers: Biobibliographical
          Studies, Vol. 8, pp. 35-38.

B-817.   Yugai, R. L.   1984.   "Sergei Semyonovich
          Neustruev, 1874-1928," Geographers:
          Biobibliographical Studies, Vol. 8, pp. 77-80.

B-818.   Yugai, R. L.   1985.   "Peter Iranovich Rychkov,
         1712-1777," Geographers: Biobibliographical
         Studies, Vol. 9, pp. 109-112.

B-819.   Zabelin, I. M.   1981.   "Andrei Alexandrovich
         Grigoryev, 1883-1968," Geographers:
         Biobibliographical Studies, Vol. 5, pp. 55-62.

B-820.   Zaidi, Iqtidar H.   1971.   "Kazi S. Ahmad,
         1904-1970," Pakistan Geographical Review, Vol.
         25, pp. 50-54.

B-821.   Zhongming, Sun.   1986.   The Contribution of Xu
         Xiake's Famous Work - 'Travel Note for Tracing to
         River Source - to Geography," Scientific
         Geographica Sinica, Vol. 6, pp. 64-69 [English
         Summary].

B-822.   Zimmerman, Frances.   1930.   "Geography as a Life
         Career," Journal of Geography, Vol. 29, pp.
         30-34.

B-823.   Zimmermann, Susanne and Dorflinger, Johannes.
         1983.   "Eugen Oberhummer,   1859-1944,"
         Geographers: Biobibliographical Studies, Vol. 7,
         pp. 93-100.

Geography and Other Disciplines

C-1. Ackerman, Edward A. 1962. "Public Policy Issues for the Professional Geographer," _Annals of the Association of American Geographers_, Vol. 52, pp. 292-298.

C-2. Adams, John S. 1979. "A Geographical Basis for Urban Public Policy," _Professional Geographer_, Vol. 31, pp. 135-145.

C-3. Agafonov, N. T., _et al_. 1976. "Population Geography and Socio-Economic Planning," _Soviet Geography_: _Review and Translation_, Vol. 17, pp. 377-383.

C-4. Agafonov, N. T., _et al_. 1982. "The Tasks of Geography in Connection With the Perfecting of Economic Planning," _Soviet Geography_: _Review and Translation_, Vol. 23, pp. 270-276.

C-5. Agnew, J. A., and Duncan, J. S. 1981. "The Transfer of Ideas into Anglo-American Human Geography," _Progress in Human Geography_, Vol. 5, pp. 42-57.

C-6. Alexander, John W. 1959. "Geography: As Some Others See It," _Professional Geographer_, Vol. 11, pp. 2-5.

C-7. Allen, Lyman R. 1903. "The Correlation of Geography and History," _Journal of Geography_, Vol. 2, pp. 404-415.

C-8. Alpert, Harry. 1957. "Geography, Social Science, and the National Science Foundation," _Professional Geographer_, Vol. 9, pp. 7-9.

C-9.   Anderson, James R. 1979. "Geographers in
        Government," Professional Geographer, Vol. 31,
        pp. 265-270.

C-10.   Andrews, A. W. 1897. "The Teaching of Geography
        in Relation to History," Geographical Journal,
        Vol. 9, pp. 427-441.

C-11.   Anonymous. 1918. "The Aim of Geography,"
        Journal of Geography, Vol. 17, pp. 111-112.

C-12.   Appleton, J. 1978. "What Makes a Place
        Beautiful," Horizon, Vol. 26, pp. 37-41.

C-13.   Aschmann, Homer. 1958. "Geography and the
        Liberal Arts College," Professional Geographer,
        Vol. 10, pp. 2-6.

C-14.   Avsyuk, G. A., et al. 1963. "Geography in the
        System of Earth Sciences," Soviet Geography:
        Review and Translation, Vol. 4, No. 8, pp. 3-14.

C-15.   Bergstrom, Roger C. and Ehrenberger, Donald S.
        1975. "Geography and English: An
        Interdisciplinary Approach to the City," Journal
        of Geography, Vol. 74, pp. 463-468.

C-16.   Blunden, J. R. 1983. "Andrew Learnmonth and the
        Evaluation of Medical Geography, in Geographical
        Aspects of Health, N. D. McGlashan & J. R.
        Blunden, eds., (Academic Press), pp. 15-32.

C-17.   Boggs, S. W. 1948. "Geographic and Other
        Scientific Techniques for Political Science,"
        American Political Science Review, Vol. 42, pp.
        223-238.

C-18.   Boggs, S. W. 1948. "Geographic Techniques in
        Political Science," Annals of the Association of
        American Geographers, Vol. 38, pp. 93-94.

C-19.   Bose, N. K. 1953. "The Role of Social Science,"
        Geographical Review of India, Vol. 15, No. 1,
        n.p.

C-20.   Bouwer, K. 1985. "Ecological and Spatial
        Traditions in Geography, and the Study of
        Environmental Problems," GeoJournal, Vol. 11, pp.
        307-312.

C-21.   Bowen, M. 1985. "The Ecology of Knowledge:
        Linking the Natural and Social Sciences,"
        Geoforum, Vol. 16, pp. 213-226.

C-22.   Branom, Mendel E. 1926. "Geography and the
        Social Sciences," Journal of Geography, Vol. 25,
        pp. 161-168.

C-23.   Brown, Robert M.   1924.   "The Bounds of Racial
         Geography," _Journal of Geography_, Vol. 23, pp.
         41-48.

C-24.   Brown, W. G.   1931.   "Modern Geography and Its
         Relation to Sociology," _Sociological Bureau_, Vol.
         23, pp. 188-194.

C-25.   Brown, Wendell J.   1961.   "A Lawyer Looks at the
         Name Geography," _Professional Geographer_, Vol.
         13, No. 3, pp. 16-19.

C-26.   Buchanan, J. Y.   1895.   "A Retrospect of
         Oceanography During the Last Twenty Years,"
         _Proceedings - Sixth International Geographical
         Congress_, pp. 403-435.

C-27.   Burgess, Jacqueline and Lee, Roger.   1985.   "Only
         Connect? Thoughts on Geography, Social Science
         and the Media," _Area_, Vol. 17, pp. 247-250.

C-28.   Buttimer, Anne.   1969.   "Social Space in
         Interdisciplinary Perspective," _Geographical
         Review_, Vol. 59, pp. 417-426.

C-29.   Carey, Everett P.   1911.   "General Science in
         Relation to Physical Geography," _Journal of
         Geography_, Vol. 10, pp. 62-66.

C-30.   Carney, Frank.   1908.   "State Geological Surveys
         and Practical Geography," _Bulletin of the
         American Geographical Society_, Vol. 40, pp.
         530-535.

C-31.   Chakkaborty, Satyesh C.   1973.   "Meaning of
         Regions in Social Science Research: A
         Geographer's Point of View," _Geographical Review
         of India_, Vol. 35, pp. 1-14.

C-32.   Chandler, T. J.   1976.   "Geographers in Public
         Science," _Area_, Vol. 8, pp. 87-93.

C-33.   Chapman, Conrad and Brooks, Charles F.   1944.
         "Meteorology in the Warring Forties: A Review,"
         Geographical Review, Vol. 34, pp. 466-475.

C-34.   Chisholm, Michael.   1969.   "Social Science
         Research in Geography," _Area_, Vol. 1, pp. 8-9.

C-35.   Chisholm, Michael.   1973.   "The Corridors of
         Geography," _Area_, Vol. 5, p. 43.

C-36.   Christensen, David E.   1977.   "Geography and
         Planning: Some Perspectives," _Professional
         Geographer_, Vol. 29, pp. 148-152.

C-37.   Clark, Austin H.   1929.   "Geography and Zoology,"
        Annals of the Association of American
        Geographers, Vol. 17, pp. 101-146.

C-38.   Clarkson, James D.   1970.   "Ecology and Spatial
        Analysis," Annals of the Association of American
        Geographers, Vol. 60, pp. 700-716.

C-39.   Cooper, Sherwin H.   1966.   "Theoretical
        Geography, Applied Geography and Planning,"
        Professional Geographer, Vol. 18, pp. 1-2.

C-40.   Cowen, Joel B.   1971.   "The Place of Geography in
        the Liberal Arts," Journal of Geography, Vol.
        70, pp. 135-136.

C-41.   Cox, K.   1976.   "American Geography: Social
        Science Emergent," Social Science Quarterly, Vol.
        57, pp. 182-207.

C-42.   Dann, E. W.   1906.   "Orography and History,"
        Journal of the Manchester Geographical Society,
        Vol. 22, pp. 56-64.

C-43.   Darby, H. C.   1953.   "On the Relations of
        Geography and History," Transactions and Papers -
        Institute of British Geographers, No. 19, pp.
        1-12.

C-44.   Daysh, G. H. J. and O'Dell, A. C.   1947.
        "Geography and Planning," Geographical Journal,
        Vol. 109, pp. 103-107.

C-45.   Dodoo, Robert, Jr.   1971.   "The Use of
        Speculative Social Thought in Geographic
        Research," Professional Geographer, Vol. 23, pp.
        295-297.

C-46.   Doerr, Arthur H. and Sieve, Kenneth.   1971.
        "Nonsense Geography--Or Is It?" Journal of
        Geography, Vol. 70, pp. 169-174.

C-47.   Duke of Argyll.   1890.   "Border Lands Between
        Geology and Geography," Scottish Geographical
        Magazine, Vol. 6, pp. 169-182.

C-48.   Dunbar, G. S.   1983.   "Geography Rides, Geology
        Walks: The Barrett- Huntington Expedition to
        Central Asia in 1905." Yearbook, Association of
        Pacific Coast Geographers, Vol. 45, pp. 7-23.

C-49.   Dury, G. H.   1983.   "Geography and Geomor-
        phology: the Last Fifty Years," Transactions -
        Institute of British Geographers, Vol. 8, pp.
        90-99.

C-50.   Eliot Hurst, Michael E.   1971.   "Geography and
         the Contemporary Urban   Scene," Journal of
         Geography, Vol. 70, pp. 110-114.

C-51.   Eliot Hurst, Michael E.   1980.   "Geography,
         Social Science and Society," Australian
         Geographical Studies, Vol. 18, pp. 3-21.

C-52.   Ellen, Roy.   1988.   "Persistence and Change in
         the Relationship Between Anthropology and Human
         Geography," Progress in Human Geography, Vol. 12,
         pp. 229-269.

C-53.   Englebert, Ernest.   1954.   "The Contributions of
         Political Science to the Theory and Methodology
         of Regionalism," Professional Geographer, Vol. 6,
         No. 5, pp. 15-19.

C-54.   Fahy, G.   1974.   "Geography in the Early Irish
         Monastic Schools: A Brief Review of MacCosse's
         Geographical Poems," Geographical Viewpoint, Vol.
         3, pp. 31-45.

C-55.   Fenneman, Nevin M.   1922.   "Functions of the
         Division of Geology and Geography in the National
         Research Council," Science, Vol. 56, pp. 620-624.

C-56.   Fenneman, Nevin M.   1922.   "The Place of
         Physiography in Geography," Journal of
         Geography, Vol. 21, pp. 20-23.

C-57.   Floyd, B. and O'Brien, D.   1976.   "Whither
         Geography? A Cautionary Tale From Economics,"
         Area, Vol. 8, pp. 15-23.

C-58.   Fosberg, F. R.   1976.   "Geography, Ecology, and
         Biogeography," Annals of the Association of
         American Geographers, Vol. 66, pp. 117-128.

C-59.   Gamble, Cline.   1987.   "Archaeology, Geography
         and Time," Progress in Human Geography, Vol. 11,
         pp. 227-246.

C-60.   Geddes, Arthur.   1948.   "Geography, Sociology,
         and Psychology: A Plea for Coordinators,"
         Geographical Review, Vol. 38, pp. 590-597.

C-61.   Gilg, A. W.   1978.   "Geography and Landscape
         Architecture," Progress in Human Geography, Vol.
         2, pp. 183-185.

C-62.   Glassner, Martin Ira.   1977.   "Geographers and
         the Law of the Sea," Geographical Survey, Vol. 6,
         pp. 9-13.

C-63.   Gray, Fred.   1976.   "Radical Geography and the
         Study of Education," Antipode, Vol. 8, pp. 38-44.

C-64.   Griffin, Donald W.   1965.   "Some Comments on
         Urban Planning and the   Geographer," Professional
         Geographer, Vol. 17, pp. 4-6.

C-65.   Grossman, Larry.   1977.   "Man-Environmental
         Relationships in Anthropology and Geography,"
         Annals of the Association of American
         Geographers, Vol. 67, pp. 126-144.

C-66.   Harris, Britton.   1983.   "Interdisciplinary
         Disciplines," Geographical Analysis, Vol. 15, pp.
         47-50.

C-67.   Harrison, James D.   1977.   "Geography and
         Planning: Convenient Relationship or Necessary
         Marriage?," Geographical Survey, Vol. 6, pp.
         11-24.

C-68.   Harrison, James D. and Larsen, Robert D.   1977.
         "Geography and Planning: The Need for an Applied
         Interface," Professional Geographer, Vol. 29, pp.
         139-147.

C-69.   Hayden, Robert S.   1982.   "The Place of Geography
         in the Sciences,"   Virginia Geographer, Vol. 24,
         pp. 57-62.

C-70.   Hayes, E. S.   1908.   "Sociology, Psychology and
         Geography," American Journal of Sociology, Vol.
         14, pp. 371-407.

C-71.   Hicks, D.   1981.   "The Contribution of Geography
         to Multi-Cultural Misunderstanding," Teaching
         Geography, Vol. 7, pp. 64-67.

C-72.   Hoy, Don R.   1970.   "Geographic Research in
         Development of Guatemala,"   East Lakes
         Geographer, Vol. 6, pp. 74-80.

C-73.   Huckle, John.   1978.   "Geography and Values in
         Higher Education," Journal of Geography in Higher
         Education, Vol. 2, pp. 57-67.

C-74.   Hunt, J.   1980.   "Cartography and Geography:
         Some Interactions and Developments," Bulletin:
         Society of University Cartographers, Vol. 14, pp.
         35-37.

C-75.   Huntington, Ellsworth.   1914.   "The Geographer
         and History," Geographical Journal, Vol. 43, pp.
         19-32.

C-76.   Huntington, Ellsworth.   1937.   "Geography and
         History," Canadian Journal of Economics and
         Political Science, Vol. 3, pp. 565-572.

C-77.   Il'yina, R. P. 1981. "Geographical Problems in
         Bioresource Science," Soviet Geography: Review
         and Translation, Vol. 22, pp. 30-42.

C-78.   Inskeep, Edward L. 1962. "The Geographer in
         Planning," Professional Geographer, Vol. 14, pp.
         22-24.

C-79.   Iyer, S. S. 1953. "Social Studies Versus
         Geography," Bombay Geographical Magazine, Vol. 1,
         pp. 69-72.

C-80.   Jackson, John N. 1967. "Geography and
         Planning: Two Subjects, or One?" Canadian
         Geographer, Vol. 11, pp. 357-365.

C-81.   Jeffries, Ella. 1926. "The Dependence of the
         Social Sciences Upon Geographic Principles,"
         Journal of Geography, Vol. 25, pp. 228-236.

C-82.   Johnston, R. J. 1972. "Geography, the Social
         Sciences and Social Studies," New Zealand Journal
         of Geography, Vol. 52, pp. 18-21.

C-83.   Johnston, Ron. 1977. "On Geography and the
         Organization of Education," Journal of Geography
         in Higher Education, Vol. 1, pp. 5-12.

C-84.   Johnston, Ron. 1978. "More on the Structure of
         British Education and the Role of Geography,"
         Journal of Geography in Higher Education, Vol. 2,
         pp. 6-13.

C-85.   Jones, H. 1979. "Population Policies and the
         Geographer," Area, Vol. 11, pp. 175-176.

C-86.   Karpinski, Louis C. 1923. "The Contribution of
         Mathematicians and Astronomers to Scientific
         Cartography," Annals of the Association of
         American Geographers, Vol. 13, pp. 211-212.

C-87.   Kirkby, Richard. 1977. "Geography and Planning
         at Nanking University: Winter 1977," China
         Geographer, No. 2, pp. 51-58.

C-88.   Kirwan, L. P. 1965. "Geography as a Social
         Study: Review," Geographical Journal, Vol. 131,
         pp. 373-375.

C-89.   Klee, Gary A. 1975. "Future Series and
         Geography," Journal of Geography, Vol. 74, pp.
         430-436.

C-90.   Konstantinov, F. V. 1964. "Interaction Between
         Nature and Society and Modern Geography," Soviet
         Geography: Review and Translation, Vol. 5, pp.
         61-73.

C-91.   Konstantinov, O. A.   1976.   "Economic Geography
        and Regional Economics," Soviet Geography:
        Review and Translation, Vol. 17, pp. 28-37.

C-92.   Landgraf, John L.   1953.   "Cultural Anthropology
        and Human Geography," Transactions, New York
        Academy of Sciences,   ser. 2, Vol. 15, pp.
        152-156.

C-93.   Lapworth, Charles.   1903.   "The Relations of
        Geology," Scottish Geographical Magazine, Vol.
        19, pp. 393-417.

C-94.   Lillywhite, J.   1961.   "The Geographer and
        Planning," Northern Universities Geographical
        Journal, Vol. 2, pp. 65-67.

C-95.   Livingstone, D. N.   1984.   "Science and Society:
        Historical Reflections on the Geographical
        Experiment," Geoforum, Vol. 16, pp. 119-130.

C-96.   Lock, Chris.   1978.   "The Role of Ecology Within
        Geography," Geoscope, Vol. 9, pp. 51-56.

C-97.   Lukerman, F.   1961.   "The Concept of Location in
        Classical Geography," Annals of the Association
        of American Geographers, Vol. 51, pp. 194-210.

C-98.   Makunina, A. A.   1977.   "Landscape Science and
        Regional Physical Geography," Soviet Geography:
        Review and Translation, Vol. 18, pp. 68-75.

C-99.   Marchand, Bernard.   1972.   "Information Theory
        and Geography," Geographical Analysis, Vol. 4,
        pp. 234-257.

C-100. Markham, Clements R.   1893.   "The Limits Between
        Geology and Physical Geography," Scottish
        Geographical Magazine, Vol. 9, pp. 633-639.

C-101. Mason, Col. Charles H.   1948.   "The Role of the
        Geographer in Military Planning," Annals of the
        Association of American Geographers, Vol. 38, pp.
        104-105.

C-102. Mason, Peter F. and Kuhn, Michael W.   1971.
        "Geography and Environmental Studies: The Fifth
        Tradition," Journal of Geography, Vol. 70, pp.
        91-94.

C-103. Mathes, Francois E.   1933.   "The Committee on
        Glaciers of the American Geophysical Union, and
        Its Work," Annals of the Association of American
        Geographers, Vol. 23, pp. 49-50.

C-104. Matley, Ian. 1966. "The Marxist Approach to the
        Geographical Environment," Annals of the
        Association of American Geographers, Vol. 56, pp.
        97-111.

C-105. McKinney, William M. 1961. "Geography and the
        Social Sciences -- A New Approach," Journal of
        Geography, Vol. 60, pp. 66-70.

C-106. McNee, Robert B. 1959. "The Changing
        Relationships of Economics and Economic
        Geography," Economic Geography, Vol. 35, pp.
        189-198.

C-107. McNee, Robert B. 1966. "The Structure of
        Geography and Its Potential Contribution to
        Generalist Education for Planning," Professional
        Geographer, Vol. 18, pp. 63-68.

C-108. McNee, Robert B. 1970. "Regional Planning,
        Bureaucracy and Geography," Economic Geography,
        Vol. 46, pp. 190-198.

C-109. Mercer, David. 1972. "Behavioural Geography and
        the Sociology of Social Action," Area, Vol. 4,
        pp. 48-52.

C-110. Mikesell, Marvin W. 1967. "Geographic
        Perspectives in Anthropology," Annals of the
        Association of American Geographers, Vol. 57, pp.
        617-634.

C-111. Mikesell, Marvin W. 1969. "Geography and Its
        Neighbors: Comments on the International
        Encyclopedia of the Social Sciences,"
        Geographical Review, Vol. 59, pp. 276-283.

C-112. Mill, Hugh Robert. 1887. "The Relations Between
        Commerce and Geography," Scottish Geographical
        Magazine, Vol. 3, pp. 626-638.

C-113. Mitchell, L. 1934. "Social Studies and
        Geography," Progress in Education, Vol. 11, pp.
        97-105.

C-114. Mitchell, Robert B. 1961. "On Paradigms and
        Paradiddles: A City Planner Looks at Regional
        Science," Papers of the Regional Science
        Association, Vol. 7, pp. 7-15.

C-115. Morgan, W. B. and Moss, R. P. 1965. "Geography
        and Ecology: The Concept of the Community and
        Its Relationship to Environment," Annals of the
        Association of American Geographers, Vol. 55, pp.
        339-350.

C-116.   Morris, John W.   1950.   "The Role of the
          Geographers in Social Surveys," Professional
          Geographer, Vol. 2, pp. 23-27.

C-117.   Mosley, J. G.   1977.   "Geography and
          Conservation," Australian Geographical Studies,
          Vol. 15, pp. 95-103.

C-118.   Nash, P.   1977.   "Future Studies and the
          Geo-Bio-Sciences," GeoJournal,   Vol. 1, pp.
          13-16.

C-119.   Nolan, M. Olive.   1928.   "Correlation of
          Geography, History, Civics and Economics,"
          Journal of Geography, Vol. 27, pp. 76-81.

C-120.   Norton, W. H.   1918.   "Earth Science in American
          Colleges and Universities," School and Society,
          Vol. 8, pp. 702-706.

C-121.   Nowak, W. S.   1970.   "On the Interdisciplinary
          Approach to Geography," Journal of Geography,
          Vol. 69, pp. 401-403.

C-122.   Nowak, W. S. W.   1963.   "Economic Oceanography as
          a Geographic Science," Professional Geographer,
          Vol. 15, No. 1, pp. 1-4.

C-123.   Ogden, Philip E.   1986.   "Demographers in Need of
          Geographers," Area, Vol. 18, pp. 33-34.

C-124.   Ogilvie, Alan G.   1938.   "The Relations of
          Geology and Geography," Geography, Vol. 23, pp.
          75-82.

C-125.   Olson, John Alden.   1975.   "A Geographical Basis
          for Educational Planning," Journal of Geography,
          Vol. 74, pp. 279-284.

C-126.   O'Riordan, Timothy.   1970.   "New Conservation and
          Geography," Area,   Vol. 2, pp. 33-36.

C-127.   Parker, Frances W.   1893. "Relations of Geography
          to History," National Geographic Magazine, Vol.
          5, p. 125.

C-128.   Parson, Ruben L.   1961.   "Geography and Resource
          Management," Journal of Geography, Vol. 60, pp.
          399-406.

C-129.   Parsons, James J.   1985.   "On Bioregionalism and
          Watershed Consciousness," Professional
          Geographer, Vol. 37, pp. 1-5.

C-130.   Peattie, Roderick.   1940.   "The Fields of
          Environmentalism," Annals of the Association of
          American Geographers, Vol. 30, pp. 68.

C-131.   Pocock, Douglas C. D.   1988.   "Geography and
         Literature," Progress in Human Geography, Vol.
         12, pp. 87-102.

C-132.   Pokshishevskiy, V. V.   1976.   "Interpenetration
         and Interaction Between Geography and
         Ethnography," Soviet Geography: Review and
         Translation, Vol. 17, pp. 665-679.

C-133.   Portugali, Juval.   1984.   "Location Theory in
         Geography and Archaeology," Geography Research
         Forum, Vol. 7, pp. 43-60.

C-134.   Pruitt, Amy M.   1947.   "The Geographer in Public
         Health Research," Professional Geographer, Vol.
         6, pp. 15-16.

C-135.   Raup, Hugh M.   1942.   "Trends in the Development
         of Geographic Botany," Annals of the Association
         of American Geographers, Vol. 32, pp. 319-354.

C-136.   Renfrew, C.   1976.   "Archaeology and the Earth
         Sciences," in Davidson, D. A. and M. L.
         Schachley, eds., Geoarchaeology, London:
         Duckworth, pp. 1-5.

C-137.   Renfrew, Colin, Wagstaff, J. M. and Tharnes,
         J. B.   1983.   "Geology, Archaeology and
         Environment," Geographical Journal, Vol. 149, pp.
         316-333.

C-138.   Renner, G. T.   1926.   "Geography's Affiliations,"
         Journal of Geography, Vol. 25, pp. 267-272.

C-139.   Renner, G. T.   1943.   "Air Age Geography,"
         Harper, Vol. 187, pp. 38-41, July.

C-140.   Rich, John L.   1948.   "Goals and Trends of
         Research in Geology and Geography," Science, Vol.
         107, pp. 581-584.

C-141.   Richards, Greg.   1984.   "Common Ground:
         Geomorphology and Archaeology," Bloomsburg
         Geographer, Vol. 12, pp. 76-79.

C-142.   Robinson, J. Lewis.   1956.   "Geography and
         Regional Planning," Canadian Geographer, Vol. 8,
         pp. 1-8.

C-143.   Rorabacher, J. Albert.   1973.   "Geo-historical
         Approaches to Environment: The Evolution of
         Environmental Thought in Western Civilization,"
         Journal of Geography, Vol. 72, pp. 31-41.

C-144.   Rowley, Gwyn.   1984.   "Foreign Languages and
         American Geography: A View from the Field,"
         Professional Geographer, Vol. 36, p. 76.

C-145.   Ryabchikov, A. M. 1964. "On the Interaction of the Geographic Sciences," _Soviet Geography: Review and Translation_, Vol. 5, pp. 45-61.

C-146.   Saha, Suranjit. 1978. "Explanation in Regional Planning," _Oriental Geographer_, Vol. 22, pp. 37-56.

C-147.   Saushkin, Yu. G. 1976. "Economic Geography Among the Cognate Disciplines," _Soviet Geography: Review and Translation_, Vol. 17, pp. 655-664.

C-148.   Schnore, Leo F. 1961. "Geography and Human Ecology," _Economic Geography_, Vol. 37, pp. 207-217.

C-149.   Senger, L. W. and Chang, S. 1975. "A Matter of Terminology -- the Ecological Approach in Geography: A Re-Examination of Basic Concepts," _Geoforum_, Vol. 6, pp. 164-167.

C-150.   Sheail, J. 1986. "Nature Conservation and the Agricultural Historian," _Agricultural History_, Vol. 34, pp. 1-11.

C-151.   Shearer, M. H. 1930. "Aviators Need Geography," _Journal of Geography_, Vol. 29, pp. 371-380.

C-152.   Sims, John H. and Baumann, Duane D. 1975. "Interdisciplinary, Cross- Cultural Research: Double Trouble," _Professional Geographer_, Vol. 27, pp. 153-159.

C-153.   Skinner, A. W. 1905. "Geography, Relations to History," _Education_, Vol. 25, pp. 597-601.

C-154.   Smith, J. Russell. 1907. "Economic Geography and Its Relation to Economic Theory and Higher Education," _Bulletin of the American Geographical Society of New York_, Vol. 39, pp. 472-481.

C-155.   Smith, P. J. 1975. "Geography and Urban Planning: Links and Departures," _Canadian Geographer_, Vol. 19, pp. 267-278.

C-156.   Sochava, V. B. 1971. "Geography and Ecology," _Soviet Geography: Review and Translation_, Vol. 12, pp. 277-293.

C-157.   Sparks, Edwin E. 1908. "Report of Conference on the Relations of History and Geography," _American Historical Association Annual Report_, Vol. 1, pp. 57-61.

C-158.   Spencer, Christopher and Blades, Mark. 1986.
          "Pattern and Process: A Review Essay on the
          Relationship Between Geography and Environmental
          Psychology," Progress in Human Geography, Vol.
          10, pp. 230-248.

C-159.   Speth, William. 1975. "Friedrich Ratzel and the
          Shaping of American Anthropology," Proceedings of
          the Twenty-Second International Geographical
          Congress, Vol. 7, pp. 230-233.

C-160.   Stafford, John H. 1963. "Why Planners Fail,"
          Landscape, Vol. 13, pp. 8-11.

C-161.   Stolberg, Irving. 1965. "Geography and Peace
          Research," Professional Geographer, Vol. 17, pp.
          9-12.

C-162.   Strate, Jessie B. 1924. "Mark Twain and
          Geography," Journal of Geography, Vol. 23, pp.
          81-92.

C-163.   Sugden, David E. 1983. "Geography and
          Geomorphology: Alternatives to G. H. Dury,"
          Area, Vol. 15, pp. 122-125.

C-164.   Sweet, David C. 1969. "The Geographer's Role in
          the Urban Planning Process," Southeastern
          Geographer, Vol. 9, pp. 25-35.

C-165.   Towler, John O. and Brenchley, David L. 1975.
          "Geography and Environmental Education--Why
          Aren't We Involved?" Journal of Geography, Vol.
          74, pp. 520-524.

C-166.   Tuan, Yi-Fu. 1971. "Geography, Phenomenology,
          and the Study of Human Nature," Canadian
          Geographer, Vol. 15, pp. 181-192.

C-167.   Turner, F. J. 1907. "Report of the Conference
          on the Relations of Geography and History,"
          American Historical Association Report, Vol. 1,
          pp. 45-48.

C-168.   Ullman, Edward L. 1953. "Human Geography and
          Area Research," Annals of the Association of
          American Geographers, Vol. 43, pp. 54-66.

C-169.   Unstead, J. F. 1906. "Geographical Novels,"
          Geographical Teacher, Vol. 3, pp. 147-152.

C-170.   Valentey, D. I. and Koval'skaya, N. Ya. 1967.
          "The Place of Population Geography in the System
          of Population Sciences," Soviet Geography:
          Review and Translation, Vol. 8, pp. 629-641.

C-171.   Van Cleef, Eugene. 1960. "Geography as an Earth Science," Professional Geographer, Vol. 12, No. 6, pp. 8-11.

C-172.   Van Passen, Christiaan. 1981. "Human Geography in Terms of Existential Anthropology," Tijdschrift voor Economische en Sociale Geografie, Vol. 67, pp. 324-341.

C-173.   Vining, James W. 1983. "Astronomical Geography: An Examination of the Early American Literature," Geographical Bulletin, Vol. 23, pp. 30-40.

C-174.   Wagstaff, J. M. 1976. "Some Thoughts About Geography and Catastrophe Theory," Area, Vol. 8, pp. 316-320.

C-175.   Warntz, William. 1967. "Global Science and the Tyranny of Space," Papers of the Regional Science Association, Vol. 19, pp. 7-19.

C-176.   Waters, Roy. 1970. "Geography As a Social Science: A More Functional Geography for Latin America," East Lakes Geographer, Vol. 6, pp. 5-25.

C-177.   Watson, J. Wreford. 1953. "Geography in Relation to the Physical and Social Sciences," Journal of Geography, Vol. 52, pp. 313-323.

C-178.   Watson, J. Wreford. 1962. "Geography and History Versus 'Social Studies,'" Journal of Geography, Vol. 61, pp. 125-129.

C-179.   Webb, Walter Prescott. 1960. "Geographical-Historical Concepts in American History," Annals of the Association of American Geographers, Vol. 50, pp. 85-92.

C-180.   Weir, Thomas. 1892. "Astronomy in Relation to Geography," Journal of the Manchester Geographical Society, Vol. 8, pp. 211-225.

C-181.   Whitaker, J. R. 1943. "The Place of Geography in the Social Studies: From the Viewpoint of Conservation Education," Journal of Geography, Vol. 42, pp. 12-21.

C-182.   White, Gilbert F. 1972. "Geography and Public Policy," Professional Geographer, Vol. 24, pp. 101-104.

C-183.   White, Gilbert F., et al. 1962. "Critical Issues Concerning Geography in the Public Service," Annals of the Association of American Geographers, Vol. 52, pp. 279-298.

C-184. Wilbanks, Thomas J. and Symanski, Richard. 1968.
        "What is Systems Analysis?" _Professional_
        Geographer, Vol. 20, pp. 81-85.

C-185. Wilbanks, Thomas J. 1978. "Geographic Research
        and Energy Policy Making," _Geographical_ _Survey_,
        Vol. 7, No. 4, pp. 11-18.

C-186. Wilhelm, E. J. 1968. "Biogeography and
        Environmental Science," _Professional_ _Geographer_,
        Vol. 20, pp. 123-125.

C-187. Willatts, E. C. 1971. "Planning and Geography in
        the Last Three Decades," _Geographical_ _Journal_,
        Vol. 137, pp. 311-338.

C-188. Williams, L. 1961. "Climatology and Geographers,"
        Professional _Geographer_, Vol. 13, pp. 11-15.

C-189. Wilson, Thomas D. 1977. "Is Ambiguity Necessary
        in the Social Sciences?" _Geographical_ _Survey_, Vol.
        6, pp. 3-8.

C-190. Winkler, E. 1970. "A Possible Classification of
        Geosciences," _Geoforum_, Vol. 1, No. 1, pp. 9-18.

C-191. Winkler, Karen J. 1986. "New Breed of Scholar
        Works the Territory That Lies Between History and
        Geography," _Historical_ _Geography_, Vol. 6, pp.
        9-11.

C-192. Winsberg, Morton D. 1977. "Social Sciences in
        the United States: 1948- 1975," _Geographical_
        Review, Vol. 67, pp. 335-343.

C-193. Wright, John K. 1960. "Geography and History
        Cross-Classified," _Professional_ _Geographer_, Vol.
        12, pp. 7-10.

C-194. Wright, John Kirkland. 1940. "Where History and
        Geography Meet: Recent American Studies in the
        History of Exploration," _Proceedings_ - _Eighth_
        American _Scientific_ _Conference_, Washington, D.C.:
        Vol. 19, pp. 17-23.

C-195. Zdorkowski, Gretchen. 1977. "Geographical
        Perspectives on the Quality of Life: A
        Commentary," _Geographical_ _Survey_, Vol. 6, pp.
        9-10.

C-196. Zelinsky, Wilbur. 1970. "Beyond the
        Exponentials: The Role of Geography in the Great
        Transition," _Economic_ _Geography_, Vol. 46, pp.
        498-535.

C-197. Zelinsky, Wilbur. 1976. "Quality of Life: An
        Inquiry Into Its Utility for Geographers,"
        Geographical _Survey_, Vol. 5, pp. 8-11.

Geography in Various Countries

D-1. Abrahams, Paul P. 1975. "Academic Geography in America: An Overview," _Reviews in American History_, Vol. 3, pp. 46-52.

D-2. Adejuyigbe, O. 1970. "Re-shaping High School Geography in Nigeria," _Nigerian Geographical Journal_, Vol. 13, pp. 89-94.

D-3. Adrian, Colin and Forbes, Dean. 1984. "Australasian Human Geography: Urban Geographys' Reply," _Progress in Human Geography_, Vol. 8, pp. 562-569; Dennis Jean's Rejoinder, pp. 570-573.

D-4. Afolabi, Ojo 1978. "Thirty Years of Geographic Thought in Nigeria, _Nigerian Geographical Journal_, Vol. 21, pp. 2-23.

D-5. Agafonov, N. T., _et al_. 1976. "Population Geography and Socio-Economic Planning," _Soviet Geography: Review and Translation_, Vol. 17, pp. 377-383.

D-6. Agafonov, N. T., _et al_. 1983. "The Present Tasks of Soviet Geography," _Soviet Geography: Review and Translation_, Vol. 24, pp. 411-422.

D-7. Ahmad, Kazi S. 1950. "The Role of Geography in our National Planning," _Pakistan Geographical Review_, Vol. 5, pp. not known.

D-8. Ahmad, S. Maqbul. 1951. "Arabs' Contribution to the Science of Geography in the Middle Ages," _Geographer_, Vol. 4, No. 2, pp. 41-48.

D-9. Ahmad, S. Maqbul. 1956-57. "Arab Geography," _Geographer_, Vol. 8-9, pp. 27-36.

D-10.   Ahmad, Nafis.   1945.   "The Task Before the Indian Geographers, Geographical Review of India, Vol. 7, No. 4, n.p.

D-11.   Ahmad, Nafis.   1971.   "Some Aspects of Scientific Geographical Work in Central Asia During 9th to 13th Century," Pakistan Geographical Review, Vol 26, pp. 50-52.

D-12.   Ahnert, Frank.   1962.   "Some Reflections on the Place and Nature of Physical Geography in America," Professional Geographer, Vol. 14, pp. 1-7.

D-13.   Ahsan, Syed Reza.   1959.   "Geography and Geography Teaching in Pakistan," Memorandum Folio of the Southeastern Association of American Geographers, Vol. 11, pp. 1-4.

D-14.   Akhtar, Rais.   1988.   "Geography in Zambia," Professional Geographer, Vol. 40, pp. 100-103.

D-15.   Al-Amiri, Sami S. A.   185.   "Teaching Geomorphology in Geography Departments of Arab Universities," Geographical Perspectives, No. 56, pp. 55-57.

D-16.   Alampiyev, P. M., et al.   1963.   "Letter of Protest Regarding Yu. G. Saushkin's Article in Economic Geography [U.S.], 1962, No. 1 ["Economic Geography in the U.S.S.R."]," Soviet Geography: Review and Translation, Vol. 4, No. 1, pp. 60-62.

D-17.   Alao, N.   1978.   "Geography in Nigerian Universities," Nigerian Geographical Journal, Vol. 21, pp. 31-37.

D-18.   Alcaraz, Arturo P.   1981.   "Thirty Years of the Philippine Geographical Society," Philippine Geographical Journal, Vol. 25, pp. 8-[16].

D-19.   Alcock, F. I.   1949.   "Cartography in Canada Since 1983," Proceedings - Sixteenth International Geographical Congress, pp. 203-204.

D-20.   Ali, S. M.   1950.   "Some Geographical Ideas of Abu-Rehan Alberuni," Geographer, Vol. 2, No. 2, pp. 6-12.

D-21.   Al'tman, L. P., et al.   1968.   "Economic Geogrpahy at Leningrad University," Soviet Geography: Review and Translation, Vol. 9, pp. 1-11.

D-22.   Anderson, A. Grant.   1987.   "Communication in Geography: The Role of the New Zealand Geographical Society," New Zealand Geographer, Vol. 43, pp. 40-45.

D-23.   Andrews, H. F.   1986.   "The French View of
         Geography Teaching in Britain in 1871,"
         Geographical Journal, Vol. 152, pp. 225-231.

D-24.   Andrews, Howard F.   1987.   "Paul Vidal de la
         Blanche and the Concours de'agregation of 1866,"
         Canadian Geographer, Vol. 31, pp. 12-20.

D-25.   Annenkov, V. V. and Demko, George J.   1984.
         "Development of Relations Between Geographers of
         the United States and the U.S.S.R. from the 1950s
         to the 1980s," _Soviet Geography: Review and
         Translation_, Vol. 25, pp. 749-757.

D-26.   Annette, Mary.   1968.   "French Geography in the
         Sixties," _Professional Geographer_, Vol. 20, pp.
         92-97.

D-27.   Anonymous.   1885.   "Scotland and Geographical
         Work," _Scottish Geographical Magazine_, Vol. 1,
         pp. 17-25.

D-28.   Anonymous.   1885.   "Short Note on the Origin of
         the Manchester Geographical Society," _Journal of
         the Manchester Geographical Society_, Vol. 1, pp.
         64-66.

D-29.   Anonymous.   1886.   "Royal Geographical Society's
         Education Schemes and Its Exhibition of
         Geographical Appliances," _Scottish Geographical
         Magazine_, Vol. 2, pp. 27-31.

D-30.   Anonymous.   1893.   "The Teaching of Geography in
         Germany," _Scottish Geographical Magazine_, Vol. 9,
         pp. 366-371.

D-31.   Anonymous.   1896.   "Geography at the
         Universities," _Geographical Journal_, Vol. 8, pp.
         61-65.

D-32.   Anonymous.   1896.   "Geography at the
         Universities," _Geographical Journal_, Vol. 29, pp.
         653-655.

D-33.   Anonymous.   1896.   "Geography in the Schools,"
         Scottish Geographical Magazine, Vol. 12, pp.
         252-256.

D-34.   Anonymous.   1897.   "The Fifty Years History of
         the Russian Geographical Society," _Geographical
         Journal_, Vol. 10, pp. 53-56.

D-35.   Anonymous.   1888.   "The Oxford School of
         Geography," _Geographical Journal_, Vol. 14, pp.
         82-83.

D-36.   Anonymous. 1903. "Geographical Education at the
         British Association," Geographical Journal, Vol.
         22, pp. 549-553.

D-37.   Anonymous. 1903. "Geography in British
         Universities and University Colleges at the
         Beginning of 1903," Geographical Teacher, Vol. 2,
         pp. 33-40.

D-38.   Anonymous. 1903. "Geography in the University
         of Chicago," Bulletin of the American
         Geographical Society of New York, Vol. 35, pp.
         207-208.

D-39.   Anonymous. 1904. "Hungarian Activity in
         Geography," Bulletin of the American Geographical
         Society of New York, Vol. 36, pp. 697-699.

D-40.   Anonymous. 1905. "The Teaching of Geography in
         the Schools in Cuba," Scottish Geographical
         Magazine, Vol. 21, pp. 591-599.

D-41.   Anonymous. 1910. "Geography at Oxford,"
         Geographical Journal, Vol. 35, pp. 316-318.

D-42.   Anonymous. 1918. "The South African
         Geographical Society and Its Journal," Journal of
         Geography, Vol. 7, pp. 118-120.

D-43.   Anonymous. 1941. "Globe Trotting Artists,"
         Independent Woman, Vol. 20, pp. 67-68.

D-44.   Anonymous. 1945. "Geography in the Soviet
         Union," Geographical Journal, Vol. 106, pp.
         217-221.

D-45.   Anonymous. 1946. "Geography at Japanese
         Imperial Universities," Science, Vol. 104, pp.
         394-395.

D-46.   Anonymous. 1950. "Geography in Italy Since
         1939," Geographical Journal, Vol. 116, pp. 79-83.

D-47.   Anonymous. 1955. "American Geography: Review
         and Commentary," New Zealand Journal of
         Geography, Vol. 11, pp. 183-194.

D-48.   Anonymous. 1965. "Geography in Australian
         Universities," Australian Geographical Studies,
         Vol. 3, pp. 129-132.

D-49.   Anonymous. 1966. "Concerning the Discussion of
         Geography in Literaturnaya Gazeta," Soviet
         Geography: Review and Translation, Vol. 7, pp.
         3-9.

D-50.   Anonymous. 1966. "The Reorganized Department of
        Geography at the University of Mysore," Deccan
        Geographer, Vol. 4, pp. 84-90.

D-51.   Anonymous. 1981. "Cartographic Work in Japan,"
        Bulletin - Geographical Survey Institute, Tokyo,
        Vol. 25, pp. 1-20.

D-52.   Antonini, Gustavo and Hungrin, Jose J. 1988.
        "Geography in the Dominican Republic,"
        Professional Geographer, Vol. 40, pp. 96-100.

D-53.   Antonora, I. F. 1969. "Geographic Education and
        Research at Canadian Universities," Soviet
        Geography: Review and Translation, Vol. 10, pp.
        473-476.

D-54.   Antonora, I. F. 1979. "Economic Geography in
        Canada at the Present Stage," Soviet Geography:
        Review and Translation, Vol. 20, pp. 49-55.

D-55.   Asheim, Bjorn T. 1987. "A Critical Evaluation
        of Postwar Developments in Human Geography in
        Scandinavia," Progress in Human Geography, Vol.
        11, pp. 333-353.

D-56.   Bagchi, Kanangopal. 1976. "Role of Geographical
        Societies and Journals in National
        Developments," Geographical Review of India,
        Vol. 38, pp. 215-220.

D-57.   Bagdasaryan, A. B., et al. 1968. "The
        Development of Geography in the Soviet Republics
        of Transcaucasia," Soviet Geography: Review and
        Translation, Vol. 9, pp. 286-293.

D-58.   Bailly, Antonie S. and Greer-Wooten, Bryn.
        1983. "Behavioral Geography in Francophone
        Countries," Progress in Human Geography, Vol. 7,
        pp. 344-356.

D-59.   Baker, Alan R. H. 1986. "Historical Geography
        in Czechoslovakia," Area, Vol. 18, pp. 223-228.

D-60.   Baker, J. 1948. "Mary Somerville and Geography
        in England," Geographical Journal, Vol. 111, pp.
        207-222.

D-61.   Baker, J. N. L. 1935. "Academic Geography in
        the Seventeenth and Eighteenth Centuries,"
        Scottish Geographical Magazine, Vol. 51, pp.
        129-144.

D-62.   Baker, Marcus. 1898. "A Century of Geography in
        the United States," Bulletin - Philosophical
        Society of Washington, Vol. 13, pp. 223-239.

D-63.   Baker, Marcus. 1898. "Geographical Research in
         the United States," Geographical Journal, Vol.
         11, pp. 52-58.

D-64.   Bako, Elemer. 1957. "Organization of Hungarian
         Cartography Since 1948," Professional Geographer,
         Vol. 9, No. 1, pp. 9-12.

D-65.   Barbour, K. M. 1963. "Geography in Nigeria,"
         Nigerian Geographical Journal, Vol. 6, pp. 3-16.

D-66.   Barbour, K. M. 1973. "Process in Geography,"
         Nigerian Geographical Journal, Vol. 16, pp. 3-18.

D-67.   Barker, W. H. 1921. "Geography in the Schools
         of England and Wales," Journal of Geography, Vol.
         20, pp. 302-310.

D-68.   Barr, Brenton M. 1986. "Presidential Address:
         Canadian Geography in a Multilingual World: The
         Implosion of Relevance," Canadian Geographer,
         Vol. 30, pp. 290-301.

D-69.   Bartholomew, John. 1951. "Early Scottish
         Cartographers," Scottish Geographical Magazine,
         Vol. 67, pp. 101-104.

D-70.   Bassin, Mark. 1983. "The Russian Geographical
         Society, the 'Amur Epoch,' and the Great Siberian
         Expedition 1855-1863," Annals of the Association
         of American Geographers, Vol. 73, pp. 240-256.

D-71.   Basu, A. N. 1936. "Geography Teaching in
         India," Geographical Review of India, Vol. 1, No.
         1, n.p.

D-72.   Baugh, Ruth E. 1959. "Status and Trends of
         Geography in the United States, 1952-1957,"
         Professional Geographer, Vol. 11, pp. 2-159.

D-73.   Beavon, K. S. O. and Rogerson, C. M. 1981.
         "Trekking On: Recent Trends in Human Geography
         of South Africa," Progress in Human Geography,
         Vol. 5, pp. 159-189.

D-74.   Becker, Bertha K. 1986. "Geography in Brazil in
         the 1980's: Background and Recent Advances,"
         Progress in Human Geography, Vol. 10, pp.
         157-183.

D-75.   Becker, Chr., Maier, J., Ruppert, K., Weber, P.
         and Wolf, K. 1984. "Geographical Tourism
         Research in the Federal Republic of Germany,"
         GeoJournal, Vol. 9, pp. 37-40.

D-76.   Bennett, R. J.   1985.   "A Reappraisal of the Role
        of Spatial Science and Statistical Inference in
        Geography in Britain," Espace Geography, Vol. 14,
        pp. 23-28.

D-77.   Beukema, Col. Herman.   1948.   "The Geographical
        Factor in the Study of International Relations,"
        Annals of the Association of American
        Geographers, Vol. 102-103.

D-78.   Bishop, Avard L.   1909.   "Geography in
        Universities Abroad," Educational Review, Vol.
        37, pp. 447-481.

D-79.   Black, Lloyd D.   1948.   "Troll's Critique of
        Geographical Science in Germany from 1933 to
        1945," Annals of the Association of American
        Geographers, Vol. 38, pp. 72-73.

D-80.   Boggs, S. Whittemore.   1938.   "American
        Contributions to Geographic Knowledge of the
        Central Pacific," Annals of the Association of
        American Geographers, Vol. 28, pp. 41.

D-81.   Bolshakov, V. D.   1970.   "Higher Geodetic and
        Cartographic Education in Tsarist and Soviet
        Russia," Canadian Cartographer, Vol. 7, pp.
        116-125.

D-82.   Bone, R. M.   1961.   "The Opinion of a Canadian
        Scientist on Geography in Canada and the
        U.S.S.R.," Canadian Geographer, Vol. 5, pp.
        48-51.

D-83.   Borchert, Johan G.   1983.   "Geography across the
        Borders: On the Relationship between Urban
        Geography in the Netherlands and Germany,"
        Tijdschrift voor Economische en Sociale
        Geografie, Vol. 74, pp. 335-343.

D-84.   Bosque-Sendra, J., Rodriquez, V. and Santos, J.
        M.   1983.   "Quantitative Geography in Spain,"
        Progress in Human Geography, Vol. 7, pp. 370-385.

D-85.   Bowen, Emrys George.   1970.   "Herbert John Fleure
        and Western European Geography in the Twentieth
        Century," Geographische Zeitschrift, Vol. 58, pp.
        28-35.

D-86.   Bowie, I. J. S.   1983.   "Australian Geography: A
        Disciplinary Profile," Australian Geographical
        Studies, Vol. 21, pp. 259-265.

D-87.   Bremer, H.   1984.   "Twenty-one Years of German
        Geomorphology." Earth Surface Processes and
        Landforms, Vol. 9, pp. 281-287.

D-88.   Briggs, J. and Gray, A. 1982. "Geography in a
         Developing Country: The Case of the University
         of Dar es Salaam, Tanzania," Journal of Geography
         in Higher Education, Vol. 6, pp. 39-46.

D-89.   Brigham, Albert Perry. 1914. "Remarks on
         Geography in America," Journal of Geography, Vol.
         12, pp. 202-204.

D-90.   Brookfield, H. C. 1973. "On One Geography and a
         Third World," Transactions - Institute of British
         Geographers, Vol. 58, pp. 1-20.

D-91.   Brown, Eric H. 1964. "Geomorphology in Poland,"
         Professional Geographer, Vol. 16, No. 2, pp.
         22-26.

D-92.   Bruk, S. I., Kozolov, V. I. and Levin, M. G.
         1962. "The Present Status of Research in Ethnic
         Geography in the U.S.S.R.," Soviet Geography:
         Review and Translation, Vol. 3, No. 4, pp. 22-28.

D-93.   Campbell, Frank. 1895. "The Literature of
         Geography: How Shall It Be?," Proceedings -
         Sixth International Geographical Congress, pp.
         391-398.

D-94.   Carol, Hans. 1959. "Current Geographic Thought
         in the German Language Area," Professional
         Geographer, Vol. 11, No. 5, pp. 11-16.

D-95.   Carter, Frank. 1980. "Between East and West:
         Geography in Higher Education in Yugoslavia,"
         Journal of Geography in Higher Education, Vol. 4,
         pp. 43-53.

D-96.   Carter, Frank. 1981. "Yugoslav Geography: A
         Case of Misguided Optimism," Journal of Geography
         in Higher Education, Vol. 5, pp. 202-205.

D-97.   Castner, H. W. 1980. "Special Purpose Mapping
         in 18th Century Russia: A Search for the
         Beginning of Thematic Mapping," American
         Cartographer, Vol. 7, pp. 163-175.

D-98.   Chang, Chi-Yun. 1944. "Geographic Research in
         China," Annals of the Association of American
         Geographers, Vol. 34, pp. 47-62.

D-99.   Chang, Kvei-sheng. 1975. "The Geography of
         Contemporary China: Inventory and Prospect,"
         Professional Geographer, Vol. 27, pp. 2-6.

D-100.   Chang, Sen-dor. 1966. "The Role of the
         Agricultural Geographer in Communist China,"
         Professional Geographer, Vol. 18, pp. 125-128.

D-101.   Chao, Lin and En-Yong, Wong. 1984. "Dr. Chu
          Ko-Chen and the Department of Geography at Peking
          University," Acta Geographica Sinica, Vol. 39,
          pp. 17-19 [English Summary].

D-102.   Chapman, A. D'arcy. 1922. "Modern Geography --
          From a Canadian Teacher's Point of View," Journal
          of Geography, Vol. 21, pp. 98-105.

D-103.   Chappell, John E. 1975. "The Ecological
          Dimension: Russian and American Views," Annals
          of the Association of American Geographers, Vol.
          65, pp. 144-162.

D-104.   Chappell, John E., Jr. 1963. "Soviet
          Cartography: Comparisons and Gaps," Professional
          Geographer, Vol. 15, No. 2, pp. 1-8.

D-105.   Charlier, Roger H. 1957. "The Study of
          Geography in Belgium," Professional Geographer,
          Vol. 9, No. 3, pp. 10-14.

D-106.   Charlier, Roger H. 1970. "The Geosciences in
          Romania," Professional Geographer, Vol. 22, pp.
          31-34.

D-107.   Charlier, Roger H. and Charlier, Partricia S.
          1960. "The Place of Geography in French
          Education," Journal of Geography, Vol. 59, pp.
          322-326.

D-108.   Chatterjee, S. P. 1941. "The Place of Geography
          in National Planning," Geographical Review of
          India, Vol. 3, No. 2, n.p.

D-109.   Chatterjee, S. C. 1972. "The Growth of
          Geography in India," Proceedings - Twenty Second
          International Geographical Congress, pp. 951-954.

D-110.   Chief Directorate of Schools, USSR Ministry of
          Education. 1987. "The Geography Curriculum for
          the Secondary General Education School," Soviet
          Education, Vol. 29, pp. 10-86.

D-111.   Chien, Cheng-Siang. 1967. "Ups and Downs of
          Acta Geographica Sinica," Geographical Review,
          Vol. 57, pp. 108-111.

D-112.   Chisholm, George G. 1913. "On the Position of
          Geography in British Universities," Journal of
          Geography, Vol. 12, pp. 65-69.

D-113.   Chisholm, George G. 1916. "Geography in Italy,"
          Scottish Geographical Magazine, Vol. 32, pp.
          401-406.

D-114.   Chisholm, George G. 1916. "Geography in the
          United States," Geographical Journal, Vol. 48,
          pp. 392-403.

D-115.   Chisholm, George G. 1919. "The Edinburgh
          University Diploma in Geography," Scottish
          Geographical Magazine, Vol. 35, pp. 30-31.

D-116.   Chu, K. Y. and Sit, Victor. 1985. "Geography in
          Asia: A Review of 1982," Asian Geographer, Vol.
          4, pp. 67-69.

D-117.   Chuanjun, Wu. 1984. "Geography in China,"
          Professional Geographer, Vol. 36, pp. 479-480.

D-118.   Chung, Yuet Ping. 1968. "Geography and
          Agricultural Development in China," Professional
          Geographer, Vol. 20, pp. 163-167.

D-119.   Church, R. J. Harrison. 1948. "The Case For
          Colonial Geography," Transactions and Papers -
          Institute of British Geographers, No. 14, pp.
          15-26.

D-120.   Church, R. J. Harrison. 1957. "The French
          School of Geography: Review," Geographical
          Journal, Vol. 123, pp. 235-237.

D-121.   Church, R. J. Harrison. 1966. "Geography in
          American Universities," Horizon, Vol. 15, pp.
          7-8.

D-122.   Clark, Andrew H. 1950. "Contributions to
          Geographical Knowledge of Canada Since 1945,"
          Geographical Review, Vol. 40, pp. 285-308.

D-123.   Clarke, J. I. et al. 1970. "Letters to the
          Editor: Some Observations on Geography in
          British Universities," Area, Vol. 2, p. 8.

D-124.   Claval, Paul and Thompson, Ian. 1975. "Trends
          in Human Geography in Britain and France,"
          Geographical Journal, Vol. 141, pp. 345-354.

D-125.   Claval, Paul C. 1983. "One Hundred Years of
          Teaching Geography in French Universities,"
          Journal of Geography, Vol. 82,, pp. 110-111.

D-126.   Claval, P. 1984. "The Historical Dimension of
          French Geography," Journal of Historical
          Geography, Vol. 10, pp. 229-245.

D-127.   Clayton, Keith. 1985. "The State of Geography,"
          Transactions - Institute of British Geographers,
          Vol. 10, pp. 5-16.

D-128.   Clement, Mark.   1942.   "The Contribution of the
          Yugoslavs to Geography and Ethnography," Scottish
          Geographical Magazine, Vol. 58, pp. 113-115.

D-129.   Clout, Hugh.   1985.   "French Geography in the
          1980s," Progress in Human Geography, Vol. 9, pp.
          473-490.

D-130.   Conacher, A. J.   1980.   "Some Thoughts About
          Future Development/Directions in Environmental
          Studies by Geographers in Australia," Australian
          Geographer, Vol. 14, 1980, pp. 68-69.

D-131.   Conde, Shirley G.   1980.   "Moslem Contributions
          to Geography," Philippine Geographical Journal,
          Vol. 24, pp. 91-96.

D-132.   Conrad, Joseph.   1924.   "Geography and Some
          Explorers," National Geographic Magazine, Vol.
          45, pp. 239-274.

D-133.   Cooke, R. U. and Robson, B. T.   1976.   "Geography
          in the United Kingdom 1972-76," Geographical
          Journal, Vol. 142, pp. 81-100.

D-134.   Coones, Paul.   1983.   "A Russian Interpretation
          of Classical Geography," Geographical Review,
          Vol. 73, pp. 95-109.

D-135.   Corner, D. J.   1984.   "English Cartography in the
          Thirteenth Century: The Intellectual Context,"
          Bulletin - Society of University Cartographers,
          Vol. 17, pp. 65-73.

D-136.   Coulton, R.   1981.   "Charting of Vinland by the
          Norse," Mariner's Mirror, Vol. 67, pp. 187-192.

D-137.   Crist, Raymond E.   1960.   "Some Recent Trends in
          French Geographic Research and Thought,"
          Professional Geographer, Vol. 12, pp. 26-28.

D-138.   Cross, W. K.   1967.   "John Leland the
          Geographical Antiquary, and Others of His Like
          and Kind," Canadian Geographer, Vol. 11, pp.
          172-179.

D-139.   Crush, Jonathan and Rogerson, Christian.   1983.
          "New Wave African Historiography and African
          Historical Geography," Progress in Human
          Geography, Vol. 7, pp. 203-231.

D-140.   Cumberland, Kenneth B.   1969.   "Geography in the
          University of New Zealand," Scottish Geographical
          Magazine, Vol. 65, pp. 98-100.

D-141.   Czekenska, M. 1984. [Geography at Poznan
         University in the Period 1919- 1939], Czasopismo
         Geograficzne, Vol. 55, pp. 3-33 [English
         Summary].

D-142.   Da-Dao, Lu. 1984. "A Tentative Exploration on
         Regional Analysis in Human Geography," Acta
         Geographica Sinica, Vol. 39, pp. 397-408
         [English Summary].

D-143.   Dagenais, Pierre. 1953. "Status and Tendencies
         of Geography in Canada," Canadian Geographer, No.
         3, pp. 1-15.

D-144.   Dalgleish, W. Scott. 1894. "Geography at the
         British Association," Scottish Geographical
         Magazine, Vol. 10, pp. 463-474.

D-145.   Dalton, K. G. 1984-85. "Examining Geography in
         Northern Ireland," Geographical Viewpoint, Vol.
         13, pp. 5-13.

D-146.   Daly, Chief-Justice. 1874. "The Geographical
         Work of the World in 1872," Journal of the
         American Geographical Society of New York, Vol.
         4, pp. 63-118.

D-147.   Daly, Chief-Justice. 1874. "The Geographical
         Work of the World in 1873," Journal of the
         American Geographical Society of New York, Vol.
         5, pp. 49-94.

D-148.   Daly, Chief-Justice. 1876. "The Geographical
         Work of the World for 1873," Journal of the
         American Geographical Society of New York, Vol.
         6, pp. 53-92.

D-149.   Daly, Chief-Justice. 1876. "The Geographical
         Work of the World in 1876," Journal of the
         American Geographical Society of New York, Vol.
         8, pp. 45-95.

D-150.   Daly, Chief-Justice. 1878. "Geographical Work
         of the World in 1877," Journal of the American
         Geographical Society of New York, Vol. 10, pp.
         1-76.

D-151.   Daly, Chief-Justice. 1880. "Geographical Work
         of the World in 1878 and 1879," Journal of the
         American Geographical Society of New York, Vol.
         12, pp. 1-103.

D-152.   Daly, Charles P. 1888. "Recent Geographical Work
         of the World," Journal of the American
         Geographical Society of New York, Vol. 20, pp.
         1-93.

D-153.   Daniels, Peter W., Salt, John and Werritty.
          1987. "Research Foci in British Geography,"
          Area, Vol. 19, pp. 57-59.

D-154.   Darby, H. C. 1983. "Academic Geography in
          Britain, 1918-1946," Transactions - Institute of
          British Geography, Vol. 8, pp. 14-26.

D-155.   Darby, H. C. 1983. "Historical Geography in
          Britain, 1920-1980," Transactions - Institute of
          British Geography, Vol. 8, pp. 421-428.

D-156.   Darkoh, M. B. K. 1977. "Trends in Geography:
          Some Relatively New Thrusts in Research and
          Methodology," Journal of the Geographical
          Association of Tanzania, Vol. 15, pp. 23-47.

D-157.   Davidson, A. 1954. "The Role of Geographers in
          Saskatchewan," Canadian Geographer, No. 4, pp.
          33-38.

D-158.   Davis, C. L. 1977. "The Making of Irish
          Geography, II: Grenville Arthur James Cole,"
          Irish Geography, Vol. 10, pp. 90-94.

D-159.   Davis, Gordon L. 1966. "Early British
          Geomorphology, 1578-1705," Geographical Journal,
          Vol. 132, pp. 252-261.

D-160.   Davis, R. M. 1975. "An Approach to Trading off
          Economic and Environmental Values in Industrial
          Land-Use Planning," Geographical Analysis, Vol.
          7, pp. 397-410.

D-161.   Davis, W. M. 1924. "The Progress of Geography
          in the United States," Annals of the Association
          of American Geographers, Vol. 14, pp. 159-216.

D-162.   Dawson, George M. 1897. "Geographical Work in
          Canada, 1896," Journal of the American
          Geographical Society of New York, Vol. 29, pp.
          13-15.

D-163.   Dement'yev, V. A. 1968. "The Development of
          Geography in Belorussia During 50 Years of Soviet
          Rule," Soviet Geography: Review and Translation,
          Vol. 9, pp. 261-272.

D-164.   Deshpande, C. D. 1974. "New Perspectives in
          Indian Geography," Deccan Geographer, Vol. 12,
          pp. 56-60.

D-165.   Deshpande, C. D. 1977-78. "Discovering 'Indian
          Geography'," Geographical Outlook, Vol. 13, pp.
          1-4.

D-166.   Deskins, Donald R., Jr. and Sibert, Linda E.
         1975.   "Blacks in American Geography: 1974,"
         Professional Geographer, Vol. 27, pp. 65-72.

D-167.   Dikshit, K. 1958.   "Some Observations on the
         Techniques and Generalizations in Urban
         Geography," Indian Geographer, Vol. 3, pp.
         61-70.

D-168.   Dikshit, Om. 1986.   "The Contribution of Blacks
         in the Field of Geographic Knowledge and
         Discovery," Deccan Geographer, Vol. 24, pp. 1-10.

D-169.   Dima, Nicholas. 1978.   "University Education in
         Eastern Europe: The Case of Geography in
         Romania," Journal of Geography, Vol. 77, pp.
         149-151.

D-170.   Dingelstedt, V. 1886.   "Geographical Education
         in the Caucasus," Scottish Geographical
         Magazine, Vol. 2, pp. 274-276.

D-171.   Doerr, Arthur H. 1964.   "The United States in
         Professional Geographic Literature: A Recent
         Review," Professional Geographer, Vol. 16, No. 1,
         pp. 11-16.

D-172.   Doherty, Joe. 1982.   "Geography, Education and
         Ideology in Tanzania," Journal of Geography in
         Higher Education, Vol. 6, pp. 173-176.

D-173.   Doornkamp, J. C. and Warren, K. 1980.
         "Geography in the U.K., 1976- 1980. Report to
         the 24th L.G.C. in Tokyo, Japan in August 1980,"
         Geographical Journal, Vol. 146, pp. 94-110.

D-174.   Downes, Alan. 1971.   "The Bibliographic
         Dinosaurs of Georgia Geography (1714-1830),"
         Geographical Journal, Vol. 137, pp. 379-387.

D-175.   Doyle, Angela. 1983.   "Transfer From Primary to
         Post Primary Geography in the Republic of
         Ireland," Geographical Viewpoint, Vol. 12, pp.
         5-20.

D-176.   Drake, Christine and Horton, June. 1983.
         "Comment on Editorial Essay: Sexist Bias in
         Political Geography," Political Geography
         Quarterly, Vol. 2, pp. 329-337.

D-177.   Drummond, Robert R. 1959.   "Geography in Burma,"
         Professional Geographer, Vol. 11, No. 1, pp. 2-5.

D-178.   Dryer, Charles Redway. 1907.   "The Oxford School
         of Geography," Bulletin of the Geographical
         Society of Philadelphia, Vol. 5, pp. 30-36.

D-179. Duffield, B. S. 1984. "The Study of Tourism in
        Britain - A Geographical Perspective,"
        GeoJournal, Vol. 9, pp. 27-36.

D-180. Dumas, Wayne and Lu, William B. 1977.
        "Geography in West German Schools," Journal of
        Geography, Vol. 76, pp. 84-85.

D-181. Dunbar, G. S. 1983. "Geography Rides, Geology
        Walks: The Barrett- Huntington Expedition to
        Central Asia in 1905." Yearbook - Association of
        Pacific Coast Geographers, Vol. 45, pp. 7-23.

D-182. Dunbar, Gary S. 1985. "Harold Innis and
        Canadian Geography," Canadian Geographer, Vol.
        29, pp. 159-163.

D-183. Dury, G. H. 1970. "Inventory and Prospect:
        Griffith Taylor's Department and Geographical
        Education in New South Wales During the 1950's
        and 1960's," Australian Geographer, Vol. 11, pp.
        221-241.

D-184. Edwards, K. C. and Crone, G. R. 1960.
        "Geography in Great Britain, 1956-1960,"
        Geographical Journal, Vol. 126, pp. 427-441.

D-185. El-Bushra, El-Sayed and Ahmed, Hassan A. 1986.
        "The Status of Geography in Saudi Universities,"
        GeoJournal, Vol. 13, pp. 153-156.

D-186. Elkins, T. H. 1986. "German Social Geography,"
        Progress in Human Geography, Vol. 10, pp.
        313-344.

D-187. Elkins, T. H. 1986. "Planned Geographical
        Education at University Level in the German
        Democratic Republic," Area, Vol. 18, pp. 141-145.

D-188. Embleton, C. 1983. "21 Years of British
        Geography, Geomorphology," Progress in Physical
        Geography, Vol. 7, pp. 361-384.

D-189. Erodi, Bela. 1984. "Geographical Science in
        Hungary," Geographers: Biobibliographical
        Studies, Vol. 8, pp. 1039-1052.

D-190. Erskine, J. Y. 1942. "Report on the Teaching of
        Geography in Scottish Senior Secondary Schools,"
        Scottish Geographical Magazine, Vol. 58, pp.
        74-75.

D-191. Evenden, L. J. 1976. "The Western Division of
        the Canadian Association of Geographers,"
        Canadian Geographer, Vol. 20, pp. 329-333.

D-192.   Fahy, G. 1974. "Geography in the Early Irish
         Monastic Schools: A Brief Review of MacCosse's
         Geographical Poems," Geographical Viewpoint, Vol.
         3, pp. 31-45.

D-193.   Fahy, G. 1981. "Geography and Geographic
         Education in Ireland From Early Christian Times
         to 1960," Geographical Viewpoint, Vol. 10, pp.
         5-30.

D-194.   Faniran, Adetoye. 1973. "Geography and the
         Construction Industry in Nigeria," The Nigerian
         Geographical Journal, Vol. 16, pp. 151-165.

D-195.   Farmer, B. H. 1983. "British Geographers
         Overseas, 1933-1983," Transactions - Institute of
         British Geography, Vol. 8, pp. 70-79.

D-196.   Fayed, Youssef. 1985. "Geography in Egypt,"
         Professional Geographer, Vol. 37, pp. 475-482.

D-197.   Fedorovich, B. A. and Pal'gov, N. N. 1968.
         "Achievements of Soviet Geography in
         Kazakhstan," Soviet Geography: Review and
         Translation, Vol. 9, pp. 304-312.

D-198.   Fel, S. Ye. 1974. "Russian Cartography of the
         18th Century of the 18th Century as a Synthesis
         of Astronomic-Geodetic and Graphic Processes,"
         Canadian Geographer, Vol. 11, pp. 15-23.

D-199.   Fincher, Ruth. 1986. "Focus -- Historical
         Materialism in Canadian Human Geography,"
         Canadian Geographer, Vol. 30, pp. 265-272.

D-200.   Fischer, Eric. 1946. "German Geographical
         Literature, 1940-1945," Geographical Review, Vol.
         36, pp. 92-100.

D-201.   Fischer, Eric. 1949. "Geographic Science in
         Germany During the Period 1933-1945: A Critique
         and a Justification, by C. Troll," (Translated in
         part), Annals of the Association of American
         Geographers, Vol. 39, pp. 99-137.

D-202.   Fischer, H. 1906. "Geography in Prussia,"
         Geographical Teacher, Vol. 3, pp. 171-174.

D-203.   Fitzpatrick, Mother Stella. 1974. "The
         Significance of Geography in Irish Education,"
         Geographical Viewpoint, Vol. 3, pp. 1-14.

D-204.   Flowerdew, Robin. 1986. "Three Years in British
         Geography," Area, Vol. 18, pp. 263-264.

D-205.   Floyd, B. N.   1966.   "Some Comments on the Scope and Objectives of Geography in the Developing Areas," Nigerian Geographical Journal, Vol. 9, pp. 11-24.

D-206.   Fotheringham, A. Stewart.   1984.   "Geography in the United Kingdom," Professional Geographer, Vol. 36, pp. 482-486.

D-207.   Freeman, T. W.   1946.   "Historical Geography and the Irish Historian," Irish Historical Studies, Vol. 5, pp. 139-146.

D-208.   Freeman, T. W.   1976.   "French Geography: The Eighteenth Century Background: Review," Geographical Journal, Vol. 142, pp. 308-310.

D-209.   Freeman, T. W.   1976.   "The Scottish Geographical Magazine in War and Peace from 1914," Scottish Geographical Magazine, Vol. 92, pp. 138-147.

D-210.   Freeman, T. W.   1976.   "The Scottish Geographical Magazine: Its First Thirty Years," Scottish Geographical Magazine, Vol. 92, pp. 92-100.

D-211.   Freeman, T. W.   1984.   "The Manchester and Royal Scottish Geographical Societies," Geographical Journal, Vol. 150, pp. 55-62.

D-212.   French, R. A.   1961.   "Geography and Geographers in the Soviet Union," Geographical Journal, Vol. 127, pp. 159-167.

D-213.   French, R. A.   1968.   "Historical Geography in the U.S.S.R.," Soviet Geography: Review and Translation, Vol. 9, pp. 551-562.

D-214.   Fuchs, Roland J.   1964.   "Review Article: Soviet Urban Geography An Appraisal of Postwar Research," Annals of the Association of American Geographers, Vol. 54, pp. 276-290.

D-215.   Fuggle, Richard F.   1967.   "South African Geography: An Analysis," Professional Geographer, Vol. 19, pp. 345-351.

D-216.   Gallois, Lucren.   1913.   "The Teaching of Geography in French Universities," Journal of Geography, Vol. 12, pp. 40-44.

D-217.   Garnett, A.   1949.   "Geography and Post-war Trends in Education in Great Britain," Proceedings - Sixteenth International Geographical Congress, pp. 388-398.

D-218.   Garnier, B. J.   1947.   "The New Zealand Geographical Society: Its Progress and Purpose," New Zealand Geographer, Vol. 3, pp. 151-160.

D-219.   Gaspar, Jorge. 1985. "Portuguese Human
         Geography: From Origins to Recent Development,"
         Progress in Human Geography, Vol. 9, pp. 315-330.

D-220.   Geiger, Pedro Pinchas. 1970. "The Development
         of Geography in Brazil," East Lakes Geographer,
         Vol. 6, pp. 56-62.

D-221.   Genthe, Martha K. 1911. "Geography in Germany
         and in the United States," Journal of Geography,
         Vol. 9, pp. 215-218.

D-222.   Georgiou, Zoe. 1987. "The Development of
         Regional Studies in Greece," Antipode, Vol. 19,
         pp. 40-47.

D-223.   Gerasimov, I. P. 1956. "Role of Geography in
         Socialist Reconstruction of the U.S.S.R. and
         Modern Tendencies of Its Development,"
         Proceedings - Eighteenth International
         Geographical Congress, pp. 553-558.

D-224.   Gerasimov, I. P. 1960. "The Present Status and
         Aims of Soviet Geography," Soviet Geography:
         Review and Translation, Vol. 1, No. 1-2, pp.
         3-16.

D-225.   Gerasimov, I. P. 1961. "The Main Tasks and
         Trends of Geomorphological Research in the
         U.S.S.R.," Soviet Geography: Review and
         Translation, Vol. 2, No. 3, pp. 35-44.

D-226.   Gerasimov, I. P. 1963. "Scientific Results of
         the Trip of the Delegation of Soviet Geographers
         to the United States," Soviet Geography: Review
         and Translation, Vol. 4, No. 2, pp. 39-44.

D-227.   Gerasimov, I. P. 1964. "Comments," [on
         geography] Soviet Geography: Review and
         Translation, Vol. 5, pp. 73-76.

D-228.   Gerasimov, I. P. 1965. "Has Geography
         'Disappeared'?" Soviet Geography: Review and
         Translation, Vol. 6, pp. 38-41.

D-229.   Gerasimov, I. P. 1966. "The Past and the Future
         of Geography," Soviet Geography: Review and
         Translation, Vol. 7, pp. 3-15.

D-230.   Gerasimov, I. P. 1968. "Fifty Years of
         Development of Soviet Geographic Thought," Soviet
         Geography: Review and Translation, Vol. 9, pp.
         238-254.

D-231.   Gerasimov, I. P. 1970. "Futurology in Soviet
         Geography," Soviet Geography: Review and
         Translation, Vol. 11, pp. 521-527.

D-232.   Gerasimov, I. P.   1971.   "Scientific Technical
         Progress and Geography," Soviet Geography, Vol.
         12, pp. 205-218.

D-233.   Gerasimov, I. P., et al.   1976.   "Large Scale
         Research and Engineering Problems for the
         Transformation of Nature in the Soviet Union and
         the Role of Geography in Their Implementation,"
         Soviet Geography: Review and Translation, Vol.
         17, pp. 235-245.

D-234.   Gerasimov, I. P.   1979.   "Modern Soviet
         Geography," Geoforum, Vol. 10, pp. 219-222.

D-235.   Gerasimov, I. P. et al.   1979.   "Soviet Physical
         and Biological Geography," Geoforum, Vol. 10, pp.
         261-266.

D-236.   Gerlack, Jerry D.   1979.   "The Origins of
         Professional Geographers in the United States,"
         Professional Geographer, Vol. 31, pp. 212-216.

D-237.   Gibson, Edward M.   1986.   "Where is Here?   The
         Uses of Geography in English-Canadian
         Literature," B.C. Geographical Series, No. 37,
         pp. 132-149.

D-238.   Gilbert, Anne.   1988.   "The New Regional
         Geography in English and French-Speaking
         Countries," Progress in Human Geography, Vol. 12,
         pp. 208-228.

D-239.   Gillmore, Desmond A.   1976.   "Geographic
         Education in Ireland and the National Commission
         for the Teaching of Geography," Geographical
         Viewpoint, Vol. 5, pp. 60-73.

D-240.   Gillmore, Desmond A.   1977.   "Geographic
         Education in the Republic of Ireland," Journal of
         Geography, Vol. 77, pp. 103-107.

D-241.   Gillmore, Desmond A.   1988.   "Geography in the
         Republic of Ireland," Professional Geographer,
         Vol. 40, pp. 103-106.

D-242.   Ginkel, Hans van.   1983.   "Mirror of a Changing
         Society--The Development of a Residential
         Geography at Utrecht," Tijdschrift voor
         Economische en Sociale Geografie, Vol. 74, pp.
         358-366.

D-243.   Ginkel, Hans van and Smidt, Marc de.   1983.   "One
         Hundred Years of Human Geography at Utrecht,"
         Tijdschrift voor Economische en Sociale
         Geografie, Vol. 74, pp. 315-316.

D-244.   Gladkov, N. A. 1963. "The Defense of V. A.
          Anuchin's Doctoral Dissertation," Soviet
          Geography: Review and Translation, Vol. 4, No.
          8, pp. 34-45.

D-245.   Gokhman, V. M. 1961. "The Geography of Industry
          in the United States," Soviet Geography: Review
          and Translation, Vol. 2, No. 6, pp. 21-39.

D-246.   Gokhman, V. M., Lavrov, S. B., and Sdasyvk, G.
          V. 1980. "Socio-Economic Geography in the West
          at a Turning Point," Soviet Geography: Review
          and Translation, Vol. 21, pp. 284-293.

D-247.   Goode, J. Paul. 1925. "The Progress of
          Cartography in Poland," Annals of the Association
          of American Geographers, Vol. 15, pp. 36.

D-248.   Gottmann, Jean. 1946. "French Geography in
          Wartime," Geographical Review, Vol. 36, pp.
          80-91.

D-249.   Gottmann, Jean. 1950. "Geography and the United
          Nations," Scottish Geographical Magazine, Vol.
          66, pp. 129-134.

D-250.   Gould, P. 1974. "Some Steineresque Comments,
          and Monodian Asides on Geography in Europe,"
          Geoforum, Vol. 5, pp. 9-13

D-251.   Gould, W. T. S. 1971. "Geography and
          Educational Opportunity in Tropical Africa,"
          Tijdschrift voor Economische en Sociale Geografie
          Vol. 62, pp. 82-89.

D-252.   Grant, C. J. 1978. "Geography at the University
          of Hong Kong," in R. D. Hill and J. M. Bray,
          eds. Geography and the Environment in Southeast
          Asia. Hong Kong: Hong Kong University Press.

D-253.   Graves, N. J. 1980. "Geographical Education in
          Britain," Progress in Human Geography, Vol. 9,
          pp. 12-14.

D-254.   Gregor, Howard F.   1957. "German vs. American
          Economic Geography," Professional Geographer,
          Vol. 9, pp. 12-14.

D-255.   Gregory, D. 1981. "Human Agency and Human
          Geography," Transactions, Institute of British
          Geographers, Vol. 6, pp. 1-18.

D-256.   Gregory, Joel. 1981. "Synthesis and
          Reflections: Africanist Social Science," B.C.
          Geographical Series, No. 33, Vol. 22, pp.
          120-127.

D-257.   Gregory, S. 1983. "Quantitative Geography: The
         British Experience and the Role of the
         Institute," Transactions - Institute of British
         Geographers, Vol. 8, pp. 80-89.

D-258.   Gudonyte, M. 1968. "Geography in the Baltic
         Republics on the 50th Anniversary of the Great
         October Revolution," Soviet Geography: Review
         and Translation, Vol. 9, pp 272-280.

D-259.   Haegen, H. van Der and Van Weespe, J. 1974.
         "Urban Geography in the Low Countries: The
         Netherlands and Flanders," Tijdschrift voor
         Economische en Sociale Geografie, Vol. 65, pp.
         156-165.

D-260.   Hagerstrand, T. 1982. "Proclamations About
         Geography From the Pioneering Years in Sweden,"
         Geografiska Annaler B, Vol. 43, pp. 119-126.

D-261.   HaHari, Masauyki. 1979. "Historical Geography
         in Japan," Professional Geographer, Vol. 31, pp.
         321-326.

D-262.   Hajdu, Joseph B. 1968. "Toward a Definition of
         Post-War German Social Geography," Annals of the
         Association of American Geographers, Vol. 58, pp.
         397-410.

D-263.   Hajdú, Zoltan. 1987. "Political Geography
         Around the World VII: Administrative Geography
         and Reforms of the Administrative Areas in
         Hungary," Political Geography Quarterly, Vol. 6,
         pp. 269-278.

D-264.   Hallinan, M. 1981. "The Evolution of the
         Geography Syllabus in Irish Second-level
         Education Since 1961," Geographical Viewpoint,
         Vol. 10, pp. 56-62.

D-265.   Hare, F. Kenneth. 1964. "A Policy for
         Geographical Research in Canada," Canadian
         Geographer, Vol. 8, pp. 113-116.

D-266.   Hare, F. Kenneth. 1964. "Research in Canada,"
         Canadian Geographer, Vol. 6, pp. 1-4.

D-267.   Hare, F. Kenneth. 1974. "Geography and Public
         Policy: A Canadian View," Transactions -
         Institute of British Geographers, No. 63, pp.
         25-28.

D-268.   Harkema, Roll C. 1971. "School Geography in
         Developing Nations," Journal of Geography, Vol.
         70, pp. 71-72.

D-269.   Harris, C. D. and Edmonds, R. L. 1982. "Urban
         Geography in Japan: A Survey of Recent

D-270.   Harris, Chauncy D. 1958. "Geography in the
          Soviet Union," Professional Geographer, Vol. 10,
          No. 1, pp. 8-13.

D-271.   Harris, R. Colebrook. 1967. "Historical
          Geography in Canada," Canadian Geographer, Vol.
          11, pp. 235-250.

D-272.   Harshbarger, Herschel. 1976. "On the Need for
          an International Focus in American Geography: A
          Reply," Geographical Survey, Vol. 5, pp. 5-6.

D-273.   Hartmann, R. 1985. "Survey 3: Recent
          Development in German-Speaking Human
          Geography--Controversy, Change, and Continuity,"
          Environment and Planning D: Society and Space,
          Vol. 3, pp. 259-263.

D-274.   Hasegawa, Norio. 1980. "Geographical Literature
          in Japan," Professional Geographer, Vol. 32, pp.
          90-97.

D-275.   Hauer, J. and Veldman, J. 1983. "Rural
          Geography at Utrecht," Tijdschrift voor
          Economische en Sociale Geografie, Vol. 74, pp.
          397-406.

D-276.   Hausladen, Gary. 1979. "Soviet Historical
          Geography in the 1970s: A Preliminary
          Assessment," Syracuse University, Department of
          Geography, Discussion Paper Series, No. 60, pp.
          1-25.

D-277.   Hayward, D. F. 1965. "Purism in Geography,"
          Bulletin, Vol. 10, pp. 3-12.

D-278.   Heathcote, G. E. A. and Heathcote, R. L. 1972.
          "German Geographical Literature on Australia,
          1810-1940: A Preliminary Bibliography and
          Comment," Australian Geographer, Vol. 12, pp.
          154-176.

D-279.   Helburn, N. 1979. "An American's Perception of
          British Geography," Geography, Vol. 64, pp.
          327-333.

D-280.   Hellprin, Angelo. 1894-1895. "The Progress of
          Discovery and the Lands of Promise to the
          Explorer," Bulletin of the Geographical Club of
          Philadelphia, Vol. 1, pp. 85-120.

D-281.   Herbertson, A. J. 1898. "The Perlous Plight of
          Geography in Scottish Education," Scottish
          Geographical Magazine, Vol. 14, pp. 81-88.

D-282.   Herin, R. 1984. "Social Geography in France --
          Heritages and Perspectives," GeoJournal, Vol. 9,
          pp. 231-240.

D-283.   Hescinga, M. W. 1983. "Between German and
         French Geography - In Search of the Origins of
         the Utrecht School," Tijdschrift voor Economische
         en Sociale Geografie, Vol. 74, pp. 317-334.

D-284.   Heske, Henning. 1986. "Political Geographers of
         the Past III: German Geographic Research in the
         Nazi Period -- A Content Analysis of the Major
         Geography Journals, 1925-1945," Political
         Geography Quarterly, Vol. 5, pp. 267-282.

D-285.   Hight, J. 1906. "Geography in the University of
         New Zealand," Geographical Teacher, Vol. 3, pp.
         168-170.

D-286.   Hilling, D. 1962. "The Geographer's Region,"
         Bulletin - Ghana Geographical Association, Vol.
         7, pp. 36-40.

D-287.   Hoffman, P. P. and Kamerling, D. S. 1979.
         "Comparative Geography of Higher Education in the
         U.S. and the U.S.S.R.: An Initial
         Investigation," Soviet Geography: Review and
         Translation, Vol. 20, pp. 412-439.

D-288.   Hong, Cheng. 1984. "A Chinese View of Canadian
         Geography . . .," Operational Gegographer, No. 4,
         pp. 20-21.

D-289.   Hooson, David J. M. 1959. "Some Recent
         Developments in the Content and Theory of Soviet
         Geography," Annals of the Association of American
         Geographers, Vol. 49, pp. 73-82.

D-290.   Hooson, David J. M. 1962. "Methodological
         Clashes in Moscow," Annals of the Association of
         American Geographers, Vol. 52, pp. 469-475.

D-291.   Hooson, David J. M. 1968. "The Development of
         Geography in Pre-Soviet Russia," Annals of the
         Association of American Geographers, Vol. 58, pp.
         250-272.

D-292.   Hooson, David. 1969. Phases in the 20th Century
         Development of Russian and American Geography,"
         Proceedings - Nineteenth International
         Geographical Congress, Vol. 1, pp. 66-69.

D-293.   Hooson, D. 1977. "The Units of Geography in the
         USA and the USSR," GeoJournal, Vol. 1, pp. 5-2.

D-294.   Hooson, D. 1987. "Geography East and West,"
         GeoJournal, Vol. 14, pp. 203- 210.

D-295.   Howe, G. Melvyn. 1958. "Geography in the Soviet
         Universities," Geographical Journal, Vol. 124,
         pp. 80-84.

D-296.   Hoy, Don R.   1968.   "Geography's Role in
         Development Planning in Guatemala," Professional
         Geographer, Vol. 20, pp. 333-336.

D-297.   Hozayen, S.A.S.   1932.   "Some Contributions of
         the Arabs to Geography," Geography, Vol. 17, pp.
         117-128.

D-298.   Hsieh, Chaio-Min.   1959.   "The Status of
         Geography in Communist China," Geographical
         Review, Vol. 49, pp. 535-551.

D-299.   Hsu, Ginn-Tze.   1949.   "Some Chinese Geographical
         Works During the War," Scottish Geographical
         Magazine, Vol. 65, pp. 54-59.

D-300.   Hu, Charles Y.   1948.   "Some Basic Problems of
         Geographical Research on China," Annals of the
         Association of American Geographers, Vol. 38, pp.
         75-76.

D-301.   Hunker, Henry L.   1958.   "Geography in
         Australia," Professional Geographer, Vol.   10,
         pp. 7-12.

D-302.   Huzinec, George A.   1977.   "A Reexamination of
         Soviet Industrial Location Theory," Professional
         Geographer, Vol. 29, pp. 259-265.

D-303.   Ikhavorai, Isi A.   1986.   "The Nigerian School of
         Geography," GeoJournal Vol. 12, pp. 103-106.

D-304.   Ikhavorai, I. A.   1986.   "The Nigerian School of
         Geography," GeoJournal Vol. 12, pp. 107-110.

D-305.   Innis, Harold A. and Broek, Jan O.M.   1945.
         "Geography and Nationalism: A Discussion,"
         Geographical Review, Vol. 35, pp. 301-311.

D-306.   Isachenko, A. G.   1968.   "Fifty Years of Soviet
         Landscape Science," Soviet Geography: Review and
         Translation, Vol. 9, pp. 402-407.

D-307.   Isachenko, A. G.   1972.   "Determinism and
         Indeterminism in Foreign Geography," Soviet
         Geography: Review and Translation, Vol. 13, pp.
         421-432, pp. 544-558.

D-308.   Jackson, John N.   1964.   "Review Article:
         Geography and Planning in British Columbia,"
         Canadian Geographer, Vol. 8, pp. 92-96.

D-309.   Jackson, W. A. Douglas.   1958.   "American
         Geographic Research on Russia," Professional
         Geographer, Vol. 10, No. 6, pp. 2-6.

D-310.   Jackson, W. A. Douglas. 1964. "Geographic
          Education in Poland," Journal of Geography, Vol.
          63, pp. 418-425.

D-311.   Jahr, Anton. 1911. "Geographical Instruction in
          German Elementary Schools," Journal of Geography,
          Vol. 9, pp. 239-243.

D-312.   Jancu, M. and Baron, P. 1984. "Directions of
          Romanian Tourism and of Tourist Research,"
          GeoJournal, Vol. 9, pp. 75-76.

D-313.   Jeans, D. N. 1983. "Experiments of Fruit and
          Experiments of Light: Human Geography in
          Australia and New Zealand," Progress in Human
          Geography, Vol. 7, pp. 313-343.

D-314.   Jeans, D. N. and Davies, J. L. 1984.
          "Australian Geography 1972-1982," Australian
          Geographical Studies, Vol. 22, pp. 3-35.

D-315.   Jen, Mei-Ngo. 1948. "The Progress of Geography
          in China During the Last Thirty Years,"
          Professional Geographer, Vol. 8, pp. 46-54.

D-316.   Joerg, W. L. G. 1922. "Recent Geographical Work
          in Europe," Geographical Review, Vol. 12, pp.
          431-484.

D-317.   Joerg, W. L. G. 1933. "The Development of
          Polish Cartography Since the World War,"
          Geographical Review, Vol. 23, pp. 122-129.

D-318.   Johnson, J. H. 1979. "Postgraduate Research
          Students in British Universities," Geoforum,
          Vol. 10, pp. 251-252.

D-319.   Johnston, R. J. 1978. "Paradigms and
          Revolutions or Evolution: Observations on Human
          Geography Since the Second World War," Progress
          in Human Geography, Vol. 2, pp. 189-206.

D-320.   Johnston, R. J. 1985. "Spatial Analysis in
          British Human Geography: A Twenty-Year
          Diversion, Espace Geographique, Vol. 14, pp.
          29-32.

D-321.   Jones, Clarence F. 1959. "Status and Trends of
          Geography in the United States, 1952-1957,"
          Professional Geographer, Vol. 11, Part 2, pp.
          1-145.

D-322.   Jones, E. 1979. "Contemporary British
          Geography," Geoforum, Vol. 10, pp. 215-218.

D-323.   Jopling, A. 1970. "Recommendations on the
          Future Development of Geomorphology in Canada,"
          Canadian Geographer, Vol. 14, pp. 167-173.

D-324.   Kadar, Laszlo. 1971. "A Hundred Years of the
          Hungarian Geographical Society," Geoforum, Vol.
          2, No. 6, pp. 75-83.

D-325.   Kalesnik, S. V. 1956. "Training of Geographers
          and Geography Teachers at Soviet Universities,"
          Proceedings - Eighteenth International
          Geographical Congress, pp. 563-568.

D-326.   Kalesnik, S. V. 1962. "About Monism and
          'Dualism' in Soviet Geography," Soviet
          Geography: Review and Translation, Vol. 3, No.
          7, pp. 3-16.

D-327.   Kalesnik, S. V. 1966. "Geography Today," Soviet
          Geography: Review and Translation, Vol. 7, pp.
          15-28.

D-328.   Kalesnik, S. V. 1968. "The Development of
          General Earth Science in the U.S.S.R. During the
          Soviet Period," Soviet Geography: Review and
          Translation, Vol. 9, pp. 393-402.

D-329.   Kalesnik, S. V. 1971. "On the Significance of
          Lenin's Ideas for Soviet Geography," Soviet
          Geography: Review and Translation, Vol. 12, pp.
          196-205.

D-330.   Kalesnik, S. V. and Davitaya, F. F. 1976. "The
          Tasks of Soviet Geography in Supporting Soviet
          Economic Development During the 10th Five-Year
          Plan (1976-80)," Soviet Geography: Review and
          Translation, Vol. 17, pp. 217-234.

D-331.   Kekoni, Karl. 1926. "Geography in the Schools
          of Finland," Journal of Geography, Vol. 25, pp.
          67-71.

D-332.   Keltie, J. Scott. 1886. "Geographical Education
          on the Continent and the Appliances for Teaching
          the Subject," Journal of the Manchester
          Geographical Society, Vol. 2, pp. 241-258.

D-333.   Keltie, J. Scott. 1891. "Recent Progress of
          Geographical Education in England," Journal of
          the Manchester Geographical Society, Vol. 7, p.
          263.

D-334.   Kincer, J. B. 1936. "Organization and Work in
          Climatology and Agricultural Meteorology in Great
          Britain, France and Scandinavian Countries,
          Poland and Russia," Annals of the Association of
          American Geographers, Vol. 26, pp. 64-65.

D-335.   Kipnis, Baruch and Waterman, Stanley. 1985.
          "Geography in Israel," Professional Geographer,
          Vol. 37, pp. 214-215.

D-336.   Kirkby, Richard. 1977. "Geography and Planning
          at Nanking University: Winter 1977," China
          Geographer, No. 6, pp. 51-58.

D-337.   Kish, George. 1988. "Geography in Estonia,"
          Professional Geographer, Vol. 40, pp. 95-96.

D-338.   Kiss, George. 1942. "Political Geography into
          Geopolitics: Recent Trends in Germany,"
          Geographical Review, Vol. 32, pp. 632-645.

D-339.   Kiuchi, Shinzo. 1963. "Recent Trends in Urban
          Geography in Japan," Annals of the Association of
          American Geographers, Vol. 53, pp. 93-101.

D-340.   Kochergin, P. G. 1961. "The Scientific
          Principles of the Content of a Geography Course
          of the Soviet Eight-Year School," Soviet
          Geography: Review and Translation, Vol. 2, No.
          8, pp. 46-51.

D-341.   Kohl, Horst. 1971. "The Humboldt University,
          Berlin and Its Development in Terms of Science
          Policies," Geographical Review of India, Vol. 23,
          pp. 263-272.

D-342.   Kohn, Clyde F. 1970. "The 1960's: A Decade of
          Progress in Geographical Research and
          Instruction," Annals of the Association of
          American Geographers, Vol. 60, pp. 211-219.

D-343.   Komar, I. V. et al. 1971. "Soviet Geographic
          Literature," Soviet Geography: Review and
          Translation, Vol. 12, pp. 495-528.

D-344.   Konovalenko, V. G. 1963. "About S. V.
          Kalesnik's Article on 'Monism' and 'Dualism' in
          Soviet Geography," Soviet Geography: Review and
          Translation, Vol. 4, No. 10, pp. 20-34.

D-345.   Konstantinov, O. A. 1960. "The Present Status
          of Economic Geographic Status of Economic
          Geographic Studies on the Economic
          Regionalization of the U.S.S.R.," Soviet
          Geography: Review and Translation, Vol. 1, No.
          7, pp. 36-59.

D-346.   Konstantinov, O. A. 1965. "On the Thirtieth
          Anniversary of the Department of Economic
          Geography of the Geographical Society U.S.S.R.,"
          Soviet Geography: Review and Translation, Vol.
          7, pp. 3-11.

D-347.   Konstantinov, O. A. 1968. "Economic Geography
          in the U.S.S.R. on the 50th Anniversary of Soviet
          Power," Soviet Geography: Review and
          Translation, Vol. 9, pp. 417-425.

D-348.   Konstantinov, O. A. 1971. "125 Years of the
          Geographical Society U.S.S.R.," Soviet
          Geography: Review and Translation, Vol. 12, pp.
          226-239.

D-349.   Konstantinov, O. A. 1980. "The 1929 Meeting of
          Soviet Geography Teachers: A Key Event in the
          History of Soviet Economic Geography," Soviet
          Geography: Review and Translation, Vol. 21, pp.
          427-439.

D-350.   Koreshy, K. V. 1966. "Geography in National
          Planning, With Special Reference to Urban
          Development," Pakistan Geographical Review, Vol.
          21, pp. 21-33.

D-351.   Kostrowicki, Jerzy. 1956. "Contribution of
          Geography to Planning in Poland," Proceedings -
          Eighteenth International Geographical Congress,
          pp. 569-574.

D-352.   Kostrowicki, Jerzy. 1956. "Geography in Poland
          Since the War," Geographical Journal, Vol. 122,
          pp. 441-450.

D-353.   Kovalevskiy, V. P. 1961. "A Canadian Scholar's
          Views on Geography in Canada and in the
          U.S.S.R.," Soviet Geography: Review and
          Translation, Vol. 2, No. 1, pp. 44-47.

D-354.   Krupenikov, I. A. 1968. "Results of the
          Development of Geography in the Moldavian SSR
          Under Soviet Rule," Soviet Geography: Review and
          Translation, Vol. 9, pp. 280-286.

D-355.   Küchler, D. A. 1983. "Commentary-The Guest
          Editorial," [Geography in Australia], Australian
          Geographical Studies, Vol. 21, pp. 162-163.

D-356.   Kuklinski, A. 1983. "Studies in the History of
          Polish Geography: Observations and Reflections,"
          GeoJournal, Vol. 7, pp. 317-319.

D-357.   Kuklinski, A. 1984. "Dilemmas in Polish
          Geography," in Miscelanea Geogrpahica, B.
          Dumanowski, et al., eds. (University of Warsaw
          Faculty of Geography) pp. 11-20.

D-358.   Kuklinski, A. 1984. "[Polish Geography --
          Mechanisms of Development in the Years
          1945-1982]," Prezeglad Geograficzny, Vol. 55, pp.
          521-546 [English Summary].

D-359.   Kumm, H. K. W. 1925. "Arab Geographers and
          Africa," Scottish Geographical Magazine, Vol. 41,
          pp. 284-289.

D-360.   Kundig-Steiner W.   1949.   "Geography as a
         Profession in Switzerland," Proceedings -
         Sixteenth International Geographical Congress,
         pp. 490.

D-361.   Kunze, Donald.   1983.   "Commentary on
         Metaphorical Vision: Changes in Western
         Attitudes to the Environment," Annals of the
         Association of American Geographers, Vol. 73, pp.
         153-156.

D-362.   Kupper, V. I.   1973.   "The Contribution of German
         Geographers to Local Boundary Reforms," Area,
         Vol. 5, pp. 172-176.

D-363.   Lane, Bernard.   1970.   "Geography and Manning in
         the Republic of Ireland," Geographical Viewpoint,
         Vol. 2, pp. 117-124.

D-364.   Lattimore, O.   1978.   "Douglas Carruthers and
         Geographical Contrasts in Central Asia,"
         Geographical Journal, Vol. 144, pp. 208-217.

D-365.   Lavrov, S. B.   et al.   1979.   "Socio-Economic
         Geography in the U.S.S.R.," Geoforum, Vol. 10,
         pp. 333-344.

D-366.   Law, B. C.   1944.   "Ancient Indian Geography,"
         Indian Geographical Journal, Vol. 19, pp. 1-23.

D-367.   Lea, David A. M., Clark, Nancy and Ward, R.
         Gerard.   1975.   "Geographers in Papua New
         Guinea: A Preliminary Bibliography," Australian
         Geographer, Vol. 13, pp. 104-145.

D-368.   Learmonth, A. T. A.   1961.   "Medical Geography in
         India and Pakistan," Geographical Journal, Vol.
         127, pp. 10-26.

D-369.   Lee, Chun-Fen.   1982.   "Geographical Education in
         Higher Institutions in China: A Personal
         Viewpoint," Canadian Geographer, Vol. 26, pp.
         153-157.

D-370.   Lee, Chun-Fen and Tang, J.   1982.   "Geography in
         Higher Education in China," Journal of Geography
         in Higher Education, Vol. 6, pp. 47-56.

D-371.   Lee, David and Evans, Arthur.   1985.   "Geographers'
         Rankings of Foreign Geography and Non-Geography
         Journals," Professional Geographer, Vol. 37, pp.
         396-402.

D-372.   Lee, Ki-Suk and Un Rii, Hae.   1985.   "Geography
         in Korea," Professional Geographer, Vol. 37, pp.
         344-345.

D-373.   Leeming, F.   1980.   "On Chinese Geography,"
         Geographical Journal, Vol. 4, pp. 218-237.

D-374.   Leng, Karl.   1978.   "The Berlin Geographical
         Society, 1928-1978," Geographical Journal, Vol.
         144, pp. 218-223.

D-375.   Leighly, John.   1938.   "Methodologic Controversy
         in Nineteenth Century German Geography," Annals
         of the Association of American Geographers, Vol.
         28, pp. 238-258.

D-376.   Leont'yev, N. F.   1970.   "Some Achievements and
         Problems in Soviet Cartography," Soviet
         Geography: Review and Translation, Vol. 11, pp.
         278-288.

D-377.   Leszczycki, Stanislaw.   1960.   "The Application
         of Geography in Poland," Geographical Journal,
         Vol. 126, pp. 418-426.

D-378.   Lewis, E. W.   1973.   "The Development of
         Geography in the Polytechnics of England and
         Wales," Geographical Journal, Vol. 139, pp.
         509-515.

D-379.   Lewis, G. Malcolm.   1982.   "The Milieu of
         Geography Within Higher Education in the United
         Kingdom in the 1980s," Journal of Geography in
         Higher Education, Vol. 6, pp. 141-150.

D-380.   Liang, Pv.   1982.   "Institution Profile:
         Department of Geography,   Zhongshan University,
         Guangzhon, China," Asian Geographer, Vol. 1, pp.
         77-78.

D-381.   Lichtenberger, E.   1978.   "Quantitative Geography
         in German-Speaking Countries," Tijdschrift voor
         Economische en Sociale Geografie, Vol. 69, pp.
         362-373.

D-382.   Lichtenberger, E.   1971.   "The Impact of
         Political Systems Upon Geography: The Case of
         the Federal Republic of Germany and the German
         Democratic Republic," Professional Geographer,
         Vol. 31, pp. 201-211.

D-383.   Limbird, A.   1986.   "A Mission for Geographers in
         the Secondary Schools of Canada," Operational
         Geographer, No. 10, p. 5.

D-384.   Lincoln, David.   1979.   "Ideology and South
         African Development Geography," South African
         Geographical Journal, Vol. 61, pp. 99-110.

D-385.   Linke, M., Hoffman, M. and Hellen, J. A.   1986.
         "Two Hundred Years of the Geographical-
         Cartographical Institute in Gotha," Geographical
         Journal, Vol. 152, pp. 75-80.

D-386.   Livingstone, David N.   1984.   "Natural Theology
         and NeoLamarkism: The Changing Context of
         Nineteenth-Century Geography in the United States
         and Great Britain," Annals of the Association of
         American Geographers, Vol. 74, pp. 9-28.

D-387.   Lochhead, E. N.   1981.   "Scotland as the Cradle
         of Modern Academic Geography in Britain,"
         Scottish Geographical Magazine, Vol. 97, pp.
         98-109.

D-388.   Luchs, Roland J. and Street, John M.   1976.
         "Geography as a Discipline in Asian
         Universities," Journal of Geography, Vol. 75, pp.
         93-108.

D-389.   Ludemann, H.   1984.   "Applied Aspects of
         Geography-Experience in the German Democratic
         Republic." Sbornik-Praci-Csav, Vol. 4, pp.
         67-74.

D-390.   Luk, S. H.   1980.   "Geography in the People's
         Republic of China," Canadian Geographer, Vol.
         24, pp. 299-306.

D-391.   Lukerman, F.   1961.   "The Concept of Location in
         Classical Geography," Annals of the Association
         of American Geographers, Vol. 51, pp. 194-210.

D-392.   Lunden, Thomas.   1986.   "Political Geography
         Around the World VI: Swedish Contributions to
         Political Geography," Political Geography
         Quarterly, Vol. 5, pp. 181-186.

D-393.   Lundgrew, J. O. J.   1984.   "Geographic Concepts
         and the Development of Tourism Research in
         Canada," GeoJournal, Vol. 9, pp. 17-26.

D-394.   Lutz, H. F.   1924.   "Geographical Studies Among
         Babylonians and Egyptians," American
         Anthropologist, Vol. 26, N.S. pp. 160-174.

D-395.   Ma, L. J. C. and Noble, A. G.   1979.   "Recent
         Developments in Chinese Geographical Research,"
         Geographical Review, Vol. 69, pp. 63-78.

D-396.   Mabogunje, A. L.   1968.   "Geography and National
         Reconstruction," Nigerian Geographical Journal,
         Vol. 11, pp. 3-10.

D-397.   Mabogunje, A. L.   1968.   "Research in Urban
         Geography in Nigeria," Nigerian Geographical
         Journal, Vol. 11, pp. 101-114.

D-398.   MacAlister, Sir Donald. 1921. "Geography at the
         University of Glasgow," Scottish Geographical
         Magazine, Vol. 37, pp. 53-56.

D-399.   MacDonald, William. 1961. "Geography in the
         English School," Journal of Geography, Vol. 60,
         pp. 310-312.

D-400.   Mackinder, H. J. 1895. "Modern Geography,
         German and English," Geographical Journal, Vol.
         6, pp. 367-379.

D-401.   Mackinder, Rt.-Hon. Sir Halford. 1935.
         "Progress of Geography in the Field and in the
         Study During the Reign of His Majesty King George
         the Fifth," Geographical Journal, Vol. 86, pp.
         1-17.

D-402.   Malecki, E. J. 1980. "Technological Change:
         British and American Research Themes," Area,
         Vol. 12, pp. 253-259.

D-403.   Malley, Ian M. 1987. "Literary Geography and
         the Writer's Country," Scottish Geographical
         Magazine, Vol. 103, pp. 122-131.

D-404.   Marcus, M. G. 1979. "Coming Full Circle:
         Physical Geography in the Twentieth Century,"
         Annals of the Association of American
         Geographers, Vol. 69, pp. 521-532.

D-405.   Marinich, A. M. et al. 1968. "The Development
         of Geography in the Ukraine During the Soviet
         Period," Soviet Geography: Review and
         Translation, Vol. 9, pp. 253-261.

D-406.   Mariot, P. 1984. "Geography of Tourism in
         Czechoslovakia," GeoJournal, Vol. 9, pp. 65-68.

D-407.   Markovin, A. P. 1962. "Historical Sketch of the
         Development of Soviet Medical Geography," Soviet
         Geography: Review and Translation, Vol. 3, No.
         8, pp. 3-20.

D-408.   Mashalla, S. K. 1988. "Geography in Tanzania,"
         Professional Geographer, Vol. 40, pp. 229-232.

D-409.   Mathieson, R. S. 1970. "Quantitative Geography
         in the Soviet Union," Australian Geographer, Vol.
         11, pp. 299-305.

D-410.   Matley, Ian. 1966. "The Marxist Approach to the
         Geographical Environment," Annals of the
         Association of American Geographers, Vol. 56, pp.
         97-111.

D-411.   May, J. A. 1983. "Review Essay - Philosophy and
         Geography in the Seventeenth Century: A Review,"
         Canadian Geographer, Vol. 27, pp. 85-96 [reply to
         Sitwell, pp. 379-380] [This review was printed
         first with many errors in CG, Vol. 26, pp.
         367-376].

D-412.   Maze, W. H. 1941. "Geography in New South Wales
         1930-1940," Australian Geographer, Vol. 4, pp.
         49-56.

D-413.   Maze, W. H. 1946. "The Teaching of Geography in
         Australian and New Zealand Universities,"
         Australian Geographer, Vol. 5, pp. 77-83.

D-414.   McBain, F. C. A. 1967. "Some Observations on
         Geography Courses in Nigerian Secondary Schools,
         Nigerian Geographical Journal, Vol. 10, pp.
         56-64.

D-415.   McCune, Shannon. 1947. "Geographical Journals
         in Asia," Professional Geographer, Vol. 6, pp.
         35-36.

D-416.   McCune, Shannon. 1948. "The Training of Foreign
         Geographers in the United States," Professional
         Geographer, Vol. 8, pp. 1-3.

D-417.   McCune, Shannon. 1949. "The Geographic
         Profession in Asia [Abstract]," Annals of the
         Association of American Geographers, Vol. 39, pp.
         62-63.

D-418.   McDonald, James R. 1964. "Current Controversy
         in French Geography," Professional Geographer,
         Vol. 16, No. 6, pp. 20-23.

D-419.   McDonald, James R. 1965. "Publication Trends in
         a Major French Geographical Journal," Annals of
         the Association of American Geographers, Vol. 55,
         pp. 125-139.

D-420.   McDonald, James R. 1975. "Current Trends in
         French Geography," Professional Geographer, Vol.
         27, pp. 15-18.

D-421.   McGee, T. G. 1978. "Western Geography and the
         Third World," American Behavioral Scientist, Vol.
         22, pp. 93-114.

D-422.   McIntire, Elliott G. 1979. "Native Americans
         and Geography," Transition, Vol. 9, pp. 20-22.

D-423.   McKay, Donald Vernon. 1943. "Colonialism in the
         French Geographical Movement, 1871-1881,"
         Geographical Review, Vol. 33, pp. 214-232.

D-424.   McKay, John and Powell, Joe. 1985. "Geography
          in Australian Society - Part One: The Heritage,"
          Journal of Geography, Vol. 84, pp. 98-104.

D-425.   McKay, John and Powell, Joe. 1985. "Geography
          in Australian Society - Part Two: The Current
          Situation," Journal of Geography, Vol. 84, pp.
          148-153.

D-426.   McKim, Wayne. 1988. "Geography in Botswana,"
          Professional Geographer, Vol. 40, pp. 227-228.

D-427.   McKnight, Tom. 1962. "Academic Geography in
          Australia," Professional Geographer, Vol. 14, No.
          4, pp. 21-24.

D-428.   Meadows, M. E. 1985. "Biogeographer: A Happy
          Ending to the Fairy Tale?" South African
          Geographical Journal, Vol. 67, pp. 40-61.

D-429.   Melezin, Abraham. 1963. "Trends and Issues in
          the Soviet Geography of Population," Annals of
          the Association of American Geographers, Vol. 53,
          pp. 144-160.

D-430.   Meyer, Alfred H. 1968. "American Geography:
          Image and Challenge," Journal of Geography, Vol.
          67, pp. 460-461.

D-431.   Meyer, Henry Cord. 1946. "Mittelevropa in
          German Political Geography," Annals of the
          Association of American Geographers, Vol. 36, pp.
          178-194.

D-432.   Mihailescu, V. 1975. "Editorial: Some Remarks
          on Geographical Thought in Romania," Geoforum,
          Vol. 6, pp. 3-8.

D-433.   Mikhaylov, A. N. et al. 1976. "Dissemination of
          Geographical Knowledge by the Geographical
          Society U.S.S.R.," Soviet Geography: Review and
          Translation, Vol. 16, pp. 593-604.

D-434.   Mikos, M. J. 1984. "Joachim Lelewel: Polish
          Scholar and Map Collector." Map Collector, Vol.
          26, pp. 20-24.

D-435.   Mill, Hugh Robert. 1890. "On the Teaching of
          Geography in Russia," Journal of the Manchester
          Geographical Society, Vol. 6, pp. 239-243.

D-436.   Mill, Hugh Robert. 1893. "Geography in European
          Universities," Educational Review, Vol. 6, pp.
          417-430.

D-437.   Miller, John P. 1961. "Physical Geography in
          Poland," Professional Geographer, Vol. 13, No. 2,
          pp. 34-37.

D-438.   Miller, R.   1980.   "The Royal Geographical
          Society, 1830-1980," Scottish Geographical
          Magazine, Vol. 96, pp. 180.

D-439.   Milojevic, Borivojez.   1956.   "The Teaching of
          Regional Geography at the Universities,"
          Proceedings - Eighteenth International
          Geographical Congress, pp. 583-588.

D-440.   Minamoto, Shokyu.   1985.   "A Study of J. M. D.
          Meikle-John's A New Geography on the Comparative
          Method -- One Aspect of The History of Geography
          in the Meiji Period," Geographical Review of
          Japan, Vol. 58B, pp. 195-207.

D-441.   Minkel, C. W.   1986.   "Geography in Argentina,"
          Professional Geographer, Vol. 38, pp. 423-425.

D-442.   Minkel, Clarence W.   1970.   "Geography in Central
          America: Its States and Prospects," East Lakes
          Geographer, Vol. 6, pp. 63-73.

D-443.   Mints, Aleksey A.   1967.   "A Program of
          Development of American Geography," Soviet
          Geography: Review and Translation, Vol. 9, pp.
          46-55.

D-444.   Mitra, Sevati.   1968.   "History of the
          Geographical Society of India," Geographical
          Review of India, Vol. 30. pp. 106-112.

D-445.   Mizvoka, Fujio.   1983.   "The Development of
          Marxian Economic Geography in Japan," Antipode,
          Vol. 15, pp. 27-36.

D-446.   Momsen, Janet Henshael.   1980.   "Women in
          Canadian Geography," Canadian Geographer, Vol.
          24, pp. 177-183.

D-447.   Momsen, Janet Henshael.   1980.   "Women in
          Canadian Geography," Professional Geographer,
          Vol. 32, pp. 355-369.

D-448.   Momsen, Richard P. Jr.   1965.   "The Role of the
          Geographer in Development Surveys, with Examples
          from the South American Tropics," Professional
          Geographer, Vol. 17, No. 1, pp. 1-4.

D-449.   Monk, Janice.   1977.   "Issues Confronting
          Geographic Educators in Europe and the
          U.S.S.R.," Professional Geographer, Vol. 29, pp.
          379-385.

D-450.   Moore, E.   1964-65.   "Geography in Alberta
          Schools," Albertan Geographer,   No. 1, pp. 26-28.

D-451.   Muir, T. S. 1912. "Geography in Scottish
Schools," Scottish Geographical Magazine, Vol.
28, pp. 534-540.

D-452.   Muller, J. 1953. "History of the South African
Geographical Society," South African Geographical
Journal, Vol. 35, pp. 3-16.

D-453.   Munton, R. J. and Gouldie, A. S. 1984.
"Geography in the United Kingdom, 1980-1984
Report to the 25th IGU Congress, Paris, 1984,"
Geographical Journal, Vol. 150, pp. 27-47.

D-454.   Murphy, Raymond E. 1961. "Marketing Geography
Comes of Age," Economic Geography, Vol. 37, pp.
1.

D-455.   Murray, Malcolm A. 1964. "Medical Geography in
the United Kingdom," Geographical Review, Vol.
54, pp. 582-584.

D-456.   Murray, Nancy and Vander Velde, Ed. 1984.
"Socially and Ecologically Responsible Geography
in Kenya," Antipode, Vol. 16, pp. 39-40.

D-457.   Mvrzayev, E. M. 1960. "Results and Aims of
Physical Regional Geography in the U.S.S.R.,"
Soviet Geography: Review and Translation, Vol.
1, No. 1-2, pp. 21-28.

D-458.   Mvrzayev, E. M. 1968. "Geography in the
Republics of Central Asia," Soviet Geography:
Review and Translation, Vol. 9, pp. 312-324.

D-459.   Nesterov, A. I. 1974. "The Development of
Anthropogenic Landscape Science at the Geography
Faculty of Voronezh University, Soviet
Geography: Review and Translation, Vol. 15, pp.
463-466.

D-460.   Newbigin, Marion I. 1913. "Geography in
Scotland Since 1889," Scottish Geographical
Magazine, Vol. 29, pp. 471-480.

D-461.   Nicholson, N. L. 1959. "Canada and the
International Geographical Union," Canadian
Geographer, No. 14, pp. 37-41.

D-462.   Nicholson, N. L. 1967. "The Geographer in
Contemporary Canadian Society," Canadian
Geographer, Vol. 11, pp. 157-160.

D-463.   Nikishoov, M. I. and Terekhov, N. M. 1968. "50
Years of Soviet Cartography: Translation,"
Canadian Cartographer, Vol. 5, pp. 122-132.

D-464.   Nikitin, N. P. 1966. "A History of Economic
         Geography in Pre-Revolutionary Russia," Soviet
         Geography: Review and Translation, Vol. 7, pp.
         3-37.

D-465.   Nishioba, Hisao. 1975. "Location Theory in
         Japan," Progress in Geography, Vol. 7, pp.
         133-200.

D-466.   Noh, Toshio. 1948. "Notes on Japanese
         Geographical Periodicals," Annals of the
         Association of American Geographers, Vol. 38, pp.
         231-232.

D-467.   Nunley, Robert E. 1970. "The Role of
         Anglo-American Geographers in Latin American
         Development," East Lakes Geographer, Vol. 6, pp.
         81-89.

D-468.   Obenbrugge, Jurgen. 1983. "Political Geography
         Around the World: West Germany," Political
         Geography Quarterly, Vol. 2, pp. 71-80.

D-469.   Ocitti, J. P. 1971. "A Revolutionary School
         Geography Syllabus in East Africa," East African
         Geographical Review, No. 9, pp. 3-10.

D-470.   Ogilvie, F. G. 1913. "Geographical Studies in
         the Schools of England and Wales," Proceedings -
         Tenth International Geographical Congress, pp.
         1426-1430.

D-471.   Ogundana, B. 1978. "The Growth and
         Contributions of the Nigerian Geographical
         Association," Nigerian Geographical Journal, Vol.
         21, pp. 25-30.

D-472.   Ojo, G. J. A. 1965. "The Immediate Future of
         Geography in Nigeria - the Relative Prospects of
         Physical and Human Geography," Nigerian
         Geographical Journal, Vol. 8, pp. 3-16.

D-473.   Ojo, G. J. A. 1966. "Nigerian Geography in
         Action," Nigerian Geographical Journal, Vol. 9,
         pp. 3-10.

D-474.   Okunrotifa, P. O. 1969. "Towards a Curriculum
         Reform in High School Geography," Nigerian
         Geographical Journal, Vol. 12, pp. 155-161.

D-475.   Okunrotifa, P. O. 1971. "The Aims and
         Objectives of Geographic Education," Nigerian
         Geographical Journal, Vol. 14, pp. 221-230.

D-476.   Okunrotifa, P. O. 1974. "A Study of Geography
         Teaching in Some Welsh Secondary Schools,"
         Nigerian Geographical Journal, Vol. 17, pp.
         165-172.

D-477.   Olson, Ralph E.   1970.   "Geography in Dutch
         Universities," Professional Geographer, Vol. 22,
         pp. 161-166.

D-478.   Oman, C.   1980.   "Note on Geography as Applied to
         History in Great Britain," Historical Geography,
         Vol. 10, pp. 18-20.

D-479.   Ota, Yoko and Nogami, Michio.   1979.   "Recent
         Research in Japanese Geomorphology," Professional
         Geographer, Vol. 31, pp. 410-415.

D-480.   Otok, Stanislaw.   1985.   "Political Geography
         Around the World V: Poland," Political Geography
         Quarterly, Vol. 4, pp. 321-328.

D-481.   Otok, Stanislaw and Achmatowicz-Otok, Anna.
         1985.   "Geography in Poland," Professional
         Geographer, Vol. 37, pp. 476-479.

D-482.   Ottens, H. F. L. and ter Welle-Heethuis, J. G.
         P.   1983.   "Recent Urban Research at Utrecht."
         Tidjscrift voor Economische en Sociale Geografie,
         Vol. 74, pp. 387-396.

D-483.   Pallot, Judith.   1983.   "Recent Approaches in the
         Geography of the Soviet Union," Progress in Human
         Geography, Vol. 7, pp. 519-542.

D-484.   Papy, Louis.   1983.   "Cavailles, Arque and
         Revert: Three Geographers of Bordeaux,"
         Geographers: Biobibliographical Studies, Vol. 7,
         pp. 5-10.

D-485.   Parker, Geoffrey.   1987.   "French Geopolitical
         Thought in the Interwar Years and the Emergence
         of the European Idea," Political Geography
         Quarterly, Vol. 6, pp. 145-150.

D-486.   Parry, J. T.   1967.   "Geomorphology in Canada,"
         Canadian Geographer, Vol. 11, pp. 280-311.

D-487.   Partsch, Joseph.   1913.   "Geographical
         Instruction in Germany," Journal of Geography,
         Vol. 12, pp. 119-121.

D-488.   Paterson, J. H.   1987.   "German Geopolitics
         Reassessed," Political Geography Quarterly, Vol.
         6, pp. 107-114.

D-489.   Pattanayak, D. P. and Bayer, J. M.   1987.
         "Laponcis 'The French Language in Canada:
         Tensions Between Geography and Politics'--a
         Rejoinder," Political Geography Quarterly, Vol.
         6, pp. 261-264.

D-490.   Pedrini, L.   1984.   "The Geography of Tourism and
         Leisure in Italy," GeoJournal, Vol. 9, pp. 55-58.

D-491.   Peet, Richard and Slater, David. 1980. "Reply
         to Soviet Review of Radical Geography," Soviet
         Geography: Review and Translation, Vol. 21, pp.
         541-544.

D-492.   Pellegrini, Giacomo Corna and Zerbi, Maria
         Clara. 1983. "Urban Geography and Urban
         Problems in Italy, 1945-81," Progress in Human
         Geography, Vol. 7, pp. 357-369.

D-493.   Perpillion, A. 1946. "Geography and
         Geographical Studies in France During the War
         and the Occupation," Geographical Journal, Vol.
         107, pp. 50-57.

D-494.   Perrett, Maurice Ed., 1947. "Geography in
         Switzerland," Professional Geographer, Vol. 6,
         pp. 30-34.

D-495.   Pethybridge, Roger. 1971. "British Contribu-
         tions to the Study of Russian Geography in the
         Nineteenth Century," Scottish Geographical
         Magazine, Vol. 87, pp. 58-65.

D-496.   Phillips, Martin and Unwin, Tim. 1985. "British
         Historical Geography: Places and People," Area,
         Vol. 17, pp. 155-164.

D-497.   Piggott, C. A. 1980. "A Geography of Religion
         in Scotland," Scottish Geographical Magazine,
         Vol. 96, pp. 130-140.

D-498.   Pirie, G. H. 1985. "Geography in South Africa,"
         Professional Geographer, Vol. 37, pp. 479-482.

D-499.   Pithawalla, Maneck B. 1944. "Some Knotty
         Problems of Indian Historical Geography," Indian
         Geographical Journal, Vol. 19, pp. 78-83.

D-500.   Podanchuk, V. D., Otalenko, M. A. and Tolcarskiy,
         N. K. 1962. "The New Geography Programs for the
         Eight-Year and General Middle Schools of the
         Ukranian SSR," Soviet Geography: Review and
         Translation, Vol.3, pp. 3-13.

D-501.   Pokshishevskiy, V. V. 1966. "Relationships and
         Contacts Between Pre- Revolutionary Russian and
         Soviet Geography and Foreign Geography," Soviet
         Geography: Review and Translation, Vol. 7, pp.
         56-77.

D-502.   Pokshishevskiy, V. V. 1971. "On New Directions
         in the Development of Soviet Economic Geography,"
         Soviet Geography: Review and Translation, Vol.
         12, pp. 403-416.

D-503.   Pokshishevskiy, V. V.   1975.   "On the Soviet
         Concept of Economic   Regionalisation: A Review
         of Geographical Research in the USSR on the
         Problems of Economic Regionalisation," Progress
         in Geography, Vol. 7, pp. 1-57.

D-504.   Pokshishevskiy, V. V. and Stepanova, Ye. A.
         1966.   "Publication of Soviet Economic-Geography
         Research in Foreign Publications," Soviet
         Geography: Review and Translation, Vol. 7, pp.
         77-81.

D-505.   Polizzi, Nicholas T.   1973-74.   "A Hundred Years
         of Geography in California," California
         Geographer, Vol. 14, pp. 9-28.

D-506.   Porteous, Douglas and Dyck, Heinz.   1987.   "How
         Canadian are Canadian Geographers?"   Canadian
         Geographer 24, pp. 177-179.

D-507.   Powell, J. M.   1981.   "Wide Angles and
         Convergencies: Recent Historical- Geographical
         Interaction in Australasia," Journal of
         Historical Geography, Vol. 7, pp. 407-414.

D-508.   Prescott, J. R. V. and Najdu, J. G.   1964.   "A
         Review of Some German Post-War Contributions to
         Political Geography," Australian Geographical
         Studies, Vol. 2, pp. 35-46.

D-509.   Preston, David F.   1974.   "Geographers Among the
         Peasants: Research on Rural Societies in Latin
         America," Progress in Geography, Vol. 6, pp.
         143-178.

D-510.   Probald, F.   1981-82.   "The Status of Geographical
         Education in Hungary,"   Annales-Universitaties
         Scientiarum Budapestensis de Rolando Eotvos
         Nominatae, Sectio Geographica, Vol. 16-17, pp.
         89-97.

D-511.   Prunty, Merle C.   1979.   "Geography in the
         South," Annals of the Association of American
         Geographers, Vol. 69, pp. 53-58.

D-512.   Pulle, Count Francesco L.   1902.   "Geography in
         Italy in 1901," Scottish Geographical Magazine,
         Vol. 18, pp. 471-479.

D-513.   Raisz, Erwin.   1964.   "Geography in Hungary,"
         Professional Geographer, Vol. 16, No. 3, pp.
         36-37.

D-514.   Reborahi, Carlos E.   1982.   "Human Geography in
         Latin America,"   Progress in Human Geography,
         Vol. 6, pp. 397-408.

D-515.   Reitsma, Hendrik-Jan A. 1983. "Foreign
          Languages: Some Comments," Professional
          Geographer, Vol. 36, p. 77.

D-516.   Richards, Paul. 1974. "Kant's Geography and
          Mental Maps," Transactions - Institute of British
          Geographers, Vol. 61, pp. 1-16.

D-517.   Riddell, J. Barry. 1981. "Human Geography and
          the Study of Africa," B. C. Geographical Series,
          No. 33, Vol. 2, pp. 109-119.

D-518.   Rizvi, A. I. H. 1969. "Pakistani
          Geomorphology," Pakistan Geographical Review,
          Vol. 24, pp. 142-146.

D-519.   Roberts, S. H. 1933. "Regionalism in France,"
          Australian Geographer, Vol. 2, pp. 11-16.

D-520.   Robertson, C. J. 1973. "Scottish Geographers:
          The First Hundred Years," Scottish Geographical
          Magazine, Vol. 89, pp. 5-18.

D-521.   Robinson, J. Lewis. 1951. "The Development and
          Status of Geography in Universities and
          Government in Canada," Yearbook of the
          Association of Pacific Coast Geographers, Vol.
          13, pp. 3-13.

D-522.   Robinson, J. Lewis. 1966. "Geography in the
          Canadian Universities," Professional Geographer,
          Vol. 18, pp. 69-74.

D-523.   Robinson, J. Lewis. 1967. "Growth and Trends in
          Geography in Canadian Universities," Canadian
          Geographer, Vol. 11, pp. 216-229.

D-524.   Robinson, J. Lewis. 1977. "The Production and
          Employment of Geographers in Canada,"
          Professional Geographer, Vol. 29, pp. 208-214.

D-525.   Robinson, J. Lewis. 1984. "The Employment of
          Ph.D. Geographers in Canada," Operational
          Geographer, No. 3, pp. 20-22.

D-526.   Robinson, J. Lewis. 1985. "The Production of
          Graduate Geographers from Canadian Universities,"
          Operational Geographer, No. 8, pp. 51-53.

D-527.   Robinson, J. Lewis. 1986. "Geography in
          Canada," Professional Geographer, Vol. 38, pp.
          411-417.

D-528.   Robinson, J. L. 1986. "Trends in Geography in
          Canada as Illustrated by Articles in the Canadian
          Geographer," Operational Geographer, No. 9, pp.
          15-18.

D-529.   Rodgers, Allan. 1975. "Some Observations on the
         Current Status of Geography in the People's
         Republic of China," China Geographer, No.2, pp.
         13-23.

D-530.   Rogers, Garry F. 1983. "Growth of Biogeography
         in Canadian and U. S. Geography Departments,"
         Professional Geographer, Vol. 35, pp. 219-226.

D-531.   Roglic, J. 1952. "Geography in Yugoslavia,"
         Geographical Journal, Vol. 118, pp. 205-208.

D-532.   Roglic, J. 1980. "The Postwar Development of
         Geographical Thought in Yugoslavia," Geographica
         Iugoslavica, Vol. 2, pp. 9-18.

D-533.   Rumley, Dennis. 1984. "Australian Geography,
         quo vadis," Australian Geographical Studies,
         Vol. 22, pp. 313-314.

D-534.   Ryabchikov, A. M. 1968. "Geography at Moscow
         University Over the Last 50 Years," Soviet
         Geography: Review and Translation, Vol. 9, pp.
         343-358.

D-535.   Sada, P. O. 1978. "Growth and Trends of
         Geographic Research in Nigeria," Nigerian
         Geographical Journal, Vol. 21, pp. 39-61.

D-536.   Sada, P. O. 1982. "Geography in Nigeria:
         Perspectives and Prospects," Presidential
         Address, 25th Annual Conference, Nigerian
         Geographical Association, Idadan.

D-537.   Saenz de la Calzada, C. 1972. "Academic
         Training in Mexico of Medical Geography
         Specialists," Proceedings - Twenty Second
         International Geographical Congress, pp.
         1225-1226.

D-538.   Salan, Ademola T. 1986. "Geography in Nigeria,"
         Professional Geographer, Vol. 38, pp. 417-419.

D-539.   Saleh, Nassir A. 1985. "Geography in Saudi
         Arabia," Professional Geographer, Vol. 37, pp.
         216-218.

D-540.   Salishchev, K. A. 1971. "Present Problems in
         Soviet Cartography and the Tasks of the
         Geographical Society," Soviet Geography: Review
         and Translation, Vol. 12, pp. 428-434.

D-541.   Salita, Domingo C. 1980. "Geography and
         Environmental Problems in the Philippines,"
         Philippine Geographical Journal, Vol. 234, pp.
         153-[158].

D-542. Sandru, I. and Cucu, V. 1966. "The Development of Geographical Studies in Rumania," Geographical Journal, Vol. 132, pp. 43-47.

D-543. Sandru, Ion and Cucu, Vasile. 1966. "Some Considerations on the Development of Geography in the Socialist Republic of Rumania," Professional Geographer, Vol. 18, pp. 219-223.

D-544. Sanguin, Andre-Louis. 1983. "Political Geography Around the World II: Whither the Geography of Power Among French Geographers?" Political Geography Quarterly, Vol. 2, pp. 319-328.

D-545. Saushkin, Julian G. 1960. "Geography in the Schools, Universities, and Everyday Life of the Soviet Union," Canadian Geographer, Vol. 17, pp. 41-47.

D-546. Saushkin, Yu G. 1962. "Geography in American Universities," Soviet Geography: Review and Translation, Vol. 3, No. 2, pp. 64-74, No. 3, pp. 74-81.

D-547. Saushkin, Yu. G. 1964. "Methodological Problems of Soviet Geography as Interpreted by Some Foreign Geographers," Soviet Geography: Review and Translation, Vol. 5, pp. 50-66.

D-548. Saushkin, Y. G. 1976. "The Role of Geography in the Definition and Solution of the Problems Associated with the Soviet Economy," Geoforum, Vol. 7, pp. 159-166.

D-549. Scarfe, N. V. 1955. "The Teaching of Geography in Canada," Canadian Geographer, No. 5, pp. 1-8.

D-550. Scargill, D. I. 1976. "The RGS and the Foundations of Geography at Oxford," Geographical Journal, Vol. 142, pp. 438-44.

D-551. Schoy, Carl. 1924. "The Geography of the Moslems of the Middle Ages," Geographic Review, Vol. 14, pp. 257-269.

D-552. Schroeder, Klaus. 1956. "The Study of Geography in Germany," Professional Geographer, Vol. 8, No. 4, pp. 13-16.

D-553. Scott, D. 1986. "Time, Structuration and the Potential for South African Historical Geography," South African Geographical Journal, Vol. 68, pp. 45-66.

D-554.   Sellors, Richard Pickering. 1913. "Geography.
         The Courses of Instruction in the Schools of New
         South Wales," Proceedings - Tenth International
         Geographical Congress, pp. 1479-1498.

D-555.   Semevskiy, B. N. 1960. "Some Impressions From a
         Visit to the United States," Soviet Geography:
         Review and Translation, Vol. 1, No. 3, pp. 62-68.

D-556.   Semevskiy, B. N. 1963. "Geography at the
         University of Havana," Soviet Geography: Review
         and Translation, Vol. 4, No. 9, pp. 52-55.

D-557.   Semevskiy, B. N. 1970. "Propaganda for a
         'Unified Geography'," Soviet Geography: Review
         and Translation, Vol. 11, pp. 501-509.

D-558.   Semevskiy, B. N. 1973. "Problems in the Theory
         of Geography ... [report of IGU conference],"
         Soviet Geography: Review and Translation, Vol.
         14, pp. 625-633.

D-559.   Semevskiy, Boris N. 1967. "Geography Teaching
         in Cuba," Soviet Geography: Review and
         Translation, Vol. 8, pp. 40-44.

D-560.   Senda, H. 1982. "Progress in Japanese
         Historical Geography," Journal of Historical
         Geography, Vol. 8, pp. 170-181.

D-561.   Sereno, Paola. 1983. "New Trends and Past
         Traditions in Historical Geography in Italy,"
         Historical Geography Newsletter, Vol. 13, pp.
         11-12.

D-562.   Shafi, Mohammad. 1967. "Applied Geography,"
         Indian Journal of Geography, Vol. 2, pp. 9-12.

D-563.   Shaw, Dennis. 1977. "Geography in Higher
         Education in the U.S.S.R.," Journal of Geography
         in Higher Education, Vol. 1, pp. 35-40.

D-564.   Sheppard, Eric. 1982. "Recent Research in
         Soviet Quantitative Geography: A Brief Review,"
         Antipode, Vol. 14, pp. 11-16.

D-565.   Shibanov, F. A. 1971. "Some Aspects of the
         Cartography of the Pre-Petrine Period (16th-17th
         Centuries) and the Role of S. Yu. Remezov in the
         History of Russian Cartography," Canadian
         Cartographer, Vol. 8, pp. 84-89.

D-566.   Shibanov, F. A. 1973. "The Essence and Content
         of the History of Cartography and the Results of
         Fifty Years of Work by Soviet Scholars," Canadian
         Cartographer, Vol. 10, pp. 21-25.

D-567.   Shitara, H.   1978.   "Fifty Years of Climatology
          in Japan," Science Reports of Tohaku University,
          Vol. 28, pp. 395-430.

D-568.   Siddal, William R.   1961.   "Two Kinds of
          Geography," Economic Geography Vol. 37, pp. 189.

D-569.   Simmons, James W.   1967.   "Urban Geography in
          Canada," Canadian Geographer, Vol. 11, pp.
          341-356.

D-570.   Sindiga, Isaac and Burnett, G. Wesley.   1988.
          "Geography and Development in Kenya,"
          Professional Geographer, Vol. 40, pp. 232-237.

D-571.   Singh, C. P.   1976.   "Indian Geographers and
          Foreign Area Studies," Geographical Review of
          India, 139, pp. 134-145.

D-572.   Singh, Dina Nath.   1970.   "Review Article: A
          Review of the Works Published in the National
          Geographical Journal of India.   1955-1969,"
          National Geographical Journal of India, Vol. 16,
          pp. 288-302.

D-573.   Singh, Dina Nath.   1977.   "Transportation
          Geography in India: A Survey of Research,"
          National Geographical Journal of India, Vol. 23,
          pp. 95-114.

D-574.   Singh, Mahar.   1982.   "History of Cartography in
          India: Some Questions," Indian Geographical
          Journal, Vol. 57, pp. 79-81.

D-575.   Sit, Victor and Chu, David K. Y.   1984.
          "Geography in Asia," Asian Geographer, Vol. 3,
          pp. 69-71.

D-576.   Sit, Victor and Chu, David K. Y.   1984.
          "Geography in Asia; Review of 1981," Asian
          Geographer, Vol. 3, pp. 163-165.

D-577.   Sit, Victor and Chu, David K. Y.   1985.
          "Geography in Asia; Review of 1983," Asian
          Geographer, Vol. 4, pp. 163-165.

D-578.   Smidt, Marc de.   1983.   "Dutch Economic Geography
          in Retrospect," Tijdschrift voor Economische en
          Sociale Geografie, Vol. 74, pp. 344-357.

D-579.   Smith, J. Russell.   1902.   "Geography in
          Germany," Journal of Geography, Vol. 1, pp.
          420-430.

D-580.   Smith, J. Russell.   1902.   "Geography in Germany,
          II - The University," Journal of Geography, Vol.
          1, pp. 448-457.

D-581.   Smith, Thomas R. and Black, Lloyd D.   1946.
          "German Geography: War Work and Present Status,"
          Geographical Review, Vol. 36, pp. 398-408.

D-582.   Smole, William J.   1964.   "Professional Geography
          in Venezuela," Professional Geographer, Vol. 16,
          No. 3, pp. 32-35.

D-583.   Sochava, V. B.   1968.   "Modern Geography and Its
          Tasks in Siberia and the Soviet Far East," Soviet
          Geography: Review and Translation, Vol. 9, pp.
          80-95.

D-584.   Sommers, Lawrence M.   1961.   "Geography in
          Denmark: Instruction and   Research,"
          Professional Geographer, Vol. 13, No. 2, pp.
          32-33.

D-585.   Soulsby, Eve M.   1976.   "Innovation in Scottish
          School Geography," Geographical Viewpoint, Vol.
          5, pp. 48-59.

D-586.   Spate, O. H. K.   1963.   "Theory and Practice in
          Soviet Geography," Australian Geographical
          Studies, Vol. 1, pp. 18-30.

D-587.   Spate, O. H. K.   1972.   "Australian Geography,
          1951-1971," Australian Geographical Studies, Vol.
          10, pp. 113-140.

D-588.   Stander, E.   1970.   "South African Geography -
          Trends and Prospects," South African Geographical
          Journal, Vol. 52, pp. 3-12.

D-589.   Stanley, H. M.   1885.   "Central African and the
          Congo Basin; on the   Importance of the Scientific
          Studies of Geography," Journal of the Manchester
          Geographical Society, Vol. 1, pp. 6-25.

D-590.   Steel, Robert.   1969.   "Geography in Ghana,"
          Bulletin - Ghana Geographical   Association, Vol.
          14, pp. 4-6.

D-591.   Steel, Robert W.   1952.   "The Progress of
          Geogrpahy in British Tropical Africa,"
          Proceedings - Seventeenth International
          Geographical Congress, pp. 93-97.

D-592.   Steel, Robert W. and Watson, J. Wreford.   1972.
          "Geography in the United Kingdom, 1968-72,"
          Geographical Journal, Vol. 138, pp. 395-430.

D-593.   Steers, Harriet.   1974.   "A History of Geography
          in Europe: Review," Geographical Journal, Vol.
          140, pp. 121-123.

D-594.   Sternberg, Hilgard O'Reilly.   1951.   "The Status
          of Geography in Brazil," Professional Geographer,
          Vol. 3, pp. 23-29.

D-595.   Sternberg, Hilgard O'Reilly.   1959.   "Geographic
          Thought and Development in Brazil," Professional
          Geographer, Vol. 11, No. 6, pp. 12-17.

D-596.   Stoddart, D. R.   1978.   "Geomorphology in China,"
          Progress in Physical Geography, Vol. 2, pp.
          514-551.

D-597.   Stone, Adolf.   1953.   "Geopolitics as Haushofer
          Taught It," Journal of Geography, Vol. 52, pp.
          167-171.

D-598.   Suizu, Ichiro.   1984.   "The Codes of Japanese
          Landscapes - An Attempt to Topological
          Geography," Geographical Review of Japan, Vol.
          57B, pp. 1-21.

D-599.   Sukhwal, Bheru.   1984.   "Geography in Indian
          Secondary Schools," National Geographical Journal
          of India, Vol. 30, pp. 223-230.

D-600.   Sullivan, Michael E.   1976.   "On the Need for an
          International Focus in American Geography,"
          Geographical Survey, Vol. 5, No. 1, pp. 4-5.

D-601.   Sun, Pan-Shou.   1982.   "Current Research in Urban
          Geography in China: A Review," Asian
          Geographer, Vol. 1, pp. 67-69.

D-602.   Sutton, K. and Lawless, R. I.   1987.   "Progress
          in the Human Geography of Maghreb," Progress in
          Human Geography, Vol. 11, 60-105.

D-603.   Sweeting, M. M., et al.   1978.   "British
          Geographers in China," Geographical Journal, Vol.
          144, pp. 187-207.

D-604.   Szekely, Beatrice Bench.   1987.   "The New Soviet
          Secondary School Geography Curriculum: Editor's
          Introduction," Soviet Education, Vol. 29, pp. 3-9
          [entire volume devoted to curriculum study, pp.
          3-99]

D-605.   Tait, John B.   1945.   "Oceanography: Scotland's
          Interest in its Progress," Scottish Geographical
          Magazine, Vol. 61, pp. 1-9.

D-606.   Takeuchi, K.   1984.   "Some Remarks on the
          Geography of Tourism in Japan," GeoJournal, Vol.
          9, pp. 85-90.

D-607.   Takeuchi, K.   1980.   "Some Remarks on the History
         of Regional Description and the Tradition of
         Regionalism in Modern Japan," _Progress in Human
         Geography_, Vol. 4, pp. 238-248.

D-608.   Tamaskar, B. G.   1981.   "Historical
         Maps--Prospects of Historical Cartography in
         India," _Deccan Geographer_, Vol. 19, pp. 137-144.

D-609.   Tang, Jianzhang, et al.   1983.   "Geography in
         Higher Education in China," _Journal of Geography
         in Higher Education_, Vol. 7, pp. 77-84.

D-610.   Taylor, Bruce.   1986.   "Geography in Hong Kong,"
         Professional Geographer, Vol. 38, pp. 419-423.

D-611.   Taylor, D. R. F.   1983.   "Geography and the
         Developing Nations," _Canadian Geographer_, Vol.
         27, pp. 1-3.

D-612.   Taylor, D. R. F.   1985.   "The Educational
         Challenges of New Cartography," _Cartographica_,
         Vol. 22, pp. 19-37.

D-613.   Taylor, Peter J.   1975.   "An Interpretation of
         the Quantification Debate in British Geography,"
         Department of Geography Seminar Paper No. 29,
         University of Newcastle Upon Tyne.

D-614.   Taylor, Peter J.   1976.   "An Interpretation of
         the Quantification Debate in British Geography,"
         Transactions - Institute of British Geographers,
         New Series, Vol. 1, pp. 129-142.

D-615.   Taylor, Peter J.   1986.   "Locating the Question
         of Unity," _Transactions - Institute of British
         Geographers_, Vol. 11, pp. 443-448.

D-616.   Taylor, S. Martin.   1979.   "Personal Dispositions
         and Human Spatial Behavior." _Economic
         Geography_, Vol. 55, pp. 184-195.

D-617.   Taylor, Zbigniew.   1985.   "Geography as an
         Academic Discipline in Poland," _Journal of
         Geography in Higher Education_, Vol. 9, pp. 45-54.

D-618.   Teggart, F. J.   1919.   "Geography as an Aid to
         Statecraft: An   Appreciation of Mackinder's
         'Democratic Ideals and Reality'," _Geographical
         Review_, Vol. 8, pp. 227-242.

D-619.   Teggart, Frederick J.   1919.   "Human Geography
         and the University, An Opportunity for the
         University," _Journal of Geography_, Vol. 18, pp.
         142-148.

D-620.   Teller, James T. 1983. "Jean de Charpentier,
          1786-1855," Geographers: Biobibliographical
          Studies, Vol. 7, pp. 17-22.

D-621.   Temple, Paul. 1977. "Obituary: Professor Harry
          Thorpe O.B.E., M.A., M. Litt., Ph.D., F.S.A.,
          1913-1977," Transactions - Institute of British
          Geographers, Vol. 2, pp. 255-256.

D-622.   Tewari, A. K. 1984-85. "Geography in Indian
          Universities: Past, Present and Future -- A
          Review," Indian Journal of Geography, Vol. 14,
          pp. 85-94.

D-623.   Thirunaranan, B. M. 1983. "J. A. Yates: The
          Link Between Geography at Oxford and at Madras,"
          Indian Geographical Journal, Vol. 58, pp.
          93-[96].

D-624.   Thomale, E. 1984. "Social Geographical Research
          in Germany - a Balance Sheet for the Years
          1950-1980," GeoJournal, Vol. 9, pp. 223-230.

D-625.   Thoman, Richard S. 1958. "Recent Methodological
          Contributions to German Economic Geography,"
          Annals of the Association of American
          Geographers, Vol. 48, pp. 92-96.

D-626.   Thoman, Richard S. 1967. "Economic Geography in
          Canada," Canadian Geographer, Vol. 11, pp.
          366-371.

D-627.   Thomas, Benjamin E. 1949. "College Geography in
          the Rocky Mountain States," Journal of
          Geography, Vol. 48, pp. 160-170.

D-628.   Thomas, Benjamin E. 1962. "Exclusionism in
          American Geography," Yearbook - Association of
          Pacific Coast Geographers, Vol. 24, pp. 7-14.

D-629.   Thomas, Oline J. 1917. "The Development and
          Present Organization of Elementary School
          Geography in the United States," Journal of
          Geography, Vol. 15, pp. 213-220.

D-630.   Thomas, Colin. 1981. "Yugoslav Geography: A
          Case of Mistaken Identity," Journal of Geography
          in Higher Education, Vol. 5, pp. 199-201.

D-631.   Thompson, Rev. Joseph P. 1859. "The Value of
          Geography to the Scholar, the Merchant, and the
          Philanthropist," Journal of the American
          Geographical and Statistical Society, Vol. 1, pp.
          98-107.

D-632.   Thornes, J. B. 1979. "Research and Application
          in British Geomorphology," Geoforum, Vol. 10,
          pp. 253-260.

D-633.   Thornes, John E.   1978.   "Applied Climatology
         [Great Britain]," Progress in Physical Geography,
         Vol. 2, pp. 481-493.

D-634.   Thornes, John E.   1979.   "Applied Climatology
         [Europe]," Progress in Physical Geography, Vol.
         3, pp. 427-442.

D-635.   Thornthwaite, C. W.   1961.   "American
         Geographers: A Critical Evaluation,"
         Professional Geographer, Vol. 13, pp. 10-13.

D-636.   Thorpe, D.   1978.   "Progress in the Study of the
         Geography of Retailing and Wholesaling in
         Britain," Geoforum, Vol. 9, pp. 83-106.

D-637.   Thorpe, Harry.   1955.   "Geography in the Danish
         Universities," Geographical Studies, Vol. 2, pp.
         58-61.

D-638.   Thrift, Nigel.   1983.   "Literature, the
         Production of Culture and the Politics of Place,"
         Antipode, Vol. 15, pp. 12-23.

D-639.   Thrower, Norman J. W.   1964.   "Geomorphology in
         Strabo's Geography," California Geographer, Vol.
         5, pp. 11-16.

D-640.   Tomkins, G. A.   1972.   "Griffith Taylor and the
         Beginnings of Academic Geography in Canada,"
         Proceedings of the Twenty Second International
         Geographical Congress, pp. 939-941.

D-641.   Tomkins, George S.   1986.   "Understanding
         Ourselves: The Origin and   Development of
         Canadian Studies," B. C. Geographical Series, No.
         43, pp. 75-94.

D-642.   Towler, J.   1981.   "Geography and Environmental
         Education: A Canadian Perspective," Journal of
         Geography, Vol. 80, pp. 132-135.

D-643.   Tripathi, Shri Maya Prasad.   1964.   "Was
         Geography a Separate Systematic Science in
         Ancient India?" National Geographical Journal of
         India, Vol. 10, pp. 82-91.

D-644.   Trusov, Yu. P.   1969.   "The Concept of the Noo
         Sphere," Soviet Geography: Review and
         Translation, Vol. 10, pp. 220-237.

D-645.   Tsegmid, Sh.   1968.   "Geography in the Mongolian
         Peoples Republic," Soviet Geography: Review and
         Translation, Vol. 9, pp. 324-333.

D-646.   Turnock, D.   1982.   "Romanian Geography Reunited
          - The Integrative Approach Demonstrated by the
          Conservation Movement," GeoJournal, Vol. 6, pp.
          419-432.

D-647.   Turnock, D.   1987.   "Urban Geography and Urban
          Development in Romania: The Contribution of
          Vintila Mihailescu," GeoJournal, Vol. 14, pp.
          181-202.

D-648.   Uchida, Kan-ichi.   1952.   "Present-day Geography
          Education in Japan," Proceedings of the
          Seventeeth International Geographical Congress,
          pp. 709-712.

D-649.   Ulack, Richard.   1983.   "Geography in the
          Philippines," Philippine Geographical Journal,
          Vol. 27, 143-   .

D-650.   Ulack, Richard.   1984.   "Geography in the
          Philippines," Professional Geographer, Vol. 36,
          pp. 480-482.

D-651.   UNESCO.   1951.   The Teaching of Geography -- and
          International Understanding, Australian
          Geographer, No. 9, pp. 250-253.

D-652.   Unwin, J. W.   1978.   "Quantative and Theoretical
          Geography in the United Kingdom," Area, Vol. 10,
          pp. 337-344.

D-653.   Unwin, Dr. J. W.   1979.   "Theoretical and
          Quantitative Geography in North- West Europe,"
          Area, Vol. 11, pp. 164-166.

D-654.   Uren, P. C.   1950.   "The Status of Military
          Geography in Canada," Canadian Geographer, No.
          1, pp. 11-14.

D-655.   Valentey, D. I. and Koval'skaya, N. Ya.   1967.
          "The Place of Population Geography in the System
          of Population Sciences," Soviet Geography:
          Review and Translation, Vol. 8, pp. 629-641.

D-656.   Vascovic, M.   1984.   "Some Views on the Geography
          of Tourism and Recreation in Yugoslavia,"
          GeoJournal Vol. 9, pp. 77-82.

D-657.   Vasilevskiy, L. I.   1964.   "Basic Research
          Problems in the Geography of Transportation of
          Capitalist and Underdeveloped Countries," Soviet
          Geography: Review and Translation, Vol. 4, No.
          7, pp. 36-59.

D-658.   Veen, Arthur W. L. 1976. "Geography Between the
          Devil and the Deep Blue Sea," Tijdscrift voor
          Economische en Sociale Geografie, Vol. 67, pp.
          369-380.

D-659.   Vink, A. P. A. 1968. "The Role of Physical
          Geography in Integrated Surveys of Developing
          Countries," Tijdschrift voor Economische en
          Sociale Geografie, Vol. 59, pp. 294-312.

D-660.   Vol'f, M. B. et al. 1976. "Geography Education
          in the U.S.S.R. and Ways of Improving It," Soviet
          Geography: Review and Translation, Vol. 17, pp.
          581-593.

D-661.   Von Engeln, O. D. 1912. "Emil Von Sydon and the
          Development of German School Cartography,"
          Bulletin of the American Geographical Society,
          Vol. 44, pp. 846-848.

D-662.   Voronov, A. G. 1968. "Biogeography Today and
          Tomorrow," Soviet Geography: Review and
          Translation, Vol. 9, pp. 367-378.

D-663.   Vovil, Robert J. 1950. "Cartographer in
          Government," Professional Geographer, Vol. 2, pp.
          29-32.

D-664.   Wadley, David. 1983. "Postgraduate Education
          and Thesis Writing in Australian Geography: A
          Critique," Australian Geographical Studies, Vol.
          21, pp. 109-120.

D-665.   Wagner, P. 1971. "Geography as Criticism," B.
          C. Geographical Series, No. 12, pp. 32-40.

D-666.   Wagner, Philip. 1963. "America Emerging,"
          Landscape, Vol. 13, pp. 22-26.

D-667.   Wagner, Philip L. 1970. "The Hemisphere
          Revisited," East Lakes Geographer, Vol. 6, pp.
          26-36.

D-668.   Wagner, Philip L. 1975. "The Themes of Cultural
          Geography Rethought," Yearbook - Association of
          Pacific Coast Geographers, Vol. 37, pp. 7-14.

D-669.   Walford, Rex. 1982. "British School Geography
          in the 1980s: An Easy Test?" Journal of
          Geography in Higher Education, Vol. 6, pp.
          151-160.

D-670.   Ward, Roy. 1979. "The Changing Scope of
          Geographical Hydrology in Great Britain,"
          Progress in Geography, Vol. 3, pp. 392-412.

D-671.   Warszynska, J. 1984. "Geography of Tourism in
          Poland," GeoJournal, Vol. 9, pp. 69-70.

D-672.   Waterman, S. 1979. "Developments in Geographic
         Education in Israel," Geographical Viewpoint,
         Vol. 8, pp. 60-66.

D-673.   Waterman, Stanley. 1985. "Not Just Milk and
         Honey -- Now a Way of Life: Israeli Human
         Geography," Progress in Human Geography, Vol. 9,
         pp. 194-234.

D-674.   Waters, Roy. 1970. "Geography as a Social
         Science: A More Functional Geography for Latin
         America," East Lakes Geographer, Vol. 6, pp.
         5-25.

D-675.   Watson, J. Wreford. 1950. "Geography in
         Canada," Scottish Geographical Magazine, Vol. 66,
         pp. 170-172.

D-676.   Wellings, P. 1986. "Editor's Introduction.
         Geography and Development Studies in Southern
         Africa: A Progressive Prospectus," Geoforum,
         Vol. 17, pp. 119-132.

D-677.   Wellings, P. A. and McCarthy, J. J. 1983.
         "Whither South African Human Geography?" Area,
         Vol. 15, pp. 337-345.

D-678.   Welsted, John. 1988. "Twenty-five Years of
         Geography at Brandon University," Operational
         Geographer, No. 14, pp. 33-37.

D-679.   White, Arthur Silva. 1889. "On the Achievements
         of Scotsmen During the Nineteenth Century in the
         Fields of Geographical Exploration and Research,"
         Scottish Geographical Magazine, Vol. 5, pp.
         595-605.

D-680.   Wilheim, Eugene J. Jr. 1972. "Geography and
         Environmental Education in Virginia," Virginia
         Geographer, Vol. 7, pp. 17-19.

D-681.   Williams, J. F. 1978. "Two Observations on the
         State of Geography in the People's Republic of
         China: I) Economic Geography; II) Cartography,"
         China Geographer, Special Issue No. 9, pp. 17-31.

D-682.   Williams, Jack F. and Chung, Ch'ang-yi. 1985.
         "Geography in Taiwan," Professional Geographer,
         Vol. 37, pp. 219-220.

D-683.   Winid, Bogodar, et al. 1956. "The Polish
         University System of Teaching Geography,"
         Proceedings - Eighteenth International
         Geographical Congress, pp. 611-616.

D-684.   Wise, M. 1980. "Geographers in Japan," Area,
         Vol. 12, pp. 259-261.

D-685.   Wolforth, John.   1986.   "School Geography --
         Alive and Well in Canada?" Annals of the
         Association of American Geographers, Vol. 76, pp.
         17-24.

D-686.   Wood, J. D.   1964-65.   "Historical Geography in
         Alberta," Albertan Geographer, No. 1, pp. 17-19.

D-687.   Worth, C.   1982.   "Cartography and Portsmouth
         Polytechnic," South Hampshire Geographer, Vol.
         14, pp. 2-7.

D-688.   Wright, J. K.   1952.   "British Geography and the
         American Geographical Society," Geographical
         Journal, Vol. 118, pp. 153-167.

D-689.   Wright, John K.   1948.   "The Educational
         Functions of the Geographical Societies of the
         United States," Journal of Geography, Vol. 47,
         pp. 165-173.

D-690.   Wright, John K.   1950.   "American Geography in
         the Eighteen Fifties and Sixties," Annals of the
         Association of American Geographers, Vol. 40, p.
         151.

D-691.   Wright, John K.   1950.   "The Society's Beginning,"
         Geographical Review,   Vol. 40, pp. 350-352.

D-692.   Wright, John K.   1952.   "Protean Geography,"
         Geographical Review, Vol. 42, pp. 175-176.

D-693.   Wyckoff, William L.   1979.   "On the Louisiana School
         of Historical Geography and the Case of the Upland
         South," Syracuse University, Department of Geogra-
         phy, Discussion Paper Series, No. 54, pp. 1-34.

D-694.   Wynn, Graeme.   1977.   "Discovering the Antipodes,
         A Review of Historical Geography in Australia and
         New Zealand, 1969-1975, With a Bibliography,"
         Journal of Historical Geography, Vol. 3, pp.
         251-266.

D-695.   Yefremov, Yu K., Kalinin, F. P. and Yun'yev, I.
         S.   1962." The Importance of Home-Area Studies
         for Soviet Geography," Soviet Geography: Review
         and Translation, Vol. 3, No. 1, pp. 14-26.

D-696.   Younghusband, Lieut. Colonel Sir Francis.   1917.
         "Geographical Work in India for This Society,"
         Geographical Journal, Vol. 49, pp. 401-418.

D-697.   Yunns, M.   1952.   "Post-Graduate Teaching in
         Indian Universities," Geographer, Vol. 5, No. 1,
         pp. 44-50, No. 2, pp. 48-52.

D-698.   Zhirmunskiy, M. M. and Yanitskiy, N. F.   1964.
         "Methodological Clashes in Moscow as Misinter-
         preted by an American Geographer," <u>Soviet
         Geography</u>:   <u>Review</u> <u>and</u> <u>Translation</u>, Vol. 5, pp.
         85-91.

D-699.   Zinyama, Lovemare M.   1988.   "Geography in
         Zimbabwe," <u>Professional</u> <u>Geographer</u>, Vol. 40, pp.
         223-227.

Geographic Techniques and Models

E-1. Adams, Cyrus C. 1906. "Map-Making in the United States," _Bulletin of the American Geographical Society of New York_, Vol. 38, pp. 123-125.

E-2. Al'Brut, M. I. 1961. "Let Us Clear Up, Once and For All, Differences on Methodological Questions in Economic Geography," _Soviet Geography: Review and Translation_, Vol. 2, No. 3, pp. 23-26.

E-3. Alexander, John W. 1943. "An Isarithmic-Dot Population Map," _Economic Geography_, Vol. 19, pp. 431-432.

E-4. Allan, J. A. 1978. "Remote Sensing in Physical Geography," _Progress in Physical Geography_, Vol. 2, pp. 36-54.

E-5. Allan, J. A. 1984. "The Role and Future of Remote Sensing," _Satellite Remote Sensing_, Proc. 10th Anniversary Conference, Reading, 1984, pp. 23-39.

E-6. Angel, Shlomo, and Hyman, Geoffrey M. 1972. "Transformations and Geographic Theory," _Geographic Analysis_, Vol. 4, pp. 350-372.

E-7. Anonymous. 1896. "Lord Kelvin's Services to Geography," _Geographical Journal_, Vol. 8, pp. 68-70.

E-8. Anonymous. 1905. "On Geographical Method," _Scottish Geographical Magazine_, Vol. 21, pp. 309-312.

E-9. Anonymous. 1983. "Commentaries on Automated Geography," _Professional Geographer_, Vol. 35, pp. 339-353.

E-10.   Anuchin, V. A.   1970.   "Mathematization and the Geographic Method," _Soviet Geography: Review and Translation_, Vol. 11, pp. 71-81.

E-11.   Applebaum, William.   1952.   "A Technique for Constructing a Population and Urban Land Use Map." _Economic Geography_, Vol. 28, pp. 240-243.

E-12.   Archer, J. Clarke and Lavin, Stephen.   1981.   "Computer Assisted Instruction in Geography," _Geographical Perspectives_, Vol. 47, pp. 16-29.

E-13.   Armand, A. D. and Tarqul'yan, V. O.   1976.   "Some Fundamental Limitations on Experimentation and Model-Building in Geography," _Soviet Geography: Review and Translation_, Vol. 17, pp. 197-207.

E-14.   Bartholomew, J. G.   1902.   "The Philosophy of Map-Making, and the Evolution of a Great German Atlas," _Scottish Geographical Magazine_, Vol. 18, pp. 34-39.

E-15.   Beaumont, John.   1980.   "Data Collection and Analysis for Geographic Research: A Post Graduate Training Course," _Journal of Geography in Higher Education_, Vol. 4, pp. 72-80.

E-16.   Beguin, Hubert and Thisei, Jacques-Francois.   1979.   "An Axiomatic Approach Geographical Space," _Geographical Analysis_, Vol. 11, pp. 325-341.

E-17.   Bennett, R. J., Haining, R. P. and Griffith, D. A.   1984.   "The Problem of Missing Data on Spatial Surfaces," _Annals of the Association of American Geographers_, Vol. 74, pp. 138-156.

E-18.   Berry, Brian J. L.   1960.   "The Quantitative Bogey-man," _Economic Geography_, Vol. 36, (facing) pp. 283.

E-19.   Berry, Brian J. L.   1964.   "Approaches to Regional Analysis: A Synthesis," _Annals of the Association of American Geographers_, Vol. 54, pp. 2-12.

E-20.   Berry, Brian J. L.   1968.   "Interdependency of Spatial Structure and Spatial Behavior: A General Field Theory Formulation," _Papers of the Regional Science Association_, Vol. 21, pp. 205-228.

E-21.   Berry, Brian J. L.   1971.   "Problems of Data Organization and Analytical Methods in Geography," _Journal of the American Statistical Association_, Vol. 66, pp. 510-523.

E-22.   Beyers, William B. 1980. "Migration and the
        Development of Multiregional Economic Systems,"
        Economic Geography, Vol. 56, pp. 320-334.

E-23.   Bird, J. 1978. "Methodology and Philosophy,"
        Progress in Human Geography, Vol. 2, pp. 133-140.

E-24.   Bird, J. 1979. "Methodology and Philosophy,"
        Progress in Human Geography, Vol. 3, pp. 117-125.

E-25.   Blakemore, Michael. 1986. "Cartography and
        Geographic Information Systems," Progress in
        Human Geography, Vol. 10, pp. 553-563.

E-26.   Blaut, J. M. 1959. "Microgeographic Sampling:
        A Quantitative Approach to Regional Agricultural
        Geography," Economic Geography, Vol. 35, pp.
        79-88.

E-27.   Blaut, J. M. and Stea, David. 1971. "Studies of
        Geographic Learning," Annals of the Association
        of American Geographers, Vol. 61, pp. 387-393.

E-28.   Boots, B. N. 1980. "Weighting Thiessen
        Polygons," Economic Geography, Vol. 56, pp.
        248-259.

E-29.   Borchert, John R. 1968. "Remote Sensors and
        Geographical Science," Professional Geographer,
        Vol. 20, pp. 371-375.

E-30.   Bowen, M. J. 1979. "Scientific Method After
        Positivism," Australian Geographical Studies,
        Vol. 17, pp. 210-216.

E-31.   Bowie, William. 1923. "The Board of Surveys and
        Maps of the Federal Government," Annals of the
        Association of American Geographers, Vol. 13, pp.
        207-208.

E-32.   Boyce, Ronald R. and Clark, W. A. V. 1964. "The
        Concept of Shape in Geography," Geographical
        Review, Vol. 54, pp. 561-572.

E-33.   Briggs, D. J. 1981. "The Principles and
        Practice of Applied Geography," Applied
        Geography, Vol. 1, pp. 1-8.

E-34.   Browett, J. 1980. "Development, the
        Diffusionist Paradigm and Geography," Progress in
        Human Geography, Vol. 4, pp. 57-80.

E-35.   Bryan, M. Leonard. 1979. "Remote Sensing
        Applications: An Overview," Geographical Survey,
        Vol. 8, No. 4, pp. 23-28.

E-36.   Bunge, William W.   1961.   "The Structure of
        Contemporary American Geographic Research,"
        Professional Geographer, Vol. 13, pp. 19-23.

E-37.   Bunge, William W.   1973.   "Spatial Prediction,"
        Annals of the Association of American
        Geographers, Vol. 63, pp. 566-568.

E-38.   Bunting, Trudi E. and Guelke, Leonard.   1979.
        "Behavioral and Perception Geography: A Critical
        Appraisal," Annals of the Association of American
        Geographers, Vol. 69, pp. 448-462.

E-39.   Burton, Ian.   1963.   "The Quantitative Revolution
        and Theoretical Geography," Canadian Geographer,
        Vol. 7, pp. 151-162.

E-40.   Campbell, Robert D.   1968.   "Personality as an
        Element of Regional Geography," Annals of the
        Association of American Geographers, Vol. 58, pp.
        748-759.

E-41.   Chapman, G. P.   1970.   "The Application of
        Information Theory to the Analysis of Population
        Distributions in Space," Economic Geography, Vol.
        46, pp. 317-331.

E-42.   Chappell, John E. Jr.   1969.   "On Causation in
        Geographical Theory," Proceedings of the
        Nineteenth International Geographical Congress,
        Vol. 11, pp. 34-38.

E-43.   Chisholm, Michael.   1972.   "Macro- and
        Micro-Approaches to Urban Systems Research,"
        Geographical Journal, Vol. 138, pp. 60-63.

E-44.   Chojnicki, Zbyszko.   1970.   "Prediction in
        Economic Geography," Economic Geography, Vol. 46,
        pp. 213-222.

E-45.   Chojnicki, Zbyszko.   1979.   "The Methodological
        Bases of Prediction in Economic Geography,"
        Quaestiones Geographicae, Vol. 5, pp. 23-34.

E-46.   Chorley, Richard J.   1964.   "Geography and
        Analogue Theory," Annals of the Association of
        American Geographers, Vol. 54, pp. 127-137.

E-47.   Clarkson, James D.   1970.   "Ecology and Spatial
        Analysis," Annals of the Association of American
        Geographers, Vol. 60, pp. 700-716.

E-48.   Claval, P.   1981.   "Methodology and Geography,"
        Progress in Human Geography, Vol. 5, pp. 97-104.

E-49.   Cliff, A. D.   1980.   "Quantitative Methods,"
        Progress in Human Geography, Vol. 4, pp. 568-576.

E-50.   Cliff, Andrew D. and Ord, Keith. 1970. "Spatial
        Autocorrelation: a Review of Existing and New
        Measures with Applications," Economic Geography,
        Vol. 46, pp. 269-292.

E-51.   Coleman, G. 1971. "Computers and the
        Geographer," Dziko (Malawi), No. 3, pp. 11-18.

E-52.   Coppock, J. T. 1962. "Electronic Data
        Processing in Geographical Research,"
        Professional Geographer, Vol. 14, pp. 1-4.

E-53.   Coppock, J. T. and Johnson, J. H. 1962.
        "Measurement in Human Geography," Economic
        Geography, Vol. 38, pp. 130-137.

E-54.   Cosgrove, D. E. 1979. "Geography and the Past:
        States and Change," Area, Vol. 11, pp. 304-306.

E-55.   Couclelis, Helen. 1983. "Some Second Thoughts
        About Theory in the Social Sciences,"
        Geographical Analysis, Vol. 15, pp. 28-33.

E-56.   Cox, Nicholas and Anderson, Evan. 1978.
        "Teaching Geographical Data Analysis: Problems
        and Possible Solutions," Journal of Geography in
        Higher Education, Vol. 2, pp. 29-37.

E-57.   Crary, Douglas. 1959. "A Geographer Looks at
        the Landscape," Landscape, Vol. 9, pp. 22-25.

E-58.   Curry, Leslie. 1967. "Quantitative Geography,
        1967," Canadian Geographer, Vol. 11, pp. 265-279.

E-59.   Davis, D. H. 1926. "Objectives in a Geographic
        Field Study of a Community," Annals of the
        Association of American Geographers, Vol. 16, pp.
        24-25.

E-60.   De Souza, Anthony R. 1984. "A Crisis in
        Geographical Education," Journal of Geography,
        Vol. 83, p. 3.

E-61.   Dorigo, Guido and Tobler, Waldo. 1983.
        "Push-Pull Migration Laws," Annals of the
        Association of American Geographers, Vol. 73, pp.
        1-17.

E-62.   Downs, R. M. 1981. "Maps and Metaphors,"
        Professional Geographer, Vol. 33, pp. 287-293.

E-63.   Dziewonski, Kazimierz. 1965. "On Integration of
        Statistical Cartographic Analysis for Research
        Purposes," Papers of the Regional Science
        Association, Vol. 15, pp. 119-129.

E-64.   Dziewonski, Kazimierz. 1966. "A New Approach to the Theory and Empirical Analysis of Location," _Papers of the Regional Science Association_, Vol. 16, pp. 17-26.

E-65.   Eichenbaum, Jack and Gale, Stephen. 1971. "Form, Function, and Process: A Methodological Inquiry," _Economic Geography_, Vol. 47, pp. 525-544.

E-66.   Elliott, Francis E. 1948. "Locational Factors Affecting Industrial Plants," _Economic Geography_, Vol. 24, pp. 283-285.

E-67.   Estes, John E. 1974. "Recent Growth of Aerial Photographic Interpretation\Remote Sensing in Geography in The United States," _Professional Geographer_, Vol. 26, pp. 48-55.

E-68.   Eyles, J. and Lee, R. 1982. "Human Geography in Explanation," _Transactions - Institute of British Geographers_, Vol. 7, pp. 117-122.

E-69.   Farrington, I and S. M. Zuckerman. 1971. "The Logical Function of 'Models' in Geographical Methodology," _Bloomsbury Geographer_, Vol. 4, pp. 5-9.

E-70.   Fitzgerald, Walter. 1944. "Progress in Geographical Method," _Nature_, Vol. 153, No. 3886, pp. 481-483.

E-71.   Floyd, Barry N. 1962. "The Pleasures Ahead: A Geographic Meditation," _Professional Geographer_, Vol. 14, pp. 1-4.

E-72.   Floyd, Barry N. 1963. "Quantification--A Geographic Deviation?" _Professional Geographer_, Vol. 15, pp. 15-17.

E-73.   Friberg, Justin C. 1975. "Field Techniques and the Training of the American Geographer," Syracuse University, Department of Geography, _Discussion Paper Series_, No. 5.

E-74.   Frolov, Yu. S. 1975. "Measuring the Shape of Geographical Phenomena: A History of the Issue," _Soviet Geography: Review and Translation_, Vol. 16, pp. 676-687.

E-75.   Gale, N. and Golledge, R. G. 1982. "On the Subjective Partitioning of Space," _Annals of the Association of American Geographers_, Vol. 72, pp. 60-67.

E-76.   Gale, Stephen. 1972. "Inexactness, Fuzzy Sets, and the Foundations of Behavioral Geography," _Geographical Analysis_, Vol. 4, pp. 337-349.

E-77.   Gale, Stephen. 1972. "On the Heterodoxy of
        Explanations: A Review of David Harvey's
        Explanation in Geography," Geographical Analysis,
        Vol. 4, pp. 285-322.

E-78.   Garrison, William L. 1959.   "Spatial Structure
        of the Economy: I," Annals of the Association of
        American Geographers, Vol. 49, pp. 232-239.

E-79.   Garrison, William L. 1979. "Playing With
        Ideas," Annals of the Association of American
        Geographers," Vol. 69, pp. 118-120.

E-80.   Gates, N. C. 1979. "The Potential of Aviation
        Geography," Horizon, Vol. 29, pp. 50-58.

E-81.   Gatrell, A. C. 1984. "Describing the Structure
        of a Research Literature: Spatial Diffusion
        Modelling in Geography," Environment and Planning
        B, Vol. 11, pp. 29-45.

E-82.   Gatrell, Anthony C. 1984.   "The Geometry of a
        Research Specialty: Spatial Diffusion Modeling,"
        Annals of the Association of American
        Geographers, Vol. 74, pp. 437-453.

E-83.   Gauthier, Howard L. 1970. "Geography,
        Transportation, and Regional Development,"
        Economic Geography, Vol. 46, pp. 612-619.

E-84.   Gerasimov, I. P. 1978. "The Integrative
        Potential of Modern Geographic Research," Soviet
        Geography: Review and Translation, Vol. 19, pp.
        137-148.

E-85.   Gill, Don and Ironside, R. G. 1969. "The Role
        of Field Training in Canadian Geography,"
        Canadian Geographer, Vol. 13, pp. 373-380.

E-86.   Golledge, Reginald. 1966. "Geography and
        Quantitative Methods," B.C. Geographical Series,
        No. 3, pp. 29-34.

E-87.   Golledge, Reginald G. 1979. "The Development of
        Geographical Analysis," Annals of the Association
        of American Geographers, Vol. 69, pp. 151-154.

E-88.   Golledge, Reginald G., and Amadeo, Douglas.
        1966. "Some Introductory Notes on Regional
        Division and Set Theory," Professional
        Geographer, Vol. 18, pp. 14-19.

E-89.   Golledge, Reginald G., Brown, L. A., and
        Williamson, Frank. 1972.   "Behavioural
        Approaches in Geographer: An Overview,"
        Australian Geographer, Vol. 12, pp. 59-79.

E-90. Golledge, R. G. 1970. "Some Equilibrium Models
       of Consumer Behavior," Economic Geography, Vol.
       46, pp. 417-423.

E-91. Golledge, R. G. and Amadeo, Douglas. 1968. "On
       Laws in Geography," Annals of the Association of
       American Geographers, Vol. 58, pp. 760-774.

E-92. Goodchild, Michael F. 1985. "Geographic
       Information Systems in Undergraduate Geography:
       A Contemporary Dilemma," Operational Geographer,
       No. 8, pp. 34-38.

E-93. Goode, J. Paul. 1927. "The Map as a Record of
       Progress in Geography," Annals of the
       Association of American Geographers, Vol. 17, pp.
       1-15.

E-94. Gould, Peter. 1969. "Methodological Development
       Since the Fifties," Progress in Geography, Vol.
       1, pp. 1-50.

E-95. Gould, Peter. 1970. "Is Statestix Inferens the
       Geographical Name for a Wild Goose?", Economic
       Geography, Vol. 46, pp. 439-448.

E-96. Gould, P. 1970. "Computers and Spatial
       Analysis: Extension of Geographic Research,"
       Geoforum, [Vol. 1], No. 1, pp. 53-70.

E-97. Gould, Peter. 1979. "Geography 1957-1977: The
       Angean Period," Annals of the Association of
       American Geographers, Vol. 69, pp. 139-151.

E-98. Gould, Peter. 1981. "Letting the Data Speak for
       Themselves," Annals of the Association of
       American Geographers, Vol. 71, pp. 166-176.

E-99. Gregory, Derek. 1980. "The Ideology of
       Control: Systems Theory and Geography,"
       Tijdschrift voor Economische en Sociale
       Geografie, Vol. 71, pp. 327-342.

E-100. Gregory, S. 1976. "On Geographical Myths and
       Statistical Fables," Transactions - Institute of
       British Geographers, New series Vol. 1, pp.
       385-400.

E-101. Griffeth, Daniel A. 1976. "Spatial
       Autocorrelation Problems: Some Preliminary
       Sketches of a Structural Taxonomy," East Lakes
       Geographer, Vol. 11, pp. 59-68.

E-102. Grigg, David. 1965. "The Logic of Regional
       Systems," Annals of the Association of American
       Geographers, Vol. 55, pp. 465-491.

E-103.   Grigoryev, A. A. 1946. "The Theory of
         Physical-Geographic Processes," Annals of the
         Association of American Geographers, Vol. 36, pp.
         75-78.

E-104.   Guelke, Leonard. 1971. "Problems of Scientific
         Explanation in Geography," Canadian Geographer,
         Vol. 15, pp. 38-53.

E-105.   Guelke, Leonard. 1979. "Objectives of
         Philosophical Analysis in Geography," Canadian
         Geographer, Vol. 23, pp. 170-171.

E-106.   Gurevich, B. L. and Saushkin, Yu. G. 1966. "The
         Mathematical Method in Geography," Soviet
         Geography: Review and Translation, Vol. 7, pp.
         3-35.

E-107.   Hagerstrand, T. 1967. "The Computer and the
         Geographer," Transactions - Institute of British
         Geographers, No. 42, pp. 1-19.

E-108.   Haggett, Peter. 1969. "On Geographic Research
         in a Computer Environment," Geographical Journal,
         Vol. 135, pp. 497-507.

E-109.   Harley, J. B. 1973. "Change in Historical
         Geography: A Qualitative Impression of
         Quantitative Methods," Area, Vol. 5, pp. 69-74.

E-110.   Harris, B. 1978. "Some Questions of Philosophy,
         Methodology and Explanation in Geography,"
         London School of Economics, Graduate School of
         Geography, Discussion Papers, Vol. 64, 15 pp.

E-111.   Hart, John Fraser. 1954. "Central Tendency in
         Areal Distributions," Economic Geography, Vol.
         30, pp. 48-59.

E-112.   Hartshorne, Richard. 1950. "The Functional
         Approach in Political Geography," Annals of the
         Association of American Geographers, Vol. 40, pp.
         95-130.

E-113.   Hartshorne, Richard. 1979. "Notes Toward a
         Bibliobiography of 'the Nature of Geography',"
         Annals of the Association of American
         Geographers, Vol. 69, pp. 63-76.

E-114.   Heawood, Edward. 1905. "Glareanus: His
         Geography and Maps," Geographical Journal, Vol.
         25, pp. 647-654.

E-115.   Hewitt, Kenneth. 1970. "Probabilistic
         Approaches to Discrete Natural Events: A Review
         and Theoretical Discussion," Economic Geography,
         Vol. 46, pp. 332-349.

E-116. Hey, R. D. 1979. "Causal and Functional Relations in Fluvial Geomorphology," Earth Surface Processes, Vol. 4, pp. 179-182.

E-117. Hong-Key, Y. 1980. "The Image of Nature in Geomancy," GeoJournal, Vol. 4, pp. 341-348.

E-118. Hong-Key, Y. 1982. "Environmental Determinism and Geomancy: Two Cultures, Two Concepts," GeoJournal, Vol. 6, pp. 77-80.

E-119. Horvath, R. J. and Gibson, K. D. 1984. "Abstraction in Marx's Method," Antipode, Vol. 16, pp. 12-25.

E-120. Hotles, Ruth. 1983. "Walter Christaller," Annals of the Association of American Geographers, Vol. 73, pp. 51-54.

E-121. Hudson, G. Donald. 1936. "Methods Employed by Geographers in Regional Surveys," Economic Geography, Vol. 12, pp. 98-104.

E-122. Hudson, J. C. 1979. "A Diamond Anniversary," Annals of the Association of American Geographers, Vol. 69, pp. 1-3.

E-123. Hufferd, James. 1980. "Toward a Transcendental Human Geography of Places," Antipode, Vol. 12, pp. 18-23.

E-124. Hultquist, Nancy B. 1970. "Quantitative Geography Course Offering," Professional Geographer, Vol. 22, pp. 37-40.

E-125. Huntington, Ellsworth. 1927. "The Quantitative Phases of Human Geography," Scientific Monthly, Vol. 25, pp. 289-305.

E-126. Irving, Henry W. 1975. "A Geographer Looks at Personality," Area, Vol. 7, pp. 207-212.

E-127. Isard, Walter. 1969. "Some Notes on the Linkage of Ecologic and Economic Systems," Papers of the Regional Science Association, Vol. 22, pp. 85-96.

E-128. Isard, Walter and Tung, Tze Hsiung. 1963. "Some Concepts for the Analysis of Spatial Organization: Part I," Papers of the Regional Science Association, Vol. 12, pp. 237-240.

E-129. Isard, Walter and Tung, Tze Hsuing. 1964. "Some Concepts for the Analysis of Spatial Organization: Part II," Papers of the Regional Science Association, Vol. 12, pp. 1-26.

E-130. Jackson, P. 1981. "Phenomenology and Social Geography," Area, Vol. 13, pp. 299-305.

E-131.   Johnson, J. H. and Farrell, W. C., Jr.   1979.
          "Phenomenology in Geography," Geographical
          Survey, Vol. 8, pp. 3-9.

E-132.   Johnston, R. J.   1970.   "Grouping and
          Regionalizing: Some Methodological and Technical
          Observations," Economic Geography, Vol. 46, pp.
          293-305.

E-133.   Johnston, R. J.   1973.   "On Fractions of Distance
          and Regression Coefficients," Area, Vol. 5, pp.
          187-191.

E-134.   Johnston, R. J.   1978.   "Paradigms and
          Revolutions or Evolution: Observations on Human
          Geography Since the Second World War," Progress
          in Human Geography, Vol. 2, pp. 189-206.

E-135.   Johnston, R. J.   1980.   "Geography Is What
          Geographers Do -- and Did," Progress in Human
          Geography, Vol. 4, pp. 277-283.

E-136.   Johnston, R. J.   1980.   "On the Nature of
          Explanation in Human Geography," Transactions -
          Institute of British Geographers, Vol. 5, pp.
          402-412.

E-137.   Johnston, R. J.   1981.   "Applied Geography,
          Quantitative Analysis and Ideology," Applied
          Geography, Vol. 1, pp. 213-220.

E-138.   Johnston, R. J.   1985.   "Spatial Analysis in
          British Human Geography: A Twenty-Year
          Diversion," Espace Geographique, Vol. 14, pp.
          29-32.

E-139.   Jones, Emrys.   1956.   "Cause and Effect in Human
          Geography," Annals of the Association of American
          Geographers, Vol. 46, pp. 369-377.

E-140.   Jones, Stephen B.   1953.   "A Unified Field Theory
          of Political Geography," Annals of the
          Association of American Geographers, Vol. 43, pp.
          111-123.

E-141.   Jones, W. D. and Sauer, C. O.   1915.   "Outline
          for Field Work in Geography," Bulletin of the
          American Geographical Society, Vol. 47, pp.
          520-525.

E-142.   Kalesnik, S. Y.   1964.   "General Geographic
          Regularities of the Earth," Annals of the
          Association of American Geographers, Vol. 54, pp.
          160-164.

E-143.   Kilchenmann, A.   1971.   "Statistical-Analytical
          Methods in Theoretical Regional Geography,"
          Geoforum, Vol. 2, pp. 39-53.

E-144.   Kilchenmann, A.   1974.   "Editorial: Quantitative and Theoretical Geography," Geoforum, Vol. 5, pp. 3-8.

E-145.   King, Leslie J.   1970.   "Discriminant Analysis: A Review of Recent Theoretical Contributions and Applications," Economic Geography, Vol. 46, pp. 367-378.

E-146.   King, Leslie J.   1978.   "Numerical Techniques and Human Geography," Progress in Human Geography, Vol. 2, pp. 179-181.

E-147.   King, Leslie J.   1979.   "Areal Associations and Regressions," Annals of the Association of American Geographers, Vol. 69, pp. 124-127.

E-148.   King, Leslie J.   1979.   "The Seventies: Disillusionment and Consolidation," Annals of the Association of American Geographers, Vol. 69, pp. 155-156.

E-149.   King, Russell.   1982.   "On Geography, Cartography and the Fourth Language," Geographical Research Forum, No. 5, pp. 42-56.

E-150.   Kirby, Andrew.   1980.   "An Approach to Ideology," Journal of Geography in Higher Education, Vol. 4, pp. 16-26.

E-151.   Kirkpatrick, J. B.   1974.   "The Use of Differential Systematics in Geographical Research," Area, Vol. 6, pp. 52-53.

E-152.   Knight, C. Gregory.   1971.   "Ethnogeography and Change," Journal of Geography, Vol. 70, pp. 47-51.

E-153.   Kohn, Clyde F.   1970.   "The 1960's: A Decade of Progress in Geographical Research and Instruction," Annals of the Association of American Geographers, Vol. 60, pp. 211-219.

E-154.   Krzysztof, Porwit.   1969.   "Theoretical and Methodological Questions in the Construction of Comprehensive Models for Regional Planning," Papers of the Regional Science Association, Vol. 22, pp. 203-214.

E-155.   Latham, J. P.   1963.   "Methodology for an Instrumented Geographic Analysis," Annals of the Association of American Geographers, Vol. 53, pp. 194-209.

E-156.   LaValle, Placido, et al., 1967.   "Certain Aspects of the Expansion of Quantitative Methodology in American Geography," Annals of the Association of American Geographers, Vol. 57, pp. 423-436.

E-157. Lavrov, S. B., Preobrazhenskiy, V. S., and
Sdasyuk, G. V. 1980. "Radical Geography: Its
Roots, History and Positions," Soviet Geography:
Review and Translation, Vol. 21, pp. 308-321.

E-158. LeHeron, R. B. and Williams, D. B. 1981.
"Geography Is Not What Geographers Do, It's What
They Learn," New Zealand Journal of Geography,
Vol. 70, pp. 9-13.

E-159. Leighly, John. 1937. "Some Comments on
Contemporary Geographic Method," Annals of the
Association of American Geographers, Vol. 27, pp.
125-141.

E-160. Leighly, John. 1938. "Methodologic Controversy
in Nineteenth Century German Geography," Annals
of the Association of American Geographers, Vol.
28, pp. 238-258.

E-161. Lichtenberger, E. 1978. "Quantitative Geography
in German-Speaking Countries," Tijdschrift voor
Economische en Sociale Geografie, Vol. 69, pp.
362-373.

E-162. Lieber, Stanley R. 1977. "Behavioral Approaches
and Geographic Prediction," Great Plains - Rocky
Mountain Geographical Journal, Vol. 6, pp. 4-12.

E-163. Lipetz, G. Yu. 1974. "The Application of
Mathematical Methods in Economic Geography,"
Theoretical Problems in Physical and Economic
Geography, Vol. 1, pp. 129-139.

E-164. Livingstone, D. N. 1979. "Some Methodological
Problems in the History of Geographical Thought,"
Tijdschrift Voor Economische en Sociale
Geografie, Vol. 70, pp. 226-231.

E-165. Livingstone, David N. and Harrison, Richard T.
1981. "Meaning Through Metaphor: Analogy as
Epistemology," Annals of the Association of
American Geographers, Vol. 71, pp. 95-107.

E-166. Lowenthal, David. 1961. "Geography, Experience,
and Imagination: Towards a Geographical
Epistemology," Annals of the Association of
American Geographers, Vol. 51, pp. 241-260.

E-167. Maceachren, A. M. 1979. "The Evolution of
Thematic Cartography--A Research Methodology and
Historical Review," Canadian Cartographer, Vol.
16, pp. 17-33.

E-168. Mackay, J. Ross. 1951. "Some Problems and
Techniques on Isopleth Mapping," Economic
Geography, Vol. 27, pp. 1-9.

E-169.   Mackay, J. Ross. 1953. "A New Projection for
          Cubic Symbols on Economic Maps," Economic
          Geography, Vol. 29, pp. 60-62.

E-170.   Mackay, J. Ross. 1953. "Percentage Dot Maps,"
          Economic Geography, Vol. 29, pp. 263-266.

E-171.   Mackay, J. Ross. 1955. "An Analysis of Isopleth
          and Choropleth Class Intervals," Economic
          Geography, Vol. 31, pp. 71-81.

E-172.   MacKinnon, Ross D. 1970. "Dynamic Programming
          and Geographical Settings," Economic Geography,
          Vol. 46, pp. 350-366.

E-173.   Manion, T. and Whitelegg, J. 1979. "Comment:
          Radical Geography and Marxism," Area, Vol. 11,
          pp. 122-124.

E-174.   Marantz, H. and Warren, A. 1976. "Harvey on the
          Implications of Methodology," Area, Vol. 8, pp.
          175-178.

E-175.   Marchand, B. 1974. "Quantitative Geography:
          Revolution or Counter- revolution," Geoforum,
          Vol. 5, No. 15, pp. 15-24.

E-176.   Marchand, Bernard. 1978. "A Dialectical
          Approach to Geography," Geographical Analysis,
          Vol. 10, pp. 105-119.

E-177.   Marcus, Melvin G. 1978. "Directions in Applied
          Physical Geography," Geographical Survey, Vol. 7,
          pp. 19-25.

E-178.   Marcus, Melvin G. 1979. "Coming Full Circle:
          Physical Geography in the Twentieth Century,"
          Annals of the Association of American
          Geographers, Vol. 69, pp. 521-532.

E-179.   Marschner, F. J. 1943. "Maps and a Mapping
          Program for the United States," Annals of the
          Association of American Geographers, Vol. 33, pp.
          119-219.

E-180.   Mathieson, R. S. 1970. "Quantitative Geography
          in the Soviet Union," Australian Geographer, Vol.
          11, pp. 299-305.

E-181.   Mather, Paul M. 1979. "Theory and Quantitative
          Methods in Gemorphology," Progress in Physical
          Geography, Vol. 3, pp. 471-487.

E-182.   McAdie, Alexander. 1916. "Geography and
          Aerography," Annals of the Association of
          American Geographers, Vol. 6, pp. 129.

E-183.   McCarty, Harold H.   1979.   "Geography at Iowa,"
         Annals of the Association of American
         Geographers, Vol. 69, pp. 121-123.

E-184.   McGee, T. G.   1978.   "Western Geography and the
         Third World," American Behavioral Scientist, Vol.
         22, pp. 93-114.

E-185.   McNee, R. B.   1981.   "Perspective--Use It or Lose
         It," Professional Geographer, Vol. 33, pp. 12-15.

E-186.   Meir, A.   1982.   "The Urgency of Teaching History
         and Philosophy of Geography," Professional
         Geographer, Vol. 34, pp. 6-10.

E-187.   Mikhaylov, Yu. P.   1981.   "On the Question of the
         Subject and the Object of Geography," Soviet
         Geography: Review and Translation, Vol. 22, pp.
         331-340.

E-188.   Mints, A. A. and Preobrazenskiy, V. S.   1975.
         "Timely and Controversial Problems in the Systems
         Orientation of Geography," Soviet Geography:
         Review and Translation, Vol. 26, pp. 61-74.

E-189.   Monk, J. and Hanson, S.   1982.   "On Not Excluding
         Half of the Human in Human Geography,"
         Professional Geographer, Vol. 34, pp. 11-23.

E-190.   Morgan, W. B.   1973.   "The Doctrine of the
         Rings," Geography, Vol. 58, pp. 301-312.

E-191.   Morrill, R. L.   1978.   "Geography as Spatial
         Interaction," Dept. of Geography, University of
         North Carolina, Studies in Geography, Vol. 11,
         pp. 16-29.

E-192.   Morrill, Richard L.   1987.   "A Theoretical
         Imperative," Annals of the Association of
         American Geographers, Vol. 77, pp. 535-541.

E-193.   Morris, John W.   1950.   "The Role of the
         Geographer in Social Surveys," Professional
         Geographer, Vol. 2, pp. 23-27.

E-194.   Moss, R. P.   1978.   "Ideology and Science: Some
         Preliminary Reflections," Area, Vol. 10, pp.
         371-377.

E-195.   Moss, R. P.   1979.   "On Geography as Science,"
         Geoforum, Vol. 10, pp. 223- 234.

E-196.   Muller, J. C.   1985.   "Geographic Information
         Systems: A Unifying Force for Geography,"
         Operational Geographer, Vol. 8, pp. 41-43.

E-197.   Murphy, Raymond E.   1979.   "Economic Geography and Clark University," Annals of the Association of American Geographers, Vol. 69, pp. 39-41.

E-198.   Newman, James L.   1973.   "The Use of the Term 'Hypothesis' in Geography," Annals of the Association of American Geographers, Vol. 63, pp. 22-27.

E-199.   Nordstrom, Karl F.   1979.   "The Field Course in Geography: A Conceptual Framework," Journal of Geography, Vol. 78, pp. 267-272.

E-200.   Nunley, Robert E.   1979.   "Changing Technology: A 1990 Tour of a Computerized Geography Department," Geographical Perspective, No. 44, pp. 1-4.

E-201.   Nystuen, John D.   1984.   "'Artificial Intelligence and Geographical Problem Solving'" [comment] Professional Geographer, Vol. 36, pp. 358-360.

E-202.   Openshaw, S.   1973.   "GISP: Towards a Geographic Information System," Area, Vol. 5, pp. 25-27.

E-203.   Overton, J. D.   1981.   "A Theory of Exploration," Journal of Historical Geography, Vol. 7, pp. 53-70.

E-204.   Pattison, William.   1964.   "The Four Traditions of Geography," Journal of Geography, Vol. 63, pp. 211-216.

E-205.   Peet, R.   1978.   "The Dialectics of Radical Geography: A Reply to Gordon Clark and Michael Dear," Professional Geographer, Vol. 30, pp. 360-364.

E-206.   Peet, Richard.   1979.   "Societal Contradiction and Marxist Geography," Annals of the Association of American Geographers, Vol. 69, pp. 164-168.

E-207.   Peet, Richard.   1981.   "Spatial Dialectics and Marxist Geography," Progress in Human Geography, Vol. 5, pp. 105-110.

E-208.   Peet, Richard and Slater, David.   1980.   "Reply to Soviet Review of Radical Geography," Soviet Geography: Review and Translation, Vol. 21, pp. 541-544.

E-209.   Pike, Richard J.   1987.   "Geography on the Planets: Gift of Remote Sensing," Professional Geographer, Vol. 39, pp. 131-145.

E-210.   Pitts, Forrest R.   1962.   "Chorology
         Revisited--Computerwise," Professional
         Geographer, Vol. 14, pp. 8-12.

E-211.   Platt, Robert S.   1935.   "Field Approach to
         Regions," Annals of the Association of American
         Geographers, Vol. 25, pp. 153-174.

E-212.   Pocock, D.   1983.   "Geographical Fieldwork: An
         Experiential Perspective," Geography, Vol. 60,
         pp. 319-325.

E-213.   Poiker, T. K.   1982.   "Looking at Computer
         Cartography," Geojournal, Vol. 6, pp. 241-250.

E-214.   Porter, P. W.   1978.   "Geography as Human
         Ecology: A Decade of Progress in a Quarter
         Century," American Behavioral Scientist, Vol. 22,
         pp. 15-39.

E-215.   Pred, Allan.   1977.   "The Choreography of
         Existence: Comments on Hagerstrand's
         Time-Geography and Its Usefulness," Economic
         Geographer, Vol. 53, pp. 207-221.

E-216.   Pred, Allan.   1979.   "The Academic Past Through a
         Time-Geographic Looking Glass," Annals of the
         Association of American Geographers, Vol. 69, pp.
         175-179.

E-217.   Pye, Norman.   1955.   "Object and Method in
         Geographical Studies," An Inaugural Lecture
         Delivered at University College, Leicester, 2
         June 1955.   19 p.

E-218.   Raisz, Erwin.   1937.   "Time Charts of Historical
         Cartography," Imago Mundi, Vol. 2, pp. 9-16.

E-219.   Raisz, Erwin.   1939.   "Block-Pile System of
         Statistical Maps," Economic Geography, Vol. 15,
         pp. 185-188.

E-220.   Rasmussen, K. and Reenberg, A.   1980.
         "Ecological Human Geography: Some Considerations
         of Concepts and Methods," Geografisk Tijdschrift,
         Vol. 80, pp. 81-88.

E-221.   Reeder, Edwin H.   1933.   "Method in Geography,"
         Journal of Geography, Vol. 32, pp. 152-158.

E-222.   Relph, E. C.   1976.   "The Phenomenological
         Foundations of Geography," Discussion Paper No.
         21, Toronto: University of Toronto: Department
         of Geography, December 1976.

E-223.   Renfrew, Colin.   1981.   "Space, Time, and Man,"
         Transactions: Institute of British Geographers,
         Vol. 6, pp. 257-278.

E-224.   Renner, George T.   1943.   "Air Age Geography,"
         Harpers Magazine, Vol. 187, No. 1117, pp. 38-41.

E-225.   Rhind, David.   1975.   "A Task Outstanding: The
         Reform of Area Units," Area, Vol. 7, pp. 1-3.

E-226.   Rhind, David.   1976.   "Whither Analogy?   (Reply
         to Floyd & O'Brien)," Area, Vol. 8, pp. 256-257.

E-227.   Robertson, Douglas L.   1980.   "Participant
         Observation and Geographical   Research,"
         Geographical Survey, Vol. 9, pp. 3-12.

E-228.   Robinson, Arthur H.   1961.   "On Perks and Pokes,"
         Economic Geography, Vol. 37, pp. 181-183.

E-229.   Robinson, Brian S.   1971.   "A Note on
         Geographical Description in the Age of
         Discoveries," Professional Geographer, Vol. 23,
         pp. 208-211.

E-230.   Roterus, Victor and Calef, Wesley.   1955.   "Notes
         on the Basic-Nonbasic Employment Ratio," Economic
         Geography, Vol. 31, pp. 17-20.

E-231.   Sack, R.   1980.   "Conceptions of Geographic
         Space," Progress in Human Geography, Vol. 4, pp.
         313-345.

E-232.   Sack, Robert David.   1972.   "Geography, Geometry,
         and Explanation," Annals of the Association of
         American Geographers, Vol. 62, pp. 61-78.

E-233.   Salikov, N. A.   1977.   "Methodological Problems
         in the Geography of Labor Resources," Soviet
         Geography: Review and Translation, Vol. 18, pp.
         396-402.

E-234.   Saushkin, Yu. G.   1971.   "Results and Prospects
         of the Use of Mathematical Methods in Economic
         Geography," Soviet Geography: Review and
         Translation, Vol. 12, pp. 416-427.

E-235.   Sayer, Andrew.   1979.   "Epistemology and
         Conceptions of People and Nature in Geography,"
         Geoforum, Vol. 10, pp. 19-44.

E-236.   Sayer, Andrew.   1982.   "Explanation in Economic
         Geography: Abstraction   Versus Generalization,"
         Progress in Human Geography, Vol. 6, pp. 68-88.

E-237.   Schaefer, Fred K.   1953.   "Exceptionalism in
         Geography: A Methodological Examination," Annals
         of the Association of American Geographers, Vol.
         43, pp. 226-249.

E-238.   Semevskiy, B. N.   1972.   "Theoretical Foundations
          of the Geographical Science," Proceedings -
          Twenty-second International Geographical
          Congress, pp. 931-933.

E-239.   Senger, Leslie W. and Chang, Stephen.   1975.   "A
          Matter of Terminology--The Ecological Approach in
          Geography: A Re-Examination of Basic Concepts,"
          Geoforum, Vol. 6, pp. 164-167.

E-240.   Singh, R. P. B.   1978.   "Emerging Frontiers in
          Geography: A Review.   New Trends in Geographic
          Thought and Methodology," National Geographical
          Journal of India, Special Issue, Vol. 24, pp.
          186-202.

E-241.   Sitwell, O. F. G.   1980.   "Where to Begin?   A
          Methodological Problem for the Writers of
          'Special' Geography in the Seventeenth and
          Eighteenth Centuries," Canadian Geographer, Vol.
          24, pp. 294-299.

E-242.   Slater, F.   1981.   "What is Your View of People?
          Some Comments on Recently Changing Viewpoints in
          Geographical Research," New Zealand Journal of
          Geography, No. 71, pp. 6-9.

E-243.   Smirnov, L. Ye.   1968.   "The Role and
          Significance of Objective [Mathematical] Methods
          in Geographic Research," Soviet Geography:
          Review and Translation, Vol. 9, pp. 55-68.

E-244.   Smith, Guy-Harold.   1932.   "Cartography in
          Philately," Annals of the Association of American
          Geographers, Vol. 22, p. 76.

E-245.   Smith, N.   1979.   "Geography, Science and Post
          Positivist Modes of Explanation," Progress in
          Human Geography, Vol. 3, pp. 356-385.

E-246.   Smith, Neil and Phil O'Keefe.   1980.   "Geography,
          Marx and the Concept of Nature," Antipode, Vol.
          12, pp. 30-39.

E-247.   Smith, S. J.   1981.   "Humanistic Method in
          Contemporary Social Geography," Area, Vol. 13,
          pp. 293-298.

E-248.   Smith, Terence R.   1984.   "Artificial
          Intelligence and Its Applicability to
          Geographical Problem Solving," Professional
          Geographer, Vol. 36, pp. 147-158.

E-249.   Sochava, V. B. et al.   1976.   "Theoretical Bases
          of Modern Landscape Science," Proceedings -
          Twenty-Third International Geographical Congress,
          pp. 27-30.

E-250.   Sonnenfeld, J. 1982. "Egocentric Perspectives on Geographic Orientation," _Annals of the Association of American Geographers_, Vol. 72, pp. 68-76.

E-251.   Srivastava, M. P. 1962. "Statistical Methods in Geography," _Deccan Geographer_, Vol. 1, pp. 68-70.

E-252.   Steel, R. W. 1982. "Regional Geography in Practice," _Geography_, Vol. 67, pp. 2-8.

E-253.   Stone, Kirk H. 1972. "A Geographer's Strength: The Multiple-Scale Approach," _Journal of Geography_, Vol. 71, pp. 354-362.

E-254.   Strahler, Arthur. 1954. "Empirical and Explanatory Methods in Physical Geography," _Professional Geographer_, Vol. 6, No. 1, pp. 4-9.

E-255.   Su-Fen, Lu. 1984. "The Relation Between Geography and Cartography," _Acta Geographica Sinica_, Vol. 39, pp. 314-320 [English Summary].

E-256.   Swain, P. H. 1983. "Remote Sensing: Surveying the Frontiers in the Information Age." _South African Journal of Photogrammetry, Remote Sensing & Cartography_, Vol. 13, pp. 305-313.

E-257.   Taylor, James A. 1958. "The Geographic Method," _Weather_, Vol. 13, pp. 303-307.

E-258.   Taylor, Peter J. 1969. "The Location Variable in Taxonomy," _Geographical Analysis_, Vol. 1, pp. 181-195.

E-259.   Taylor, Peter J. 1976. "An Interpretation of the Quantification Debate in British Geography," _Transactions - Institute of British Geographers_, New Series Vol. 1, pp. 129-142.

E-260.   Thong, Lee Boon. 1979. "On Quantification of Geographical Ideas," _Journal Geographica_, Vol. 13, pp. 19-24.

E-261.   Tinkler, K. J. 1969. "Uniqueness in Geographical Interactions," _Area_, Vol. 3, pp. 27-30.

E-262.   Tinkler, K. J. 1979. "Graph Theory," _Progress in Human Geography_, Vol. 3, p. 85-116.

E-263.   Tomlinson, Roger F. 1984. "Geographic Information Systems -- A New Frontier," _Operational Geographer_, No. 5, pp. 31-36.

E-264.   Tuan, Yi-Fu. 1957. "Use of Simile and Metaphor in Geographical Descriptions," _Professional Geographer_, Vol. 9, No. 5, pp. 8-11.

E-265. Tuan, Yi-Fu. 1969. "Uniqueness in Geographical
        Interactions," _Area_, Vol. 3, pp. 411-423.

E-266. Uhlig, H. 1971. "Organization and System of
        Geography," _Geoforum_, Vol 2, pp.7-38.

E-267. Unstead, J. F. 1916.   "A Synthetic Method of
        Determining Geographical Regions," _Geographical
        Journal_, Vol. 48, pp. 230-249.

E-268. Unwin, J. W. 1978. "Quantitative and
        Theoretical Geography in the United Kingdom,"
        Area, Vol. 10, pp. 337-344.

E-269. Unwin, J. W. 1979. "Theoretical and
        Quantitative Geography in North-West Europe,"
        Area, Vol. 11, pp. 164-166.

E-270. Walker, R. A. 1981. "Left-Wing Liberianism, An
        Academic Disorder: A Response to David Sibley,"
        Professional Geographer, Vol. 33, pp. 5-9.

E-271. Wallis, B. C. 1912. "Measurement in Economic
        Geography: Its Principles and Practices,"
        Geographical Journal, Vol. 39, pp. 22-26.

E-272. Walmsley, D. J. 1974. "Positivism and
        Phenomenology in Human Geography," _Canadian
        Geographer_, Vol. 18, pp. 95-107.

E-273. Walsmley, D. J. 1979. "Time and Human
        Geography," _Australian Geographical Studies_, Vol.
        17, pp. 223-230.

E-274. Webber, M. J. 1980. "Literature for Teaching
        Quantitative Geography: Techniques By, For, But
        Not of Geographers," _Environment and Planning A_,
        Vol. 12, pp. 1083-1090.

E-275. Whittlesey, D. S. 1927. "Devices for
        Accumulating Geographic Data in the Field,"
        _Annals of the Association of American
        Geographers_, Vol. 17, pp. 72-78.

E-276. Widdis, R. W. 1980. "Science and Humanism in
        Geography: The Dilemma of the Dialectic,"
        Ontario Geography, Vol. 15, pp. 53-64.

E-277. Wilbanks, Thomas J. and Symanski, Richard.
        1968. "What Is Systems Analysis," _Professional
        Geographer_, Vol. 20, pp. 81-85.

E-278. Williams, Stephen Wyn. 1981. "Realism, Marxism
        and Human Geography," _Antipode_, Vol. 13, pp.
        31-38.

E-279.   Wilson, Alan G. 1969. "The Use of Analogies in Geography," Geographical Analysis, Vol. 1, pp. 225-233.

E-280.   Wilson, Alan G. 1978. "Mathematical Education for Geographers," Journal of Geography in Higher Education, Vol. 2, pp. 17-28.

E-281.   Wolforth, J. 1976. "The New Geography--And After?" Geography, Vol. 61, pp. 143-149.

E-282.   Wood, P. A. 1977. "Information for Geography -- Cause for Alarm," Area, Vol. 9, pp. 109-113.

E-283.   Wrigley, N. 1979. "Developments in the Statistical Analysis of Categorical Data," Progress in Human Geography, Vol. 3, pp. 315-355.

E-284.   Wrigley, N. 1979. "Research in Quanitative Geography," Area, Vol. 11, pp. 66-68.

E-285.   Wrigley, N. 1981. "Quantitative Methods: A View on the Wider Scene," Progress in Human Geography, Vol. 5, pp. 545-561.

E-286.   Wrigley, Neil. 1987. "Quantitative Methods: Gearing Up for 1991," Progress in Human Geography, Vol. 11, pp. 565-579.

E-287.   Young, R. W. 1979. "Paradigms in Geography: Implications of Kuhn's Interpretation of Scientificc Inquiry," Australian Geographical Studies, Vol. 17, pp. 204-209.

E-288.   Zelinsky, Wilbur. 1970. "Beyond the Exponentials: The Role of Geography in the Great Transition," Economic Geography, Vol. 46, pp. 498-535.

Philosophy in Geography

F-1. Aay, Hank. 1972. "A Re-examination: Geography--The Science of Space," <u>Monadnock</u>, Vol. 46, pp. 20-31.

F-2. Abler, Ronald F. 1987. "What Shall We Say? To Whom Shall We Speak?" <u>Annals of the Association of American Geographers</u>, Vol. 77, pp. 511-524.

F-3. Ackerman, Edward A. 1953. "Regional Research--Emerging Concepts and Techniques in the Field of Geography," <u>Economic Geography</u>, Vol. 29, pp. 189-197.

F-4. Ackerman, Edward A. 1963. "Where is a Research Frontier?" <u>Annals of the Association of American Geographers</u>, Vol. 53, pp. 429-440.

F-5. Adams, John S. 1979. "Future Prospects," <u>Professional Geographer</u>, Vol. 31, pp. 360-363.

F-6. Agnew, J. A. 1979. "Instrumentalism, Realism, and Research on the Diffusion of Innovation," <u>Professional Geographer</u>, Vol. 31, pp. 364-370.

F-7. Agnew, J. A. and Duncan, J. S. 1981. "The Transfer of Ideas into Anglo- American Human Geography," <u>Progress in Human Geography</u>, Vol. 5, pp. 42-57.

F-8. Ahmad, Aijazuddin. 1983. "Nature of Dichotomy in Geography: General and Particular," <u>Indian Geographical Journal</u>, Vol. 58, pp. 97-106.

F-9. Ahmad, G. Munir. 1952. "Geography as a Social Science," <u>Geographer</u>, Vol. 5, pp. 17-23.

F-10.   Ahmad, Kazi S. 1964. "Geography Through the
         Ages," Pakistan Geographical Review, Vol. 19, pp.
         1-30.

F-11.   Ahnert, Frank. 1962. "On the Concept of Areal
         Differentiation: A Reply," Professional
         Geographer, Vol. 14, No. 6, pp. 16-18.

F-12.   Ahnert, Frank. 1962. "Some Reflections on the
         Place and Nature of Physical Geography in
         America," Professional Geographer, Vol. 14, No.
         1, pp. 1-7.

F-13.   Aiyar, T. S. Sundaram. 1933. "Human Geography,"
         Journal of the Madras Geographical Association,
         Vol. 8, pp. 64-77.

F-14.   Alexander, John W. 1959. "Geography: As Some
         Others See It," Professional Geographer, Vol. 11,
         No. 4, pp. 2-5.

F-15.   Allen, Lyman R. 1903. "The Correlation of
         Geography and History," Journal of Geography,
         Vol. 2, pp. 404-415.

F-16.   Allix, Andre. 1948. "Man in Human Geography,"
         Scottish Geographical Magazine, Vol. 64, pp. 1-8.

F-17.   Altengarten, J. 1975. "An Old Game for New
         Geographers," Professional Geographer, Vol. 27,
         pp. 121-123.

F-18.   Amad, Kazi S. 1964. "Geography Through the
         Ages," Pakistan Geographical Review, Vol. 19, pp.
         1-30.

F-19.   Amadeus de Nossa Senhora, Father. 1950. "The
         Geographical Spirit -- Creator of the Modern
         Scientific Spirit," [English Summary] Boletim da
         Sociedade de Geografia de Lisboa, Serie 68, pp.
         264-265. [article pp. 185-202].

F-20.   Anderson, J. 1978. "Geography, Political
         Economy and the State," Antipode, Vol. 10, pp.
         87-93.

F-21.   Anderson, J. 1980. "Towards a Materialist
         Conception of Geography," Geoforum, Vol. 11, pp.
         171-178.

F-22.   Anderson, James. 1964-65. "Geography and the
         World to Come," Albertan Geographer, No. 1, pp.
         47-51.

F-23.   Anderson, J. H. 1983. "Thomas Aisken Larcom,
         1801-1879," Geographers: Biobibliographical
         Studies, Vol. 7, pp. 71-74.

F-24.   Anderson, James R. 1973. "Arch G. Gerlach
         (1911-1972)," Geographical Review, Vol. 63, pp.
         577-578.

F-25.   Andrews, H. F. 1984. "The Durkheimians and
         Human Geography: Some Contextural Problems in
         the Socialogy of Knowledge," Transactions --
         Iurtitute of British Geographers, Vol. 9, pp.
         315-336.

F-26.   Angel, Shlomo and Hyman, Geoffrey M. 1972.
         "Transformations and Geographic Theory,"
         Geographical Analysis, Vol. 4, pp. 350-372.

F-27.   Anonymous. 1893. "The Limits between Geology
         and Physical Geography," Geographical Journal,
         Vol. 2, pp. 518-534.

F-28.   Anonymous. 1911. "What Is Geography?" Journal
         of Geography, Vol. 10, pp. 59-60.

F-29.   Anonymous. 1918. "The Aim of Geography,"
         Journal of Geography, Vol. 17, pp. 111-112.

F-30.   Anonymous. 1920. "Current Opinions on the
         Function of Geography," Journal of Geography,
         Vol. 19, pp. 33-37.

F-31.   Anonymous. 1921. "Can You Justify Geography?"
         Journal of Geography, Vol. 20, pp. 22-23.

F-32.   Anonymous. 1924. "Geography, Evolution,
         Confusion," Journal of Geography, Vol. 23, pp.
         265-266.

F-33.   Anonymous. 1927. "New Geography," Saturday
         Evening Post, Vol. 199, p. 20.

F-34.   Anonymous. 1936. "Decorative Geography,"
         Country Life, Vol. 70, pp. 42-44.

F-35.   Anonymous. 1941. "War, Peace, and Geography --
         An Editorial Forward," Annals of the Association
         of American Geographers, Vol. 31, pp. 77-82.

F-36.   Anonymous. 1944. "Geography Needs a Brush-up
         Too," Saturday Evening Post, Vol. 216, pp. 104.

F-37.   Anonymous. 1948. "The Far-Off Hills,"
         Geographical Review, Vol. 38, pp. 352-354.

F-38.   Anonymous. 1952. "Some Science! [Geography],"
         Life, Vol. 33, p. 20.

F-39.   Anonymous. 1961. "Review and Discussion of V.
        A. Anuchin's Book on Theory of Geography," Soviet
        Geography: Review and Translation, Vol. 2, No.
        10, pp. 12-31.

F-40.   Anonymous. 1966. "The Development of Theory of
        Geography and Landscape Science in East and West
        Germany," Soviet Geography: Review and
        Translation, Vol. 7, pp. 40-47.

F-41.   Anonymous. 1967. "Editorial: An Evolutionary
        Approach in Geography," Scottish Geographical
        Magazine, Vol. 83, pp. 75-77.

F-42.   Anonymous. 1973. "Editorial: Geog and Mammon,"
        Area, Vol. 5, pp. 81-82.

F-43.   Anuchin, V. A. 1962. "On the Criticism of the
        Unity of Geography," Soviet Geography: Review
        and Translation, Vol. 3, No. 7, pp. 22-39.

F-44.   Anuchin, V. A. 1964. "The Problem of Synthesis
        in Geographic Science," Soviet Geography: Review
        and Translation, Vol. 5, pp. 34-46.

F-45.   Anuchin, V. A. 1965. "A Sad Tale About
        Geography," Soviet Geography: Review and
        Translation, Vol. 6, pp. 27-31.

F-46.   Anuchin, V. A. 1970. "Mathematization and the
        Geographic Method," Soviet Geography: Review and
        Translation, Vol. 11, pp. 71-81.

F-47.   Anuchin, V. A. 1970. "On the Problems of
        Geography and the Tasks of Popularizing
        Geographical Knowledge," Soviet Geography:
        Review and Translation, Vol. 11, pp. 82-112.

F-48.   Anuchin, V. A. 1972. "Straddling the Boundaries
        Between Science," Soviet Geography: Review and
        Translation, Vol. 13, pp. 432-441.

F-49.   Armand, D. L., Gerasimov, I. P. and
        Preobrazhenskiy, V. S. 1975. "Elements of a
        Forecast of the Evolution of Geography as a
        Scientific Discipline," Soviet Geography: Review
        and Translation, Vol. 26, pp. 421-427.

F-50.   Asheim, B. T. 1979. "Social Geography-Welfare
        State Ideology or Critical Social Science,"
        Geoforum, Vol. 10, pp. 5-18.

F-51.   Atwood, Wallace W. 1940. "The Fundamental Bases
        for the Study of Geography," Annals of the
        Association of American Geographers, Vol. 30, pp.
        44-45.

F-52. Atwood, Wallace W. 1940. "Geography and the
       Great Human Dramas," Journal of Geography, Vol.
       39, pp. 337-343.

F-53. Augelli, John P. 1975. "Geographic Concepts and
       the Caribbean Crises Area," Journal of Geography,
       Vol. 74, pp. 393-402.

F-54. Baber, Zonia. 1904. "Scope of Geography,"
       Elementary School Teacher, Vol. 4, pp. 257-270.

F-55. Baber, Zonia. 1905. "The Scope of Geography,"
       Journal of Geography, Vol. 4, pp. 386-396.

F-56. Back, Catherine D. J. 1942. "Geography: An
       Arts or Science Subject?" Australian Journal of
       Science, Vol. 5, pp. 56-57.

F-57. Bagchi, K. 1975. "Geography at the Cross
       Roads," Geographical Review of India, Vol. 37,
       pp. 201-206.

F-58. Bagchi, K. 1983. "New Emphasis in Geography,"
       Geographical Review of India, Vol. 45, pp. 1-3.

F-59. Bailly, A. S., Racine, J. B. and Weiss-Altaner,
       E. 1978. "Which Way is North? Directions for
       Human Geography," Geoforum, Vol. 9, pp. 341-348.

F-60. Baker, A. R. H. 1985. "Maps, Models and
       Marxism: Methodological Motivation in British
       Historical Geography," Espace Geographique, Vol.
       14, pp. 9-15.

F-61. Baker, Alan R. H. et al. 1969. "The Future of
       the Past," Area, Vol. 1, pp. 46-51.

F-62. Baker, David. 1986. "Core, Periphery and Focus
       for Geography," Area, Vol. 18, pp. 157-160.

F-63. Baker, J. N. L. 1955. "Geography and Its
       History," Advancement of Science, Vol. 12, pp.
       188-198.

F-64. Balchin, W. G. V. 1955. "Research in
       Geography," Inaugural lecture of the Professor of
       Geography, delivered at University College of
       Swansea, 1955, 23 pp.

F-65. Bale, J. R. 1981. "Geography, Sport and
       Geographical Education," Geography, Vol. 66, pp.
       104-115.

F-66. Balfour, Henry. 1937. "Address at the Annual
       General Meeting," Geographical Journal, Vol. 90,
       pp. 489-498.

F-67.   Balfour, Henry. 1938. "Address at the General
        Meeting," Geographical Journal, Vol. 91, pp.
        97-107.

F-68.   Baranskiy, N. N. 1961. "Theoretical Problems in
        Geography [a review]," Soviet Geography: Review
        and Translation, Vol. 2, No. 8, pp. 81-84.

F-69.   Barbour, George B. 1967. "In Honor of Times
        Past," Isoline, Vol. 3, pp. 5-7.

F-70.   Barns, Burton, A. 1922. "Geography - A Social
        Science," Journal of Geography, Vol. 21, pp.
        156-158.

F-71.   Barnes, Harry E. 1921. "The Relation of
        Geography to the Writing and Interpretation of
        History," Journal of Geography, Vol. 20, pp.
        321-337.

F-72.   Barnes, Trevor and Curry, Michael. 1983.
        "Towards a Contextual Approach to Geographical
        Knowledge," Transactions - Institute of British
        Geographers, Vol. 8, pp. 467-482.

F-73.   Barrows, Harlan H. 1923. "Geography as Human
        Ecology," Annals of the Association of American
        Geographers, Vol. 13, pp. 1-14.

F-74.   Barton, B. 1978. "Geographical Inquiry in a
        Hypothetical World," Professional Geographer,
        Vol. 30, No. 4, pp. 397-406.

F-75.   Beasley, C. R. 1902. "Dawn of Modern
        Geography," Atheneaum, Vol. 1, pp. 227.

F-76.   Beck, C. W. 1985. "Trouble in the Hedgerows,"
        Journal of Archaeological Science, Vol. 12, pp.
        405-409.

F-77.   Beel, Morag and Roberts, Neil. 1986.
        "Development Theory and Practice in Human and
        Physical Geography," Area, Vol. 18, pp. 3-8.

F-78.   Begvin, H. 1985. "La theorie Mans démarche
        geographique," [Mans' Theoretical Approach to
        Geography] Espace Geographique, Vol. 14, pp.
        65-68 [English Summary].

F-79.   Berdoulay, Vincent. 1976. "French Possibilism
        as a Form of Neo-Kantian Philosophy," Proceeding
        - Twenty Third International Geographical
        Congress, Vol. 8, pp. 176-179.

F-80.   Berkner, Lloyd V. 1959. "Geography and Space,"
        Geographical Review, Vol. 49, pp. 305-314.

F-81.   Berry, Brian J. L.   1959.   "Recent Studies
        Concerning the Role of Transportation in the
        Space Economy," Annals of the Association of
        American Geographers, Vol. 49, pp. 328-342.

F-82.   Berry, Brian J. L.   1960.   "The Quantitative
        Bogey-Man," Economic Geography, Vol. 36, Guest
        Editorial, front piece.

F-83.   Berry, Brian J. L.   1964.   "Approaches to
        Regional Analysis: A Synthesis," Annals of the
        Association of American Geographers, Vol. 54, pp.
        2-12.

F-84.   Berry, Brian J. L.   1968.   "Interdependency of
        Spatial Structure and Spatial Behavior: A
        General Field Theory Formulation," Papers of the
        Regional Science Association, Vol. 21, pp.
        205-228.

F-85.   Berry, Brian J. L.   1980.   "Creating Future
        Geographies," Annals of the Association of
        American Geographers, Vol. 70, pp. 449-458.

F-86.   Berry, William J.   1933.   "Some Opinions Relative
        to the Content and Grouping of Geography,"
        Journal of Geography, Vol. 32, pp. 236-241.

F-87.   Bhattacharyya, Anima.   1974.   "Region,
        Regionalism, Regionalisation," Geographical
        Review of India, Vol. 36, pp. 131-137.

F-88.   Billinge, Mark.   1977.   "In Search of
        Negativism: Phenomenology and Historical
        Geography," Journal of Historical Geography, Vol.
        3, pp. 55-67.

F-89.   Bird, J.   1978.   "Methodology and Philosophy,"
        Progress in Human Geography, Vol. 2, pp. 133-140.

F-90.   Bird, J.   1979.   "Methodology and Philosophy,"
        Progress in Human Geography, Vol. 3, pp. 117-125.

F-91.   Bird, J. H.   1973.   "Desiderata for a Definition;
        or is Geography What Geographers Do?" Area, Vol.
        5, pp. 201-203.

F-92.   Bird, James.   1981.   "The Target of Space and the
        Arrow of Time," Transactions - Institute of
        British Geographers, Vol. 6, pp. 129-151.

F-93.   Bird, James H.   1975.   "Methodological
        Implications for Geography from the Philosophy of
        K. R. Popper," Scottish Geographical Magazine,
        Vol. 91, pp. 153-163.

F-94.   Bird, James H. 1985.   "Geography in Three
         Worlds: How Popper's System Can Help Elucidate
         Dichotomies and Changes in the Discipline,"
         Professional Geographer, Vol. 37, pp. 403-409.

F-95.   Bishop, A. 1978.   "Human Geography: A
         Nomothetic Science," Area, Vol. 10, pp. 149-151.

F-96.   Blair, Alexander M. 1967.   "One Geographer's
         Views on the Geographer's Existing and Potential
         Roles," Canadian Geographer, Vol. 11, pp.
         160-162.

F-97.   Bland, F. A. 1944.   "A Note on Regionalism,"
         Australian Geographer, Vol. 4, pp. 212-216.

F-98.   Blaut, J. M. 1961.   "Space and Process,"
         Professional Geographer, Vol. 13, No. 4, pp. 1-7.

F-99.   Blaut, J. M. 1962.   "Object and Relationship,"
         Professional Geographer, Vol. 14, No. 6, pp. 1-7.

F-100.   Blaut, J. M. 1971.   "Space, Structure and Maps,"
         Tijdschrift voor Economische en Sociale
         Geographie, Vol. 62, pp. 18-21.

F-101.   Blaut, James M. 1961.   "Space and Process,"
         Professional Geographer, Vol. 13, pp. 1-7.

F-102.   Blaut, James M. 1962.   "Object and
         Relationship," Professional Geographer, Vol. 14,
         pp. 1-7.

F-103.   Blaut, James M. 1979.   "The Dissenting
         Tradition," Annals of the Association of American
         Geographers, Vol. 69, pp. 157-163.

F-104.   Blaut, James M. 1980.   "A Radical Critique of
         Cultural Geography," Antipode, Vol. 12, pp.
         25-29.

F-105.   Blaut, James M. 1987.   "Diffusionism: A
         Uniformitarian Critique," Annals of the
         Association of American Geographers, Vol. 77, pp.
         30-47.

F-106.   Blowers, Andrew T. 1974.   "Relevance, Research,
         and the Political Process," Area, Vol. 6, pp.
         32-36.

F-107.   Boas, Franz. 1887.   "The Study of Geography,"
         Science, Vol. 9, p. 140.

F-108.   Boateng, E. A. 1964.   "Is Geography a Science?"
         Bulletin - Ghana Geographical Association, Vol.
         9, pp. 4-12.

F-109.   Boesch, Hans and Carol, Hans. 1956. "Principles
          of the Concept 'Landscape'," Proceedings -
          Eighteenth International Geographical Congress,
          pp. 541-544.

F-110.   Borchert, John R. 1960. "A Statement Favoring
          Support of the Term Geography," Professional
          Geographer, Vol. 12, No. 4, pp. 14-16.

F-111.   Bowen, E. G. 1983. "Some Early Impressions,"
          Transactions - Institute of British Geographers,
          Vol. 8, pp. 38-40.

F-112.   Bowen, M. J. 1979. "Scientific Method - After
          Positivism," Australian Geographical Studies,
          Vol. 17, pp. 210-216.

F-113.   Bowlby, S., Foord, J. and Mackenzie, S. 1982.
          "Feminism and Geography," Area, Vol. 14, pp.
          19-25.

F-114.   Bowman, I. 1929. "Geography, Modern Style,"
          Outlook, Vol. 152, p. 461.

F-115.   Bowman, Isaiah. 1938. "Geography in the
          Creative Experiment," Geographical Review, Vol.
          28, pp. 1-19.

F-116.   Bowman, Isaiah. 1947. "The New Geography,"
          Journal of Geography, Vol. 44, pp. 213-216.

F-117.   Bowman, Isaiah. 1947. "The New Geography," in
          The Scientists Speak, W. Weaner, ed. New York,
          pp. 291-294.

F-118.   Bowman, Isaiah. 1949. "Geographical
          Interpretation," Geographical Review, Vol. 39,
          pp. 355-370.

F-119.   Branom, M. E. 1929. "Recent Tendencies in the
          Field of Geography," Historical Outlook, Vol. 20,
          pp. 399-402.

F-120.   Brigham, Albert Perry. 1910. "The Organic Side
          of Geography: Its Nature and Limits," Bulletin
          of the American Geographical Society, Vol. 42,
          pp. 442-452.

F-121.   Brigham, Albert Perry. 1915. "The Problems of
          Geographic Influence," Annals of the Association
          of American Geographers, Vol. 5, pp. 3-26.

F-122.   Brigham, Albert Perry. 1916. "A Type of
          Geographic Description," Annals of the
          Association of American Geographers, Vol. 6, pp.
          122.

F-123.   Brigham, Albert Perry.   1922.   "A Quarter-Century in Geography," Journal of Geography, Vol. 21, pp. 12-17.

F-124.   Brookfield, H. C.   1964.   "Questions on the Human Frontiers of Geography," Economic Geography, Vol. 40, pp. 283-303.

F-125.   Brookfield, H. C.   1985.   "Revolutionary and Evolutionary Change in Geography: A Comment with Dirty Boots, Dusty Sandals or Filthy Feet," Australian Geographical Studies, Vol. 23, pp. 172-173.

F-126.   Brooks, C. F.   1924.   "Trends in Modern Geography: Reply," Science, Vol. 60 N.S., Nov. 7, p. 429.

F-127.   Brow, Carole.   1972.   "The Role Systems Analysis in Geography: Education of a Geographer, 1970," California Geographer, Vol. 13, pp. 26-31.

F-128.   Browett, J.   1980.   "Development, the Diffusionist Paradigm and Geography," Progress in Human Geography, Vol. 4, pp. 57-80.

F-129.   Browett, John.   1984.   "Revolutionary and Evolutionary Change in Geography: A Personal Assessment," Australian Geographical Studies, Vol. 22, pp. 163-191.

F-130.   Brown, R. N. Rudmose.   1914.   "The Province of the Geographer," Scottish Geographical Magazine, Vol. 30, pp. 467-480.

F-131.   Brown, Wendell, J.   1961.   "A Lawyer Looks at the Name Geography," Professional Geographer, Vol. 17, pp. 16-19.

F-132.   Browne, W. A.   1940.   "A New Prospectus for Geography," Journal of Geography, Vol. 39, pp. 17-25.

F-133.   Browning, Clyde E.   1974.   "The Question, 'But Is It Geography?'-- Revisited Or Are There Criteria for Establishing the Geographic Content of Topics?" Professional Geographer, Vol. 26, pp. 137-139.

F-134.   Brunhes, Jean.   1913.   "The Specific Characteristics and Complex Character of the Subject Matter of Human Geography," Scottish Geographical Magazine, Vol. 29, pp. 304-322, 358-374.

F-135.   Brunhes, Jean. 1925. "Human Geography," in H.
          E. Barns (ed.), The History and Prospects of the
          Social Sciences, New York: Alfred A. Knopf, pp.
          55-105.

F-136.   Brunsolen, Dengs. 1987. "The Science of the
          Unknown," Geography, Vol. 72, pp. 193-208.

F-137.   Bryan, P. W. 1958. "Geography and Landscape,"
          Geography, Vol. 43, pp. 1-9.

F-138.   Bryant, J. 1966. "New Geography," Science
          Digest, Vol. 60, pp. 62-65.

F-139.   Bunge, W. 1969. "Simplicity," Geographical
          Analysis, Vol. 1, pp. 388- 391.

F-140.   Bunge, W. 1974. "Simplicity Again,"
          Geographical Analysis, Vol. 6, pp. 85-88.

F-141.   Bunge, William. 1961. "The Structure of
          Contemporary American Geographic Research,"
          Professional Geographer, Vol. 13, No. 3, pp.
          19-23.

F-142.   Bunge, William 1964. "Geographical Dialectics,"
          Professional Geographer, Vol. 16, No. 4, pp.
          28-29.

F-143.   Bunge, William. 1966. "Appendix to Theoretical
          Geography," Lund Series in Geography, Series C,
          entire volume 6.

F-144.   Bunge, William. 1966. "Commentary: Locations
          are Not Unique," Annals of the Association of
          American Geographers, Vol. 56, pp. 375-376.
          [Reply, pp. 376-377].

F-145.   Bunge, William. 1977. "The Conservation of
          Geography," Area, Vol. 9, pp. 93-95.

F-146.   Bunge, William. 1979. "Perspective on
          Theoretical Geography," Annals of the Association
          of American Geographers, Vol. 69, pp. 169-174.

F-147.   Bunge, William. 1983. "Geography as a Field
          Subject," Area, Vol. 15, pp. 208-210.

F-148.   Bunge, William W. 1961. "The Structure of
          Contemporary American Geographic Research,"
          Professional Geographer, Vol. 13, pp. 19-23.

F-149.   Bunge, William W. 1967. "Theoretical
          Geography," in Introduction to Geography:
          Selected Readings, Dohrs and Sommers (eds.), New
          York: Crowell Co.

F-150.   Bunge, William W.   1973.   "The Geography,"
Professional Geographer, Vol. 25, pp. 331-337.

F-151.   Bunge, William W.   1973.   "Spatial Prediction,"
Annals of the Association of American
Geographers, Vol. 63, pp. 566-568.

F-152.   Bunge, William W.   1974.   "Regions Are Sort of
Unique," Area, Vol. 6, pp. 92-99.

F-153.   Burgess, R.   1978.   "The Concept of Nature in
Geography and Marxism," Antipode, Vol. 10, pp.
1-11.

F-154.   Burns, Nancy.   1972.   "A Philosophy for Geography
Today," Monadnock, Vol. 46, pp. 8-19.

F-155.   Burrill, Meredith.   1953.   "The Significance of
Theory in Geography," Professional Geographer,
Vol. 5, No. 3, p. 5.

F-156.   Burrill, Meredith.   1968.   "The Language of
Geography," Annals of the Association of American
Geographers, Vol. 58, pp. 1-11.

F-157.   Burrill, Meredith F.   1970.   "Context as a Fifth
Dimension in Geography," Journal of Geography,
Vol. 69, pp. 518-521.

F-158.   Burton, Ian.   1963.   "The Quantitative Revolution
and Theoretical Geography," Canadian Geographer,
Vol. 7, pp. 151-162.

F-159.   Burton, Ian.   1968.   "The Quality of the
Environment: A Review," Geographical Review,
Vol. 58, pp. 472-481.

F-160.   Buttimer, A.   1982.   "Musing on Helcon: Root
Metaphors and Geography," Geografiska Annaler,
Vol.64B, pp. 89-96.

F-161.   Buttimer, Anne.   1976.   "Grasping the Dynamism of
Lifeworld," Annals of the Association of American
Geographers, Vol. 66, pp. 277-292.

F-162.   Buttimer, Anne.   1983.   "Teoria, Ryoanji, and the
Place Pompidor," Geographical Analysis, Vol. 15,
pp. 42-46.

F-163.   Buttimer, Anne. 1984.   "Musing on Helicon: Root
Metaphors and Geography," Geoscience & Man, Vol.
24, pp. 55-62.

F-164.   Büttner, M.   1979.   "The Significance of the
Reformation for the Reorientation of Geography in
Lutheran Germany," History of Science, Vol. 17,
pp. 151-169.

F-165.   Buursink, J. 1975. "Hierarchy: A Concept
          Between Theoretical and Applied Geography,"
          Tijdschrift voor Economische en Sociale
          Geografie, Vol. 66, pp. 194-203.

F-166.   Byrd, Donald V. 1971. "Sailing Off to
          Jerusalem: Toward a Philosophy of Geographic
          Research," Virginia Geographer, Vol. 6, pp. 3-7.

F-167.   Cahnman, Werner J. 1948. "Outline of a Theory
          of Area Studies," Annals of the Association of
          American Geographers, Vol. 38, pp. 233-243.

F-168.   Calvin, D. D. 1934. "Apology for Geography,"
          Queen's Quarterly, Vol. 41, pp. 218-225.

F-169.   Campbell, Marius R. 1928. "Geographic
          Terminology," Annals of the Association of
          American Geographers, Vol. 17, pp. 25-40.

F-170.   Capelle, Russell B., Jr. 1979. "On the
          Periphery of Geography," Journal of Geography,
          Vol. 78, pp. 64-67.

F-171.   Carchedi, G. 1987. "Popular Movements and
          Socialism," Antipode, Vol. 19, pp. 216-221.

F-172.   Caris, S. 1978. "Geographic Perspectives on
          Women: A Review," Transition, Vol. 8, pp.
          10-14.

F-173.   Carol, Hans. 1961. "Geography of the Future,"
          Professional Geographer, Vol. 13, No. 1, pp.
          14-18.

F-174.   Carpenter, C. C. 1978. "Expanding Geographic
          Dimensions: A Geographic Epistemology," Journal
          of the Tennessee Academy of Science, Nashville,
          Vol. 53, pp. 16-22.

F-175.   Carter, George F. 1976. "An Epigraphic
          Geography or Kilroy (amongst others) Was Here,"
          Geographical Bulletin, Vol. 12, pp. 6-23.

F-176.   Chamberlain, James F. 1906. "Some Essentials in
          Geography," Journal of Geography, Vol. 5, pp.
          369-375.

F-177.   Chapman, J. D. 1966. "Geographical Dialogue,"
          B.C. Geographical Series, No. 3, pp. 41-60.

F-178.   Chapman, J. D. 1966. "The Status of Geography,"
          Canadian Geographer, Vol. 10, pp. 133-144.

F-179.   Chapman, J. D. 1971. "Relevance to What? A
          Review of Some Contemporary Forces for Change and
          Their Impact Upon Geography," B.C. Geographical
          Series, No. 12, pp. 21-31.

F-180.   Chappell, J. E. 1980. "Crucial Deficiencies in
          Cultural Determinism," Geographical Survey, Vol.
          9, pp. 3-18.

F-181.   Chappell, John E. 1967. "Comment: Marxism and
          Environmentalism," Annals of the Association of
          American Geographers, Vol. 57, pp. 203-206 [reply
          pp. 206-207].

F-182.   Chardon, Roland E. 1962. "Geography: A Working
          Definition," Journal of Geography, Vol. 61, pp.
          71-75.

F-183.   Chatterjee, S. P. 1963. "Presidential Address,"
          Geographical Review of India, Vol. 25, pp. 1-10.

F-184.   Chatterjee, S. P. 1964. "Presidential Address,"
          Geographical Review of India, Vol. 26, pp. 1-10.

F-185.   Chatterjee, S. P. 1966. "Presidential Address,"
          Geographical Review of India, Vol. 28, pp. 1-8.

F-186.   Chatterjee, S. P. 1967. "Presidential Address,"
          Geographical Review of India, Vol. 29, pp. 1-13.

F-187.   Chaudhuri, M. R. 1948. "The Scientific Basis of
          Geographic Regionalism," Geographical Review of
          India, Vol. 10, No. 1, n.p.

F-188.   Chisholm, George. 1908. "The Meaning and Scope
          of Geography," Scottish Geographical Magazine,
          Vol. 24, pp. 561-575.

F-189.   Chisholm, George C. 1911. "Some Recent
          Contributions to Geography," Scottish
          Geographical Magazine, Vol. 27, pp. 561-574.

F-190.   Chisholm, George G. 1916. "Geography in Italy,"
          Scottish Geographical Magazine, Vol. 32, pp.
          401-406.

F-191.   Chisholm, M. 1978. "Theory Construction in
          Geography," South African Geographer, Vol. 6, pp.
          113-122.

F-192.   Chisholm, Michael. 1986. "Beyond 1984 - the
          Image of Geography," Area, Vol. 16, p. 337.

F-193.   Chojnicki, Z. 1979. "The Methodological Bases
          of Prediction in Economic Geography," Quaestiones
          Geographicae, Vol. 5, pp. 23-34.

F-194.   Chovinard, Vera and Fincher, Ruth. 1983. "A
          Critique of 'Structural Marxism and Human
          Geography,'" Annals of the Association of
          American Geographers, Vol. 73, pp. 137-150.

F-195.   Chovinard, Vera, Fincher, Ruth and Webber,
         Michael. 1984. "Empirical Research in
         Scientific Human Geography," _Progress in Human
         Geography_, Vol. 8, pp. 347-380.

F-196.   Christensen, K. 1982. "Geography As a Human
         Science: A Philosophic Critique of the
         Positivist - Humanist Split," _A Search for Common
         Ground_, P. Gould and G. Olsson eds., Pion,
         London, pp. 37-57.

F-197.   Christie, P. 1973. "Poetry of Today and
         Geography," _South Hampshire Geographer_, No. 6,
         pp. 86-89.

F-198.   Claeson, C. F. 1982. "Integrated Development
         and Integrative Geography -- Some Reflections and
         Impulses," _Geografiska Annaler_, Vol. 64B, pp.
         97-104.

F-199.   Clark, Andrew. 1962. "Praemia Geographiae: The
         Incidental Rewards of a Professional Career,"
         _Annals of the Association of American
         Geographers_, Vol. 52, pp. 229-241.

F-200.   Clark, Andrew Hill. 1963. "Honing the Edge of
         Curiosity," _Canadian Geographer_, Vol. 4, pp. 1-2.

F-201.   Clark, Andrew. 1968. "What Geographers Did: A
         Review," _Economic Geography_, Vol. 44, pp. 83-86.

F-202.   Clark, Gordon L. 1984. "A Theory of Local
         Autonomy," _Annals of the Association of American
         Geographers_, Vol. 74, pp. 195-208.

F-203.   Clark, Gordon L. and Dear, Michael. 1978. "The
         Future of Radical Geography," _Professional
         Geographer_, Vol. 30, pp. 356-359.

F-204.   Clark, K. G. T. 1950. "Certain Underpinning of
         Our Arguments in Human Geography," _Transactions
         and Papers - Institute of British Geographers_,
         No. 16, pp. 13-22.

F-205.   Clark, K. G. T. 1952. "Certain Underpinnings of
         our arguments in Human Geography," Institute of
         British Geographers, _Publication_ No. 16, pp.
         13-22.

F-206.   Clarke, M. and Wilson, A. G. 1987. "Towards an
         Applicable Human Geography: Some Developments
         and Observations," _Environment and Planning A_,
         Vol. 19, pp. 1525-1542.

F-207.   Claval, P. 1980. "Epistemology and the History
         of Geographical Thought," _Progress in Human
         Geography_, Vol. 4, pp. 371-384.

F-208.   Claval, P.   1985.   "Les Ideologie Spatiales
         (Spatial Ideologies)," Cahiers de Geographie du
         Quebec, Vol. 29, pp. 261-269 [English Summary].

F-209.   Claval, Paul.   1967.   "Ou'est-CE Que La
         Geographie?," Geographical Journal, Vol. 133, pp.
         33-38.

F-210.   Claval, Paul.   1982.   "Methodology and
         Philosophy," Progress in Human Geography, Vol. 6,
         pp. 449-458.

F-211.   Claval, Paul C.   1983.   "One Hundred Years of
         Teaching Geography in French Universities,"
         Journal of Geography, Vol. 82,, pp. 110-111.

F-212.   Clayton, K. M.   1972.   "Tradition and
         Experiment," Horizon, Vol. 21, pp. 6-7.

F-213.   Clayton, K. M.   1985.   "The State of Geography,"
         Transactions - Institute of British Geographers,
         Vol. 10, pp. 5-16.

F-214.   Clayton, Keith.   1971.   "Geographical Reference
         Systems," Geographical Journal, Vol. 137, pp.
         1-13.

F-215.   Close, Colonel C. F.   1911.   "The Purpose and
         Position of Geography," Bulletin of the American
         Geographical Society, Vol. 43, pp. 740-753.

F-216.   Close, Colonel C. F.   1911.   "The Purpose and
         Position of Geography," Journal of the Manchester
         Geographical Society, Vol. 27, pp. 84-100.

F-217.   Close, Colonel Sir Charles.   1928.   "Address at
         the Anniversary General Meeting," Geographical
         Journal, Vol. 72, pp. 97-117.

F-218.   Close, Colonel Sir Charles.   1929.   "Address at
         the Annual General Meeting," Geographical
         Journal, Vol. 74, pp. 97-109.

F-219.   Colby, Charles C.   1936.   "Changing Currents of
         Geographic Thought in America," Annals of the
         Association of American Geographers, Vol. 26, pp.
         1-37.

F-220.   Committee of Fifteen.   1895.   "Report on
         Geography," Proceedings of the N.E.A. for 1895,
         pp. 232-237.

F-221.   Cooke, Philip.   1987.   "Clinical Inference and
         Geographic Theory," Antipode, Vol. 19, pp.
         69-78.

F-222.   Cooke, R. V. 1985. "Cooke's Second Law -
         Prolegomenon to a Paradigm," _Area_, Vol. 17, pp.
         324-326.

F-223.   Cooper, Sherwin H. 1966. "Theoretical
         Geography, Applied Geography and Planning,"
         Professional Geographer, Vol. 18, pp. 1-2.

F-224.   Corpoz, Min. Onofre D. 1981. "Geography and Its
         Development in the 80's: A Challenge," _Philippine
         Geographical Journal_, Vol. 25, pp. 4-[7].

F-225.   Cosgrove, D. 1985. "Prospect, Perspective and
         the Evolution of the Landscape Idea,"
         Transactions - Institute of British Geographers,
         Vol. 10, pp. 45-62.

F-226.   Couclelis, H. 1982. "Philosophy in the
         Construction of Geographic Reality," _A Search for
         Common Ground_, P. Gould and G. Olsson, eds.,
         Pion, London, pp. 105-138.

F-227.   Couclelis, Helen. 1983. "Some Second Thoughs
         About Theory in the Social Sciences,"
         Geographical Analysis, Vol. 15, pp. 28-33.

F-228.   Couclelis, H. and Gale, N. 1986. "Space and
         Spaces," _Geografiska Annaler_, Vol. 68B, pp. 1-12.

F-229.   Couclelis, Helen and Golledge, Reginald. 1983.
         "Analytic Research, Positivism, and Behavioral
         Geography," _Annals of the Association of American
         Geographers_, Vol. 73, pp. 331-339.

F-230.   Coulter, John Wesley. 1949. "The Method of
         Science in Human Geography," _Annals of the
         Association of American Geographers_, Vol. 39, pp.
         60-61.

F-231.   Coulter, John Wesley. 1953. "Comments on Human
         Geography and Physical Geography," _Journal of
         Geography_, Vol. 52, pp. 202-205.

F-232.   Coulter, John Wesley. 1956. "The Significance
         of Human Geography Today," _Education_, Vol. 77,
         pp. 5-10.

F-233.   Cowen, Joel B. 1971. "The Place of Geography in
         the Liberal Arts," _Journal of Geography_, Vol.
         20, pp. 135-136.

F-234.   Cressey, G. B. 1936. "Current Trends in
         Geography," _Science_, Vol. 84 October 2, N.S.,
         pp. 311-314.

F-235.   Crist, Raymond E. 1969. "Geography,"
         Professional Geographer, Vol. 21, pp. 305-307.

F-236.   Crone, G. R.   1964.   "Geography in the Twentieth Century," Geographical Journal, Vol. 130, pp. 197-220.

F-237.   Crone, G. R.   1965.   "More Thoughts on the Nature of Geography: Review," Geographical Journal, Vol. 131, pp. 256-259.

F-238.   Crowe, P. R.   1938.   "On Progress in Geography," Scottish Geographical Journal, Vol. 54, pp. 1-19.

F-239.   Culling, W. E. H.   1987.   "Equifinality: Modern Approaches to Dynamical Systems and Their Potential for Geographical Thought," Transaction - Institute of British Geographers, Vol. 12, pp. 57-72.

F-240.   Cumberland, K. B.   1955.   "American Geography: Review and Commentary," New Zealand Geographer, Vol. 11, pp. 183-194.

F-241.   Cumberland, K. B.   1956.   "Why Geography?" Proceedings of the First Geography Conference, New Zealand Geographical Society, 1955, pp. 1-8.

F-242.   Cumberland, Kenneth B.   1946.   "The Geographer's Point of View," An Inaugural lecture delivered 2 April 1946, New Zealand, Auckland University College, 1946, 24 p.

F-243.   Cunningham, Frank F.   1977.   "The Revolution in Landscape Science," B.C. Geographical Series, No. 25, pp. 1-136.

F-244.   Curry, Leslie.   1967.   "Quantitative Geography, 1967," Canadian Geographer, Vol. 11, pp. 265-279.

F-245.   Curry, Michael.   1985.   "Contemporary Geography and the Ideal of Scientific Expertise," Operational Geographer, No. 7, pp. 15-16.

F-246.   Curry, M.   1982.   "The Idealist Dispute in Anglo-American Geography," Canadian Geographer, Vol. 26, pp. 37-50.

F-247.   Curry, M.   1982.   "The Idealist Dispute in Anglo-American Geography: A Reply," Canadian Geographer, Vol. 26, pp. 57-59.

F-248.   Curry, M.   1985.   "On Relationality: Contemporary Geography and the Search for the Foolproof Method," Geoforum, Vol. 16, pp. 109-118.

F-249.   Cutter, Susan Curtis and Renwick, Hilary.   1980. "The Myth of the Women's Session," Transition, Vol. 10, pp. 14-17.

F-250.   Dann, E. W.   1904.   "What is Geography?"   _Journal_
         of the Manchester Geographical Society, Vol. 20,
         pp. 130-139.

F-251.   Dann, E. W.   1905.   "What is Geography?"
         Geographical Teacher, Vol. 3, pp. 97-103.

F-252.   Darby, H. C.   1935.   "The Geographical Ideas of
         the Venerable Bede," _Scottish Geographical_
         Magazine, Vol. 51, pp. 84-89.

F-253.   Darby, H. C.   1946.   "The Theory and Practice of
         Geography," An Inaugural lecture delivered at
         Liverpool on 7 February 1946.   Liverpool: The
         University Press, 22 pp.

F-254.   Darwin, Major Leonard.   1909.   "Address to the
         Royal Geographical Society, 1909," _Geographical_
         Journal, Vol. 34, pp. 1-5.

F-255.   Darwin, Major Leonard.   1910.   "Address to the
         Royal Geographical Society, 1910," _Geographical_
         Journal, Vol. 36, pp. 1-11.

F-256.   Darwin, Major Leonard.   1911.   "Address to the
         Royal Geographical Society, _Geographical Journal_,
         Vol. 38, pp. 1-8.

F-257.   Davgun, Satish K.   1980.   "Humanism in
         Geography," _Geographical Review of India_, Vol.
         42, pp. 211-215.

F-258.   David, T.   1958.   "Against Geography,"
         Universities Quarterly, Vol. 13, pp. 261-273.

F-259.   Davies, R. J.   1974.   "Geography and Society,"
         South African Geographical Journal, Vol. 56, pp.
         3-14.

F-260.   Davies, W. K. D.   1966.   "Theory, Science and
         Geography," _Tijdschrift voor Economische en_
         Sociale Geografie, Vol. 57, pp. 125-130.

F-261.   Davis, W.   1903.   "A Scheme of Geography,"
         Geographical Journal, Vol. 22, pp. 413-423.

F-262.   Davis, W. M.   1906.   "An Inductive Study of the
         Content of Geography," _Bulletin of the American_
         Geographical Society, Vol. 38, pp. 67-84.

F-263.   Davis, W. M.   1906.   "An Inductive Study of the
         Content of Geography," _Journal of Geography_,
         Vol. 5, pp. 145-160.

F-264.   Davis, W. M.   1910.   "Experiments in Geographical
         Description," _Bulletin of the American_
         Geographical Society, Vol. 42, pp. 401-435.

F-265.   Davis, W. M. 1914. "The Principles of Regional
         Exposition," Annals of the Association of
         American Geographers, Vol. 4, pp. 141-142.

F-266.   Davis, W. M. 1915. "The Principles of
         Geographical Description," Annals of the
         Association of American Geographers, Vol. 5, pp.
         61-106.

F-267.   Davis, W. M. 1932. "A Retrospect of Geography,"
         Annals of the Association of American
         Geographers, Vol. 22, pp. 211-230.

F-268.   Davis, William M. 1887. "The Study of
         Geography," Science, Vol. 10, pp. 131-137.

F-269.   Davis, William M. 1899. "The Rational Element
         in Geography," National Geographic Magazine, Vol.
         10, p. 466.

F-270.   Davis, William M. 1904. "A Scheme of
         Geography," Journal of Geography, Vol. 3, pp.
         20-31.

F-271.   Davis, William M. 1904. "The Essential in
         Geography," Bulletin of the American Geographical
         Society of New York, Vol. 36, pp. 470-473.

F-272.   Davis, William M. 1906. "An Inductive Study of
         the Content of Geography," Bulletin of the
         American Geographical Society of New York, Vol.
         38, pp. 67-84.

F-273.   Day, M. D. 1980. "Dialectical Materialism and
         Geography," Area, Vol. 12, pp. 142-146.

F-274.   Day, M. D. and Tineis, J. 1979. "Catastrophe
         Theory and Geography: A Marxist Critique," Area,
         Vol. 11, pp. 54-58.

F-275.   Dear, Michael. 1975. "The Nature of Socialist
         Geography," Antipode, Vol. 7, pp. 87-89.

F-276.   de Blij, Harm J. 1977. "Visual Evidence in
         Geography," Professional Geographer, Vol. 29, pp.
         66-69.

F-277.   de Freetas, C. R. and Woolmington, E. 1980.
         "Catastrophe Theory and Catastasis," Area, Vol.
         12, pp. 191-194.

F-278.   DeGeer, S. 1923. "On the Definition, Method and
         Classification of Geography," Geografiska
         Annaler, Vol. 5, pp. 1-37.

F-279.   De Silva, S. F. 1956. "The Meaning of
         Geography," Bulletin of the Ceylon Geographical
         Society, Vol. 10, pp. 1-8.

F-280. de Souza, Anthony R. and Vogeler, Ingolf. 1980.
        "Teaching Ideological Alternatives," Geographical
        Perspectives, Vol. 46, pp. 56-60.

F-281. Dickinson, J. P. and Clarke, C. G. 1972.
        "Relevance and the Newest Geography," Area, Vol.
        4, pp. 25-27.

F-282. Dickinson, Robert E. 1939. "Landscape and
        Society," Scottish Geographical Magazine, Vol.
        55, pp. 1-15.

F-283. Dickinson, John P. 1986. "Irreverence and
        Another New Geography," Area, Vol. 18, pp.
        52-54.

F-284. Dikshit, K. 1958. "Some Observations on the
        Techniques and Generalizations in Urban
        Geography," Indian Geographer, Vol. 3, pp.
        61-70.

F-285. Dodge, R. E. 1896. "Geography from Nature,"
        Journal of the American Geographical Society of
        New York, Vol. 28, pp. 146-156.

F-286. Dodge, Stanley D. 1960. "Geography: What to
        Call It," Professional Geographer, Vol. 12, No.
        4, pp. 13-14.

F-287. Dodoo, Robert, Jr. 1971. "The Use of
        Speculative Social Thought in Geographical
        Research," Professional Geographer, Vol. 23, pp.
        295-297.

F-288. Dollfus, O. and Dastes, F. Durand. 1975. "Some
        Remarks on the Notions of 'Structure' and
        'System' in Geography," Geoforum, Vol. 6, pp.
        83-94.

F-289. Doughty, R. W. 1981. "Environmental Theology:
        Trends and Prospects in Christian Thought,"
        Progress in Human Geography, Vol. 5, pp. 234-248.

F-290. Douglas, Ian. 1987. "The Influence of Human
        Geography on Physical Geography," Progress in
        Human Geography, Vol. 11, pp. 517-540.

F-291. Downs, R. M. 1981. "Maps and Metaphors,"
        Professional Geographer, Vol. 33, pp. 287-293.

F-292. Driver, Felix and Philo, Christopher. 1986.
        "The Implications of 'Scientific Geography',"
        Area, Vol. 18, pp. 161-162.

F-293. Dryer, C. R. 1905. "What is Geography?"
        Journal of Geography, Vol. 4, pp. 348-360.

F-294.   Dryer, Charles R. 1912. "Regional Geography,"
          Journal of Geography, Vol. 11, pp. 73-75.

F-295.   Duncan, J. S. 1980. "The Superorganic in
          American Cultural Geography," Annals of the
          Association of American Geographers, Vol. 70, pp.
          181-198.

F-296.   Duncan, J. S. and Ley, D. 1982. "Structural
          Marxism and Human Geography," Annals of the
          Association of American Geographers, Vol. 72, pp.
          30-59.

F-297.   Duncan, S. S. 1979. "Qualitative Change in
          Human Geography -- An Introduction," Geoforum,
          Vol. 10, pp. 1-4.

F-298.   Duncan, S. S. and Sager, R. A. 1980. "Debate on
          Geography and the Vampire Trick," Area, Vol. 12,
          pp. 195-197.

F-299.   Dziewonski, Kazimierz. 1966. "A New Approach to
          the Theory and Empirical Analysis of Location,"
          Papers of the Regional Science Association, Vol.
          16, pp. 17-26.

F-300.   Eichenbaum, Jack and Gale, Stephen. 1971.
          "Form, Function, and Process: A Methodological
          Inquiry," Economic Geography, Vol. 47, pp.
          525-544.

F-301.   Entrikin, J. N. 1977. "Geography's Spatial
          Perspective and the Philosophy of Ernst
          Cassiver," Canadian Geographer, Vol. 21, pp.
          209-222.

F-302.   Entrikin, J. Nicholas. 1976. "Contemporary
          Humanism in Geography," Annals of the Association
          of American Geographers, Vol. 66, pp. 615-632.

F-303.   Entrikin, J. Nicholas. 1985. "Humanism,
          Naturalism, and Geographical Thought,"
          Geographical Analysis, Vol. 17, pp. 243-247.

F-304.   Ernst, J. A. and Merrens, H. R. 1978. "Praxeis
          and Theory in the Writing of American Historical
          Geography," Journal of Historical Geography, Vol.
          4, pp. 277-290.

F-305.   Eyles, J. 1981. "Why Geography Cannot Be
          Marxist: Towards an Understanding of Lived
          Experience," Environment and Planning A, Vol. 13,
          pp. 1371-1388.

F-306.   Eyles, J., and Lee, R. 1982. "Human Geography
          in Explanation," Transactions - Institute of
          British Geographers, Vol. 7, pp. 117-122.

F-307. Eyles, John. 1973. "Geography and Relevance,"
        Area, Vol. 158-160.

F-308. Eyles, John. 1984. "An Outsider on the Inside:
        Fear and Loathing from Wollongong," Australian
        Geographical Studies, Vol. 22, pp. 306-312.

F-309. Fairbanks, H. W. 1919. "A New Definition of
        Geography," Journal of Geography, Vol. 18, pp.
        185-188.

F-310. Farmer, B. H. 1973. "Geography, Area Studies
        and the Study of Area," Transactions - Institute
        of British Geographers, No. 60, pp. 1-16.

F-311. Fellmann, Jerome D. 1986. "Myth and Reality in
        the Origin of American Economic Geography,"
        Annals of the Asociation of American Geographers,
        Vol. 76, pp. 313-330.

F-312. Fenneman, N. M. 1919. "The Circumference of
        Geography," Geographical Review, Vol. 7, pp.
        168-175.

F-313. Fenneman, Nevin. 1919. "The Circumference of
        Geography," Annals of the Association of American
        Geographers, Vol. 9, pp. 3-12.

F-314. Fifer, J. Valerie. 1978. "Geography and
        Politics: Concepts of Space, Distance and
        Connection," Geoforum, Vol. 9, pp. 331-339.

F-315. Finch, V. C. 1934. "Written Structures for
        Presenting the Geography of Regions," Annals of
        the Association of American Geographers, Vol. 24,
        pp. 113-122.

F-316. Finch, V. C. 1939. "Geographical Science and
        Social Philosophy," Annals of the Association of
        American Geographers, Vol. 29, pp. 1-28.

F-317. Finch, V. C. 1944. "Training for Research in
        Economic Geography," Annals of the Association
        of American Geographers, Vol. 34, pp. 207-215.

F-318. Fisher, C. A. 1959. "The Compleat Geographer,"
        [Inaugural Lecture] Sheffield: University of
        Sheffield, 18 pp.

F-319. Fitzgerald, Walter. 1943. "The Regional Concept
        in Geography," Nature, Vol. 152, pp. 740-741.

F-320. Fitzsimmons, M. 1985. "Hidden Philosophies:
        How Geographic Thought Has Been Limited by Its
        Theoretical Models," Geoforum, Vol. 16, pp.
        139-150.

F-321.   Fleure, H. J. 1931. "Geographical Outlook," New
         Era, Vol. 12, pp. 221- 223.

F-322.   Fleure, H. J. 1938. "Geography and the
         Scientific Movement," Calcutta Geographical
         Review, Vol. 2, pp. 33-37.

F-323.   Fleure, H. J. 1938. "Geography and the
         Scientific Movement," Geographical Review of
         India, Vol. 2, No. 1, n.p.

F-324.   Fleure, H. J. 1938. "Geography and the
         Scientific Movement," Journal of the Madras
         Geographical Association, Vol. 13, pp. 10-15.

F-325.   Fleure, H. J. 1944. "Geographical Thought in
         the Changing World," Geographical Review, Vol.
         34, pp. 515-528.

F-326.   Flowers, Rick. 1984. "What is the Use of
         Geography?" Bloomsbury Geographer, Vol. 12, pp.
         58-61.; Peter Jackson replies, pp. 61-62; final
         word from Flowers, pp. 62-63.

F-327.   Floyd, B. N. 1966. "Some Comments on the Scope
         and Objectives of Geography in the Developing
         Areas," Nigerian Geographical Journal, Vol. 9,
         pp. 11-24.

F-328.   Floyd, B. N. 1967. "A Niche for Verbalizers in
         the 'New School':   Geography as Polite
         Literature," Nigerian Geographical Journal, Vol.
         10, pp. 133-136.

F-329.   Floyd, Barry. 1963. "Quantification -- A
         Geographic Deviation?" Professional Geographer,
         Vol. 15, No. 6, pp. 15-17.

F-330.   Floyd, Barry N. 1961. "Towards a More Literary
         Geography," Professional Geographer, Vol. 13, No.
         4, pp. 7-11.

F-331.   Floyd, Barry N. 1962. "The Pleasures Ahead: A
         Geographic Meditation," Professional Geographer,
         Vol. 14, No. 5, pp. 1-4.

F-332.   Floyd, Barry N. 1971. "On Reversing the Image
         of a Simplistic Geography: The Task of
         Socio-Economic Geography (Geonomics)," Journal of
         Geography, Vol. 70, pp. 84-90.

F-333.   Floyd, Barry and O'Brien, Dennis. 1976.
         "Whither Geography? A Cautionary Tale from
         Economics," Area, Vol. 8, pp. 15-23.

F-334.   Ford, D. 1983. "Isotope Geography,"
         Operational Geographer, Vol. 1, pp. 5-7.

F-335.   Ford, L. R.   1982.   "Beware of New Geographies,"
         Professional Geographer, Vol. 34, pp. 131-135.

F-336.   Ford, Larry R.   1984.   "A Core of Geography:
         What Geographers Do Best," Journal of Geography,
         Vol. 83, pp. 102-106.

F-337.   Forde, C. Daryll.   1925.   "Values in Human
         Geography," Geographical Teacher, Vol. 13, pp.
         216-221.

F-338.   Forer, P. C. and Owens, I. F.   1979.   "The
         Frontiers of Geography in the 1980's," New
         Zealand Journal of Geography, Vol. 67, pp. 2-5.

F-339.   Foresta, Ronald.   1976.   "Entitivity and Regional
         Geography," Geographical Survey, Vol. 5, No. 1,
         pp. 6-13.

F-340.   Fox, G. C.   1969.   "Geography: Sighted Subject,
         Sank Same," Clearing House, Vol. 44, pp. 35-36.

F-341.   Francaviglia, Richard V.   1972.   "Phenomenology,
         Experience, and Geographic Tradition,"
         Geographical Survey, Vol. 1, No. 4, pp. 1-9.

F-342.   Freeman, Otis W.   1951.   "Geography Among the
         Sciences," Journal of Geography, Vol. 50, pp.
         202-210.

F-343.   Freeman, T. W.   1986.   "The Unity of Geography:
         Introduction," Transactions - Institute of
         British Geographers, Vol. 11, pp. 441-443.

F-344.   Friis, H.   1960.   "Geography -- What to Call
         It," Professional Geographer, Vol. 12, pp. 8-16.

F-345.   Furman, A. Ye.   1962.   "On Interrelationships
         Between Natural and Social," Soviet Geography:
         Review and Translation, Vol. 3, No. 7, pp. 49-55.

F-346.   Gaile, G. L., Barber, D. and Ferguson, A.   1982.
         "Deflouring Sandwich Geography," Area, Vol. 14,
         pp. 201-202.

F-347.   Gale, N., and Golledge, R. G.   1982.   "On the
         Subjective Partitioning of Space," Annals of the
         Association of American Geographers, Vol. 72, pp.
         60-67.

F-348.   Gale, S.   1976.   "Geography: from Form and
         Function to Process and Design," Proceedings -
         Twenty-Third International Geographical Congress,
         pp. 27-29.

F-349.   Gale, Stephen.   1970.   "Simplicity Isn't That
         Simple," Geographical Analysis, Vol. 2, pp.
         400-402.

F-350.   Gale, Stephen. 1972. "On the Heterodoxy of
          Explanations: A Review of David Harvey's
          Explanation in Geography," Geographical Analysis,
          Vol. 4, pp. 285-322.

F-351.   Gale, Stephen. 1975. "Simplicity, Again, Isn't
          That Simple," Geographical Analysis, Vol. 7, pp.
          451-455.

F-352.   Gale, Stephen. 1977. "Ideological Man in a
          Nonideological Society," Annals of the
          Association of American Geographers, Vol. 67, pp.
          267-272.

F-353.   Gananathan, V. S. 1954. "The Meaning of
          Landscape in Geography," Indian Geographical
          Journal, Vol. 29, pp. 28-29.

F-354.   Gannett, Henry. 1901. "Certain Persistent
          Errors in Geography," Bulletin of the American
          Geographical Society of New York, Vol. 33, pp.
          259-264.

F-355.   Gardner, J. 1968-69. "Location and Place in
          Geography," Albertan Geographer, No. 5, pp.
          21-24.

F-356.   Garnier, B. J. 1952. "The Contribution of
          Geography," An Inaugural Lecture Delivered at
          University College, Ibadan, 17 November 1951.
          Ibadan: Ibadan University Press, 20 p.

F-357.   Garrison, William L. 1964. "Values of Regional
          Science," Papers of the Regional Science
          Association, Vol. 13, pp. 7-11.

F-358.   Garrison, William L. 1979. "Playing with
          Ideas," Annals of the Association of American
          Geographers, Vol. 69, pp. 118-120.

F-359.   Gatrell, A. C. 1984. "Describing the Structure
          of a Research Literature: Spatial Diffusion
          Modelling in Geography," Environment and Planning
          B: Vol. 11, pp. 29-45.

F-360.   Gatrell, Anthony. 1983. "Saving Space: A
          Perspective for Geographical Enquiry," Area, Vol.
          15, pp. 251-256.

F-361.   Gatrell, Anthony C. 1984. "The Geometry of a
          Research Specialty: Spatial Diffusion Modeling,"
          Annals of the Association of American
          Geographers, Vol. 74, pp. 437-453.

F-362.   Genthe, M. K.   1912.   "Comment on Colonel Close's Address on the Purpose and Position of Geography," Bulletin of the American Geographical Society, Vol. 44, pp. 27-38.

F-363.   Gerasimov, I. P.   1962.   "Soviet Geographic Science and Problems of the Transformation of Nature," Soviet Geography: Review and Translation, Vol. 3, pp. 27-38.

F-364.   Gerasimov, I. P.   1968.   "Constructive Geography: Aims, Methods, and Results," Soviet Geography: Review and Translation, Vol. 7, pp. 739-755.

F-365.   Gerasimov, I. P.   1978.   "The Integrative Potential of Modern Geographic Research," Soviet Geography: Review and Translation, Vol. 19, pp. 137-148.

F-366.   Gerenchuk, K. I.   1979.   "Results of a Soviet Symposium on Theoretical Aspects of Geography," Soviet Geography: Review and Translation, Vol. 20, pp. 329-331.

F-367.   Gerenchuk, K. I.   1980.   "On Theoretical Geography," Soviet Geography: Review and Translation, Vol. 21, pp. 42-47.

F-368.   Gibson, Lyle E.   1961.   "Geography as an Area Social Science," California Geographer, Vol. 2, pp. 57-64.

F-369.   Gier, Jaclyn and Walton, John.   1987.   "Some Problems with Reconceptualising Patriarchy," Antipode, Vol. 19, pp. 54-58.

F-370.   Giffard, E. O.   1951.   "Geography in the Service of Mankind," Nature, Vol. 168, No. 4269, pp. 314-317.

F-371.   Gilbert, A.   1971.   "Some Thoughts on the 'New Geography' and the Study of Development," Area, Vol. 3, pp. 123-128.

F-372.   Gilbert, E. W.   1960.   "The Idea of Region," Geography, Vol. 45, pp. 157-175.

F-373.   Gilbert, Edmund W.   1962.   "Geographie Is Better Than Divinitie," Geographical Journal, Vol. 128, pp. 494-497.

F-374.   Gill, D. and Cook, I.   1984.   "Power: the Fourth Dimension," Contemporary Issues in Geography and Education, Vol. 1, pp. 10-12.

F-375.   Gillman, C.   1945.   "The Place of Geography in
          Western Culture," Records of the Dar es Salaam
          Society, No. 3, N.P.

F-376.   Ginsburg, Norton.   1972.   "The Mission of a
          Scholarly Society," Professional Geographer, Vol.
          24, pp. 1-6.

F-377.   Glick, Thomas F.   1984.   "History and Philosophy
          of Geography," Progress in Human Geography, Vol.
          8, pp. 275-283.

F-378.   Glick, Thomas F.   1985.   "History and Philosophy
          of Geography," Progress in Human Geography, Vol.
          9, pp. 424-431.

F-379.   Glick, Thomas F.   1986.   "History and Philosophy
          of Geography," Progress in Human Geography, Vol.
          10, pp. 267-278.

F-380.   Glowacki, Walter.   1971.   "The Demon's Demise,"
          Geographical Journal, Vol. 70, pp. 517-518.

F-381.   Gokhman, V. M., Gurevich, B. L. and Snushkin, Yu
          G.   1969.   "Problems of Metageography," Soviet
          Geography: Review and Translation, Vol. 10, pp.
          355-364.

F-382.   Gokhman, V. M. and Saushkin, Yu. G.   1972.
          "Present Problems in Theoretical Geography,"
          Soviet Geography: Review and Translation, Vol.
          13, pp. 499-517.

F-383.   Goldberg, M. A.   1985.   "Flexibility and
          Adaptation: Some Cues for Social Systems from
          Nature," Geoforum, Vol. 16, pp. 179-190.

F-384.   Goldie, Rt. Hon. Sir George Taubman.   1907.
          "Geographical Ideals," Geographical Journal, Vol.
          29, pp. 1-15.

F-385.   Golledge, R. G.   1981.   "Misconceptions,
          Misinterpretations, and Misrepresentations of
          Behavioural Approaches in Human Geography,"
          Environment and Planning A, Vol. 13, pp.
          1325-1344.

F-386.   Golledge, R. G., and Amadeo, Douglas.   1968.   "On
          Laws in Geography," Annals of the Association of
          American Geographers, Vol. 58, pp. 760-774.

F-387.   Golledge, Reginald G.   1983.   "Models of Man,
          Points of View, and Theory in Social Science,"
          Geographical Analysis, Vol. 15, pp. 57-60.

F-388. Golledge, Reginald G., et al.   1982.
        "Commentary on 'The Highest Form of the
        Geographers Art,'" Annals of the Association of
        American Geographers, Vol. 72, pp. 557-558.

F-389. Golledge, Reginald G. and Halperin, William C.
        1983.   "On the Status of Women in Geography,"
        Professional Geographer, Vol. 35, pp. 214-218.

F-390. Golledge, Reginald G.   1983.   "The Reality of
        Modern Geography," Journal of Geography, Vol. 82,
        pp. 5-6.

F-391. Goodchild, M. F.   1985.   "Questions, Tools or
        Paradigms: Scientific Geography in the 1980s,"
        Ontario Geography, Vol. 25, pp. 3-14.

F-392. Goodchild, Michael F. and Janelle, Donald G.
        1988.   "Specialization in the Structure and
        Organization of Geography," Annals of the
        Association of American Geographers, Vol. 78, pp.
        1-28.

F-393. Goodenough, Admiral Sir William.   1931.   "Address
        at the Annual General Meeting," Geographical
        Journal, Vol. 78, pp. 97-102.

F-394. Goudie, A. S.   1986.   "The Integration of Human
        and Physical Geography," Transactions - Institute
        of British Geography, Vol. 11, pp. 454-458.

F-395. Gould, P.   1979.   "Geography 1959-1977: The
        Angean Period," Annals of the Association of
        American Geographers, Vol. 69, pp. 139-151.

F-396. Gould, P.   1982.   "Things I Do Not Understand
        Very Well: 3.   Are Algebraic Operations Laws?"
        Environment and Planning A, Vol. 14, pp.
        1567-1569.

F-397. Gould, Peter.   1969.   "Methodological Development
        Since the Fifties," Progress in Geography, Vol.
        1, pp. 1-50.

F-398. Gould, P. R.   1969.   "New Geography: Central
        Place Theory," Harper's, Vol. 238, pp. 91-100
        [Reply R. E. Crist, Vol. 239, pp. 6+].

F-399. Gould, Peter.   1983.   "On the Road to Colonus:
        Or Theory and Perversity in the Social Sciences,"
        Geographical Analysis, Vol. 15, p. 35-40.

F-400. Gourou, P.   1984.   "La Geographie Comme
        Divertissement?"   (Geography reviewed as
        'diversion'), Herodote, Vol. 33-34, pp. 50-72
        [English Summary].

F-401.   Graham, Elspeth. 1986. "The Unity of
         Geography: A Comment," Transactions - Institute
         of British Geographers, Vol. 11, pp. 464-467.

F-402.   Graham, Julie. 1988. "Post-Modernism and
         Marxism," Antipode, Vol. 20, pp. 60-66.

F-403.   Graves, N. and Simons, M. 1966. "Geography and
         Philosophy," University of London Institute of
         Education Bulletin, N.V., pp. 11-14.

F-404.   Graves, N. J. 1968. "Geography, Social Science
         and Inter-Disciplinary Enquiry," Geographical
         Journal, Vol. 134, pp. 390-393.

F-405.   Gray, Fred. 1976. "Radical Geography and the
         Study of Education," Antipode, Vol. 8, pp. 38-44.

F-406.   Green, D. G. 1982. "The Spatial Sciences and
         the State," Environment and Planning A, Vol. 14,
         pp. 1541-1550.

F-407.   Green, F. H. W. 1971. "Back to the Heartland,"
         Area, Vol. 3, pp. 129-130.

F-408.   Gregory, S. 1976. "On Geographical Myths and
         Statistical Fables," Transactions - Institute of
         British Geographers, Vol. 1, N.S. pp. 385-400.

F-409.   Gregson, Nicky. 1986. "On Duality and Dualism:
         The Case of Structuration and Time Geography,"
         Progress in Human Geography, Vol. 10, pp.
         184-205.

F-410.   Griffith, Daniel A. 1984. "Reexamining the
         Question 'Are Locations Unique?'" Progress in
         Human Geography, Vol. 8, pp. 82-94.

F-411.   Grigg, David. 1965. "The Logic of Regional
         Systems," Annals of the Association of American
         Geographers, Vol. 55, pp. 465-491.

F-412.   Grigor'yev, A. A, and Kondrat'yev, K. Ya. 1982.
         "Outer Space and Geography," Soviet Geography:
         Review and Translation, Vol. 23, pp. 353-359.

F-413.   Guelke, L. 1974. "An Idealist Alternative in
         Human Geography," Annals of the Association of
         American Geographers, Vol. 64, pp. 193-202.

F-414.   Guelke, L. 1978. "Geography and Logical
         Positivism," In Geography and the Urban
         Environment, Vol. 1, D. Herbert and R. Johnston,
         eds., Chuceiter: Wiley, 35-61.

F-415.   Guelke, L. 1979. "Idealist Human Geography?"
         Area, Vol. 11, pp. 80-81.

F-416.   Guelke, L. 1985. "On the Role of Evidence in
         Physical and Human Geography," Geoforum, Vol. 16,
         pp. 131-138.

F-417.   Guelke, Len. 1988. "Commentary on 'Geography,
         Social Science, and Public Policy," [see G.
         Steed, 1988] Recognizing the Historical
         Foundation of Geographical Knowledge," Canadian
         Geographer, Vol. 32, pp. 14-17.

F-418.   Guelke, Leonard. 1971. "Problems of Scientific
         Explanation in Geography," Canadian Geographer,
         Vol. 15, pp. 38-53.

F-419.   Guelke, Leonard. 1974. "An Idealist Alternative
         in Human Geography," Annals of the Association of
         American Geographers, Vol. 64, pp. 193-202.

F-420.   Guelke, Leonard. 1977. "Regional Geography,"
         Professional Geographer, Vol. 29, pp. 1-7.

F-421.   Guelke, Leonard. 1979. "Objectives of
         Philosophical Analysis in Geography," Canadian
         Geographer, Vol. 23, pp. 170-171.

F-422.   Guelke, Leonard. 1979. "There and Back Again,"
         Area, Vol. 11, pp. 214-215.

F-423.   Guelke, Leonard. 1982. "The Idealist Dispute in
         Anglo-American Geography: A Comment," Canadian
         Geographer, Vol. 26, pp. 51-56.

F-424.   Gumilev, L. N. 1968. "On the Subject of the
         'Unified' Geography (Landscape and Ethnos, VI),"
         Soviet Geography: Review and Translation, Vol.
         9, pp. 36-47.

F-425.   Haas, William H. 1934. "Foundations and Limits
         in Geography [Abstract]," Annals of the
         Association of American Geographers, Vol. 24, pp.
         53.

F-426.   Hägerstrand, Torsten. 1982. "Dioramu, Patha and
         Project," [Response to Van Poassen's review of
         time-geography, 1976] Tijdschrift voor
         Economische en Sociale Geografie, Vol. 73, pp.
         323-339.

F-427.   Haigh, M. J. 1985. "Geography and General
         System Theory, Philosophical Homologies and
         Current Practice," Geoforum, Vol. 16, pp.
         191-204.

F-428.   Haines-Young, R. H. 1983. "Revolutions and
         Research Programmes," Area, Vol. 15, pp.
         125-130.

F-429.   Haken, H.   1985.   "Synergetics - an
         Interdisciplinary Approach to Phenomena of
         Self-Organization," Geoforum, Vol. 16, pp.
         205-212.

F-430.   Hall, Robert Burnett.   1935.   "The Geographic
         Region: A Resume," Annals of the Association of
         American Geographers, Vol. 25, pp. 137-152.

F-431.   Hall, Robin.   1980.   "Teaching Humanistic
         Geography," Australian Geographer, Vol. 14, pp.
         7-14.

F-432.   Hanson, Ravs M.   1959.   "What Geography Do You
         Want?" Journal of Geography, Vol. 58, pp. 33-43.

F-433.   Hanson, Susan.   1983.   "The World is Not a Stone
         Garden," Geographical Analysis, Vol. 15, pp.
         33-35.

F-434.   Hardwick, Walter G.   1966.   "Views on Human
         Geography," B.C. Geographical Series, No. 3, pp.
         23-28.

F-435.   Hare, F. K.   1971.   "The Environmental
         Imperative," Horizon, Vol. 20, pp. 6-9.

F-436.   Hare, F. K.   1977.   "Man's World and
         Geographers: A Secular Sermon," In: Humanism,
         Analysis and Social Action.   D. R. Deskins, et
         al. ed., Ann Arbor, University of Michigan, Dept.
         of Geography, Michigan Geographical Publication,
         Vol. 17, pp. 261-273.

F-437.   Hare, F. Kenneth.   1985.   "Future Environments:
         Can They be Predicted?" Transactions - Institute
         of British Geographers, Vol. 10, pp. 131-137.

F-438.   Harries, Keith D.   1975.   "Rejoinder to Richard
         Peet: 'The Geography of Crime: A Political
         Critique,'" Professional Geographer, Vol. 27, pp.
         280-282.

F-439.   Harris, B.   1978.   "Some Questions of Philosophy,
         Methodology and Explanation in Geography," London
         School of Economics, Graduate School of
         Geography, Discussion Papers, Vol. 64, 15 pp.

F-440.   Harris, Britton.   1968.   "Problems in Regional
         Science," Papers of the Regional Science
         Association, Vol. 21, pp. 7-18.

F-441.   Harris, Cole.   1971.   "Theory and Synthesis in
         Historical Geography," Canadian Geographer, Vol.
         15, pp. 157-172.

F-442.   Harrison, James D. 1977. "What is Applied
          Geography?" Professional Geographer, Vol. 29,
          pp. 297-300.

F-443.   Harrison, R. T. and Livingstone, D. N. 1979.
          "There and Back Again--Towards A Critique of
          Idealist Human Geography," Area, Vol. 11, pp.
          75-79.

F-444.   Harrison, R. T. and Livingstone, D. N. 1980.
          "Philosophy and Problems in Human Geography: A
          Presuppositional Approach," Area, Vol. 12, pp.
          25-31.

F-445.   Harshbarger, Herschel. 1976. "On the Need for
          an International Focus in American Geography,"
          Geographical Survey, Vol. 5, No. 2, pp. 5-6.

F-446.   Hart, J. F. 1982. "The Highest Form of the
          Geographer's Art," Annals of the Association of
          American Geographers, Vol. 72, pp. 1-30.

F-447.   Hartshorne, Richard. 1927. "Location as a
          Factor in Geography," Annals of the Association
          of American Geographers, Vol. 17, pp. 92-100.

F-448.   Hartshorne, Richard. 1928. "Location Factors in
          the Iron and Steel Industry," Economic
          Geography, Vol. 4, pp. 241-252.

F-449.   Hartshorne, Richard. 1939. "The Nature of
          Geography," Annals of the Association of American
          Geographers, Vol. 29, pp. 171-658.

F-450.   Hartshorne, Richard. 1942. "The Role of
          Geography, I," in Education for Citizen
          Responsibilities, F. L. Buidette, ed., pp. 39-43.

F-451.   Hartshorne, Richard. 1948. "On the Mores of
          Methodological Discussion in American Geography,"
          Annals of the Association of American
          Geographers, Vol. 38, pp. 74-75.

F-452.   Hartshorne, Richard. 1948. "On the Mores of
          Methodological Discussion in American Geography,"
          Annals of the Association of American
          Geographers, Vol. 38, pp. 113-125.

F-453.   Hartshorne, Richard. 1955. "Exceptionalism in
          Geography: Re-Examined," Annals of the
          Association of American Geographers, Vol. 45, pp.
          204-244.

F-454.   Hartshorne, Richard. 1958. "The Concept of
          Geography as a Science of Space, from Kant and
          Humboldt to Hettner," Annals of the Association
          of American Geographers, Vol. 48, pp. 97-108.

F-455.   Hartshorne, Richard. 1962. "On the Concept of
          Areal Differentiation," Professional Geographer,
          Vol. 14, pp. 10-12.

F-456.   Harsthorne, Richard. 1966. "Why Study
          Geography?" Journal of Geography, Vol. 65, pp.
          100-102.

F-457.   Hartshorne, Richard. 1968. "Geography--The
          Field," International Encyclopedia of the Social
          Sciences, Vol. 6 (New York: Macmillan), pp.
          115-116.

F-458.   Hartshorne, Richard. 1979. "Notes Toward a
          Bibliography of The Nature of Geography," Annals
          of the Association of American Geographers, Vol.
          69, pp. 63-76.

F-459.   Harvey, David. 1974.   "Population, Resources,
          and the Ideology of Science," Economic Geography,
          Vol. 50, pp. 256-276.

F-460.   Harvey, David. 1974. "What Kind of Geography
          for What Kind of Public Policy?" Transactions -
          Institute of British Geographers, No. 63, pp.
          18-24.

F-461.   Harvey, David. 1984. "On the History and
          Present Condition of Geography: An Historical
          Materialist Manifesto," Professional Geographer,
          Vol. 36, pp. 1-11.

F-462.   Hasson, Shlomo. 1984. "Humanistic Geography
          from the Perspective of Martin Buber's
          Philosophy," Professional Geographer, Vol. 36,
          pp. 11-18.

F-463.   Hay, A. 1979. "Positivism in Human Geography:
          Response to Critics," In Geography and the Urban
          Environment, Vol. 2, D. Herbert and R. Johnston,
          eds. Chicester: Wiley, pp. 1-26.

F-464.   Hay, Iain. 1987. "Optical Analysis: (Pr)isms
          in Geographic Thought," New Zealand Journal of
          Geography, No. 83, pp. 2-8.

F-465.   Healey, R. G. 1983. "Regional Geography in the
          Computer Age: A Further Commentary on 'The
          Highest Form of the Geographer's Art," Annals of
          the Association of American Geographers, Vol. 73,
          pp. 439-441.

F-466.   Helburn, Nicholas. 1982. "Geography and the
          Quality of Life," Annals of the Association of
          American Geographers, Vol. 72, 445-456.

F-467.   Hellen, J. A.   1978.   "The Future of German
          Geography," Geographical Journal, Vol. 144, pp.
          118-120.

F-468.   Henry, J. T. and Dikshit, Om.   1971.   "The
          Temporal Process in Geographic Thought," Deccan
          Geographer, Vol. 9, pp. 217-230.

F-469.   Herbertson, A. J.   1911.   "The New Science of
          Geography," Scientific American, Vol. 72, pp.
          62-67.

F-470.   Hewitt, Kenneth.   1983.   "Place Annihilation:
          Area Bombing and the Fate of Urban Places,"
          Annals of the Association of American
          Geographers, Vol. 73, pp. 257-284.

F-471.   Hill, A. D.   1982.   "Another View of the
          Sixteen-Million-Dollar Question," Professional
          Geographer, Vol. 34, pp. 1-5.

F-472.   Hilling, D.   1962.   "The Geographer's Region,"
          Bulletin - Ghana Geographical Association, Vol.
          7, No. 1-2, pp. 36-40.

F-473.   Hinderink, J.   1968.   "Purpose and Scope of the
          Human Geography of Non-Western Countries."
          Tijdschrift voor Economische en Sociale
          Geografie, Vol. 59, pp. 289-293.

F-474.   Hines, Howard H.   1977.   "Trends in Geographical
          Research and the Role of the National Science
          Foundation in Assisting Geographical Research,"
          Geographical Survey, Vol. 6, pp. 11-17.

F-475.   Hogarth, D. G.   1927. "Address at the Anniversary
          General Meeting, 20 June, 1927," Geographical
          Journal, Vol. 70, pp. 97-105.

F-476.   Hoggart, Keith.   1974.   "Geography Published
          Underground(?) -- The Output from British
          Polytechnics and Cognate Disciplines," Area, Vol.
          6, pp. 128-129.

F-477.   Hohnholz, J. H.   1985.   "The Dynamic Principle of
          Regional Geography," Universitas, Vol. 27, pp.
          175-182.

F-478.   Holcomb, Brivel.   1974.   "Geography in the
          Competitive Academic Market Place," Journal of
          Geography, Vol. 73, pp. 40-43.

F-479.   Holdich, Colonel Sir T. H.   1902.   "The Progress
          of Geographical Knowledge," Scottish Geographical
          Magazine, Vol. 18, pp. 525-535.

F-480. Hong-Key, Y. 1982. "Environmental Determinism
        and Geomancy: Two Cultures, Two Concepts,"
        GeoJournal, Vol. 6, pp. 77-80.

F-481. Hoover, Edgar M. 1963. "Whence Regional
        Scientists?" Papers of the Regional Science
        Association, Vol. 11, pp. 7-16.

F-482. Hornbeck, David. 1979. "Applied Geography: Is
        it Really Needed?" Journal of Geography, Vol. 78,
        pp. 47-49.

F-483. Hubbard, George D. 1904. "Geographic Influence,
        a Field for Investigation," Proceedings - Eight
        International Geographical Congress, pp. 992-996.

F-484. Hubbard, George D. 1930. "More Exact
        Geography," Bulletin of the Geographical Society
        of Philadelphia, Vol. 28, pp. 174-178.

F-485. Hudman, Lloyd E. 1971. "Geographic Concepts: A
        Need to be Explicit," Journal of Geography, Vol.
        71, pp. 520-525.

F-486. Hudson, J. C. 1979. "A Diamond Anniversary,"
        Annals of the Association of American
        Geographers, Vol. 69, pp. 1-3.

F-487. Hudson, John C. 1984. "Geography's Image
        Crisis," Journal of Geography, Vol. 83, pp.
        100-101.

F-488. Hudson, R. 1980. "Culture and Theory in Human
        Geography," Progress in Human Geography, Vol. 4,
        pp. 292-295.

F-489. Hufferd, James. 1980. "Towards a Transcendental
        Human Geography of Places," Antipode, Vol. 12,
        pp. 18-23.

F-490. Huggett, R. J. 1976. "A Schema for the Science
        of Geography, Its Systems, Laws, and Models,"
        Area, Vol. 8, pp. 25-30.

F-491. Hunter, John M. 1971. "The Structure of
        Geography: Note on an Introductory Model,"
        Journal of Geography, Vol. 70, pp. 332-336.

F-492. Huntington, C. C. 1926. "The Main Divisions in
        the Classification of Geography," Annals of the
        Association of American Geographers, Vol. 16, pp.
        28-29.

F-493. Huntington, C. C. 1928. "Geography as a Social
        Science," Annals of the Association of American
        Geographers, Vol. 18, pp. 62-63.

F-494.   Huntington, E.   1913.   "The New Science of
         Geography," Bulletin of the American Geographical
         Society, Vol. 45, pp. 641-652.

F-495.   Huntington, E.   1934.   "Problems of Geography,"
         Saturday Review, Vol. 11, pp. 242-243.

F-496.   Huntington, Ellsworth.   1912.   "The New Science
         of Geography," Yale Review, Vol. 2, pp. 82-96.

F-497.   Huntington, Ellsworth.   1914.   "The Geographer
         and History," Geographical Journal, Vol. 43, pp.
         19-32.

F-498.   Huntington, Ellsworth.   1916.   "Geographic
         Variables," Annals of the Association of American
         Geographers, Vol. 6, p. 127.

F-499.   Huntington, Ellsworth.   1924.   "Geography and
         Natural Selection," Annals of the Association of
         American Geographers, Vol. 14, pp. 1-16.

F-500.   Huntington, Ellsworth.   1927.   "The Quantitative
         Phases of Human Geography," Scientific Monthly,
         Vol. 25, pp. 289-305.

F-501.   Huntington, Ellsworth.   1942.   "What Next in
         Geography? Journal of Geography, Vol. 41, pp.
         1-9.

F-502.   Ilyichev, L. F.   1964.   "Remarks About a Unified
         Geography," Soviet Geography: Review and
         Translation, Vol. 5, pp. 32-34.

F-503.   Innis, Harold A. and Broek, Jan O. M.   1945.
         "Geography and Nationalism: A Discussion,"
         Geographical Review, Vol. 35, pp. 301-311.

F-504.   Isachenko, A. G.   1970.   "Problems and Trends in
         American Geography," [a review] Soviet
         Geography: Review and Translation, Vol. 11, pp.
         678-681.

F-505.   Isachenko, A. G.   1972.   "On the Unity of
         Geography," Soviet Geography: Review and
         Translation, Vol. 13, pp. 195-220.

F-506.   Isachenko, A. G.   1974.   "On the So-Called
         Anthropogenic Landscapes," Soviet Geography:
         Review and Translation, Vol. 15, pp. 467-475.

F-507.   Isachenko, A. G.   1974.   "On the Study of the
         History of Ideas (A Rebuttal)," Soviet
         Geography: Review and Translation, Vol. 15, pp.
         367-373.

F-508.   Isard, Walter and Reiner, Thomas A.   1962.
         "Regional Science and Planning," Papers of the
         Regional Science Association, Vol. 8, pp. 1-36.

F-509.   Isard, Walter and Reiner, Thomas A.   1966.
         "Regional Science: Retrospect and Prospect,"
         Papers of the Regional Science Association, Vol.
         16, pp. 1-16.

F-510.   Iyer, S. S.   1953.   "Social Studies Versus
         Geography," Bombay Geographical Magazine, Vol. 1,
         pp. 69-72.

F-511.   Jackson, J. B. J.   1952.   "Human, All Too Human
         Geography," Landscape, Vol. 2, pp. 2-7.

F-512.   Jackson, J.   1964.   "The Meaning of 'Landscape,'"
         Saetryk af Okulturgeografl, Vol. 88, pp. 47-50.

F-513.   Jackson, J. B.   1979.   "Landscape as Theater,"
         Landscape, Vol. 23, pp. 3-7.

F-514.   Jackson, Col. J. R.   1834.   "Hints on the Subject
         of Geographical Arrangement and Nomenclature,"
         Journal of the Royal Geographical Society of
         London, Vol. 4, pp. 72-88.

F-515.   Jackson, P.   1981.   "Phenomenology and Social
         Geography," Area, Vol. 13, pp. 299-305.

F-516.   Jackson, Peter.   1988.   "Social Geography:
         Social Struggles and Spatial Strategies,"
         Progress in Human Geography, Vol. 12, pp.
         263-269.

F-517.   Jackson, W. A. Douglas.   1958.   "Whither
         Political Geography?" Annals of the Association
         of American Geographers, Vol. 48, pp. 178-183.

F-518.   James, P.   1969.   "The Significance of Geography
         in American Education," Journal of Geography,
         Vol. 68, pp. 473-483.

F-519.   James, Preston E.   1947.   "Developments in the
         Field of Geography and Their Implications for the
         Geography Curriculum," Journal of Geography, Vol.
         46, pp. 221-226.

F-520.   James, Preston E.   1948.   "Formulating Objectives
         of Geographic Research," Annals of the
         Association of American Geographers, Vol. 38, pp.
         271-276.

F-521.   James, Preston E.   1949.   "Formulating the
         Objectives of Geographic Research," Annals of the
         Association of American Geographers, Vol. 39, pp.
         62-63.

F-522.   James, Preston E.   1963.   "Geography in an Age of Revolution," Journal of Geography, Vol. 62, pp. 97-103.

F-523.   James, Preston E.   1965.   "A Conceptual Structure for Geography," Journal of Geography, Vol. 64, pp. 292-298.

F-524.   James, Preston E.   1967.   "On the Origin and Persistence of Error in Geography," Annals of the Association of American Geographers, Vol. 57, pp. 1-24.

F-525.   James, Preston E.   1972.   "Geography," in Encyclopaedia Britannica (Chicago: The Company), Vol. 10, pp. 144-160.

F-526.   James, Preston E.   1974.   "The Nature and Scope of Geography," Geographical Perspectives, No. 33, pp. 5-19.

F-527.   James, Preston E.   1975.   "Geographic Concepts and World Crises," Journal of Geography, Vol. 74, pp. 8-15.

F-528.   James, Preston E.   1976.   "The Process of Competitive Discussion," Professional Geographer, Vol. 28, pp. 1-7.

F-529.   James, Preston E. and Martin, Geoffrey J.   1979. "On AAG History," Professional Geographer, Vol. 31, pp. 353-357.

F-530.   Jansen, Adviaan C. M.   1976.   "On Theoretical Foundations of Policy- Oriented Geography." Tijdschrift voor Economische en Sociale Geografie, Vol. 67, pp. 342-351.

F-531.   Jeans, D. N.   1974.   "Changing Formulations of the Man-Environment Relationship in Anglo-American Geography," Journal of Geography, Vol. 73, pp. 36-40.

F-532.   Jeans, D. N.   1983.   "Wilderness, Nature and Society: Contributions to the History of an Environmental Attitude," Australian Geographical Studies, Vol. 21, pp. 170-182.

F-533.   Jeffries, Ella.   1926.   "The Dependence of the Social Sciences Upon Geographic Principles," Journal of Geography, Vol. 25, pp. 228-236.

F-534.   Jennings, J. N.   1978.   "Apostasy or Apologetics? Confessions of a Natural Geographer," Monash Publications in Geography, Vol. 20, 29 p.

F-535.   Jinazali, M.   1973.   "The Nature and Subject
          Matter of Geography," Dziko, (Malawi), No. 4,
          pp. 1-11.

F-536.   Joerg, W. L. G.   1916.   "The Geographic Center:
          Its Definition and Determination," Annals of the
          Association of American Geographers, Vol. 6, pp.
          127-128.

F-537.   John, B. S.   1972.   "Guide to the Perception of
          New Geography," Area, Vol. 4, pp. 122-124.

F-538.   Johnson, C.   1903.   "First American Geography,"
          New England Magazine, Vol. 28, N.S. pp. 516-524.

F-539.   Johnson, C.   1903.   "Geographies of Our
          Forefathers," New England Magazine, Vol. 29,
          N.S., pp. 61-72.

F-540.   Johnson, Clifton.   1904.   "The First American
          Geography," Journal of Geography, Vol. 3, pp.
          311-321.

F-541.   Johnson, Clifton.   1904.   "Later Geographies,"
          Journal of Geography, Vol. 3, pp. 467-485.

F-542.   Johnson, D.   1934.   "Monumental Reference Work on
          Geography: The Geographie Universelle,"
          Science, Vol. 79, N.S., pp. 305-11, April 6.

F-543.   Johnson, Douglas.   1922.   "The Geography of
          History," Geographical Review, Vol. 12, pp.
          278-293.

F-544.   Johnson, Douglas.   1929.   "The Geographic
          Prospect," Annals of the Association of American
          Geographers, Vol. 19, pp. 167-231.

F-545.   Johnson, Hildegard B.   1961.   "Geography in the
          Realm of Wissenschaft," Southeastern Geographer,
          Vol. 1, pp. 9-20.

F-546.   Johnson, Hildegard B.   1967.   "Values in
          Geography," Journal of Geography, Vol. 66, pp.
          102-107.

F-547.   Johnson, James H. and Farrell, Walter C., Jr.
          1979.   Phenomenology in Geography," Geographical
          Survey, Vol. 8, pp. 3-9.

F-548.   Johnson, Louise.   1983.   "Bracketing Lifeworlds:
          Husserlean Phenomenology as Geographical Method,"
          Australian Geographical Studies, Vol. 21, pp.
          102-108.

F-549.   Johnson, Louise.   1987.   "Patriarchy and Feminist
          Challenges," Antipode, Vol. 19, pp. 210-215.

F-550.   Johnston, R. J. 1972. "Geography, the Social
         Sciences and Social Studies," New Zealand Journal
         of Geography, Vol. 52, pp. 18-21.

F-551.   Johnston, R. J. 1976. "Anarchy, Conspiracy,
         Apathy: The Three 'Conditions' of Geography,"
         Area, Vol. 8, pp. 1-3.

F-552.   Johnston, R. J. 1976. "Areal Studies,
         Ecological Studies, and Social Patterns in
         Cities," Transactions - Institute of British
         Geographers, Vol. 1, pp. 118-122.

F-553.   Johnston, R. J. 1976. "Population Distributions
         and the Essentials of Human Geography," South
         African Geographical Journal, Vol. 58, pp.
         93-106.

F-554.   Johnston, R. J. 1978. "Paradigms and
         Revolutions or Evolution: Observations on Human
         Geography Since the Second World War," Progress
         in Human Geography, Vol. 2, pp. 189-206.

F-555.   Johnston, R. J. 1980. "Geography is What
         Geographers Do--and Did," Progress in Human
         Geography, Vol. 4, pp. 277-283.

F-556.   Johnston, R. J. 1980. "On the Nature of
         Explanation in Human Geography," Transactions:
         Institute of British Geographers, Vol. 5, pp.
         402-412.

F-557.   Johnston, R. J. 1981. "Applied Geography,
         Quantitative Analysis and Ideology," Applied
         Geography, Vol. 1, pp. 213-220.

F-558.   Johnston, R. J. 1983. "It Must Remain One
         World," Environment and Planning A, Vol. 15, pp.
         143-146.

F-559.   Johnston, R. J. 1983. "Resource Analysis,
         Resource Management and the Integration of
         Physical and Human Geography," Progress in
         Physical Geography, Vol. 7, pp. 127-146.

F-560.   Johnston, R. J. 1984. "Marxist Political
         Economy, the State and Political Geography,"
         Progress in Human Geography, Vol. 8, pp. 473-492.

F-561.   Johnston, R. J. 1984. "The World is Our
         Oyster," Transactions - Institute of British
         Geographers, Vol. 9, pp. 443-459.

F-562.   Johnston, R. J. 1986. "Four Fixations and the
         Quest for Unity in Geography," Transactions -
         Institute of British Geographers, Vol. 11, pp.
         449-453.

F-563.   Johnston, R. J. 1987. "Geography, the State of
          the World and the Study of Places," New Zealand
          Journal of Geography, No. 84, pp. 4-8.

F-564.   Jones, Emrys. 1956. "Cause and Effect in Human
          Geography," Annals of the Association of American
          Geographers, Vol. 46, pp. 369-377.

F-565.   Jones, Emrys. 1984. "On the Specific Nature of
          Space," Geoforum, Vol. 15, pp. 5-9.

F-566.   Jones, Stephen B. 1952. "The Enjoyment of
          Geography," Geographical Review, Vol. 42, pp.
          543-550.

F-567.   Jones, Stephen B. 1955. "Geographical Thought
          in the United States," Perspectives USA, No. 12,
          pp. 59-76.

F-568.   Jones, Stephen B. 1959. "Boundary Concepts in
          the Setting of Place and Time," Annals of the
          Association of American Geographers, Vol. 49, pp.
          241-255.

F-569.   Kalesnik, S. V. 1964. "General Geographic
          Regularities of the Earth," Annals of the
          Association of American Geographers, Vol. 54, pp.
          160-164.

F-570.   Kalesnik, S. V. 1965. "Some Results of the New
          Discussion About a Unified Geography," Soviet
          Geography: Review and Translation, Vol. 6, pp.
          11-27.

F-571.   Kalesnik, S. V. 1966. "Geography Today," Soviet
          Geography: Review and Translation, Vol. 7, pp.
          15-28.

F-572.   Kalesnik, S. V. 1974. "The Subject, System and
          Classification of the Geographical Sciences,"
          Theoretical Problems on Physical and Economic
          Geography, Vol. 1, pp. 1-14.

F-573.   Kariel, Herbert G. 1967. "Scope of Geographic
          Study," Journal of Geography, Vol. 66, pp.
          150-154.

F-574.   Kariya, Paul. 1978-79. "Commentary:
          Ruminations on Humanistic Geography," Monadnock,
          Vol. 52-53, pp. 55-60.

F-575.   Kasperson, R. 1971. "The Post-Behavioural
          Revolution," Geographical Series, No. 12, pp.
          5-20.

F-576.   Kates, Robert W. 1987. "The Human Environment:
          The Road Not Taken, The Road Still Beckoning,"
          Annals of the Association of American
          Geographers, Vol. 77, pp. 525-534.

F-577.   Keelerman, Aharon. 1981. "Time-Space Approaches
          and Regional Study," Tijdschrift voor Economische
          en Sociale Geografie, Vol. 72, pp. 17-27.

F-578.   Kennedy, Barbara. 1980. "Outrageous Hypotheses
          in Geography," Journal Geographica, Vol. 15, pp.
          14-18.

F-579.   Kenzer, Martin S. 1987. "Geographic Thought,"
          Canadian Geographer, Vol. 31, pp. 70-81.

F-580.   Keuning, H. J. 1977. "Aims and Scope of Modern
          Human Geography, A Personal Contribution to
          Geographical Theory," Tijdschrift voor Economishe
          en Sociale Geografie, Vol. 68, pp. 266-274.

F-581.   Khan, Mohammad Aslam. 1974. "Nuclear
          Geography: A Conceptual Framework," Pakistan
          Geographical Review, Vol. 29, pp. 65-74.

F-582.   Khan, Sharafat. 1984. "A Primer in Scientific
          Geographic Research Terminology: Implications
          for Teaching Geography Majors," Geographical
          Bulletin, Vol. 26, pp. 29-34.

F-583.   Kibria, K. F. Md. 1972. "Regional Methods as a
          Means of Geographical Investigation of the
          World," Oriental Geographer, Vol. 16, pp.
          107-117.

F-584.   Kimble, George H. T. 1944. "The Geographer in
          the Modern World," Geographical Magazine, Vol.
          17, pp. 96-100.

F-585.   Kimble, George H. T. 1951. "Raising our
          Sights," Geographical Review, Vol. 41, pp. 1-3.

F-586.   Kimble, George H. T. 1951. "The Role of
          Geography at the Mid-Century," Journal of
          Geography, Vol. 50, pp. 45-54.

F-587.   Kimble, George H. T. 1952. "Expanding Horizons
          in a Shrinking World," Geographical Review, Vol.
          42, pp. 1-3.

F-588.   Kimble, George H. T. 1952. "The Comity of the
          Geographical Minded," Geographical Review, Vol.
          42, pp. 333-334.

F-589.   Kimble, George H. T. 1952. "The Uses of
          Geography," Geographical Review, Vol. 42, pp.
          507-509.

F-590.   King, Leslie J.   1960.   "A Note on Theory and
         Reality," Professional Geographer, Vol. 12, No.
         3, pp. 4-6.

F-591.   King, Leslie J.   1966.   "Approaches to Locational
         Analysis: An Overview," East Lakes Geographer,
         Vol. 2, pp. 1-16.

F-592.   King, Leslie J.   1976.   "Alternatives to a
         Positive Economic Geography," Annals of the
         Association of American Geographers, Vol. 66, pp.
         293-308.

F-593.   King, Leslie J.   1979.   "Areal Associations and
         Regressions," Annals of the Association of
         American Geographers, Vol. 69, pp. 124-127.

F-594.   King, Leslie J.   1979.   "The Seventies:
         Disillusionment and Consolidation," Annals of the
         Association of American Geographers, Vol. 69, pp.
         155-156.

F-595.   King, Russell   1984.   "Geography: Continuity,
         Change and a Return to the Roots," Geography,
         Vol. 69, pp. 1-2.

F-596.   Kinvig, R. H.   1953.   "The Geographer as
         Humanist," Advancement of Science, Vol. 10, pp.
         157-168.

F-597.   Kirby, Andrew.   1980.   "An Approach to Ideology,"
         Journal of Geography in Higher Education, Vol. 4,
         pp. 16-26.

F-598.   Kirk, William.   1963.   "Problems of Geography,"
         Geography, Vol. 48, pp. 357-371.

F-599.   Kirk, William.   1978.   "The Road from Mandalay:
         Towards a Geographical Philosophy," Transactions
         - Institute of British Geographers, Vol. 3, pp.
         381-394.

F-600.   Kirkpatrick, J. B.   1974.   "The Use of
         Differential Systematics in   Geographical
         Research," Area, Vol. 6, pp. 52-53.

F-601.   Kirwan, L. P.   1965.   "Geography as a Social
         Study: Review," Geographical Journal, Vol. 131,
         pp. 373-375.

F-602.   Kish, George.   1964.   "Mirror for the American
         Geographer," Professional Geographer, Vol. 16,
         pp. 1-4.

F-603.   Kitts, D. B.   1980.   "Analogies in G. K.
         Gilbert's Philosophy of Science," Geological
         Society of America, Special Paper, Vol. 183, pp.
         143-148.

F-604.   Klimm, L. 1947. "Comments on the Nature of
          Geography," Geographical Review, Vol. 37, pp.
          486-490.

F-605.   Knight, D. B. 1971. "Impress of Authority and
          Ideology on Landscape: A Review of Some
          Unanswered Questions," Tijdschrift voor
          Economische en Sociale Geografie, Vol. 62, pp.
          383-387.

F-606.   Knight, David B. 1982. "Identity and
          Territory: Geographical Perspec- tives on
          Nationalism and Regionalism," Annals of the
          Association of American Geographers, Vol. 72, pp.
          514-531.

F-607.   Knight, Peter. 1987. "Why Doesn't Geography Do
          Something?" Operational Geographer, No. 12, p.
          38.

F-608.   Knopp, Lawrence and Lauria, Mickey. 1987.
          "Gender Relations and Social Relations,"
          Antipode, Vol. 19, pp. 48-53.

F-609.   Koerner, Grace E. 1957. "The Vital Role and
          Scope of Geography," Journal of Geography, Vol.
          56, pp. 177-180.

F-610.   Kollmorgan, Walter M. 1945. "Crucial
          Deficiences of Regionalism," American Economic
          Review, Vol. 35, pp. 377-389.

F-611.   Kolosovskiy, N. N. 1962. "On the Concept of the
          Unity of Geography," Soviet Geography: Review
          and Translation, Vol. 3, No. 7, pp. 39-45.

F-612.   Konovalenko, V. G. 1962. "The Concept of the
          Unity of Geography in the Solution of Basic
          Problems in Geography," Soviet Geography: Review
          and Translation, Vol. 3, No. 7, pp. 45-49.

F-613.   Konstantinov, F. V. 1964. "Interaction Between
          Nature and Society and Modern Geography," Soviet
          Geography: Review and Translation, Vol. 5, pp.
          61-73.

F-614.   Konstantinov, O. A. 1961. "A Methodological
          Jumble in Theoretical Problems of Geography,"
          Soviet Geography: Review and Translation, Vol.
          2, No. 10, pp. 12-18.

F-615.   Kostbade, J. Trenton. 1965. "A Brief for
          Regional Geography," Journal of Geography, Vol.
          64, pp. 262-266.

F-616.   Kostbade, J. Trenton. 1968. "The Regional
          Concept and Geographic Education," Journal of
          Geography, Vol. 67, pp. 6-12.

F-617.   Krackowizer, A. M.   1929.   "Geography and Life,"
         Journal of Education,   Vol. 110, pp. 9-12.

F-618.   Krone, P.   1979.   "The Humanistic Perspective in
         Historical Geography: Willa Cather's Nebraska,
         1880-1920," Ohio Geographers, Vol. 7, pp. 41-46.

F-619.   Kropotkin, Prince.   1889.   "What Geography Ought
         to Be," Journal of the Manchester Geographical
         Society, Vol. 5, pp. 356-358.

F-620.   Kropotkin, Peter Alexcivich.   1885.   "What
         Geography Ought to Be," Nineteenth Century, Vol.
         18, No. 106, pp. 940-956.

F-621.   Kropotkin, Peter.   1979.   "What Geography Ought
         to Be," Antipode, Vol. 10, pp. 6-15.

F-622.   Kruczala, Jerry.   1963.   "The Attempt to
         Formulate the Theoretical Base of Regional
         Science," Papers of the Regional Science
         Association, Vol. 10, pp. 47-50.

F-623.   Küchler, A. W.   1940.   "The Chorologic Aspect,"
         Yearbook - Association of Pacific Coast
         Geographers, Vol. 6, pp. 32-36.

F-624.   Küchler, A. W.   1953.   "The Trinity of
         Geography," Professional Geographer, Vol. 5, No.
         1, pp. 3-4.

F-625.   Laborde, E. D.   1931.   "New Geography," New Era,
         Vol. 12, pp. 242-244.

F-626.   Lackey, E. E.   1924.   "The Classification and Use
         of Geographic Principles," Journal of Geography,
         Vol. 13, pp. 64-71.

F-627.   Ladylea, C. A. and Simpson-Housely, P.   1984.   "A
         Framework for Positivist and Phenomonological
         Methodologies," Cahiers de Geographie du Quebec,
         Vol. 28, pp. 479-483.

F-628.   Laity, Alan L.   1984.   "Perceiving Regions as
         Scattered Objects," Professional Geographer,
         Vol. 36, pp. 285-292.

F-629.   Langton, John.   1972.   "Potentialities and
         Problems of Adopting a Systems Approach to the
         Study of Change in Human Geography," Progress in
         Geography, Vol. 4, pp. 125-180.

F-630.   Lankiewicz, Donald.   1986.   "The First American
         Geography," Early American Life, Vol. 17, p. 67+.

F-631.   Lavrov, S. B. and Dmitrevskiy, Yu. D. 1978.
         "Problems in the History of Geographical Thought
         at the 23rd International Geographical Congress,"
         Soviet Geography: Review and Translation, Vol.
         19, pp. 54-59.

F-632.   Lavrov, S. B., Preobrazhenskiy, V. S. and
         Sdasyuk, G. V. 1980. "Radical Geography: Its
         Roots, History and Positions," Soviet Geography:
         Review and Translation, Vol. 21, pp. 308-321.

F-633.   Lawton, R. 1983. "Space, Place and Time,"
         Geography, Vol. 68, pp. pp. 193-207.

F-634.   Lawton, Richard. 1986. "Unity or Diversity,"
         Area, Vol. 18, p. 1.

F-635.   Leach, B. 1978. "Geography, Behavior and
         Marxist Philosophy," Antipode, Vol. 10, pp.
         33-37.

F-636.   Lee, David R. 1974. "Existentialism in
         Geographic Education," Journal of Geography, Vol.
         73, pp. 13-19.

F-637.   LeHeron, R. B. and Williams, D. B. 1981.
         "Geography is Not What Geographers Do, It's What
         they Learn," New Zealand Journal of Geography,
         Vol. 70, pp. 9-13.

F-638.   le Lannou, Maurice. 1951. "The Vocation of
         Human Geography," Landscape, Vol. 1, p. 41.

F-639.   Leighly, John. 1940. "Environmentalism in the
         History of Thought," Annals of the Association of
         American Geographers, Vol. 30, pp. 64-65.

F-640.   Lennon, Ian. 1969. "History, Geography, and
         Anarchy," in: Michael Horovitz, ed. Children of
         Albion, (London: Renquin), p. 93.

F-641.   Leszczycki, Stanislaw. 1960. "The Latest
         Approaches and Concepts in Geography," Soviet
         Geography: Review and Translation, Vol. 1, No.
         4, pp. 3-17.

F-642.   Lewis, Peter W. 1965. "Three Related Problems
         in the Formulation of Laws in Geography,"
         Professional Geographer, Vol. 17, No. 5, pp.
         24-27.

F-643.   Lewthwaite, Gordon R. 1966. "Environmentalism
         and Determinism: A Search for Clarification,"
         Annals of the Association of American
         Geographers, Vol. 56, pp. 1-23.

F-644.   Lewthwaite, Gordon. 1979. "Geography,"
         Encyclopedia Americana, Vol. 12, pp. 437-443.

F-645.   Ley, D.   1980.   "Geography Without Man: A
         Humanistic Critique," Oxford University, School
         of Geography, Research Paper No. 24.

F-646.   Ley, David.   1977.   "The Personality of a
         Geographical Fact," Professional Geographer, Vol.
         29, pp. 8-13.

F-647.   Ley, David.   1982.   "Rediscovering Man's Place,"
         Transactions - Institute of British Geographers,
         Vol. 7, pp. 248-253.

F-648.   Ley, David and Pratt, Geraldine.   1983.   "Is
         Philosophy Necessary?"   Geographical Analysis,
         Vol. 15, pp. 64-69.

F-649.   Ley, David.   1985.   "Cultural/Humanistic
         Geography," Progress in Human Geography, Vol. 9,
         pp. 415-423.

F-650.   Light, Richard U.   1949.   "Geography in This
         Crowded World,"   Geographical Review, Vol. 39,
         pp. 1-3.

F-651.   Limbird, A.   1986.   "On Being a Geographer,"
         Operational Geographer,   No. 11, p. 5.

F-652.   Lincoln, David.   1979.   "Ideology and South
         African Development Geography," South African
         Geographical Journal, Vol. 61, pp. 99-110.

F-653.   Lindsay, Sir Harry.   1949-50.   "The Scope and
         Pattern of Geography," Journal of the Manchester
         Geographical Society, Vol. 55, pp. 33-44.

F-654.   Lindsay, Sir Harry.   1951.   "The Presidential
         Address," [Geography: Theory and Practice]
         Geographical Journal, Vol. 117, pp. 257-262.

F-655.   Livingstone, D. N.   1984.   "Science and Society:
         Historical Reflections on the Geographical
         Experiment," Geoforum, Vol. 16, pp. 119-130.

F-656.   Livingstone, D. N. and Harrison, R. T.   1981.
         "Hunting the Snark: Perspectives on Geographical
         Investigation," Geografiska Annaler, Vol. 63B,
         pp. 69-72.

F-657.   Livingstone, David N.   1979.   "Some
         Methodological Problems in the History of
         Geographical Thought," Tijdschrift voor
         Economische en Sociale Geografie, Vol. 70, pp.
         226-231.

F-658.   Livingstone, David N. and Harrison, Richard T.
         1981.   "Meaning Through Metaphor: Analogy as
         Epistemology," Annals of the Association of
         American Geographers, Vol. 71, pp. 95-107.

F-659.   Lochhead, E. N. 1981. "Scotland as the Cradle
          of Modern Academic Geography in Britain,"
          Scottish Geographical Magazine, Vol. 97, pp.
          98-109.

F-660.   Lock, C. 1978. "The Role of Ecology Within
          Geographical Thought," Geoscope, Vol. 9, pp.
          51-56.

F-661.   Lowenthal, D. 1953. "George Perkins Marsh and
          the American Geographical Tradition,"
          Geographical Review, Vol. 43, pp. 207-213.

F-662.   Lowenthal, David. 1960. "In Defense of the Name
          Geography," Professional Geographer, Vol. 12, No.
          4, pp. 11-12.

F-663.   Lowenthal, David. 1961. "Geography, Experience,
          and Imagination: Towards a Geographical
          Epistemology," Annals of the Association of
          American Geographers, Vol. 51, pp. 241-260.

F-664.   Lowenthal, David. 1984. "Preserving the Old,
          Creating the New: Conflict or Synthesis,"
          Bloomsbury Geographer, Vol. 12, pp. 13-15.

F-665.   Lukerman, F. 1960. "On Explanation, Model, and
          Description," Professional Geographer, Vol. 12,
          No. 1, pp. 1-2.

F-666.   Lukerman, F. 1961. "The Concept of Location in
          Classical Geography," Annals of the Association
          of American Geographers, Vol. 51, pp. 194-210.

F-667.   Lukerman, F. 1961. "The Role of Theory in
          Geographical Inquiry," Professional Geographer,
          Vol. 13, No. 2, pp. 1-6.

F-668.   Lukerman, F. 1964. "Geography as a Formal
          Intellectual Discipline and the Way in Which it
          Contributes to Human Knowledge," Canadian
          Geographer, Vol. 8, pp. 167-172.

F-669.   Lyons, E. 1942. "New Geography," American
          Mercury, Vol. 54, April, pp. 461-462.

F-670.   MacDonald, James R. 1966. "The Region: Its
          Conception, Designs and Limitations," Annals of
          the Association of American Geographers, Vol. 56,
          pp. 516-528.

F-671.   Mackinder, H. 1887. "On the Scope and Methods
          of Geography," Proceedings - Royal Geographical
          Society, N.S. Vol. 9, pp. 140-160.

F-672.   Mackinder, H.   1930.   "The Content of
          Philosophical Geography,"   International
          Geographical Congress, Cambridge, 1928.   Report
          of the Proceedings.   Cambridge: Cambridge
          University Press, n.p.

F-673.   Mackinder, H. J.   1890.   "On the Necessity of
          Thorough Teaching in General Geography as a
          Preliminary to the Teaching of Commercial
          Geography," Journal of the Manchester
          Geographical Society, Vol. 6, pp. 1-6.

F-674.   Mackinder, H. J.   1895.   "Modern Geography,
          German and English," Geographical Journal, Vol.
          6, pp. 367-379.

F-675.   Mackinder, Halford.   1928.   "The Content of
          Philosophical Geography," Proceedings - Twelfth
          International Geographical Congress, pp. 305-311.

F-676.   Mackinder, Sir Halford.   1930.   "The Content of
          Philosophical Geography," International
          Geographical Congress, Cambridge, 1928.   Report
          of the Proceedings, pp. 305-311.

F-677.   Mackinder, Sir Halford.   1942.   "Geography, an
          Art and a Philosophy," Geography, Vol. 27, pp.
          122-130.

F-678.   Mair, Andrew.   1986.   "Thomas Kuhn and
          Understanding Geography," Progress in Human
          Geography, Vol. 10, pp. 345-370.

F-679.   Manion, T. and Whitelegg, J.   1979.   "Comment:
          Radical Geography and   Marxism," Area, Vol. 11,
          pp. 122-124.

F-680.   Manzie, A. A. and Sitwell, O. F. G.   1977.   "A
          Middle Way Between the Positivist and Humanist
          Approaches to Knowledge," Albertan Geographer,
          Vo. 13, pp. 57-68.

F-681.   Marantz, H. and Warren, A.   1976.   "Harvey on the
          Implications of Methodology," Area, Vol. 8, pp.
          175-178.

F-682.   Marchand, Bernard.   1978.   "A Dialectical
          Approach to Geography," Geographical Analysis,
          Vol. 10, pp. 105-119.

F-683.   Marcus, M. G.   1979.   "Coming Full Circle:
          Physical Geography in the Twentieth Century,"
          Annals of the Association of American
          Geographers, Vol. 69, pp. 521-532.

F-684.   Martin, A. F. 1951. "The Necessity for
          Determinism: A Metaphysical Problem Confronting
          Geographers," <u>Transactions and Papers, Institute
          of British Geographers</u>, No. 17, pp. 1-12.

F-685.   Martin, A. F. 1960. "Second Thoughts on the
          Nature of Geography," <u>Geographical Journal</u>, Vol.
          126, pp. 205-206.

F-686.   Martin, Geoffrey J. 1987. "The Ecologic
          Tradition in American Geography 1895-1925,"
          <u>Canadian Geographer</u>, Vol. 31, pp. 74-77.

F-687.   Martin, J. E. 1982. "Location Theory and
          Spatial Analysis," <u>Progress in Human Geography</u>,
          Vol. 6, pp. 260-264.

F-688.   Mason, Peter F. and Kuhn, Michael W. 1971.
          "Geography and Environmental Studies: The Fifth
          Tradition," <u>Journal of Geography</u>, Vol. 70, pp.
          91-94.

F-689.   Mather, D. B. 1965. "The New Age of Reason in
          Geography," <u>Australian Geographer</u>, Vol. 9, pp.
          259-268.

F-690.   Matley, Ian. 1966. "The Marxist Approach to the
          Geographical Environment," <u>Annals of the
          Association of American Geographers</u>, Vol. 56, pp.
          97-111.

F-691.   Matley, Ian M. 1987. "Literary Geography and
          the Writer's Country," <u>Scottish Geographical
          Magazine</u>, Vol. 103, pp. 122-131.

F-692.   Matore, Georges. 1966. "Existential Space,"
          <u>Landscape</u>, Vol. 15, pp. 5-6.

F-693.   Matsui, Taketoshi. 1952. "An Essay on the
          Nature of Geogarphy," [English Summary], <u>Human
          Geography/Jinbunchiri</u>, Vol. 4, pp. 279-280.
          [Article pp. 175-183].

F-694.   Mazur, E. 1983. "Space in Geography,"
          <u>GeoJournal</u>, Vol. 7, pp. 139-143.

F-695.   McAdie, Alexander. 1929. "The Third Estate of
          Geography," <u>Annals of the Association of
          American Geographers</u>, Vol. 19, pp. 38-39.

F-696.   McCarty, H. H. 1954. "An Approach to a Theory
          of Economic Geography," <u>Economic Geography</u>, Vol.
          30, pp. 99-101.

F-697.   McCarty, H. H. 1959. "Toward a More General
          Economic Geography," <u>Economic Geography</u>, Vol. 35,
          pp. 283-289.

F-698.   McCarty, H. H.   1963.   "The Geographer and His Intellectual Environment," New Zealand Journal of Geography, Vol. 19, pp. 1-6.

F-699.   McCourt, W. E.   1912.   "Philosophy of Geography," Popular Science, Vol. 80, pp. 587-596.

F-700.   McCune, Shannon.   1970.   "Geography: Where? Why? So What?"   Journal of Geography, Vol. 69, pp. 454-457.

F-701.   McLaughlin, Jim.   1986.   "State-centered Social Science and the Anarchist Critique," Antipode, Vol. 18, pp. 5-10.

F-702.   McNee, R. B.   1981.   "Perspective - Use It or Lose It," Professional Geographer, Vol. 33, pp. 12-15.

F-703.   McNee, Robert B.   1960.   "Toward a More Humanistic Economic Geography: The Geography of Enterprise," Tijdschrift voor Economische en Sociale Geografie, Vol. 51, pp. 201-206.

F-704.   McQueen, A. E.   1977.   "On Geography," New Zealand Geographer, Vol. 33, pp. 2-3.

F-705.   Medvedkov. Yu. V.   1965.   "Trends in Economic-Geographic Research on Regions of the Capitalist World," Soviet Geography: Review and Translation, Vol. 6, pp. 41-49.

F-706.   Meinig, D. W.   1983.   "Geography as an Art," Transactions, Institute of British Geographers, Vol. 8, pp. 314-328.

F-707.   Meir, A.   1979.   "The Nature and Mutual Complementarity of Humanism and Positivism in Geography," Geographical Research Forum, No. 1, pp. 21-36.

F-708.   Meir, A.   1982.   "The Urgency of Teaching History and Philosophy of Geography," Professional Geographer, Vol. 34, pp. 6-10.

F-709.   Meir, Avinoam.   1981.   "Humanistic Geography and Education for Human and Environmental Values," Geographical Research Forum, No. 4, pp. 55-60.

F-710.   Mercer, David.   1972.   "Behavioural Geography and the Sociology of Social Action," Area, Vol. 4, pp. 48-52.

F-711.   Mercer, David.   1985.   "On Marx, Moral, Method, and Meaning," [Review Article] Australian Geographical Studies, Vol. 23, pp. 139-157.

F-712.   Meston, Lord. 1933. "Geography as Mental
          Equipment," <u>Scottish Geographical Magazine</u>, Vol.
          49, pp. 253-273.

F-713.   Middleton, C. 1984. "The Concept of the 'Ivory
          Tower' and Its Relevance in Human Geography,"
          <u>Bloomsbury Geographer</u>, Vol. 12, pp. 6-8.

F-714.   Mihailescu, V. 1975. "Editorial: Some Remarks
          on Geographical Thought in Romania," <u>Geoforum</u>,
          Vol. 6, pp. 3-8.

F-715.   Mikhaylov, Yu. P. 1981. "On the Question of the
          Subject and the Object of Geography," <u>Soviet
          Geography</u>: <u>Review and Translation</u>, Vol. 22, pp.
          331-340.

F-716.   Mill, H. R. 1912. "Further Comment [on Colonel
          Close's Address on the Purpose and Position of
          Geography," <u>Bulletin of the American Geographical
          Society</u>, Vol. 44, pp. 38-39.

F-717.   Mill, Hugh Robert. 1892. "The Principles of
          Geography," <u>Scottish Geographical Magazine</u>, Vol.
          8, pp. 87-93.

F-718.   Mill, Hugh Robert. 1895. "The Geographical Work
          of the Future," <u>Scottish Geographical Journal</u>,
          Vol. 11, pp. 49-56.

F-719.   Mill, Hugh Robert. 1898. "The Classification of
          Geography," <u>Geographical Journal</u>, Vol. 11, pp.
          145-152.

F-720.   Mill, Hugh Robert. 1901. "On Research in
          Geographical Science," <u>Geographical Journal</u>,
          Vol. 18, pp. 407-424.

F-721.   Mill, Hugh Robert. 1904. "The Present Problems
          of Geography," <u>Bulletin of the American
          Geographical Society of New York</u>, Vol. 36, pp.
          657-675.

F-722.   Mill, Hugh Robert. 1905. "The Present Problems
          of Geography," <u>Geographical Journal</u>, Vol. 25,
          pp. 1-17.

F-723.   Miller, David H. 1965. "Geography, Physical and
          Unified," <u>Professional Geographer</u>, Vol. 17, No.
          2, pp. 1-4.

F-724.   Miller, E. Willard. 1950. "A Short History of
          the American Society for Professional
          Geographers," <u>Professional Geographer</u>, Vol. 2,
          pp. 29-40.

F-725.   Miller, E. Willard. 1952. "Geography--A Dynamic
          Earth Science," Mineral Industries, Vol. 22, pp.
          1-6.

F-726.   Miller, G. J. 1915. "Essentials of Modern
          Geography and Criteria for Their Determination,"
          Journal of Geography, Vol. 13, pp. 129-134.

F-727.   Miller, Geo. J. 1922. "The Past and Future,"
          Journal of Geography, Vol. 21, pp. 32-33.

F-728.   [Miller, George J.] 1925. "Geography's
          Distinctive Character," Journal of Geography,
          Vol. 24, pp. 121-122.

F-729.   Mills, W. J. 1982. "Metaphorical Vision:
          Changes in Western Attitudes to the Environment,"
          Annals of the Association of American
          Geographers, Vol. 72, pp. 237-253.

F-730.   Mills, W. J. 1982. "Positivism Reversed: The
          Relevance of Giambattista Vico," Transactions -
          Institute of British Geographers, Vol. 7, pp.
          1-14.

F-731.   Mills, William J. 1983. "Vico, Kunze, and the
          Theory of Metaphorical Vision," Annals of the
          Association of American Geographers, Vol. 73, pp.
          157-159.

F-732.   Mints, A. A. and Preobrazhenskiy, V. S. 1975.
          "Timely and Controversial Problems in the Systems
          Orientation of Geography," Soviet Geography:
          Review and Translation, Vol. 26, pp. 61-74.

F-733.   Mintz, A. A. 1974. "The History of Geographical
          Thought [A Survey of Soviet Literature,
          1961-1970]," Theoretical Problems in Physical and
          Economic Geography, Vol. 1, pp. 15-32.

F-734.   Misra, A. B. 1961. "The Scope and Nature of
          Geography," National Geographical Journal of
          India, Vol. 7, pp. 1-11.

F-735.   Mitchell, B. and Draper, D. 1973. "A
          Perspective on the Nature and Development of
          Behavioural Geography," Geographical Viewpoint,
          Vol. 2, pp. 353-374.

F-736.   Mitchell, J. B. and Davies, W. K. D. 1980.
          "Geography," The New Encyclopedia Britannica,
          15th ed., Vol. 7, pp. 1035-1053.

F-737.   Mitchell, James K. 1975. "Man-Environment
          Research Preferences Among Geographers," Journal
          of Geography, Vol. 234, pp. 525-530.

F-738.   Mitchell, L. S.   1931.   "Geographic Thinking,"
          New Era, Vol. 12, pp. 245-248.

F-739.   Mizvoka, Fujio.   1983.   "The Development of
          Marxian Economic Geography in Japan," Antipode,
          Vol. 15, pp. 27-36.

F-740.   Monk, J. and Hanson, S.   1982.   "On Not Excluding
          Half of the Human in Human Geography,"
          Professional Geographer, Vol. 34, pp. 11-23.

F-741.   Monkhouse, F. J.   1955.   "The Concept and Content
          of Modern Geography," an inaugural lecture
          delivered at the University of South Hampton, 24
          February 1955, 31 p.

F-742.   Montefiore, A. C. and Williams, W. M.   1955.
          "Determinism and Possibilism," Geographical
          Studies, Vol. 2, pp. 1-11.

F-743.   Mookarjee, Sitanshu.   1963.   "Whither
          Geography?" Deccan Geographer, Vol. 1, pp.
          181-184.

F-744.   Mookerjee, S.   1972.   "Renaming the Field,"
          Proceedings - Twenty- Second International
          Geographical Congress, pp. 915-917.

F-745.   Morrill, Richard L.   1975.   "The Future of
          Geography," Professional Geographer, Vol. 27, p.
          1.

F-746.   Morrill, Richard L.   1977.   "Geographic Scale and
          the Public Interest," Geographical Survey, Vol.
          6, pp. 3-10.

F-747.   Morrill, Richard L.   1978.   "Geography as Spatial
          Interaction," Department of Geography, University
          of North Carolina, Studies in Geography, Vol. 11,
          pp. 16-29.

F-748.   Morrill, Richard.   1979.   "On the Spatial
          Organization of the Landscape," Lund Studies in
          Geography, Series B, entire volume 46.

F-749.   Morrill, Richard.   1983.   "The Nature, Unity and
          Value of Geography," Professional Geographer,
          Vol. 35, pp. 1-9.

F-750.   Morris, J. W.   1981.   "An Age of Reality,"
          Journal of Geography, Vol. 80, pp. 4-6.

F-751.   Moss, R. P.   1978.   "Ideology and Science: Some
          Preliminary Reflections," Area, Vol. 10, pp.
          371-377.

F-752.   Moss, R. P.   1979.   "On Geography as a Science,"
          Geoforum, Vol. 10, pp. 223-234.

F-753.   Mugerauer, R.   1981.   "Concerning Regional
         Geography as a Hermenetical Discipline,
         Geographische Zeitschrift, Vol. 69, pp. 57-67.

F-754.   Murphy, Raymond E.   1979.   "Economic Geography
         and Clark University," Annals of the Association
         of American Geographers, Vol. 69, pp. 39-41.

F-755.   Murphy, Richard E.   1960.   "Geography: How
         Adequate is the Term?" Professional Geographer,
         Vol. 12, No. 4, pp. 8-10.

F-756.   Nakand, T.   1976.   "Natural Environment as
         Historic-Geographical System," Proceedings -
         Twenty-Third International Geographical Congress,
         pp. 18-21.

F-757.   Newbigin, Marion I.   1922.   "Human Geography:
         First Principles and Some Applications," Scottish
         Geographical Magazine, Vol. 38, pp. 209-221.

F-758.   Neyfakh, A. M.   1963.   "New Trends in Bourgeois
         Science on the Location of Production," Soviet
         Geography: Review and Translation, Vol. 4, No.
         3, pp. 12-21.

F-759.   Nickerson, M. G.   1978.   "The Humanistic
         Tradition in Geography," Ohio Geographers:
         Recent Research Themes, Vol. 6, pp. 65-76.

F-760.   Norton, W. and Pouliot, D. F.   1984.   "A Critical
         Appraisal of Contemporary Human Geography,"
         Geographical Perspectives, Vol. 54, pp. 62-66.

F-761.   Ogg, F. A.   1901.   "Geography from Homer to
         Columbus," Chatauquan, Vol. 32, pp. 473-478.

F-762.   Ogilvie, A. G.   1952.   "The Time-Element in
         Geography," Transactions and Papers - Institute
         of British Geographers, No. 18, pp. 1-16.

F-763.   O'Keefe, Phil.   1982.   "Revisionist Geography,"
         Antipode, Vol. 14, p. 49.

F-764.   Oldham, R. D.   1909.   "The New Geography,"
         Geographical Journal, Vol. 34, pp. 156-166.

F-765.   Olsson, Gunnar and Gale, Stephen.   1968.
         "Spatial Theory and Human Behavior," Papers of
         the Regional Science Association, Vol. 21, pp.
         229-241.

F-766.   Orata, P. T.   1927.   "The Humanizing of
         Geographical Knowledge," Journal of Geography,
         Vol. 26, pp. 281-284.

F-767.   Orme, Antony R.   1980.   "The Need for Physical
         Geography," Professional Geographer, Vol. 32, pp.
         141-148.

F-768.   Osterhart, Harry John.   1949.   "The Place of
         Geography," Journal of Geography, Vol. 48, pp.
         171-173.

F-769.   Overton, D. J. B.   1976.   "Towards a Discussion
         of the Nature of Radical Geography," Antipode,
         Vol. 8, pp. 86-87.

F-770.   Owen, E. E.   1965-66.   "The Structure of
         Geography," Albertan Geographer, No. 2, pp. 1-4.

F-771.   Paddock, Miner H.   1894.   "The New Geography,"
         Education, Vol. 14, pp. 482- 487.

F-772.   Papageorgiou, G. J.   1980.   "Social Values and
         Social Justice."   Economic Geography, Vol. 56,
         pp. 110-119.

F-773.   Page, Colonel Robert W., Jr.   1962.   "The
         Heavenly View: Geographic Thought at the Dawn of
         America's Air Age," Memorandum Folio of the
         Southeastern Association of American Geographers,
         Vol. 14, pp. 104-110.

F-774.   Palm, Risa.   1986.   "Coming Home," Annals of the
         Association of American Geographers, Vol. 76, pp.
         469-479.

F-775.   Parsons, James J.   1977.   "Geography as
         Exploration and Discovery," Annals of the
         Association of American Geographers, Vol. 67, pp.
         1-16.

F-776.   Paterson, John H.   1960.   "On the Nature of
         Geography: A Review," Scottish Geographical
         Magazine, Vol. 76, pp. 182-184.

F-777.   Patmore, J. Allan.   1980.   "Geography and
         Relevance," Geography, Vol. 65, pp. 265-283.

F-778.   Patten, J. H. C.   1970.   "The Past and Geography
         Reconsidered," Area, Vol. 2, pp. 37-39.

F-779.   Pattison, William D.   1964.   "The Four Traditions
         of Geography," Journal of Geography, Vol. 63, pp.
         211-216.

F-780.   Pattison, William D.   1978.   "Goode's Proposal of
         1902: An Interpretation," Professional
         Geographer, Vol. 30, pp. 3-8.

F-781.   Patton, Orin C.   1970.   "Cause and Effect In
          Geographic Analysis: Anachronism or Useful
          Concept," Southeastern Geographer, Vol. 10, pp.
          4-13.

F-782.   Peattie, Roderick.   1921.   "Introductory
          Geography for Colleges," Journal of Geography,
          Vol. 20, pp. 318-320.

F-783.   Peet, R.   1978.   "The Dialectics of Radical
          Geography: A Reply to Gordon Clark and Michael
          Dear," Professional Geographer, Vol. 30, pp.
          360-364.

F-784.   Peet, R.   1979.   "Societal Contradiction and
          Marxist Geography," Annals of the Association of
          American Geographers, Vol. 69, pp. 164-168.

F-785.   Peet, R.   1979.   "The Geography of Human
          Liberation," Antipode, Vol. 10 and Vol. 11, pp.
          119-134.

F-786.   Peet, R.   1981.   "Spatial Dialectics and Marxist
          Geography," Progress in Human Geography, Vol. 5,
          pp. 105-110.

F-787.   Peet, Richard and Slater, David.   1980.   "Reply
          to Soviet Review of Radical Geography," Soviet
          Geography: Review and Translation, Vol. 21, pp.
          541-544.

F-788.   Peet, Richard.   1985.   "An Introduction to
          Marxist Geography," Journal of Geography, Vol.
          84, pp. 5-10.

F-789.   Perkins, W. L.   1933.   "Frontiers of Science:
          Geography," Teachers College Journal, Vol. 4, pp.
          249-251.

F-790.   Perry, Allen.   1985.   "Hazardology - a Bridge
          Between Physical and Human Geography," Manchester
          Geographer, Vol. 6, pp. 58-62.

F-791.   Philips, Philip D.   1975.   "Radical Theory,
          Relevance, and the Geography of Crime,"
          Professional Geographer, Vol. 27, pp. 283-284.

F-792.   Pike, Richard J.   1974.   "Why Not an
          Extraterrestrial Geography?" Professional
          Geographer, Vol. 26, pp. 258-261.

F-793.   Pinchemel, Ph.   1974.   "Sur la situation actuelle
          de la Geographie," Tijdschrift voor Economische
          en Sociale Geografie, Vol. 65, pp. 97-101
          [English abstract, p. 71].

F-794.   Piveteau, J. L.   1975.   "The Problem of
         Regionalization Among Geographers: The Case of
         Switzerland," Geoforum, Vol. 6, pp. 105-112.

F-795.   Plakhotnik, A. F.   1974.   "The Subject and
         Structure of Geosystems Theory," Soviet
         Geography: Review and Translation, Vol. 15, pp.
         429-436.

F-796.   Pletnikov, Yu. K.   1969.   "The Subject of
         Geography and the Science of the Man-Nature
         Relationship," Soviet Geography: Review and
         Translation, Vol. 10, pp. 256-265.

F-797.   Platt, R. S.   1948.   "Environmentalism Versus
         Geography," American Journal of Sociology, Vol.
         53, pp. 351-358.

F-798.   Platt, Robert S.   1943.   "Regionalism in World
         Order," Annals of the Association of American
         Geographers, Vol. 33, pp. 230-231.

F-799.   Platt, Robert S.   1946.   "Problems of our Time,"
         Annals of the Association of American
         Geographers, Vol. 36, pp. 1-43.

F-800.   Platt, Robert S.   1948.   "Can We Avoid
         Determinism?" Annals of the Association of
         American Geographers, Vol. 38, pp. 76-77.

F-801.   Platt, Robert S.   1948.   "Determinism in
         Geography," Annals of the Association of American
         Geographers, Vol. 38, pp. 126-132.

F-802.   Pleat, H.   1929.   "What is Geography?"
         Pennsylvania School Journal, Vol. 78, p. 148.

F-803.   Pocock, D.   1983.   "Geographical Fieldwork: An
         Experiential Perspective," Geography, Vol. 60,
         pp. 319-325.

F-804.   Pocock, D. C. D.   1983.   "The Paradox of
         Humanistic Geography," Area, Vol. 15, pp.
         355-358.

F-805.   Pocock, Douglas.   1986.   "Literature and Humanist
         Geography," [comment] Area, Vol. 18, pp. 55-56.

F-806.   Pokshishevskiy, V. V.   1961.   "The Place of
         Regional Economic Geography in the System of
         Geographical Sciences," Soviet Geography: Review
         and Translation, Vol. 2, No. 5, pp. 13-23.

F-807.   Pokshishevskiy, V. V.   1963.   "On the Character
         of the Laws in Economic Geography," Soviet
         Geography: Review and Translation, Vol. 4, No.
         4, pp. 3-17.

F-808. Polyan, Pavel Markovich and Treyvish, A. I.
        1984. "Book Review - Theoretical Issues in
        Geography as Reflected in the Work of Estonian
        Geographers," Soviet Geography: Review and
        Translation, Vol. 25, pp. 122-131.

F-809. Porteous, J. Douglas. 1985.   "Literature and
        Humanist Geography," Area, Vol. 17, pp. 117-122.

F-810. Porter, Philip W. 1960. "Earnest and the
        Orephagrans - A Fable for The Instruction of
        Young Geographers," Annals of the Association of
        American Geographers, Vol. 50, pp. 297-299.

F-811. Porter, P. W. 1978. "Geography as Human
        Ecology: A Decade of Progress in a Quarter
        Century," American Behavioral Scientist, Vol. 22,
        pp. 15-39.

F-812. Portmann, Adolf. 1958. "Man and Nature,"
        Landscape, Vol. 8, pp. 1-4.

F-813. Powell, J. M. 1980. "The Haunting of Salomad's
        House: Geography and the Limits of Science,"
        Australian Geographer, Vol. 14, pp. 327-341.

F-814. Prasad, Har. 1984. "A Note on the Quest for
        Geographic Theory," National Journal of India,
        Vol. 30, pp. 231-235.

F-815. Pred, Allan. 1967. "Behavior and Location:
        Foundations for a Geographic and Dynamic Location
        Theory," Lund Studies in Geography, Series B, No.
        27, Introduction, pp. 5-20.

F-816. Pred, Allan. 1977. "The Choreography of
        Existence: Comments on Hägerstrand's
        Time-Geography and Its Usefulness," Economic
        Geographer, Vol. 53, pp. 207-221.

F-817. Pred, Allan. 1979. "The Academic Past Through A
        Time-Geographic Looking Glass," Annals of the
        Association of American Geographers, Vol. 69, pp.
        175-179.

F-818. Pred, Allan, 1984. "Place as Historically
        Contingent Process: Structuration and the
        Time-Geography of Becoming Places," Annals of the
        Association of American Geographers, Vol. 74, pp.
        279-297.

F-819. Preobrazhenskiy, V. S. 1983. "Geosystem as an
        Object of Landscape Study," GeoJournal, Vol. 7,
        pp. 131-134.

F-820. Preston, D. A. 1984. "The Rise and Fall of
        Regional Studies," University of Leeds, School
        of Geography, Working Paper, 12 p.

F-821.   Preston-Whyte, R. A.   1983.   "Environmentalism in
         Geography: The Missing Link," South African
         Geographical Society, Vol. 65, pp. 2-12.

F-822.   Price, Edward T.   1963.   "Aspects of Cause in
         Human Geography," Association of Pacific Coast
         Geographers Yearbook, Vol. 25, pp. 7-20.

F-823.   Prince, Hugh C.   1961.   "The Geographical
         Imagination," Landscape, Vol. 11, pp. 22-25.

F-824.   Prince, Hugh C.   1971.   "Real, Imagined and
         Abstract Worlds of the Past," Progress in
         Geography, Vol. 3, pp. 1-86.

F-825.   Pryde, Philip R.   1982.   "Welcome New
         Geographies," Professional Geographer, Vol. 34,
         pp. 440-442.

F-826.   Pulyarki, V. A.   1969.   "On the Content of the
         Concept 'Geographical Environment' and the
         Influence of the Environment on Society," Soviet
         Geography: Review and Translation, Vol. 10, pp.
         237-247.

F-827.   Pye, Norman.   1955.   "Object and Method in
         Geographical Studies," An Inaugural Lecture
         Delivered at University College, Leicester, 2
         June 1955.   19 p.

F-828.   Quirk, Barry.   1975.   "A Polemic or Perception
         and Experience in Geographic Research," South
         Hampshire Geographer, Vol. 7.

F-829.   Rafiullah, S. M.   1967.   "Regionalism in
         Geography," Geographer, Vol. 14, pp. 55-62.

F-830.   Raman, K.   1976.   "An Attempt to Interpret
         Geocomplex as a Spatial polystructural Unity,"
         Proceedings - Twenty Third International
         Geographical Congress, pp. 21-26.

F-831.   Rasmussen, K. and Reenberg, A.   1980.
         "Ecological Human Geography: Some Considerations
         of Concepts and Methods," Geografisk Tijdschrift,
         Vol. 80, pp. 81-88.

F-832.   Reclus, Elisée.   1898.   "A Great Globe,"
         Geographical Journal, Vol. 12, pp. 401-409.

F-833.   Redclift, Michael.   1987.   "The Production of
         Nature," Antipode, Vol. 19, pp. 222-230.

F-834.   Reed, Andrew.   1981.   "Innovation Evolution and
         Entropy," Geoscope, Vol. 12, pp. 1-6.

F-835.   Reed, Henry H., Jr.   1954-55.   "The Architecture
          of Humanism," Landscape, Vol. 4, pp. 16-20.

F-836.   Reitsma, H. A.   1982.   "Development Geography
          Dependency Relations and the Capitalist
          Scapegoat," Professional Geographer, Vol. 34, pp.
          125-130.

F-837.   Reitsma, H. A.   1982.   "Geography and
          Dependency: A Rejoinder," Professional
          Geographer, Vol. 34, pp. 337-341.

F-838.   Relph, E. C.   1976.   "The Phenomenological
          Foundations of Geography," Discussion Paper No.
          21, Toronto: University of Toronto; Department
          of Geography, December 1976.

F-839.   Relph, Edward.   1970.   "An Inquiry into the
          Relations Between Phenomenology and Geography,"
          Canadian Geographer, Vol. 14, pp. 193-201.

F-840.   Renfrew, Colin.   1981.   "Space, Time and Man,"
          Transactions - Institute of British Geographers,
          Vol. 6, pp. 257-278.

F-841.   Renner, G. T.   1927.   "Contribution of Geography
          to Vocabulary," Journal of Geography, Vol. 26,
          pp. 263-270.

F-842.   Renner, George T.   1947.   "Geography of
          Industrial Localization," Economic Geography,
          Vol. 23, pp. 167-190.

F-843.   Rich, J. L.   1948.   "Goals and Trends of Research
          in GeoCogyard Geography," Science, Vol. 107, pp.
          581-584.

F-844.   Ridgley, Douglas C.   1914.   "The Problem of Place
          Geography," Journal of Geography, Vol. 12, pp.
          333-340.

F-845.   Robertson, S.   1901.   "Science of Distances,"
          Popular Science, Vol. 58, pp. 526-539.

F-846.   Robinson, Arthur H.   1961.   "On Perks and Pokes,"
          Economic Geography, Vol. 37, pp. 181-183.

F-847.   Robinson, G. W. S.   1953.   "The Geographical
          Region: Form and Function," Scottish
          Geographical Magazine, Vol. 69, pp. 49-58.

F-848.   Robinson, J. Lewis.   1976.   "A New Look at the
          Four Traditions of Geography," Journal of
          Geography, Vol. 75, pp. 520-530.

F-849.   Robinson, M. E.   1983.   "Explanation and Human
          Geography," Transactions, Institute of British
          Geographers, Vol. 8, pp. 231-234.

F-850.   Roglic, J.   1972.   "The Spatial Viewpoint is the
          Essence and Prospect of Geography," Proceedings -
          Twenty-Second International Geographical
          Congress, pp. 926-928.

F-851.   Romanowski, J.   1965-66.   "Some Unfulfilled
          Promises of a More Economic Geography," Albertan
          Geographer, No. 2, pp. 50-55.

F-852.   Roorbach, G. B.   1914.   "The Trend of Modern
          Geography: A Symposium," Bulletin of the
          American Geographical Society, Vol. 46, pp.
          801-816.

F-853.   Rorabacher, J. Albert.   1973.   "Geo-historical
          Approaches to Environment: The Evolution of
          Environmental Thought in Western Civilization,"
          Journal of Geography, Vol. 72, pp. 31-41.

F-854.   Rountree, Lester.   1987.   "Cultural/Humanistic
          Geography," Progress in Human Geography, Vol. 11,
          pp. 558-564.

F-855.   Roxby, P. M.   1930.   "The Scope and Aims of Human
          Geography," Scottish Geographical Magazine, Vol.
          47, pp. 276-290; Nature, Vol. 126, pp. 650-654.

F-856.   Roxby, Percy M.   1907.   "What is a Natural
          Region?" Geographical Teacher, Vol. 4, pp.
          123-129.

F-857.   Roxby, Percy M.   1910.   "The Theory of Natural
          Regions," Geographical Teacher, Vol. 13, pp.
          376-382.

F-858.   Rushton, Gerard.   1984.   "Schaefer and the
          Influence of Spatial Arrangements on Social and
          Economic Behavior Patterns," Geographical
          Perspectives, No. 54, pp. 1-6.

F-859.   Ryan, Bruce.   1971.   "Geography and Futurology,"
          Australian Geographer, Vol. 11, pp. 510-521.

F-860.   Sack, Robert.   1985.   "Spatial Analysis Since
          Schaefer," Geographical Perspectives, No. 55, pp.
          1-5.

F-861.   Sack, Robert D.   1974.   "The Spatial Separatist
          Theme in Geography," Economic Geography, Vol. 50,
          pp. 1-19.

F-862.   Sack, Robert D.   1983.   "Human Territoriality: A
          Theory," Annals of the Association of American
          Geographers, Vol. 73, pp. 55-74.

F-863.   Sack, Robert David.   1972.   "Geography, Geometry,
          and Explanation," Annals of the Association of
          American Geographers, Vol. 62, pp. 61-78.

F-864.   Sack, Robert David. 1973. "A Concept of
          Physical Space in Geography," Geographical
          Analysis, Vol. 5, pp. 16-31.

F-865.   Sack, Robert David. 1976. "Magic and Space,"
          Annals of the Association of American
          Geographers, Vol. 66, pp. 309-322.

F-866.   Sack, Robert David. 1980. "Conceptions of
          Geographic Space," Progress in Human Geography,
          Vol. 4, pp. 313-345.

F-867.   Sack, Robert David. 1980. "Teaching the
          Philosophy of Geography," Journal of Geography in
          Higher Education, Vol. 4, pp. 3-9.

F-868.   Sack, Robert David. 1982. "Realism and
          Realistic Geography," Transactions - Institute
          of British Geographers, Vol. 7, pp. 504-509.

F-869.   Salter, Christopher L. 1969. "The Five
          Co-Traditions of Geography," California
          Geographer, Vol. 10, pp. 1-6.

F-870.   Sauer, Carl O. 1921. "Geography as Regional
          Economics," Annals of the Association of American
          Geographers, Vol. 11, pp. 130-131.

F-871.   Sauer, Carl O. 1924. "The Survey Method in
          Geography and Its Objectives," Annals of the
          Association of American Geographers, Vol. 14, pp.
          17-34.

F-872.   Sauer, Carl O. 1940. "Foreword to Historical
          Geography," Annals of the Association of American
          Geographers, Vol. 31, pp. 1-24.

F-873.   Sauer, Carl O. 1970. "The Duality of
          Geography," California Geographer, Vol. 11, pp.
          5-10.

F-874.   Sauer, Carl O. 1974. "Regional Reality in
          Economy," Yearbook of the Association of Pacific
          Coast Geographers, Vol. 64, pp. 35-50.

F-875.   Sauer, Carl O. 1974. "The Fourth Dimension of
          Geography," Annals of the Association of American
          Geographers, Vol. 64, pp. 189-192.

F-876.   Saushkin, Yu. G. 1964. "Methodological Problems
          of Soviet Geography as Interpreted by Some
          Foreign Geographers," Soviet Geography: Review
          and Translation, Vol. 5, pp. 50-66.

F-877.   Saushkin, Yu. G. 1965. "The Today and Tomorrow
          of Geography," Soviet Geography: Review and
          Translation, Vol. 6, pp. 50-56.

F-878.   Saushkin, Yu. G. 1966. "A History of Soviet
          Economic Geography," Soviet Geography: Review
          and Translation, Vol. 7, pp. 3-104.

F-879.   Saushkin, Yu. G. 1974. "Study of the History of
          Geographical Ideas," Soviet Geography: Review
          and Translation, Vol. 15, pp. 42-50.

F-880.   Saushkin, Yu. G. and Smirnov, A. M. 1971. "The
          Role of Lenin's Ideas in the Development of
          Theoretical Geography," Soviet Geography: Review
          and Translation, Vol. 12, pp. 559-569.

F-881.   Sautler, G. 1985. "La Geographie Comme
          Ideology?" (Geography as idealogy?), Cahiers de
          Geographie de Quebec, Vol. 29, pp. 193-203
          [English summary].

F-882.   Sayer, A. 1979. "Epistemology and Conceptions
          of People and Nature in Geography," Geoforum,
          Vol. 10, pp. 19-44.

F-883.   Sayer, Andrew. 1982. "Explanation in Economic
          Geography: Abstraction Versus Generalization,"
          Progress in Human Geography, Vol. 6, pp. 68-88.

F-884.   Sayer, R. A. 1982. "Misconceptions of Space in
          Social Thought," Transactions - Institute of
          British Geographers, Vol. 7, pp. 494-503.

F-885.   Scarfe, Neville V. 1962. "What Is Geography?"
          Journal of Geography, Vol. 61, pp. 84-85.

F-886.   Scargill, D. I. 1985. "Space, Place and
          Region: Towards a Transformed Regional
          Geography," Geography, Vol. 70, pp. 138-141.

F-887.   Schaefer, Fred K. 1953. "Exceptionalism in
          Geography: A Methodological Examination," Annals
          of the Association of American Geographers, Vol.
          43, pp. 226-249.

F-888.   Schick, Manfred. 1982. "O. Schluter,
          1872-1959," Geographers: Biobibliographical
          Studies, Vol. 6, pp. 115-122.

F-889.   Schultz, Ronald R. 1985. "The Meaning and
          Importance of Geographic Knowledge." Florida
          Geographer, pp. 1-3.

F-890.   Scott, D. 1986. "Time, Structuration and the
          Potential for South African Historical
          Geography," South African Geographical Journal,
          Vol. 68, pp. 45-66.

F-891.   Seamon, D. 1984. "Philosophical Directions in
          Behavioral Geography with an Emphasis on the
          Phenomenological Contribution," Research Paper -
          University of Chicago, Department of Geography,
          No. 209, pp. 167-178.

F-892.   Seamon, David. 1979. "Phenomenology, Geography
          and Geographic Education," Journal of Geography
          in Higher Education, Vol. 3, pp. 40-50.

F-893.   Seamon, David. 1984. "The Question of Reliable
          Knowledge: The Irony and Tragedy of Positivist
          Research," Professional Geographer, Vol. 36, pp.
          216-218.

F-894.   Seleg, John E. and Wolport, Julian. 1985. "The
          Savings Harm Tableau for Social Impact Assessment
          of Retrenchment Policies," Economic Geography,
          Vol. 61, pp. 158-171.

F-895.   Semple, Ellen Churchill. 1904. "Emphasis Upon
          Anthropogeography in School," Proceedings -
          Eighth International Geographical Congress, pp.
          657-663.

F-896.   Senger, Leslie W. and Chang, Stephen. 1975. "A
          Matter of Terminology--The Ecological Approach in
          Geography: A Re-Examination of Basic Concepts,"
          Geoforum, Vol. 6, pp. 164-167.

F-897.   Sheppard, E. 1980. "The Ideology of Spatial
          Choice," Papers of the Regional Science
          Association, Vol. 45, pp. 197-213.

F-898.   Siddall, William R. 1961. "Two Kinds of
          Geography," Economic Geography, Vol. 37, pp. 189.

F-899.   Silk, John. 1982. "Comment on 'On the Nature of
          Explanation in Human Geography,'" Transactions -
          Institute of British Geographers, Vol. 7, pp.
          380-384.

F-900.   Simmons, Ian, Smith, David M., Colenutt, Bob, and
          Mead, W. R. 1976. "To What Extent is the
          Geographer's World the 'Real' World?" Area, Vol.
          8, pp. 82-87.

F-901.   Singh, R. L. 1960. "Geographical Concepts and
          Methods of Research Work," National Geographical
          Journal of India, Vol. 6, pp. 127-136.

F-902.   Singh, R. L. 1961. "Meaning Objectives and
          Scope of Settlement Geography," National
          Geographical Journal of India, Vol. 7, pp. 12-20.

F-903.   Singh, R. L. and Singh, Rana P. B.   1978.
          "Concept of Morphological Analysis: Some
          Theoretical Postulations," National Geographical
          Journal of India, Vol. 24, pp. 1-16.

F-904.   Singh, R. P. B. 1978. "Emerging Frontiers in
          Geography: A Review. New Trends in Geographic
          Thought and Methodology," National Geographical
          Journal of India, Special Issue, Vol. 24, pp.
          186-202.

F-905.   Sitwell, O. F. G. 1980. "Where to Begin? A
          Methodological Problem for the Writers of
          'Special' Geography in the Seventeenth and
          Eighteenth Centuries," Canadian Geographer, Vol.
          24, pp. 294-299.

F-906.   Skinner, A. W. 1905. "Geography, Relations to
          History," Education, Vol. 25, pp. 597-601.

F-907.   Slater, David. 1975. "The Poverty of Modern
          Geographical Enquiry," Pacific Viewpoint, Vol.
          16, pp. 159-176.

F-908.   Slater, F. 1981. "What Is Your View of People?
          Some Comments on Recently Changing Viewpoints in
          Geographical Research," New Zealand Journal of
          Geography, Vol. 71, pp. 6-9.

F-909.   Slaymaker, Olav. 1934. "The New Geography:
          Review," Geographical Journal, Vol. 134, pp.
          405-407.

F-910.   Smirnov, A. M. 1972. "General Geographic
          Concepts," Soviet Geography: Review and
          Translation, Vol. 13, pp. 517-543.

F-911.   Smirnov, L. Ye. 1968. "The Role and
          Significance of Objective [Mathematical] Methods
          in Geographic Research," Soviet Geography:
          Review and Translation, Vol. 9, pp. 55-68.

F-912.   Smith, Christopher J. 1976. "Geography and
          Public Consciousness Raising," Geographical
          Survey, Vol. 5, pp. 27-31.

F-913.   Smith, David M. 1976. "Welfare as a Quality of
          Life Concept," Geographical Survey, Vol. 5, pp.
          19-26.

F-914.   Smith, J. Russell. 1907. "Geography with a
          Purpose," Bulletin of the Geographical Society of
          Philadelphia, Vol. 5, No. 4, pp. 61-66.

F-915.   Smith, J. Russell. 1935. "Are We Free to Coin
          New Terms?" Annals of the Association of American
          Geographers, Vol. 25, pp. 17-22.

F-916.   Smith, J. Russell. 1952. "American Geography, 1900-1904," <u>Professional Geographer</u>, Vol. 4, No. 4, pp. 4-7.

F-917.   Smith, N. 1979. "Geography, Science and Post Positivist Modes of Explanation," <u>Progress in Human Geography</u>, Vol. 3, pp. 356-385.

F-918.   Smith, N. 1982. "Theories of Underdevelopment: A Response to Reitsma," <u>Professional Geographer</u>, Vol. 34, pp. 332-336.

F-919.   Smith, Neil and O'Keefe, Phil. 1980. "Geography, Marx and the Concept of Nature," <u>Antipode</u>, Vol. 12, pp. 30-39.

F-920.   Smith, S. J. 1981. "Humanistic Method in Contemporary Social Geography," <u>Area</u>, Vol. 13, pp. 293-298.

F-921.   Smith, Susan J. 1984. "Practicing Humanistic Geography," <u>Annals of the Association of American Geographers</u>, Vol. 74, pp. 353-374.

F-922.   Smith, Terence R. 1983. "More Thoughts on Theory in the Social Sciences," <u>Geographical Analysis</u>, Vol. 15, pp. 40-42.

F-923.   Sochava, V. B. 1971. "Geography and Ecology," <u>Soviet Geography: Review and Translation</u>, Vol. 12, pp. 277-293.

F-924.   Sochava, V. B. 1974. "A New Work on Theoretical Geography (review of David Harvey's <u>Explanation in Geography</u>)," <u>Soviet Geography: Review and Translation</u>, Vol. 15, pp. 311-320.

F-925.   Soja, Edward W. 1980. "The Socio-Spatial Dialectic," <u>Annals of the Association of American Geographers</u>, Vol. 70, pp. 207-225.

F-926.   Soja, Edward and Hadjimichalis, C. 1979. "Between Geographicl Materialism and Spatial Fetishism: Some Observations on the Development of Marxist Spatial Analysis," <u>Antipode</u>, Vol. 11, pp. 3-11.

F-927.   Solntsev, V. A. 1962. "Basic Problems in Soviet Landscape Science," <u>Soviet Geography: Review and Translation</u>, Vol. 5, No. 6, pp. 3-15.

F-928.   Solntsev, V. N. 1976. "Spatial and Temporal Structure of the Geosystem," <u>Proceedings - Twenty Third International Geographical Congress</u>, pp. 30-34.

F-929.   Sommers, Lawrence M. and Vinge, Clarence L.
         1957. "The Geographer's Quest," _Centennial
         Review_, Vol. 1, pp. 386-403.

F-930.   Sonnenfeld, J. 1982. "Egocentric Perspectives
         on Geographic Orientation," _Annals of the
         Association of American Geographers_, Vol. 72, pp.
         68-76.

F-931.   Sopher, David E. and Duncan, James S. 1975.
         "Brahman and Untouchables: The Transactional
         Ranking of American Geography Departments,"
         Syracuse University, Department of Geography,
         Discussion Paper Series, No. 10.

F-932.   Spate, O. H. K. 1957. "How Determined is
         Possibilism?" _Geographical Studies_, Vol. 3, pp.
         3-12.

F-933.   Spate, O. H. K. 1960. "Lord Kelvin Rides
         Again," _Economic Geography_, Vol. 36, (facing) p.
         95.

F-934.   Spate, O. H. K. 1960. "Quantity and Quality of
         Geography," _Annals of the Association of American
         Geographers_, Vol. 50, pp. 377-394.

F-935.   Spate, O. H. K. 1960. "New Perspectives in
         Geography," _Australian Journal of Science_, Vol.
         22, pp. 436-439.

F-936.   Spate, O. H. K. 1980. "Palaeoclimates of
         Geographical Thought," _Australian Geographer_,
         Vol. 14, pp. 1-7.

F-937.   Spencer, J. E. 1974. "The Evolution of the
         Discipline of Geography in the Twentieth
         Century," _Geographical Perspectives_, No. 33, pp.
         20-36.

F-938.   Speth, William W. 1987. "On the Discrimination
         of Anthropo Geographies," _Canadian Geographer_,
         Vol. 31, pp. 72-74.

F-939.   Spilhaus, M. W. 1931. "Significance of
         Geography," _New Era_, Vol. 12, pp. 249-250.

F-940.   Spoehr, Alexander. 1966. "Part and the Whole:
         Reflections on the Study of a Region," _American
         Anthropologist_, Vol. 68, pp. 629-640.

F-941.   Stamp, Sir Josiah. 1937. "Geography and
         Economic Theory," _Nature_, Vol. 139, No. 3512, pp.
         311-314; _Geography_, Vol. 22, pp. 1-14.

F-942.   Stamp, L. Dudley. 1966. "Ten Years On,"
         Transactions - Institute of British Geographers,
         No. 40, pp. 11-20.

F-943.   Stamp, R. M.   1983.   "Where Does Geography End
          and Literature Begin?" _Operational Geographer_,
          Vol. 1, pp. 33-35.

F-944.   Stanley, Carleton.   1953.   "Some Threads in the
          Web of Geography,"   _Transactions of the Royal
          Society of Canada_, Vol. 47, 3rd sec., pp. 49-60.

F-945.   Steed, Guy P. F.   1988.   "Geography, Social
          Science, and Public Policy: Regeneration Through
          Interpretation," _Canadian Geographer_, Vol. 32,
          pp. 2-14.

F-946.   Steel, R. W.   1982.   "Regional Geography in
          Practice," _Geography_, Vol. 67, pp. 2-8.

F-947.   Steinhauser, Frederic R.   1967.   "The Study of
          Geography," _Journal of Geography_, Vol. 66, pp.
          350-359.

F-948.   Stephenson, Daphne P.   1948, 1949.
          "Regionalism," _Journal of King's College
          Geographical Society_, No. 1, pp. 4-7; No. 2, pp.
          7-12.

F-949.   Stevens, A.   1939.   "The Natural Geographical
          Region," _Scottish Geographical Magazine_, Vol. 55,
          pp. 305-317.

F-950.   Stewart, John Q. and Wartnz, William.   1958.
          "Macrogeography and Social Science," _Geographical
          Review_, Vol. 48, pp. 167-184.

F-951.   Stoddart, D. R.   1967.   "Growth and Structure of
          Geography," _Transactions - Institute of British
          Geographers_, Vol. 41, pp. 1-19.

F-952.   Stoddart, D. R.   1975.   "Kropotkin, Reclus, and
          'Relevant' Geography," _Area_, Vol. 7, pp. 188-190.

F-953.   Stoddart, D. R.   1975.   "'That Victorian
          Science': Huxley's _Physiography_ and Its Impact
          on Geography," _Transactions - Institute of
          British Geographers_, No. 66, pp. 17-40.

F-954.   Stoddart, D. R.   1975.   "The RGS and the
          Foundations of Geography at Cambridge,"
          Geographical Journal, Vol. 141, pp. 216-239.

F-955.   Stoddart, D. R.   1978.   "Biogeography," _Progress
          in Physical Geography_, Vol. 2, pp. 514-551.

F-956.   Stoddart, D. R.   1978.   "Geomorphology in China,"
          Progress in Physical Geography, Vol. 2, pp.
          514-551.

F-957.   Stoddart, D. R.   1987.   "To Claim the High
          Ground: Geography for the End of the Century,"
          Transactions - Institute of British Geographers,
          Vol. 12, pp. 327-336.

F-958.   Stone, Kirk H.   1970.   "Has the GEO Gone Out of
          Geography," Professional Geographer, Vol. 22, pp.
          5-7.

F-959.   Storper, Michael.   1985.   "Oligopoly and the
          Product Cycle: Essentialism in Economic
          Geography," Economic Geography, Vol. 61, pp.
          260-282.

F-960.   Strong, Helen M.   1931.   "How Business is Using
          and Might Use the Science of Geography," Annals
          of the Association of American Geographers, Vol.
          21, pp. 138-139.

F-961.   Strong, Helen M.   1936.   "Regionalism: Its
          Cultural Significance," Economic Geography, Vol.
          12, pp. 392-410.

F-962.   Sugden, J. F. and Gibbons, A. F.   1960.   "On
          Geography," Journal of King's College
          Geographical Society, Vol. 12, pp. 1-7.

F-963.   Suizu, Ichiro.   1958.   "Functionalism in a
          Regional Concept," [English Summary] Geographical
          Review of Japan/Chirigaku-Hyoron, Vol. 31, pp.
          589-590 [article, pp. 577-590].

F-964.   Sullivan, Michael E.   1976.   "On the Need for an
          International Focus in American Geography,"
          Geographical Survey, Vol. 5, No. 1, pp. 4-5.

F-965.   Sutherland, W. J.   1905.   "The Rational Element
          as an Organizing Principle in Geography," Journal
          of Geography, Vol. 4, pp. 97-105.

F-966.   Sutherland, W. J.   1906.   "Geography and Life,"
          Journal of Geography, Vol. 5, pp. 121-126.

F-967.   Szava-Kovats, E.   1966.   "The Present State of
          Landscape Theory and Its Main Philosophical
          Problems," Soviet Geography: Review and
          Translation, Vol. 7, pp. 28-40.

F-968.   Taaffe, Edward J.   1974.   "The Spatial View in
          Context," Annals of the Association of American
          Geographers, Vol. 64, pp. 1-16.

F-969.   Taaffe, Edward J.   1985.   "Comments on Regional
          Geography," Journal of Geography, Vol. 84, pp.
          96-97.

F-970.   Takevchi, K. and Nozawa, H., eds. 1985.
         "Diffusion, Succession and Innovation in the
         History of Geographical Thought in Japan,"
         Geographical Review of Japan, Series A, Vol. 58,
         pp. 103-112 [English Summary].

F-971.   Talarchek, G. M. 1977. "Phenomenology as a New
         Paradigm in Human Geography," Department of
         Geography, Syracuse University, Discussion Paper
         Series, No. 39, pp. 1-39.

F-972.   Tata, Robert J. 1970. "Geographic Thought:
         Progress Through Evolution, Not Reaction,"
         Southeastern Geographer, Vol. 10, pp. 14-20.

F-973.   Taylor, E. G. R. 1931. "Imago Mundi," Scottish
         Geographical Magazine, Vol. 47, pp. 78-80.

F-974.   Taylor, E. G. R. 1937. "The Geographical Ideas
         of Robert Hooke," Geographical Journal, Vol. 89,
         pp. 525-539.

F-975.   Taylor, E. G. R. 1937. "Whither Geography? A
         Review of Some Recent Geographical Texts,"
         Geographical Review, Vol. 27, pp. 129-135.

F-976.   Taylor, E. G. R. 1948. "The English Worldmakers
         of the Seventeenth Century and Their Influence on
         the Earth Sciences," Geographical Review, Vol.
         38, pp. 104-112.

F-977.   Taylor, Griffith. 1935. "Geography, the
         Correlative Science," Canadian Journal of
         Economics and Political Science, Vol. 1, pp.
         535-550.

F-978.   Taylor, Griffith. 1938. "Correlations and
         Culture: A Study in Technique," Scottish
         Geographical Magazine, Vol. 54, pp. 321-344.

F-979.   Taylor, Griffith. 1942. "The Role of Geography
         II," in Education for Citizen Responsibilities,
         F. L. Burderte, ed., pp. 44-61.

F-980.   Taylor, Griffith. 1963. "Geography and World
         Peace," Australian Geographical Studies, Vol. 1,
         pp. 1-17.

F-981.   Taylor, Peter J. 1969. "The Location Variable
         in Taxonomy," Geographical Analysis, Vol. 1, pp.
         181-195.

F-982.   Taylor, Peter J. 1986. "Locating the Question
         of Unity," Transactions - Institute of British
         Geographers, Vol. 11, pp. 443-448.

F-983.   Thom, B. G.   1987.   "The Man/Land Theme in
          Geography: A Sidney University Perspective,"
          Australian Geographer, Vol. 18, pp. 8-18.

F-984.   Thoman, Richard S.   1965.   "Some Comments on The
          Science of Geography," Professional Geographer,
          Vol. 17, No. 6, pp. 8-11.

F-985.   Thomas, Benjamin E.   1962.   "Exclusionism in
          American Geography," Yearbook of the Association
          of Pacific Coast Geographers, Vol. 24, pp. 7-14.

F-986.   Thompson, Kenneth.   1960.   "Geography - A
          Problem in Nomenclature," Professional
          Geographer, Vol. 12, No. 2, pp. 4-7.

F-987.   Thornthwaite, C. W.   1961.   "The Task Ahead,"
          Annals of the Association of American
          Geographers, Vol. 51, pp. 345-356.

F-988.   Thrall, Grant Ian.   1986.   "Reply to Felix
          Driver and Christopher Philo," [re: Scientific
          Geography] Area, Vol. 18, pp. 162-163.

F-989.   Thrift, N. and Pred, A.   1981.   "Time
          Geography: A New Beginning," Progress in Human
          Geography, Vol. 5, pp. 277-286.

F-990.   Thrift, N. J.   1982.   "Editorial: Towards a
          Human Geography," Environment and Planning A,
          Vol. 14, pp. 1280-1282.

F-991.   Thrift, Nigel.   1981.   "Owner's Time and Own
          Time: The Making of a Capitalist Time
          Consciousness, 1300-1880," Lund Studies in
          Geography, Series B, Vol. 48, pp. 56-84.

F-992.   Thrift, Nigel.   1983.   "Literature, the
          Production of Culture and the Politics of
          Place," Antipode, Vol. 15, pp. 12-23.

F-993.   Tietz, Wolf.   1972.   "Geographer's Role In
          Clarifying Environmental Problems," Proceedings
          - Twenty-Second International Geographical
          Congress, pp. 1175-1177.

F-994.   Tinkler, K. J.   1969.   "Uniqueness in
          Geographical Interactions," Area, Vol. 3, pp.
          27-30.

F-995.   Tobin, Graham A.   1985.   "Environmental Ethics
          and Geography: Some Thoughts," Geographical
          Perspectives, No. 55, pp. 6-14.

F-996.   Tomkins, George S.   1966.   "Towards a Continuing
          Geographic Dialogue," B. C. Geographical Series,
          No. 3, pp. 7-10.

F-997.   Tornquist, Gunnar. 1979. "On Fragmentation and
          Coherence in Regional Research," Lund Studies
          in Geography, Series B, Entire Volume 45.

F-998.   Tornquist, Gunnar. 1981. "On Arenas and
          Systems," Lund Studies in Geography, Series B,
          Vol. 48, pp. 109-120.

F-999.   Tower, Walter S. 1906. "A Field for Studies in
          Regional Geography," Bulletin of the American
          Geographical Society of New York, Vol. 38, pp.
          481-489.

F-1000.   Tower, Walter S. 1914. "The Question of Field
          Work in Geography," Journal of Geography, Vol.
          12, pp. 345-349.

F-1001.   Tower, Walter Sheldon. 1908. "The Human Side
          of Systematic Geography," Bulletin of the
          American Geographical Society, Vol. 40, pp.
          522-530.

F-1002.   Tower, Walter Sheldon. 1910. "Scientific
          Geography: The Relation of its Content to its
          Subdivisions," Bulletin of the American
          Geographical Society, Vol. 42, pp. 801-825.

F-1003.   Tuan, Yi-Fu. 1957. "Use of Simile and Metaphor
          in Geographical Descriptions," Professional
          Geographer, Vol. 9, No. 5, pp. 8-11.

F-1004.   Tuan, Yi-Fu. 1963. "Architecture and Human
          Nature," Landscape, Vol. 13, pp. 16-19.

F-1005.   Tuan, Yi-Fu. 1971. "Geography, Phenomenology,
          and the Study of Human Nature," Canadian
          Geographer, Vol. 15, pp. 181-192.

F-1006.   Tuan, Yi-Fu. 1973. "Ambiguity in Attitudes
          Toward Environment," Annals of the Association
          of American Geographers, Vol. 63, pp. 411-423.

F-1007.   Tuan, Yi-Fu. 1974. "Space and Place:
          Humanistic Perspective," Progress in Geography,
          Vol. 6, pp. 211-252.

F-1008.   Tuan, Yi-Fu. 1975. "Images and Mental Maps,"
          Annals of the Association of American
          Geographers, Vol. 65, pp. 205-213.

F-1009.   Tuan, Yi-Fu. 1975. "Place: An Experiential
          Perspective," Geographical Review, Vol. 65, pp.
          151-165.

F-1010.   Tuan, Yi-Fu. 1976. "Humanistic Geography,"
          Annals of the Association of Geographers, Vol.
          66, pp. 266-276.

F-1011.   Tuan, Yi-Fu. 1978. "Sign and Metaphor," Annals
           of the Association of American Geographers, Vol.
           68, pp. 363-371.

F-1012.   Tuan, Yi-Fu. 1983. "Geographical Theory:
           Queries from a Cultural Geographer,"
           Geographical Analysis, Vol. 15, pp. 69-72.

F-1013.   Tuan, Yi-Fu. 1983. "Orientation: An Approach
           to Human Geography," Journal of Geography, Vol.
           82, pp. 11-14.

F-1014.   Tuan, Yi-Fu. 1984. "Continuity and
           Discontinuity," Geographical Review, Vol. 74,
           pp. 245-256.

F-1015.   Uhlig, H. 1971. "Organization and System of
           Geography," Geoforum, Vol. 2, No. 7, pp. 7-38.

F-1016.   Unstead, J. F. 1907. "The Meaning of
           Geography," Geographical Teacher, Vol. 4, pp.
           19-28.

F-1017.   Unstead, J. F. 1916. "A Synthetic Method of
           Determining Geographical Regions," Geographical
           Journal, Vol. 48, pp. 230-249.

F-1018.   Unwin, D. J. 1978. "Quantitative and
           Theoretical Geography in the United Kingdom,"
           Area, Vol. 10, pp. 337-344.

F-1019.   Unwin, D. J. 1979. "Theoretical and
           Quantitative Geography in North-West Europe,"
           Area, Vol. 11, pp. 164-166.

F-1020.   Unwin, Tim. 1984. "Through a Glass Darkly,"
           [Book Review Essay] Progress in Human Geography,
           Vol. 8, pp. 423-454.

F-1021.   Van Cleef, Eugene. 1913. "The Language of
           Geography," Journal of Geography, Vol. 11, pp.
           235-238.

F-1022.   Van Cleef, E. 1936. "Stratigraphic View of
           Geography," Science, Vol. 83, pp. 313-317.

F-1023.   Van Cleef, Eugene. 1952. "Areal Differentia-
           tion and the 'Science' of Geography," Science,
           Vol. 115, No. 2998, pp. 654-655.

F-1024.   Van Cleef, Eugene. 1955. "Must Geographers
           Apologize?" Annals of the Association of
           American Geographers, Vol. 45, pp. 105-108.

F-1025.   Van Cleef, Eugene. 1960. "Geography as an
           Earth Science," Professional Geographer, Vol.
           12, pp. 8-11.

F-1026.   Van Cleef, Eugene. 1964. "Confusion or
          Revolution?" Professional Geographer, Vol. 16,
          No. 5, pp. 1-5.

F-1027.   Van Cleef, Eugene. 1971. "Whither Geography?"
          Professional Geographer, Vol. 23, pp. 344-346.

F-1028.   Van Der Laan, L. and Piersma, A. 1982. "The
          Image of Man: Paradigmatic Cornerstone in Human
          Geography," Annals of the Association of
          American Geographers, Vol. 72, pp. 411-526.

F-1029.   Van Passen, Christiaan. 1981. "The Philosophy
          of Geography: From Vidal to Hägerstrand," Lund
          Studies in Geography, Series B, Vol. 48, pp.
          17-29.

F-1030.   Vance, Rupert B. 1929. "The Concept of the
          Region," Social Forces, Vol. 8, pp. 208-218.

F-1031.   Varlas, V. Ya. et al. 1970. "Teoretich-eskaya
          Geografiya," [a review] Soviet Geography:
          Review and Translation, Vol. 11, pp. 138-143.

F-1032.   Vaughn, Nigel. 1978. "Geography, an
          Integrating Subject?" Teaching Geography, Vol.
          4, pp. 50-51.

F-1033.   Veen, Arthur W. L. 1976. "Geography Between
          the Devil and the Deep Blue Sea," Tijdschrift
          voor Economische en Sociale Geografie, Vol. 67,
          pp. 369-380.

F-1034.   Vinge, Clarence L. 1952. "Specialism,
          Evolution, and Geography," Social Studies, Vol.
          43, pp. 282-284.

F-1035.   Visher, S. S. 1932. "Recent Trends in
          Geography," Science Monthly, Vol. 35, pp.
          439-442.

F-1036.   Visher, Stephen S. 1923. "Modern Geography:
          Its Aspects, Aims, and Methods," Educational
          Review, Vol. 65, pp. 295-298.

F-1037.   Visher, Stephen Sargent. 1932. "Recent Trends
          in Geography," Scientific Monthly, Vol. 35, pp.
          439-442.

F-1038.   Von Engeln, O. D. 1919. "A Campaign for
          Geography," Journal of Geography, Vol. 18, pp.
          28-31.

F-1039.   Von Richthofen, Baron F. 1904. "The Impetus
          and Direction of Geography in the Nineteenth
          Century," Geographical Journal, Vol. 23, pp.
          229-234.

F-1040.   Wagner, P. 1971. "Geography as Criticism," <u>B. C. Geographical Series</u>, No. 12, pp. 32-40.

F-1041.   Wagner, P. L. 1976. "Reflections on a Radical Geography," <u>Antipode</u>, Vol. 8, pp. 83-85.

F-1042.   Wagner, Philip L. 1958. "Remarks on the Geography of Language," <u>Geographical Review</u>, Vol. 48, pp. 86-97.

F-1043.   Wagstaff, J. M. 1979. "Dealectical Materialism, Geography and Catastrophe Theory," <u>Area</u>, Vol. 11, pp. 326-332.

F-1044.   Wagstaff, J. M. 1979. "Etymology and Geography," <u>Area</u>, Vol. 11, pp.   219-220.

F-1045.   Wagstaff, J. M. 1979. "Etymology and Urban Geography," <u>Area</u>, Vol. 11, pp. 93-94.

F-1046.   Walford, Rex. 1984. "Geography and the Future," <u>Geography</u>, Vol. 69, pp. 193-208.

F-1047.   Walker, David. 1985. "From Laurel Creek and Back Again," <u>Bloomsbury</u>, <u>Geographer</u>, Vol. 13, pp. 75-78.

F-1048.   Walker, R. A. 1981. "Left-Wing Libertarianism, An Academic Disorder: A Response to David Sibley," <u>Professional Geographer</u>, Vol. 33, pp. 5-9.

F-1049.   Walker, Richard A. and Greenberg, Douglas A. 1982. "A Guide for the Lay Reader of Marxist Criticism," <u>Antipode</u>, Vol. 14, pp. 38-43.

F-1050.   Walmsley, D. J. 1974. "Positivism and Phenomenology in Human Geography," <u>Canadian Geographer</u>, Vol. 18, pp. 95-107.

F-1051.   Walmsley, D. J. 1979. "Time and Human Geography," <u>Australian Geological Studies</u>, Vol. 17, pp. 223-230.

F-1052.   Walmsley, D. J. and Sorenson, A. D. 1980. "What Marx for the Radicals? An Antipodean Viewpoint," <u>Area</u>, Vol. 12, pp. 137-141.

F-1053.   Walter, Bob J. and Bernard, Frank E. 1973. "A Thematic Approach to Regional Geography," <u>Journal of Geography</u>, Vol. 14-28.

F-1054.   Ward, David. 1966. "The Changing Heritage of Geography," <u>B. C. Geographical Series</u>, No. 3, pp. 11-14.

F-1055.   Warf, Barney. 1986. "Ideology, Everyday Life
           and Emancipatory Phenomenology," Antipode, Vol.
           18, pp. 268-283.

F-1056.   Warf, Barney. 1987. "Comments on 'Rethinking
           Cultural Adaptation,'" Professional Geographer,
           Vol. 39, pp. 65-66.

F-1057.   Warman, Henry J. 1970. "Perpetual
           Transformation: A Concept of Change and
           Choice," Journal of Geography, Vol. 69, pp.
           531-538.

F-1058.   Warntz, William. 1957. "Contributions Toward a
           Macroeconomic Geography: A Review," Geographical
           Journal, Vol. 47, pp. 420-424.

F-1059.   Warntz, William. 1967. "Global Science and the
           Tyranny of Space," Papers of the Regional
           Science Association, Vol. 19, pp. 7-19.

F-1060.   Warntz, William. 1958. "The Unity of
           Knowledge, Social Science and the Role of
           Geography," [address: National Council for the
           Social Studies, Pittsburgh, 1957] New York.

F-1061.   Warntz, William. 1974. "Conceptual
           Breakthroughs in Geography," Geographical
           Perspectives, No. 33, pp. 37-40.

F-1062.   Watson, C. 1969. "This Geography is Something
           to Sing About," American Education, Vol. 5, pp.
           14-18.

F-1063.   Watson, J. W. 1955. "Geography - A Discipline
           in Distance," Scottish Geographical Magazine,
           Vol. 71, pp. 1-13.

F-1064.   Watson, J. Wreford. 1983. "The Soul of
           Geography," Transactions - Institute of British
           Geographers, Vol. 8, pp. 385-399.

F-1065.   Watson, M. K. 1981. "The Scale Problem in
           Human Geography," Geografiska Annaler, Vol. 60B,
           pp. 36-47.

F-1066.   Watts, Sheldon J. and Watts, Susan J. 1978.
           "The Idealist Alternative in Geography and
           History," Professional Geographer, Vol. 30, pp.
           123-127.

F-1067.   Weaver, C. 1978. "Regional Theory and
           Regionalism: Towards Rethinking the Regional
           Question," Geoforum, Vol. 9, pp. 397-414.

F-1068.   West, H. G. 1954-55. "An Another Point of
           View," [of the Architecture of Humanism]
           Landscape, Vol. 4, pp. 20-24.

F-1069.   Wharton, Rear-Admiral Sir W. J. L.   1905.   "The
           Field of Geography and Some of Its Problems,"
           Geographical Journal, Vol. 26, pp. 429-443.

F-1070.   Wheatley, Paul.   1972.   "Great Expectations,"
           Bloomsbury Geographer, Vol. 5, pp. 8-13.

F-1071.   Wheeler, James O.   1975.   "Trends in the
           Philosophy and Methodology of Geography,
           1950-1974: An Overview," Mississippi
           Geographer, Vol. 3, pp. 9-16.

F-1072.   Wheeler, James O.   1986.   "Notes on the Rise of
           the Area Studies Tradition in U.S. Geography,
           1910-1929," Professional Geographer, Vol. 38,
           pp. 53-62.

F-1073.   Whipple, G.   1941.   "Human Geography: From
           Slogan to Actuality," Elementary School
           Journal, Vol. 41, pp. 337-346.

F-1074.   Whitaker, J. Russell.   1954.   "The Way Lies
           Open," Annals of the Association of American
           Geographers, Vol. 44, pp. 231-244.

F-1075.   Whitbeck, R. H.   1906.   "The Fundamental and the
           Incidental in Geography," Journal of Geography,
           Vol. 5, pp. 66-73.

F-1076.   Whitbeck, R. H.   1910.   "The Present Trend of
           Geography in the United States," Geographical
           Journal, Vol. 35, pp. 419-425.

F-1077.   Whitbeck, R. H.   1915.   "An Important Movement
           in Geography," Journal of Geography, Vol. 13,
           pp. 270-273.

F-1078.   Whitbeck, R. H.   1920.   "Rejuvenation of
           Geography," School and Society, Vol. 12, pp.
           415-420.

F-1079.   Whitbeck, R. H.   1921.   "Thirty Years of
           Geography in the United States," Journal of
           Geography, Vol. 20, pp. 121-128.

F-1080.   Whitbeck, R. H.   1923.   "Fact and Fiction in
           Geography by Natural Regions," Journal of
           Geography, Vol. 22, pp. 86-94.

F-1081.   Whitbeck, R. H.   1924.   "Traditional Geography
           and the Present Trend," Journal of Geography,
           Vol. 23, pp. 59-63.

F-1082.   White, Stephen E.   1980.   "A Philosophical
           Dichotomy in Migration Research," Professional
           Geographer, Vol. 32, pp. 6-13.

F-1083.   White, Stuart.   1984.   "Landscape of Events,"
          Journal _of_ _Cultural_ _Geography_, Vol. 4, pp.
          100-108.

F-1084.   White, Wayne R.   1967.   "Geography and the
          Organization of Knowledge," _Journal_ _of_
          Geography, Vol. 66, pp. 496-499.

F-1085.   Whitehand, J. W. R.   1970.   "Innovation
          Diffusion in An Academic Discipline: The Case
          of the 'New' Geography," _Area_, Vol. 2, pp.
          19-30.

F-1086.   Whitehand, J. W. R.   1970.   "Letter . . ., The
          Case of the 'New' Geography," _Area_, Vol. 2, pp.
          71-72.

F-1087.   Whitehand, J. W. R.   1971.   "In-Words Outwards:
          The Diffusion of the 'New' Geography, 1968-70,"
          Area, Vol. 3, pp. 158-163.

F-1088.   Whitehand, J. W. R.   1973.   "Radicalism and
          Conservatism in University Courses," _Area_, Vol.
          5, pp. 193-199.

F-1089.   Whittlesey, D.   1932.   "Environment and the
          Student of Human Geography," _Science_ _Monthly_,
          Vol. 35, pp. 265-267.

F-1090.   Whittlesey, Derwent.   1942.   "Geography into
          Politics," _Annals_ _of_ _the_ _Association_ _of_
          American _Geographers_, Vol. 32, pp. 142-143.

F-1091.   Whittlesey, Derwent.   1945.   "The Horizon of
          Geography," _Annals_ _of_ _the_ _Association_ _of_
          American _Geographers_, Vol. 35, pp. 1-36.

F-1092.   Widdis, R. W.   1980.   "Science and Humanism in
          Geography: The Dilemma of the Dialectic,"
          Ontario _Geography_, Vol. 15, pp. 53-64.

F-1093.   Wilbanks, Thomas J. and Szymanski, Richard.
          1968.   "What is Systems Analysis," _Professional_
          Geographer, Vol. 20, pp. 81-85.

F-1094.   Wilcock, A. A.   1972.   "Redefinition?" _Area_,
          Vol. 4, pp. 149-151.

F-1095.   Wilcock, Arthur A.   1975.   "The Geography Before
          1800," _Area_, Vol. 7, pp. 45-46.

F-1096.   Williams, Michael.   1985.   "The Geographical
          Association and the Great Debate," _Geography_,
          Vol. 70, pp. 129-137.

F-1097.   Williams, Michael.   1987.   "Editorial: Can the
          Centre Hold?" _Transactions_ -_Institute_ _of_
          British _Geographers_, Vol. 12, pp. 387-390.

F-1098.   Williams, S. W.   1983.   "The Concept of Culture
          and Human Geography: A Review and Reassessment,"
          Occasional Paper - University of Keele,
          Department of Geography, Vol. 5.

F-1099.   Williams, Stephen Wyn.   1981.   "Realism, Marxism
          and Human Geography," Antipode, Vol. 13, pp.
          31-38.

F-1100.   Williams, Trevor C.   1981.   "Maps and
          Matchboxes," Horizon, Vol. 29, pp. 59-62.

F-1101.   Wilson, A. G.   1972.   "Theoretical Geography:
          Some Speculations," Transactions - Institute of
          British Geographers, No. 57, pp. 31-44.

F-1102.   Wilson, Alan G.   1969.   "The Use of Analogies in
          Geography," Geographical Analysis, Vol. 1, pp.
          225-233.

F-1103.   Wilson, Alan G.   1979.   "Theory in Human
          Geography: A Review Essay," University of
          Leeds, School of Geography, Working Paper, Vol.
          253, 23 pp.

F-1104.   Wilson, Henry.   1918.   "The Geography of Culture
          and the Culture of Geography," Geographical
          Teacher, Vol. 9, N.P.

F-1105.   Wilson, Martha.   1925.   "Our Geographical
          Ignorance," Education, Vol. 45, pp. 547-549.

F-1106.   Wilson, Thomas D.   1977.   "Is Ambiguity
          Necessary in the Social Sciences?" Geographical
          Survey, Vol. 6, No. 2, pp. 3-8.

F-1107.   Winkler, E.   1970.   "A Possible Classification
          of Geosciences," Geoforum, Vol. 1, No. 1, pp.
          9-18.

F-1108.   Winsberg, Morton D.   1977.   "Social Sciences in
          the United States, 1948 to 1975," Geographical
          Review, Vol. 67, pp. 335-343.

F-1109.   Wirth, E.   1984.   "Geographie als moderne
          theorieorientierte Sozialwissenschaft?"
          (Geography - a modern Social Science?) Erdkunde,
          Vol. 38, pp. 73-79 [English Summary].

F-1110.   Wise, M. J.   1962.   "On the Writing of Regional
          Economic Geography," Economic Geography, Vol.
          38, p. 1.

F-1111.   Wisner, Ben.   1978.   "Does Radical Geography
          Lack an Approach to Environmental Relations?"
          Antipode, Vol. 10, pp. 349-95.

F-1112.   Wisner, Ben. 1986. "Geography: War or Peace
          Studies?" Antipode, Vol. 18, pp. 212-217.

F-1113.   Witfogel, Karl. 1985. "Geopolitics,
          Geographical Materialism, and Marxism," [trans.
          G. L. Ulmen] Antipode, Vol. 17, pp. 21-72.

F-1114.   Wolfe, Lloyd E. 1903. "The Human Side of
          Geography," National Education Association,
          Proceedings, pp. 143-153.

F-1115.   Wolforth, J. 1976. "The New Geography--And
          After?" Geography, Vol. 61, pp. 143-149.

F-1116.   Wood, L. J. 1970. "Perception Studies in
          Geography," Transactions - Institute of British
          Geographers, No. 50, pp. 129-142.

F-1117.   Wood, Tim F. 1987. "Thinking in Geography,"
          Geography, Vol. 72, pp. 289-299.

F-1118.   Wright, John K. 1925. "The History of
          Geography: A Point of View," Annals of the
          Association of American Geographers, Vol. 15,
          pp. 192-201.

F-1119.   Wright, John K. 1926. "A Plea for the History
          of Geography," Isis, Vol. 8, pp. 477-491.

F-1120.   Wright, John K. 1947. "Terrae Incognitae: The
          Place of the Imagination in Geography," Annals
          of the Association of American Geographers, Vol.
          37, pp. 1-15.

F-1121.   Wrobel, Andrzej. 1962. "Regional Analysis and
          the Geographic Concept of Region," Papers of the
          Regional Science Association, Vol. 8, pp. 37-42.

F-1122.   Yates, John. 1984. "Editorial: Social
          Geography," GeoJournal, Vol. 9, pp. 215-222.

F-1123.   Yefremov, Yu. K. 1961. "An Approach to
          Integrated Physical-Geographic Description of an
          Area," Soviet Geography: Review and
          Translation, Vol. 2, No. 7, pp. 42-47.

F-1124.   Yefremov, Yu. K. 1964. "The Place of Physical
          Geography Among the Natural Sciences," Soviet
          Geography: Review and Translation, Vol. 5, pp.
          3-11.

F-1125.   Yeomans, E. 1920. "Geography," Atlantic, Vol.
          125, pp. 167-172.

F-1126.   Yermolayev, M. M. 1969. "Geographical Space
          and Its Future," Soviet Geography: Review and
          Translation, Vol. 10, pp. 23-34.

F-1127.   Young, R. W.   1979.   "Paradigms in Geography:
          Implications of Kuhn's Interpretation of
          Scientific Inquiry," Australian Geographical
          Studies, Vol. 17, pp. 204-209.

F-1128.   Zabelin, I.   1965.   "What is the Matter with
          Geography?"   Soviet Geography: Review and
          Translation, Vol. 6, pp. 47-50.

F-1129.   Zaborski, Jerzy.   1972.   "On Metageography,"
          Proceedings - Twenty- Second International
          Geographical Congress, pp. 945-947.

F-1130.   Zakharov, N. D.   1962.   "Scholastics Instead of
          Science," Soviet Geography: Review and
          Translation, Vol. 3, No. 7, pp. 16-22.

F-1131.   Zelinsky, Wilbur.   1970.   "Beyond the
          Exponentials: The Role of Geography in the
          Great Transition," Economic Geography, Vol. 46,
          pp. 498-535.

F-1132.   Zelinsky, Wilbur.   1975.   "The Demigod's
          Dilemma," Annals of the Association of American
          Geographers, Vol. 65, pp. 123-143.

F-1133.   Zelinsky, Wilbur.   1976.   "Quality of Life: An
          Inquiry Into its Utility for Geographers,"
          Geographical Survey, Vol. 5, No. 4, pp. 8-11.

F-1134.   Zhirmunskiy, M. M. and Yanitskiy, N. F.   1964.
          "Methodological Clashes in Moscow as
          Misinterpreted by an American Geographer,"
          Soviet Geography: Review and Translation, Vol.
          5, pp. 85-91.

F-1135.   Zonneveld, J. I. S.   1983.   "Some Basic Notions
          in Geographical Synthesis," GeoJournal, Vol. 7,
          pp. 121-130.

F-1136.   Zvonkova, T. V. and Saushkin, Yu. G.   1977.
          "Interaction Between Physical and Economic
          Geography," Soviet Geography: Review and
          Translation, Vol. 18, pp. 245-250.

The Profession of Geography

G-1.   Abler, Ronald F. 1988. "Awards, Rewards, and
       Excellence: Keeping Geography Alive and Well,"
       Professional Geographer, Vol. 40, pp. 135-140.

G-2.   Ackerman, Edward A. 1967. "Gilbert Hovey
       Grosvenor, 1875-1966," Annals of the Association
       of American Geographers, Vol. 57, p. 197.

G-3.   Adams, Cyrus C. 1907. "Some Phases of Future
       Geographical Work in America," Bulletin of the
       American Geographical Society of New York, Vol.
       39, pp. 1-12.

G-4.   Adams, Cyrus C. 1914. "Geographical Book
       Reviewing," Bulletin of the American Geographical
       Society, Vol. 46, pp. 917-919.

G-5.   Afable, Engr. Pedro G. 1981. "Geography in the
       1980's," Philippine Geographical Journal, Vol.
       25, pp. 1-3.

G-6.   Akande, M. D. 1981. "Withdrawal from the
       Geography Class: A Study of the 'Push' and
       'Pull' Factors," Nigerian Geographical Journal,
       Vol. 25, pp. 105-118.

G-7.   Alpert, Harry. 1957. "Geography, Social
       Science, and the National Science Foundation,"
       Professional Geographer, Vol. 9, No. 6, pp. 7-9.

G-8.   Anderson, James R. 1979. "Geographers in
       Government," Professional Geographer, Vol. 31,
       pp. 265-270.

G-9.   Andrews, Alice C. 1974. "Some Demographic and
       Geographic Aspects of Community Colleges,"
       Journal of Geography, Vol. 73, pp. 10-16.

G-10.   Andrews, Alice C. and Moy, Kay. 1986. "Women
        Geographers in Business and Government: A
        Survey," Professional Geographer, Vol. 38, pp.
        406-410.

G-11.   Andrews, D. J. 1940. "Address at the Annual
        Meeting," Australian Geographer, Vol. 3, pp.
        3-14.

G-12.   Annenkov, V. V. 1981. "The Organization and
        Effectiveness of Commissions in International
        Geographical Union," Soviet Geography: Review
        and Translation, Vol. 22, pp. 194-204.

G-13.   Anokhin, A. A. 1982. "The 26th Party Congress
        and the Tasks of Socioeconomic Geography," Soviet
        Geography: Review and Translation, Vol. 23, pp.
        303-310.

G-14.   Anonymous. 1846. "The Royal Geographical
        Society and Its Labors," Royal Geographical
        Society Journal, Vol 16, pp. 1-32.

G-15.   Anonymous. 1891. "Geography in Newspapers and
        Periodicals," Journal of the Manchester
        Geographical Society, Vol. 7, pp. 124-126.

G-16.   Anonymous. 1893. "The Geographical Journal,"
        Geographical Journal, Vol. 1, pp. 58-61.

G-17.   Anonymous. 1894. "Geography at the
        Universities," Geographical Journal, Vol. 4, pp.
        29-31.

G-18.   Anonymous. 1895. "Geography at the
        Universities," Geographical Journal, Vol. 6, pp.
        25-27.

G-19.   Anonymous. 1897. "Conference of Missionaries on
        Geography," Journal of the Manchester
        Geographical Society, Vol. 13, pp. 189-202.

G-20.   Anonymous. 1902. "Geography and the War
        Office," Scottish Geographical Magazine, Vol. 18,
        pp. 423-425.

G-21.   Anonymous. 1903. "Geography in the University
        of Chicago," Bulletin of the American
        Geographical Society of New York, Vol. 35, pp.
        207-208.

G-22.   Anonymous. 1905. "The Annual Meeting of the
        Geographical Association," Geographical Teacher,
        Vol 3, pp. 1-11.

G-23.   Anonymous. 1907. "Geography and the Public
        Service," Geographical Journal, Vol. 29, pp.
        73-74.

G-24. Anonymous. 1916. "The National Council of
       Geography Teachers," School and Society, Vol. 3,
       pp. 754-756.

G-25. Anonymous. 1918. "Meteorology and the War,"
       Scottish Geographical Magazine, Vol. 34, pp.
       263-265.

G-26. Anonymous. 1919. "War Services of Members of
       the Association of American Geographers," Annals
       of the Association of American Geographers, Vol.
       9, pp. 49-70.

G-27. Anonymous. 1920. "A Proposal for an
       International Geographical Union," Geographical
       Journal, Vol. 55, pp. 139-143.

G-28. Anonymous. 1926. "News Items from Members [of
       the AAG]," Annals of the Association of American
       Geographers, Vol. 16, pp. 40-62.

G-29. Anonymous. 1928. "The Centenary of the Berlin
       Geographical Society," Geographical Journal,
       Vol. 72, pp. 159-162.

G-30. Anonymous. 1930. "The Centenary Meeting:
       Addresses on the History of the Society,"
       Geographical Journal, Vol. 76, pp. 455-476.

G-31. Anonymous. 1932. "Geography at the 1932 Annual
       Meeting of the Division of Geology and Geography
       of the National Research Council," Annals of the
       Association of American Geographers, Vol. 22, pp.
       231-236.

G-32. Anonymous. 1932. "Geography: Beginning of
       Popularization," Nation Vol. 135, p. 205.

G-33. Anonymous. 1933. "Titles and Abstracts of
       Papers Presented Before the Association at
       Washington, D.C., December, 1932," Annals of the
       Association of American Geographers, Vol. 23, pp.
       33-56.

G-34. Anonymous. 1940. "Publishers Plans for
       Geographical Series," Publisher's Weekly, Vol.
       138, pp. 1101-1103.

G-35. Anonymous. 1942. "Renaissance in Geography,"
       Christian Science Monitor, p. 13.

G-36. Anonymous. 1943. "The First Hundred Volumes,"
       [of the Geographical Journal] Geographical
       Journal, Vol. 101, pp. 30-33.

G-37. Anonymous. 1950. "Careers for Geographers,"
       Geographical Journal, Vol. 116, pp. 93-95.

G-38.   Anonymous. 1952. "The American Geographical
        Society: 1851-1957," Scottish Geographical
        Magazine, Vol. 68, pp. 128-130.

G-39.   Anonymous. 1954. "A Selected Bibliography on
        Careers in Geography," Professional Geographer,
        Vol. 6, No. 3, pp. 29-35.

G-40.   Anonymous. 1960. "Careers For Geographers,"
        Geographical Journal, Vol. 126, pp. 451-454.

G-41.   Anonymous. 1964. "The Development of
        International Contacts in the Field of Geography
        and Preparations for the 20th International
        Geographical Congress," Soviet Geography: Review
        and Translation, Vol. 5, pp. 72-85.

G-42.   Anonymous. 1965. "Editorial: Geography and the
        Changing Scottish Scene," Scottish Geographical
        Magazine, Vol. 81, pp. 75-77.

G-43.   Anrick, Carl Julius. 1923. "A Popular
        Geographic Club of Sweden: The Swedish Touring
        Club and Its Activities," Annals of the
        Association of American Geographers, Vol. 13, pp.
        608-612.

G-44.   Anuchin, V. A. 1970. "On the Problems of
        Geography and the Tasks of Popularizing
        Geographical Knowledge," Soviet Geography:
        Review and Translation, Vol. 11, pp. 82-112.

G-45.   Asley, W. B. 1921. "Jogging Up Jography,"
        Outlook, Vol. 128, pp. 651-653.

G-46.   Atwood, W. W. 1919. "Geography in America,"
        Geographical Review, Vol. 7, pp. 36-43.

G-47.   Atwood, Wallace W. 1919. "The Call for
        Geographers," Annals of the Association of
        American Geographers, Vol. 9, pp. 71.

G-48.   Atwood, Wallace W. 1921. "The Development of
        Productive Scholarship among American
        Geographers," Annals of the Association of
        American Geographers, Vol. 11, pp. 119-120.

G-49.   Atwood, Wallace W. 1925. "Geographical
        Research," Annals of the Association of American
        Geographers, Vol. 15, pp. 31.

G-50.   Augelli, John P. 1987. "On 'Academic War Over
        the Field of Geography'," [see N. Smith, 1987]
        Annals of the Association of American
        Geographers, Vol. 78, pp. 145-147.

G-51. Bagchi, I. 1983. "Golden Jubilee Welcome Address," _Geographical Review of India_, Vol. 45, pp. 7-10.

G-52. Bailey, Patrick. 1983. "Evolution of a British Professional Journal for Geography Teachers," _Journal of Geography_, Vol. 82, pp. 7-10.

G-53. Bailly, Antoine S. 1978. "Which Way is North? Directions for Human Geography," _Geoforum_, Vol. 9, pp. 341-348.

G-54. Balchin, W. G. V. 1983. "Careers for Graduate Geographers," _Geographical Journal_, Vol. 149, pp. 334-341.

G-55. Barker, D. 1981. "Observation: Sandwich Geography--a Bread and Butter Course," _Area_, Vol. 13, pp. 242-244.

G-56. Barr, William. 1983. "Geographical Aspects of the First International Polar Year, 1882-1883," _Annals of the Association of American Geographers_, Vol. 73, pp. 463-484.

G-57. Bartholomew, J. G. 1902. "A Plea for a National Institute of Geography," _Scottish Geographical Magazine_, Vol. 18, pp. 144-148.

G-58. Barton, Thomas Frank. 1964. "Leadership in the Early Years of the National Council of Geography Teachers, 1916-1935," _Journal of Geography_, Vol. 63, pp. 355-366.

G-59. Beaner, S. H. 1983. "Recollections of a Founder Member," _Transactions - Institute of British Geographers_, Vol. 8, pp. 36-37.

G-60. Beard, Daniel P. 1976. "Professional Problems of Nonacademic Geographers," _Professional Geographer_, Vol. 28, pp. 127-131.

G-61. Beaumont, John. 1980. "Data Collection and Analysis for Geographic Research: A Post Graduate Training Course," _Journal of Geography in Higher Education_, Vol. 4, pp. 72-80.

G-62. Beaver, S. H. 1978. "The Student Geographical," _Area_, Vol. 10, p. 135.

G-63. Beaver, S. H. 1982. "Geography in the British Association for the Advancement of Science," _Geographical Journal_, Vol. 148, pp. 173-181.

G-64. Beck, A. D. 1974. "Geography in the American Community College," _Geography_, Vol. 59, pp. 333-335.

G-65.   Bein, F. L.   1984.   "Geography Extension at
         IUPUI," Professional Geographer, Vol. 36, pp.
         238-240.

G-66.   Beishlag, George.   1949.   "What's Wrong With
         Geographic Writing?" Annals of the Association of
         American Geographers, Vol. 39, pp. 60.

G-67.   Bengston, Nels A.   1961.   "The Geographic
         Expert," Professional Geographer, Vol. 13, No. 2,
         pp. 10-13.

G-68.   Bennet, Robert.   1978.   "Teaching Mathematics in
         Geography Degrees," Journal of Geography in
         Higher Education, Vol. 2, pp. 38-46.

G-69.   Bentham, Graham.   1987.   "An Evaluation of the
         U.G.C.'s Rating of the Research of British
         University Geography Departments," Area, Vol. 19,
         pp. 147-154.

G-70.   Bergen, John V.   1972.   "Geographers, Maps, and
         Campus Map Collections," Professional Geographer,
         Vol. 24, pp. 310-316.

G-71.   Berman, Mildred.   1977.   "Facts and Attitudes on
         Discrimination as Perceived by AAG Members:
         Survey Results," Professional Geographer, Vol.
         29, pp. 70-76.

G-72.   Berman, Mildred.   1984.   "On Being a Woman in
         American Geography: A Personal Perspective,"
         Antipode, Vol. 16, pp. 61-68.

G-73.   Berry, B. J. L.   1981.   "Applied Geography at the
         Public-Private Interface," Applied Geography
         Conference, Vol. 4, pp. 3-5.

G-74.   Berry, B. J. L.   1981.   "Challenges of the
         Numbers Game," Professional Geographer, Vol. 33,
         pp. 161-162.

G-75.   Birch, William.   1977.   "On Excellence and
         Problem Solving in Geography," Transactions -
         Institute of British Geographers, Vol. 2, pp.
         417-429.

G-76.   Bird, James.   1983.   "Transactions of Ideas: A
         Subjective Survey of the Transactions During the
         Last Fifty Years of the Institute," Transactions
         - Institute of British Geographers, Vol. 8, pp.
         55-69.

G-77.   Birtles, Terry G.   1985.   "A Plea for a
         'Professional' Institute of Australian
         Geographers," Australian Geographical Studies,
         Vol. 23, pp. 338-346.

G-78.   Bishop, Avard L.   1909.   "Geography in
        Universities Abroad," Educational Review, Vol.
        37, pp. 447-481.

G-79.   Bishop, Sir George.   1985.   "The Presidential
        Address," Geographical Journal, Vol. 151, pp.
        311-317.

G-80.   Bishop, Sir George.   1986.   "The Presidential
        Address," Geographical Journal, Vol. 152, pp.
        307-313.

G-81.   Blaut, J. M.   1984.   "Modesty and the Movement:
        A Commentary," Research Paper - University of
        Chicago, Department of Geography, No. 209, pp.
        149-163.

G-82.   Bleasdale, Sue.   1977.   "After the Graduation
        Ceremony: Some Thoughts on Geography Graduate
        Careers," Journal of Geography in Higher
        Education, Vol. 1, pp. 71-77.

G-83.   Blowers, A. T.   1972.   "Relevance - Bleeding
        Hearts and Open Valves," Area, Vol. 4, pp.
        290-292.

G-84.   Bodman, A. R.   1987.   "In Plain Cite," Area, Vol.
        19, pp. 284-287.

G-85.   Boehm, Richard G.   1984.   "On Prejudice in
        Geography," Journal of Geography, Vol. 83, pp.
        52-53.

G-86.   Boggs, S. Whittemore.   1937.   "Library
        Classification and Cataloguing of Geographic
        Material," Annals of the Association of American
        Geographers, Vol. 27, pp. 49-93.

G-87.   Bombay Society.   1833.   "Bombay Geographical
        Society," Journal of the Royal Geographical
        Society of London, Vol. 3, pp. vii-xi.

G-88.   Borchert, John R.   1987.   "Maps, Geography, and
        Geographers," Professional Geographer, Vol. 39,
        pp. 387-389.

G-89.   Bowen, E. G.   1968.   "Regional Geography at
        Aberystwyth," in E. G. Bowen, et al., eds.,
        Geography at Aberystwyth (Cardiff: University of
        Wales Press), pp. 270-276.

G-90.   Bowlby, S., Foord, J. and Mackenzie, S.   1982.
        "Feminism and Geography," Area, Vol. 14, pp.
        19-25.

G-91.   Bowlby, S. R. et al. 1982. "Guest Editorial: Environment Planning, and Feminist Theory: A British Perspective," _Environment and Planning A_, Vol. 14, pp. 711-716.

G-92.   Bowman, Isaiah. 1908. "Geography at Yale University," _Journal of Geography_, Vol. 7, pp. 59-61.

G-93.   Bradshaw, Michael J. 1985. "Geography and Peace Studies," _Operational Geographer_, Vol. 6, pp. 41-43.

G-94.   Brandes, Donald. 1986. "Humor: A Frank and Ernest Look at Geographers," _Florida Geographer_, Vol. 20, pp. 48-49.

G-95.   Breitbart, Myrna Margulies. 1984. "Feminist Perspectives in Geographic Theory and Methodology," _Antipode_, Vol. 16, pp. 72-74.

G-96.   Bridges, Roy C. 1985. "The Foundation and Early Years of the Aberdeen Centre of the Royal Scottish Geographical Society," _Scottish Geographical Magazine_, Vol. 101, pp. 77-84.

G-97.   Briggs, John. 1988. "Jobs for Geographers: Some Hard Evidence," _Geography_, Vol. 73, pp. 137-140.

G-98.   Brigham, Albert Perry. 1920. "Geography and the War," _Journal of Geography_, Vol. 19, pp. 19-103.

G-99.   Brigham, Albert Perry. 1924. "The Association of American Geographers," _Annals of the Association of American Geographers_, Vol. 14, pp. 109-116.

G-100.   Brigham, Albert Perry. 1931. "The Centenary of the Royal Geographical Society," _Geographical Review_, Vol. 21, pp. 142-145.

G-101.   Brigham, Albert Perry. 1932. "Research by American Geographers Since 1900," _Annals of the Association of American Geographers_, Vol. 22, pp. 49-50.

G-102.   Britton, Robert L. 1944. "Some Impacts of War on Geography," _Journal of Geography_, Vol. 43, pp. 34-36.

G-103.   Broek, Jan O. M. 1959. "Progress in Human Geography," _Yearbook - National Council for the Social Studies_, Washington, D.C., Vol. 29, pp. 34-53.

G-104.   Broude, Henry W. 1960. "The Significance of
          Regional Studies for the Elaboration of National
          Economic History," Journal of Economic History,
          Vol. 20, pp. 588-596.

G-105.   Brown, R. N. R. 1915. "The Geographer's Need of
          Travel," Journal of Geography, Vol. 13, p. 301.

G-106.   Brunn, Stanley D. 1988. "The Manuscript Review
          Process and Advice to Prospective Authors,"
          Professional Geographer, Vol. 40, pp. 8-14.

G-107.   Bryce, Rt. Hon. Viscount. 1915. "The Mental
          Training of a Traveller," Geographical Journal,
          Vol. 45, pp. 110-126.

G-108.   Buchanan, R. Ogilvie. 1948. "Geography and the
          Community," New Zealand Geographer, Vol. 4, pp.
          115-126.

G-109.   Buchanan, R. Ogilvie. 1984. "The I.B.G.:
          Retrospect and Prospect," Transactions and
          Papers - Institute of British Geographers, No.
          20, pp. 1-14.

G-110.   Bunge, William. 1961. "The Structure of
          Contemporary American Geographic Research,"
          Professional Geographer, Vol. 13, No. 3, pp.
          19-23.

G-111.   Bunge, William. 1967. "Theoretical Geography,"
          in Introduction to Geography: Selected Readings,
          Dohrs and Sommers, eds. (New York: Crowell Co.),
          1967.

G-112.   Bunge, William. 1973. "Spatial Prediction,"
          Annals of the Association of American
          Geographers, Vol. 63, pp. 556-568.

G-113.   Bunge, William. 1974. "Regions Are Sort of
          Unique," Area, Vol. 6, pp. 92-99.

G-114.   Bunge, William. 1979. "Perspective on
          Theoretical Geography," Annals of the Association
          of American Geographers, Vol. 69, pp. 169-174.

G-115.   Burghardt, Andrew F. 1988. "On Academic War
          over the Field of Geography," [see N. Smith,
          1987] Annals of the Association of American
          Geographers, Vol. 78, p. 144.

G-116.   Bushong, Allen D. 1974. "Some Aspects of the
          Membership and Meetings of the Association of
          American Geographers Before 1949," Geographical
          Journal, Vol. 26, pp. 435-439.

G-117.   Butler, G. 1879. "Geography in the
         Universities," Contemporary Review, Vol. 35, p.
         671.

G-118.   Campbell, Frank. 1895. "The Literature of
         Geography: How Shall It Be?" Proceedings - Sixth
         International Geographical Congress, pp. 391-398.

G-119.   Cantor, L. M. 1962. "The Royal Geographical
         Society and the Projected London Institute of
         Geography, 1892-99," Geographical Journal, Vol.
         128, pp. 30-37.

G-120.   Caris, S. 1978. "Geographic Perspectives on
         Women: A Review," Transition, Vol. 8, pp. 10-14.

G-121.   Carthew, Arthur. 1965.   "A Brief History of the
         California Council of Geography Teachers,"
         California Geographer, Vol. 6, pp. 11-16.

G-122.   Chapman, General. 1905. "The Proposed Chair of
         Geography in the University of Edinburgh,"
         Scottish Geographical Magazine, Vol. 21, pp.
         197-198.

G-123.   Chapman, J. 1971. "Relevance to What? A Review
         of Some Contemporary Forces for Change and Their
         Impact Upon Geography," B.C. Geographical Series,
         pp. 21-31.

G-124.   Chih-hai, Hua. 1977. "Learn Some Geography,"
         China Geographer, No. 5, pp. 19-25.

G-125.   Chisholm, M. 1973. "Post-graduate Training in
         Geography," Area, Vol. 5, pp. 83-87.

G-126.   Clark, Andrew. 1962. "Praemia Geographiae: The
         Incidential Rewards of a Professional Career,"
         Annals of the Association of American
         Geographers, Vol. 52, pp. 229-241.

G-127.   Clark, Colin. 1985. "Geography Must Be Alive
         and Kicking," Area, Vol. 17, pp. 174-175.

G-128.   Clark, Michael. 1983. "Institutional Threats to
         Research and Academic Merit," Area, Vol. 15, pp.
         174-176.

G-129.   Claval, Paul. 1980. "Integrating Concepts in
         the Teaching of Geography in Higher Education,"
         Journal of Geography in Higher Education, Vol. 4,
         pp. 10-15.

G-130.   Clayton, K. M. and Riordan, T. O. 1977. "The
         Readership of Transactions and the Role of the
         IBG," Area, Vol. 9, pp. 96-98.

G-131.   Clerk, Rt. Hon. Sir George. 1943. "Address at
          the Annual General Meeting," Geographical
          Journal, Vol. 102, pp. 1-6.

G-132.   Clerk, Rt. Hon. Sir George. 1944. "Address at
          the Annual General Meeting," Geographical
          Journal, Vol. 104, pp. 1-7.

G-133.   Clerk, Rt. Hon. Sir George. 1945. "Address at
          the Annual General Meeting," Geographic Journal,
          Vol. 105, pp. 153-159.

G-134.   Clerk, Sir George. 1942. "Address at the Annual
          General Meeting," Geographical Journal, Vol.
          100, pp. 1-5.

G-135.   Close, Lieut.-Colonel C. F. 1909. "Recent
          Progress in Geographical Work," Geographical
          Journal, Vol. 33, pp. 573-579.

G-136.   Coates, Bryan and White, Paul. 1985. "The
          Catchment For University Geography," Geography,
          Vol. 70, pp. 343-346.

G-137.   Cohen, Saul B. 1987. "Reflections on the
          Elimination of Geography at Harvard," Annals of
          the Association of American Geographers, Vol. 78,
          pp. 149-151.

G-138.   Colby, Charles C. 1929. "Twenty-five Years of
          the Association of American Geographers: A
          Secretarial Review," Annals of the Association of
          American Geographers, Vol. 19, pp. 59-61.

G-139.   Connell, John. 1974. "Geography Published
          Underground (1). The Output from British
          Universities," Area, Vol. 6, pp. 121-127.

G-140.   Cooper, A. D. 1976. "Geography as Taught,"
          Area, Vol. 8, pp. 9-10.

G-141.   Cosgrove, D. 1981. "Teaching Geographical
          Thought Through Student Interviews," Journal of
          Geography in Higher Education, Vol. 5, pp. 19-22.

G-142.   Cosgrove, D., et al. 1983. "Changing Geography
          and Writing a Ph.D.," Area, Vol. 15, pp. 47-51.

G-143.   Cosgrove, Denis. 1985. "Present Fears for the
          Future of the Past: Report of a Survey into
          Academic Recruitment of Historical Geographers,"
          Area, Vol. 17, pp. 243-246.

G-144.   Cosgrove, Denis. 1987. "U.G.C. Rankings, I.B.G.
          Council and the Future of Geography in the
          Universities," Area, Vol. 19, pp. 155-159.

G-145.   Cox, Percy. 1934. "Address at the Annual
          General Meeting," Geographical Journal, Vol. 84,
          pp. 97-104.

G-146.   Cox, P. Z. 1935. "Address at the Annual General
          Meeting," Geographical Journal, Vol. 86, pp.
          89-97.

G-147.   Cox, Percy. 1936. "Address at the Annual
          General Meeting," Geographical Journal, Vol. 88,
          pp. 481-491.

G-148.   Cox, Nicholas and Anderson, Evan. 1978.
          "Teaching Geographical Data Analysis Problems and
          Possible Solutions," Journal of Geography in
          Higher Education, Vol. 2, pp. 29-37.

G-149.   Cramer, R. E. and Gritzner, C. F., Jr. 1963.
          "Let's Sell Geography," Journal of Geography,
          Vol. 62, pp. 3-11.

G-150.   Creary, John P. 1979. "So You Want to Be a
          Planner ... Notes and Thoughts on the Role of
          Geography in Planning," Geoscope, Vol. 10, pp.
          1-6.

G-151.   Cressey, George B. 1948. "The International
          Geographical Union," Annals of the Association
          of American Geographers, Vol. 38, pp. 73-74.

G-152.   Cross, Clark I. 1960. "Geography and the
          Exploration of Space," Memorandum Folio of the
          Southeastern Association of American Geographers,
          Vol. 12, pp. 18-21.

G-153.   Currey, Bruce. 1984. "Professional Geography
          Versus Public Policy," Australian Geographical
          Studies, Vol. 22, pp. 153-155.

G-154.   Cutshall, Alden. 1942. "The Geographer in War
          Time," Journal of Geography, Vol. 41, pp.
          252-258.

G-155.   Cutter, Susan Curtis and Renwick, Hilary. 1980.
          "The Myth of the Women's Session," Transition,
          Vol. 10, pp. 14-17.

G-156.   Daish, John B. 1988. "The Study of Geography,"
          Education, Vol. 8, pp. 313-320.

G-157.   Darby, N. C. 1932. "Geography in a Medieval
          Text-Book," Scottish Geographical Magazine, Vol.
          49, pp. 323-331.

G-158.   Davies, D. H. 1978. "From Rhodesia to
          Zimbabwe: The Geographer and the Road Ahead,"
          Area, Vol. 10, pp. 286-288.

G-159.   Davis, Bruce E.   1975.   "The Cosmos: A New Frontier for Geography,"   Mississippi Geographer, Vol. 3, pp. 17-20.

G-160.   Davis, D. F.   1985.   "The 'Metropolitan Thesis' and the Writing of Canadian Urban History,"   Urban History Review, Vol. 14, pp. 95-113.

G-161.   Davis, W. M.   1905.   "Home Geography,"   Journal of Geography, Vol. 4, pp. 1-5.

G-162.   Davis, W. M.   1920.   "Geography at Cambridge University, England,"   Journal of Geography, Vol. 19, pp. 207-211.

G-163.   Davis, William M.   1911.   "Disciplinary Value of Geography,"   Popular Science Monthly, Vol. 78, pp. 105-119 and pp. 223-246.

G-164.   Dean, C. B.   1939.   "That's a Subject for Fathers!   Relationships of Life to Earth," American Home, Vol. 21, January, pp. 22+.

G-165.   Dean, W. G.   1967.   "Canadian Geography, 1967," Canadian Geographer, Vol. 11, pp. 195-196.

G-166.   Deasy, George F.   1947.   "Training, Professional Work, and Military Experience of Geographers, 1942-1947,"   Professional Geographer, Vol. 6, pp. 1-14.

G-167.   Deasy, George F.   1948.   "The Geographer's Salary,"   Professional Geographer, Vol. 8, pp. 4-17.

G-168.   Deasy, George F.   1948.   "War-time Changes in Occupation of Geographers,"   Professional Geographer, Vol. 7, pp. 33-41.

G-169.   Deshpande, C. D.   1974.   "New Perspectives in Indian Geography,"   Deccan Geographer, Vol. 12, pp. 56-60.

G-170.   Deskins, Donald.   1980.   "Comments on Geography, Change and the Future,"   Geographical Perspectives, Vol. 46, pp. 1-5.

G-171.   Deskins, Donald R., Jr. and Sibert, Linda E. 1975.   "Blacks in American Geography: 1974," Professional Geographer, Vol. 27, pp. 65-72.

G-172.   Deskins, Donald R., Jr. and Speil, Linda J. 1971.   "The Status of Blacks   in American Geography: 1970,"   Professional Geographer, Vol. 23, pp. 283-289.

G-173.   Deskins, Donald R., Jr. and Speil, Linda J.
         1972. "Geography and Black America,"
         Professional Geographer, Vol. 24, pp. 45-47.

G-174.   de Souza, Anthony R. 1988. "Writing Matters,"
         Professional Geographer, Vol. 40, pp. 1-3.

G-175.   de Souza, Anthony R., and Vogeler, Ingolf.
         1980. "Teaching Ideological Alternatives,"
         Geographical Perspectives, Vol. 46, pp. 55-60.

G-176.   Dikshit, Ramesh Dutta. 1984. "The Changing
         Professional Concerns in Geography: A Review,"
         Geographical Review of India, Vol. 46, pp. 1-15.

G-177.   Dima, Nicholas. 1978. "University Education in
         Eastern Europe: The Case of Geography in
         Romania," Journal of Geography, Vol. 77, pp.
         149-151.

G-178.   Dohrs, Fred E. 1962. "A Public Information
         Program for the Association of American
         Geographers," Professional Geographer, Vol. 14,
         pp. 44-47.

G-179.   Doran, Michael T. 1978. "The Supply and Demand
         of Doctorates in Geography," Professional
         Geographer, Vol. 30, pp. 48-54.

G-180.   Dow, Maynard Weston. 1974. "The Oral History of
         Geography," Professional Geographer, Vol. 26, pp.
         430-435.

G-181.   Drake, Christine and Horton, June. 1983.
         "Comment on Editorial Essay: Sexist Bias in
         Political Geography," Political Geography
         Quarterly, Vol. 2, pp. 329-337.

G-182.   Dryer, Charles R. 1913. "The New Departure in
         Geography," Journal of Geography, Vol. 11, pp.
         145-151, 177-180.

G-183.   Duff, Hon. Sir Mountstuart E. 1983. "The Annual
         Address on the Progress of Geography, 1892-93,"
         Geographical Journal, Vol. 2, pp. 1-25.

G-184.   Dugdale, G. S. 1967. "The Motto of the Royal
         Geographical Society and William Richard
         Hamilton," Geographical Journal, Vol. 133, pp.
         51-53.

G-185.   Dunbar, G. S. 1978. "The Rival Geographical
         Societies of Fin-de-Siecle," Yearbook -
         Association of Pacific Coast Geographers, Vol.
         40, pp. 57-64.

G-186. Dunbar, G. S. 1981. "The Prospects for
        Geography at Mont Eagle University in 1871,"
        California Geographer, Vol. 21, pp. 95-99.

G-187. Dunbar, G. S. 1986. "Geography in the
        Bellweather Universities of the United States,"
        Area, Vol. 18, pp. 25-33.

G-188. Dunbar, Gary S. 1985. "Mining the Archives:
        The Richmond College Geographical and Historical
        Society," Virginia Geographer, Vol. 17,
        Spring/Summer, pp. 42-43.

G-189. Dunbar, Gary S. 1986. "The Fiftieth Anniversary
        Banquet: Messages from Charter Members of the
        Association of Pacific Coast Geographers,"
        Yearbook - Association of Pacific Coast
        Geographers, Vol. 48, pp. 168-188.

G-190. Dury, George Harry. 1972. "Some Recent Views on
        the Nature, Location, Needs, and Potential of
        Geomorphology," Professional Geographer, Vol. 24,
        pp. 199-202.

G-191. Earl of Ronaldshay, Rt. Hon. 1923. "Address at
        the Anniversary General Meeting, 28 May 1923,"
        Geographical Journal, Vol. 62, pp. 1-6.

G-192. Earl of Ronaldshay, Rt. Hon. 1924. "Address at
        the Anniversary General Meeting, 26 May 1924,"
        Geographical Journal, Vol. 64, pp. 1-6.

G-193. Earl of Ronaldshay, Rt. Hon. 1925. "Address at
        the Anniversary General Meeting, 15 June 1925,"
        Geographical Journal, Vol. 66, pp. 1-9.

G-194. Earley, Albert. 1917. "Geographies of the
        Eighteenth Century," Journal of Geography, Vol.
        16, pp. 17-18.

G-195. East, W. Gordon. 1973. "The Joint School:
        Early Days," Horizon, Vol. 22, pp. 6-10.

G-196. Eder, Herbert M. 1964. "The Biography of a
        Periodical: Geographische Zeitschrift,
        1895-1963," Professional Geographer, Vol. 16, No.
        3, pp. 1-5.

G-197. Enedy, J. and Gustafson, G. 1983. "Examples of
        Academic Geographers and Geography in Local
        Government," Papers and Proceedings of Applied
        Geography Conference, Vol. 6, pp. 177-184.

G-198. Evenden, L. J. 1976. "The Western Division of
        the Canadian Association of Geographers,"
        Canadian Geographer, Vol. 20, pp. 329-333.

G-199.   Eyles, John. 1977. "After the Revelance
         Debate: The Teaching of Social Geography,"
         Journal of Geography in Higher Education, Vol. 1,
         pp. 3-12.

G-200.   Fairchild, Wilma B. 1966. "Adventures in
         Longevity: Fifty Years of the Geographical
         Review," Geographical Review, Vol. 56, pp. 1-11.

G-201.   Fairchild, Wilma B. 1977. "The Geographical
         Review and The American Geographical Society,"
         Annals of the Association of American
         Geographers, Vol. 69, pp. 33-38.

G-202.   Farrell, Bryan H. 1956. "Cultural or Human
         Geography?" New Zealand Geographical Society.
         Proceedings of the First Geography Conference,
         Auckland, 1955, pp. A1/9-16.

G-203.   Fealman, J. D. 1986. "Myth and Reality in the
         Origin of American Economic Geography," Annals of
         the Association of American Geographers, Vol. 76,
         pp. 313-330.

G-204.   Fink, L. D. 1984. "First Year on the Faculty:
         Being There," Journal of Geography in Higher
         Education, Vol. 8, pp. 11-25.

G-205.   Fink, L. Dee. 1979. "The Changing Location of
         Academic Geographers in the United States,"
         Professional Geographer, Vol. 31, pp. 217-226.

G-206.   Fink, L. Dee. 1983. "First Year on the
         Faculty: Getting There," Journal of Geography in
         Higher Education, Vol. 7, pp. 45-56.

G-207.   Fink, L. Dee. 1985. "First Year on the
         Faculty: The Quality of Their Teaching," Journal
         of Geography in Higher Education, Vol. 9, pp.
         129-146.

G-208.   Fisher, C. A. 1959. "The Compleat Geographer"
         [Inaugural Lecture], Sheffield: University of
         Sheffield, 18 p.

G-209.   Fleure, H. J. 1931. "Geographical Outlook," New
         Era, Vol. 12, pp. 221- 223.

G-210.   Floyd, B. N. 1967. "A Niche for Verbalizers in
         the 'New School': Geography as Polite
         Literature," Nigerian Geographical Journal, Vol.
         10, pp. 133-136.

G-211.   Floyd, Barry. 1973. "The Jargoneers in
         Geography," Area, Vol. 5, pp. 207-211.

G-212.   Forbes, D. K., Rimmer, P. J. 1983. "Please
         Sir! Can We Have More? Geography and the
         Australian Research Grants Scheme, 1983,"
         Australian Geographical Studies, Vol. 21, pp.
         167-169.

G-213.   Forbes, D. K., Thrift, N. J. and Williams, P.
         1983. "The Institute of Australian Geographers:
         Blueprint for the 1980s," Australian Geographical
         Studies, Vol. 21, pp. 3-7.

G-214.   Forde, C. Caryll. 1939. "Human Geography,
         History and Sociology," Scottish Geographical
         Magazine, Vol. 55, pp. 217-235.

G-215.   Forer, P. C. 1978. "Homo Geographicus and the
         School Computer," New Zealand Journal of
         Geography, Vol. 65, pp. 22-30.

G-216.   Forer, P. C. and Owens, I. F. 1979. "The
         Frontiers of Geography in The 1980's," New
         Zealand Journal of Geography, Vol. 68, pp. 2-5.

G-217.   Foster, L. T. and Jones, K. G. 1977. "Applied
         Geography: An Educational Alternative,"
         Professional Geographer, Vol. 29, pp. 300-304.

G-218.   Foster, Les, Jones, Ken, and Mock, Dennis.
         1979. "Internships in the Applied Geography
         Curriculum," Journal of Geography in Higher
         Education, Vol. 3, pp. 8-14.

G-219.   Frazer, W. J. 1980. "The California
         Geographer: The First 20 Years," California
         Geographer, Vol. 20, pp. 1-9.

G-220.   Freeman, T. 1968. "Forty Years of Geography,"
         Irish Geography, Vol. 5, pp. 355-371.

G-221.   Freeman, T. W. 1979. "Twenty-five Years of 'The
         East Midland Geographer' 1954-1979," East Midland
         Geographer, Vol. 7, pp. 95-99.

G-222.   Freeman, T. W. 1984. "The Manchester and Royal
         Scottish Geographical Societies," Geographical
         Journal, Vol. 150, pp. 55-62.

G-223.   Freeman, T. W. 1985. "Geography Then and Now,"
         Espace Geographique, Vol. 14, pp. 16-22.

G-224.   French, R. A. 1979. "Possibilities for Future
         British-Soviet Cooperation in Geography,"
         Geoforum, Vol. 10, pp. 349-350.

G-225.   Friis, Herman. 1954. "The Distribution of
         Members of the AAG and of the Middle Atlantic
         Division, December 1953: A Cartographic
         Representation," Professional Geographer, Vol. 6,
         No. 5, pp. 6-15.

G-226.   Fuller, G., Murton, B. and Lewis, N. D. 1984.
         "Crisis in Graduate Student Foreign Area Field
         Study," Geographical Perspectives, Vol. 53, pp.
         15-26.

G-227.   Fuller, Gary, Murton, Brian and Davis, Nancy
         Lewis. 1984. "Crisis in Graduate Student
         Foreign Area Field Study," Geographical
         Perspectives, No. 53, pp. 15-26.

G-228.   Fuson, Robert H. 1959. "Toward a Geographic
         Orientation of America's Geography Departments,"
         Journal of Geography, Vol. 58, pp. 243-245.

G-229.   Fyson, A. 1979. "Environmental Education:
         Swinging Geography," Town and Country Planning,
         Vol. 48, pp. 99-100.

G-230.   Gade, Daniel W. 1983. "Foreign Languages and
         American Geography," Professional Geographer,
         Vol. 35, pp. 261-266.

G-231.   Gaile, Gary L. 1985. "Rankling at Rankings,"
         Professional Geographer, Vol. 37, pp. 62.

G-232.   Gananathan, V. S. 1951. "The Evaluation of a
         Good Geography Graduate," Geographer, Vol. 4, No.
         2, pp. 35-40.

G-233.   Garnett, Alice. 1983. "I.B.G.: the Formative
         Years -- Some Reflections," Transactions -
         Institute of British Geographers, Vol. 8, pp.
         27-35.

G-234.   Garnier, B. J. 1947. "The New Zealand
         Geographical Society: Its Progress and Purpose,"
         New Zealand Geographer, Vol. 3, pp. 151-160.

G-235.   Garofaco, Donald and Nichols, David A. 1984.
         "The Role of the Geographer on Multidisciplinary
         Resource Surveys," Professional Geographer, Vol.
         36, pp. 362-366.

G-236.   Garrison, William L. 1979. "Playing with
         Ideas," Annals of the Association of American
         Geographers, Vol. 69, pp. 118-120.

G-237.   Gatrell, Anthony C. and Smith, Anthony. 1984.
         "Networks of Relations among a Set of
         Geographical Journals," Professional Geographer,
         Vol. 36, pp. 300-307.

G-238.   Gault, F. B.   1899.   "A Geographical Retrospect,"
         Education, Vol. 20, pp. 95-99.

G-239.   Geddes, Patrick. 1902. "Note on a Draft Plan
         for Institute of Geography," Scottish
         Geographical Magazine, Vol. 18, pp. 142-144.

G-240.   Geddes, Professor. 1903. "A Naturalists'
         Society and Its Work," Scottish Geographical
         Magazine, Vol. 19, pp. 89-95, 141-147.

G-241.   Gentilli, J. 1971. "A Statistical View of
         Australian Geographers," Australian Geographical
         Studies, Vol. 9, pp. 177-184.

G-242.   George, P. 1984. "La 'Geographie Active'
         Reflexions sur les Responsibili- ties de
         Geographes.' (On 'active geography.' Reflections
         on the responsibility of geographers)," Herodote,
         Vol. 33-34, pp. 213-221.

G-243.   Gerald, Albert C. and Warman, Henry J. 1954.
         "Most Cited Periodicals in Geography,"
         Professional Geographer, Vol. 6, No. 2, pp. 6-13.

G-244.   Gerasimov, I. P. 1963. "Scientific Results of
         the Trip of the Delegation of Soviet Geographers
         to the United States," Soviet Geography: Review
         and Translation, Vol. 4, No. 2, pp. 39-44.

G-245.   Gerasimov, I. P. 1964. "Comments," [on
         geography] Soviet Geography: Review and
         Translation, Vol. 5, pp. 73-76.

G-246.   Gerasimov, I. P. 1965. "Has Geography
         'Disappeared?" Soviet Geography: Review and
         Translation, Vol. 6, pp. 38-41.

G-247.   Gerasimov, I. P. 1966. "The Past and the Future
         of Geography," Soviet Geography: Review and
         Translation, Vol. 7, pp. 3-15.

G-248.   Gerasimov, I. P. 1978. "Scientific Results and
         Organizational Lessions of the 23rd International
         Geographical Congress," Soviet Geography: Review
         and Translation, Vol. 19, pp. 435-442.

G-249.   Gerenchuk, K. I. 1979. "Results of a Soviet
         Symposium on Theoretical Aspects of Geography,"
         Soviet Geography: Review and Translation, Vol.
         20, pp. 329-331.

G-250.   Gerlach, Jerry. 1976. "Is There a Ph.D. Surplus
         in Geography?" Virginia Geographer, Vol. 11, pp.
         3-5.

G-251.   Gerlach, Jerry D. 1979. "The Origins of
          Professional Geographers in the United States,"
          Professional Geographer, Vol. 31, pp. 212-216.

G-252.   Gibbs, David. 1907. "The Pedagogy of
          Geography," Pedagogical Seminary, Vol. 14, pp.
          39-100.

G-253.   Gibson, Edward M. 1986. "Where is Here? The
          Uses of Geography in English-Canadian
          Literature," B.C. Geographical Series, No. 37,
          pp. 132-149.

G-254.   Gibson, Lyle E. 1966. "Planning Geography in
          the Curriculum of a New College," California
          Geographer, Vol. 7, pp. 13-18.

G-255.   Gillmor, Desmond. 1978. "Geographic Education
          in the Republic of Ireland," Journal of
          Geography, Vol. 77, pp. 103-107.

G-256.   Gilman, Daniel C. 1873. "The Last Ten Years of
          Geographical Work in this Country," Journal of
          the American Geographical Society of New York,
          Vol. 3, pp. 111-133.

G-257.   Gilman, Daniel C. 1874. "Geographical Work in
          the United States During 1871," Journal of the
          American Geographical Society of New York, Vol.
          4, pp. 119-144.

G-258.   Ginsburg, Norton. 1972. "The Mission of a
          Scholarly Society," Professional Geographer, Vol.
          24, pp. 1-6.

G-259.   Gold, John R. 1977. "Teaching Behavioral
          Geography," Journal of Geography in Higher
          Education, Vol. 1, pp. 37-46.

G-260.   Goldie, Rt. Hon. Sir George Taubman. 1906.
          "Address to the Royal Geographical Society,
          1906," Geographical Journal, Vol. 28, pp. 1-7.

G-261.   Goldie, Rt. Hon. Sir George Taubman. 1906.
          "Twenty-five Years' Geographical Progress,"
          Geographical Journal, Vol. 28, pp. 377-384.

G-262.   Goldie, Rt. Hon. Sir George Taubman. 1907.
          "Geography and the Civil Services," Geographical
          Journal, Vol. 30, pp. 1-6.

G-263.   Goldie, Rt. Hon. Sir George Taubman. 1908.
          "Address to the Royal Geographical Society,
          1908," Geographical Journal, Vol. 32, pp. 1-6.

G-264.   Golledge, Reginald G. 1979. "The Development of
          Geographical Analysis," Annals of the Association
          of American Geographers, Vol. 69, pp. 151-154.

G-265.   Golledge, Reginald G. and William C. Halperin.
         1983. "On the Status of Women in Geography,"
         Professional Geographer, Vol. 35, pp. 214-218.

G-266.   Goodchild, Michael F. 1986. "The Issue of
         Professional Standing in Geography," Ontario
         Geography, No. 27, pp. 5-13.

G-267.   Goodchild, Michael F. and Janelle, Donald G.
         1988. "Specialization in the Structure and
         Organization of Geography," Annals of the
         Association of American Geographers, Vol. 78, pp.
         1-28.

G-268.   Goode, J. Paul. 1903. "Geographical Societies
         of America," Journal of Geography, Vol. 2, pp.
         343-350.

G-269.   Goode, J. Paul. 1919. "What the War Should Do
         for Our Methods in Geography," Journal of
         Geography, Vol. 18, pp. 179-185.

G-270.   Goodenough, Admiral Sir William. 1932. "Address
         at the Annual General Meeting," Geographical
         Journal, Vol. 80, pp. 97-101.

G-271.   Goodenough, Admiral Sir William. 1933. "Address
         at the Annual General Meeting," Geographical
         Journal, Vol. 82, pp. 97-103.

G-272.   Goodey, Brian. 1985. "Rescue Geography:
         Specific Actions," [comment] Area, Vol. 17, pp.
         55-57.

G-273.   Goodridge, J. C. 1978. "Environmental
         Science/Studies," Area, Vol. 10, pp. 315-317.

G-274.   Gordon, Marvin F. and Fonseca, James W. 1980.
         "Geography in the Federal Government,"
         Geographical Survey, Vol. 9, No. 3, pp. 3-15.

G-275.   Gould, Peter. 1980. "What is Worth Teaching in
         Geography?" Journal of Geography, Vol. 1, pp.
         20-36.

G-276.   Gould, Peter. 1981. "Beginning Geography: A
         Human and Technical Perspective," Journal of
         Geography in Higher Education, Vol. 5, pp. 45-52.

G-277.   Graves, N. J. 1978. "Changes in Attitude
         Towards the Training of Teachers in Geography,"
         Geography, Vol. 63, pp. 75-84.

G-278.   Graves, N. J. 1979. "Contrasts and
         Contradictions in Geographical Education,"
         Geography, Vol. 64, pp. 259-267.

G-279.   Graves, N. J. 1980. "Geographical Education in Britain," Progress in Human Geography, Vol. 4, pp. 560-567.

G-280.   Graves, N. J. 1981. "Geographical Education," Progress in Human Geography, Vol. 5, pp. 562-571.

G-281.   Graves, N. J. 1981. "International Aspects of Geographical Education," Journal of Geography, Vol. 80, pp. 84-86.

G-282.   Gray, Fred. 1976. "Radical Geography and the Study of Education," Antipode Vol. 8, pp. 38-44.

G-283.   Green, F. H. W. 1982. "Observation: Fifty Years of the IBG," Area, Vol. 14, pp. 319-321.

G-284.   Greenough, G. B. 1840. "Address at the Anniversary Meeting, 25th May, 1840," Journal of Royal Geographical Society of London, Vol. 10, pp. xliii-lxxxv.

G-285.   Greenough, G. B. 1841. "Address at the Anniversary Meeting, May 24, 1841," Journal of Royal Geographical Society of London, Vol. 11, pp. xxxix-lxxvii.

G-286.   Gregory, Derek. 1981. "Human Agency and Human Geography," Transactions - Institute of British Geographers, Vol. 6, pp. 1-18.

G-287.   Gregory, Nicky. 1983. "Training in Human Geography," Area, Vol. 15, pp. 45-47.

G-288.   Gregory, S. 1974. "The Geographer and Natural Resources Research," South African Geographer, Vol. 4, pp. 371-382.

G-289.   Gregory, S. 1983. "Quantitative Geography: The British Experience and the Role of the Institute," Transactions - Institute of British Geographers, Vol. 8, pp. 80-89.

G-290.   Gregory, Stanley. 1978. "Objectives and Methods in our Statistical Teaching," Journal of Geography in Higher Education, Vol. 63, pp. 251-264.

G-291.   Gregory, Stanley. 1978. "The Role of Physical Geography in the Curriculum," Geography, Vol. 63, pp. 251-264.

G-292.   Grosvenor, G. H. 1912. "Progress in Geography," Chatauquan, Vol. 41, pp. 148-158.

G-293.   Grosvenor, G. M. 1984. "The Society and the Discipline," Professional Geographer, Vol. 36, pp. 413-418.

G-294.   Grosvenor, Gilbert M.   1985.   "The Society and
          the Discipline,"   Journal of Geography, Vol. 84,
          pp. 52-55.

G-295.   Grosvenor, Gilbert M.   1985.   "What Happens When
          America Flunks Geography," Vital Speeches of the
          Day, Vol. 51, pp. 533-535 [July 15].

G-296.   Guelke, Leonard.   1983.   "Scholarship in
          Geography: An Intellectual Challenge,"
          Professional Geographer, Vol. 35, pp. 336-338.

G-297.   Hägerstrand, Torsten.   1982.   "Proclamations
          About Geography from the Pioneering Years in
          Sweden," Geografiska Annaler, Vol. 64B, pp.
          119-125.

G-298.   Haigh, Martin J.   1987.   "Citation Levels in
          Geography," Area, Vol. 19, pp. 169-170.

G-299.   Hall, Peter.   1981.   "The Geographer and
          Society," Geographical Journal, Vol. 147, pp.
          154-152.

G-300.   Hall, Peter, et al.   1987.   "Horizons and
          Opportunities in Research," Area, Vol. 19, pp.
          266-272.

G-301.   Hall, Robin.   1980.   "Teaching Humanistic
          Geography," Australian Geographer, Vol. 14, pp.
          7-14.

G-302.   Hall, R.   1982.   "Commentary: Theory and
          Practice in Geographical Education," Australian
          Geographical Studies, Vol. 20, pp. 122-128.

G-303.   Hamill, Louis.   1964.   "The Training of
          Geographers for Business," Canadian Geographer,
          Vol. 8, pp. 42-45.

G-304.   Hamilton, W. R.   1838.   "Address at the
          Anniversary Meeting, May 15, 1838," Journal of
          the Royal Geographical Society of London, Vol. 8,
          pp. xxxvii-lxi.

G-305.   Hamilton, W. R.   1839.   "Address at the
          Anniversary Meeting, May 27, 1839," Journal of
          the Royal Geographical Society of London, Vol. 9,
          pp. xlvii-lxxxvi.

G-306.   Hamilton, William Richard.   1843.   "Address to
          the Royal Geographical Society of London,"
          Journal of the Royal Geographical Society of
          London, Vol. 13, pp. xli-cv.

G-307.   Hansen, Walter.   1928.   "Suggestions for Writing
          Geographic Principles," Journal of Geography,
          Vol. 27, p. 219.

G-308.   Hanson, Susan. 1988. "Soaring," _Professional Geographer_, Vol. 40, pp. 4-7.

G-309.   Harkema, Roll C. 1971. "School Geography in Developing Nations," _Journal of Geography_, Vol. 70, pp. 71-72.

G-310.   Harris, Chauncy D. 1959. "English, French, German, and Russian as Supplementary Languages in Geographical Serials," _Geographical Review_, Vol. 49, pp. 397-405.

G-311.   Harris, Chauncy D. 1979. "Geography at Chicago in the 1930s and 1940s," _Annals of the Association of American Geographers_, Vol. 69, pp. 21-32.

G-312.   Harris, Chauncy D. and Fellmann, Jerome D. 1950. "Geographical Serials," _Geographical Review_, Vol. 40, pp. 649-656.

G-313.   Harris, Chauncy D. and Fellmann, Jerome D. 1961. "Current Geographical Serials," _Geographical Review_, Vol. 40, pp. 649-656.

G-314.   Harris, Chauncy D. and Fellmann, Jerome D. 1973. "Current Geographical Serials, 1970," _Geographical Review_, Vol. 63, pp. 99-105.

G-315.   Harris, F. D. 1935. "The Claims of Geography to be Considered as a Science, and Consequent Implications as to Methods of Teaching the Subject," _Geography_, Vol. 20, No. 107, pp. 38-46.

G-316.   Hart, J. F. 1979. "The 1950's," _Annals of the Association of American Geographers_, Vol. 69, pp. 109-114.

G-317.   Hart, J. F. 1982. "The Highest Form of the Geographer's Art," _Annals of the Association of American Geographers_, Vol. 72, pp. 1-30.

G-318.   Hart, John Fraser. 1976. "Ruminations of a Dyspeptic Ex-Editor," _Professional Geographer_, Vol. 28, pp. 225-232.

G-319.   Hart, John Fraser. 1982. "A Reply," [to Golledge, et al.] _Annals of the Association of American Geographers_, Vol. 72, pp. 559.

G-320.   Hart, John Fraser. 1983. "More Gnashing of False Teeth," _Annals of the Association of American Geographers_, Vol. 73, pp. 441-443.

G-321.   Hausladen, Gary and Wyckoff, William. 1985.
         "Our Discipline's Demographic Futures:
         Retirements, Vacancies, and Appointment
         Priorities," Professional Geographer, Vol. 37,
         pp. 339-343.

G-322.   Hawley, Claude E. and Dexter, Lewis A. 1952. "A
         Basis for Studying the Supply of Geographers,"
         Journal of Geography, Vol. 51, pp. 163-164.

G-323.   Hay, A. M. 1985. "Some Differences in Citation
         Between Articles Based on Thesis Work and Those
         Written by Established Researchers: Human
         Geography in the UK, 1974-84," Social Science
         Information Studies, Vol. 5, pp. 81-85.

G-324.   Heiges, Harvey E. 1976. "Academics and
         Practical Geographic Training," Geographical
         Survey, Vol. 5, No. 3, pp. 3-6.

G-325.   Heiges, Harvey E. 1979. "Development of a
         Student Internship Programme," Journal of
         Geography in Higher Education, Vol. 3, pp. 29-39.

G-326.   Helburn, Nicholas. 1962. "On Levels of Regional
         Specialization," Professional Geographer, Vol.
         14, No. 6, pp. 14-16.

G-327.   Helleiner, F. M. 1977. "Careers for
         Geographers: The Case of Ontario 1953 to 1972,"
         Canadian Geographer, Vol. 21, pp. 182-189.

G-328.   Henderson, H. C. K. 1968. "Geography's Balance
         Sheet," Transactions - Institute of British
         Geographers, No. 45, pp. 1-10.

G-329.   Herbert, Francis. 1983. "The Royal Geographical
         Society's Membership, the Map Trade, and
         Geographical Publishing in Britain 1830 to c.
         1930: An Introductory Essay with Listing of Some
         250 Fellows in Related Professions," Imago Mundi,
         Vol. 35, pp. 67-95.

G-330.   Herman, Theodore. 1960. "Undergraduate
         Preparation for a Planning Career," Professional
         Geographer, Vol. 12, pp. 10-12.

G-331.   Hewes, Leslie. 1954. "The Graduate Student in
         Geography," Professional Geographer, Vol. 6, No.
         3, pp. 13-19.

G-332.   Hewland, J. L. 1965. "A Century of Geography
         Texts," New Zealand Geographer, Vol. 21, pp.
         156-167.

G-333.   Hickox, David H. 1984. "Rank and Distinction in
         Geography," Transition, Vol. 14, No. 1, pp.
         18-19.

G-334.   Hills, Major E. H.   1908.   "The Present and
         Future Work of the Geographer," Geographical
         Journal, Vol. 32, pp. 390-405.

G-335.   Hines, Howard H.   1977.   "Trends in Geographical
         Research and the Role of the National Science
         Foundation in Assisting Geographical Research,"
         Geographical Survey, Vol. 6, No. 1, pp. 11-17.

G-336.   Hoffman, P. P. and Kamerling, D. S.   1979.
         "Comparative Geography of Higher Education in the
         U.S. and the U.S.S.R.:   An Initial Investiga-
         tion," Soviet Geography: Review and Translation,
         Vol. 20, pp. 412-439.

G-337.   Holdich, Colonel Sir T. H.   1902.   "Some
         Geographical Problems," Geographical Journal,
         Vol. 20, pp. 411-427.

G-338.   Holdich, Colonel Sir T. H.   1904.   "Geographical
         Research," Geographical Journal, Vol. 23, pp.
         29-32.

G-339.   Holdich, Colonel Sir Thomas.   1918.   "Address at
         the Anniversary General Meeting, 27 May 1918,"
         Geographical Journal, Vol. 52, pp. 1-12.

G-340.   Holdich, Colonel Sir Thomas.   1919.   "Address at
         the Anniversary Meeting, 2 June 1919,"
         Geographical Journal, Vol. 52, pp. 1-12.

G-341.   Holmes, E. E.   1922.   "The Kind of Geography the
         Working World Needs," Journal of Geography, Vol.
         21, pp. 72-77.

G-342.   Holmes, J. MacDonald.   1935.   "The Content of
         Geographical Study," Report, Melborne (1935)
         Meeting of the Australian and New Zealand
         Association for the Advancement of Science, pp.
         401-433.

G-343.   Hones, Gerald H. and Ryba, Raymond H.   1972.
         "Why Not a Geography of Education?" Journal of
         Geography, Vol. 71, pp. 135-139.

G-344.   Horne, William R.   1984.   "Geographers: An
         Endangered Species," Area, Vol. 16, pp. 252-254.

G-345.   Howarth, O. J. R.   1951.   "The Centenary of
         Section E. (Geography) in the British
         Association," Scottish Geographical Magazine,
         Vol. 67, pp. 145-160.

G-346.   Horvath, Ronald J., Deskins, Donald R., Jr., and
         Larimore, Ann E. 1969.   "Activity Concerning
         Black America in University Departments Graning
         M.A. and Ph.D. Degrees in Geography,"
         Professional Geographer, Vol. 21, pp. 137-139.

G-347.   Hudman, Lloyd E.   1971.   "Geographical Concepts:
         A Need to be Explicit," _Journal of Geography_,
         Vol. 71, pp. 520-525.

G-348.   Hudson, G. Donald.   1951.   "Professional Training
         of the Membership of the Association of American
         Geographers," _Annals of the Association of
         American Geographers_, Vol. 41, pp. 97-115.

G-349.   Hultquist, Nancy B.   1970.   "Quantitative
         Geography Course Offering," _Professional
         Geographer_, Vol. 22, pp. 37-40.

G-350.   Hutchinson, Captain H. B.   1948.   "Navy Interest
         in Geographic Exploration," _Annals of the
         Association of American Geographers_, Vol. 38, p.
         103.

G-351.   Hutton, J. F.   1885.   "Inaugural Address to the
         Society," _Journal of the Manchester Geographical
         Society_, Vol. 1, p. 1-6.

G-352.   Hyland, Gerry.   1970.   "Geotherapy," _Monadnock_,
         Vol. 44, pp. 56-57.

G-353.   Jackson, Peter.   1982.   "Comments on Special
         Feature on Women," _Professional Geographer_, Vol.
         34, p. 440.

G-354.   Jackson, S. P.   1969.   "Geography as
         Environmental Science and the Training of
         Geographers," _South African Geographical Journal_,
         Vol. 51, pp. 3-18.

G-355.   Jackson, S. P.   1978.   "The South African
         Geographical Society, 1917- 1977," _South African
         Geographical Journal_, Vol. 60, pp. 3-12.

G-356.   James, Preston E.   1974.   "The Association of
         American Geographers: A Summary of the Annual
         Meetings, Officers, and the Presidential
         Addresses," _Professional Geographer_, Vol. 26, pp.
         187-195.

G-357.   James, Preston E.   1974.   "The Southern Studies
         Project: A Paragraph in the History of American
         Geography," _Southeastern Geographer_, Vol. 14, pp.
         1-6.

G-358.   James, Preston E. and Martin, Geoffrey J.   1979.
         "On AAG History," _Professional Geographer_, Vol.
         31, pp. 353-357.

G-359.   Jenkins, Herman.   1972.   "Symposium: Black
         Perspectives on Geography," _Monadnock_, Vol. 46,
         pp. 55-56.

G-360.   Jennings, J. N.   1973.   "'Any Millenniums Today,
          Lady?' The Geomorphic Bandwagon Parade,"
          Australian Geographical Studies, Vol. 11, pp.
          115-130.

G-361.   Jewel, William.   1979.   "Geographic Application
          and the Geographic Practitioner," Geographical
          Perspectives, Vol. 44, pp. 37-42.

G-362.   Johnson, Brian A.   1963.   "The Use of Theoretical
          Models in Geography Teaching," Journal of
          Geography, Vol. 57, pp. 237-240.

G-363.   Johnson, H. G.   1979.   "Geography's Role in
          Alabama Education," Alabama Geographer, Vol. 11,
          p. 3.

G-364.   Johnson, H. G.   1981.   "What Future for
          Geography," Alabama Geographer, Vol. 13, p. 1.

G-365.   Johnson, Lane J.   1961.   "Some Thoughts on
          Geography of the Future," Professional
          Geographer, Vol. 13, No. 4, pp. 30-32.

G-366.   Johnson, Louise.   1985.   "Gender, Genetics and
          the Possibility of Feminist Geography,"
          Australian Geographical Studies, Vol. 23, pp.
          161-171.

G-367.   Johnston, R. J. and Brack, E. V.   1983.
          "Appointment and Promotion in the Academic Labor
          Market: A Preliminary Survey of British
          University Departments of Geography, 1933-1983,
          Transactions - Institute of British Geographers,
          Vol. 8, pp. 100-111.

G-368.   Johnston, Ron J.   1976.   "Anarchy, Conspiracy,
          Apathy: The Three 'Conditions' of Geography,"
          Area, Vol. 8, pp. 1-3.

G-369.   Johnston, Ron J.   1977.   "On Geography and the
          Organization of Education," Journal of Geography
          in Higher Education, Vol. 1, pp. 5-12.

G-370.   Johnston, Ron J.   1978.   "More on the Structure
          of British Education and the Role of Geography,"
          Journal of Geography in Higher Education, Vol. 2,
          pp. 6-13.

G-371.   Johnston, Ron J.   1980.   "After 150 Years,"
          Geographical Magazine, Vol. 52, pp. 601-603.

G-372.   Johnston, Ron J.   1981.   "Applied Geography,
          Quantitative Analysis Ideology," Applied
          Geography, Vol. 1, pp. 213-220.

G-373.   Jones, Clarence F.   1957.   "Presidents' Analysis
          of the State of the Association," _Professional
          Geographer_, Vol. 9, No. 3, pp. 16-20.

G-374.   Jones, E. Lester.   1928.   "The National
          Geographic Society," _Proceedings - Twelfth
          International Geographical Congress_, pp. 500-508.

G-375.   Jones, G. W.   1974.   "Children's Choice of
          Geography," _Geography_, Vol. 59, pp. 351-354.

G-376.   Jones, M.   1981.   "Putting Geography on the
          Air,"   _Teaching Geography_,   Vol. 7, pp. 29-31.

G-377.   Jones, Rodwell.   1926.   "Geography and the
          University," _Scottish Geographical Magazine_, Vol.
          42, pp. 65-77.

G-378.   Juillard, Etienne and Klein, Claude.   1980.
          "Henri Baulig, 1877-1962,"   _Geographers_:
          Biobibliographical Studies, Vol. 4, pp. 7-18.

G-379.   Jumper, Sidney R.   1975.   "Going to the Well,"
          Professional Geographer, Vol. 27, pp. 419-425.

G-380.   Jumper, Sidney R.   1984.   "A Call for Strong
          State Geographical Societies," _Journal of
          Geography_, Vol. 83, pp. 263-264.

G-381.   Jumper, Sidney R.   1984.   "Departmental
          Relationships and Images Within the University,"
          Journal of Geography in Higher Education, Vol. 8,
          pp. 41-48.

G-382.   Jumper, Sidney R. and Harrison, Ivar Glen.
          1986.   "Characteristics of the AAG Membership in
          1982," _Professional Geographer_, Vol. 38, pp.
          390-396.

G-383.   Kalesnik, S. V. and Gerasimov, I. P.   1965.   "The
          Geographical Society, Its Past, Present, and
          Future," _Soviet Geography_: _Review and
          Translation_, Vol. 6, pp. 3-14.

G-384.   Kalinin, G. P. and Saushkin, Yu. G.   1971.   "The
          Present Level of Candidates and Doctoral
          Dissertations in Geography and Ways of Improving
          Them," _Soviet Geography_: _Review and Translation_,
          Vol. 12, pp. 611-615.

G-385.   Kay, Jeanne.   1982.   "Comments on Status-of-Women
          Measures,"   _Professional Geographer_, Vol. 34, pp.
          438-449.

G-386.   Kay, Jeanne.   1982.   "Job Sharing in Geography,"
          Transition, Vol. 12, pp. 19-22.

G-387.   Kedleston, Rt. Hon. Earl Curzon of. 1912.
          "Address to the Royal Geographical Society,"
          Geographical Journal, Vol. 40, pp. 1-8.

G-388.   Kedleston, Rt. Hon. Earl Curzon of. 1913.
          "Address to the Royal Geographical Society,"
          Geographical Journal, Vol. 42, pp. 1-8.

G-389.   Kedleston, Rt. Hon. Earl Curzon of. 1914.
          "Address to the Royal Geographical Society,"
          Geographical Journal, Vol. 44, pp. 1-12.

G-390.   Keltie, J. Scott. 1897. "Address to the
          Geographical Section of the British Association,"
          Scottish Geographical Magazine, Vol. 13, pp.
          449-466.

G-391.   Keltie, J. Scott. 1897. "Some Geographical
          Problems," Geographical Journal, Vol. 10, pp.
          308-323.

G-392.   Keltie, J. Scott. 1915. "A Half-Century of
          Geographical Progress," Scottish Geographical
          Magazine, Vol. 31, pp. 617-636.

G-393.   Keltie, J. Scott. 1917. "A Half Century of
          Geographical Progress: Smithsonian Report for
          1916, Publication 2471, pp. 501-521.

G-394.   Keltie, J. Scott. 1917. "Thirty Years' Work of
          the Royal Geographical Society," Geographical
          Journal, Vol. 47, pp. 350-376.

G-395.   Kemp, Richard. 1979. "Editorial: The
          Geographer's Contribution," Teaching Geography,
          Vol. 5, pp. 50-52.

G-396.   Kennamer, Lorrin G., Jr. 1968. "The National
          Council for Geographic Education: Purpose and
          Perspective," Journal of Geography, Vol. 67, pp.
          288-292.

G-397.   Kent, R. B. 1982. "Academic Geographer/
          Cartographers in the U.S.: Their Training and
          Professional Activity in Cartography," American
          Cartographer, Vol. 7, pp. 59-66.

G-398.   Kermea, T. 1974. "Human Geography Research and
          Postgraduate Training in Further Education: The
          Role of the SSRC," Area, Vol. 6, pp. 24-28.

G-399.   Khan, Sharafat and Vuicich, George. 1984.
          "Effective Leadership in Geography: The Role of
          the Department Chairperson," Professional
          Geographer, Vol. 36, pp. 158-164.

G-400.   Kimble, George H. T.   1964.   "The United States
         Geography Project of the Twentieth Century Fund,"
         Annals of the Association of American
         Geographers, Vol. 54, pp. 19-23.

G-401.   Kirwan, L. P.   1964.   "The R. G. S. and British
         Exploration: A Review of Recent Trends,"
         Geographical Journal, Vol. 130, pp. 221-225.

G-402.   Kish, George.   1964.   "Mirror for the American
         Geographer," Professional Geographer, Vol. 16,
         No. 1, pp. 1-5.

G-403.   Kissling, C. C.   1984.   "Guest Editorial:
         Membership Blues," Australian Geographical
         Studies, Vol. 22, pp. 304-305.

G-404.   Kniffen, Fred B.   1983.   "On Becoming a
         Geographer," Journal of Geography, Vol. 82, pp.
         48-49.

G-405.   Knight, Peter G.   1986.   "Why Doesn't Geography
         Do Something," Area, Vol. 18, pp. 333-334.

G-406.   Knight, Peter G.   1987.   "The Relationship
         Between Teaching and Research," Area, Vol. 19,
         pp. 350-352.

G-407.   Knopp, Lawrence and Lauria, Mickey.   1987.
         "Gender Relations and Social Relations,"
         Antipode, Vol. 19, pp. 48-53.

G-408.   Knos, Duane C.   1977.   "Problems of Education in
         Geography," Journal of Geography, Vol. 1, pp.
         13-19.

G-409.   Koelsch, W. A.   1981.   "Better Than Thou: The
         Rating of Geography Departments in the U.S.,
         1924-80," Journal of Geography, Vol. 80, pp.
         164-169.

G-410.   Konstantinov, O. A.   1971.   "125 Years of the
         Geographical Society U.S.S.R.," Soviet
         Geography: Review and Translation, Vol. 12, pp.
         226-239.

G-411.   Konstantinov, O. A.   1980.   "The 1929 Meeting of
         Soviet Geography Teachers: A Key Event in the
         History of Soviet Economic Geography," Soviet
         Geography: Review and Translation, Vol. 21, pp.
         427-439.

G-412.   Lacoste, S.   1984.   "Editorial: les geographes,
         l'action et le politique," [Geographers, action
         and politics] Herodote, pp. 3-32 [English
         summary].

G-413.   Larimore, Ann E., Scott, Earl P. and Deskins,
          Donald R.. 1969. "Geographic Activity at
          Predominately Negro Colleges and Universities: A
          Survey," Professional Geographer, Vol. 21, pp.
          140-144.

G-414.   Larkham, Peter J. 1987. "Geographical
          Literature Undergound," Area, Vol. 19, pp.
          321-326.

G-415.   Larkin, Robert. 1980. "Learning Through
          Teaching," Journal of Geography in Higher
          Education, Vol. 4, pp. 33-34.

G-416.   LaValle, Placido, et al. 1967. "Certain Aspects
          of the Expansion of Quantitative Methodology in
          American Geography," Annals of the Association of
          American Geographers, Vol. 57, pp. 423-426.

G-417.   Law, B. C. 1941. "Geography in National Life,"
          Geographical Review of India, Vol. 3, No. 3, N.P.

G-418.   Lawton, R. 1978. "Changes in University
          Geography," Geography, Vol. 63, pp. 1-13.

G-419.   Lawton, R. 1980. "Career Opportunities for
          Geographers," Geography, Vol. 65, pp. 236-247.

G-420.   Leach, Bridget. 1974. "Race, Problems and
          Geography," Transactions - Institute of British
          Geographers, Vol. 63, pp. 41-47.

G-421.   Leacock, S. 1943. "Plea for Geographical
          Science," Queen's Quarterly, Vol. 50, pp. 1-13.

G-422.   Lee, D. R. and Evans, A. S. 1985. "Reply to
          Comments on American Geographers' Ranking of
          American Geography Journals," Professional
          Geographer, Vol. 37, pp. 62-63.

G-423.   Lee, David. 1973. "Existentialsim in Geographic
          Education," Journal of Geography, Vol. 73, pp.
          13-19.

G-424.   Lee, David. 1984. "Women and Geography, 1984:
          A Bibliography," Transition, Vol. 14, No. 4, pp.
          20-26.

G-425.   Lee, David and Evans, Arthur. 1984. "American
          Geographers' Rankings of American Geography
          Journals," Professional Geographer, Vol. 36, pp.
          292-300.

G-426.   Lee, David and Evans, Arthur. 1985.
          "Geographers' Rankings of Foreign Geography and
          Non-Geography Journals," Professional Geographer,
          Vol. 37, pp. 396-402.

G-427.   Lee, David R. 1978.   "Feminist Approaches in
          Teaching Geography," Journal of Geography, Vol.
          77, pp. 180-183.

G-428.   Lee, Roger. 1985.   "Where Have All the
          Geographers Gone," Geography,   Vol. 70, pp.
          45-59.

G-429.   LeHeron, R. B. and Williams, D. B. 1980.   "Which
          School Geography Would the Consumers' Institute
          Approve," New Zealand Journal of Geography, Vol.
          68, pp. 2-3.

G-430.   Leigh, Myee D. 1980.   "The Manchester
          Geographical Society: 1884-1979," Manchester
          Geographer, Vol. 1, pp. 7-14.

G-431.   Leighly, John. 1979.   "Drifting into Geography
          in the Twenties," Annals of the Association of
          American Geographers, Vol. 69, pp. 4-8.

G-432.   Lemon, Jim. 1979.   "Reflections on Work
          Experience and Community," Journal of Geography
          in Higher Education, Vol. 3, pp. 24-28.

G-433.   Leng, Karl. 1978.   "The Berlin Geographical
          Society, 1828-1978," Geographical Journal, Vol.
          144, pp. 218-223.

G-434.   Lentz, Peggy. 1980.   "High-Priority Research
          Areas in HUD's Office of Policy Development and
          Research," Professional Geographer, Vol. 32, pp.
          205-208.

G-435.   Lewis, Lawrence T. 1974.   "The Geography of
          Black America: The Growth of the Subdiscipline,"
          Journal of Geography, Vol. 73, pp. 38-43.

G-436.   Lewis, Peirce and Zelinsky, Wilbur. 1987.   "The
          Coffee Hour at Penn State," Professional
          Geographer, Vol. 39, pp. 75-79.

G-437.   Libbe, Michael. 1980.   "Geographic Research and
          Women," Transition, Vol. 9, pp. 2-5.

G-438.   Libbe, Michael. 1982.   "Problems Encountered by
          Women in Completing Graduate School,"
          Transition, Vol. 11, No. 1, pp. 12-14.

G-439.   Libbe, Michael and Wilbanks, Thomas. 1982.
         "Program Evaluation as a Strategy for Program
         Enhancement," Professional Geographer, Vol. 34,
         pp. 381-387.

G-440.   Lier, John. 1983. "The Reticent Geographer, The
         Popular Image, and Pre- University Education:
         Perceptions From a Recent Inter-Disciplinary
         Conference," California Geographer, Vol. 23, pp.
         1-13.

G-441.   Lier, John. 1984. "Comments on Industry-
         Government-Academic Cooperation," Professional
         Geographer, Vol. 36, pp. 219-221.

G-442.   Light, Richard U. 1948. "A Library for
         Geographers," Geographical Review, Vol. 38, pp.
         523-525.

G-443.   Lindsay, Sir Harry. 1949. "Address at the
         Annual General Meeting," Geographical Journal,
         Vol. 113, pp. 1-6.

G-444.   Lindsay, Sir Harry. 1950. "Address at the
         Annual General Meeting, [Geography: Scope and
         Pattern]," Geographical Journal, Vol. 116, pp.
         1-6.

G-445.   Little, H. P. 1922. "Geography as a
         Profession," Science, Vol. 55, No. 1423, pp.
         319-321.

G-446.   Livingstone, D. N. and Harrison, R. T. 1981.
         "Hunting the Snark: Perspectives on Geographical
         Investigation," Geografiska Annaler, Vol.63B, pp.
         69-72.

G-447.   Lloyd, Trevor. 1959. "The Geographer as
         Citizen," Canadian Geographer, No. 13, pp. 1-13.

G-448.   Lochhead, E. N. 1984. "The Royal Scottish
         Geographical Society: The Setting and Sources of
         Its Success," Scottish Geographical Magazine,
         Vol. 100, pp. 69-80.

G-449.   Logsdon, John W. 1963. "We Are Selling
         Geography?" Journal of Geography, Vol. 62, pp.
         361-365.

G-450.   Lounsbury, John F. 1968. "College Geography in
         the United States," Journal of Geography, Vol.
         67, pp. 282-287.

G-451.   Lowenthal, David. 1960. "In Defense of the Name
         Geography," Professional Geographer, Vol. 12, No.
         4, pp. 11-12.

G-452.   Lukerman, F. 1964. "Geography as a Formal
         Intellectual Discipline and the Way in Which It
         Contributes to Human Knowledge," Canadian
         Geographer, Vol. 8, pp. 167-172.

G-453.   Lyde, L. W. and Hosgood, B. 1926. "Geography at
         the Imperial Institute," Geographical Journal,
         Vol. 68, pp. 418-427.

G-454.   Lyons, Major H. G. 1915. "The Importance of
         Geographical Research," Geographical Journal,
         Vol. 46, pp. 254-269.

G-455.   Macalla, Robert J. 1983. "On Running Harder:
         Some Reflections From a Geography Dept.
         Chairperson," Operational Geographer, No. 2, pp.
         23-25.

G-456.   Mackenzie, Sir Leslie. 1932. "A Health
         Administrator's Attitude To Geography,"
         Geography, Vol. 17, pp. 1-10.

G-457.   Mackinder, H. J. 1895. "Address to the
         Geography Section of the British Association,"
         Scottish Geographical Magazine, Vol. 11, pp.
         497-511.

G-458.   Mackinder, H. J. et al. 1893. "Reports on
         Geography at the Universities," Geographical
         Journal, Vol. 2, pp. 25-28.

G-459.   Mackinder, Rt.-Hon. Sir Halford. 1935.
         "Progress of Geography in the Field and in the
         Study During the Reign of His Majesty King George
         the Fifth," Geographical Journal, Vol. 86, pp.
         1-17.

G-460.   Manson, G. 1981. "Notes on the Status of
         Geography in American Schools," Journal of
         Geography, Vol. 80, pp. 244-248.

G-461.   Marcus, Melvin G. 1978. "The Association of
         American Geographers: Planning for the Future,"
         Professional Geographer, Vol. 30, pp. 113-122.

G-462.   Marcus, Melvin G. 1979. "Coming Full Circle:
         Physical Geography in the Twentieth Century,"
         Annals of the Association of American
         Geographers, Vol. 69, pp. 521-532.

G-463.   Markham, Clements R. 1880. "The Fifty Years
         Work of the Royal Geographical Society," Royal
         Geographical Society Journal, Vol. 50, pp. 1-126.

G-464.   Markham, Clements R. 1893. "The Present
         Standpoint of Geography," Geographical Journal,
         Vol. 2, pp. 481-505.

G-465.   Markham, Clements R.   1894.   "Address to the
          Royal Geographical Society," Geographical
          Journal, Vol. 4, pp. 1-26.

G-466.   Markham, Clements R.   1895.   "Address to the
          Royal Geographical Society," Geographical
          Journal, Vol. 6, pp. 1-22.

G-467.   Markham, Sir Clements.   1896.   "Address to the
          Royal Geographical Society," Geographical
          Journal, Vol. 8, pp. 1-15.

G-468.   Markham, Sir Clements.   1897.   "Anniversary
          Address, 1897," Geographical Journal, Vol. 9, pp.
          589-604.

G-469.   Markham, Sir Clements R.   1898.   "Anniversary
          Address, 1898," Geographical Journal, Vol. 12,
          pp. 1-10.

G-470.   Markham, Sir Clements R.   1898.   "The Field of
          Geography," Geographical Journal, Vol. 11, pp.
          1-15.

G-471.   Markham, Sir Clements.   1899.   "Address to the
          Royal Geographical Society," Geographical
          Journal, Vol. 14, pp. 1-14.

G-472.   Markham, Sir Clements R.   1899.   "The Presidents
          Opening Address Session 1898-99," Geographical
          Journal, Vol. 13, pp. 1-17.

G-473.   Markham, Sir Clements R.   1900.   "Address to the
          Royal Geographical Society," Geographical
          Journal, Vol. 16, pp. 1-14.

G-474.   Markham, Sir Clements R.   1901.   "Address to the
          Royal Geographical Society," Geographical
          Journal, Vol. 18, pp. 1-13.

G-475.   Markham, Sir Clements R.   1901.   "Address to the
          Royal Geographical Society," Scottish
          Geographical Magazine, Vol. 17, pp. 337-347.

G-476.   Markham, Sir Clements R.   1902.   "Address to the
          Royal Geographical Society," Geographical
          Journal, Vol. 20, pp. 1-13.

G-477.   Markham, Sir Clements R.   1903.   "Address to the
          Royal Geographical Society," Geographical
          Journal, Vol. 22, pp. 1-13.

G-478.   Markham, Sir Clements R.   1904.   "Address to the
          Royal Geographical Society," Geographical
          Journal, Vol. 24, pp. 1-17.

G-479.   Markham, Sir Clements R.   1905.   "Address to the
          Royal Geographical Society, 1905," Geographical
          Journal, Vol. 26, pp. 1-28.

G-480.   Markham, Sir Clements R.   1905.   "The Sphere and
          Uses of Geography," Geographical Journal, Vol.
          26, pp. 593-604.

G-481.   Markham, Sir Clements R.   1908.   "Admiral Sir
          Leopald M'Clintoch K. C. B.," Geographical
          Journal, Vol. 31, pp. 1-12.

G-482.   Marotz, Glen A.   1983.   "Industry-Government-
          Academic Cooperation: Possible Benefits for
          Geography," Professional Geographer, Vol. 35, pp.
          407-416.

G-483.   Marston, Sallie A.   1986.   "Putting Women on the
          Agenda: A New Perspective for Geographers,"
          Urban Resources, Vol. 3, pp. 60-62.

G-484.   Martin, Geoffrey J.   1985.   "Preservation of the
          History of Geography," Journal of Geography, Vol.
          84, pp. 186-188.

G-485.   Martinson, Tom L.   1980.   "Editing for the
          Geographical Survey, 1975-1980," Geographical
          Survey, Vol. 9, No. 4, pp. 3-7.

G-486.   Mayer, H. M.   1979.   "Urban Geography and Chicago
          in Retrospect," Annals of the Association of
          American Geographers, Vol. 69, pp. 114-118.

G-487.   McBoyle, G.   1983.   "The Operational Geographer:
          An Appropriate Training," Operational Geographer,
          No. 2, pp. 26-29.

G-488.   McCarty, Harold H.   1979.   "Geography at Iowa,"
          Annals of the Association of American
          Geographers, Vol. 69, pp. 121-123.

G-489.   McConnell, R. J.   1979.   "The Geography Teacher
          and Outdoor Education," New Zealand Journal of
          Geography, Vol. 66, pp. 9-12.

G-490.   McCune, Shannon.   1947.   "Geographical Journals
          in Asia," Professional Geographer, Vol. 6, pp.
          35-36.

G-491.   McCune, Shannon.   1948.   "The Training of Foreign
          Geographers in the United States," Professional
          Geographer, Vol. 8, pp. 1-3.

G-492.   McCune, Shannon.   1949.   "The Geographic
          Profession in Asia," Annals of the Association of
          American Geographers, Vol. 39, pp. 62-63.

G-493.   McCune, Shannon. 1960.   "Thoughts on Reading
         Applications for Grants in Geography,"
         Professional Geographer, Vol. 12, No. 3, pp.
         11-12.

G-494.   McCune, Shannon. 1986. "The Young Geographers
         and Their Research: 1936-1943," Professional
         Geographer, Vol. 38, pp. 359-365.

G-495.   McDowell, L. 1979. "Women in British
         Geography," Area, Vol. 11, pp. 151-154.

G-496.   McDowell, Linda. 1986. "Beyond Patriarchy: A
         Class-Based Explanation of Women's
         Subordination," Antipode, Vol. 18, pp. 311-321.

G-497.   McDowell, Linda and Bowlby, Sophia. 1983.
         "Teaching Feminist Geography," Journal of
         Geography in Higher Education, Vol. 7, pp.
         97-108.

G-498.   McKee, Jesse O. 1982. "The Mississippi Council
         for Geographic Education: 1962-1982,"
         Mississippi Geographer, Vol. 10, pp. 66-68.

G-499.   McNally, Andrew, III. 1987. "'You Can't Get
         There from Here' with Today's Approach to
         Geography," Professional Geographer, Vol. 39, pp.
         389-392.

G-500.   McNee, Robert B. 1966. "The Structure of
         Geography and Its Potential Contribution to
         Generalist Education for Planning," Professional
         Geographer, Vol. 18, pp. 63-68.

G-501.   McNee, Robert B. 1968. "The Education of a
         Geographer: 1962-1967," Journal of Geography,
         Vol. 67, pp. 70-75.

G-502.   Mead, Bill. 1987. "Citation Classics and
         Citation Levels: A Further Comment," Area, Vol.
         19, pp. 168-169.

G-503.   Meir, A. 1982. "The Urgency of Teaching History
         and Philosophy of Geography," Professional
         Geographer, Vol. 34, pp. 6-10.

G-504.   Mercer, David. 1983. "Freedom of Information
         and Geographical Practice," Australian
         Geographical Studies, Vol. 21, pp. 8-32.

G-505.   Meyer, Alfred H. 1947. "A Geographic
         Classification of Geography Material as Based on
         the Dewey Classification System," Annals of the
         Association of American Geographers, Vol. 37, pp.
         209-222.

G-506.   Meyer, Alfred H.   1961.   "The Stature of
         Geography: Stake and Status," _Journal of
         Geography_, Vol. 50, pp. 301-309.

G-507.   Meyer, Alfred H.   1968.   "American Geography:
         Image and Challenge," _Journal of Geography_, Vol.
         67, pp. 460-461.

G-508.   Mikesell, Marvin W.   1979.   "The AAG at 75:
         Current Status," _Professional Geographer_, Vol.
         31, pp. 358-359.

G-509.   Mikesell, Marvin W.   1980.   "The Sixteen-Million-
         Hour Question," _Professional Geographer_, Vol. 32,
         pp. 263-268.

G-510.   Mikesell, Marvin W.   1986.   "Year One of the
         Geographical Review," _Geographical Review_, Vol.
         76, pp. 2-9.

G-511.   Mikhaylov, A. N. et al.   1976.   "Dissemination of
         Geographical Knowledge by the Geographical
         Society U.S.S.R.," _Soviet Geography: Review and
         Translation_, Vol. 16, pp. 593-604.

G-512.   Mill, Hugh Robert.   1931.   "Geography at the
         British Association: A Retrospect," _Scottish
         Geographical Magazine_, Vol. 47, pp. 336-353.

G-513.   Mill, Hugh Robert.   1933.   "The First London
         Professor of Geography," _Geographical Journal_,
         Vol. 81, pp. 536-538.

G-514.   Mill, Hugh Robert.   1934.   "Recollections of the
         Society's Early Years," _Scottish Geographical
         Magazine_, Vol. 50, pp. 269-280.

G-515.   Miller, E. Willard.   1950.   "A Short History of
         the American Society for Professional
         Geographers," _Professional Geographer_, Vol. 2,
         pp. 29-40.

G-516.   Miller, Geo. J.   1922.   "Twenty-five Years Growth
         in Collegiate Geography," _Journal of Geography_,
         Vol. 21, pp. 34-37.

G-517.   Miller, George J.   1920.   "The National Council
         of Geography Teachers," _Journal of Geography_,
         Vol. 19, pp. 69-75.

G-518.   Miller, George J.   1922.   "Twenty-five Years'
         Growth in Collegiate Geography," _Annals of the
         Association of American Geographers_, Vol. 12, pp.
         159-160.

G-519.   Miller, R.   1980.   "The Royal Geographical
         Society, 1830-1980," _Scottish Geographical
         Magazine_, Vol. 96, p. 180.

G-520.   Minkel, C. W. 1981. "Women in the Development
          of Geography in Latin America," in: Papers in
          Latin American Geography in Honor of Lucia C.
          Harrison, O. H. Horst, ed. (Conference of Latin
          Americanist Geographers, Special Publication),
          pp. 88-89.

G-521.   Mitchell, Bruce and Draper, Dianne. 1983.
          "Ethics in Geographical Research," Professional
          Geographer, Vol. 35, pp. 9-17.

G-522.   Mitchelson, Ronald L. and Hoy, Don R. 1984.
          "Problems in Predicting Graduate Student
          Success," Journal of Geography, Vol. 83, pp.
          54-57.

G-523.   Moir, Donald G. 1959. "Royal Scottish
          Geographical Society 1884-1959: Early Days of the
          Society," Scottish Geographical Magazine, Vol.
          75, pp. 131-143.

G-524.   Moles, Richard. 1977. "Geography and Values in
          Higher Education: 1," Journal of Geography in
          Higher Education, Vol. 1, pp. 13-19.

G-525.   Momsen, J. H. 1980. "Women in Canadian
          Geography," Canadian Geographer, Vol. 24, pp.
          177-183.

G-526.   Momsen, Janet Henshael. 1980. "Women in
          Canadian Geography," Professional Geographer,
          Vol. 32, pp. 365-369.

G-527.   Monk, Janice. 1983. "Integrating Women into the
          Geography Curriculum," Journal of Geography, Vol.
          82, pp. 271-273.

G-528.   Monk, Janice. 1985. "Feminist Transformation:
          How Can It Be Accomplished," Journal of
          Geography in Higher Education, Vol. 9, pp.
          101-105.

G-529.   Monk, J., and Hanson, S. 1982. "On Not
          Excluding Half of the Human in Human Geography,"
          Professional Geographer, Vol. 34, pp. 11-23.

G-530.   Monte, J. A. 1982. "My Career in Geography -
          From Academia to Private Industry," Newsletter -
          Committee on the Status of Women in Geography,
          AAG, Vol. 3, No. 4, pp. 1-3.

G-531.   Monte, Judith A. 1983. "The Job Market for
          Geographers in Private Industry in the
          Washington, D.C. Area," Professional Geographer,
          Vol. 35, pp. 90-94.

G-532.   Mookherjee, Debnath. 1968. "Membership Patterns
         of the Association of American Geographers,"
         Professional Geographer, Vol. 20, pp. 346-352.

G-533.   Moriarty, Barry M. 1965. "Current Status of
         Cartographic Education in American Colleges and
         Universities," Professional Geographer, Vol. 17,
         pp. 7-11.

G-534.   Moriarty, Barry M. 1978. "Making Employees
         Aware of the Job Skills Geographers,"
         Professional Geographer, Vol. 30, pp. 315-318.

G-535.   Moriarty, Barry M. 1983. "'Science' and the
         Funding of Geographic Research: The Pursuit of
         Reliable Knowledge," [comment] Professional
         Geographer, Vol. 35, pp. 332-336.

G-536.   Morrill, Richard L. 1977. "Geographic Scale and
         the Public Interest," Geographical Survey, Vol.
         6, No. 1, pp. 3-10.

G-537.   Morrill, Richard L. 1978. "Geography as Spatial
         Interaction," Department of Geography,
         University of North Carolina, Studies in
         Geography, Vol. 11, pp. 16-29.

G-538.   Morrill, Richard L. 1980. "Productivity of
         American Ph.D. - Granting Departments,"
         Professional Geographer, Vol. 32, pp. 85-89.

G-539.   Morrill, Richard. 1984. "The Responsibility of
         Geography," Annals of the Association of
         American Geographers, Vol. 74, pp. 1-8.

G-540.   Morrill, Richard. 1985. "Some Important
         Geographic Questions," Professional Geographer,
         Vol. 37, pp. 263-271.

G-541.   Morrisey, Mike and Barke, David. 1983.
         "Introducing Caribbean Geography," Caribbean
         Geography, Vol. 1, pp. 1-2.

G-542.   Morrison, Carolyn. 1982. "Options for Women in
         Geography: Some Experiences Shared," Canadian
         Geographer, Vol. 26, pp. 360-366.

G-543.   [Morrison, Philip S.] 1984. "Pacific Viewpoint
         - Twenty-Five Years On," Pacific Viewpoint, Vol.
         25, pp. 113-116.

G-544.   Moss, R. P. 1970. "Authority and Charisma:
         Criteria of Validity in Geographical Method,"
         South African Geographical Journal, Vol. 52, pp.
         13-37.

G-545.   Mote, Victor L.   1972.   "Sixty-Six Years of
          Presidential Addresses," <u>Professional
          Geographer</u>," Vol. 24, pp. 149-153.

G-546.   Mugerauer, R.   1984.   "Mapping the Movement of
          Geographical Inquiry: A Commentary." <u>Research
          Paper</u> - University of Chicago, Department of
          Geography, Vol. 209, pp. 235-243.

G-547.   Muir, R.   1978.   "Radical Geography or a New
          Orthodoxy?" <u>Area</u>, Vol. 10, pp. 322-327.

G-548.   Muller, J.   1953.   "History of the South African
          Geographical Society," <u>South African Geographical
          Journal</u>, Vol. 35, pp. 3-16.

G-549.   Mumford, J.   1982.   "Is the British Cartographic
          Society in the Doldrums," <u>Cartographic Journal</u>,
          Vol. 18, pp. 128-129.

G-550.   Munn, Alvin A.   1980.   "The Role of Geographers
          in the Department of Defense," <u>Professional
          Geographer</u>, Vol. 32, pp. 361-364.

G-551.   Munski, Douglas C.   1984.   "Geography Academic
          Advisors as Foreign Language and Area Studies
          Advocates," <u>Professional Geographer</u>, Vol. 36, p.
          462-464.

G-552.   Murphy, Raymond E.   1962.   "Report to the
          Profession at the Close of 1962," <u>Economic
          Geography</u>, Vol. 38, p. 283.

G-553.   Murphy, Raymond E.   1977.   "American Geography as
          I Have Known It," <u>Journal of Geography</u>, Vol. 76,
          pp. 244-249.

G-554.   Murphy, Raymond E.   1979.   "<u>Economic Geography</u>
          and Clark University," <u>Annals of the Association
          of American Geographers</u>, Vol. 69, pp. 39-41.

G-555.   Musk, L. F. and Tout, D. G.   1979.
          "Climatological Teaching in British Universities
          and Polytechnics," <u>Geography</u>, Vol. 64, pp. 21-25.

G-556.   Myers, Sarah K.   1976.   "Geography in Action: An
          Editorial," <u>Geographical Review</u>, Vol. 66, pp.
          467-468.

G-557.   Natoli, Salvatore.   1984.   "The Invisible
          Geography Teachers and the Profession,"
          <u>Professional Geographer</u>, Vol. 36, pp. 89-92.

G-558.   Natoli, Salvatore.   1986.   "The Importance of
          Redundancy and External Vigilance," <u>Professional
          Geographer</u>, Vol. 38, pp. 75-76.

G-559.   Nelson, J. G.   1977.   "The Joy of Geography,"
          Canadian Geographer, Vol. 21, pp. 303-310.

G-560.   Newbigin, Marion I.   1925.   "The Training of the
          Geographer: Actual and Ideal," Scottish
          Geographical Magazine, Vol. 41, pp. 27-37.

G-561.   Newbigin, Marion Isabel.   1934.   "The Royal
          Scottish Geographical Society: The First Fifty
          Years," Scottish Geographical Years, Vol. 50, pp.
          257-269.

G-562.   Newcomb, Robert M.   1961.   "Departmental Status
          of Geography," Professional Geographer, Vol. 13,
          No. 2, p. 41.

G-563.   Nicholson, N. L.   1957.   "The Geographical
          Branch, 1947-1957," Canadian Geographer, No. 10,
          pp. 61-68.

G-564.   Nicholson, N. L.   1959.   "Canada and the
          International Geographical Union," Canadian
          Geographer, No. 14, pp. 37-41.

G-565.   Nicol, I.G.   1974.   "Geography Teaching for the
          Seventies," The South African Geographical
          Journal, Vol. 56, pp. 105-110.

G-566.   Nijim, Basheer K.   1974.   "Geographic Data and
          Concepts: An Introductory Exercise," Journal of
          Geography, Vol. 73, pp. 44-49.

G-567.   Nikiforoff, C. C.   1947.   "Biography of the
          Russian Geographical Society [a book review],"
          Annals of the Association of American
          Geographers, Vol. 37, pp. 225-226.

G-568.   Noh, Toshio.   1948.   "Notes on Japanese
          Geographical Periodicals," Annals of the
          Association of American Geographers, Vol. 38, pp.
          231-232.

G-569.   Norton, W.   1981.   "Cultural Analysis in
          Geography: A Course Outline," Journal of
          Geography, Vol. 80, pp. 46-50.

G-570.   Ogilvie, Alan G. 1934.   "Co-operative Research in
          Geography: With An African Example," Scottish
          Geographical Magazine, Vol. 50, See pp. 353-356.

G-571.   Ogundana, B.   1978.   "The Growth and
          Contributions of the Nigerian Geographical
          Association," Nigerian Geographical Journal, Vol.
          21, pp. 25-30.

G-572.   Ojo, G. J. A.   1972.   "Geography in Contemporary
          Society - Presidential Address," Nigerian
          Geographical Journal, Vol. 15, pp. 3-12.

G-573.   Ologe, K. O. 1978. "Career Outlets of Geography
          Graduates from A.B.V.," Proceedings - 21st Annual
          Conference of the Nigerian Geographical
          Association, University of Jos, pp. 256-258.

G-574.   Olmstead, A. T. 1913. "Geographic
          Visualization," Bulletin of the American
          Geographical Society, Vol. 45, pp. 921-923.

G-575.   Openshaw, Stan, Rhind, David and Goddard, John.
          1986. "Geography, Geographers and the BBC
          Domesday Project," Area, Vol. 18, pp. 9-13.

G-576.   O'Riordan, T. 1981. "Environmentalism and
          Education," Journal of Geography in Higher
          Education, Vol. 5, pp. 3-18.

G-577.   Orme, Antony R. 1980. "The Need for Physical
          Geography," Professional Geographer, Vol. 32, pp.
          141-148.

G-578.   Parker, W. 1958-59. "Geography Defended,"
          Universities Quarterly, Vol. 14, pp. 34-44.

G-579.   Parkins, A. E. 1934. "The Geography of American
          Geographers," Journal of Geography, Vol. 33, pp.
          221-230.

G-580.   Patmore, J. Allan. 1980. "Geography and
          Relevance," Geography, Vol. 65, pp. 265-283.

G-581.   Pattison, William D. 1960. "The Star of the
          AAG," Professional Geographer, Vol. 12, No. 5, p.
          18-19.

G-582.   Pattison, William D. 1962. "Geography in the
          High School," Annals of the Association of
          American Geographers, Vol. 52, pp. 280-284.

G-583.   Pattison, William D. 1978. "Goode's Proposal of
          1902: An Interpretation," Professional
          Geographer, Vol. 30, pp. 3-8.

G-584.   Pauly, Philip J. 1979. "The World and All That
          Is in It: The National Geographic Society,
          1888-1918," American Quarterly, Vol. 31, Fall,
          1979, pp. 517-532.

G-585.   Peake, Linda. 1985. "Teaching Feminist
          Geography: Another Perspective," Journal of
          Geography in Higher Education, Vol. 9, pp.
          186-190.

G-586.   Peet, Richard. 1985. "Evaluating the
          Discipline's Journals: A Critique of Lee and
          Evans," Professional Geographer, Vol. 37, pp.
          59-62.

G-587.   Peet, Richard. 1985. "Introduction to the
         Thought of Karl Wittfogel," Antipode, Vol. 17,
         pp. 3-20.

G-588.   Pemberton, Dixie A., et al. 1974. "Implications
         of Methodology in Training Teachers of
         Geography: A Micro Lab Session Using a Process
         Model," Journal of Geography, Vol. 73, pp. 26-38.

G-589.   Petersen, Albert J. and Wayne L. Hoffman. 1972.
         "The Status of Geography: An 'Attitude-Opinion'
         Survey of the AAG Membership," Professional
         Geographer, Vol. 24, pp. 146-149.

G-590.   Phelps, Jewel. 1969. "Needed: Geographers,"
         Journal of Geography, Vol. 68, pp. 68-69.

G-591.   Pickles, John. 1982. "'Science' and the Funding
         of Geography," Professional Geographer, Vol. 34,
         pp. 387-393.

G-592.   Pickles, John. 1986. "Geographic Theory and
         Educating For Democracy," Antipode, Vol. 18, pp.
         136-154.

G-593.   Pinchemel, Philippe. 1982. "De La Geographie
         Eclatee a Une Geographie Recentree," Tijdschrift
         voor Economische en Sociale Geography, Vol. 73,
         pp. 362-369 [English abstract, p. 322].

G-594.   Platt, R. S. 1948. "Environmentalism Versus
         Geography," American Journal of Sociology, Vol.
         53, pp. 351-358.

G-595.   Pokshishevskiy, V. V. 1980. "Editorial: Social
         Geography in the Soviet Union and Its Demographic
         Sources," GeoJournal Supplementary Issue 1, pp.
         3-6.

G-596.   Pontius, Steven K. 1973. "Jobs in Geography?"
         Professional Geographer, Vol. 25, pp. 277-279.

G-597.   Porteous, J. D. 1986. "Geography as a Personal
         Art," Operational Geographer, No. 10, pp. 43-44.

G-598.   Powell, J. M. 1983. "Prescient Pasts? A Plea
         for Geography, 1928," Australian Geographical
         Studies, Vol. 21, pp. 121-128.

G-599.   Powers, Pauline R. 1938. "Ah! Geography,"
         Journal of Geography, Vol. 37, pp. 274-277.

G-600.   Pred, Allan. 1979. "The Academic Past Through a
         Time-Geographic Looking Glass," Annals of the
         Association of American Geographers, Vol. 69, pp.
         175-179.

G-601.   Pred, Allan.   1981.   "Power, Everyday Practice
         and the Discipline of Human Geography," Lund
         Studies in Geography, Series B, Vol. 48, pp.
         30-55.

G-602.   Prince, Hugh.   1971.   "Questions of Social
         Relevance," Area, Vol. 3, pp. 150-153.

G-603.   Proctor, Nigel.   1986.   "The Pioneers of
         Geography: A New and Currently Relevant
         Perspective," Transactions - Institute of British
         Geographers, Vol. 11, pp. 75-85.

G-604.   Pruitt, Evelyn L.   1979.   "The Office of Naval
         Research and Geography," Annals of the
         Association of American Geographers, Vol. 69, pp.
         103-108.

G-605.   Prunty, M. C.   1979.   "Clark in the Early 1940s,"
         Annals of the Association of American
         Geographers, Vol. 69, pp. 42-45.

G-606.   Prunty, M. C.   1979.   "Geography in the South,"
         Annals of the Association of American
         Geographers, Vol. 69, pp. 53-58.

G-607.   Qualthrough, Miss Kate.   1910.   "The Fascination
         of Geography," Journal of the Manchester
         Geographical Society, Vol. 26, pp. 78-96.

G-608.   Quirk, B. and Trim, V.   1978.   "Childspace:
         Piaget and Cognitive Geography," South Hampshire
         Geographer, Vol. 10, pp. 9-17.

G-609.   Quirk, Barry.   1975.   "A Polemic on Perception
         and Experience in Geographic Research," South
         Hampshire Geographer, Vol. 7, pp. 1-8.

G-610.   Ramsaur, Robert T.   1958.   "Geography at the
         United States Air Force Academy," Journal of
         Geography, Vol. 57, pp. 450-454.

G-611.   Raup, H. F.   1956.   "The United States in
         Professional Geographic Literature," Annals of
         the Association of American Geographers, Vol. 46,
         pp. 140-149.

G-612.   Raup, H. F.   1961.   "Where Shall I Go From the
         Ph.D.?" Professional Geographer, Vol. 13, No. 3,
         pp. 27-30.

G-613.   Rechlin, Alice T. M.   1983.   "Geography:
         Academic Cross Stitching," Geographical Bulletin,
         Vol. 24, pp. 5-10.

G-614.   Reed, J. Howard.   1909.   "Kingston-Upon-Hull
         Geographical Society," Journal of the Manchester
         Geographical Society, Vol. 23, pp. 124-133.

G-615.   Relph, Edward, 1974. "Graduate Education in
         Geography: A Critique and a Proposal,"
         Professional Geographer, Vol. 26, pp. 4-8.

G-616.   Rennell of Rodd, Rt. Hon. Lord. 1946. "Address
         at the Annual General Meeting," Geographical
         Journal, Vol. 107, pp. 81-90.

G-617.   Rennell of Rodd, Rt. Hon. Lord. 1947. "Address
         at the Annual General Meeting," Geographical
         Journal, Vol. 109, pp. 161-165.

G-618.   Rennell of Rodd, Rt. Hon. Lord. 1948. "Address
         at the Annual General Meeting," Geographical
         Journal, Vol. 111, pp. 153-158.

G-619.   Reynolds, T. C. 1981. "Research Training for
         Young Historical Geographers," Journal of
         Historical Geography, Vol. 7, pp. 415-416.

G-620.   Richards, Peter S. 1977. "What is Geography
         Anyway? A Survey of Professional Views,"
         Teaching Geography, Vol. 3, pp. 68-69.

G-621.   Richason, Benjamin F. 1972. "An Analysis of
         NCGE Membership," Journal of Geography, Vol. 71,
         pp. 73-86.

G-622.   Richling, A. 1983. "Subject of Study in Complex
         Physical Geography," GeoJournal, Vol. 7, pp.
         185-187.

G-623.   Riddel, J. Barry. 1987. "Geography and the
         Study of Third World Underdevelopment," Progress
         in Human Geography, Vol. 11, pp. 264-274.

G-624.   Rimmer, P. J. and Forbes, D. K. 1984. "Now
         Gods, Stand Up for Geographers," Australian
         Geographical Studies, Vol. 22, pp. 36-38.

G-625.   Robertson, Kent A. 1980. "The Status of
         Geography in Graduate Urban Affairs Programs,"
         Professional Geographer, Vol. 32, pp. 133-137.

G-626.   Robertson, Sir George S. 1900. "Address to the
         Geographical Section of the British Association,
         1900," Scottish Geographical Magazine, Vol. 16,
         pp. 561-573.

G-627.   Robinson, Arthur H. 1961. "On Perks and Pokes,"
         Economic Geography, Vol. 37, pp. 181-183.

G-628.   Robinson, Arthur H. 1979. "Geography and
         Cartography Then and Now," Annals of the
         Association of American Geographers, Vol. 69, pp.
         97-102.

G-629. Robinson, J. Lewis. 1951. "The Development and
        Status of Geography in Universities and
        Government in Canada," Yearbook of the
        Association of Pacific Coast Geographers, Vol.
        13, pp. 3-13.

G-630. Robinson, J. Lewis. 1967. "Trends in Geography
        in Canadian Universities," B. C. Geographical
        Series, No. 8, pp. 47-56.

G-631. Robinson, J. Lewis. 1977. "The Production and
        Employment of Geographers in Canada,"
        Professional Geographer, Vol. 29, pp. 208-214.

G-632. Robinson, J. Lewis. 1984. "The Employment of
        Ph.D. Geographers in Canada," Operational
        Geographer, No. 3, pp. 20-22.

G-633. Robinson, J. Lewis. 1985. "The Production of
        Graduate Geographers from Canadian Universities,"
        Operational Geographer, No. 8, pp. 51-53.

G-634. Robinson, J. L. 1986. "Trends in Geography in
        Canada as Illustrated by Articles in the Canadian
        Geographer," Operational Geographer, No. 9, pp.
        15-18.

G-635. Robinson, K. W. 1970. "Diversity, Conflict and
        Change - The Meeting Place of Geography and
        Politics," Australian Geographical Studies, Vol.
        8, pp. 1-5.

G-636. Roepke, Howard G. 1977. "Applied Geography:
        Should We, Must We, Can We?" Geographical
        Review, Vol. 67, pp. 481-482.

G-637. Rowley, Gwyn. 1984. "Foreign Languages and
        American Geography: A View from the Field,"
        Professional Geographer, Vol. 36, p. 76.

G-638. Rubin, Barbara. 1979. "'Women in Geography'
        Revisted: Present Status, New Opinions,"
        Professional Geographer, Vol. 31, pp. 125-134.

G-639. Rubin, Barbara. 1981. "Earned Doctorates In
        Geography By Sex, 1970- 1979," Transition, Vol.
        10, No. 4, p. 32.

G-640. Rushton, G. 1980. "Exceptionalism in Social
        Geography: A Heretics View," University of Iowa,
        Department of Geography, Discussion Paper, No.
        32, pp. 18-30.

G-641. Rushton, G. 1987. "Writing a Classic," Area,
        Vol. 19, pp. 167-168.

G-642.   Russell, Israel. 1895. "Reports of a Conference
         on Geography," _Journal of the American
         Geographical Society of New York_, Vol. 27, pp.
         30-41.

G-643.   Russell, Joseph A., ed. 1958. "Trends in
         Placement and Training of American Geographers,"
         Professional Geographer, Vol. 10, No. 3, pp.
         32-36.

G-644.   Russell, Joseph A. 1977. "Modern Geography:
         Foundation of Corporate Strategy," _Professional
         Geographer_, Vol. 29, pp. 200-207.

G-645.   Russell, Richard Joel. 1945. "Post-War
         Geography," _Journal of Geography_, Vol. 44, pp.
         301-312.

G-646.   Ruthren, Alexander G. 1921. "Geography in
         Museums of Zoology," _Annals of the Association
         of American Geographers_, Vol. 11, pp. 130.

G-647.   Sack, Robert David. 1980. "Teaching the
         Philosophy of Geography," _Journal of Geography in
         Higher Education_, Vol. 4, pp. 3-9.

G-648.   Salisbury, R. 1903. "Geography in the
         University of Chicago," _Geographical Teacher_,
         Vol. 2, pp. 81-82.

G-649.   Salter, Christopher L. 1976. "Geography in the
         K-12 Curriculum: Where to Locate It and How to
         Get It There," _California Geographer_, Vol. 16,
         pp. 73-83.

G-650.   Salter, Christopher L. 1977. "The Convenience
         of Environmental Ignorance," _Professional
         Geographer_, Vol. 29, pp. 249-253.

G-651.   Salter, Christopher L. 1983. "What Can I Do
         With Geography?" _Professional Geographer_, Vol.
         35, pp. 266-273.

G-652.   Salter, Christopher L. 1983. "What Geographers
         See," _Journal of Geography_, Vol. 82, pp. 50-53.

G-653.   Sauer, Carl O. 1921. "Geography as Regional
         Economics," _Annals of the Association of
         American Geographers_, Vol. 11, pp. 130-131.

G-654.   Sauer, Carl O. 1956. "The Education of a
         Geographer," _Annals of the Association of
         American Geographers_, Vol. 46, pp. 287-299.

G-655.   Sauer, Carl O. 1976. "The Seminar as
         Exploration," _Historical Geography Newsletter_,
         Vol. 6, pp. 31-34.

G-656.   Saushkin, Yu G. 1961. "Fifty Volumes of the
          Serial," Voprosy Geografii, Vol. 2, No. 8, pp.
          18-27.

G-657.   Saushkin, Yu G. 1963. "On the Subject Matter of
          Doctoral Dissertations in Geography," Soviet
          Geography: Review and Translation, Vol. 4, No.
          1, pp. 47-53.

G-658.   Saushkin, Yu G. 1963. "...Reply to a Letter of
          Protest by Nine Soviet Geographers," Soviet
          Geography: Review and Translation, Vol. 4, No.
          8, pp. 25-31.   Rebuttal, pp. 31-34.

G-659.   Saushkin, Yu G. 1963. "V. A. Anuchin's Doctoral
          Dissertation Defense," Soviet Geography: Review
          and Translation, Vol. 4, No. 1, pp. 53-59.

G-660.   Saushkin, Yu. G. and A. M. Smirnov. 1970.
          "Geosystems and Geostructures," Soviet
          Geography: Review and Translation, Vol. 11, pp.
          149-154.

G-661.   Saveland, R. N. 1962. "Whatever Happened to
          Geography?" Saturday Review, Vol. 45, pp. 56+,
          Nov. 17.

G-662.   Sayer, Andrew. 1982. "Explanation in Economic
          Geography. Abstraction Versus Generalization,"
          Progress in Human Geography, Vol. 6, pp. 68-88.

G-663.   Schofer, Jerry P. 1975. "Computer Cartography
          and Professional Geographers," Professional
          Geographer, Vol. 27, pp. 335-340.

G-664.   Schwendeman, J. R. 1952. "Meet the Modern
          Challenge to Geography," Memorandum Folio of the
          Southeastern Association of American Geographers,
          Vol. 3, pp. 108-126.

G-665.   Scully, M. G. 1982. "Academic Geography: Few
          Students, Closed Departments, Fuzzy Image,"
          Chronicle of Higher Education, Vol. 24, No. 13,
          May, p. 1.

G-666.   Seamon, David. 1979. "Phenomenology, Geography
          and Geographic Education," Journal of Geography
          in Higher Education, Vol. 3, pp. 40-50.

G-667.   Secretary, The. 1837. "Sketch of the Progress
          of Geography During the Past Year and the
          Labours of the Society," Journal of the Royal
          Geographical Society of London, Vol. 7, pp.
          172-195.

G-668.   Semple, Ellen Churchill. 1904. "Emphasis Upon
          Anthropo-Geography in Schools," Journal of
          Geography, Vol. 3, pp. 366-374.

G-669.   Shaw, Dennis. 1977. "Geography in Higher
         Education in the U.S.S.R.," Journal of Geography
         in Higher Education, Vol. 1, pp. 35-40.

G-670.   Sheperd, Ifan. 1979. "Internships and the
         Education of Geographers," Journal of Geography
         in Higher Education, Vol. 3, pp. 5-7.

G-671.   Shnitnikov, A. V. 1968. "Geographical Problems
         in Climatology, Hydrology and Glaciology Over
         the Last 50 Years," Soviet Geography: Review and
         Translation, Vol. 9, pp. 407-417.

G-672.   Sibley, David. 1987. "Racism and Sexism in
         Geographic Practice," Area, Vol. 19, p. 273.

G-673.   Singh, R. L. and Singh, Rana P. B. 1984.
         "Lifeworld and Lifecycle in India: A Search in
         Geographical Understanding," National
         Geographical Journal of India, Vol. 30, pp.
         207-222.

G-674.   Slater, David. 1975. "The Poverty of Modern
         Geographical Enquiry," Pacific Viewpoint, Vol.
         16, pp. 159-176.

G-675.   Slater, F. 1981. "What is Your View of People?
         Some Comments on Recently Changing Viewpoints in
         Geographical Research," New Zealand Journal of
         Geography, No. 71, pp. 6-9.

G-676.   Slaymaker, Olav. 1934. "The New Geography:
         Review," Geographical Journal, Vol. 134, pp.
         405-407.

G-677.   Smith, Bruce W. and Hiltner, John. 1983. "Where
         Non-Academic Geographers Are Employed,"
         Professional Geographer, Vol. 35, pp. 210-213.

G-678.   Smith, Bruce W. and Spinelli, Joseph G. 1979.
         "A Development Program for Applied Geographers:
         Planning in the Present for the Future," Journal
         of Geography, Vol. 78, pp. 45-47.

G-679.   Smith, Christopher J. 1976. "Geography and
         Public Consciousness Raising," Geographical
         Survey, Vol. 5, No. 4, pp. 27-31.

G-680.   Smith, D. M. 1972. "Geography and Social
         Indicators," South African Geographical Journal,
         Vol. 54, pp. 43-57.

G-681.   Smith, D. M. 1973. "Alternative 'Relevant'
         Professional Roles," Area, Vol. 5, pp. 1-4.

G-682.   Smith, David M. 1971. "Radical Geography - The
         Next Revolution," Area, Vol. 3, pp. 153-157.

G-683.   Smith, F.   1934.   "Intimate Geography,"
         Commonweal, Vol. 21, pp. 116-117, Nov. 23.

G-684.   Smith, Guy-Harold.   1959.   "Meeting the Needs for
         Geographers," Professional Geographer, Vol. 11,
         No. 1, pp. 5-9.

G-685.   Smith, Guy-Harold.   1960.   "Salaries of
         Geographers in the Universities," Professional
         Geographer, Vol. 12, No. 3, pp. 15-18.

G-686.   Smith, Guy-Harold.   1961.   "Geography Teaching
         Loads in American Universities," Professional
         Geographer, Vol. 13, No. 3, pp. 11-16.

G-687.   Smith, Neil.   1987.   "Academic War Over the Field
         of Geography: The Elimination of Geography at
         Harvard, 1947-1951," Annals of the Association of
         American Geographers, Vol. 77, pp. 155-172.

G-688.   Smith, Neil.   1987.   "For a History of
         Geography: A Response to Comments [On Academic
         War . . .]," Annals of the Association of
         American Geographers, Vol. 78, pp. 159-163.

G-689.   Smith, J. Russell.   1935.   "Are We Free to Coin
         New Terms," Annals of the Association of American
         Geographers, Vol. 25, pp. 17-22.

G-690.   Snaden, J.   1978.   "Fifty Years of Service to
         Geography (The Founding of Gamma Theta Upsilon),"
         Geographical Bulletin, Vol. 16, pp. 7-10.

G-691.   Sochava, V. B.   1968.   "The Development of
         Geographic Science in Siberia and the Soviet Far
         East Over the Last 50 Years (1917-67)," Soviet
         Geography: Review and Translation, Vol. 9, pp.
         293-304.

G-692.   Solomon, R. J.   1965.   "Ourselves as Others See
         Us: An Antipodean View," Professional
         Geographer, Vol. 17, No. 1, pp. 7-10.

G-693.   Solov'yer, A. I.   1965.   "The Present State and
         Tasks of Higher Geography Education," Soviet
         Geography: Review and Translation, Vol. 6, pp.
         28-46.

G-694.   Sopher, David E. and Duncan, James S.   1975.
         "Brahman and Untouchables: The Transactional
         Ranking of American Geography Departments,"
         Syracuse University, Department of Geography,
         Discussion Paper Series, No. 10.

G-695.   Spata, Carolyn D.   1975.   "The Supply, Demand,
         and Mobility of Ph.D. Geographers," Professional
         Geographer, Vol. 27, pp. 480-485.

G-696.   Spate, O. H. T.   1940.   "Old and New Approaches
         to Human Geography," Calcutta Geographical
         Review, Vol. 3, pp. 6-16.

G-697.   Speigner, Theodore R.   1969.   "Critical Shortage
         of Black Geography Teachers," Journal of
         Geography, Vol. 68, pp. 388-389.

G-698.   Spencer, J. E.   1979.   "A Geographer West of the
         Sierra Nevada," Annals of the Association of
         American Geographers, Vol. 69, pp. 46-52.

G-699.   Spencer, Joseph E.   1976.   "What's in a Name? -
         The Berkeley School," Historical Geography
         Newsletter, Vol. 6, pp. 7-12.

G-700.   Spetz, Dennis L.   1986.   "Strengthening Geography
         in Kentucky," Professional Geographer, Vol. 38,
         pp. 256-257.

G-701.   Stoltman, Joseph P.   1980.   "Round One for HSGP:
         A Report on Acceptance and Diffusion,"
         Professional Geographer, Vol. 32, pp. 209-215.

G-702.   Steers, J. A.   1982.   "A. R. Hinks and the Royal
         Geographical Society," Geographical Journal, Vol.
         148, pp. 1-7.

G-703.   Stephenson, Larry K.   1979.   "Geographic
         Education and Community Development," Journal of
         Geography in Higher Education, Vol. 3, pp. 93-97.

G-704.   Stevens, Joseph A.   1984.   "A Student's Assess-
         ment of the Employment Future for Geographers,"
         Geographical Bulletin, Vol. 25, pp. 5-8.

G-705.   Stoddart, D. R.   1980.   "The RGS and the 'New
         Geography': Changing Aims and Changing Roles in
         Nineteenth Century Science," Geographical
         Journal, Vol. 146, pp. 190-202.

G-706.   Stoddart, D. R.   1981.   "Geography, Education and
         Research," Geographical Journal, Vol. 147, pp.
         287-297.

G-707.   Stoddart, D. R.   1983.   "Progress in Geography:
         The Record of the I.B.G.," Transactions -
         Institute of British Geographers, Vol. 8, pp.
         1-13.

G-708.   Stokes, E.   1979.   "The Assessment of Geography
         Students at University," New Zealand Journal of
         Geography, Vol. 67, pp. 10-15.

G-709.   Stokes, Evelyn, et al.   1987.   "Feminist
         Perspectives in Geography: A Collective
         Statement," New Zealand Journal of Geography,
         Vol. 43, pp. 139-149.

G-710.   Stolberg, Irving. 1965. "Geography and Peace
          Research," Professional Geographer, Vol. 17, No.
          4, pp. 9-13.

G-711.   Stone, Kirk H. 1963. "A Colloquium for
          Undergraduate Majors in Geography," Professional
          Geographer, Vol. 15, pp. 8-11.

G-712.   Stone, Kirk H. 1979. "Geography's War-Time
          Service," Annals of the Association of American
          Geographers, Vol. 69, pp. 89-96.

G-713.   Struve, A. W. von. 1940. "Geography in the
          Census Bureau." Economic Geography, Vol. 16, pp.
          275-280.

G-714.   Stutz, Frederick P. 1980. "Applied Geographic
          Research for State and Local Government:
          Problems and Prospects," Professional Geographer,
          Vol. 32, pp. 393-399.

G-715.   Sugen, David and Hamilton, Patrick. 1978.
          "Teaching Geography at the University," Journal
          of Geography in Higher Education, Vol. 2, pp.
          14-22.

G-716.   Sutherland, W. J. 1914. "The Vocational Aspect
          of Regional Geography," Journal of Geography,
          Vol. 12, pp. 308-312.

G-717.   Swearington, Will D. 1984. "Foreign Languages
          and the Terrae Incognitae," Professional
          Geographer, Vol. 36, pp. 73-75.

G-718.   Taaffe, E. J. 1979. "Geography of the Sixties:
          In the Chicago Area," Annals of the Association
          of American Geographers, Vol. 69, pp. 133-138.

G-719.   Tamsicar, B. G. 1973. "Silver Jubilee of
          Geography Department Nagpur Maitavidyacay,"
          Deccan Geographer, Vol. 13, pp. 247-249.

G-720.   Taylor, E. G. R. 1947. "Geography in War and
          Peace," Scottish Geographical Magazine, Vol. 63,
          pp. 97-108.

G-721.   Taylor, E. G. R. 1948. "Geography in War and
          Peace," Geographical Review, Vol. 38, pp.
          132-141.

G-722.   Taylor, Zbigniew. 1985. "Geography as an
          Academic Discipline in Poland," Journal of
          Geography in Higher Education, Vol. 9, pp. 45-54.

G-723.   Thirunaranan, B. M. 1983. "J. A. Yates: The
          Link Between Geography at Oxford and at Madras,"
          Indian Geographical Journal, Vol. 58, pp. 93-96.

G-724.   Thomas, Frank H. 1962. "Economically Distressed
         Areas and the Role of the Academic Geographer,"
         Professional Geographer, Vol. 14, No. 2, pp.
         12-16.

G-725.   Thompson, Keith W. 1961. "An Assessment of
         Graduate Schools of Geography in the United
         States of America," Australian Geographer, Vol.
         8, pp. 138-139.

G-726.   Thompson, Kenneth. 1959. "The Academic Outlook
         for Geographers," Journal of Geography, Vol. 58,
         pp. 226-233.

G-727.   Thorpe, David. 1963. "The Non-Traditional Jobs
         of Geographers," Education for Business, No. 42,
         pp. 20-22.

G-728.   Thrall, Grant Ian. 1986. "Reply to Felix Driver
         and Christopher Philo," [re: Scientific
         Geography], Area, Vol. 18, pp. 162-163.

G-729.   Tinkler, Keith J. 1969. "Uniqueness in
         Geographic Interactions," Area, Vol. 1, pp.
         27-30.

G-730.   Tomkins, George S. 1986. "Understanding
         Ourselves: The Origin and Development of
         Canadian Studies," B. C. Geographical Series, No.
         43, pp. 75-94.

G-731.   Towler, J. 1971. "Geography's Decline--Some
         Preventive Guidelines," Journal of Geography,
         Vol. 70, pp. 133-135.

G-732.   Towler, J. 1981. "Geography and Environmental
         Education: A Canadian Perspective," Journal of
         Geography, Vol. 80, pp. 132-135.

G-733.   Treshnikov, A. F., et al. 1982. "Basic Trends
         in the Development of Geography in the Era of
         Developed Socialism," Soviet Geography: Review
         and Translation, Vol. 23, pp. 164-177.

G-734.   Trewartha, Glenn T. 1979. "Geography at
         Wisconsin," Annals of the Association of American
         Geographers, Vol. 69, pp. 16-20.

G-735.   Trimble, Stanley W. 1986. "Declining Student
         Performance in College Geography and the
         Down-Writing of Texts," Professional Geographer,
         Vol. 38, pp. 270-273.

G-736.   Trimble, Stanley W. 1987. "The Use of Citation
         Indices in Comparing Geography Programs: an
         Exploratory Study: Some Comments," Professional
         Geographer, Vol. 39, pp. 202-203.

G-737.   Tripathi, Shri Maya Prasad. 1964. "Was
          Geography a Separate Systematic Science in
          Ancient India," National Geographical Journal of
          India, Vol. 10, pp. 82-91.

G-738.   Turner, B. L., II. 1988. "Whether to Publish in
          Geography Journals," Professional Geographer,
          Vol. 40, pp. 15-18.

G-739.   Turner, B. L., II and Meyer, William B.
          "Response to Trimble," Professional Geographer,
          Vol. 39, pp. 203-204.

G-740.   Unstead, J. F. 1906. "Geographical Novels,"
          Geographical Teacher, Vol. 3, pp. 147-152.

G-741.   Van Cleef, E. 1936. "Stratigraphic View of
          Geography," Science, Vol. 83, pp. 313-317.

G-742.   Van Cleef, Eugene. 1944. "Training for
          Geographic Research: A Symposium," Annals of the
          Association of American Geographers, Vol. 34, pp.
          181-182.

G-743.   Vaniria, Louis M. 1959. "Geography Associations
          and the Teacher," Journal of Geography, Vol. 58,
          pp. 238-243.

G-744.   Varma, Dilip. 1986. "Geography and
          Accountancy: Figuring Out the Links," Bloomsbury
          Geographer, Vol. 14, pp. 71-74.

G-745.   Vent, Herbert. 1955. "Eminence Among
          Geographers," Professional Geographer, Vol. 7,
          No. 5, pp. 5-7.

G-746.   Vinge, Clarence L. 1953. "The Language of
          Geography," Professional Geographer, Vol. 5, pp.
          8-9.

G-747.   Visher, Stephen S. 1950. "The Presidents and
          Vice-Presidents of the AAG (1904-1948): Where
          They Received Their College and Graduate
          Training," Professional Geographer, Vol. 2, pp.
          41-46.

G-748.   Volif, M. D., et al. 1976. "Geography Education
          in the U.S.S.R. and Ways of Improving It,"
          Soviet Geography: Review and Translation, Vol.
          17, pp. 581-592.

G-749.   Wadley, D. and East, J. 1980. "The Employment
          Market for Geographers," Australian Geographer,
          Vol. 18, pp. 96-103.

G-750.   Wadley, David and Lindgren, Elise. 1987.
          "Strategic Planning for Geography Departments?"
          Professional Geographer, Vol. 39, pp. 392-404.

G-751. Wako, Tatsuo. 1975. "An Essay of the Landform
        Study in Schools and Universities," Science
        Reports of the Tohoku University, Seventh Series
        (Geography), Vol. 25, pp. 209-217.

G-752. Walford, Rex. 1986. "Finding Grenada on the
        Map," Area, Vol. 18, pp. 56-57.

G-753. Walker, David. 1985. "From Laurel Creek and
        Back Again," Bloomsbury Geographer, Vol. 13, pp.
        75-78.

G-754. Ward, A. W. 1886. "A Professor of Geography,"
        Journal of the Manchester Geographical Society,
        Vol. 2, pp. 119-129.

G-755. Ward, Peter. 1986. "Geography at U.C.L.A.: A
        Ten Year Perspective," Bloomsbury Geographer,
        Vol. 14, pp. 65-68.

G-756. Ward, R. Gerard. 1985. "On Cooke's Second Law,"
        Area, Vol. 17, pp. 322-324.

G-757. Ward, Robert DeC. 1909. "Geography at Harvard
        University," Journal of Geography, Vol. 7, pp.
        105-108.

G-758. Ware, Amy E. 1924. "Building Up the New
        Organization," Journal of Geography, Vol. 23, pp.
        106-112.

G-759. Warner, C. 1972. "Careers for Geographers: A
        Note on Recent Trends," South Hampshire
        Geographer, No. 5, pp. 69-70.

G-760. Washington, Captain. 1838. "Sketch of the
        Progress of Geography and of the Labours of the
        Royal Geographical Society in 1837-8," Journal of
        the Royal Geographical Society of London, Vol. 8,
        pp. 235-266.

G-761. Watson, J. W. 1950. "The Canadian Association
        of Geographers: A Sketch of the Preliminaries,"
        Canadian Geographer, No. 1, pp. 1-3.

G-762. Watson, J. Wreford. 1984. "Guest Editorial:
        The Royal Scottish Geographical Society and the
        Progress of Geography," Scottish Geographical
        Magazine, Vol. 100, pp. 66-68.

G-763. Watson, Mary K. 1978. "The Scale Problem in
        Human Geography," Geografiska Annaler, Vol. 60B,
        pp. 36-47.

G-764. Webb, Robert M. 1972. "Place Location in
        Geographic Education: Anathema or Exigency,"
        Ecumene, Vol. 4, pp. 18-21.

G-765. Wheeler, P. B. 1981. "Revolutions, Research Programmes and Human Geography," _Area_, Vol. 13, pp. 1-6.

G-766. Whitaker, J. Russell. 1954. "The Way Lies Open," _Annals of the Association of American Geographers_, Vol. 44, pp. 231-244.

G-767. Whitaker, P. D. 1971. "A Brief History of the Department," [Geography at Sheffield University] _Don_, No. 14, pp. 6-8.

G-768. Whitbeck, R. H. 1918. "Editorial: The American Geographical Society and the _Journal of Geography_," _Journal of Geography_, Vol. 17, pp. 166-167.

G-769. Whitbeck, R. H. 1919. "Country's Call for Geographers To-Day and To-Morrow," _School and Society_, Vol. 9, pp. 223-228.

G-770. Whitbeck, R. H. 1920. "Rejuvenation to Geography," _School and Society_, Vol. 12, pp. 415-420.

G-771. Whitbeck, R. H. 1921. "Thirty Years of Geography in the United States," _Journal of Geography_, Vol. 20, pp. 121-128.

G-772. White, C. Langdon. 1942. "Geography and a World at War," _Denison University, Bulletin, Journal of the Scientific Laboratories_, Vol. 37, pp. 133-139.

G-773. White, Gilbert F. 1958. "Introductory Graduate Work for Geographers," _Professional Geographer_, Vol. 10, No. 2, pp. 6-8.

G-774. White, Robert C. 1968. "Early Geographical Dictionaries," _Geographical Review_, Vol. 58, pp. 652-659.

G-775. Whitehand, J. W. R. 1984. "The Impact of Geographical Journals: A Look at the ISI Data," _Area_, Vol. 16, pp. 185-187.

G-776. Whitehand, J. W. R. 1985. "Contributors to the Recent Development and Influence of Human Geography: What Citation Analysis Suggests," _Transactions - Institute of British Geographers_, Vol. 10, pp. 222-234.

G-777. Whitehand, J. W. R. 1987. "What's in a Citation?" _Area_, Vol. 19, pp. 170-171.

G-778. Whitehead, J. 1972. "Poem -- Haggettwocky or Berry-My-Boots-'Neath-the-Hartshorne-Tree-Wocky," _Bloomsbury Geographer_, Vol. 5, p. 72.

G-779. Whitehead, J. 1973. "Haggettwocky or
        Berry-My-Books-'neath-the- Hartshorne-Tree,"
        Area, Vol. 5, pp. 24.

G-780. Whitelegg, John. 1986. "Publicity for
        Geography," Area, Vol. 18, p. 97.

G-781. Whittlemore, Katheryne Thomas. 1964. "The
        National Council for Geographic Education: To
        Foster Geographic Education," Journal of
        Geography, Vol. 63, pp. 197-204.

G-782. Whittlemore, Katheryne Thomas. 1972.
        "Celebrating Seventy-Five Years of the Journal of
        Geography," Journal of Geography, Vol. 71, pp.
        7-18.

G-783. Whittlesey, Derwent. 1931. "Field Study of
        Human Geography in the United States,"
        Proceedings - Thirteenth International
        Geographical Congress, pp. 774-777.

G-784. Wilbanks, Thomas J. 1981. "Geography and Jobs
        in the Nonacademic World," Geographical
        Perspective, Vol. 47, pp. 1-5.

G-785. Wilbanks, Thomas J. and Libbee, Michael. 1978.
        "A Departmental Approach to Professional Growth
        for Faculty Members," Professional Geographer,
        Vol. 30, pp. 349-355.

G-786. Wilbanks, Thomas J. and Libbee, Michael. 1979.
        "Avoiding the Demise of Geography in the United
        States," Professional Geographer, Vol. 31, pp.
        1-7.

G-787. Wilcock, Arther A. 1975. "The Geographer Before
        1800," Area, Vol. 7, pp. 45-46.

G-788. Willes, Richard. 1947. "On Geographers,"
        [quotation] Geographical Journal, Vol. 109, p.
        228.

G-789. Williams, Michael. 1985. "The Geographical
        Association and the Great Debate," Geography,
        Vol. 70, pp. 129-137.

G-790. Wilson, Alan. 1978. "Mathematical Education for
        Geographers," Journal of Geography in Higher
        Education, Vol. 2, pp. 17-28.

G-791. Wilson, Leonard S. 1946. "Some Observations on
        Wartime Geography in England," Geographical
        Review, Vol. 36, pp. 597-612.

G-792. Wilson, Leonard S. 1948. "Geographical Training
        for the Postwar World: A Proposal," Geographical
        Review, Vol. 38, pp. 575-589.

G-793.   Winsberg, Morton D.   1977.   "Social Sciences in
         the United States: 1948-1975," Geographical
         Review, Vol. 67, pp. 335-343.

G-794.   Wise, Donald A.   1970.   "Opportunities for
         Geographers in the Federal Government,"
         Professional Geographer, Vol. 22, pp. 94-96.

G-795.   Wise, M. J.   1978.   "Postgraduate Training in
         Human Geography, Area, Vol. 10, pp. 43-44.

G-796.   Wise, M. J.   1982.   "The Presidential Address,"
         Geographical Journal, Vol. 148, pp. 301-307.

G-797.   Wise, M. J.   1983.   "Three Founder Members of the
         I.B.G.:   R. Ogilvie Buchanan, Sir Dudley Stamp,
         S. W. Wooldridge. A Personal Tribute,"
         Transactions - Institute of British Geographers,
         Vol. 8, pp. 41-54.

G-798.   Wood, P. A.   1977.   "Information for Geography -
         Cause for Alarm," Area, Vol. 9, pp. 109-113.

G-799.   Wright, J. K.   1952.   "British Geography and the
         American Geographical Society," Geographical
         Journal, Vol. 118, pp. 153-167.

G-800.   Wright, John K.   1925.   "The History of
         Geography: A Point of View," Annals of the
         Association of American Geographers, Vol. 15, pp.
         192-201.

G-801.   Wright, John K.   1926.   "A Plea for the History
         of Geography," Isis, Vol. 8, pp. 477-491.

G-802.   Wright, John K.   1948.   "The Educational
         Functions of the Geographical Societies of the
         United States," Journal of Geography, Vol. 47,
         pp. 165-173.

G-803.   Wright, John K.   1950.   "American Geography in
         the Eighteen Fifties and Sixties," Annals of the
         Association of American Geographers, Vol. 40, p.
         151.

G-804.   Wright, John K.   1950.   "The Society's
         Beginning," Geographical Review,   Vol. 40, pp.
         350-352.

G-805.   Wright, John K.   1952.   "Protean Geography,"
         Geographical Review, Vol. 42, pp. 175-176.

G-806.   Wright, John K.   1954.   "AAG Programs and
         Program-Making, 1904-1954 ...," Professional
         Geographer, Vol. 6, No. 6, pp. 6-11.

G-807.   Wright, John K. 1960. "Geography and History
          Cross-Classified," _Professional Geographer_, Vol.
          12, No. 5, pp. 7-10.

G-808.   Wrigley, Gladys M. 1952. "Adventures in
          Serendipity: Thirty Years of the _Geographical
          Review_," _Geographical Review_, Vol. 42, pp.
          511-542.

G-809.   Wrigley, N. 1985. "Guest Editorial: Citation
          Classics in Urban and Regional Research,"
          Environment and Planning A, Vol. 17, 147-149.

G-810.   Wrigley, Neil and Matthews, Stephen. 1986.
          "Citation Classics Citation Levels in
          Geography," _Area_, Vol. 18, pp. 185-194.

G-811.   Wrigley, Neil and Matthews, Stephen. 1987.
          "Citation Classics in Geography and the New
          Centurions: A Response to Haigh, Mead and
          Whitehand," _Area_, Vol. 19, pp. 279-284.

G-812.   Wusten, Herman van der and O'Loughlin, John.
          1986. "Claiming New Territory for a Stable
          Place: How Geography Can Contribute,"
          Professional Geographer, Vol. 38, pp. 18-28.

G-813.   Wyckoff, William L. 1979. "On the Louisiana
          School of Historical Geography and the Case of
          the Upland South," _Discussion Paper Series_,
          Syracuse University, Department of Geography, No.
          54, pp. 1-34.

G-814.   Yermakov, Yurity G. 1978. "Some Observations on
          Geographic Education in American Universities,"
          Soviet Geography: Review and Translation, Vol.
          19, pp. 206-213.

G-815.   Young, Ann. 1983. "Post-Graduate Education,"
          Australian Geographical Studies, Vol. 21, pp.
          296-297.

G-816.   Younghusband, Francis. 1917. "Geographical Work
          in India for This Society," _Geographical
          Journal_, Vol. 49, pp. 401-418.

G-817.   Younghusband, Lieutenant-Colonel Sir Francis.
          1920. "Address at the Anniversary Meeting, 31
          May 1920," _Geographical Journal_, Vol. 56, pp.
          1-13.

G-818.   Younghusband, Lieutenant-Colonel Sir Francis.
          1921. "Address at the Anniversary General
          Meeting, 30 May 1921," _Geographical Journal_, Vol.
          58, pp. 1-8.

G-819.   Younghusband, Lieutenant-Colonel Sir Francis.
          1922. "Address at the Anniversary General
          Meeting, 29 May 1922," Geographical Journal, Vol.
          60, pp. 1-5.

G-820.   Zaidi, Qaiser Husain. 1951. "Geography for the
          Citizen," Geographer, Vol. 4, No. 2, pp. 23-34.

G-821.   Zakharov, N. D. 1962. "Scholastics Instead of
          Science," Soviet Geography: Review and
          Translation, Vol. 3, No. 7, pp. 16-22.

G-822.   Zelinsky, Wilbur. 1970. "Beyond the
          Exponentials: The Role of Geography in the Great
          Transition," Economic Geography, Vol. 46, pp.
          151-165.

G-823.   Zelinsky, Wilbur. 1973. "The Strange Case of
          the Missing Female Geographer," Professional
          Geographer, Vol. 25, pp. 101-105.

G-824.   Zelinsky, Wilbur. 1973. "Women in Geography: A
          Brief Factual Account," Professional Geographer,
          Vol. 25, pp. 151-165.

G-825.   Zimmerman, Frances. 1930. "Geography as a Life
          Career," Journal of Geography, Vol. 29, pp.
          30-34.

Subdisciplines in Geography

H-1.   Abbe, Cleveland. 1906. "The Importance of
        Sustaining a Special Journal of Geophysics in the
        English Language as Representing the Highest
        Development of Physical Geography [Abstract],"
        Bulletin of the American Geographical Society of
        New York, Vol. 38, p. 101-102.

H-2.   Adams, Charles C. 1926. "The Status of
        Zoogeography in North American," Annals of the
        Association of American Geographers, Vol. 16, pp.
        22.

H-3.   Adrian, Colin. 1984. "'Touring' Urban Studies:
        A Review Article," Australian Geographical
        Studies, Vol. 22, pp. 142-145.

H-4.   Adrian, Colin and Forbes, Dean. 1984.
        "Australasian Human Geography: Urban Geographys'
        Reply," Progress in Human Geography, Vol. 8, pp.
        562-569; Dennis Jean's Rejoinder, pp. 570-573.

H-5.   Agafonov, N. T. and Lavrov, S. B. 1974.
        "Ekonomicheskaya Geografiya: Istoriya, Teoriya,
        Metody, Praktika," [a review] Soviet Geography:
        Review and Translation, Vol. 15, pp. 582-587.

H-6.   Agafonov, N. T. and Mozgalin, S. E. 1975. "On
        Social-Geographic Requirements Addressed to
        Medical-Geographic Research," Geographea Medica,
        Vol. 14, pp. 264-273.

H-7.   Agafonov, N. T., et al. 1976. "Population
        Geography and Socio-Economic Planning," Soviet
        Geography: Review and Translation, Vol. 18. pp.
        377-383.

H-8.   Aitchinson, Alison E.   1918.   "Physiography as a
       Basis for Commercial Geography, Botany, and
       History," Journal of Geography, Vol. 16, pp.
       215-218.

H-9.   Al-Amiri, Sami S. A.   1985.   "Teaching
       Geomorphology in Geography Departments of Arab
       Universities," Geographical Perspectives, No. 56,
       pp. 55-57.

H-10. Alampiyev, P. M.   1961.   "The Objective Basics of
       Economic Regionalization and Its Long-Range
       Prospects," Soviet Geography: Review and
       Translation, Vol. 2, no. 8, pp. 64-74.

H-11. Alampiyev, P. M., et al.   1976.   "The
       Scientific-Technical Progress and New Problems in
       Economic Geography," Proceedings - Twenty-third
       International Geographical Congress, pp. 19-23.

H-12. Alampiyev, P. M. and Feygin, Ya. G.   1963.
       "Methodological Problems in Economic Geography,"
       Soviet Geography: Review and Translation, Vol.
       4, No. 10, pp. 34-71 [review, pp. 71-72].

H-13. Al'Brut, M. I.   1961.   "Let Us Clear Up, Once and
       For All, Differences on Methodological Questions
       in Economic Geography," Soviet Geography: Review
       and Translation, Vol. 2, pp. 23-26.

H-14. Al'Brut, M. I.   1977.   "Geographical Systems and
       Economic-Geographical Systems," Soviet
       Geography: Review and Translation, Vol. 18, pp.
       115-119.

H-15. Al'Brut, M. I.   1980.   "Against the Notion of
       Taking the "Economic" Out of Economic Geography,"
       Soviet Geography: Review and Translation, Vol.
       21, pp. 364-369.

H-16. Al'Brut, M. I.   1983.   "On the Issue of Defining
       the Subject of Economic and Social Geography,"
       Soviet Geography: Review and Translation, Vol.
       24, pp. 734-738.

H-17. Allan, J. A.   1978.   "Remote Sensing in Physical
       Geography," Progress in Physical Geography, Vol.
       2, pp. 36-54.

H-18. Alcock, F. I.   1949.   "Cartography in Canada
       Since 1939," Proceedings of the Sixteenth
       International Geographical Congress, pp. 203-204.

H-19. Al'tman, L. P. et al.   1968.   "Economic Geogrpahy
       at Leningrad University," Soviet Geography:
       Review and Translation, Vol. 9, pp. 1-11.

H-20.   Anderson, J., et al. (eds.). 1978. "New
         Approaches to Geography and Planning," Institute
         of British Geographers, Social Geography Group,
         51 p.

H-21.   Anderson, S. Axel. 1934. "Location Factor in
         the Choice of Free Port Sites," Economic
         Geography, Vol. 10, pp. 147-159.

H-22.   Anokhin, A. A. 1982. "The 26th Party Congress
         and the Tasks of Socioeconomic Geography," Soviet
         Geography: Review and Translation, Vol. 23, pp.
         303-310.

H-23.   Anonymous. 1891. "Political Geography," Journal
         of the Manchester Geographical Society, Vol. 7,
         p. 403.

H-24.   Anonymous. 1903. "The New Zoogeography,"
         Scottish Geographical Magazine, Vol. 19, pp.
         253-258.

H-25.   Anonymous. 1911. "Educational: The Teaching of
         Geography," Scottish Geographical Magazine, Vol.
         27, pp. 317-321.

H-26.   Anonymous. 1919. "Relations Between Economic
         and General Geography," Journal of Geography,
         Vol. 18, pp. 94-86.

H-27.   Anonymous. 1926. "Economics and Geography;
         Round Table Discussion," American Economic
         Review, Vol. 16, pp. 112-133.

H-28.   Anonymous. 1937. "Round Table on Problems in
         Cultural Geography," Annals of the Association
         of American Geographers, Vol. 27, pp. 155-176.

H-29.   Anonymous. 1951. "Cartography Round Table,"
         Professional Geographer, Vol. 3, pp. 3-12.

H-30.   Anonymous. 1952. "A Plea for Social
         Geography." South African Geographical Journal,
         Vol. 34, pp. 61-62.

H-31.   Anonymous. 1982. "Editorial Essay: Political
         Geography - Research Agendas for the Nineteen
         Eighties," Political Geography Quarterly, Vol. 1,
         pp. 1-18.

H-32.   Anonymous. 1982. "Research Agendas for the
         1980s: Comments, Additions and Critiques,"
         Political Geography Quarterly, Vol. 1, pp.
         167-180.

H-33.   Anonymous. 1983. "The Limits between Geology
         and Physical Geography," Geographical Journal,
         Vol. 2, pp. 518-534.

H-34.   Anonymous.   1984.   "The Geo-Economists: A New
        Profession for the Market Jobs," _Futurist_, Vol.
        18, p. 58.

H-35.   Antonova, I. F.   1979.   "Economic Geography in
        Canada at the Present Stage," _Soviet Geography_:
        Review and Translation, Vol. 20, pp. 49-55.

H-36.   Appleton, Jay.   1975.   "Landscape Evaluation:
        The Theoretical Vacuum," _Transactions - Institute
        of British Geographers_, Vol. 66, pp. 120-123.

H-37.   Archer, J. Clark.   1982.   "Political Geography,"
        Progress in Human Geography, Vol. 6, pp. 231-241.

H-38.   Armitage, Ernest.   1972.   "The Teaching of
        Biogeography in Post-Primary Schools,"
        Geographical Viewpoint, Vol. 2, pp. 227-286.

H-39.   Asheim, B. T.   1979.   "Social Geography-Welfare
        State Ideology or Critical Social Science,"
        Geoforum, Vol. 10, pp. 5-18.

H-40.   Ashworth, G. J.   1971.   "The Geography of Outdoor
        Recreation," _South Hampshire Geographer_, No. 4,
        pp. 14-22.

H-41.   Atwood, W. W.   1935.   "Pan American Institute of
        Geography and History," _Science_, Vol. 81 NS,
        March 22, pp. 285-286.

H-42.   Augelli, John P.   1968.   "Regional Geography in
        Revolution," _Journal of Geography_, Vol. 67, pp.
        68-69.

H-43.   Aurousseau, M.   1924.   "Recent Contributions to
        Urban Geography: A Review," _Geographical Review_,
        Vol. 14, pp. 444-455.

H-44.   Bailly, Antonie S. and Greer-Wooten, Bryn.
        1983.   "Behavioral Geography in Francophone
        Countries," _Progress in Human Geography_, Vol. 7,
        pp. 344-356.

H-45.   Baker, A. R. H.   1978.   "Historical Geography,"
        Progress in Human Geography, Vol. 2, pp. 495-504.

H-46.   Baker, A. R. H.   1979.   "Historical Geography: A
        New Beginning," _Progress in Human Geography_, Vol.
        3, pp. 560-570.

H-47.   Baker, Alan R. H.   1987.   "The Practice of
        Historical Geography," _Journal of Historical
        Geography_, Vol. 13, pp. 1-2.

H-48.   Baker, Alan R. W.   1974.   "In Pursuit of Wilbur
         Zelinsky and Other Historical Geographers,"
         Historical Geography Newsletter, Vol. 4, pp.
         17-19.

H-49.   Baker, P. R.   1973.   "Geography in Development
         Studies at the University of East Anglia," Area,
         Vol. 5, pp. 279-281.

H-50.   Baker, V. R.   1984.   "Planetary Geomorphology."
         Journal of Geological Education, Vol. 32, pp.
         236-246.

H-51.   Baker, V. R. and Pyne, S.   1978.   "G. K. Gilbert
         and Modern Geomorphology," American Journal of
         Science, Vol. 278, pp. 97-123.

H-52.   Bakis, Henry.   1981.   "Elements for a Geography
         of Telecommunication," Geographical Research
         Forum, No. 4, pp. 31-45.

H-53.   Bako, Elemer.   1957.   "Organization of Hungarian
         Cartography Since 1948," Professional Geographer,
         Vol. 9, No. 1, pp. 9-12.

H-54.   Balbour, K. M.   1982.   "Africa and the
         Development of Geography," Geographical Journal,
         Vol. 148, pp. 317-326.

H-55.   Bale, J. R.   1981.   "Geography, Sport and
         Geographical Education,"   Geography, Vol. 66, pp.
         104-115.

H-56.   Ballas, Donald J.   1980.   "Cultural Geography,"
         International Yearbook of Popular Culture, Vol.
         1, pp. 43-45.

H-57.   Ballas, Donald J. and King, Margaret J.   1981.
         "Cultural Geography and Popular Culture:
         Proposal for a Creative Merger," Journal of
         Cultural Geography, Vol. 2, pp. 154-163.

H-58.   Barbier, B. and Pearce, D. G.   1984.   "The
         Geography of Tourism in France: Definition, Scope
         and Themes," GeoJournal, Vol. 9, pp. 47-54.

H-59.   Barker, W. H.   1923-24.   "The History of
         Cartography," Journal of the Manchester
         Geographical Society, Vol. 39-40, p. 1-17.

H-60.   Barnes, Trevor.   1987.   "Home Economics, Physical
         Metaphors, and Universal Models in Economic
         Geography," Canadian Geographer, Vol. 31, pp.
         299-308.

H-61.   Bascom, Johnathan.   1982.   "The Historical and
         Philosophical Emergence of Radical Geography,"
         Geographical Bulletin, Vol. 22, pp. 7-13.

H-62.   Beesley, K.   1978.   "Urban Fringe Geography,"
        Bloomsbury Geographer, Vol. 9, pp. 23-29.

H-63.   Belov, M. I.   1978.   "Problems in the Study of
        the Historical-Geographic Environment," Soviet
        Geography: Review and Translation, Vol. 19, pp.
        165-169.

H-64.   Bennett, Charles F., Jr.   1960.   "Cultural Animal
        Geography: An Inviting Field of Research,"
        Professional Geographer, Vol. 12, No. 5, pp.
        12-14.

H-65.   Bennett, Charles F., Jr.   1961.   "Animal
        Geography in Geography Textbooks," Professional
        Geographer, Vol. 13, No. 2, pp. 13-16.

H-66.   Bennett, D.   1980.   "The Future of Welfare
        Geography--Review Essay," Canadian Geographer,
        Vol. 24, pp. 88-98.

H-67.   Benthien, B.   1984.   "Recreational Geography in
        the German Democratic Republic," GeoJournal, Vol.
        9, pp. 59-64.

H-68.   van den Berg, G. J.   1972.   "On the Relation
        Between Geography and Physical Planning in the
        Netherlands," Tijdschrift voor Economische en
        Sociale Geografie, Vol. 63, pp. 124-128.

H-69.   Berry, Brian J. L.   1959.   "Further Comments
        Concerning 'Geographic' and 'Economic' Economic
        Geography," Professional Geographer, Vol. 11, No.
        1, pp. 11-13.

H-70.   Berry, Brian J. L.   1959.   "Recent Studies
        Concerning the Role of Transportation in the
        Space Economy," Annals of the Association of
        American Geographers, Vol. 49, pp. 328-342.

H-71.   Billinge, Mark.   1977.   "In Search of
        Negativism: Phenomenology and Historical
        Geography," Journal of Historical Geography, Vol.
        3, pp. 55-67.

H-72.   Binatarto, R.   1982.   "Geographical Relevance to
        the Study of Development," Indonesian Journal of
        Geography, Vol. 12, pp. 51-56.

H-73.   Blakemore, M. J. and Harley, J. B.   1980.
        "Concepts of the History of Cartography: A
        Review and Perspective," Cartographica, Vol. 17,
        pp. 1-20.

H-74.   Blakemore, Michael.   1987.   "Cartography and
        Geographic Information Systems," Progress in
        Human Geography, Vol. 11, pp. 590-606.

H-75.   Blaut, J. M.   1980.   "A Radical Critique of
         Cultural Geography," _Antipode_, Vol. 12, pp.
         25-29.

H-76.   Blyn, George.   1961.   "Controversial Views on the
         Geography of Nutrition," _Economic Geography_, Vol.
         37, pp. 72-74.

H-77.   Board, Christopher.   1982.   "Maps and Mapping,"
         Progress in Human Geography, Vol. 6, pp. 106-114.

H-78.   Bohland, James.   1976.   "Geographic Perspectives
         on Quality of Life: An Introduction,"
         Geographical Survey, Vol. 5, No. 4, pp. 3-7.

H-79.   Borchert, Johan G.   1983.   "Geography Across the
         Borders: On the Relationship Between Urban
         Geography in the Netherlands and Germany,"
         _Tijdschrift voor Economische en Sociale
         Geografie_, Vol. 74, pp. 335-343.

H-80.   Borchert, John R.   1968.   "Remote Sensors and
         Geographical Science," _Professional Geographer_,
         Vol. 20, pp. 371-375.

H-81.   Bosque-Sendra, J., Rodriquez, V. and Santos, J.
         M.   1983.   "Quantitative Geography in Spain,"
         Progress in Human Geography, Vol. 7, pp. 370-385.

H-82.   Bowler, I. R.   1987.   "Agricultural Geography,"
         Progress in Human Geography, Vol. 11, pp.
         425-432.

H-83.   Bradshaw, M.   1982.   "Process, Time and the
         Physical Landscape: Gemorphology Today,"
         Geography, Vol. 67, pp. 15-28.

H-84.   Briggs, D. J.   1981.   "The Principles and
         Practice of Applied Geography," _Applied
         Geography_, Vol. 1, pp. 1-8.

H-85.   Britton, Robert.   1979.   "Some Notes on the
         Geography of Tourism," _Canadian Geographer_, Vol.
         23, pp. 276-282.

H-86.   Brock, E. J. and Twidace, C. R.   1984.   "J. T.
         Judson's Contributions to Geomorphological
         Thought," _Australian Journal of Earth Sciences_,
         Vol. 31, pp. 107-121.

H-87.   Broek, J. O. M.   1967.   "National Character in
         the Perspective of Cultural Geography," _Annals of
         the American Academy of Political and Social
         Science_, Vol. 370, pp. 8-15.

H-88.   Broek, Jan O. M.   1941.   "Discourse on Economic
         Geography," _Geographical Review_, Vol. 31, pp.
         663-674.

H-89.   Brookfield, H. C.   1963.   "On Training
         Geographers," Australian Geographical Studies,
         Vol. 1, pp. 100-114.

H-90.   Brookfield, H. C.   1969.   "On the Environment as
         Perceived," Progress in Geography, Vol. 1, pp.
         51-80.

H-91.   Brooks, Charles F.   1951.   "What Does Geography
         Need From Climatology," Professional Geographer,
         Vol. 3, p. 39.

H-92.   Browett, John.   1981.   "The Role of Geography in
         Development Geography," Tijdschrift voor
         Economische en Sociale Geografie, Vol. 72, pp.
         155-161.

H-93.   Brown, Eric H.   1964.   "Geomorphology in Poland,"
         Professional Geographer, Vol. 16, No. 2, pp.
         22-26.

H-94.   Brown, Eric H.   1975.   "The Concept and
         Relationships of Physical Geography,"
         Geographical Journal, Vol. 141, pp. 35-48.

H-95.   Brown, Eric H.   1980.   "Historical Geomorphology
         - Principles and Practice," Zeitschrift fur
         Geomorphologie, Supplementband, Vol. 36, pp.
         9-15.

H-96.   Brown, L. A. and Moore, E. G.   1969.   "Diffusion
         Research in Geography: A Perspective," Progress
         in Geography, Vol. 1, pp. 119-158.

H-97.   Brown, Robert C. and Eliot Hurst, Michael E.
         1969.   "Recent Change in Economic Geography,"
         Journal of Geography, Vol. 68, pp. 41-45.

H-98.   Brown, Stephen.   1987.   "Institutional Change in
         Retailing: A Geographical Interpretation,"
         Progress in Human Geography, Vol. 11, pp.
         181-206.

H-99.   Bruk, S. I., Kozolov, V. I. and Levin, M. G.
         1962.   "The Present Status of Research in Ethnic
         Geography in the U.S.S.R.," Soviet Geography:
         Review and Translation, Vol. 3, No. 4, pp. 22-28.

H-100.   Bryan, Kirk.   1950.   "The Place of Gemorphology
         in the Geographic Sciences," Annals of the
         Association of American Geographers, Vol. 40, pp.
         196-208.

H-101.   Bryan, M. Leonard.   1979.   "Remote Sensing
         Applications: An Overview," Geographical Survey,
         Vol. 8, No. 4, pp. 23-28.

H-102. Budin, M. 1981. "An Evaluation of Applied
        Geography: A Social Scientists Viewpoint,"
        Applied Geography Conference, Vol. 4, pp.
        200-213.

H-103. Bunting, Trudi E. and Guelke, Leonard. 1979.
        "Behavioral and Perception Geography: A Critical
        Appraisal," Annals of the Association of American
        Geographers, Vol. 69, pp. 448-462.

H-104. Burghardt, Andrew. 1969. "The Core Concept in
        Political Geography: A Definition of Terms,"
        Canadian Geographer, Vol. 13, pp. 349-353.

H-105. Burley, Terence M. 1962. "A Note on the
        Geography of Sport," Professional Geographer,
        Vol. 14, No. 1, pp. 55-56.

H-106. Burnett, A. 1978. "Political Geography: Dead
        Duck or Phoenix?" Area, Vol. 10, pp. 209-211.

H-107. Burnett, P. 1976. "Behavioral Geography and the
        Philosophy of Mind," in: Spatial Choice and
        Spatial Behavior, R. Golledge and G. Rushton,
        eds., (Ohio State University Press, Columbus),
        pp. 23-48.

H-108. Burnett, Pat. 1981. "Theoretical Advances in
        Modeling Economic and Social Behaviors:
        Applications to Geographical, Policy-Oriented
        Models," Economic Geography, Vol. 57, pp.
        291-303.

H-109. Burton, Ian. 1968. "Quality of the
        Environment: A Review," Geographical Review,
        Vol. 58, pp. 472-481.

H-110. Butler, Richard W. and Wall, Geoffrey. 1985.
        "Themes in Research on the Evolution of Tourism,"
        Annals of the Association of American
        Geographers, Vol. 12, pp. 287-298.

H-111. Butler-Adam, J. F. 1981. "Literature and the
        Night-Time Geography of Cities," South African
        Geographical Journal, Vol. 63, pp. 47-59.

H-112. Buttimeer, A (Sister Mary Annette). 1968.
        "Social Geography," in International Encyclopedia
        of the Social Sciences, D. Sills, ed.,(New York:
        Macmillan and the Free Press), Vol 6, pp.
        134-142.

H-113. Buttner, Manfred. 1985. "Geography of
        Religion," Geographca Religionum, Vol. 1, pp.
        13-121.

H-114.   Butzer, Karl W.   1973.   "Pluralism in
          Geomorphology," Proceedings - Twentieth
          International Geographical Congress, Vol. 5, pp.
          39-44.

H-115.   Calkins, R. D.   1918.   "Commercial Geography from
          the Regional Point of View," Journal of
          Geography, Vol. 17, pp. 18-25.

H-116.   Campbell, Colin K.   1966.   "An Approach to
          Research in Recreational Geography," B.C.
          Geographical Series, No. 7, pp. 85-90.

H-117.   Campbell, James B. and Edmonds, William J.
          1984.   "The Missing Geographic Dimension to Soil
          Taxonomy," Annals of the Association of American
          Geographers, Vol. 74, pp. 83-97.

H-118.   Carlson, Alvar W.   1975.   "Cultural Geography and
          Popular Culture," Journal of Popular Culture,
          Vol. 9, pp. 482-483.

H-119.   Carlson, Alvar W.   1978.   "Contributions of
          Cultural Geographers to Popular Culture," Journal
          of Popular Culture, Vol. 11, pp. 830-831.

H-120.   Carlson, Alvar W.   1980.   "Geographical Research
          on International and Domestic Tourism," Journal
          of Cultural Geography, Vol. 1, pp. 149-160.

H-121.   Carpenter, F. O.   1903.   "Commercial
          Geography--the New Science," School Review, Vol.
          11, pp. 593-605.

H-122.   Carpenter, Frank O.   1908-1909.   "Teaching
          Commercial Geography," Education, Vol. 29, pp.
          345-350.

H-123.   Carrega, P.   1983.   "Global Physical Geography:
          A Wager? Analyse Spatiale Quantitative et
          Appliquie, Vol. 16, pp. 9-14.

H-124.   Carter, George F.   1946.   "The Role of Plants in
          Geography," Geographical Review, Vol. 36, pp.
          121-131.

H-125.   Carter, Ronald L. and Steinbrink, John E.   1974.
          "Geography: From the Product Concept to the
          Marketing," Professional Geographer, Vol. 26, pp.
          1-4.

H-126.   Castner, H. W.   1980.   "Special Purpose Mapping
          in 18th Century Russia: A Search for the
          Beginning of Thematic Mapping," American
          Cartographer, Vol. 7, pp. 163-175.

H-127.   Chambers, William T.   1931.   "Geographic Areas of
          Cities," Economic Geography, Vol. 7, pp. 177-188.

H-128.   Chang, Sen-dor. 1966. "The Role of the
          Agricultural Geographer in Communist China,"
          Professional Geographer, Vol. 18, pp. 125-128.

H-129.   Chapman, J. D. 1960. "The Geography of Energy
          -- An Emerging Field of Study," Canadian
          Geographer, No. 1, pp. 31-40.

H-130.   Chapman, J. D. 1976. "Geographers and Energy,"
          B.C. Geographical Series, No. 22, pp. 15-24.

H-131.   Chapman, John D. 1961. "A Geography of Energy:
          An Emerging Field of Study," Canadian Geographer,
          Vol. 5, pp. 10-15.

H-132.   Chappell, John E., Jr. 1963. "Soviet
          Cartography: Comparisons and Gaps," Professional
          Geographer, Vol. 15, No. 2, pp. 1-8.

H-133.   Chappell, John E., Jr. 1980. "Crucial
          Deficiencies in Cultural Determinism,"
          Geographical Survey, Vol. 9, No. 2, pp. 3-18.

H-134.   Chatterjee, S. P. 1964. "Historical Geography,"
          in Fifty Years of Sciences in India: Progress of
          Geography, Indian Science Congress Association,
          Calcutta, pp. 331-347.

H-135.   Cheng-Siang, C. 1978. "The Historical
          Development of Cartography in China," Progress in
          Human Geography, Vol. 2, pp. 101-120.

H-136.   Chisholm, George. 1908. "Economic Geography,"
          Scottish Geographical Magazine, Vol. 24, pp.
          113-133.

H-137.   Chisholm, George G. 1921. "The Drift of
          Economic Geography: A Review," Scottish
          Geographical Magazine, Vol. 37, pp. 184-186.

H-138.   Chisholm, M. 1971. "Geography and the Question
          of Relevance," Area, Vol. 3, pp. 65-68.

H-139.   Chisholm, Michael. 1972. "Macro- and
          Micro-Approaches to Urban Systems Research,"
          Geographical Journal, Vol. 138, pp. 60-63.

H-140.   Chisholm, Michael. 1981. "Political Geography
          Without Prejudice," Progress in Human Geography,
          Vol. 5, pp. 593-594.

H-141.   Chojnicki, Zbyszko. 1970. "Prediction in
          Economic Geography," Economic Geography, Vol.
          46, pp. 213-222.

H-142.   Chojnicki, Zbyszko. 1979. "The Methodological
          Bases of Prediction in Economic Geography,"
          Quaestiones Geographicae, Vol. 5, pp. 23-34.

H-143.   Chokor, B. A.   1986.   "Research Policy and Review
         7.   Developments in Environment-Behavior-Design
         Research: A Critical Assessment in the Context
         of Geography and Planning with Special Reference
         to the Third World," Environment and Planning A,
         Vol. 18, pp. 5-26.

H-144.   Chorley, Richard J.   1971.   "The Role and
         Relations of Physical Geography," Progress in
         Geography, Vol. 3, pp. 87-110.

H-145.   Chorley, R. J. and Beckinsale, R. P.   1980.   "G.
         K. Gilbert's Geomorphology," Geological Survey of
         America, Special Paper, Vol. 183, pp. 129-142.

H-146.   Clark, Andrew H.   1946.   "Field Research in
         Historical Geography,"   Professional Geographer,
         Vol. 4, pp. 13-23.

H-147.   Clark, G.   1978.   "Current Research in Rural
         Geography," Area, Vol. 10,   pp. 51-52.

H-148.   Clark, G.   1979.   "Current Research in Rural
         Geography," Area, Vol. 11,   pp. 51-52.

H-149.   Clark, G.   1982.   "Developments in Rural
         Geography," Area, Vol. 14,   pp. 249-254.

H-150.   Clark, G. L.   1988.   "Time, Events, and Places:
         Reflections on Economic Analysis," Environment
         and Planning A, Vol. 20, pp. 187-194.

H-151.   Clarke, J. I.   1978.   "Population Geography,"
         Progress in Human Geography, Vol. 2, pp. 163-169.

H-152.   Clarke, J. I.   1980.   "Population Geography,"
         Progress in Human Geography, Vol. 4, pp. 385-391.

H-153.   Clayton, K.   1976.   "Environmental Sciences/
         Studies: A Decade of Attempts to Discover a
         Curriculum," Area, Vol. 8, pp. 78-101.

H-154.   Clayton, K. M.   1980.   "Geomorphology," in
         Geography Yesterday and Tomorrow, E. H. Brown,
         ed., (Oxford: Oxford University Press), pp.
         167-180.

H-155.   Clayton, Keith.   1970.   "Environmental Science,"
         Area, Vol. 2, pp. 5-6.

H-156.   Clenerly, P.   1978.   "The Role of Physical
         Geography," Area, Vol. 10, p. 285.

H-157.   Cloke, P. J.   1980.   "New Emphases for Applied
         Rural Geography,"   Progress in Human Geography,
         Vol. 4, pp. 181-217.

H-158.   Cloke, P. J. 1985. "Whither Rural Studies,"
          Journal of Rural Studies, Vol. 1, pp. 1-9.

H-159.   Cloke, Paul. 1985. "Essay Review: Studies of
          Land and Society in Rural Geography," Applied
          Geography, Vol. 5, pp. 259-263.

H-160.   Collins, Michael F. and Pattmore, J. Allan.
          1982. "Recreation and Leisure," Progress in
          Human Geography, Vol. 6, pp. 254-259.

H-161.   Collinson, A. S. 1981. "Is Cartography in the
          Doldrums?--A Personal View," Cartographic
          Journal, Vol. 18, pp. 58-59.

H-162.   Colten, Craig E. 1988. "Are There Options for
          Historical Geographers?" Historical Geography,
          Vol. 17, No. 2, pp. 5-6, 20.

H-163.   Conacher, A. J. 1980. "Some Thoughts About
          Future Development/Directions in Environmental
          Studies by Geographers in Australia," Australian
          Geographer, Vol. 14, pp. 68-69.

H-164.   Conkling, E. C. and McConnell, J. E. 1981.
          "Toward An Integrated Approach to the Geography
          of International Trade," Professional Geographer,
          Vol. 33, pp. 16-25.

H-165.   Conzen, M. P. 1980. "Historical Geography:
          North American Progress During the 1970s,"
          Progress in Human Geography, Vol. 4, pp. 549-559.

H-166.   Conzen, M. P. 1980. "Possibilities for the
          Future," Historical Geography, Vol. 10, pp. 4-6.

H-167.   Conzen, Michael P. 1977. "Bibliographic Aid to
          Navel Contemplation for Historical Geographers,"
          Historical Geography Newsletter, Vol. 7, pp.
          13-20.

H-168.   Coppock, J. T. 1964. "Agricultural Geography in
          Nigeria," Nigerian Geographical Journal, Vol. 7,
          pp. 67-90.

H-169.   Coppock, J. T. 1970. "Geographers and
          Conservation," Area, Vol. 2, pp. 24-26.

H-170.   Coppock, J. T. 1974. "Geography and Public
          Policy: Challenges, Opportunities and
          Implications," Transactions - Institute of
          British Geographers, Vol. 54, pp. 1-16.

H-171.   Corner, D. J. 1984. "English Cartography in the
          Thirteenth Century: The Intellectual Context,"
          Bulletin - Society of University Cartographers,
          Vol. 17, pp. 65-73.

H-172.   Cosgrove, D. E. 1979. "Geography and the Past:
          Status and Change," _Area_, Vol. 11, pp. 304-306.

H-173.   Cosgrove, Denis. 1983. "Towards a Radical
          Cultural Geography: Problems of Theory,"
          Antipode, Vol. 15, pp. 1-11.

H-174.   Cosgrove, Denis. 1985. "Present Fears for the
          Future of the Part: Report of a Survey into
          Academic Recruitment of Historical Geogrpahers,"
          Area, Vol. 17, pp. 243-246.

H-175.   Cosgrove, Denis and Jackson, Peter. 1987. "New
          Directions in Cultural Geography," _Area_, Vol. 19,
          pp. 95-101.

H-176.   Costa, John E. and Graf, William L. 1984. "The
          Geography of Geomorphologists in the United
          Status," _Professional Geographer_, Vol. 36, pp.
          82-89.

H-177.   Coull, J. R., Smith, J. P., Springett, J., Jones,
          J. A. C. and Jackson, P. 1980. "Observations:
          A Future for Cultural Geography," _Area_, Vol. 12,
          pp. 105-108.

H-178.   Cox, Kevin R. 1974. "The Behavioral Revolution
          in Geography: Definition and Evaluation,"
          Geographical Perspectives, No. 33, pp. 41-50.

H-179.   Cribin, J. A. and Turner, M. E. 1970.
          "Perception as Methodology in Historical
          Geography," _Bloomsbury Geographer_, Vol. 3, pp.
          44-49.

H-180.   Critzner, C. 1966. "The Scope of Cultural
          Geography," _Journal of Geography_, Vol. 65, pp.
          4-11.

H-181.   Crone, G. R., Campbell, E. M. J., and Skelton, R.
          A. 1962. "Landmarks in British Cartography,"
          Geographical Journal, Vol. 128, pp. 406-430.

H-182.   Crowley, John M. 1967. "Biogeography," _Canadian
          Geographer_, Vol. 11, pp. 312-326.

H-183.   Crush, Jonathan and Rogerson, Christian. 1983.
          "New Wave African Historiography and African
          Historical Geography," _Progress in Human
          Geography_, Vol. 7, pp. 203-231.

H-184.   Cuary, Douglas. 1959. "A Geographer Looks at
          the Landscape," _Landscape_, Vol. 9, pp. 22-25.

H-185.   Cullen, I. G. 1976. "Human Geography, Regional
          Science and the Study of Individual Behaviour,"
          Environment and Planning A, Vol. 8, pp. 397-410.

H-186. Cundall, L. B. 1938. "The Nature and Extent of
the Teaching of Physical Geography in Britain,"
Proceedings - Fifteenth International
Geographical Congress, pp. 59-68.

H-187. Curry, Leslie. 1970. "Univariate Spatial
Forecasting," Economic Geography, Vol. 46, pp.
241-258.

H-188. Curry, M. and Barnes, T. 1988. "Time and
Narrative in Economic Geography," Environment and
Planning A, Vol. 20, pp. 141-149.

H-189. Daly, Chief-Justice. 1879. "The Early History
of Cartography; or, What We Know of Maps and
Map-Making Before the Time of Mercator," Journal
of the American Geographical Society of New York,
Vol. 11, pp. 1-40.

H-190. Daly, Charles P. 1890. "The History of Physical
Geography," Journal of the American Geographical
Society of New York, Vol. 22, pp. 1-55.

H-191. Darby, H. C. 1962. "Historical Geography," in
Approaches to History, H. P. R. Finburg (ed.),
pp. 127-156.

H-192. Darby, H. C. 1979. "Some Reflections on
Historical Geography," Historical Geography, Vol.
9, pp. 9-14.

H-193. Darby, H. C. 1983. "Historical Geography in
Britain, 1920-1980," Transactions - Institute of
British Geographers, Vol. 8, pp. 421-428.

H-194. Davies, D. H. 1979. "Concerning Human Geography
Today," Proceedings - Geographical Association
of Zimbabwe, Proceedings, Vol. 12, pp. 5-12.

H-195. Davies, G. L. H. 1983. "Field Evidence in the
Earth Sciences," Irish Geography, Vol. 16, pp.
95-107.

H-196. Davies, J. L. 1961. "Aim and Method in
Zoogeography," Geographical Review, Vol. 51, pp.
412-417.

H-197. Davis, Gordon L. 1966. "Early British
Geomorphology, 1578-1705," Geographical Journal,
Vol. 132, pp. 252-261.

H-198. Davis, W. M. 1919. "Passargis Principles of
Landscape Description," Geographical Review, Vol.
8, pp. 266-273.

H-199. Dawkins, W. Boyd. 1892. "Geology in Relation to
Geography," Journal of the Manchester
Geographical Society, Vol. 8, pp. 226-230.

H-200.   Dean, K. G. 1984. "Social Theory and Prospects
          in Social Geography," GeoJournal, Vol. 9, pp.
          287-302.

H-201.   Dearden, Philip. 1985. "Landscape Aesthetics,"
          Canadian Geographer, Vol. 29, pp. 263-273.

H-202.   DeBres, Karen. 1986. "Political Geographers of
          the Past IV: George Renner and the Great Map
          Scandal," Political Geography Quarterly, Vol. 5,
          pp. 385-394.

H-203.   Demek, J. 1976. "Theory of the Cultural
          Landscape," Proceedings - Twenty-Third
          International Geographical Congress, Vol. 5, pp.
          11-14.

H-204.   Denevan, William M. 1983. "Adaptation,
          Variation, and Cultural Geography," Professional
          Geographer, Vol. 35, pp. 399-406.

H-205.   Dennis, Richard. 1983. "Rethinking Historical
          Geography," Progress in Human Geography, Vol. 7,
          pp. 587-594.

H-206.   Dennis, Richard. 1984. "Historical Geography:
          Theory and Progress," Progress in Human
          Geography, Vol. 8, pp. 536-543.

H-207.   Dennis, Richard. 1985. "Historical Geography:
          Landscape With Figures," Progress in Human
          Geography, Vol. 9, pp. 576-585.

H-208.   Derbyshire, Edward. 1983. "Geography and
          Geomorphology: Alternatives to G. H. Dury,"
          Area, Vol. 15, pp. 118-121.

H-209   Dever, G. E. Alan. 1972. "Training a Medical
          Geographer," Proceedings - Twenty-Second
          International Geographical Congress, pp.
          1212-1214.

H-210.   De Vos, A. 1967. "The Ecologist-Biogeographer
          in Resource Analysis and Environmental
          Planning," Canadian Geographer, Vol. 11, pp.
          162-165.

H-211.   Dickinson, R. E. 1948. "Scope and Status of
          Urban Geography: An Assessment," Land Economics,
          Vol. 24, pp. 220-238.

H-212.   Dickson, H. N. 1897. "Recent Researchers on
          Climate," Geographical Journal, Vol. 10, pp.
          303-307.

H-213.   Dickson, K. B. 1972. "Historical Geography
          Reconsidered," Proceedings - Twenty-Second
          International Geographical Congress, pp. 412-415.

H-214.   Dikshit, R. D.   1970.   "Toward a Generic Approach in Political Geography," _Tijdschrift voor Economische en Sociale Geografie_, Vol. 61, pp. 242-254.

H-215.   Dikshit, R. D.   1977.   "The Retreat from Political Geography," _Area_, Vol. 9, pp. 234-240.

H-216.   Dixey, F.   1962.   "Applied Geomorphology," _South African Geographical Journal_, Vol. 44, pp. 3-24.

H-217.   Doerr, Arthur H.   1957.   "Progress Report on Physical Geography at the University of Oklahoma," _Professional Geographer_, Vol. 9, No. 3, pp. 14-16.

H-218.   Doornkamp, J. C., and Sugden, D. E.   1979. "Whither Geomorphology?" _Area_, Vol. 11, pp. 307-312.

H-219.   Doughty, R. W.   1981.   "Environmental Theology: Trends and Prospects in Christian Thought," _Progress in Human Geography_, Vol. 5, pp. 234-248.

H-220.   Douglas, I.   1980.   "Future Trends in Geographical Hydrology and Climatology," _Australian Geographer_, Vol. 14, pp. 65-66.

H-221.   Douglas, J. Neville.   1984.   "Political Geography: From Comprehensive Empiricism to Tentative Theory," [Book Review Essay] _Progress in Human Geography_, Vol. 8, pp. 418-422.

H-222.   Downs, R. M. and Meyer, J. T.   1978.   "Geography and the Mind: An Exploration of Perceptual Geography," _American Behavioral Scientist_, Vol. 22, pp. 59-77.

H-223.   Downs, Roger M.   1980.   "Geographic Space Perception: Past Approaches and Future Prospects," _Progress in Geography_, Vol. 2, pp. 65-108.

H-224.   Doyle, F. J.   1983.   "Surveyors, Cartographers Photogrammetrists, Identification: Friends or Foes," _Cartography_, Vol. 13, pp. 88-95.

H-225.   Drdos, J.   1983.   "Landscape Research and Its Anthropocentric Orientation," _GeoJournal_, Vol. 7, pp. 155-160.

H-226.   Duffield, B. S.   1984. "The Study of Tourism in Britain - A Geographical Perspective," _GeoJournal_, Vol. 9, pp. 27-36.

H-227.   Dunbar, G. S.   1977.   "Some Early Occurrences of the Term 'Social Geography,'" _Scottish Geographical Magazine_, Vol. 93, pp. 15-20.

H-228.   Dunbar, G. S.   1978.   "What Was Applied
         Geography?" Professional Geographer, Vol. 30,
         pp. 238-239.

H-229.   Dunbar, G. S.   1980.   "Geogophy, Geohistory, and
         Historical Geography: A Study in Terminology,"
         Historical Geography, Vol. 10, pp. 1-8.

H-230.   Duncan, S. S.   1976.   "Research Directions in
         Social Geography: Housing Opportunities and
         Constraints," Transactions - Institute of British
         Geographers, Vol. 1, pp. 10-19.

H-231.   Durden, Dennis.   1959.   "Economic Geographers as
         Investment Consultants, Professional Geographer,
         Vol. 9, No. 1, pp. 14-16.

H-232.   Dury, G. H.   1980.   "Neocatastrophism? A Further
         Look," Progress in Physical Geography, Vol. 4,
         pp. 391-13.

H-233.   Dury, G. H.   1983.   "Geography and
         Geomorphology: the Last Fifty Years,"
         Transactions - Institute of British Geographers,
         Vol. 8, pp. 90-99.

H-234.   Dury, George Harry.   1972.   "Some Recent Views on
         the Nature, Location, Needs, and Potential of
         Geomorphology," Professional Geographer, Vol. 24,
         pp. 199-202.

H-235.   Dwyer, D. J.   1979.   "Urban Geography and the
         Urban Future," Geography, Vol. 64, pp. 86-95.

H-236.   Dziewonski, Kazimierz.   1965.   "On Integration of
         Statistical Cartographic Analysis for Research
         Purposes," Papers of the Regional Science
         Association, Vol. 15, pp. 119-129.

H-237.   Dzik, A. K.   1979.   "A Brief Review of the
         Development of Medical Geography," Bulletin -
         Illinois Geographical Society, Vol. 21, pp.
         18-23.

H-238.   Earth Science Committee of the NCGE.   1964.   "The
         Role of Geography in the Earth Sciences," Journal
         of Geography, Vol. 63, pp. 101-108.

H-239.   East, W. G.   1933.   "A Note on Historical
         Geography," Geography, Vol. 18, pp. 282-292.

H-240.   Eckert, Max.   1907.   "The New Fields of
         Geography, Especially Commercial Geography,"
         Scottish Geographical Magazine, Vol. 23, pp.
         561-568.

H-241.   Edwards, K. J.   1982.   "Palynology and
         Biogeography," Area, Vol. 14, pp. 241-248.

H-242. Eliot Hurst, Michael E. 1973. "Transportation
        and the Societal Framework," Economic Geography,
        Vol. 49, pp. 163-184.

H-243. Elkins, T. H. 1986. "German Social Geography,"
        Progress in Human Geography, Vol. 10, pp.
        313-344.

H-244. Embleton, C. 1983. "21 Years of British
        Geographic Geomorphology," Progress in Physical
        Geography, Vol. 7, pp. 361-384.

H-245. Epstein, Bart J. 1978. "Marketing Geography: A
        Chronicle of 45 Years," Applied Geography
        Conference, Vol. 1, pp. 372-379.

H-246. Ericksen, Neil J. 1976. "Behavioural
        Geography: A Bulb for the Black Box?" New
        Zealand Journal of Geography, No. 61, pp. 19-29.

H-247. Ernst, J. A. and Merrens, H. R. 1978. "Praxeis
        and Theory in the Writing of American Historical
        Geography," Journal of Historical Geography, Vol.
        4, pp. 277-290.

H-248. Estes, John E. 1974. "Recent Growth of Aerial
        Photographic Interpretation/Remote Sensing in
        Geography in The United States," Professional
        Geographer, Vol. 26, pp. 48-55.

H-249. Ettema, W. A. 1979. "Geographers and
        Development," Tijdschrift voor Economische en
        Sociale Geografie, Vol. 70, pp. 66-74.

H-250. Evenden, L. J. 1983. "A Preface to Themes in
        Social Geography," B.C. Geographical Series, No.
        36, pp. 9-16.

H-251. Eyles, J. 1984. "The Examination of Social
        Relationships in Space: Its Territorial,
        Empirical and Practical Parameters," GeoJournal,
        Vol. 9, pp. 247-253.

H-252. Eyles, J. D. 1974. "Social Theory and Social
        Geography," Progress in Geography, Vol. 6, pp.
        27-88.

H-253. Eyles, J. D. and Smith, D. M. 1978. "Social
        Geography," American Behavioral Scientist, Vol.
        22, pp. 41-58.

H-254. Eyles, John. 1977. "After the Relevance
        Debate: The Teaching of Social Geography,"
        Journal of Geography in Higher Education, Vol. 1,
        pp. 3-12.

H-255.   Eyles, John. 1978. "Social Geography and the
          Study of the Capitalist City: A Review,"
          Tijdschrift voor Economische en Sociale
          Geografie, Vol. 69, pp. 296-305.

H-256.   Fairbanks, H. W. 1929. "Industrialized
          Geography," Journal of Geography, Vol. 28, pp.
          202-206.

H-257.   Falconer, J. D. 1914. "The Progress of Physical
          Geography," Scottish Geographical Magazine, Vol.
          30, pp. 537-542.

H-258.   Falick, Abraham J. 1966. "Maritime Geography
          and Oceanography," Professional Geographer, Vol.
          18, pp. 283-286.

H-259.   Farley, A. L. 1954. "Applied Geography in
          British Columbia," Canadian Geographer, No. 4,
          pp. 15-20.

H-260.   Farrell, W. C. 1979. "Recent Methodological
          Developments and the Geography of Black America,"
          Pennsylvania Geographer, Vol. 17, pp. 19-30.

H-261.   Fel, S. Ye. 1974. "Russian Cartography of the
          18th Century as a Synthesis of Astronomic-
          Geodetic and Graphic Processes," Canadian
          Geographer, Vol. 11, pp. 15-23.

H-262.   Fellmann, Jerome D. 1986. "The Rise and Fall of
          High-School Economic Geography," Geographical
          Review, Vol. 76, pp. 424-437.

H-263.   Fenneman, Nevin M. 1922. "Functions of the
          Division of Geology and Geography in the National
          Research Council," Science, Vol. 56, pp. 620-624.

H-264.   Fenneman, Nevin M. 1922. "The Place of
          Physiography in Geography," Journal of
          Geography, Vol. 21, pp. 20-23.

H-265.   Fenneman, Nevin M. 1939. "The Rise of
          Physiography," Bulletin of the Geological
          Society of America, Vol. 50, pp. 349-360.

H-266.   Ferguson, Alan and Alley, Jamie. 1984.
          "Resource Geography: Is There Shape to the
          Terrain," Operational Geographer, No. 5, pp.
          36-38.

H-267.   Fifer, J. V. 1978. "Geography and Politics:
          Concepts of Space, Distance and Connection,"
          Geoforum, Vol. 9, pp. 331-340.

H-268.   Finch, V. C. 1944. "Training for Research in
          Economic Geography," Annals of the Association
          of American Geographers, Vol. 34, pp. 207-215.

H-269.   Fincher, Ruth. 1986. "Focus -- Historical
         Materialism in Canadian Human Geography,"
         <u>Canadian Geographer</u>, Vol. 30, pp. 265-272.

H-270.   Fincher, Ruth. 1987. "Social Theory and the
         Future of Urban Geography," <u>Professional
         Geographer</u>, Vol. 39, pp. 9-12.

H-271.   Fink, L. Dee. 1979. "The Changing Location of
         Academic Geographers in the United States,"
         <u>Professional Geographer</u>, Vol. 31, pp. 217-226.

H-272.   Finke, Leonard Ludwig. 1946. "On the Different
         Kinds of Geographies but Chiefly on Medical
         Topographies, and How to Compose Them," <u>Bulletin
         of the History of Medicine</u>, Vol. 20, pp. 527-538.

H-273.   Fisher, C. A. 1949. "Economic Geography in a
         Changing World," <u>Transactions and Papers -
         Institute of British Geographers</u>, No. 14, pp.
         69-84.

H-274.   Floyd, B. and O'Brien, D. 1976. "Whither
         Geography? A Cautionary Tale From Economics,"
         <u>Area</u>, Vol. 8, pp. 15-23.

H-275.   Floyd, Barry. 1970. "No Easy Harvest: The
         Challenge to Agricultural Geographers," <u>East
         Lakes Geographer</u>, Vol. 6, pp. 48-55.

H-276.   Floyd, Barry N. 1971. "On Reversing the Image
         of a Simplistic Geography: The Task of
         Socio-Economic Geography (Geonomics)," <u>Journal of
         Geography</u>, Vol. 70, pp. 84-90.

H-277.   Fonaroff, L. Schuyler. 1963. "Malaria
         Geography: Problems and Potential for the
         Profession," <u>Professional Geographer</u>, Vol. 15,
         No. 6, pp. 1-7.

H-278.   Fonaroff, L. Schuyler. 1976. "To a Young
         Medical Geographer," <u>Professional Geographer</u>,
         Vol. 28, pp. 331-335.

H-279.   Foord, Jo. 1980. "Some Notes on Women and
         Space," <u>Horizon</u>, Vol. 28, pp. 41-45.

H-280.   Foord, Jo and Gregson, Nicky. 1986.
         "Patriarchy: Towards a Reconceptualisation,"
         <u>Antipode</u>, Vol. 18, pp. 186-211.

H-281.   Foote, Don Charles and Greer-Wootten, Bryn.
         1968. "An Approach to System Analysis in
         Cultural Geography," <u>Professional Geographer</u>,
         Vol. 20, pp. 86-91.

H-282.   Forbes, Dean. 1981. "Beyond the Geography of
          Development," Singapore Journal of Tropical
          Geography, Vol. 2, pp. 68-[80].

H-283.   Ford, Larry R. 1975. "Historic Preservation and
          the Stream of Time: The Role of the Geographer,"
          Historical Geography Newsletter, Vol. 5, pp.
          1-15.

H-284.   Ford, Larry. 1984. "Architecture and
          Geography: Toward a Mutual Concern for Space and
          Place," Yearbook - Association of Pacific Coast
          Geographers, Vol. 46, pp. 7-34.

H-285.   Fosberg, F. R. 1976. "Geography, Ecology, and
          Biogeography," Annals of the Association of
          American Geographers, Vol. 66, pp. 117-128.

H-286.   Foster, Les, Jones, Ken and Mock, Dennis. 1979.
          "Internships in the Applied Geography
          Curriculum," Journal of Geography in Higher
          Education, Vol. 3, pp. 8-14.

H-287.   Foster, Harold D. 1969. "Geomorphology:
          Academic Exercize or Social Necessity," Canadian
          Geographer, Vol. 13, pp. 283-289.

H-288.   Foster, Harold D. 1972. "The Changing Focus of
          Geomorphology," Soviet Geography: Review and
          Translation, Vol. 13, pp. 337-343.

H-289.   Fradkin, N. G. 1970. "On Scientific Hypotheses
          and Authentic Knowledge in Modern Discoveries of
          General Regularities in Physical Geography,"
          Deccan Geographer, Vol. 11, pp. 865-872.

H-290.   Frazier, John W. 1978. "Applied Geography and
          Pragmatism," Geographical Survey, Vol. 7, pp.
          3-10.

H-291.   Frazier, John W. 1978. "Communications in
          Applied Geography," Applied Geography Conference,
          Vol. 1, pp. 1-8.

H-292.   Frazier, John W. 1978. "On the Emergence of an
          Applied Geography," Professional Geographer, Vol.
          30, pp. 233-237.

H-293.   Frazier, John W. 1979. "Educational Geographers
          and Applied Geography," Journal of Geography,
          Vol. 78, pp. 44-45.

H-294.   Frazier, John W. and Henry, N. F. 1978.
          "Selected Themes in Applied Geography,"
          Geographical Survey, Vol. 7, pp. 3-10.

H-295.   Freedom, Gary S.   1976.   "Military Geography: A
          Viable Field," Geographical Bulletin, Vol. 12,
          pp. 24-27.

H-296.   Freeman, T. W.   1946.   "Historical Geography and
          the Irish Historian," Irish Historical Studies,
          Vol. 5, pp. 139-146.

H-297.   French, R. A.   1968.   "Historical Geography in
          the U.S.S.R.," Soviet Geography: Review and
          Translation, Vol. 9, pp. 551-562.

H-298.   Friends of Gramsci (The) [J. D. Pratts and T. R.
          Pringle].   1985. "Rethinking 'Studies in
          Historical Geography,'" Area, Vol. 17, pp. 50-51.

H-299.   Fuchs, Roland J.   1964.   "Review Article: Soviet
          Urban Geography: An   Appraisal of Postwar
          Research," Annals of the Association of American
          Geographers, Vol. 54, pp. 276-290.

H-300.   Gale, Stephen.   1972.   "Inexactness, Fuzzy Sets,
          and the Foundations of Behavioral Geography,"
          Geographical Analysis, Vol. 4, pp. 337-349.

H-301.   Ganssen, R.   1970.   "The Nature and Tasks of Soil
          Geography and its Place Within the Geosciences,"
          Geoforum, Vol. 1, pp. 77-94.

H-302.   Garner, Barry J.   1966.   "Aspects and Trends of
          Urban Geography," Journal of Geography, Vol. 65,
          pp. 206-211.

H-303.   Garnier, B. J.   1963.   "A Program for Physical
          Geography," Professional Geographer, Vol. 15, No.
          4, pp. 16-19.

H-304.   Geikie, James.   1887.   "Geography and Geology,"
          Scottish Geographical Magazine, Vol. 3, pp.
          398-407.

H-305.   Gelyakova, T. M.   1967.   "The Present State of
          Medical Geography in the U.S.S.R.," Soviet
          Geography: Review and Translation, Vol. 8, pp.
          228-234.

H-306.   Gerasimov, I. P.   1961.   "The Main Tasks and
          Trends of Geomorphological Research in the
          U.S.S.R.," Soviet Geography: Review and
          Translation, Vol. 2, No. 3, pp. 35-44.

H-307.   Gerasimov, I. P. et al.   1979.   "Soviet Physical
          and Biological Geography," Geforum, Vol. 10, pp.
          261-266.

H-308.   Gerasimov, I. P.   1983.   "Contemporary
          Anthropogeography at the Chorological Level,"
          Soviet Geography: Review and Translation, Vol.
          24, pp. 267-279.

H-309.   Gersmerhl, Philip J.   1976.   "An Alternative
          Biogeography," Annals of the Association of
          American Geographers, Vol. 66, pp. 223-241.

H-310.   Gertler, M. S.   1988.   "Some Problems of Time in
          Economic Geography,"   Environment and Planning A,
          Vol. 20, pp. 151-164.

H-311.   Gilbert, E. W.   1932.   "What is Historical
          Geography?"   Scottish Geographical Magazine, Vol.
          47, pp. 129-136.

H-312.   Gilbert, E. W. and Steel, R. W.   1945.   "Social
          Geography and its Place in Colonial Studies,"
          Geographical Journal, Vol. 106, pp. 118-132.

H-313.   Ginsburg, Norton S.   1948.   "Comments on Some
          Publications of the China Institute of
          Geography," Annals of the Association of American
          Geographers, Vol. 38, pp. 147-150.

H-314.   Glacken, C.   1960.   "Count Buffon on Cultural
          Changes of the Physical Environment," Annals of
          the Association of American Geographers, Vol. 50,
          pp. 1-21.

H-315.   Glick, Thomas F.   1987.   "History and Philosophy
          of Geography," Progress in Human Geography, Vol.
          11, pp. 405-416.

H-316.   Gokhman, V. M., Lavrov, S. B. and Sdasyvk, G. V.
          1980.   "Socio-Economic Geography in the West at a
          Turning Point," Soviet Geography: Review and
          Translation, Vol. 21, pp. 284-293.

H-317.   Gold, John R.   1977.   "Teaching Behavioral
          Geography," Journal of Geography in Higher
          Education, Vol. 1, pp. 37-46.

H-318.   Gold, John R. and Goodey, Brian.   1983.
          "Behavioral and Perceptual Geography," Progress
          in Human Geography, Vol. 7, pp. 578-586.

H-319.   Gold, John R. and Goodey, Brian.   1984.
          "Behavioral and Perceptual Geography: Criticisms
          and Response," Progress in Human Geography, Vol.
          8, pp. 544-550.

H-320.   Goldenberg, L. A.   1972.   "About the Place of
          Historical Geography in the System of Sciences,"
          Proceedings - Twenty-second International
          Geographical Congress, pp. 420-422.

H-321.   Golledge, R. G. 1981. "Guest Editorial: A
         Practitioner's View of Behavioral Research in
         Geography," Environment and Planning A, Vol. 13,
         pp. 1-6.

H-322.   Golledge, R. G. 1982. "Misconceptions,
         Misinterpretations, and Misrepresentations of
         Behavioral Approaches in Human Geography,"
         Environment and Planning A, Vol. 13, pp.
         1325-1344.

H-323.   Golledge, R. G., Brown, L. A. and Williamson,
         Frank. 1972. "Behavioural Approaches in
         Geography: An Overview," Australian Geographer,
         Vol. 12, pp. 59-79.

H-324.   Goode, J. Paul. 1918. "A Course in Economic
         Geography," School and Society, Vol. 7, pp.
         216-222.

H-325.   Goode, J. Paul. 1922. "The Trend in Economic
         Geography," Journal of Geography, Vol. 21, pp.
         18-20.

H-326.   Goode, J. Paul. 1925. "The Progress of
         Cartography in Poland," Annals of the Association
         of American Geographers, Vol. 15, pp. 36.

H-327.   Goode, N. J. 1968. "The Professional
         Geographer's Contribution to the Retail Food
         Industry," Professional Geographer, Vol. 20, pp.
         396-397.

H-328.   Goodey, B. and Gold, J. R. 1987. "Environmental
         Perception: The Relationship with Urban Design,"
         Progress in Human Geography, Vol. 11, pp.
         126-133.

H-329.   Goodey, Brian and Gold, John R. 1987.
         "Behavioral and Perceptual Geography: From
         Retrospect to Prospect," Progress in Human
         Geography, Vol. 9, pp. 585-596.

H-330.   Goodridge, J. C. 1978. "Environmental
         Science/Studies," Area, Vol. 10, pp. 315-317.

H-331.   Gorbatsevich, R. A. 1972. "Political Geography
         and Its Problems," Soviet Geography: Review and
         Translation, Vol. 13, pp. 220-227.

H-332.   Gottmann, Jean. 1982. "The Basic Problem of
         Political Geography: The Organization of Space
         and the Search for Stability," Tijdschrift voor
         Economische en Sociale Geografie, Vol. 73, pp.
         340-349.

H-333.   Graf, William.   1984.   "The Geography of American
          Field Geomorphology," Professional Geographer,
          Vol. 36, pp. 78-82.

H-334.   Graf, William, Tremble, Stanley W., Lay, Terrence
          J., and Costa, John E.   1980.   "Geographic
          Geomorphology in the Eighties," Professional
          Geographer, Vol. 32, pp. 279-284.

H-335.   Graves, Bruce G.   1975.   "Military Geography: An
          Investigation of Qualifications," Geographical
          Bulletin, Vol. 10, pp. 20-23.

H-336.   Graves, N. J.   1980.   "Geographical Education in
          Britain," Progress in Human Geography, Vol. 5,
          pp. 562-571.

H-337.   Graves, N. J.   1981.   "Geographical Education,"
          Progress in Human Geography, Vol. 5, pp. 562-571.

H-338.   Graves, N. J.   1981.   "International Aspects of
          Geographical Education," Journal of Geography,
          Vol. 80, pp. 84-86.

H-339.   Gray, F. and Boddy, M.   1979.   "The Origins and
          Use of Theory in Urban Geography: Household
          Mobility and Filtering Theory," Geoforum, Vol.
          10, pp. 117-127.

H-340.   Gray, F. and Duncan, S.   1978.   "Etymology,
          Mystification, and Urban Geography," Area, Vol.
          10, pp. 297-301.

H-341.   Gray, M.   1978.   "The Future of Physical
          Geography: Some Alternatives," Scottish
          Geographical Magazine, Vol. 94, pp. 183-184.

H-342.   Green, Howard L.   1967.   "The Marketing
          Geographer: His Areas of Competence,"
          Professional Geographer, Vol. 19, pp. 261-262.

H-343.   Greenberg, J.   1978.   "Psychogeography: A
          Freudian Look at Mother Earth," Science News,
          Vol. 113, pp. 90-91, Feb. 11.

H-344.   Greenwood, R. H.   1952.   "The Economic Aspects of
          Geography," Australian Geographer, Vol. 6, pp.
          17-21.

H-345.   Gregor, Howard F.   1957.   "German vs. American
          Economic Geography," Professional Geographer,
          Vol. 9, No. 1, pp. 12-14.

H-346.   Gregory, Derek.   1976.   "Rethinking Historical
          Geography," Area, Vol. 8, pp. 295-299.

H-347. Gregory, K. J. 1979. "Hydrogeomorphology: How
        Applied Should We Become?" Progress in Physical
        Geography, Vol. 3, pp. 84-101.

H-348. Gregory, S. 1978. "The Role of Physical
        Geography in the Curriculum," Geography, Vol. 63,
        pp. 251-264.

H-349. Gregory, S. 1983. "Quantitiative Geography:
        The British Experience and the Role of the
        Institute," Transactions - Institute of British
        Geographers, Vol. 8, pp. 80-89.

H-350. Gregson, Nicky. 1987. "Review Essay: Human
        Geography and Social Geography: Common Ground
        or Common Object," [D. Gregory and J. Urry,
        Social Relations and Spatial Structures]
        Political Geography Quarterly, Vol. 6, pp.
        93-101.

H-351. Griffin, Donald W. 1965. "Some Comments on
        Urban Planning and the Geographer," Professional
        Geographer, Vol. 17, No. 1, pp. 4-7.

H-352. Grigg, David. 1982. "Agricultural Geography,"
        Progress in Human Geography, Vol. 6, pp. 242-246.

H-353. Gritzner, Charles. 1986. "The South Dakota
        Experience [in High School Geography],"
        Professional Geographer, Vol. 38, pp. 252-253.

H-354. Gritzner, Charles F. 1966. "The Nature of
        Cultural Geography," Memorandum Folio,
        Southeastern Division, Association of American
        Geographers, Vol. 18, pp. 69-75.

H-355. Gritzner, Charles F. 1979. "Some Thoughts on
        Applied Geography," Journal of Geography, Vol.
        78, pp. 74-75.

H-356. Gritzner, Charles F., Jr. 1966. "The Scope of
        Cultural Geography," Journal of Geography, Vol.
        65, pp. 4-11.

H-357. Guelke, Leonard. 1975. "On Rethinking
        Historical Geography," Journal of Geography,
        Vol. 7, pp. 135-138.

H-358. Guelke, Leonard. 1976. "Interdisciplinary
        Research and Environmental Perception,"
        Proceedings - Twenty-third International
        Geographical Congress, Vol. 8, pp. 184-188.

H-359. Gulley, J. L. M. 1961. "The Practice of
        Historical Geography, A Study in the Writings of
        Professor Roger Dion," Tijdschrift voor
        Economische en Sociale Geografie, Vol. 52, pp.
        169-183.

H-360.   Guzman, Louis E.   1960.   "The Economic Geographer
          in Economic Development," _Professional_
          Geographer, Vol. 12, No. 4, pp. 16-18.

H-361.   Gvozdetskiy, N. A., et al.   1971.   "The Present
          State and Future Tasks of Physical Geography,"
          Soviet Geography: Review and Translation, Vol.
          12, pp. 257-266.

H-362.   Haase, G. and Richter, H.   1983.   "Current Trends
          in Landscape Research," _GeoJournal_, Vol. 7, pp.
          107-120.

H-363.   Haggett, P.   1978.   "The Spatial Economy,"
          American Behavioral Scientist, Vol. 22, pp.
          151-167.

H-364.   HaHari, Masayuki.   1979.   "Historical Geography
          in Japan," _Professional Geographer_, Vol. 31, pp.
          321-326.

H-365.   Hajdú, Zoltan.   1987.   "Political Geography
          Around the World: Administrative Geography and
          Reforms of the Administrative Areas in Hungary,"
          Political Geography Quarterly, Vol. 6, pp.
          269-278.

H-366.   Haines-Young, R. H. and Petch, J. R..   1980.
          "The Challenge of Critical Rationalism for
          Methodology in Physical Geography," _Progress in_
          Physical Geography, Vol. 4, pp. 63-77.

H-367.   Hall, Peter.   1974.   "The New Political
          Geography," _Transactions - Institute of British_
          Geographers, No. 63, pp. 48-52. .

H-368.   Hamill, Louis.   1965.   "Are Formal Theories
          Needed in Marketing Geography?" _Professional_
          Geographer, Vol. 17, No. 2, pp. 11-14.

H-369.   Hammond, Edwin H.   1962.   "Land Form Geography
          and Land Form Description," _California_
          Geographer, Vol. 3, pp. 69-76.

H-370.   Hampton, P.   1987.   "Economics and Human
          Geography," _Progress in Human Geography_, Vol.
          11, pp. 106-125.

H-371.   Handey, Lawrence R.   1982.   "The Rise and Demise
          of Commercial Geography," _Journal of Geography_,
          Vol. 81, pp. 174-178.

H-372.   Hans [sic], William H.   1925.   "The American
          Indian and Geographic Studies," _Annals of the_
          Association of American Geographers, Vol. 15, pp.
          86-91.

H-373. Hansis, Richard. 1984. "Comments on Adaptation, Variation, and Cultureal Geography," Professional Geographer, Vol. 36, p. 216.

H-374. Hard, Gerhard. 1976. "Physical-Geography -- Its Function and Future. A Reconsideration," Tijdschrift voor Economische en Sociale Geografie, Vol. 67, pp. 358-368.

H-375. Hardest, Donald L. 1986. "Rethinking Cultural Adaptation," Professional Geographer, Vol. 38, pp. 11-18.

H-376. Hare, F. Kenneth. 1969. "New Wings for Climatology: A Science Reborn," Yearbook - Association of Pacific Coast Geographers , Vol. 30, pp. 145-162.

H-377. Hare, F. Kenneth. 1973. "The Virtues of Requisite Variety," Horizon, Vol. 22, pp. 11-14.

H-378. Harley, J. B. 1973. "Change in Historical Geography: A Qualitative Impression of Quantitative Methods," Area, Vol. 5, pp. 69-74.

H-379. Harnapp, Vern R. 1976. "Geography: We Need Some Farm Teams," Geographical Survey, Vol. 5, No. 2, pp. 3-4.

H-380. Harris, Britton. 1985. "Synthetic Geography: The Nature of Our Understanding of Cities," Environment and Planning A, Vol. 17, pp. 443-464.

H-381. Harris, C. D. and Edmonds, R. L. 1982. "Urban Geography in Japan: A Survey of Recent Literature," Urban Geography, Vol. 3, pp. 1-21.

H-382. Harris, Cole. 1971. "Theory and Synthesis in Historical Geography," Canadian Geographer, Vol. 15, pp. 157-172.

H-383. Harris, R. Colebrook. 1967. "Historical Geography in Canada," Canadian Geographer, Vol. 11, pp. 235-250.

H-384. Harrison, James D. 1977. "What is Applied Geography?" Professional Geographer, Vol. 29, pp. 297-300.

H-385. Hartman, George W. 1949. "The Central Business District--A Study in Urban Geography," Economic Geography, Vol. 25, pp. 237-244.

H-386. Hartmann, R. 1985. "Survey 3: Recent Development in German-Speaking Human Geography-Controversy, Change, and Continuity," Environnment and Planning D: Society and Space, Vol. 3, pp. 259-263.

H-387.   Hartshorne, Richard. 1935. "Suggestions on the
          Terminology of Political Boundaries," Annals of
          the Association of American Geographers, Vol. 26,
          pp. 56-57.

H-388.   Hartshorne, Richard. 1935. "The History, Nature
          and Scope of Political Geography," Annals of the
          Association of American Geographers, Vol. 25, pp.
          40-41.

H-389.   Hartshorne, Richard. 1950. "The Functional
          Approach in Political Geography," Annals of the
          Association of American Geographers, Vol. 40, pp.
          95-130.

H-390.   Harvey, David. 1966. "Theoretical Concepts and
          the Analysis of Agricultural Land-Use Patterns in
          Geography," Annals of the Association of American
          Geographers, Vol. 56, pp. 361-374.

H-391.   Hauer, J. and Veldman, J. 1983. "Rural
          Geography at Utrecht," Tijdschrift voor
          Economische en Sociale Geografie, Vol. 74, pp.
          397-406.

H-392.   Haughton, S. H. 1952. "Conservation and the
          Geographer," South African Geographical Journal,
          Vol. 34, pp. 20-29.

H-393.   Hausladen, Gary. 1979. "Soviet Historical
          Geography in the 1970s: A Preliminary
          Assessment," Discussion Paper Series, Syracuse
          University, Department of Geography, No. 60, 25
          p.

H-394.   Hawley, A. 1968. "Environmental Perception:
          Nature and Ellen Churchill Semple," Southeastern
          Geographer, Vol. 8, pp. 54-59.

H-395.   Heenan, Brian. 1987. "Population Studies,"
          Progress in Human Geography, Vol. 11, pp.
          275-285.

H-396.   Hellen, J. A. 1978. "The Future of German
          Geography," Geographical Journal, Vol. 14, pp.
          118-120.

H-397.   Henkel, Wilhelm C. 1895. "On the Combination of
          Geography and History in the Curriculum of Modern
          Schools," Proceedings - Sixth International
          Geographical Congress, pp. 88-89.

H-398.   Hepple, Leslie W. 1986. "The Revival of
          Geopolitics," Political Geography Quarterly, Vol.
          5, Sup., pp. S21-35.

H-399.   Hepworth, Mark E.   1987.   "Information Technology as Spatial Systems," _Progress in Human Geography_, Vol. 11, pp. 157-180.

H-400.   Herbertson, A. J.   1898.   "The Position of Economic Geography in Education," _Journal of the Manchester Geographical Society_, Vol. 14, pp. 286-292.

H-401.   Herrick, Cheesman A.   1904.   "Commercial Geography in the Secondary School," _Education_, Vol. 25, pp. 129-134.

H-402.   Herrick, Cheesman A.   1904.   "Commercial Geography in the Secondary School," _Proceedings - Eighth International Geographical Congress_, pp. 987-991.

H-403.   Heske, Henning.   1986.   "Political Geographers of the Past III: German Geographic Research in the Nazi Period -- a Content Analysis of the Major Geography Journals, 1925-1945," _Political Geography Quarterly_, Vol. 5, pp. 267-282.

H-404.   Hey, R. D.   1968.   "Causal and Functional Relations in Fluvial Geomorphology," _Earth Surface Processes_, Vol. 4, pp. 179-182.

H-405.   Hight, J.   1906.   "Geography in the University of New Zealand," _Geographical Teacher_, Vol. 3, pp. 168-170.

H-406.   Hill, A. R.   1975.   "Biogeography as a Sub-Field of Geography," _Area_, Vol. 7, pp. 156-161.

H-407.   Hilton, T. E.   1961.   "Population Studies in Geography," _Bulletin - Ghana Geographical Association_, Vol. 6, No. 2, pp. 35-43.

H-408.   Hilton, T. E.   1962.   "The Study of Geomorphology," _Bulletin - Geographical Association_, Vol. 7, Nos. 1-2, pp. 21-29.

H-409.   Hinks, Arthur R.   1911.   "Recent Progress in Geodness," _Geographical Journal_, Vol. 38, pp. 181-190.

H-410.   Hodgkins, Alton R.   1925.   "The Study of Economic Geography," _Journal of Geography_, Vol. 24, pp. 226-234.

H-411.   Hodgson, H. B.   1937.   "Notes on the History of the Teaching of Geography," _Geography_, Vol. 22, pp. 44-48.

H-412.   Hoekveld, G. A.   1968.   "On the Theory and State
          of the Urban Geography in the Netherlands,"
          [English Summary] Tijdschrift voor Economische en
          Sociale Geografie, Vol. 59, pp. 11-12 [article on
          pp. 1-11].

H-413.   Hoggart, Keith.   1986.   "Geography, Political
          Control and Local Government Policy Outputs,"
          Progress in Human Geography, Vol. 10, pp. 1-23.

H-414.   Holdich, Colonel Sir T. H.   1909.   "Some Aspects
          of Political Geography," Geographical Journal,
          Vol. 34, pp. 593-608.

H-415.   Holdich, Colonel Sir Thomas.   1899.   "The Use of
          Practical Geography Illustrated by Recent
          Frontier Operations," Geographical Journal, Vol.
          13, pp. 465-477 [Discussion, pp. 477-480].

H-416.   Holland, P. G.   1982.   "Environmental Diversity:
          Review and Prospects for Biogeography," South
          African Geographical Journal, Vol. 64, pp. 51-62.

H-417.   Hooson, David J. M.   1960.   "The Distribution of
          Population as the Essential Geographical
          Expression," Canadian Geographer, No. 17, pp.
          10-20.

H-418.   Hope, Geoffrey.   1985.   "Pinning Biogeography
          Down," [Review article] Australian Geographical
          Studies, Vol. 23, pp. 136-138.

H-419.   Hornbeck, David.   1979.   "Applied Geography, Is
          It Really Needed?" Journal of Geography, Vol. 78,
          pp. 47-49.

H-420.   Hubbard, Geo. D.   1940.   "Major Objectives of
          Penck and Davis in Geomorphic Studies," Annals of
          the Association of American Geographers, Vol. 30,
          pp. 237-240.

H-421.   Hudson, G. Donald.   1935.   "Geography and
          Regional Planning," Journal of Geography, Vol.
          34, pp. 267-277.

H-422.   Hunt, J.   1980.   "Cartography and Geography:
          Some Interactions and Developments," Bulletin -
          Society of University Cartographers, Vol. 14, pp.
          35-37.

H-423.   Hunter, J. M.   1961.   "Geography in the Service
          of Economic Development," Bulletin - Ghana
          Geographical Association, Vol. 6, No. 2, pp.
          44-48.

H-424.   Huntington, C. C.   1926.   "What is Social
          Geography," Journal of Geography, Vol. 25, pp.
          90-96.

H-425.   Huntington, Ellsworth. 1923. "Influenza: An
         Example of Statistical Geography," Annals of the
         Association of American Geographers, Vol. 13, pp.
         210-211.

H-426.   Hutchinson, Lincoln. 1907. "A Plea for a
         Broader Conception of Economic Geography, Journal
         of Geography, Vol. 6, pp. 122-128.

H-427.   Huziner, George A. 1977. "A Reexamination of
         Soviet Industrial Location Theory," Professional
         Geographer, Vol. 29, pp. 259-265.

H-428.   Il'yina, L. N. 1976. "The Study of Plant
         Resources from the Point of View of Economic
         Geography," Soviet Geography: Review and
         Translation, Vol. 17, pp. 613-624.

H-429.   Inamullah, Mohd. 1962. "Oceanography Today,"
         Deccan Geographer, Vol. 1, pp. 71-81.

H-430.   Inskeep, Edward L. 1962. "The Geographer in
         Planning," Professional Geographer, Vol. 14, pp.
         22-24.

H-431.   Iofa, L. Ye. 1963. "On the Significance of
         Historical Geography," Soviet Geography: Review
         and Translation, Vol. 4, No. 1, pp. 3-13.

H-432.   Isaac, Erich. 1959-60. "Religion, Landscape and
         Space," Landscape, Vol. 9, pp. 14-18.

H-433.   Isachenko, A. G. 1961. "Landscape Mapping: Its
         Significance, Its Present State and Its Tasks,"
         Soviet Geography: Review and Translation, Vol.
         2, pp. 34-47.

H-434.   Isachenko, A. G. 1978. "Geography and
         Historical Geography," Soviet Geography: Review
         and Translation, Vol. 19, pp. 180-185.

H-435.   Ivan, A. 1983. "Some Problems in
         Geomorphological Terminology,"
         Zpravy-Geografickeho Ustavu CSAV, Vol. 20, pp.
         15-33 [English Summary].

H-436.   Jackman, Albert H. 1962. "The Nature of
         Military Geography," Professional Geographer,
         Vol. 14, No. 1, pp. 7-12.

H-437.   Jackson, John N. 1964. "Review Article:
         Geography and Planning in British Columbia,"
         Canadian Geographer, Vol. 8, pp. 92-96.

H-438.   Jackson, John N. 1967. "Geography and
         Planning: Two Subjects, or One?" Canadian
         Geographer, Vol. 11, pp. 357-365.

H-439.   Jackson, P. 1980. "A Plea for Cultural
         Geography," _Area_, Vol. 12, pp. 110-113.

H-440.   Jackson, Peter. 1983. "Social Geography:
         Convergence and Compromise," _Progress in Human
         Geography_, Vol. 8, pp. 116-121.

H-441.   Jackson, Peter. 1985. "Urban Ethnography,"
         Progress in Human Geography, Vol. 9, pp. 157-177.

H-442.   Jackson, Peter. 1986. "Social Geography: The
         Rediscovery of Place," _Progress in Human
         Geography_, Vol. 10, pp. 118-124.

H-443.   Jackson, Peter. 1987. "Social Geography:
         Politics and Place," _Progress in Human
         Geography_, Vol. 11, pp. 286-292.

H-444.   Jackson, Richard H. 1976. "The Persistence of
         Outmoded Ideas in High School Geography Texts,"
         Journal of Geography, Vol. 75, pp. 399-408.

H-445.   Jackson, S. P. 1969. "Geography as
         Environmental Science and the Training of
         Geographers," _South African Geographical Journal_,
         Vol. 51, pp. 3-18.

H-446.   Jackson, W. A. Douglas. 1958. "Whither
         Political Geography?" _Annals of the Association
         of American Geographers_, Vol. 48, pp. 178-183.

H-447.   Jacobson, Daniel. 1965. "The Role of Historical
         Geography in the American School," _Journal of
         Geography_, Vol. 64, pp. 99-105.

H-448.   Jakle, J. A. 1971. "Time, Space, and the
         Geographic Past: A Prospectus for Historical
         Geography," _American Historical Review_, Vol. 76,
         pp. 1084-1103.

H-449.   Jakle, John A. 1974. "In Pursuit of a Wild
         Goose: Historical Geography and the Geographic
         Past," _Historical Geography Newsletter_, Vol. 4,
         pp. 13-16.

H-450.   James, Preston E. 1931. "Vicksburg: A Study in
         Urban Geography," _Geographical Review_, Vol. 21,
         pp. 234-243.

H-451.   Jancu, M. and Baron, P. 1984. "Directions of
         Romanian Tourism and of Tourist Research,"
         GeoJournal, Vol. 9, pp. 75-76.

H-452.   Jansen, Adviaan C. M. 1976. "On Theoretical
         Foundations of Policy-Oriented Geography."
         _Tijdschrift voor Economische en Sociale
         Geografie_, Vol. 67, pp. 342-351.

H-453.   Jeans, D. N. 1980. "Historical Geography in the
          Future?" <u>Australian Geographer</u>, Vol. 14, pp.
          67-68.

H-454.   Jenks, George F. 1953. "An Improved Curriculum
          for Cartographic Training at the College and
          University Level," <u>Annals of the Association of
          American Geographers</u>, Vol. 43, pp. 317-331.

H-455.   Jensen, John R. 1983. "Biophysical Remote
          Sensing," <u>Annals of the Association of American
          Geographers</u>, Vol. 73, pp. 111-132.

H-456.   Joerg, W. L. G. 1933. "The Development of
          Polish Cartography Since the World War,"
          <u>Geographical Review</u>, Vol. 23, pp. 122-129.

H-457.   Johnson, Emory R. 1906. "Political Geography as
          a University Subject," <u>Bulletin of the American
          Society of New York</u>, Vol. 38, pp. 107-109.

H-458.   Johnson, P. G. 1970. "Which Way Geomorphology?"
          <u>Geoscope</u>, Vol. 1, pp. 20-26.

H-459.   Johnston, R. J. 1984. "Marxist Political
          Economy, the State and Political Geography,"
          <u>Progress in Human Geography</u>, Vol. 8, pp. 473-492.

H-460.   Johnston, R. J. 1985. "On the Practical
          Relevance of a Realist Approach to Political
          Geography," <u>Progress in Human Geography</u>, Vol. 9,
          pp. 601-604.

H-461.   Johnston, R. J. 1976. "Population Distributions
          and the Essentials of Human Geography," <u>South
          African Geographical Journal</u>, Vol. 58, pp.
          93-106.

H-462.   Johnston, R. J. 1980. "Electoral Geography and
          Political Geography," <u>Australian Geographical
          Studies</u>, Vol. 18, pp. 37-50.

H-463.   Johnston, R. J. 1980. "Political Geography
          Without Politics," <u>Progress in Human Geography</u>,
          Vol. 5, pp. 595-598.

H-464.   Johnston, R. J. 1981. "Political Geography
          Without Dogma," <u>Progress in Human Geography</u>, Vol.
          5, pp. 595-598.

H-465.   Johnston, R. J. 1983. "From Description to
          Explanation in Urban Geography," <u>Geography</u>, Vol.
          68, pp. 11-15.

H-466.   Johnston, R. J. and Lauria, Mickey. 1985.
          "Review Essays: Political Geography: Improving
          the Theoretical Base," <u>Political Geography
          Quarterly</u>, Vol. 4, pp. 251-257.

H-467.   Jones, David K. C. 1983. "Environments of
          Concern," _Transactions, Institute of British
          Geographers_, Vol. 8, pp. 429-457.

H-468.   Jones, E. 1984. "Post-positivist Social
          Geography," _GeoJournal_, Vol. 9, pp. 241-245.

H-469.   Jones, R. L. 1987. "Biogeography," _Progress in
          Human Geography_, Vol. 11, pp. 133-142.

H-470.   Jones, R. L. 1988. "Biogeography," _Progress in
          Human Geography_, Vol. 12, pp. 103-118.

H-471.   Jones, Ronald. 1967. "The Nature of Urban
          Geography," _Geographical Magazine_, Vol. 83, pp.
          147-150.

H-472.   Jones, Stephen B. 1950. "What Does Geography
          Need From Climatology," _Professional Geographer_,
          Vol. 2, pp. 41-44.

H-473.   Jones, Stephen B. 1954. "A Unified Field Theory
          of Political Geography," _Annals of the
          Association of American Geographers_, Vol. 44, pp.
          111-123.

H-474.   Jopling, A. 1970. "Recommendations on the
          Future Development of Geomorphology in Canada,"
          Canadian Geographer, Vol. 14, pp. 167-173.

H-475.   Jordan, Terry G. 1966. "On the Nature of
          Settlement Geography," _Professional Geographer_,
          Vol. 18, pp. 26-28.

H-476.   Kalesnik, S. V. 1961. "The Present State of
          Landscape Studies," _Soviet Geography: Review
          and Translation_, Vol. 2, pp. 24-34.

H-477.   Kalesnik, S. V. 1968. "The Development of
          General Earth Science in the U.S.S.R. During the
          Soviet Period," _Soviet Geography: Review and
          Translation_, Vol. 9, pp. 393-402.

H-478.   Karpinski, Louis C. 1923. "The Contribution of
          Mathematicians and Astronomers to Scientific
          Cartography," _Annals of the Association of
          American Geographers_, Vol. 13, pp. 211-212.

H-479.   Kates, Robert W. 1987. "The Human Environment:
          The Road Not Taken, The Road Still Beckoning,"
          _Annals of the Association of American
          Geographers_, Vol. 77, pp. 525-534.

H-480.   Keane, T. 1977. "Meteorology: Its Role,
          Development and Scope," _Geographical Viewpoint_,
          Vol. 6, pp. 25-35.

H-481.   Kearns, Gerry. 1986. "Historical Geography,"
          Progress in Human Geography, Vol. 10, pp.
          587-621.

H-482.   Kearns, Gerry. 1988. "Historical Geography,"
          Progress in Human Geography, Vol. 12, pp.
          103-110.

H-483.   Kearsley, G. W. and Hearn, T. J. 1981.
          "Geography and Community: Recreation Studies,"
          New Zealand Journal of Geography, Vol. 71, pp.
          18-19.

H-484.   Keasbey, L. M. 1901. "Principles of Economic
          Geography," Political Science Quarterly, Vol. 16,
          pp. 476-485.

H-485.   Keasbey, L. M. 1901. "Study of Economic
          Geography," Political Science Quarterly, Vol. 16,
          pp. 79-95.

H-486.   Keates, J. S. 1984. "The Cartographic Art,"
          Cartographica, Vol. 21, pp. 37-43.

H-487.   Keeler, Frank Lever. 1953. "Resources
          Inventory--A Basic Step in Economic Development,"
          Economic Geography, Vol. 29, pp. 39-47.

H-488.   Keelerman, Aharon. 1981. "Time-Space Approaches
          and Regional Study," Tijdschrift voor Economische
          en Sociale Geografie, Vol. 72, pp. 17-27.

H-489.   Kent, W. A. 1980. "Geography and Environmental
          Education," Geographical Viewpoint, Vol. 9, pp.
          19-28.

H-490.   Kerr, Donald P. 1960. "The Tasks of Economic
          Geography," Canadian Geographer, No. 17, pp. 1-9.

H-491.   Keuning, H. J. 1960. "Approaching Economic
          Geography from the Point of View of the
          Enterprise," Tijdschrift voor Economische en
          Sociale Geografie, Vol. 51, pp. 10-11.

H-492.   Keuning, H. J. 1960. "The Place of Social
          Geography Within Human Geography," Tijdschrift
          van het Koninklijk Nederlandsch Aardrijkskundig
          Genootscahp, Vol. 77, pp. 341-346.

H-493.   Khvalynskaya, M. S. 1984. "Economic Geography
          of Higher Education in the USSR," Soviet
          Geography: Review and Translation, Vol. 25, pp.
          381-389.

H-494.   Kincer, J. B.   1936.   "Organization and Work in
         Climatology and Agricultural Meteorology in Great
         Britain, France and Scandinavian Countries,
         Poland and Russia," Annals of the Association of
         American Geographers, Vol. 26, pp. 64-65.

H-495.   Kincer, J. B.   1936.   "Veteran Cooperative
         Observers of the U. S. Weather and the
         Organization of Climatological Observations in
         the United States," Annals of the Association of
         American Geographers, Vol. 26, pp. 65-67.

H-496.   King, Leslie J.   1976.   "Alternatives to a
         Positivist Economic Geography," Annals of the
         Association of American Geographers, Vol. 66, pp.
         293-308.

H-497.   Kirby, Andrew.   1985.   "Pseudo-Random Thoughts on
         Space, Scale and Ideology in Political
         Geography," Political Geography Quarterly, Vol.
         4, pp. 5-18.

H-498.   Kirby, Andrew.   1986.   "Where's the Theory?"
         Political Geography Quarterly, Vol. 5, pp.
         187-192.

H-499.   Kirk, W.   1952.   "Historical Geography and the
         Concept of the Behavioural Environment," Indian
         Geographical Society Silver Jubilee Souvenir, pp.
         152-160.

H-500.   Kiss, George.   1942.   "Political Geography into
         Geopolitics: Recent Trends in Germany,"
         Geographical Review, Vol. 32, pp. 632-645.

H-501.   Kiuchi, Shinzo.   1963.   "Recent Trends in Urban
         Geography in Japan," Annals of the Association of
         American Geographers, Vol. 53, pp. 93-101.

H-502.   Kliot, N.   1982.   "Recent Themes in Political
         Geography," Tijdschrift voor Economische en
         Sociale Geografie, Vol. 73, pp. 270-279.

H-503.   Kniffen, F. B.   1979.   "Why Folk Housing?" Annals
         of the Association of American Geographers, Vol.
         69, pp. 59-63.

H-504.   Knirk, Carl F.   1940.   "Industrial Geography, Its
         Meaning, Scope and Content," Journal of
         Geography, Vol. 39, pp. 141-147.

H-505.   Knox, Paul.   1987.   "Planning and Applied
         Geography," Progress in Human Geography, Vol. 11,
         pp. 540-548.

H-506. Konstantinov, O. A. 1960. "The Present Status
of Economic Geographic Studies on the Economic
Regionalization of the U.S.S.R.," Soviet
Geography: Review and Translation, Vol. 1, No.
7, pp. 36-59.

H-507. Konstantinov, O. A. 1965. "On the Thirtieth
Anniversary of the Department of Economic
Geography of the Geographical Society U.S.S.R.,"
Soviet Geography: Review and Translation, Vol.
7, pp. 3-11.

H-508. Konstantinov, O. A. 1968. "Economic Geography
in the U.S.S.R. on the 50th Anniversary of Soviet
Power," Soviet Geography: Review and
Translation, Vol. 9, pp. 417-425.

H-509. Koreshy, K. V. 1966. "Geography in National
Planning, With Special Reference to Urban
Development," Pakistan Geographical Review, Vol.
21, pp. 21-33.

H-510. Koroscil, Paul M. 1971. "Historical Geography:
A Resurrection," Journal of Geography, Vol. 70,
pp. 415-420.

H-511. Kostrowicki, Jerzy. 1956. "Contribution of
Geography to Planning in Poland," Proceedings -
Eighteenth International Geographical Congress,
pp. 569-574.

H-512. Kovalev, S. A. 1966. "A Geography of
Consumption and a Geography of Services," Soviet
Geography, Vol. 7, pp. 65-74.

H-513. Kovalev, S. A. and Pokshishevskiy, V. V. 1967.
"The Geography of Population and the Geography
of Services," Soviet Geography, Vol. 8, pp.
641-652.

H-514. Krapotkin, Prince. 1889. "What Geography Ought
to Be," Journal of the Manchester Geographical
Society, Vol. 5, pp. 356-358.

H-515. Krapotkin, P. 1893. "On the Teaching of
Physiography," Geographical Journal, Vol. 2, pp.
350-359.

H-516. Kraus, H. 1984. "Wasist Klima? (How to Define
Climate?)," Erdkunde, Vol. 38, pp. 249-258
[English Summary].

H-517. Krivolutskiy, A. Ye. 1976. "The Study Object of
Physical Geography," Soviet Geography: Review
and Translation, Vol. 17, pp. 112-121.

H-518.   Kroenig, L. 1978. "A Pragmatic Approach to
          Behavioural Research," Albertan Geographer, Vol.
          14, pp. 89-104.

H-519.   Krone, P. 1979. "The Humanistic Perspective in
          Historical Geography: Willa Cather's Nebraska,
          1880-1920," Ohio Geographers, Vol. 7, pp. 41-46.

H-520.   Krumme, Gunter. 1969. "Toward a Geography of
          Enterprise," Economic Geography, Vol. 45, pp.
          30-40.

H-521.   Kuriyan, George. N.D. "Geography and Religion,"
          Journal of the Indian Geographical Association,
          Vol. 36, N.P.

H-522.   Langdon, Keith P. 1979. "Biogeography: The
          Challenge," Geographical Survey, Vol. 8, No. 4,
          pp. 18-22.

H-523.   Laponc, J. A. 1987. "More About Languages and
          Their Territories: A Reply to Partanayak and
          Bager," Political Geography Quarterly, Vol. 6,
          pp. 265-268.

H-524.   LaValle, Placido, et al., 1967. "Certain Aspects
          of the Expansion of Quantitative Methodology in
          American Geography," Annals of the Association of
          American Geographers, Vol. 57, pp. 423-436.

H-525.   Lavrov, S. B. 1985. "Geography: Old Concepts
          and New Content," Soviet Geography: Review and
          Translation, Vol. 26, pp. 526-534.

H-526.   Lavrov, S. B. et al. 1979. "Socio-Economic
          Geography in the U.S.S.R.," Geoforum, Vol. 10,
          pp. 333-344.

H-527.   Lavrov, S. B. and Agafonov, N. T. 1978.
          "Conceptual Issues in Economic Geography at the
          23rd International Geographical Congress," Soviet
          Geography: Review and Translation, Vol. 19, pp.
          324-332.

H-528.   Lavrov, S. B. and Dmitrevskiy, Yu. D. 1978.
          "Problems in the History of Geographical Thought
          at the 23rd International Geographical Congress,"
          Soviet Geography: Review and Translation, Vol.
          19, pp. 54-59.

H-529.   Laws, K. J. 1983. "The Past as a Key to the
          Present: Historical Geography in the
          Curriculum," Geographical Education, Vol. 4, pp.
          93-106.

H-530.   Leach, B. 1978. "Geography, Behavior and
          Marxist Philosophy," Antipode, Vol. 10, pp.
          33-37.

H-531. Learmonth, A. T. A.   1961.   "Medical Geography in
        India and Pakistan," Geographical Journal, Vol.
        127, pp. 10-26.

H-532. Learmonth, A. T. A.   1975.   "Ecological Medical
        Geography," Area, Vol. 7, pp. 201-206.

H-533. Learmonth, Andrew.   1976.   "The IGU Commission on
        Medical Geography 1972-1976," Geoforum, Vol. 7,
        pp. 152-157.

H-534. Lee, Chun-Fen.   1982.   "Geographical Education in
        Higher Institutions in China: A Personal
        Viewpoint," Canadian Geographer, Vol. 26, pp.
        153-157.

H-535. Lee, C-F. and Tang, J.   1982.   "Geography in
        Higher Education," Journal of Geography in
        Higher Education, Vol. 6, pp. 47-56.

H-536. Lee, Yuk.   1975.   "A Rejoinder to 'The Geography
        of Crime: A Political Critique,'" Professional
        Geographer, Vol. 27, pp. 284-285.

H-537. Leighly, John.   1955.   "What Has Happened to
        Physical Geography?" Annals of the Association
        of American Geographers, Vol. 45, pp. 309-318.

H-538. Leighly, John.   1969.   "On the Education of
        Climatologists," Yearbook - Association of
        Pacific Coast Geographers, Vol. 30, pp. 163-174.

H-539. Leitner, Helga.   1987.   "Urban Geography:
        Undercurrents of Change," Progress in Human
        Geography, Vol. 11, pp. 134-146.

H-540. Leont'yev, N. F.   1970.   "Some Achievements and
        Problems in Soviet Cartography," Soviet
        Geography: Review and Translation, Vol. 11, pp.
        278-288.

H-541. Levine, Gregory J.   1986.   "On the Geography of
        Religion," Transactions - Institute of British
        Geographers, Vol. 11, pp. 428-440.

H-542. Lewis, Lawrence T.   1974.   "The Geography of
        Black America: The Growth of the Subdiscipline,"
        Journal of Geography, Vol. 73, pp. 38-43.

H-543. Lewthwaite, Gordon.   1969.   "A Plea for Storage
        Geography," Professional Geographer, Vol. 21, pp.
        1-4.

H-544. Ley, D.   1981.   "Cultural/Humanistic Geography,"
        Progress in Human Geography, Vol. 5, pp. 249-257.

H-545.   Ley, David.   1977.   "Social Geography and the
          Taken-for-Granted World," Transactions -
          Institute of British Geographers, Vol. 2, pp.
          498-512.

H-546.   Ley, David.   1983.   "Cultural/Humanistic
          Geography," Progress in Human Geography, Vol. 7,
          pp. 267-275.

H-547.   Ley, David.   1985.   "Cultural/Humanistic
          Geography," Progress in Human Geography, Vol. 9,
          pp. 415-423.

H-548.   Leykina, K. S. and Pokshishevskiy, V. V.   1979.
          "A Geography of the Way of Life, A Distinctive
          Subfield of Regional Economic Geography," Soviet
          Geography: Review and Translation, Vol. 20, pp.
          275-290.

H-549.   Lichtenberger, E.   1984.   "Geography of Tourism
          and the Leisure Society in Austria," GeoJournal,
          Vol. 9, pp. 41-46.

H-550.   Light, Richard Upjohn.   1944.   "The Progress of
          Medical Geography," Geographical Review, Vol.
          34, pp. 636-641.

H-551.   Lillywhite, J.   1961.   "The Geographer and
          Planning," Northern Universities Geographical
          Journal, Vol. 2, pp. 65-67.

H-552.   Lineback, Neal G.   1986.   "Physical Geography and
          the Core Curriculum: One Department's
          Experience," Professional Geographer, Vol. 38,
          pp. 274-278.

H-553.   Linge, G. J. R.   1979.   "Australian Manufacturing
          and the Role and Responsibilities of
          Geographers," Australian Geographical Studies,
          Vol. 17, pp. 193-203.

H-554.   Linke, M., Hoffman, M. and Hellen, J. A.   1986.
          "Two Hundred Years of the Geographical-
          Cartographical Institute in Gotha," Geographical
          Journal, Vol. 152, pp. 75-80.

H-555.   Lipetz, G. Yu   1974.   "The Application of
          Mathematical Methods in Economic Geography,"
          Theoretical Problems in Physical and Economic
          Geography, Vol. 1, pp. 129-139.

H-556.   Lock, Chris.   1977.   "Economics, Value, and
          Society," Geoscope, Vol. 13, pp. 19-25.

H-557.   Lock, Chris.   1978.   "The Role of Ecology Within
          Geographical Thought," Geoscope, Vol. 9, pp.
          51-56.

H-558.   Logan, M. I. 1980. "Future Developments in
          Urban Geography," Australian Geographer, Vol. 14,
          pp. 66-67.

H-559.   Lonaroff, L. Schugler. 1976. "To a Young
          Medical Geographer," Professional Geographer,
          Vol. 28, pp. 331-335.

H-560.   Lornell, Christopher and Mealor, Theodore, Jr.
          1983. "Traditions and Research Opportunities in
          Folk Geography," Professional Geographer, Vol.
          35, pp. 51.

H-561.   Losberg, F. R. 1976. "Geography, Ecology and
          Biogeography," Annals of the Association of
          American Geographers, Vol. 66, pp. 117-128.

H-562.   Lounsbury, John. 1980. "The Case for Applied
          Geography," Geographical Perspective, Vol. 45,
          pp. 1-5.

H-563.   Lovell, W. George. 1976. "The Place of
          Synthesis in Geographical Investigation and
          Study of Historical Geography," Albertan
          Geographer, No. 12, pp. 71-81.

H-564.   Lowman, John. 1986. "Conceptual Issues in the
          Geography of Crime: Toward a Geography of Social
          Control," Annals of the Association of American
          Geographers, Vol. 76, pp. 81-94.

H-565.   Lowther, G. R. 1959. "Idealist History and
          Historical Geography," Canadian Geographer, No.
          14, pp. 31-36.

H-566.   Lukerman, F. 1958. "Toward a More Geographic
          Economic Geography," Professional Geographer,
          Vol. 10, No. 4, pp. 2-11.

H-567.   Lunden, Thomas. 1986. "Political Geography
          Around the World VI: Swedish Contributions to
          Political Geography," Political Geography
          Quarterly, Vol. 5, pp. 181-186.

H-568.   Lundgrew, J. O. J. 1984. "Geographic Concepts
          and the Development of Tourism Research in
          Canada," GeoJournal, Vol. 9, pp. 17-26.

H-569.   Lydolph, Paul E. 1957. "How Many Climatologies
          Are There?" Professional Geographer, Vol. 9, No.
          6, pp. 5-7.

H-570.   Lynam, Edward. 1950. "English Maps and
          Map-Makers of The Sixteenth Century,"
          Geographical Journal, Vol. 116, pp. 7-28.

H-571.   Maboqunje, A. L.   1968.   "Research in Urban
Geography in Nigeria," Nigerian Geographical
Journal, Vol. 11, pp. 101-114.

H-572.   MacEachren, Alan M.   1979.   "The Evolution of
Thematic Cartography: A Research Methodology and
Historical Review," Canadian Cartographer, Vol.
16, pp. 17-33.

H-573.   MacEachren, Alan M.   1982.   "The Role of
Complexity and Symbolization Method in Thematic
Map Effectiveness," Annals of the Association of
American Geographers, Vol. 72, pp. 495-513.

H-574.   Mackay, J. Ross.   1951.   "Some Problems and
Techniques on Isopleth Mapping," Economic
Geography, Vol. 27, pp. 1-9.

H-575.   Mackay, J. Ross.   1953.   "A New Projection for
Cubic Symbols on Economic Maps," Economic
Geography, Vol. 29, pp. 60-62.

H-576.   Mackay, J. Ross.   1953.   "Percentage Dot Maps,"
Economic Geography, Vol. 29, pp. 263-266.

H-577.   Mackay, J. Ross.   1954.   "Geographic
Cartography," Canadian Geographer, No. 4, pp.
1-14.

H-578.   Mackay, J. Ross.   1955.   "An Analysis of Isopleth
and Choropleth Class Intervals," Economic
Geography, Vol. 31, pp. 71-81.

H-579.   Makunina, A. A.   1977.   "Landscape Science and
Regional Physical Geography, Soviet Geography:
Review and Translation, Vol. 18, pp. 68-75.

H-580.   Malecki, E. J.   1980.   "Technological Change:
British and American Research Themes," Area,
Vol. 12, pp. 253-259.

H-581.   Malecki, E. J.   1982.   "Industrial Geography:
Introduction to the Special Issue," Environment
and Planning A, Vol. 14, pp. 1571-1576.

H-582.   Malmberg, G. and Nilsson, P.   1985.
"Tidsgeografins Mojligheter Och Restriktioner,"
[The Possibilities and Restrictions of Time --
Geography] Svensk Geografisk Arsbok, Vol. 61, pp.
255-265 [English Summary].

H-583.   Marbut, C. F.   1904.   "Physiography in the
University," Proceedings - Eighth International
Geographical Congress, pp. 997-1004.

H-584.   Marbut, C. F.   1905.   "Physiography in the
University," Journal of Geography, Vol. 4, pp.
23-30.

H-585.   Marbut, C. F.   1925.   "The Rise, Decline and
         Revival of Malthusianism in Relation to Geography
         and Character of Soils," Annals of the
         Association of American Geographers, Vol. 15, pp.
         1-29.

H-586.   Marcus, M. G.   1979.   "Coming Full Circle:
         Physical Geography in the Twentieth Century,"
         Annals of the Association of American
         Geographers, Vol. 69, pp. 521-532.

H-587.   Marcus, Melvin G.   1978.   "Directions in Applied
         Physical Geography," Geographical Survey, Vol. 7,
         No. 4, pp. 19-25.

H-588.   Marcus, Melvin G.   1979.   "The Range of
         Opportunity in Applied Physical Geography,"
         Geographical Survey, Vol. 8, No. 4, pp. 3-4.

H-589.   Mardin, O.   1981.   "Piri Reis: Turkish Admiral
         and Cartographer," Map Collector, Vol. 16, pp.
         16-21.

H-590.   Mariot, P.   1984.   "Geography of Tourism in
         Czechoslovakia," GeoJournal, Vol. 9, pp. 65-68.

H-591.   Markov, K. K.   1971.   "Marine Geography," Soviet
         Geography: Review and Translation, Vol. 12, pp.
         346-350.

H-592.   Markov, K. K.   1972.   "Geography Today and
         Tomorrow," Izvestiya Akademii Nauk, Vol. 3, pp.
         20-26.

H-593.   Markov, K. K.   et al.   1976.   "The Geography of
         Oceans and Its Basic Problems," Soviet
         Geography: Review and Translation, Vol. 17, pp.
         437-446.

H-594.   Markovin, A. P.   1962.   "Historical Sketch of the
         Development of Soviet Medical Geography," Soviet
         Geography: Review and Translation, Vol. 3, No.
         8, pp. 3-20.

H-595.   Marotz, Glen A.   1979.   "Climatology: Love It or
         Apply It?" Geographical Survey, Vol. 8, No. 4,
         pp. 5-8.

H-596.   Marschner, F. J.   1943.   "Maps and a Mapping
         Program for the United States," Annals of the
         Association of American Geographers, Vol. 33, pp.
         119-219.

H-597.   Martin, Geoffrey J.   1959.   "Political Geography
         and Geopolitics," Journal of Geography, Vol. 58,
         pp. 441-444.

H-598.   Martin, J. E. 1982. "Location Theory and
          Spatial Analysis," Progress in Human Geography,
          Vol. 6, pp. 260-264.

H-599.   Massam, Bryan. 1974. "Political Geography and
          the Provision of Public Services," Progress in
          Geography, Vol. 6, pp. 179-210.

H-600.   Mather, John R., Field, Richard T., Kalkstein,
          Laurence S. and Willmot, Cort J. 1980.
          "Climatology: The Challenge for the Eighties,"
          Professional Geographer, Vol. 32, pp. 285-292.

H-601.   Mather, Paul M. 1979. "Theory and Quantitative
          Methods in Geomorphology," Progress in Physical
          Geography, Vol. 3, pp. 471-487.

H-602.   Matthes, Francois E. 1933. "The Committee on
          Glaciers of the American Geophysical Union, and
          Its Work," Annals of the Association of American
          Geographers, Vol. 23, pp. 49-50.

H-603.   May, Jacques. 1950. "Medical Geography: Its
          Methods and Objectives," Geographical Review,
          Vol. 40, pp. 9-41.

H-604.   May, Jacques M. 1951. "The Geography of
          Pathology," Scientific Monthly, Vol. 72, pp.
          128-131.

H-605.   May, Jacques M. 1954. "The Geography of
          Disease: The American Geographical Society's
          Approach to the Problem," Methodological
          Monographs, Vol. 2, pp. 104-110.

H-606.   Mayer, Harold M. 1954. "Geographers in City and
          Regional Planning," Professional Geographer, Vol.
          6, No. 3, pp. 7-13.

H-607.   Mayer, Harold M. 1978. "Applications of
          Geography in City and Regional Planning," Applied
          Geography Conference, Vol. 1, pp. 122-129.

H-608.   Mayer, J. D. 1982. "Medical Geography: Some
          Unresolved Problems," Professional Geographer,
          Vol. 34, pp. 261-269.

H-609.   Mayergoyz, J. M. 1979. "Problems in the Study
          of Economic-Geographic Situation," Soviet
          Geography: Review and Translation, Vol. 20, pp.
          489-495.

H-610.   Mazur, E. 1983. "Landscape Syntheses -
          Objectives and Tasks," GeoJournal, Vol. 7, pp.
          101-106.

H-611.   McArthur, J. L. 1978. "Environmental Science,
          Environmental Studies, Earth Science and Physical
          Geography: A Comparative Review," New Zealand
          Journal of Geography, Vol. 65, pp. 13-21.

H-612.   McArthur, J. L. 1980. "Environmental Science,
          Environmental Studies, Earth Science and Physical
          Geography: A Comparative Review," Philippine
          Geographical Journal, Vol. 24, pp. 21-32.

H-613.   McCarty, H. H. 1954. "An Approach to a Theory
          of Economic Geography," Economic Geography, Vol.
          30, pp. 99-101.

H-614.   McCarty, H. H. 1959. "Toward a More General
          Economic Geography," Economic Geography, Vol. 35,
          pp. 283-289.

H-615.   McColl, Robert W. 1966. "Political Geography as
          Political Ecology," Professional Geographer, Vol.
          18, pp. 143-145.

H-616.   McConnell, James E. 1986. "Geography of
          International Trade," Progress in Human
          Geography, Vol. 10, pp. 471-483.

H-617.   McGlashan, N. D. 1965. "The Scope of Medical
          Geography," South African Geographical Journal,
          Vol. 47, pp. 35-40.

H-618.   McGlashan, N. D. 1969. "The Nature of Medical
          Geography," Pacific Viewpoint, Vol. 10, pp.
          60-65.

H-619.   McHugh, Kevin E. 1984. "Commentary on Spatial
          Constraints on Behavior," Annals of the
          Association of American Geographers, Vol. 74, pp.
          326-330.

H-620.   McLennon, Marshall. 1984. "New Opportunities in
          Historical Geography," Geographical Bulletin,
          Vol. 26, pp. 5-9.

H-621.   McMurray, K. C. 1916. "Geographic Contributions
          to Land-Use Planning," Annals of the Association
          of American Geographers, Vol. 26, pp. 91-98.

H-622.   McNee, Robert B. 1959. "The Changing
          Relationships of Economics and Economic
          Geography," Economic Geography, Vol. 35, pp.
          189-198.

H-623.   McNee, Robert B. 1960. "Toward a More
          Humanistic Economic Geography: The Geography of
          Enterprise," Tijdschrift voor Economische en
          Sociale Geografie, Vol. 51, pp. 201-206.

H-624.   Meadows, M. E.   1985.   "Biogeographer: A Happy
         Ending to the Fairy Tale?" South African
         Geographical Society, Vol. 67, pp. 40-61.

H-625.   Mears, Eliot.   1931.   "The Geography of
         Economics," Annals of the Association of American
         Geographers, Vol. 21, pp. 132-133.

H-626.   Medvedkov, Yu. V.   1965.   "Trends in
         Economic-Geographic Research on Regions of the
         Capitalist World," Soviet Geography: Review and
         Translation, Vol. 6, pp. 41-49.

H-627.   Medvedkov, Yuri V.   1976.   "Geography of Urban
         Environment: Current Results and Prospects,"
         Geoforum, Vol. 7, pp. 295-300.

H-628.   Meinzer, Oscar Edward.   1934.   "The History and
         Development of Ground-water Hydrology," Journal
         of the Washington Academy, Vol. 24, pp. 6-32.

H-629.   Melezin, Abraham.   1963.   "Trends and Issues in
         the Soviet Geography of Population," Annals of
         the Association of American Geographers, Vol. 53,
         pp. 144-160.

H-630.   Mensching, H. G.   1984.   "Julius Budel and His
         Concept of Climatic Geomorphology--Retrospect and
         Appreciation," Erdkunde, Vol. 38, pp. 157-166
         [English Summary].

H-631.   Mercer, David.   1972.   "Behavioural Geography and
         the Sociology of Social Action," Area, Vol. 4,
         pp. 48-52.

H-632.   Mercer, David.   1983.   "Freedom of Information
         and Geographical Practice," Australian
         Geographical Studies, Vol. 21, pp. 8-32.

H-633.   Meyer, Henry Cord.   1946.   "Mitteleuropa in
         German Political Geography," Annals of the
         Association of American Geographers, Vol. 36, pp.
         178-194.

H-634.   Mikesell, M. W.   1978.   "Tradition and Innovation
         in Cultural Geography," Annals of the Association
         of American Geographers, Vol. 68, pp. 1-16.

H-635.   Mil'kov, F. N.   1977.   "Ideas, Names and
         Scientific Schools in Physical Geography," Soviet
         Geography: Review and Translation, Vol. 18, pp.
         575-582.

H-636.   Miller, David H.   1965.   "Geography, Physical and
         Unified," Professional Geographer, Vol. 17, No.
         2, pp. 1-4.

H-637.   Miller, John P.   1961.   "Physical Geography in
         Poland," _Professional Geographer_, Vol. 13, No. 2,
         pp. 34-37.

H-638.   Miller, Vincent P., Jr.   1971.   "Some
         Observations on the Science of Cultural
         Geography," _Journal of Geography_, Vol. 70, pp.
         27-35.

H-639.   Mills, W. J.   1982.   "Metaphorical Vision:
         Changes in Western Attitudes to the Environment,"
         _Annals of the Association of American
         Geographers_, Vol. 72, pp. 237-253.

H-640.   Mintz, A. A.   1974.   "Economic Geography (A
         Survey of Basic Tendencies, 1966-1970),"
         _Theoretical Problems in Physical and Economic
         Geography_, Vol. 1, pp. 79-128.

H-641.   Mitchell, L. S.   1984.   "Tourism Research in the
         United States: A Geographic Perspective,"
         GeoJournal, Vol. 9, pp. 5-16.

H-642.   Mitchell, Lisle S. and Smith, Richard V.   1985.
         "Recreational Geography: Inventory and Prospect,"
         Professional Geographer, Vol. 37, pp. 6-14.

H-643.   Mock, D. R.   1979.   "Internships: A Fundamental
         Component of Applied Geography," _Applied
         Geography Conference_, Vol. 2, pp. 317-321.

H-644.   Monk, J. and Hanson, S.   1982.   "On Not Excluding
         Half of the Human in Human Geography,"
         Professional Geographer, Vol. 34, pp. 11-23.

H-645.   Monmonier, Mark S.   1982.   "Cartography,
         Geographic Information, and Public Policy,"
         Journal of Geography in Higher Education, Vol. 6,
         pp. 99-108.

H-646.   Moodie, D. W. and Lehr, John C.   1976.   "Fact and
         Theory in Historical Geography," _Professional
         Geographer_, Vol. 28, pp. 132-135.

H-647.   Moodie, D. W., _et al_.   1974.   "Zelinsky's
         Pursuit: Wild Goose or Canard?" _Historical
         Geography Newsletter_, Vol. 4, pp. 18-21.

H-648.   Mookarjee, Sitanshu.   1972.   "A Trend-Report in
         Political Geography," _Deccan Geographer_, Vol. 10,
         pp. 80-93.

H-649.   Morrill, Richard.   1987.   "Redistricting Region
         and Representation," _Political Geography
         Quarterly_, Vol. 6, pp. 241-260.

H-650.   Morrison, J. L.   1978.   "Towards a Functional
         Definition of the Science of Cartography With
         Emphasis on Map Reading," American Cartographer,
         Vol. 5, pp. 97-110.

H-651.   Morris, Joseph Acton.   1938.   "On the Teaching of
         Physical Geography," Proceedings - Fifteenth
         International Geographical Congress, pp. 84-88.

H-652.   Moscheles, Julie.   1930.   "Social Geography and
         Its Desirability in Schools of Divinity,"
         Sociological Review, Vol. 22, pp. 309-314.

H-653.   Muehrcke, P. C.   1981.   "Whatever Happened to
         Geographic Cartography?" Professional Geographer,
         Vol. 33, pp. 397-405.

H-654.   Muir, Richard.   1976.   "Political Geography:
         Dead Duck or Phoenix?" Area, Vol. 8, pp. 195-200.

H-655.   Muir, Richard.   1978.   "Radical Geography or a
         New Orthodoxy?" Area, Vol. 10, pp. 322-327.

H-656.   Muller, J. C.   1985.   "Geographic Information
         Systems: A Unifying Force for Geography,"
         Operational Geographer, Vol. 8, pp. 41-43.

H-657.   Muller, Peter O.   1976.   "Transportation
         Geography II: Social Transportation," Progress
         in Geography, Vol. 8, pp. 208-231.

H-658.   Mulliner, Beulah A.   1912.   "The Development of
         Physiography in American Textbooks," Journal of
         Geography, Vol. 10, pp. 319-324.

H-659.   Mumford, J.   1982.   "Is the British Cartographic
         Society in the Doldrums?" Cartographic Journal,
         Vol. 18, pp. 128-129.

H-660.   Murphy, E. A. C.   1933.   "What Good is
         Physiography?" School Science and Mathematics,
         Vol. 33, pp. 767-772.

H-661.   Murphy, Raymond E.   1961.   "Marketing Geography
         Comes of Age," Economic Geography, Vol. 37, p. 1.

H-662.   Murphy, Raymond E.   1979.   "Economic Geography
         and Clark University," Annals of the Association
         of American Geographers, Vol. 69, pp. 39-41.

H-663.   Murray, Malcolm A.   1964.   "Medical Geography in
         the United Kingdom," Geographical Review, Vol.
         54, pp. 582-584.

H-664.   Murzayev, E. M.   1960.   "Results and Aims of
         Physical Regional Geography in the U.S.S.R.,"
         Soviet Geography: Review and Translation, Vol.
         1, No. 1-2, pp. 21-28.

H-665.   Murzayev, E. M. 1977. "Things That Are Almost
          But Not Quite Well Known in Physical Geography,"
          Soviet Geography: Review and Translation, Vol.
          18, pp. 287-301.

H-666.   Muschett, F. Douglas. 1979. "The Environment
          for Environmental Geography," Geographical
          Survey, Vol. 8, No. 4, pp. 29-34.

H-667.   Musk, L. F. and Tout, D. G. 1979.
          Climatological Teaching in British Universities
          and Polytechnics," Geography, Vol. 64, pp. 21-25.

H-668.   Musk, Leslie F. 1983. "Applied Climatology,"
          Progress in Physical Geography, Vol. 7, pp.
          404-412.

H-669.   Musk, Leslie F. 1984. "Applied Climatology,"
          Progress in Physical Geography, Vol. 8, pp.
          450-468.

H-670.   Musk, Leslie F. 1985. "Applied Climatology,"
          Progress in Physical Geography, Vol. 9, pp.
          442-459.

H-671.   Musk, Leslie F. 1986. "Applied Climatology,"
          Progress in Physical Geography, Vol. 10, pp.
          563-575.

H-672.   Nader, G. A. 1972. "Urban Geography or Urban
          Studies?" Proceedings - Twenty Second
          International Geographical Congress, Vol. 2, pp.
          832-834.

H-673.   Newcomb, Robert M. 1969. "Twelve Working
          Approaches to Historical Geography," Yearbook -
          Association of Pacific Coast Geographers, Vol.
          31, pp. 27-50.

H-674.   Newson, Linda. 1976. "Cultural Evolution: A
          Basic Concept for Human and Historical
          Geography," Journal of Historical Geography, Vol.
          2, pp. 239-255.

H-675.   Neyfakh, A. M. 1963. "New Trends in Bourgeoris
          Science on the Location of Production," Soviet
          Geography: Review and Translation, Vol.4, No. 3,
          pp. 12-21.

H-676.   Nientied, Peter. 1985. "A New Political
          Geography: On What Basis?," Progress in Human
          Geography, Vol. 9, pp. 597-600.

H-677.   Nikishoov, M. I. and Terekhov, N. M. 1968. "50
          Years of Soviet Cartography: Translation,"
          Canadian Cartographer, Vol. 5, pp. 122-132.

H-678.   Nikitin, N. P. 1966. "A History of Economic
         Geography in Pre-Revolutionary Russia," _Soviet
         Geography_: Review and Translation, Vol. 7, pp.
         3-37.

H-679.   Nordstrom, Karl F. 1979. "The Field Course in
         Geography: A Conceptual Framework," _Journal of
         Geography_, Vol. 78, pp. 267-272.

H-680.   Nordstrom, Karl F. 1983. "Science and the
         Funding of Physical Geographers," _Professional
         Geographer_, Vol. 35, pp. 469-470.

H-681.   Norton, W. 1981. "The Analysis of Progress in
         Historical Geography," _South African Geographical
         Journal_, Vol. 63, pp. 3-21.

H-682.   Norton, W. H. 1918. "Earth Science in American
         Colleges and Universities," _School and Society_,
         Vol. 8, pp. 702-706.

H-683.   Norton, William. 1984. "The Meaning of Culture
         in Cultural Geography: An Appraisal," _Journal of
         Geography_, Vol. 83, pp. 145-148.

H-684.   Norton, William. 1987. "Humans, Land, and
         Landscape: A Proposal for Cultural Geography,"
         Canadian Geographer, Vol. 31, pp. 21-30; "Reply
         to Norton, 1987, p. 33.

H-685.   Nunn, Patrick. 1981. "Palissy, de'Maillet and
         Voltaire: Some Incipient Ideas in the Philosophy
         of Geomorphology," _Bloomsbury Geographer_, Vol.
         10, pp. 17-21.

H-686.   Obenbrugge, Jurgen. 1983. "Political Geography
         Around the World: West Germany," _Political
         Geography Quarterly_, Vol. 2, pp. 71-80.

H-687.   Ogilvie, Alan G. 1915. "Cartographic Needs of
         Physical Geography," _Geographical Journal_, Vol.
         45, pp. 46-68.

H-688.   O'Loughlin, John. 1986. "Political Geography:
         Filling the Fallow Field," _Progress in Human
         Geography_, Vol. 10, pp. 69-83.

H-689.   O'Loughlin, John. 1987. "Political Geography:
         Marching to the Beats of Different Drummers,"
         Progress in Human Geography, Vol. 11, pp.
         247-263.

H-690.   O'Loughlin, John. 1988. "Political Geography:
         Bringing the Context Back," _Progress in Human
         Geography_, Vol. 12, pp. 121-138.

H-691.   Olson, Ralph E. and Doerr, Arthur H.   1955.
          "Physical Geography at the University of
          Oklahoma," Professional Geographer, Vol. 7, No.
          3, 2-7.

H-692.   Oman, C.   1980.   "Note on Geography as Applied to
          History in Great Britain," Historical Geography,
          Vol. 10, pp. 18-20.

H-693.   Orme, Antony R.   1980.   "The Need for Physical
          Geography," Professional Geographer, Vol. 32, pp.
          141-148.

H-694.   Orton, W.   1981.   "The Analysis of Process in
          Historical Geography," South African
          Geographical Journal, Vol. 63, pp. 24-34.

H-695.   Ota, Yoko and Nogami, Michio.   1979.   "Recent
          Research in Japanese Geomorphology,"
          Professional Geographer, Vol. 31, pp. 410-415.

H-696.   Otok, Stanislaw.   1985.   "Political Geography
          Around the World V: Poland," Political
          Geography Quarterly, Vol. 4, pp. 321-328.

H-697.   Ottens, H. F. L. and ter Welle-Heethuis, J. G.
          P.   1983.   "Recent Urban Research at Utrecht,"
          Tijdscrift voor Economische en Sociale Geografie,
          Vol. 74, pp. 387-396.

H-698.   Overton, J. D.   1981.   "A Theory of Exploration,"
          Journal of Historical Geography, Vol. 7, pp.
          53-70.

H-699.   Paasi, A.   1984.   "Connection Between J. G.
          Granos' Geographical Thinking and Behavioural and
          Humanistic Geography," Fennia, Vol. 162, pp.
          21-31.

H-700.   Paddock, Miner H.   1904.   "Physical Geography in
          Our Public Schools," Education, Vol. 25, pp.
          162-163.

H-701.   Padgett, Herbert R.   1961.   "Sea Industries: A
          Neglected Field of Geography," Professional
          Geographer, Vol. 13, No. 6, pp. 26-28.

H-702.   Paine, Alasclair D. M.   1985.   "'Engodic'
          Reasoning in Geomorphology: Time for a Review of
          the Term?" Progress in Physical Geography, Vol.
          9, pp. 1-15.

H-703.   Pal, S. K.   1974.   "Scope of Integrating Field
          Work in Geomorphology," Geographical Review of
          India, Vol. 36, pp. 309-312.

H-704.   Parker, Geoffrey. 1987. "French Geopolitical
          Thought in the Interwar Years and the Emergence
          of the European Idea," Political Geography
          Quarterly, Vol. 6, pp. 145-150.

H-705.   Parry, J. T. 1967. "Geomorphology in Canada,"
          Canadian Geographer, Vol. 11, pp. 280-311.

H-706.   Pasqualetti, Martin J. 1979. "Energy,"
          Geographical Survey, Vol. 8, No. 4, pp. 35-40.

H-707.   Pearce, D. G. and Mings, R. C. 1984.
          "Geography, Tourism and Recreation in the
          Antipodes," GeoJournal, Vol. 9, pp. 91-95.

H-708.   Pearcy, G. E. 1965. "Geography and Foreign
          Affairs," Department of State Bulletin, Vol. 52,
          July 28, pp. 1035-1041.

H-709.   Pedrini, L. 1984. "The Geography of Tourism and
          Leisure in Italy," GeoJournal, Vol. 9, pp. 55-58.

H-710.   Peet, J. Richard. 1985. "An Introduction to
          Marxist Geography," Journal of Geography, Vol.
          84, pp. 5-10.

H-711.   Pellegrini, Giacomo Corna and Zerki, Maria
          Chiara. 1983. "Urban Geography and Urban
          Problems in Italy, 1945-81," Progress in Human
          Geography, Vol. 7, pp. 357-369.

H-712.   Peltier, Louis C. 1961. "The Potential of
          Military Geography," Professional Geographer,
          Vol. 13, No. 6, pp. 1-5.

H-713.   Penck, A. 1897. "Potamology as a Branch of
          Physical Geography," Geographical Journal, Vol.
          10, pp. 619-623.

H-714.   Pepper, David and Jenkins, Alan. 1983. "A Call
          to Arms: Geography and Peace Studies," Area,
          Vol. 15, pp. 202-208.

H-715.   Phillips, Mary Viola. 1965. "Zoe Agnes
          Thralls," Journal of Geography, Vol. 64, p. 299.

H-716.   Phlipponnenau, M. 1981. "The Rise of Applied
          Geography," International Social Science Journal,
          Vol. 33, pp. 133-159.

H-717.   Piggott, C. A. 1980. "A Geography of Religion
          in Scotland," Scottish Geographical Magazine,
          Vol. 96, pp. 130-140.

H-718.   Pithawalla, Maneck B. 1944. "Some Knoty
          Problems of Indian Historical Geography," Indian
          Geographical Journal, Vol. 19, pp. 78-83.

H-719.   Pitts, Forrest R.   1956.   "What One Geographer
         Wants from Climatology," _Professional Geographer_,
         Vol. 8, No. 5, pp. 8-10.

H-720.   Platt, Raye R.   1932.   "Adventures in Map
         Making," _Annals of the Association of American
         Geographers_, Vol. 22, pp. 70-72.

H-721.   Podolyau, V. Y.   1984.   "Development of
         Medico-Geographical Ideas in the Epoch of the
         Developed Socialism and Scientific and
         Technological Progress," _Geographia Medica_, Vol.
         14, pp. 284-293.

H-722.   Poiiac Pollock, N. C.   1952.   "A Plea for Social
         Geography," _South African Geographical Journal_,
         Vol. 34, pp. 61-62.

H-723.   Poiker, T. K.   1982.   "Looking at Computer
         Cartography," _GeoJournal_, Vol. 6, pp. 241-250.

H-724.   Poiker, Thomas K.   1985.   "Geographic Information
         Systems in the Geographic Curriculums,"
         Operational Geographer, No. 8, pp. 38-41.

H-725.   Pokshishevskiy, V. V.   1961.   "The Place of
         Regional Economic Geography in the System of
         Geographical Sciences," _Soviet Geography: Review
         and Translation_, Vol. 2, No. 5, pp. 13-23.

H-726.   Pokshishevskiy, V. V.   1962.   "Geography of
         Population and Its Tasks," _Soviet Geography:
         Review and Translation_, Vol. 3, No. 9, pp. 3-14.

H-727.   Pokshishevskiy, V. V.   1963.   "On the Character
         of the Laws in Economic Geography," _Soviet
         Geography: Review and Translation_, Vol. 4, No.
         4, pp. 3-17.

H-728.   Pokshishevskiy, V. V.   1971.   "On New Directions
         in the Development of Soviet Economic Geography,"
         Soviet Geography: Review and Translation, Vol.
         12, pp. 403-416.

H-729.   Pokshishevskiy, V. V.   1975.   "On the Soviet
         Concept of Economic Regionalisation: A Review
         of Geographical Research in the USSR on the
         Problems of Economic Regionalisation," _Progress
         in Geography_, Vol. 7, pp. 1-57.

H-730.   Pokshishevskiy, V. V.   1979.   "Soviet Economic
         Geography: Six Decades of Development and
         Contemporary Problems," _Soviet Geography: Review
         and Translation_, Vol. 20, pp. 131-139.

H-731.   Pokshishevskiy, V. V. and Ye. A. Stepanova.
         1966. "Publication of Soviet Economic-Geography
         Research in Foreign Publications," Soviet
         Geography: Review and Translation, Vol. 7, pp.
         77-81.

H-732.   Polyan, P. M. 1985. "Geography and the
         Inspirational Resources of Nature," Soviet
         Geography: Review and Translation, Vol. 26, pp.
         229-238.

H-733.   Porter, P. W. 1978. "Geography as Human
         Ecology: A Decade of Progress in a Quarter
         Century," American Behavioral Scientist, Vol. 22,
         pp. 15-39.

H-734.   Pravada, J. 1980. "The Paradoxes and Trends in
         the Development of Thematic Cartography,"
         Geograficky Casopis, Vol. 32, pp. 200-209.

H-735.   Preobrashenskiy, V. S., Vedenin, Yu. A. and
         Stupina, V. M. 1984. "Development of
         Recreational Geography in the USSR," GeoJournal,
         Vol. 9, pp. 83-84.

H-736.   Preobrazhenskiy, A. I. 1966. "Economic
         Cartography," Soviet Geography, Review and
         Translation, Vol. 7, pp. 37-56.

H-737.   Prescott, J. R. V. 1959. "The Function and
         Methods of Electoral Geography," Annals of the
         Association of American Geographers, Vol. 49, pp.
         296-304.

H-738.   Prescott, J. R. V. and Najdu, J. G. 1964. "A
         Review of Some German Post-War Contributions to
         Political Geography," Australian Geographical
         Studies, Vol. 2, pp. 35-46.

H-739.   Price, R. J. 1978. "The Future of Physical
         Geography: Disintegration or Integration,"
         Scottish Geographical Magazine, Vol. 94, pp.
         24-30.

H-740.   Prince, H. 1982. "Trends in Historical
         Geography," Area, Vol. 14, pp. 235-239.

H-741.   Pryde, Philip R. 1985. "Energy Courses in
         American Geography Departments," Journal of
         Geography, Vol. 84, pp. 154-157.

H-742.   Pyle, Gerald F. 1976. "Introduction:
         Foundations to Medical Geography," Economic
         Geography, Vol. 52, pp. 95-102.

H-743.   Raisz, Erwin. 1937. "Time Charts of Historical
         Cartography," Imagio Mundi, Vol. 2, pp. 9-16.

H-744.   Raisz, Erwin, 1939. "Block-Pile System of
         Statistical Maps," Economic Geography, Vol. 15,
         pp. 185-188.

H-745.   Raitviir, T. 1986. "Social Geography: Its
         Place and Formation," Geoforum, Vol. 17, pp.
         89-96.

H-746.   Ramsey, E. E. 1911-1912. "Physical Geography in
         High Schools," School Science and Mathematics,
         Vol. 11, pp. 838-848; Vol. 12, pp. 45-54,
         114-125.

H-747.   Raup, Hugh M. 1942. "Trends in the Development
         of Geographic Botany," Annals of the Association
         of American Geographers, Vol. 32, pp. 319-354.

H-748.   Reeds, Lloyd G. 1964. "Agricultural Geography:
         Progress and Prospects," Canadian Geographer,
         Vol. 8, pp. 51-63.

H-749.   Renner, G. T. 1926. "Some Principles of
         Commercial Geography," Journal of Geography, Vol.
         25, pp. 337-342.

H-750.   Reynolds, T. C. 1981. "Research Training for
         Young Historical Geographers," Journal of
         Historical Geography, Vol. 7, pp. 415-416.

H-751.   Richards, Paul. 1974. "Kant's Geography and
         Mental Maps," Transactions - Institute of British
         Geographers, No. 61, pp. 1-16.

H-752.   Richling, A. 1983. "Subject of Study in Complex
         Physical Geography," GeoJournal, Vol. 7, pp.
         185-187.

H-753.   Richter, G. 1981. "Recent Trends of
         Experimental Geomorphology in the Field," Earth
         Surface Processes, Vol. 6, pp. 215-220.

H-754.   Riddell, J. Bary. 1987. "Geography and the
         Study of Third World Underdevelopment," Progress
         in Human Geography, Vol. 11, pp. 264-274.

H-755.   Rigdon, Vera E. 1935. "Physiographic
         Nonmenclature à la William Morris Davis," Annals
         of the Association of American Geographers, Vol.
         25, pp. 52-53.

H-756.   Rimmer, P. J. 1978. "Redirections in Transport
         Geography," Progress in Human Geography, Vol. 2,
         pp. 76-100.

H-757.   Rimmer, Peter J. 1988. "Transport Geography,"
         Progress in Human Geography, Vol. 12, pp.
         270-281.

H-758.   Rizvi, A. I. H. 1969. "Pakistani
Geomorphology," Pakistan Geographical Review,
Vol. 24, pp. 142-146.

H-759.   Rizvi, S. Q. A. 1958. "A Survey of Urban
Geography," Geographer, Vol. 10, pp. 26-42.

H-760.   Robinson, Arthur H. 1979. "Geography and
Cartography Then and Now," Annals of the
Association of American Geographers, Vol. 69, pp.
97-102.

H-761.   Robinson, Edward Van Dyke. 1913. "Editorial --
Commercial Geography," Journal of Geography, Vol.
11, pp. 203-206.

H-762.   Robinson, Geoffrey. 1963. "A Consideration of
the Relations of Geomorphology and Geography,"
Professional Geographer, Vol. 15, No. 2, pp.
13-18.

H-763.   Robinson, Guy and Parten, John. 1980. "Edmund
W. Gilbert and the Development of Historical
Geography, With a Bibliography of His Work,"
Journal of Historical Geography, Vol. 6, pp.
409-420.

H-764.   Robinson, J. Lewis. 1956. "Geography and
Regional Planning," Canadian Geographer, Vol. 8,
pp. 1-8.

H-765.   Robinson, J. Lewis. 1966. "The Need for Urban
Geography in Our High Schools," Journal of
Geography, Vol. 65, pp. 236-240.

H-766.   Robson, B. T. 1982. "Social Geography,"
Progress in Human Geography, Vol. 6, pp. 96-101.

H-767.   Rogers, Garry F. 1983. "Growth of Biogeography
in Canadian and U. S. Geography Departments,"
Professional Geographer, Vol. 35, pp. 219-226.

H-768.   Romanowski, J. 1965-66. "Some Unfulfilled
Promises of a More Economic Geography," Albertan
Geographer, No. 2, pp. 50-55.

H-769.   Rowntree, Lester. 1986. "Cultural/Humanistic
Geography," Progress in Human Geography, Vol. 10,
pp. 580-586.

H-770.   Rowntree, Lester. 1987. "Cultural/Humanistic
Geography," Progress in Human Geography, Vol. 11,
pp. 558-564.

H-771.   Ruppert, K. 1984. "The Concept of Social
Geography," GeoJournal, Vol. 9, pp. 255-260.

H-772. Rushton, G. 1979. "On Behavioral and Perceptual
        Geography," _Annals of the Association of American
        Geographers_, Vol. 69, pp. 463-464.

H-773. Russell, Richard Joel. 1949. "Geographical
        Morphology," _Annals of the Association of
        American Geographers_, Vol. 39, pp. 1-11.

H-774. Saarinen, T. F. and Sell, J. L. 1980.
        "Environmental Perception," _Progress in Human
        Geography_, Vol. 4, pp. 525-548.

H-775. Saenz de la Calzada, C. 1972. "Academic
        Training in Mexico of Medical Geography
        Specialists," _Proceedings of the Twenty Second
        International Geographical Congress_, pp.
        1225-1226.

H-776. Sakamoto, Masako. 1956. "Methods and Objectives
        of Medical Geography," _Proceedings of the
        Eighteenth International Geographical Congress_,
        pp. 630-635.

H-777. Salichtchev, K. A. 1970. "The Subject and
        Method of Cartography: Contemporary Views,"
        Canadian Cartographer, Vol. 7, pp. 77-87.

H-778. Salichtchev, K. A. 1978. "Cartographic
        Communication/Its Place in the Theory of
        Science," _Canadian Cartographer_, Vol. 1, pp.
        5-14.

H-779. Salishchev, K. A. 1962. "Cartography in the
        Universities of the United States," _Soviet
        Geography_: _Review and Translation_, Vol. 3, No.
        4, pp. 58-64.

H-780. Salishchev, K. A. 1971. "Present Problems in
        Soviet Cartography and the Tasks of the
        Geographical Society," _Soviet Geography_: _Review
        and Translation_, Vol. 12, pp. 428-434.

H-781. Sanderson, M. 1974. "Mary Somerville: Her Work
        in Physical Geography," _Geographical Review_, Vol.
        64, pp. 410-420.

H-782. Sauer, Carl O. 1921. "Geography as Regional
        Economics [Abstract]," _Annals of the Association
        of American Geographers_, Vol. 11, pp. 130-131.

H-783. Sauer, Carl O. 1934. "Cultural Geography," in
        Encyclopedia of the Social Sciences, E. Seligman
        and A. Johnson, eds., New York: Macmillan, Vol.
        6, pp. 621-624.

H-784. Sauer, Carl O. 1974. "The Fourth Dimension of
        Geography," _Annals of the Association of American
        Geographers_, Vol. 64, pp. 189-192.

H-785.   Saushkin, Yu. G. 1966. "A History of Soviet
          Economic Geography," Soviet Geography: Review
          and Translation, Vol. 7, pp. 3-104.

H-786.   Saushkin, Yu. G. 1968. "Forecasting in
          Economic Geography," Soviet Geography: Review
          and Translation, Vol. 9, pp. 384-393.

H-787.   Saushkin, Yu. G. 1971. "Results and Prospects
          of the Use of Mathematical Methods in Economic
          Geography," Soviet Geography: Review and
          Translation, Vol. 12, pp. 416-427.

H-788.   Saxena, Hari Mohan. 1977. "Marketing
          Geography: A Review," Deccan Geographer, pp.
          250-260.

H-789.   Sayer, Andrew. 1982. "Explanation in Economic
          Geography: Abstraction Versus Generalization,"
          Progress in Human Geography, Vol. 6, pp. 68-88.

H-790.   Schofer, Jerry P. 1975. "Computer Cartography
          and Professional Geographers," Professional
          Geographer, Vol. 27, pp. 335-340.

H-791.   Schroder, P. 1979. "Current Problems of
          Cartography and Their Treatment," Universitas,
          Vol. 21, pp. 303-310.

H-792.   Scott, D. 1986. "Time, Structuration and the
          Potential for South African Historical
          Geography," South African Geographical Journal,
          Vol. 68, pp. 45-66.

H-793.   Seager, Joni and Steinitz, Michael. 1980-81.
          "Preserving the Past: Some Recent Contributions
          in Applied Historical Geography," Monadnock,
          Vol. 54-55, pp. 27-42.

H-794.   Seamon, D. 1984. "Philosophical Directions in
          Behavioral Geography with an Emphasis on the
          Phenomenological Contribution," Research Paper -
          University of Chicago, Department of Geography,
          No. 209, pp. 167-178.

H-795.   Senda, H. 1982. "Progress in Japanese
          Historical Geography," Journal of Historical
          Geography, Vol. 8, pp. 170-181.

H-796.   Sereno, Paola. 1983. "New Trends and Past
          Traditions in Historical Geography in Italy,"
          Historical Geography Newsletter, Vol. 13, pp.
          11-12.

H-797.   Shabad, Theodore. 1954. "Status of Geography
          in Communist China," Professional Geographer,
          Vol. 6, No. 4, pp. 5-9.

H-798.   Shanklin, G. 1979. "Reflections on Applied
         Geography: A Position Paper," Kansas
         Geographer, Vol. 14, pp. 13-16.

H-799.   Shchukin, I. S. 1960. "The Place of
         Geomorphology in the System of Natural Sciences
         and Its Relationships With Integrated Physical
         Geography," Soviet Geography: Review and
         Translation, Vol. 1, No. 9, pp. 35-43.

H-800.   Sheppard, Eric. 1982. "Recent Research in
         Soviet Quantitative Geography: A Brief Review,"
         Antipode, Vol. 14, pp. 11-16.

H-801.   Shibanov, F. A. 1971. "Some Aspects of the
         Cartography of the Pre- Petrine Period
         (16th-17th Centuries) and the Role of S. Yu.
         Remezov in the History of Russian Cartography,"
         Canadian Cartographer, Vol. 8, pp. 84-89.

H-802.   Shibanov, F. A. 1973. "The Essence and Content
         of the History of Cartography and the Results
         of Fifty Years of Work by Soviet Scholars,"
         Canadian Cartographer, Vol. 10, pp. 21-25.

H-803.   Shitara, H. 1978. "Fifty Years of Climatology
         in Japan," Science Reports of Tohaku University,
         Vol. 28, pp. 395-430.

H-804.   Shlemon, Roy J. 1979. "Applications of
         Physical Geography: Quaternary,
         Soil-Stratigraphy, and Geomorphology,"
         Geographical Survey, Vol. 8, No. 4, pp. 9-17.

H-805.   Shnitnikov, A. V. 1968. "Geographical Problems
         in Climatology, Hydrology and Glaciology Over
         the Last 50 Years," Soviet Geography: Review
         and Translation, Vol. 9, pp. 407-417.

H-806.   Shul'gin, A. M. 1960. "Bioclimatology as a
         Scientific Discipline and Its Current
         Objectives," Soviet Geography: Review and
         Translation, Vol. 1, No. 9, pp. 67-74.

H-807.   Sidorenko, A. V. 1972. "Geomorphology and the
         National Economy," Soviet Geography: Review and
         Translation, Vol. 13, pp. 344-352.

H-808.   Silvernail, Richard G. 1966. "A Geography of
         Recreation: A Status Report," Memorandum Folio
         of the Southeastern Association of American
         Geographers, Vol. 18, pp. 195-200.

H-809.   Simmons, I. G. 1952. "Resource Management and
         Conservation," Progress in Human Geography, Vol.
         6, pp. 102-105.

H-810.   Simmons, I. G.   1978.   "Physical Geography in
          Environmental Science," Geography, Vol. 63, pp.
          314-323.

H-811.   Simmons, James W.   1967.   "Urban Geography in
          Canada," Canadian Geographer, Vol. 11, pp.
          341-356.

H-812.   Singh, Dina Nath.   1977.   "Transportation
          Geography in India: A Survey of Research,"
          National Geographical Journal of India, Vol. 23,
          pp. 95-114.

H-813.   Singh, Jagdish.   1965. "Fundamental Concepts in
          Economic Geography," National Geographical
          Journal of India, Vol. 11, pp. 63-73.

H-814.   Singh, Mahar.   1982.   "History of Cartography in
          India: Some Questions," Indian Geographical
          Journal, Vol. 57, pp. 79-81.

H-815.   Singh, R., Singh, L. and Duke, B. 1966.   "The
          Contribution to Cartography," National
          Geographical Journal of India, Vol. 12, pp.
          24-37.

H-816.   Singh, Ram Galo.   1965.   "Historical Geography:
          Place Names and Settlements - A Review of
          Studies," National Geographical Journal of
          India, Vol. 11, pp. 101-124.

H-817.   Sitwell, O. F. G. and Latham, G. R.   1979.
          "Behavioural Geography and the Cultural
          Landscape," Geografiska Annaler, Vol. 61B, pp.
          61-63.

H-818.   Small, R. J. 1978.   "The Revolution in
          Geomorphology--A Retrospect," Geography, Vol.
          63, pp. 265-272.

H-819.   de Smidt, Marc.   1983.   "Dutch Economic
          Geography in Retrospect," Tijdschrift voor
          Economische en Sociale Geografie, Vol. 74, pp.
          344-357.

H-820.   Smita, H. T.   1935.   "The History and
          Development of Organized Marine Meteorology,"
          Marine Observer, Vol. 12, pp. 19-22, 65-69,
          107-110.

H-821.   Smith, Bruce W. and Spinelli, Joseph G. 1979.
          "A Development Program for Applied
          Geographers: Planning in the Present for the
          Future," Journal of Geography, Vol. 78, pp.
          45-47.

H-822.   Smith, David M. 1971. "Radical Geography --
          The Next Revolution," Area, Vol. 3, pp.
          153-157.

H-823.   Smith, Guy-Harold. 1960. "Salaries of
          Geographers in the Universities," Professional
          Geographer, Vol. 12, No. 3, pp. 15-18.

H-824.   Smith, J. P., et al. 1980. "Towards the
          Renaissance of the Cultural Perspective," Area,
          Vol. 12, pp. 108-110.

H-825.   Smith, J. Russell. 1907. "Economic Geography
          and Its Relation to Economic Theory and Higher
          Education," Bulletin of the American
          Geographical Society of New York, Vol. 39, pp.
          472-481.

H-826.   Smith, Keith. 1983. "Training in Physical
          Geography: the NERC Connection," Area, Vol. 15,
          pp. 289-293.

H-827.   Smith, Neil. 1984. "Political Geographers of
          the Past. Isaiah Bowman: Political Geography
          and Geopolitics," Political Geography Quarterly,
          Vol. 3, pp. 69-76.

H-828.   Smith, S. J. 1981. "Humanistic Method in
          Contemporary Social Geography," Area, Vol. 13,
          pp. 293-298.

H-829.   Smith, T. Alford. 1908. "Physical Geography as
          an Essential Part of School Geography,"
          Geographical Teacher, Vol. 4, pp. 221-229.

H-830.   Smyth, W. J. 1974. "The Development and Scope
          of Social Geography: A Review," Geographical
          Viewpoint, Vol. 3, pp. 67-86.

H-831.   Sochava, V. B. 1968. "Modern Geography and Its
          Tasks in Siberia and the Soviet Far East,"
          Soviet Geography: Review and Translation, Vol.
          9, pp. 80-95.

H-832.   Spate, O. H. K. 1950. "On the Marchlands of
          Geography: Some Reflections on Method in
          Historical and Economic Geography," Geographer,
          Vol. 2, pp. 1-5.

H-833.   Spencer, Donald S. 1988. "A Short History of
          Geopolitics," Journal of Geography, Vol. 87, pp.
          42-48.

H-834.   Spencer, J. E. 1978. "The Growth of Cultural
          Geography," American Behavioral Scientist, Vol.
          22, pp. 79-92.

H-835.   Spinelli, J. G. 1978. "Notes on the Concept of
          Population Geography," East Lakes Geographer,
          Vol. 13, pp. 1-2.

H-836.   Spiridonov, A. I. 1975. "Some Theoretical
          Problems in Geomorphology," Soviet Geography:
          Review and Translation, Vol. 26, pp. 395-402.

H-837.   Stablein, G. 1983. "Alfred Wegner, from
          Research in Greenland to Plate Techtonics,"
          GeoJournal, Vol. 7, pp. 361-368.

H-838.   Stager, John K. 1966. "The Physical Side of
          Geography," B. C. Geographical Series, No. 3,
          pp. 15-22.

H-839.   Stoddart, D. R. 1978. "Geomorphology in
          China," Progress in Physical Geography, Vol. 2,
          pp. 514-551.

H-840.   Stoddart, D. R. 1983. "Biogeography: Darwin
          Devalued or Darwin Revalued," Progress in
          Physical Geography, Vol. 7, pp. 256-264.

H-841.   Storper, M. 1988. "Big Structures, Small
          Events and Large Processes in Economic
          Geography," Environment and Planning A, Vol. 20,
          pp. 165-185.

H-842.   Storper, Michael. 1985. "Oligopoly and the
          Product Cycle: Essentialism in Economic
          Geography," Economic Geography, Vol. 61, pp.
          260-282.

H-843.   Strahler, Arthur. 1954. "Empirical and
          Explanatory Methods in Physical Geography,"
          Professional Geographer, Vol. 6, No. 1, pp. 4-9.

H-844.   Stutz, Frederick and Heiges, Harvey E. 1983.
          "Developing Courses in Applied Geography for
          Transportation Planners," Professional
          Geographer, Vol. 35, pp. 206-210.

H-845.   Sugden, David E. 1983. "Geography and
          Geomorphology: Alternatives to G. H. Dury,"
          Area, Vol. 15, pp. 122-125.

H-846.   Sun, Pan-Shou. 1982. "Current Research in
          Urban Geography in China: A Review," Asian
          Geographer, Vol. 1, pp. 67-69.

H-847.   Sweet, David C. 1969. "The Geographer's Role
          in the Urban Planning Process," Southeastern
          Geographer, Vol. 9, pp. 25-35.

H-848.   Tait, John B. 1945. "Oceanography: Scotland's
          Interest in its Progress," Scottish Geographical
          Magazine, Vol. 61, pp. 1-9.

H-849.   Takeuchi, K.   1984.   "Some Remarks on the
          Geography of Tourism in Japan," _GeoJournal_, Vol.
          9, pp. 85-90.

H-850.   Tamaskar, B. G.   1981.   "Historical
          Maps--Prospects of Historical Cartography in
          India," _Deccan Geographer_, Vol. 19, pp. 137-144.

H-851.   Taylor, D. R. F.   1985.   "The Educational
          Challenges of a New Cartography,"
          Cartographica, Vol. 22, pp. 19-37.

H-852.   Taylor, J. A.   1984.   "Biogeography," _Progress
          in Physical Geography_, Vol. 8, pp. 94-101.

H-853.   Taylor, J. A.   1985.   "Biogeography," _Progress
          in Physical Geography_, Vol. 9, pp. 104-112.

H-854.   Taylor, J. A.   1986.   "Biogeography," _Progress
          in Physical Geography_, Vol. 10, pp. 239-248.

H-855.   Taylor, P. J.   1978.   "Political Geography,"
          Progress in Human Geography, Vol. 2, pp.
          153-162.

H-856.   Taylor, P. J.   1982.   "A Materialist Framework
          for Political Geography," _Transactions -
          Institute of British Geographers_, Vol. 7, pp.
          15-34.

H-857.   Taylor, Z.   1980.   "Some Comments on Social
          Transport Geography," _Progress in Human
          Geography_, Vol. 4, pp. 99-104.

H-858.   Terjung, Werner H.   1976.   "Climatology for
          Geographers," _Annals of the Association of
          American Geographers_, Vol. 66, pp. 199-222.

H-859.   Thom, B. J.   1980.   "Future Trends in Coastal
          Geomorphology," _Australian Geographer_, Vol. 14,
          pp. 64-65.

H-860.   Thomale, E.   1984.   "Social Geographical
          Research in Germany - a Balance Sheet for the
          Years 1950-1980," _GeoJournal_, Vol. 9, pp.
          223-230.

H-861.   Thoman, Richard S.   1958.   "Recent
          Methodological Contributions to German Economic
          Geography," _Annals of the Association of
          American Geographers_, Vol. 48, pp. 92-96.

H-862.   Thoman, Richard S.   1962.   "Economic Geography
          and Economic Underdevelopment," _Economic
          Geography_, Vol. 38, p. 189.

H-863.   Thoman, Richard S.   1967.   "Economic Geography in Canada," _Canadian Geographer_, Vol. 11, pp. 366-371.

H-864.   Thomas, Benjamin E.   1956.   "Methods and Objectives in Transportation Geography," _Professional Geographer_, Vol. 8, No. 4, pp. 2-5.

H-865.   Thomas, M. J.   1978.   "City Planning in Soviet Russia (1917-1932)," _Geoforum_, Vol. 9, pp. 269-278.

H-866.   Thompson, Donald J.   1966.   "Future Directions in Retail Area Research," _Economic Geography_, Vol. 42, pp. 1-18.

H-867.   Thornes, J. B.   1979.   "Research and Application in British Geomorphology," _Geoforum_, Vol. 10, pp. 253-260.

H-868.   Thornes, John E.   1978.   "Applied Climatology," [Great Britain] _Progress in Physical Geography_, Vol. 2, pp. 481-493.

H-869.   Thornes, John E.   1979.   "Applied Climatology," [Europe] _Progress in Physical Geography_, Vol. 3, pp. 427-442.

H-870.   Thornes, John E.   1981.   "A Paradigmatic Shift in Atmospheric Studies," _Progress in Physical Geography_, Vol. 5, pp. 429-447.

H-871.   Thorpe, D.   1978.   "Progress in the Study of the Geography of Retailing and Wholesaling in Britain," _Geoforum_, Vol. 9, pp. 83-106.

H-872.   Thrift, N. and Pred, A.   1981.   "Time Geography: A New Beginning," _Progress in Human Geography_, Vol. 5, pp. 277-286.

H-873.   Thrower, Norman.   1964.   "Geomorphology in Strabo's Geography," _California Geographer_, Vol. 5, pp. 11-15.

H-874.   Tietze, Wolf.   1973.   "A New Orientation for Economic Geography," _Geoforum_, Vol. 5, p. 3.

H-875.   Timar, Lajos.   1987.   "Some Special Directions of Research in U.S. Historical Geography From an East-Central European Point of View," _Historical Geography_, Vol. 17, No. 2, pp. 1-11.

H-876.   Tobler, W. R.   1979.   "A Transformational View of Cartography," _American Cartographer_, Vol. 6, pp. 101-106.

H-877.   Tornquist, Gunnar. 1977. "The Geography of
          Economic Activities: Some Critical Viewpoints
          on Theory and Application," Economic Geography,
          Vol. 53, pp. 153-162.

H-878.   Trewartha, Glenn. 1953. "A Case for Population
          Geography," Annals of the Association of
          American Geographers, Vol. 43, pp. 71-97.

H-879.   Trudgill, Peter. 1975. "Linguistic Geography
          and Geographical Linguistics," Progress in
          Geography, Vol. 7, pp. 227-234.

H-880.   Trudgill, Stephen T. 1977. "Environmental
          Sciences/Studies: Depth and Breadth in the
          Curriculum," Area, Vol. 9, pp. 266-269.

H-881.   Tuan, Yi-Fu. 1983. "Geographical Theory:
          Queries from a Cultural Geographer,"
          Geographical Analysis, Vol. 15, pp. 69-72.

H-882.   Turnock, D. 1987. "Urban Geography and Urban
          Development in Romania: The Contribution of
          Vintila Mihailescu," GeoJournal Vol. 14, pp.
          181-202.

H-883.   Ullman, Edward L. 1973. "Ecology and Spatial
          Analysis," Annals of the Association of American
          Geographers, Vol. 63, pp. 272-274.

H-884.   Unstead, J. F. 1922. "Geography and Historical
          Geography," Geographical Journal, Vol. 59, pp.
          55-60.

H-885.   Uren, P. C. 1950. "The Status of Military
          Geography in Canada," Canadian Geographer, No.
          1, pp. 11-14.

H-886.   Vale, Thomas R. and Parker, Albert J. 1980.
          "Biogeography: Research Opportunities for
          Geographers," Professional Geographer, Vol. 32,
          pp. 149-157.

H-887.   Van Burkalow, A. 1976. "Biogeography's
          Contribution to Medical Geography," Proceedings
          - Twenty-Third International Geographical
          Congress, pp. 142-145.

H-888.   Van Cleef, Eugene. 1960. "Geography as an
          Earth Science," Professional Geographer, Vol.
          12, No. 6, pp. 8-11.

H-889.   Van Cleef, Eugene. 1969. "'Things Are Not
          Always What They Seem' for the Economic
          Geographer," Economic Geography, Vol. 45, pp.
          41-44.

H-890.   Vance, J. E., Jr. 1978. "Geography and the
          Study of Cities," _American Behavioral Scientist_,
          Vol. 22, pp. 131-149.

H-891.   Vander Wusten, H. and O'Loughlin, J. 1987.
          "Back to the Future of Political Geography: A
          Rejoinder to O'Tuathail," _Annals of the
          Association of American Geographers_, Vol. 39,
          pp. 198-199.

H-892.   Vanderhill, Burke G. and Malik, Rashey A.
          1979. "Historical Perspective on Rural
          Settlement Geography," _Pakistan Geographical
          Review_, Vol. 34, pp. 11-32.

H-893.   Van Royen, William. 1947. "Resources Appraisal
          and Development Planning," _Professional
          Geographer_, Vol. 5, pp. 9-12.

H-894.   Valkenburg, S. Van. 1960. "A Political
          Geographer Looks at the World," _Professional
          Geographer_, Vol. 12, No. 4, pp. 6-8.

H-895.   Varjo, U. 1981. "Social Geography in the
          System of Geography," _Fennia_, Vol. 59, pp.
          229-235.

H-896.   Vascovic, M. 1984. "Some Views on the
          Geography of Tourism and Recreation in
          Yugoslavia," _GeoJournal_, Vol. 9, pp. 77-82.

H-897.   Vasilevskiy, L. I. 1964. "Basic Research
          Problems in the Geography of Transportation of
          Capitalist and Underdeveloped Countries," _Soviet
          Geography_: _Review and Translation_, Vol. 4, No.
          7, pp. 36-59.

H-898.   Vink, A. P. A. 1968. "The Role of Physical
          Geography in Integrated Surveys of Developing
          Countries," _Tijdschrift voor Economische en
          Sociale Geografie_, Vol. 59, pp. 294-312.

H-899.   Visher, S. S. 1915. "Notes on the Significance
          of the Biota and of Biogeography," _Bulletin of
          the American Geographical Society_, Vol. 47, pp.
          509-520.

H-900.   Visher, Stephen Sargent. 1932. "Social
          Geography," _Social Forces_, Vol. 10, pp.
          351-354.

H-901.   Vol'skiy, V. V. 1963. "On Some Problems of
          Theory and Practice in Economic Geography,"
          Soviet Geography: _Review and Translation_, Vol.
          4, No. 8, pp. 14-25.

H-902.   Von Engeln, O. D.   1912.   "Emil Von Sydon and
          the Development of German School Cartography,"
          <u>Bulletin</u> <u>of</u> <u>the</u> <u>American</u> <u>Geographical</u> <u>Society</u>,
          Vol. 44, pp. 846-848.

H-903.   Voronov, A. G.   1968.   "Biogeography Today and
          Tomorrow," <u>Soviet</u> <u>Geography</u>:   <u>Review</u> <u>and</u>
          <u>Translation</u>, Vol. 9, pp. 367-378.

H-904.   Wagner, Philip L.   1975.   "The Themes of
          Cultural Geography Rethought," <u>Yearbook</u> -
          <u>Association</u> <u>of</u> <u>Pacific</u> <u>Coast</u> <u>Geographers</u>, Vol.
          37, pp. 7-14.

H-905.   Wagner, Philip L.   1981.   "Sport: Culture and
          Geography," <u>Lund</u> <u>Studies</u> <u>in</u> <u>Geography</u>, <u>Series</u> <u>B</u>,
          Vol. 48, pp. 85-108.

H-906.   Walker, Gerald.   1987.   "Commentary on Humans,
          Land and Landscape: A Proposal for Cultural
          Geography," <u>Canadian</u> <u>Geographer</u>, Vol. 31, pp.
          30-32.

H-907.   Wallis, B. C.   1912.   "Measurement in Economic
          Geography: Its Principles and Practices,"
          <u>Geographical</u> <u>Journal</u>, Vol. 39, pp. 22-26.

H-908.   Wallis, H.   1981.   "The History of Land Use
          Mapping," <u>Cartographic</u> <u>Journal</u>, Vol. 18, pp.
          45-47.

H-909.   Walsh, F.   1979.   "Time-lag in Political
          Geography," <u>Area</u>, Vol. 11, pp. 91-92.

H-910.   Ward, David.   1966.   "The Changing Heritage of
          Geography," <u>B. C.</u> <u>Geographical</u> <u>Series</u>, No. 3,
          pp. 11-14.

H-911.   Ward, David.   1966.   "The Changing Heritage of
          Geography," <u>B. C.</u> <u>Geographical</u> <u>Series</u>, No. 3,
          pp. 35-40.

H-912.   Ward, Robert DeCourcy.   1895.   "Meteorology As a
          University Course," <u>Science</u>, n.s. Vol. 2, p.
          817.

H-913.   Ward, Robert DeCourcy.   1897.   "The Teaching of
          Climatology in Medical Schools," <u>Boston</u> <u>Medical</u>
          <u>and</u> <u>Surgical</u> <u>Journal</u>, Vol. 136, pp. 103-106.

H-914.   Ward, Robert DeCourcy.   1921.   "Instruction in
          Climatology in Medical Schools," <u>Boston</u> <u>Medical</u>
          <u>and</u> <u>Surgical</u> <u>Journal</u>, Vol. 184, pp. 477-479.

H-915.   Ward, Robert DeCourcy.   1931.   "The Literature
          of Climatology," <u>Annals</u> <u>of</u> <u>the</u> <u>Association</u> <u>of</u>
          <u>American</u> <u>Geographers</u>, Vol. 21, pp. 34-51.

H-916.   Ward, Roy.   1979.   "The Changing Scope of
         Geographical Hydrology in Great Britain,"
         Progress in Geography, Vol. 3, pp. 392-412.

H-917.   Warnes, A. M.   1980.   "Toward Geographical
         Contribution to Gerontology," Progress in Human
         Geography, Vol. 5, pp. 317-341.

H-918.   Warnes, A. M.   1984.   "Places and People:
         Reflections on Their Study in Social Geography,"
         GeoJournal, Vol. 9, pp. 261-271.

H-919.   Warnes, A. M. and Daniels, P. W.   1980.   "Urban
         Retail Distributions: An Appraisal of the
         Empirical Foundations of Retail Geography,"
         Geoforum, Vol. 11, pp. 133-146.

H-920.   Warntz, William.   1957.   "Contributions Toward a
         Macroeconomic Geography: A Review," Geographical
         Journal, Vol. 47, pp. 420-424.

H-921.   Warntz, William.   1959.   "Progress in Economic
         Geography," Yearbook, National Council of the
         Social Studies, Washington, D.C., Vol. 29, pp.
         54-75.

H-922.   Warren, A. and Harrison, C. M.   1984.   "People
         and the Ecosystem: Biogeography as a Study of
         Ecology and Culture," Geoforum, Vol. 15, pp.
         365-381.

H-923.   Warszynska, J.   1984.   "Geography of Tourism in
         Poland," GeoJournal, Vol. 9, pp. 69-70.

H-924.   Warszynska, J. and Jackowski, A.   1986.
         "Studies on the Geography of Tourism," Annals
         of Tourism Research, Vol. 13, pp. 655-658.

H-925.   Wasserman, W.   1978.   "Cartography as a
         Science," Cartography, Vol. 10, pp. 142-144.

H-926.   Waterman, Stanley.   1987.   "Partitioned States,"
         Political Geography Quarterly, Vol. 6, pp.
         151-170.

H-927.   Watts, D.   1978.   "The New Biogeography and Its
         Niche in Physical Geography Research,"
         Geography, Vol. 63, pp. 324-337.

H-928.   Weaver, John C.   1958.   "A Design for Research
         in the Geography of Agriculture," Professional
         Geographer, Vol. 10, No. 1, pp. 2-8.

H-929.   Webb, Martyn J.   1961.   "Economic Geography: A
         Framework for a Disciplinary Definition,"
         Economic Geography, Vol. 37, pp. 254-257.

H-930.   Wellings, P. 1986. "Editor's Introduction.
          Geography and Development Studies in Southern
          Africa: A Progressive Prospectus," Geoforum,
          Vol. 17, pp. 119-132.

H-931.   Wescoat, James L., Jr. 1987. "The 'Practical
          Range of Choice' in Water Resources Geography,"
          Progress in Human Geography, Vol. 11, pp. 41-59.

H-932.   Wessinger, Esther. 1918. "The Value of Place
          Geography in a Commercial Geography Course,"
          Journal of Geography, Vol. 17, pp. 162-163.

H-933.   Wheeler, James O. 1971. "An Overview of
          Research in Transportation Geography," East
          Lakes Geographer, Vol. 7, pp. 3-12.

H-934.   Wheeler, James O. 1973. "Introduction:
          Societal and Policy Perspectives in
          Transportation Geography," Economic Geography,
          Vol. 49, pp. ii-181-184.

H-935.   Wheeler, James O. 1976. "A Prologue to
          Transportation Geography Research,"
          Southeastern Geographer, Vol. 16, pp. 1-8.

H-936.   Whitaker, J. Russell. 1951. "Conservation and
          the College Professor," Memorandum Folio of the
          Southeastern Association of American
          Geographers, Vol. 2, pp. 1-6.

H-937.   Whitbeck, R. H. 1913. "Commercial Geography as
          a Secondary School Study," Journal of Geography,
          Vol. 11, pp. 49-55.

H-938.   Whitbeck, R. H. 1915. "Economic Geography:
          Its Growth and Possibilities," Journal of
          Geography, Vol. 14, pp. 284-290.

H-939.   White, Stephen E. 1980. "A Philosophical
          Dichotomy in Migration Research," Professional
          Geographer, Vol. 32, pp. 6-13.

H-940.   White, Stuart. 1984. "Landscape of Events,"
          Journal of Cultural Geography, Vol. 4, pp.
          100-108.

H-941.   Whitehand, J. W. R. 1977. "The Basis for an
          Historico-Geographical Theory of Urban Form,"
          Transactions - Institute of British Geographers,
          Vol. 2, pp. 400-416.

H-942.   Whitehand, J. W. R. 1986. "Taking Stock of
          Urban Geography," Area, Vol. 18, pp. 147-151.

H-943.   Whitehand, J. W. R. 1986. "Urban Geography:
          Within the City," Progress in Human Geography,
          Vol. 10, pp. 118-124.

H-944.   Whitmore, Frank C. 1948. "Military Geography,"
         Professional Geographer, Vol. 7, pp. 7-16.

H-945.   Whitney, Rev. J. P. 1886. "The Place of
         Historical Geography in Higher Education,"
         Journal of the Manchester Geographical Society,
         Vol. 2, pp. 106-107.

H-946.   Whittlesey, Derwent. 1942. "Geography into
         Politics," Annals of the Association of American
         Geographers, Vol. 32, pp. 142-143.

H-947.   Whittlesey, Derwent. 1943. "Geopolitics, a
         Program for Action," Annals of the Association
         of American Geographers, Vol. 33, pp. 97-98.

H-948.   Wilbanks, Thomas J. 1978. "Geographic Research
         and Energy Policy Making," Geographical Survey,
         Vol. 7, No. 4, pp. 11-18.

H-949.   Wilhelm, E. J. 1968. "Biogeography and
         Environmental Science," Professional Geographer,
         Vol. 20, pp. 123-125.

H-950.   Wilhelm, E. J. Jr. 1968. "The Role of
         Biogeography in Education," Journal of
         Geography, Vol. 67, pp. 526-529.

H-951.   Williams, J. F. 1978. "Two Observations on the
         State of Geography in the People's Republic of
         China: I) Economic Geography; II) Cartography,"
         China Geographer, Special Issue, Vol. 9, pp.
         17-31.

H-952.   Williams, Llewelyn. 1961. "Climatology and
         Geographers," Professional
         Geographer, Vol. 13, No. 4, pp. 11-15.

H-953.   Williams, Martin. 1980. "Whither Australian
         Geomorphology?" Australian Geographer, Vol. 14,
         pp. 63-64.

H-954.   Williams, Michael. 1970. "Places, Periods, and
         Themes: A Review and Prospect of Australian
         Historical Geography," Australian Geographer,
         Vol. 11, pp. 403-416.

H-955.   Williams, Michael. 1983. "'The Apple of My
         Eye': Carl Sauer and Historical Geography,"
         Journal of Historical Geography, Vol. 9, pp.
         1-28.

H-956.   Williams, S. W. 1983. "The Concept of Culture
         and Human Geography: A Review and Reassessment,"
         Occasional Paper - University of Keele,
         Department of Geography, Vol. 5.

H-957.   Wilson, Colonel C. W.   1888.   "Commercial
          Geography," Journal of the Manchester
          Geographical Society, Vol. 4, pp. 273-282.

H-958.   Wilson, Henry.   1918.   "The Geography of Culture
          and the Culture of Geography," Geographical
          Teacher, Vol. 9, p.

H-959.   Winchester, S. W. C.   1978.   "Two Suggestions
          for Developing the Geographical Study of Crime,"
          Area, Vol. 10, pp. 116-120.

H-960.   Wise, M. J.   1962.   "On the Writing of Regional
          Economic Geography," Economic Geography, Vol.
          38, p. 1.

H-961.   Wise, M. J.   1973.   "Environmental Studies:
          Geographical Studies," Geography, Vol. 58, pp.
          293-300.

H-962.   Wisner, Ben.   1978.   "Does Radical Geography
          Lack an Approach to Environmental Relations?"
          Antipode, Vol. 10, pp. 84-95.

H-963.   Wolfe, Roy I.   1967.   "The Geography of Outdoor
          Recreation: A Dynamic Approach," B. C.
          Geographical Series, No. 8, pp. 7-12.

H-964.   Wood, Harold A.   1977.   "Toward a Geographical
          Concept of Development," Geographical Review,
          Vol. 67, pp. 462-468.

H-965.   Wood, J. D.   1964-65.   "Historical Geography in
          Alberta," Albertan Geographer, No. 1, pp. 17-19.

H-966.   Wood, L. J.   1970.   "Perception Studies in
          Geography," Transactions - Institute of British
          Geographers, No. 50, pp. 129-142.

H-967.   Wood, P.   1978.   "Industrial Geography Revived:
          Space and Corporate Strategy," Bloomsbury
          Geographer, Vol. 9, pp. 2-5.

H-968.   Wood, P. A.   1979.   "Priorities in Industrial
          Location Research," Area, Vol. 11, pp. 253-256.

H-969.   Wood, P. A., 1980.   "Industrial Geography,"
          Progress in Human Geography, Vol. 4, pp.
          406-416.

H-970.   Woods, Robert.   1982.   "Population Studies,"
          Progress in Human Geography, Vol. 6, pp.
          247-253.

H-971.   Woolstencraft, R. P.   1980.   "Electoral
          Geography: Retrospect and Prospect,"
          International Political Science Journal, Vol. 1,
          pp. 540-560.

H-972.   Worley, Lillian.   1950.   "The Geographer's
         Contribution to Education for Resource
         Management," Annals of the Association of
         American Geographers, Vol. 40, pp. 131-132.

H-973.   Worsley, P.   1979.   Whither Geomorphology,"
         Area, Vol. 11, pp. 97-101.

H-974.   Worth, C.   1982.   "Cartography and Portsmouth
         Polytechnic," South Hampshire Geographer, Vol.
         14, pp. 2-7.

H-975.   Wright, J.   1926.   "A Plea for the History of
         Geography," Isis, Vol. 8, pp. 477-491.

H-976.   Wright, John K.   1942.   "Map Makers are Human:
         Comments on the Subjective in Maps,"
         Geographical Review, Vol. 32, pp. 526-544.

H-977.   Wright, John K.   1944.   "Training for Research
         in Political Geography," Annals of the
         Association of American Geographers, Vol. 34,
         pp. 190-201.

H-978.   Wright, John K.   1949.   "Highlights in American
         Cartography 1939-1949," Proceedings - Sixteenth
         International Geographical Congress, pp.
         298-314.

H-979.   Wright, John Kirtland.   1926.   "A Plea for the
         History of Geography," Isis, Vol. 8, pp.
         477-491.

H-980.   Wrigley, N.   1979.   "Developments in the
         Statistical Analysis of Categorical Data,"
         Progress in Human Geography, Vol. 3, pp.
         315-355.

H-981.   Wynn, Graeme.   1977.   "Discovering the
         Antipodes, A Review of Historical Geography in
         Australia and New Zealand, 1969-1975, with a
         Bibliography," Journal of Historical Geography,
         Vol. 3, pp. 251-266.

H-982.   Yates, T.   1984.   "Editorial: Social
         Geography," GeoJournal, Vol. 9, pp. 215-222.

H-983.   Yeates, John.   1886.   "The Relations Between
         Commercial History and Geography," Journal of
         the Manchester Geographical Society, Vol. 2, pp.
         181-198.

H-984.   Yefremov, Yu. K.   1961.   "An Approach to Inte-
         grated Physical-Geographic Description of an
         Area," Soviet Geography: Review and
         Translation, Vol. 2, No. 7, pp. 42-47.

H-985.   Yefremov, Yu. K. 1961. "The Concept of Land-
          scape and Landscapes of Different Orders,"
          Soviet Geography: Review and Translation, Vol.
          2, No. 10, pp. 32-43.

H-986.   Yefremov, Yu. K. 1964. "The Place of Physical
          Geography Among the Natural Sciences," Soviet
          Geography: Review and Translation, Vol. 5, pp.
          3-11.

H-987.   Yefremov, Yu. K. 1969. "The Landscape Sphere
          and the Geographical Environment," Soviet
          Geography: Review and Translation, Vol. 10, pp.
          248-256.

H-988.   Yefremov, Yu. K. 1975. "Geography and
          Tourism," Soviet Geography: Review and
          Translation, Vol. 16, pp. 205-217.

H-989.   Young, Baroness J. 1987. "Geography and
          Politics," Transactions - Institute of British
          Geographers, Vol. 12, pp. 391-397.

H-990.   Yugay, R. L. 1978. "The Time Frame of
          Historical Geography," Soviet Geography: Review
          and Translation, Vol. 19, pp. 186-195.

H-991.   Zakrzewska, Barbara. 1967. "Trends and Methods
          in Landform Geography," Annals of the
          Association of American Geographers, Vol. 57,
          pp. 128-167.

H-992.   Zakrzewska, Barbara. 1971. "Nature of Land
          Form Geography," Professional Geographer, Vol.
          23, pp. 351-354.

H-993.   Zdorkowski, Gretchen. 1977. "Geographical Per-
          spectives on the Quality of Life: A
          Commentary," Geographical Survey, Vol. 6, No. 2,
          pp. 9-10.

H-994.   Zeben, Leo J. 1960. "The Other Street:
          Geography in Planning," Memorandum Folio of the
          Southeastern Association of American
          Geographers, Vol. 12, pp. 105-107.

H-995.   Zekkel', Ya. D. 1960. "On the Courses of
          Development and the Next Tasks of
          Geomorphology," Soviet Geography: Review and
          Translation, Vol. 1, No. 1-2, pp. 28-33.

H-996.   Zelinsky, Wilbur. 1973. "In Pursuit of
          Historical Geography and Other Wild Geese,"
          Historical Geography Newsletter, Vol. 3, pp.
          1-5.

H-997.   Zelinsky, Wilbur. 1976. "Quality of Life: An Inquiry Into its Utility for Geographers," Geographical Survey, Vol. 5, No. 4, pp. 8-11.

H-998.   Zhekulin, V. S. 1968. "Some Thoughts on the Subject of Historical Geography," Soviet Geography: Review and Translation, Vol. 9, pp. 570-575.

H-999.   Zimmerman, R. C. and Thom, B. G. 1982. "Physiographic Plant Geography," Progress in Physical Geography, Vol. 6, pp. 45-59.

H-1000.   Zobler, Leonard. 1962. "An Economic-Historical View of Natural Resource Use and Conservation," Economic Geography, Vol. 38, pp. 189-194.

H-1001.   Zonn, Leo E. 1978. "Community and Action: An Alternative Approach to Social Geography, Research in Contemporary and Applied Geography, Vol. 2, No. 2, pp. 46-66.

H-1002.   Zonneveld, J. I. S. 1979. "Physical Geography in the Netherlands," Erdkunde, Vol. 33, pp. 1-10.

H-1003.   Zubakov, V. A. 1978. "On the Content and the Tasks of Historical Geography (as the History of Nature Management), Soviet Geography: Review and Translation, Vol. 19, pp. 170-179.

H-1004.   Zvonkova, T. V. 1968. "Practical Problems in Physical Geography," Soviet Geography: Review and Translation, Vol. 9, pp. 378-384.

H-1005.   Zvonkova, T. V. and Saushkin, Yu. G. 1977. "Interaction Between Physical and Economic Geography," Soviet Geography: Review and Translation, Vol. 18, pp. 245-250.

Applied Geography

I-1. Adams, John S. 1984. "The Meaning of Housing in
      America," Annals of the Association of American
      Geographers, Vol. 74, pp. 515-526.

I-2. Ahmad, Kazi S. 1950. "The Role of Geography in
      our National Planning," Pakistan Geographical
      Review, Vol. 5, pp. not known.

I-3. Anderson, James R., Hallam, Cheryl A. and Witmer,
      Richard E. 1979. "Applied Geography in the
      United States Geological Survey," Research in
      Contemporary and Applied Geography: A Discussion
      Series, Vol. 3, No. 3, pp. 40-73.

I-4. Anonymous. 1920. "Geography's Debt to the
      Missionary," Literary Digest, Vol. 64, March 13,
      p. 38.

I-5. Anonymous. 1984. "The Geo-Economists: A New
      Profession for the Jobs Market," Futurist, Vol.
      18, p. 58.

I-6. Applebaum, William. 1947. "The Geographer in
      Business and His Requisite Training,"
      Professional Geographer, Vol. 5, pp. 1-4.

I-7. Applebaum, William. 1951. "A Selected
      Bibliography of Careers in Geography,"
      Professional Geographer, Vol. 3, pp. 31-37.

I-8. Applebaum, William. 1956. "What Are Geographers
      Doing in Business?" Professional Geographer, Vol.
      8, pp. 2-4.

I-9. Appleton, John B. 1932. "Geography in Relation
      to Business," Journal of Geography, Vol. 31, pp.
      253-260.

I-10.   Appleton, John B. 1947. "Geographic Research
        and World Affairs," Yearbook of the Association
        of Pacific Coast Geographers, Vol. 9, pp. 3-7.

I-11.   Bagchi, Kanan G. 1973. "Geography and Its
        Social Application," Geographical Review of
        India, Vol. 35, pp. 107-112.

I-12.   Baker, Emily V. 1965. "Opportunity Still Knocks
        at the Door of the Geographer," California
        Geographer, Vol. 6, pp. 1-10.

I-13.   Barton, Thomas F. 1969. "Emphasizing Applied
        Geography," Journal of Geography, Vol. 68, pp.
        196-197.

I-14.   Beck, Richard C. 1984. "Opportunities for
        Geographers in the Cooperative Extension
        Service," Professional Geographer, Vol. 36, pp.
        234-235.

I-15.   Berry, Brian J. L. 1972. "More on Relevance and
        Policy Analysis," Area, Vol. 4, pp. 77-80.

I-16.   Berry, L. and Kates, R. W. 1973. "Applied
        Geographical Research in East Africa,"
        Professional Geographer, Vol. 25, pp. 267-271.

I-17.   Bowman, Isaiah. 1934. "William Morris Davis,"
        Geographical Review, Vol. 24, pp. 177-181.

I-18.   Brooks, Edwin. 1974. "Government
        Decision-Making," Transactions - Institute of
        British Geographers, Vol. 63, pp. 29-40.

I-19.   Clayton, K. M. 1985. "New Blood by (Government)
        Order," Area, Vol. 17, pp. 321-322.

I-20.   Common, R. 1985. "Some Reflections on the
        Practice of Applied Geography," Scottish
        Geographical Magazine, Vol. 101, pp. 4-15.

I-21.   Common, Robert. 1984. "Ends and Means in
        Applied Geography," Scottish Geographical
        Magazine, Vol. 100, pp. 4-11.

I-22.   Common, Robert. 1986. "The Quiet Influences of
        Applied Geography," Scottish Geographical
        Magazine, Vol. 102, pp. 42-45.

I-23.   Cooper, Sherwin H. 1966. "Theoretical
        Geography, Applied Geography and Planning,"
        Professional Geographer, Vol. 18, pp. 1-2.

I-24.   Cutshall, Alden. 1942. "The Geographer in War
        Time," Journal of Geography, Vol. 41, pp.
        252-258.

I-25.   Cutter, Susan L. 1988. "Geographers and Nuclear
         War: Why We Lack Influence on Public Policy,"
         Annals of the Association of American
         Geographers, Vol. 78, pp. 132-143.

I-26.   Dickinson, Joshua C., III. 1977. "An Applied
         Geographer in Latin America," Geographical
         Review, Vol. 67, pp. 232-234.

I-27.   Dobson, Jeffrey R. 1981. "The Product Needs of
         the Geographic Practitioner," Research in
         Contemporary and Applied Geography: A Discussion
         Series, Vol. 5, No. 3, pp. 43-62.

I-28.   Dobson, Jerome. 1983. "Automated Geography,"
         Professional Geographer, Vol. 35, pp. 135-143.

I-29.   Douglas, Ian. 1986. "The Unity of Geography is
         OBVIOUS ...," Transactions, Institute of British
         Geographers, Vol. 11, pp. 459-463.

I-30.   Durden, Dennis. 1959. "Economic Geographers as
         Investment Consultants, Professional Geographer,
         Vol. 9, No. 1, pp. 14-16.

I-31.   Elder, Phillip D. 1975. "The Value of the
         Geographer to the Real Estate Industry,"
         Geographical Perspectives, No. 35, pp. 21-25.

I-32.   Enedy, J. and Gustafson, G. 1983. "Examples of
         Academic Geographers and Geography in Local
         Government," Papers and Proceedings of Applied
         Geography Conferences, Vol. 6, pp. 177-184.

I-33.   Epstein, Bart J. 1984. "Applied Geography in
         Higher Education," Research in Contemporary and
         Applied Geography: A Discussion Series, Vol. 8,
         No. 2, pp. 1-16.

I-34.   Fair, T. J. D. 1956. "Geography and Physical
         Planning," South African Geographical Journal,
         Vol. 38, pp. 12-29.

I-35.   Farley, A. L. 1954. "Applied Geography in
         British Columbia," Canadian Geographer, No. 4,
         pp. 15-20.

I-36.   Foster, Alice. 1945. "Geography in Off-Duty
         Educational Opportunity for Armed Forces," Annals
         of the Association of American Geographers, Vol.
         35, pp. 167-180.

I-37.   Foster, L. T. 1982. "Applied Geography
         Internships: Operational Canadian Models,"
         Journal of Geography, Vol. 81, pp. 210-214.

I-38.   Foster, L. T. and Jones, K. G.   1977.   "Applied
         Geography: An Educational Alternative,"
         Professional Geographer, Vol. 29, pp. 300-304.

I-39.   Frazier, J. W.   1981.   "Applied Geography:
         Challenge of the 1980s," Applied Geography
         Conference, Vol. 4, pp. 169-178.

I-40.   Frazier, John W.   1978.   "Applied Geography and
         Pragmatism," Geographical Survey, Vol. 7, No. 3,
         pp. 3-10.

I-41.   Frazier, John W. and Henry, Norah F.   1978.
         "Select Themes in Applied Geography,"
         Geographical Survey, Vol. 7, No. 4, pp. 3-10.

I-42.   Garnier, B. J.   1957.   "Geography and National
         Development," Nigerian Geographical Journal, Vol.
         1, pp. 3-6.

I-43.   Gentilli, J.   1948.   "A Task for Geography in
         Building a Nation," Scope,   July, pp. 18-20.

I-44.   Gerasimov, I. P.   1984.   "The Contribution of
         Constructive Geography to the Problem of
         Optimization of Society's Impact on the
         Environment," Geoforum, Vol. 15, pp. 95-99.

I-45.   Gibson, Edward M.   1985.   "Crossing Over:
         Geographers in University and Government,"
         Operational Geographer, No. 7, pp. 22-24.

I-46.   Gillman, C.   1937.   "Geography and the Civil
         Engineer," Scottish Geographical Magazine, Vol.
         53, pp. 242-248.

I-47.   Glassner, Martin Ira.   1977.   "A Geographer Among
         Diplomats," Geographical Review, Vol. 67, pp.
         236-237.

I-48.   Glassner, Martin Ira.   1977.   "Geographers and
         the Law of the Sea," Geographical Survey, Vol. 6,
         No. 6, pp. 9-13.

I-49.   Gomes, H.   1984.   "Geografia e planjamento
         (Geography and Planning)," Boletim Paulista de
         Geografia, Vol. 61, pp. 119-132 [English
         summary].

I-50.   Gregory, K. J.   1979.   "Hydrogeomorphology: How
         Applied Should We Become?" Progress in Physical
         Geography, Vol. 3, pp. 84-101.

I-51.   Haigh, Martin J.   1987.   "Citation Levels in
         Geography," Area, Vol. 19, pp. 169-170.

I-52. Hare, F. Kenneth. 1974. "Geography and Public Policy: A Canadian View," Transactions - Institute of British Geographers, No. 63, pp. 25-28.

I-53. Harrison, James D. 1977. "Geography and Planning: Convenient Relationship or Necessary Marriage?" Geographical Survey, Vol. 6, No. 2, pp. 11-24.

I-54. Harrison, James D. and Larsen, Robert D. 1977. "Geography and Planning: The Need for an Applied Interface," Professional Geographer, Vol. 29, pp. 139-147.

I-55. Hartshorne, Richard. 1928. "Location Factors in the Iron and Steel Industry," Economic Geography, Vol. 4, pp. 241-252.

I-56. Henry, Norah F. and Budin, Morris. 1983. "Education and Applied Geography," Research in Contemporary and Applied Geography: A Discussion Series, Vol. 7, No. 4, pp. 43-52.

I-57. Herbertson, A. J. 1898. "Report on the Teaching of Applied Geography," Journal of the Manchester Geographical Society, Vol. 14, pp. 264-285.

I-58. Higbee, Edward C. 1966. "The Geographer and the Public Environment," B.C. Geographical Series, No. 7, pp. 5-8.

I-59. Highsmith, Richard M. Jr. 1965. "Geography and 'The Great Society,'" Yearbook - Association of Pacific Coast Geographers, Vol. 27, pp. 5-16.

I-60. Hirst, P. and Woolley, P. 1985. "Nature and Culture in Social Science: the Demarcation of Domains of Being in Eighteenth Century and Modern Discourses," Geoforum, Vol. 16, pp. 151-162.

I-61. Hodge, Gerald. 1965. "A New Vista for Regional Planning: What Role for the Geographer? Canadian Geographer, Vol. 9, pp. 122-127.

I-62. Hogarth, D. G. 1921. "Applied Geography," Scientific Monthly, Vol. 13, pp. 322-327.

I-63. Hogarth, D. G. 1922. "Applied Geography," Scottish Geographical Magazine, Vol. 38, pp. 10-19.

I-64. Hotles, Karlheinz, Hotles, Ruth, and Scholler, Peter. 1983. "Walter Christaller, 1893-1969," Geographers: Biobibliographical Studies, Vol. 7, pp. 11-16.

I-65.   House, J. W.   1977.   "The Applied Geographer and
         the Steady State Society," GeoJournal, Vol. 1,
         pp. 15-24.

I-66.   Hunter, J. M.   1961.   "Geography in the Service
         of Economic Development," Bulletin - Ghana
         Geographical Association, Vol. 6, No. 2, pp.
         44-48.

I-67.   Kaatz, Martin R.   1971.   "The Geography Behind
         the News," Yearbook - Association of Pacific
         Coast Geographers, Vol. 33, pp. 7-18.

I-68.   Kataria, M. S.   1975.   "Applied Geography:
         Concept, Technique and Scope," Geographical
         Review of India, Vol. 37, pp. 1-6.

I-69.   Knox, Paul.   1985.   "Planning and Applied
         Geography," Progress in Human Geography, Vol. 9,
         pp. 559-560.

I-70.   Knox, Paul.   1987.   "Planning and Applied
         Geography," Progress in Human Geography, Vol. 11,
         pp. 540-548.

I-71.   LaRocque, Alex J.   1953.   "The Role of Geography
         in Military Planning," Canadian Geographer, No.
         3, pp. 69-72.

I-72.   Lee, A. Grant.   1988.   "Professional Design Firms
         Provide Career Opportunities for Geographers,"
         Operational Geographer, No. 15, pp. 37.

I-73.   Lemons, Hoyt.   1948.   "Geography as an Applied
         Science in Quatermaster Research," Annals of the
         Association of American Geographers, Vol. 38, pp.
         104.

I-74.   Lounsbury, John F.   1983.   "Applied Geography:
         The Basic Academic Program," Research in
         Contemporary and Applied Geography, Vol. 7, No.
         2, pp. 23-31.

I-75.   Lounsbury, J. and Stutz, F.   1981.   "Training of
         the Applied Geographer," Proceedings of Applied
         Geography Conferences, Vol. 4, pp. 189-199.

I-76.   Ludemann, H.   1984.   "Applied Aspects of
         Geography - Experience in the German Democratic
         Republic," Sbornik-Praci-Csav, Vol. 4, pp.
         67-74.

I-77.   Ludwig, Gail S.   1984.   "Extension Geography:
         Applied Geography in Action," Professional
         Geographer, Vol. 36, pp. 236-238.

I-78.   Manning, E. W. 1984. "Developing Geographers
        for Public and Private Sector Research,"
        Operational Geographer, Vol. 1, pp. 15-23.

I-79.   Manshord, W. 1975. "Geographers in Public
        Service (1)," Area, Vol. 7, pp. 147-156.

I-80.   Marcus, Melvin G. 1978. "Directions in Applied
        Physical Geography," Geographical Survey, Vol. 7,
        No. 4, pp. 19-25.

I-81.   Marcus, Melvin G. 1979. "The Range of
        Opportunity in Applied Physical Geography,"
        Geographical Survey, Vol. 8, No. 4, pp. 3-4.

I-82.   Marotz, Glen A. 1983.
        "Industry-Government-Academic Cooperation:
        Possible Benefits for Geography," Professional
        Geographer, Vol. 35, pp. 407-416.

I-83.   Massam, Bryan H. 1988. "The Geographer as
        Consultant," Operational Geographer, No. 14, pp.
        39-40.

I-84.   Mayer, Harold M. 1954. "Geographers in City and
        Regional Planning," Professional Geographer, Vol.
        6, No. 3, pp. 7-13.

I-85.   McDaniel, Robt. 1957. "Geographers in Business
        and Industry," Canadian Geographer, No. 10, pp.
        72-73.

I-86.   McLellan, A. G. 1983. "The Geographer as
        Practitioner: The Challenges, Opportunities, and
        Difficulties Faced by the Academic Consultant,"
        Canadian Geographer, Vol. 27, pp. 62-66.

I-87.   Mill, Hugh Robert. 1887. "The Relations Between
        Commerce and Geography," Scottish Geographical
        Magazine, Vol. 3, pp. 626-638.

I-88.   Milner, Rt. Hon. Viscount. 1907. "Geography and
        Statecraft," Scottish Geographical Magazine, Vol.
        23, pp. 617-627.

I-89.   Mock, Dennis R. 1983. "Implementing an Applied
        Geography Program," Research in Contemporary and
        Applied Geography: A Discussion Series, Vol. 7,
        No. 3, pp. 32-42.

I-90.   Monmonier, Mark S. 1982. "Cartography,
        Geographic Information, and Public Policy,"
        Journal of Geography in Higher Education, Vol. 6,
        pp. 99-108.

I-91.   Moolag, Susan. 1983. "Applied Geography and New
        Geographies," Professional Geographer, Vol. 35,
        pp. 88-89.

I-92. Morley, David. 1983. "Applied Geography as
       Action Research: The St. Lucia Energy Future
       Project," Geographical Research Forum, No. 6, pp.
       3-23.

I-93. Morrill, Richard L. 1977. "Geographic Scale and
       the Public Interest," Geographical Survey, Vol.
       6, No. 1, pp. 3-10.

I-94. Naughton, Patrick W. 1984. "Geographers in
       Agricultural Extension," Professional Geographer,
       Vol. 36, p. 467.

I-95. Patton, Orin C. 1976. "Policies Research and
       Geography: Missed Opportunities," Mississippi
       Geographer, Vol. 4, pp. 15-24.

I-96. Pico, Rafael. 1968. "Notes on Geography and
       Development in the Tropics," Professional
       Geographer, Vol. 20, pp. 227-230.

I-97. Poole, Sidman P. 1935. "The Role of Geography
       in State Planning," Annals of the Association of
       American Geographers, Vol. 25, pp. 51-52.

I-98. Poole, Sidman P. 1944. "The Training of
       Military Geographers," Annals of the Association
       of American Geographers, Vol. 34, pp. 202-206.

I-99. Roepke, Howard G. 1977. "Applied Geography:
       Should We, Must We, Can We?" Geographical
       Review, Vol. 67, pp. 481-482.

I-100. Rose, John Kerr. 1954. "Opportunities for
       Geographers in Government," Professional
       Geographer, Vol. 6, No. 3, pp. 1-7.

I-101. Rrothero, R. Mansell. 1962. "A Geographer with
       the World Health Organization," Geographical
       Journal, Vol. 128, pp. 479-493.

I-102. Russell, Joseph A. 1954. "The Theory and
       Practice of Applied Geography," Annals of the
       Association of American Geographers, Vol. 44, pp.
       279-280.

I-103. Russell, Joseph A. 1958. "Trends in Placement
       and Training of American Geographers,"
       Professional Geographer, Vol. 10, No. 3, pp.
       32-36.

I-104. Russell, Joseph A. 1983. "Specialty Fields of
       Applied Geographers," Professional Geographer,
       Vol. 35, pp. 471-475.

I-105. Sanderson, Marie. 1987. "The Geographer as
       Director of a Multi- Disciplinary Institute,"
       Operational Gegorapher, No. 12, pp. 40.

I-106.   Saushkin, Yu. G.   1977.   "Excerpts From Letters
          by Berg on Theoretical Problems in Geography,"
          Soviet Geography: Review and Translation, Vol.
          18, pp. 23-32.

I-107.   Schoolmaster, F. Andrew.   1980.   "Improving
          Applied Geographical Research," Research in
          Contemporary and Applied Geography: A Discussion
          Series, Vol. 4, No. 3, pp. 47-64.

I-108.   Schreuders, H.   1960.   "Economic and Social
          Geography as a Basis for Market Research,"
          Tijdschrift voor Economische en Sociale
          Geografie, Vol. 51, pp. 158-160.

I-109.   Seager, Joni and Steinitz, Michael.   1980-81.
          "Perserving the Past: Some Recent Contributions
          in Applied Historical Geograpy," Monadnock, Vol.
          54-55, pp. 27-42.

I-110.   Sewell, W. R. Derrick and Mitchell, Bruce.
          1984.   "Geographers, The Policy Process and
          Education," Operational Geographer, No. 5, pp.
          23-28.

I-111.   Shabad, Theodore.   1954.   "Status of Geography in
          Communist China," Professional Geographer, Vol.
          6, No. 4, pp. 5-9.

I-112.   Shafi, Mohammad.   1967.   "Applied Geography,"
          Indian Journal of Geography, Vol. 2, pp. 9-12.

I-113.   Sigeriest, Henry E.   1933.   "Problems of
          Historical - Geographical Pathology," Bulletin of
          the Institute of the History of Medicine, Vol. 1,
          pp. 10-18.

I-114.   Siple, Paul A.   1948.   "The Application of
          Geographic Research to U. S. Army Needs,"
          Professional Geographer, Vol. 7, pp. 1-3.

I-115.   Smith, Bruce W. and Hiltner, John.   1983.   "Where
          Non-Academic Geographers Are Employed,"
          Professional Geographer, Vol. 35, pp. 210-213.

I-116.   Smith, D. M.   1973.   "Alternative 'Relevant'
          Professional Roles," Area, Vol. 5, pp. 1-4.

I-117.   Smith, David M.   1985.   "The 'New Blood' Scheme
          and Its Application to Geography," Area, Vol. 17,
          pp. 237-243.

I-118.   Smith, Neil.   1986.   "Bowman's New World and the
          Council on Foreign Relations," Geographical
          Review, Vol. 76, pp. 438-460.

I-119.   Sochava, V. B. 1970. "The Training of
         Geographers for Work in Applied Geography,"
         Soviet Geography: Review and Translation, Vol.
         11, pp. 730-736.

I-120.   Sommers, Lawrence S. 1983. "The Significance of
         Regional Analysis in Applied Geography," Research
         in Contemporary and Applied Geography: A
         Dicussion Series, Vol. 7, No. 1, pp. 1-22.

I-121.   Sowerbutts, Eli. 1898. "Geographical Education
         and Commercial Museums," Journal of the
         Manchester Geographical Society, Vol. 14, pp.
         293-296.

I-122.   Stamp, L. Dudley. 1931. "The Geographical
         Approach to the Study of Some Business Problems,"
         Harvard Business Review, Vol. 10, pp. 69-77.

I-123.   Stamp, L. Dudley. 1959. "The Scope of Applied
         Geography," International Geographical Union.
         Regional Conference, 1957 Proceedings, pp. 89-95.

I-124.   Straw, Thomas F. 1945. "A Practical Approach to
         Postwar Geography," Journal of Geography, Vol.
         44, pp. 137-144.

I-125.   Straszewicz, Ludwik. 1972. "University
         Programme and Requirements of Applied Geography,"
         Proceedings - Twenty-Second International
         Geographical Congress, pp. 1173-1175.

I-126.   Strong, Helen M. 1927. "Maps and Business,"
         Annals of the Association of American
         Geographers, Vol. 17, pp. 15-20.

I-127.   Strong, Helen M. 1929. "Geography in Business,"
         Annals of the Association of American
         Geographers, Vol. 19, pp. 48-49.

I-128.   Strong, Helen M. 1930. "Geography Essential,"
         Journal of Geography, Vol. 29, pp. 210-214.

I-129.   Strong, Helen M. 1931. "How Business is Using
         and Might Use the Science of Geography," Annals
         of the Association of American Geographers, Vol.
         21, pp. 138-139.

I-130.   Stutz, Frederick and Heiges, Harvey E. 1983.
         "Developing Courses in Applied Geography for
         Transportation Planners," Professional
         Geographer, Vol. 35, pp. 206-210.

I-131.   Taylor, Griffith. 1932. "The Geographer's Aid
         in Nation-Planning," Scottish Geographical
         Magazine, Vol. 48, pp. 1-20.

I-132.   Teggart, F. J.   1919.   "Geography as an Aid to
          Statecraft: An   Appreciation of Mackinder's
          'Democratic Ideals and Reality,'" Geographical
          Review, Vol. 8, pp. 227-242.

I-133.   Thomas, Frank H.   1962.   "Economically Distressed
          Areas and the Role of the Academic Geographer,"
          Professional Geographer, Vol. 14, No. 2, pp.
          12-16.

I-134.   Thompson, Joseph P.   1859.   "The Value of
          Geography to the Scholar, the Merchant, and the
          Philanthropist," Journal of the American
          Geographical and Statistical Society, Vol. 1, pp.
          98-107.

I-135.   Thornes, John E.   1978.   "Applied Climatology,"
          Progress in Physical Geography, Vol. 2, pp.
          481-493.

I-136.   Thornes, John E.   1979.   "Applied Climatology,"
          Progress in Physical Geography, Vol. 3, pp.
          427-442.

I-137.   Thorpe, David.   1963.   "The Non-Traditional Jobs
          of Geographers," Education for Business, No. 42,
          pp. 20-22.

I-138.   Van Cleef, Eugene.   1915.   "Geography and the
          Business Man," Annals of the Association of
          American Geographers, Vol. 5, pp. 138.

I-139.   Vovil, Robert J.   1950.   "Cartographer in
          Government," Professional Geographer, Vol. 2, pp.
          29-32.

I-140.   Warner, C.   1972.   "Careers for Geographers: A
          Note on Recent Trends," South Hampshire
          Geographer, No. 5, pp. 69-70.

I-141.   Wessinger, Esther.   1918.   "The Value of Place
          Geography in a Commercial Geography Course,"
          Journal of Geography, Vol. 17, pp. 162-163.

I-142.   Whitbeck, R. H.   1919.   "Country's Call For
          Geographers To-Day and To-Morrow," School and
          Society, Vol. 9, pp. 223-228.

I-143.   White, C. Langdon.   1942.   "Geography and a World
          at War," Denison University Bulletin, Journal of
          the Scientific Laboratories, Vol. 37, pp.
          133-139.

I-144.   Whittlesey, Derwent.   1942.   "Geography into
          Politics," Annals of the Association of American
          Geographers, Vol. 32, pp. 142-143.

I-145.   Whittlesey, Derwent. 1943. "Geopolitics, a
         Program for Action ," Annals of the Association
         of American Geographers, Vol. 33, pp. 97-98.

I-146.   Wise, Donald A. 1970. "Opportunities for
         Geographers in the Federal Government,"
         Professional Geographer, Vol. 22, pp. 94-96.

I-147.   Wisner, Ben. 1986. "Geography: War or Peace
         Studies?" Antipode, Vol. 18, pp. 212-217.

I-148.   Wright, John K. 1948. "The Educational
         Functions of the Geographical Societies of the
         United States," Journal of Geography, Vol. 47,
         pp. 165-173.

I-149.   Wusten, Herman van der and O'Loughlin, John.
         1986. "Claiming New Territory for a Stable
         Place: How Geography Can Contribute,"
         Professional Geographer, Vol. 38, pp. 18-28.

I-150.   Yeates, John. 1886. "The Relations Between
         Commercial History and Geography," Journal of
         the Manchester Geographical Society, Vol. 2, pp.
         181-198.

I-151.   Yefremov, Yu. K. 1965. "Geographers' Tasks in
         Propagandizing Knowledge, Local-Area Studies,
         and Tourism," Soviet Geography: Review and
         Translation, Vol. 6, pp. 3-17.

I-152.   Zonn, Leo E. 1978. "Community and Action: An
         Alternative Approach to Social Geography,"
         Research in Contemporary and Applied Geography,
         Vol. 2, No. 2, pp. 46-66.

Educational Geography

J-1. Adejuyigbe, O. 1970. "Re-shaping High School
      Geography in Nigeria," <u>Nigerian Geographical
      Journal</u>, Vol. 13, pp. 89-94.

J-2. Ahsan, Syed Reza. 1959. "Geography and
      Geography Teaching in Pakistan," <u>Memorandum Folio
      of the Southeastern Association of American
      Geographers</u>, Vol. 11, pp. 1-4.

J-3. Allen, Agnes M. 1933. "A Survey of Books on
      Methods of Teaching Geography," <u>Journal of
      Geography</u>, Vol. 32, pp. 285-290.

J-4. Anderson, R. C. 1966. "High School Geography:
      Retrospect and Prospect," <u>Journal of Geography</u>,
      Vol. 65, pp. 103-108.

J-5. Andrews, H. F. 1986. "The French View of
      Geography Teaching in Britain in 1871,"
      <u>Geographical Journal</u>, Vol. 152, pp. 225-231.

J-6. Anonymous. 1885. "Geographical Education,"
      <u>Journal of the Manchester Geographical Society</u>,
      Vol. 1, p. 134.

J-7. Anonymous. 1886. "Royal Geographical Society's
      Education Schemes and Its Exhibition of
      Geographical Appliances," <u>Scottish Geographical
      Magazine</u>, Vol. 2, pp. 27-31.

J-8. Anonymous. 1893. "The Teaching of Geography in
      Germany," <u>Scottish Geographical Magazine</u>, Vol. 9,
      pp. 366-371.

J-9. Anonymous. 1894. "Geography at the
      Universities," <u>Geographical Journal</u>, Vol. 4, pp.
      29-31.

J-10.   Anonymous. 1895. "Geography at the
        Universities," Geographical Journal, Vol. 6, pp.
        25-27.

J-11.   Anonymous. 1896. "Geography in the Schools,"
        Scottish Geographical Magazine, Vol. 12, pp.
        252-256.

J-12.   Anonymous. 1896. "Geography at the
        Universities," Geographical Journal, Vol. 18, pp.
        61-65.

J-13.   Anonymous. 1897. "Geography at the
        Universities," Geographical Journal, Vol. 19, pp.
        653-655.

J-14.   Anonymous. 1899. "Importance of the Study [of
        Geography," Nation, Vol. 69, December 28, p. 486.

J-15.   Anonymous. 1903. "Geographical Education at the
        British Association," Geographical Journal, Vol.
        22, pp. 549-553.

J-16.   Anonymous. 1903. "The Scope and Practical
        Teaching of Geography in Schools," Scottish
        Geographical Magazine, Vol. 19, pp. 486-490.

J-17.   Anonymous. 1905. "Geography and Education,"
        Geographical Journal, Vol. 25, pp. 17-22.

J-18.   Anonymous. 1905. "The Annual Meeting of the
        Geographical Association," Geographical Teacher,
        Vol. 3, pp. 1-11.

J-19.   Anonymous. 1905. "The Teaching of Geography in
        the Schools in Cuba," Scottish Geographical
        Magazine, Vol. 21, pp. 591-599.

J-20.   Anonymous. 1911. "Geography in the
        Encyclopaedia Britannica," Geographical Journal,
        Vol. 38, pp. 152-157.

J-21.   Anonymous. 1915. "The National Council of
        Geography Teachers," School and Society, Vol. 1,
        pp. 307-308.

J-22.   Anonymous. 1915. "The Teaching of Geography,"
        School and Society, Vol. 1, pp. 239-240.

J-23.   Anonymous. 1918. "Geographers in Pressing
        Demand for War Work," Journal of Geography, Vol.
        17, pp. 33-34.

J-24.   Anonymous. 1927. "Geography in the Junior High
        School," Journal of Geography, Vol. 26, pp.
        207-220.

J-25.   Anonymous. 1927. "Objectives of Elementary
         Education and How Geography Helps in Attaining
         Them," Journal of Geography, Vol. 26, pp. 52-57.

J-26.   Anonymous. 1951. "Geography and 'Social
         Studies' in Schools," Geographical Journal, Vol.
         116, pp. 221-224.

J-27.   Anonymous. 1959. "Even in the Space Age
         Geography is an Important Subject," Saturday
         Evening Post, Vol. 232, p. 10.

J-28.   Anonymous. 1970. "Editorial: Geography in
         Scottish Schools: A Symposium," Scottish
         Geographical Magazine, Vol. 86, pp. 83-122.

J-29.   Anonymous. 1983. "Geography in the Curriculum
         16-19," Geography, Vol. 68, pp. 149-153.

J-30.   Armitage, Ernest. 1971. "Aims and Objectives in
         Geography Teaching at Intermediate Certificate
         Level," Geographical Viewpoint, Vol. 2, pp.
         147-154.

J-31.   Armitage, Ernest. 1972. "The Teaching of
         Biogeography in Post-Primary Schools,"
         Geographical Viewpoint, Vol. 2, pp. 227-286.

J-32.   Armitage, Ernest. 1981. "The Association of
         Geography Teachers of Ireland, 1961-81,"
         Geographical Viewpoint, Vol. 10, pp. 31-43.

J-33.   Armstrong, T. H. 1903. "The Relation of
         Geography to the Other Subjects of an Elementary
         Course of Study," Education, Vol. 23, pp.
         331-336.

J-34.   Aschmann, Homer. 1958. "Geography and the
         Liberal Arts College," Professional Geographer,
         Vol. 10, No. 2, pp. 2-6.

J-35.   Aschmann, Homer. 1962. "Geography in the
         Liberal Arts College," Annals of the Association
         of American Geographers, Vol. 52, pp. 284-291.

J-36.   Atkinson, E. 1910. "World-Makers; How Geography
         is Taught Nowadays," World To-Day, Vol. 18, pp.
         313-317.

J-37.   Atwood, Rollin S. 1940. "Geography and the
         Social Sciences," Florida Academy of Sciences for
         1939, Proceedings, Vol. 4, pp. 218-224.

J-38.   Atwood, W. W. 1921. "New Meaning of Geography
         in American Education," School and Society, Vol.
         13, pp. 211-218.

J-39.   Atwood, Wallace W. 1928. "Research and
        Educational Work in Geography," Journal of
        Geography, Vol. 27, pp. 263-270.

J-40.   Atwood, Wallace W. 1928. "Research and
        Educational Work in Graduate Schools of
        Geography," Proceedings - Twelfth International
        Geographical Congress, pp. 492-499.

J-41.   Atwood, Wallace W. 1947. "The New Meaning of
        Geography in World Education," Journal of
        Geography, Vol. 46, pp. 11-15.

J-42.   Baber, Zonia. 1916. "Lost Opportunities in
        Teaching Geography," Journal of Geography, Vol.
        14, pp. 295-297.

J-43.   Bacon, H. Philip. 1955. "Fireworks in the
        Classroom: Nathaniel Southgate Shaler as a
        Teacher," Journal of Geography, Vol. 54, pp.
        349-353.

J-44.   Bagchi, Kanangopal. 1974. "Geographical
        Research in University Set-Up," Geographical
        Review of India, Vol. 36, pp. 181-187.

J-45.   Bagley, William Chandler. 1904. "The Functions
        of Geography in the Elementary School: A Study
        in Educational Values," Journal of Geography,
        Vol. 3, pp. 222-232.

J-46.   Bagley, William Chandler. 1929. "The Element of
        Adventure in Teaching and Learning Geography,"
        Journal of Geography, Vol. 28, pp. 89-100.

J-47.   Bailey, Patrick. 1983. "Evolution of a British
        Professional Journal for Geography Teachers,"
        Journal of Geography, Vol. 82, pp. 7-10.

J-48.   Bailey, Patrick. 1986. "A Geographer's View:
        Contributions of Geography to the School
        Curriculum," Geography, Vol. 71, pp. 193-206.

J-49.   Ball, John M., et al. 1972. "Experiments in
        Teaching College Geography: A Report to the
        Profession," Professional Geographer, Vol. 24,
        pp. 350-361.

J-50.   Baranskiy, N. N., Darinskiy, A. V. and Solov'yev,
        A. I. 1961. "The Reform of the System of
        Public Education in the U.S.S.R. and the
        Objectives of School Geography," Soviet
        Geography: Review and Translation, Vol. 2, No.
        10, pp. 3-12.

J-51.   Barker, W. H. 1921. "Geography in the Schools
        of England and Wales," Journal of Geography, Vol.
        20, pp. 302-310.

J-52.   Barnes, Charles C. 1934. "The Place of Social
         Geography in the High School," Journal of
         Geography, Vol. 33, pp. 178-186.

J-53.   Barrows, H. H. 1920. "The Purpose of Geography
         Teaching," Journal of Geography, Vol. 20, pp.
         151-154.

J-54.   Barrows, H. H. 1931. "Some Critical Problems in
         Teaching Elementary Geography," Journal of
         Geography, Vol. 30, pp. 353-364.

J-55.   Barton, Thomas Frank. 1965. "Publications of
         Leaders in Geographic Education: Katherine
         Thomas Whittemore," Journal of Geography, Vol.
         64, pp. 211-213.

J-56.   Basu, A. N. 1936. "Geography Teaching in
         India," Geographical Review of India, Vol. 1, No.
         1, n.p.

J-57.   Bell, A. M. 1902. "On Mr. Wilkinson's
         Critique," Geographical Teacher, Vol. 1, pp.
         109-114.

J-58.   Bell, W. S. 1972. "Geography Anaesthetized,"
         Bloomsbury Geographer, Vol. 5, pp. 61-62.

J-59.   Bellotti, Helen, Wirick, Betty C., and Menk,
         Elizabeth. 1945. "Changes in the Geography
         Taught in Teacher-Education Institutions,"
         Journal of Geography, Vol. 44, pp. 246-250.

J-60.   Bengston, N. A. 1929. "High School Geography to
         Be or Not to Be," School Science and
         Mathematics, Vol. 29, pp. 693-701.

J-61.   Bengston, Nels A. 1948. "Geography as an
         Element in General Education," Journal of
         Geography, Vol. 47, pp. 121-131.

J-62.   Bennetts, Trevor. 1985. "Geography From 5 to
         16. A View From the Inspectorate," Geography,
         Vol. 70, pp. 299-314.

J-63.   Bergen, John V. 1963. "Geography in Small
         Liberal Arts Colleges," Journal of Geography,
         Vol. 62, pp. 22-29.

J-64.   Biddle, D. S. 1963. "The Purpose of Teaching
         Geography in the Secondary School," Australian
         Geographer, Vol. 9, pp. 111-119.

J-65.   Bingham, Edgar. 1965. "Geography in the Small
         Liberal Arts College: A View From Inside,"
         Memorandum Folio of the Southeastern Association
         of American Geographers, Vol. 17, pp. 13-15.

J-66.   Bird, C. 1901. "Limitations and Possibilities
        of Geographical Teaching in Day Schools,"
        Geographical Teacher, Vol. 1, pp. 10-13.

J-67.   Bird, James. 1963. "The Noosphere: A Concept
        Possibly Useful to Geographers," Scottish
        Geographical Magazine, Vol. 79, pp. 54-56.

J-68.   Blomfield, C. J. 1930. "Some Opinions of
        Specialists in Education in Relation to the Place
        of Geography in the Social Studies," Education,
        Vol. 55, pp. 281-285.

J-69.   Boardman, David. 1983.   "Geography in British
        Schools in the 1980s," Journal of Geography, Vol.
        82, pp. 64-70.

J-70.   Boehm, Richard G. and Kracht, James B. 1986.
        "Enhancing High School Geography in Texas,"
        Journal of Geography, Vol. 38, pp. 255-256.

J-71.   Bohland, Jim and Libbee, Michael. 1977.
        "Instructional Computing in Geography: Current
        Status and Future Prospects," Professional
        Geographer, Vol. 29, pp. 385-393.

J-72.   Borchert, John R. 1965. "The Dimensions of
        Geography in the School Curriculum," Journal of
        Geography, Vol. 64, pp. 244-249.

J-73.   Bramwell, Ada. 1901. "Difficulties of Lower
        School Geography," Geographical Teacher, Vol. 1,
        pp. 14-17.

J-74.   Brereton, Clondesley. 1903. "The Teaching of
        Geography in Secondary Schools," Geographical
        Teacher, Vol. 2, pp. 107-113.

J-75.   Briel, Edith V. 1931. "What Method Shall We Use
        in Teaching Geography?" Journal of Geography,
        Vol. 30, pp. 125-131.

J-76.   Brigham, Albert Perry. 1904. "Geography and
        History in the United States," Journal of
        Geography, Vol. 3, pp. 359-366.

J-77.   Brigham, Albert Perry. 1921. "Geographic
        Education in America," Report of the Smithsonian
        Institution for 1919, pp. 487-496.

J-78.   Brigham, Albert Perry. 1921. "The Teaching of
        Geography," Journal of the New York State
        Teachers Association, (vol. and pp. not
        available).

J-79.   Brigham, Albert Perry. 1927. "Contribution of
        Geography in Senior High Schools," Journal of
        Geography, Vol. 26, pp. 165-175.

J-80.   Brigham, A. P.   1919.   "Geographic Education in
        America," Smithsonian Report, pp. 487-496.

J-81.   Bronsky, Amy.   1933.   "Elementary School
        Geography and World Problems," Journal of
        Geography, Vol. 32, pp. 316-322.

J-82.   Brooks, Leonard.   1952.   "Geography Teaching in
        School," Proceedings - Seventeenth International
        Geographical Congress, pp. 698-699.

J-83.   Brown, Robert Harold.   1966.   "Fundamentals of
        Geographic Education," Journal of Geography,
        Vol. 65, pp. 410-415.

J-84.   Bryce, Right Hon. James.   1901-02.   "The
        Importance of Geography in Education,"
        Geographical Teacher, Vol. 1, pp. 49-61.

J-85.   Bryce, Right Hon. James.   1902.   "The Importance
        of Geography in Education," Geographical Journal,
        Vol. 19, pp. 301-313.

J-86.   Buchanan, R. O.   1973.   "The Joint School: A
        Has-been Looks Back," Horizon, Vol. 22, pp.
        19-22.

J-87.   Burke, Jack D.   1983.   "Teaching Styles in
        College Geography," Journal of Geography, Vol.
        82, pp. 255-256.

J-88.   Carpenter, Frank O.   1905.   "Teaching Commercial
        Geography," Education, Vol. 29, pp. 345-350.

J-89.   Carthew, Arthur.   1965.   "A Brief History of the
        California Council of Geography Teachers,"
        California Geographer, Vol. 6, pp. 11-16.

J-90.   Casartelli, Rev. L. C.   1886.   "The Teaching of
        Commercial Geography," Journal of the Manchester
        Geographical Society, Vol. 2, pp. 328-336.

J-91.   Chamberlain, James F., et al.   1909.   "Report of
        the Committee on Secondary School Geography,"
        Journal of Geography, Vol. 8, pp. 1-10.

J-92.   Chamberlain, James F.   1912.   "Preparation for
        the Teaching of Geography," Journal of Geography,
        Vol. 11, pp. 37-40.

J-93.   Chamberlain, James F.   1918.   "Essentials in
        Geography," School and Society, Vol. 8, pp.
        220-225.

J-94.   Chamberlain, James F.   1921.   "Standardizing
        Courses of Study in Geography," Journal of
        Geography, Vol. 20, pp. 274-276.

J-95.   Chamberlain, James F.   1962.   "Report of the
         Committee on Secondary School Geography," Journal
         of Geography, Vol. 61, pp. 75-81.

J-96.   Chandler, T. J.   1971.   "Universities and the
         Sixth Form," Bloomsbury Geographer, Vol. 4, pp.
         2-4.

J-97.   Chatterjee, S. P.   1937.   "The Teaching of
         Geography," Geographical Review of India, Vol. 1,
         No. 2, n.p.

J-98.   Chestang, Ennis L.   1953.   "Some Observations on
         Introductory College Geography in the United
         States," Journal of Geography, Vol. 52, pp.
         109-114.

J-99.   Chief Directorate of Schools, USSR Ministry of
         Education.   1987.   "The Geography Curriculum for
         the Secondary General Education School," Soviet
         Education, Vol. 29, pp. 10-86.

J-100.   Chisholm, George G.   1908.   "Methods of Approach
         in Geographical Instruction," Geographical
         Teacher, Vol. 4, pp. 170-186.

J-101.   Chisholm, George G.   1915.   "Geography in
         Schools: A Review," Scottish Geographical
         Magazine, Vol. 31, pp. 406-411.

J-102.   Clark, Andrew.   1954.   "Careers for Geographers
         in Higher Education," Professional Geographer,
         Vol. 6, No. 3, pp. 19-29.

J-103.   Clark, R.   1974.   "Defining Geography: Defining
         and Doing, or Doing and Knowing," Area, Vol. 6,
         pp. 154-157.

J-104.   Clark, R.   1982.   "Objectives, Aims and the
         Design of Geography Courses," Geographical
         Viewpoint, Vol. 11, pp. 59-72.

J-105.   Claval, Paul C.   1983.   "One Hundred Years of
         Teaching Geography in French Universities,"
         Journal of Geography, Vol. 82, pp. 110-111.

J-106.   Cleverly, Pat.   1985.   "Classroom Hot Spots
         Change Again," Geography, Vol. 70, pp. 206-211.

J-107.   Coates, Bryan and White, Paul.   1985.   "The
         Catchment For University Geography," Geography,
         Vol. 70, pp. 343-346.

J-108.   Committee of Fifteen.   1895.   "Report on
         Geography," Proceedings of the N.E.A. for 1895,
         pp. 232-237.

J-109.   Committee on Training and Standards in the
          Geographic Profession, National Council. 1946.
          "Lessons from the Wartime Experience for
          Improving Graduate Training for Geographic
          Research Report." Annals of the Association of
          American Geographers, Vol. 36, pp. 195-214.

J-110.   Conn, H. 1933. "Rational Geography," School,
          Vol. 21, pp. 565-569.

J-111.   Conroy, William B. 1966. "The Misuse of
          Geography," Journal of Geography, Vol. 65, pp.
          109-113.

J-112.   Cook, E. K. and McBride, J. 1938. "Means of
          Fostering International Understanding Though the
          Teaching of Geography," Proceedings - Fifteenth
          International Geographical Congress, pp. 3-7.

J-113.   Cook, Jane Perry. 1911. "Primary Aims in
          Geography Teaching in the Grammar Grades, Journal
          of Geography, Vol. 9, pp. 203-208.

J-114.   Cooper, Clyde E. 1920. "Status of Geography in
          the Normal Schools of the Middle States," Journal
          of Geography, Vol. 19, pp. 211-223.

J-115.   Coulson, M. R. C. 1973. "Undergraduate
          Geography Care Programs: Evidence From
          University Calendars in Western Canada," B.C.
          Geographical Series, Occasional Papers in
          Geography, No. 29, pp. 9-20.

J-116.   Coulter, J. W. 1954. "Geography in Secondary
          Schools," School Life, Vol. 36, pp. 119+.

J-117.   Cowen, Joel B. 1971. "The Place of Geography in
          the Liberal Arts," Journal of Geography, Vol.
          20, pp. 135-136.

J-118.   Cowie, P. M. 1978. "Geography: A Value Laden
          Subject in Education," Geography Education, Vol.
          3, pp. 133-146.

J-119.   Coyne, John. 1984. "Geography in Area Studies:
          Have British Geographers Missed the Boat?"
          Journal of Geography in Higher Education, Vol. 8,
          pp. 3-10.

J-120.   Cranston, H. V. 1944. "The Position of
          Geography in Secondary Education," Australian
          Geographer, Vol. 4, pp. 207-211.

J-121.   Cunningham, F. F. 1975. "Teaching an
          Interdisciplinary Course About Landscape," B.C.
          Geographical Series, No. 21, pp. 112-116.

J-122.   Dakin, W. S. 1926. "Reflections on the Teaching
         of Geography," Journal of Geography, Vol. 25, pp.
         144-146, 184-192.

J-123.   Dann, E. W. 1904. "What is Geography?" Journal
         of the Manchester Geographical Society, Vol. 20,
         pp. 130-139.

J-124.   Dann, E. W. 1905. "What is Geography?"
         Geographical Teacher, Vol. 3, pp. 97-103.

J-125.   Darinskiy, A. V. 1965. "Basic Problems of
         Middle-School Geography Education in the
         U.S.S.R.," Soviet Geography: Review and
         Translation, Vol. 6, pp. 14-28.

J-126.   Darinskiy, A. V. 1971. "Problems of
         Geographical Education in the U.S.S.R.," Soviet
         Geography: Review and Translation, Vol. 12, pp.
         475-485.

J-127.   Darroch, Alex. 1906. "The Teaching of
         Geography," Scottish Geographical Magazine, Vol.
         22, pp. 484-490.

J-128.   Das, H. P. 1972. "Teaching of Geography as a
         Science Subject in Schools," Geographical Review
         of India, Vol. 34, pp. 93-96.

J-129.   Davidson, A. 1954. "The Role of Geographers in
         Saskatchewan," Canadian Geographer, No. 4, pp.
         33-38.

J-130.   Davis, William M. 1895. "Need of Geography in
         the University," Educational Review, Vol. 10,
         pp. 22-41.

J-131.   Davis, William M. 1898. "Geography as a
         University Subject," Scottish Geographical
         Magazine, Vol. 14, pp. 24-29.

J-132.   Davis, William Morris. 1922. "Home Geography,"
         Journal of Geography, Vol. 21, pp. 28-32.

J-133.   Dawson, Andrew H. 1971. "Locational Analysis
         and the Teaching of Geography," Scottish
         Geographical Magazine, Vol. 87, pp. 66-69.

J-134.   Deshpande, C. D. 1973. "'Practicals' in
         Geography: The Changing Role in Our Collegiate
         Courses of Study," Deccan Geographer, Vol. 11,
         pp. 97-100.

J-135.   de Souza, Anthony, Vogeler, Ingolf and Foust,
         Brady. 1983. "The Invisible, Overlooked
         Department of Geography," Transition, Vol. 13,
         No. 1, pp. 9-19.

J-136.   Devonshire, Brian. 1977. "Geographic Education
         - A New Course for Teachers in the Land of the
         White Cloud," California Geographer, Vol. 17, pp.
         35-38.

J-137.   Diettrich, Sigismond der. 1954. "The Status of
         Collegiate Geography Programs in the Southeast
         Division, A.A.G.," Memorandum Folio, Vol. 6, pp.
         10-21.

J-138.   Dijkink, G. J. W. 1976. "On the Foundations of
         Geographical Imagination, A Viewpoint from
         Education," Tijdschrift voor Economische en
         Sociale Geografie, Vol. 67, pp. 352-357.

J-139.   Dillion, M. A. 1977. "The Teaching of Geography
         in Primary Schools in the Republic of Ireland,"
         Geographical Viewpoint, Vol. 6, pp. 36-48.

J-140.   Dingelstedt, V. 1886. "Geographical Education
         in the Caucasus," Scottish Geographical
         Magazine, Vol. 2, pp. 274-276.

J-141.   Dodge, R. E. 1914. "A Study of Geography in
         Normal Schools," Teachers College Record, Vol.
         15, pp. 1-12.

J-142.   Dodge, R. E. 1916. "Geographic Education and
         Secondary Schools," School and Society, Vol. 4,
         pp. 253-265.

J-143.   Dodge, R. E. 1916. "Some Problems in Geographic
         Education," Journal of Geography, Vol. 14, pp.
         277-283.

J-144.   Dodge, Richard E. 1898. "Scientific Geography
         for Schools," Geographical Journal, Vol. 11, pp.
         159-163.

J-145.   Dodge, Richard E. 1897. "School Geography in
         the United States," Scottish Geographical
         Magazine, Vol. 13, pp. 523-531.

J-146.   Dodge, Richard E. 1901. "Geography in the
         Horace Mann Schools," Teacher's College Record,
         Vol. 2, pp. 3-104.

J-147.   Dodge, Richard E. 1906. "The Organization of
         School Geography," Bulletin of the American
         Geographical Society of New York, Vol. 38, pp.
         112-113.

J-148.   Dodge, Richard E. 1914. "A Study of Geography
         in Normal Schools," Teachers' College Record,
         Vol. 15, n.p.

J-149.   Dodge, Richard E.   1914.   "The Modern Point of
         View in Geography Teaching," Journal of
         Geography, Vol. 12, pp. 161-164.

J-150.   Dodge, Richard E.   1916.   "Memorial: Edward Van
         Dyke Robinson," Annals of the Association of
         American Geographers, Vol. 6, p. 120.

J-151.   Dodge, Richard E.   1916.   "Some Problems in
         Geographic Education With Special Reference to
         Secondary Schools," Annals of the Association of
         American Geographers, Vol. 6, pp. 3-18.

J-152.   Dodge, Richard E.   1918.   "Humanizing High School
         Geography," Journal of Geography, Vol. 16, pp.
         161-166.

J-153.   Dodge, Richard Elwood.   1906.   "The Opportunity
         of the Geographer in Promoting School Geography,"
         Journal of Geography, Vol. 5, pp. 385-394.

J-154.   Dodge, Richard Elwood.   1907.   "Geography for
         Secondary Schools," Journal of Geography, Vol. 6,
         pp. 241-254.

J-155.   Dodge, Richard Elwood.   1907.   "Geography in
         Secondary Schools," Journal of Geography, Vol. 6,
         pp. 273-285.

J-156.   Dodge, Richard Elwood.   1908.   "Some Suggestions
         Concerning a Course of Study in Geography,"
         Journal of Geography, Vol. 7, pp. 7-14.

J-157.   Dodge, Richard Elwood.   1910.   "Geography in
         Rural Schools," Journal of Geography, Vol. 8, pp.
         202-209.

J-158.   Dodge, Richard Elwood.   1914.   "Geography in
         Normal and Secondary Schools," Journal of
         Geography, Vol. 13, pp. 83-84.

J-159.   Dodge, Richard Elwood.   1922.   "A Glimpse at the
         Past," Journal of Geography, Vol. 21, pp. 3-7.

J-160.   Doherty, Joe.   1982.   "Geography, Education and
         Ideology in Tanzania," Journal of Geography in
         Higher Education, Vol. 6, pp. 173-176.

J-161.   Doyle, Angela.   1983.   "Transfer From Primary to
         Post Primary Geography in the Republic of
         Ireland," Geographical Viewpoint, Vol. 12, pp.
         5-20.

J-162.   Dryer, Charles R.   1905.   "Geography in the
         Normal Schools in the United States," Journal of
         Geography, Vol. 4, pp. 239-243.

J-163.   Dryer, Charles Redway. 1904. "Geography in the
         Normal Schools of the United States," Proceedings
         - Eighth International Geographical Congress, pp.
         972-976.

J-164.   Duboc, Jessie L. 1929. "What Should a Geography
         Textbook Contain?" Journal of Geography, Vol. 28,
         pp. 286-292.

J-165.   Dunbar, G. S. 1970. "Geographic Education in
         Early Charleston," Journal of Geography, Vol. 69,
         pp. 348-350.

J-166.   Earth Science Committee of the NCGE. 1964. "The
         Role of Geography in the Earth Sciences," Journal
         of Geography, Vol. 63, pp. 101-108.

J-167.   Education Committee. 1885. "Report of the
         Education Committee for the Council of the
         Manchester Geographical Society on the Subject of
         Geographical Education," Journal of the
         Manchester Geographical Society, Vol. 1, pp.
         310-341.

J-168.   Education Committee. 1890. "Geographical
         Education: Report to the Council," Journal of
         the Manchester Geographical Society, Vol. 6, pp.
         325-343.

J-169.   Eisen, Edna E. 1951. "The Geography of
         Education," Journal of Geography, Vol. 50, pp.
         374-382.

J-170.   Elam, William W. 1974. "The Needs and Scope of
         Geographic Education in America," Geographical
         Perspectives, No. 34, 14-18.

J-171.   El-Bushra, El-Sayed and Ahmed, Hassan A. 1986.
         "The Status of Geography in Saudi Universities,"
         GeoJournal Vol. 13, pp. 153-156.

J-172.   Elkins, T. H. 1986. "Planned Geographical
         Education at University Level in the German
         Democratic Republic," Area, Vol. 18, pp. 141-145.

J-173.   Emerson, Philip. 1904. "Results of an
         Elementary Course in Geography," Journal of
         Geography, Vol. 3, pp. 450-454.

J-174.   Emery, J. S., Davey, C. and Milne, A. K. 1974.
         "Environmental Education: The Geography Teacher's
         Contribution," Journal of Geography, Vol. 73, pp.
         8-18.

J-175.   Epstein, Bart J. 1984. "Applied Geography in
         Higher Education," Research in Contemporary and
         Applied Geography: A Discussion Series, Vol. 8,
         No. 2, pp. 1-16.

J-176.   Erskine, J. Y. 1942. "Report on the Teaching of
         Geography in Scottish Senior Secondary Schools,"
         Scottish Geographical Magazine, Vol. 58, pp.
         74-75.

J-177.   Fair, T. J. D. 1962. "A University Geography
         Syllabus," South African Geographical Journal,
         Vol. 44, pp. 50-53.

J-178.   Fairbanks, H. W. 1915. "What Should Elementary
         School Geography Include and in What Order Should
         Its Material Be Presented?" Journal of Geography,
         Vol. 13, pp. 201-207.

J-179.   Fairbanks, H. W. 1927. "Can the Educational
         Value of Real Geography in the Junior High School
         Be Replaced by Any Other Subject or Combination
         of Subjects?," Journal of Geography, Vol. 26, pp.
         287-293.

J-180.   Fairbanks, H. W. 1935. "The Need for a
         Harmonious and Aggressive Front on the Part of
         School Geographers," Yearbook of the Association
         of Pacific Coast Geographers, Vol. 1, p. 30.

J-181.   Fairchild, Wilma B. 1951. "On Liking
         Geography," Geographical Review, Vol. 41, pp.
         4-6.

J-182.   Farnham, Amos W. 1904. "What the Child Should
         Know of Geography at the End of His Grade
         Course," Journal of Geography, Vol. 3, pp.
         424-426.

J-183.   Farrell, Bryan H. 1956. "Cultural or Human
         Geography?" New Zealand Geographical Society.
         Proceedings - First Geography Conference,
         Auckland, 1955, pp. A1/9-16.

J-184.   Fahy, G. 1981. "Geography and Geographic
         Education in Ireland From Early Christian Times
         to 1960," Geographical Viewpoint, Vol. 10, pp.
         5-30.

J-185.   Fahy, G., Fitzpatrick, Stella, Grace, M. and
         Gillmor, D. 1977. "Teaching Regional Geography:
         A Symposium," Geographical Viewpoint, Vol. 6, pp.
         49-59.

J-186.   Fellmann, Jerome D. 1986. "The Rise and Fall of
         High-School Economic Geography," Geographical
         Review, Vol. 76, pp. 424-437.

J-187.   Finch, V. C. 1930. "An Introductory Course in
         College Geography for Liberal Arts Students,"
         Journal of Geography, Vol. 29, pp. 178-186.

J-188.   Findlay, H. J.   1914.   "The Scope of School
         Geography," Scottish Geographical Magazine, Vol.
         30, pp. 133-137.

J-189.   Fine, Benjamin.   1951.   "Geography Almost Ignored
         in Colleges, Survey Shows," Journal of Geography,
         Vol. 50, pp. 165-170.

J-190.   Fink, L. D.   1984.   "First Year on the Faculty:
         Being There," Journal of Geography in Higher
         Education, Vol. 8, pp. 11-25.

J-191.   Fink, L. Dee.   1983.   "First Year on the
         Faculty: Getting There," Journal of Geography in
         Higher Education, Vol. 7, pp. 45-56.

J-192.   Fink, L. Dee and Morgan, David.   1976.   "The
         Importance of Teaching in Academic Geography:
         Report on a National Survey," Professional
         Geographer, Vol. 28, pp. 290-297.

J-193.   Fink, L. Dee.   1985.   "First Year on the
         Faculty: The Quality of Their Teaching," Journal
         of Geography in Higher Education, Vol. 9, pp.
         129-146.

J-194.   Fish, Olive C.   1927.   "The Aims and Content of
         Junior High School Geography," Journal of
         Geography, Vol. 26, pp. 313-321.

J-195.   Fisher, W. B.   1971.   "Geography in Contemporary
         Education," South African Geographical Journal,
         Vol. 53, pp. 10-17.

J-196.   Fitzpatrick, Stella.   1974.   "The Significance of
         Geography in Irish Education," Geographical
         Viewpoint, Vol. 3, pp. 1-14.

J-197.   Fitzpatrick, S.   1980.   "Development Education
         and the Geography Teacher," Geographical
         Viewpoint, Vol. 9, pp. 49-57.

J-198.   Flowerdew, Robin.   1986.   "Three Years in British
         Geography," Area, Vol. 18, pp. 263-264.

J-199.   Foster, Alice.   1945.   "Geography in Off-Duty
         Educational Opportunity for Armed Forces," Annals
         of the Association of American Geographers, Vol.
         35, pp. 167-180.

J-200.   Foster, L. T. and Jones, K. G.   1977.   "Applied
         Geography: An Educational Alternative,"
         Professional Geographer, Vol. 29, pp. 300-304.

J-201.   Foster, T. S.   1906.   "Geography in the
         Educational Journals," Geographical Teacher, Vol.
         3, pp. 174-177.

J-202. Freshfield, Douglas W. 1901. "Introductory [to
        The Geographical Teacher]," Geographical
        Teacher, Vol. 1, pp. 1-3.

J-203. Freshfield, Douglas W. 1908. "The President's
        Address," Geographical Teacher, Vol. 4, pp.
        148-152.

J-204. Freshfield, Douglas W. 1915. "Address at the
        Anniversary General Meeting, May 17, 1915,"
        Geographical Journal, Vol. 46, pp. 1-10.

J-205. Freshfield, Douglas W. 1916. "Address at the
        Anniversary General Meeting, 22 May 1916,"
        Geographical Journal, Vol. 48, pp. 1-11.

J-206. Freshfield, Douglas W. 1917. "Address at the
        Anniversary General Meeting, 21 May 1917,"
        Geographical Journal, Vol. 50, pp. 1-12.

J-207. Frick, Mary Louise. 1965. "The Status of
        Geography in the High School Today," Journal of
        Geography, Vol. 64, pp. 317-322.

J-208. Fuchs, Vivian. 1983. "The Presidential
        Address," Geographical Journal, Vol. 149, pp.
        281-285.

J-209. Fuchs, Vivian. 1984. "The Presidential
        Address," Geographical Journal, Vol. 150, pp.
        305-310.

J-210. Fuson, Robert H. 1961. "Geography and General
        Education," Journal of Geography, Vol. 60, pp.
        422-427.

J-211. Gallois, Lucren. 1913. "The Teaching of
        Geography in French Universities," Journal of
        Geography, Vol. 12, pp. 40-44.

J-212. Gananathan, V. S. 1951. "The Evaluation of a
        Good Geography Graduate," Geographer, Vol. 4, No.
        2, pp. 35-40.

J-213. Ganzenmuller, Konrad. 1887. "How to Enlighten
        Geographical Instruction and How to Lighten It,"
        Journal of the American Geographical Society of
        New York, Vol. 17, pp. 355-382.

J-214. Gardner, David Pierpont. 1986. "Geography in
        the School Curriculum," Annals of the Association
        of American Geographers, Vol. 76, pp. 1-4.

J-215. Garfinkel, Maurice A. 1934. "Modern Tendencies
        in the Teaching of Geography," Journal of
        Geography, Vol. 33, pp. 187-194.

J-216.   Garland, John H.   1945.   "Geography in the
          Postwar Era - Are We Prepared to Teach It?"
          Journal of Geography, Vol. 44, pp. 265-273.

J-217.   Garnett, A.   1949.   "Geography and Post-War
          Trends in Education in Great Britain,"
          Proceedings - Sixteenth International
          Geographical Congress, pp. 388-398.

J-218.   Garrett, M. J.   1983.   "Geography and General
          Education: A Changing Profile (U.S.A.),"
          Bulletin - Association of North Dakota
          Geographers, Vol. 33, pp. 1-15.

J-219.   Garrett, Michael J. and Hecock, Richard D.
          1984.   "General Education and Geography: A
          Profile of Institutional Types," Journal of
          Geography, Vol. 83, pp. 273-276.

J-220.   Geddes, Patrick.   1902.   "Note on a Draft Plan
          for Institute of Geography," Scottish
          Geographical Magazine, Vol. 18, pp. 142-144.

J-221.   Genthe, Martha Krug.   1903.   "Geographical
          Teaching and Geographical Text-Books,"
          Geographical Teacher, Vol. 2, pp. 126-128.

J-222.   Genthe, Martha Krug.   1903.   "Geographical
          Textbooks and Geographical Teaching," Journal of
          Geography, Vol. 2, pp. 226-243, 360-368.

J-223.   Genthe, Martha Krug.   1904.   "School Geography in
          the United States," Education, Vol. 25, pp.
          135-141.

J-224.   Genthe, Martha Krug.   1904.   "School Geography in
          the United States," Proceedings - Eighth
          International Geographical Congress, pp. 981-986.

J-225.   Gibson, Lyle E.   1966.   "Planning Geography in
          the Curriculum of a New College," California
          Geographer, Vol. 7, pp. 13-18.

J-226.   Gillmore, D. A.   1981.   "Third Level Education in
          Geography and Career Opportunities," Geographical
          Viewpoint, Vol. 10, pp. 74-87.

J-227.   Gillmore, Desmond A.   1976.   "Geographic
          Education in Ireland and the National Commission
          for the Teaching of Geography," Geographical
          Viewpoint, Vol. 5, pp. 60-73.

J-228.   Glowacki, W.   1972.   "Rebirth of High School
          Geography," Clearing House, Vol. 46, pp. 327-331.

J-229.   Goodchild, Michael F.   1985.   "Geographic
          Information Systems in   Undergraduate Geography:
          A Contemporary Dilemma," Operational Geographer,
          No. 8, pp. 34-38.

J-230.   Goode, J. Paul.   1911.   "The Point of View in
          Elementary Geography," Journal of Geography,
          Vol. 9, pp. 155-156.

J-231.   Gordon, George.   1983.   "The Spread of the
          Ordinary Alternative Syllabuses in Geography at
          Ordinary and Higher Grades," Scottish
          Geographical Magazine, Vol. 99, pp. 31-43.

J-232.   Gould, Peter.   1970.   "Teaching and the New
          Geography," New Zealand Journal of Geography, No.
          48, pp. 1-5.

J-233.   Gould, W. T. S.   1971.   "Geography and
          Educational Opportunity in Tropical Africa,"
          Tijdschrift voor Economische en Sociale
          Geografie, Vol. 62, pp. 82-89.

J-234.   Grassmuck, E.   1927.   "Contributions to American
          Life by the Teacher of Geography," National
          Education Association, Proceedings and Addresses,
          pp. 140-142.

J-235.   Grassmuck, E.   1932.   "Geographic Education
          Whither Bound," Educational Outlook, Vol. 6, pp.
          166-178.

J-236.   Graves, N. J.   1978.   "Problems of Geographical
          Education," Geographical Viewpoint, Vol. 7, pp.
          5-19.

J-237.   Graves, N. J.   1978.   "Problems of Geographical
          Education," Geographical Viewpoint, Vol. 7, pp.
          5-19.

J-238.   Graves, Norman J.   1987.   "Research in
          Geographical Education," New Zealand Journal of
          Geography, Vol. 84, pp. 15-19.

J-239.   Gray, Fred and Tivers, Jacqueline.   1987.
          "Distant Relations and the Poor Cousins:
          Geography in University Adult Education," Area,
          Vol. 19, pp. 207-213.

J-240.   Green, J. L.   1985.   "Geography Education as a
          Field of Knowledge," Education Digest, Vol. 50,
          pp. 34-35.

J-241.   Greenwood, D. R.   1886.   "On the Teaching of
          Geography and the Proper Instruction of its
          Several Branches," Journal of the Manchester
          Geographical Society, Vol. 2, pp. 102-106.

J-242.   Greer-Wootton, Bryn. 1967. "Geography and the
          New Educational Technology," Canadian Geographer,
          Vol. 11, pp. 133-142.

J-243.   Gregory, R. A. 1908. "Scientific Methods in the
          Teaching of Geography," Geographical Teacher,
          Vol. 4, pp. 209-221.

J-244.   Gregory, S. and House, J. W. 1973. "Preliminary
          Report on Higher-Degree Graduates in Geography,"
          Area, Vol. 5, pp. 88-95.

J-245.   Gregory, W. M. 1911. "Editorial - Present
          Problems in Elementary School Geography," Journal
          of Geography, Vol. 9, pp. 193-196.

J-246.   Gregory, William M., et al. 1912. "Symposium:
          What is Most Needed in the Teaching of Elementary
          Geography?" Journal of Geography, Vol. 10, pp.
          245-263.

J-247.   Griffin, Paul F. 1953. "Secondary School
          Geography and the Needs of Our Times," Journal of
          Geography, Vol. 52, pp. 60-67.

J-248.   Gritzner, Charles. 1986. "The South Dakota
          Experience," [in High School Geography]
          Professional Geographer, Vol. 38, pp. 252-253.

J-249.   Gritzner, Charles F. 1982. "What is Right with
          Geography," Journal of Geography, Vol. 81, pp.
          237-239.

J-250.   Gross, Herbert H. 1956. "A Survey of the
          Research in Geographic Education," Proceedings -
          Eighteenth International Geographical Congress,
          pp. 548-552.

J-251.   Gross, Herbert H. 1964. "Accents in Geography,"
          Journal of Geography, Vol. 63, pp. 258-261.

J-252.   Grounds, F. Oral. 1932. "Geography in
          Elementary and Secondary Education in Germany,"
          Journal of Geography, Vol. 31, pp. 376-380.

J-253.   Gunn, Angus M. 1964. "Recent Progress in School
          Geography," Canadian Geographer, Vol. 14, No. 6,
          pp. 51-52.

J-254.   Haas, W. H. 1931. "The Teaching of Geography as
          a Science," Journal of Geography, Vol. 30, pp.
          323-329.

J-255.   Haigh, M. J. and Freeman, T. W. 1982. "The
          Crisis in American Geography," Area, Vol. 14, pp.
          185-190.

J-256.   Hall, Robin. 1983. "The Teaching of Moral
          Values in Geography," Journal of Geography in
          Higher Education, Vol. 7, pp. 3-14.

J-257.   Hallinan, M. 1977. "The Geography Teacher and
          the Integrated Curriculum," Geographical
          Viewpoint, Vol. 6, pp. 18-24.

J-258.   Hallinan, M. 1980. "New Geography Curricula and
          Teaching Opportunities," Geographical Viewpoint,
          Vol. 9, pp. 5-18.

J-259.   Hallinan, M. 1981. "The Evolution of the
          Geography Syllabus in Irish Second-level
          Education Since 1961," Geographical Viewpoint,
          Vol. 10, pp. 56-62.

J-260.   Halverson, Lynn H. 1928. "Geography in Teachers
          Colleges," Education, Vol. 49, pp. 193-205.

J-261.   Hamilton, J. W. 1950. "Geography in Education,"
          Canadian Geographer, No. 1, pp. 7-10.

J-262.   Hare, Ralph. 1984. "Geography Lessons, Past,
          Present, and Future: A Personal View,"
          Bloomsbury Geographer, Vol. 12, pp. 9-12.

J-263.   Harper, R. 1968. "More Geography, Not 'the
          Elements of ...'" Journal of Geography, Vol. 67,
          pp. 132-133.

J-264.   Harper, Robert A. 1966. "Geography's Role in
          General Education," Journal of Geography, Vol.
          65, pp. 177-185.

J-265.   Harper, Robert A. 1966. "The Minimum Essential
          Geography: Key to Teacher-Training,"
          Professional Geographer, Vol. 18, No. 3, pp.
          140-142.

J-266.   Harper, Robert A. 1982. "Geography in General
          Education: The Need to Focus on the Geography
          of the Field," Journal of Geography, Vol. 81, pp.
          122-139.

J-267.   Harper, Robert A. 1986. "New Teaching
          Opportunities and Challenges for U.S. Geography,"
          Journal of Geography, Vol. 84, pp. 3-4.

J-268.   Harris, W. T. 1902. "Place of Geography in the
          Elementary Schools," Forum, Vol. 32, pp. 539-550.

J-269.   Helgren, David M. 1983. "Place Name Ignorance
          Is National News," Journal of Geography, Vol. 82,
          pp. 176-178.

J-270.   Helleiner, Frederick. 1981. "New Directions for
         Secondary School Geography," Geoscope, Vol. 12,
         pp. 11-12.

J-271.   Henderson, Bertha. 1916. "The Cultural and
         Training Value of Geography," Journal of
         Geography, Vol. 14, pp. 97-100.

J-272.   Henkel, Wilhelm C. 1895. "On the Combination of
         Geography and History in the Curriculum of Modern
         Schools," Proceedings - Sixth International
         Geographical Congress, pp. 88-89.

J-273.   Henry, Norah F. and Budin, Morris. 1983.
         "Education and Applied Geography," Research in
         Contemporary and Applied Geography: A Discussion
         Series, Vol. 7, No. 4, pp. 43-52.

J-274.   Heppell, Roger C. 1971. "The Geography Demon,"
         Journal of Geography, Vol. 70, pp. 198-199.

J-275.   Hepple, Leslie W. 1974. "The Impact of
         Stochastic Process Theory on Spatial Analysis in
         Human Geography," Progress in Geography, Vol. 6,
         pp. 89-142.

J-276.   Herbertson, A. J. 1898. "The Parlous Plight of
         Geography in Scottish Education," Scottish
         Geographical Magazine, Vol. 14, pp. 81-88.

J-277.   Herbertson, A. J. 1898. "The Position of
         Economic Geography in Education," Journal of the
         Manchester Geographical Society, Vol. 14, pp.
         286-292.

J-278.   Herbertson, A. J. 1902. "Geography in the
         University," Scottish Geographical Magazine, Vol.
         18, pp. 124-132.

J-279.   Herbertson, A. J. 1902. "Notes on Geographical
         Education," Scottish Geographical Magazine, Vol.
         18, pp. 256-259.

J-280.   Herbertson, A. J. 1905. "Recent Discussions on
         the Scope and Educational Applications of
         Geography," Geographical Journal, Vol. 24, pp.
         417-427.

J-281.   Herbertson, A. J. 1906. "Recent Regulations and
         Syllabuses in Geography Affecting Schools,"
         Geographical Journal, Vol. 27, pp. 279-288.

J-282.   Herbertson, A. J. 1910. "Geography and Some of
         Its Present Needs," Bulletin of the American
         Geographical Society, Vol. 42, pp. 764-777.

J-283.   Herbertson, A. J. 1910. "Geography and Some of
the Present Needs," Geographical Journal, Vol.
36, pp. 468-479.

J-284.   Herbertson, A. J. 1910. "Geography and Some of
Its Present Needs," Scottish Geographical
Magazine, Vol. 26, pp. 532-544.

J-285.   Herbertson, Andrew J. 1896. "Geographical
Education," Scottish Geographical Magazine, Vol.
12, pp. 414-422, 522-529, 576-583.

J-286.   Herrick, Cheesman A. 1904. "Commercial
Geography in the Secondary School," Education,
Vol. 25, pp. 129-134.

J-287.   Hewlett, E. G. 1895. "The Position of Geography
as a School Subject," Journal of the Manchester
Geographical Society, Vol. 11, pp. 255-263.

J-288.   Hewlett, E. G. W. 1903. "Aims and Difficulties
in the Teaching of Geography," Geographical
Teacher, Vol. 2, pp. 104-107.

J-289.   High, James. 1960. "Geography: Coordinating
Element in Secondary Social Science," Journal of
Geography, Vol. 59, pp. 210-278.

J-290.   Hill, Wilhelmina. 1960. "New Development in
Geographic Education," Journal of Geography, Vol.
59, pp. 234-239.

J-291.   Hills, Theo L. 1957. "A Suggested Resolution on
the Teaching of Geography," Canadian Geographer,
No. 9, pp. 55-59.

J-292.   Hubbard, George D. 1908. "College Geography,"
Educational Review, Vol. 35, pp. 381-400.

J-293.   Hubbard, George D. 1908. "Geography in the
Secondary Schools," National Education
Association, Proceedings, pp. 978-984.

J-294.   Hubbard, George D. 1918. "Reasons for Giving
Geography a Greater Place in High Schools,"
School Science and Mathematics, Vol. 18, pp.
291-304.

J-295.   Huckle, John F. 1983. "Values Education Through
Geography: A Radical Critique," Journal of
Geography, Vol. 82, pp. 59-63.

J-296.   Huckle, John F. 1987. "What Sort of Geography
for What Sort of School Curriculum?" Area, Vol.
19, pp. 261-265.

J-297.   Hung, F.   1966.   "Comments on Frontiers of
         Geographical Teaching," Professional Geographer,
         Vol. 18, pp. 341-345.

J-298.   Huntington, Ellsworth.   1945.   "High Schools and
         Geographic Immaturity," Journal of Geography,
         Vol. 44, pp. 173-181.

J-299.   Ireland, R. P.   1904.   "What a Child Should Gain
         From Geography," Journal of Geography, Vol. 3,
         pp. 421-424.

J-300.   Jackson, Eric P.   1924.   "Geography as a
         Correlating Subject in the High School," Journal
         of Geography, Vol. 23, pp. 313-316.

J-301.   Jackson, W. A. Douglas.   1964.   "Geographic
         Education in Poland," Journal of Geography, Vol.
         63, pp. 418-425.

J-302.   Jacobson, Daniel.   1965.   "The Role of Historical
         Geography in the American School," Journal of
         Geography, Vol. 64, pp. 99-105.

J-303.   Jahr, Anton.   1911.   "Geographical Instruction in
         German Elementary Schools," Journal of Geography,
         Vol. 9, pp. 239-243.

J-304.   James, Preston E.   1947.   "Developments in the
         Field of Geography and Their Implications for the
         Geography Curriculum," Journal of Geography, Vol.
         46, pp. 221-226.

J-305.   James, Preston E.   1969.   "The Significance of
         Geography in American Education," Journal of
         Geography, Vol. 68, pp. 473-483.

J-306.   Jenks, George F.   1953.   "An Improved Curriculum
         for Cartographic Training at the College and
         University Level," Annals of the Association of
         American Geographers, Vol. 43, pp. 317-331.

J-307.   Jensen, J. Granville.   1956.   "A Professionalized
         Geography Curriculum," Professional Geographer,
         Vol. 8, No. 1, pp. 6-9.

J-308.   Jones, Stephen B.   1948.   "Geography in
         Interdepartmental Curricula," Journal of
         Geography, Vol. 47, pp. 132-140.

J-309.   Joseph, Sir Keith.   1985.   "Geography in the
         School Curriculum," Geography, Vol. 70, pp.
         290-298.

J-310.   Juillard, Etienne and Klein, Claude.   1980.
         "Henri Baulig, 1877-1962," Geographers:
         Biobibliographical Studies, Vol. 4, pp. 7-18.

J-311.   Jumper, Sidney R. 1986. "The Tennessee
          Experience [in High School Geography],"
          Professional Geographer, Vol. 38, pp. 254-255.

J-312.   Kaatz, Martin R. 1971. "The Geography Behind
          the News," Association of Pacific Coast
          Geographers Yearbook, Vol. 33, pp. 7-18.

J-313.   Kalapesi, A. S. 1960.   "The Scope and Aims of
          Geography in Modern Education," Bombay
          Geographical Magazine, Vol 1, pp. 19-23.

J-314.   Kalesnik, S. V. 1956. "Training of Geographers
          and Geography Teachers at Soviet Universities,"
          Proceedings - Eighteenth International
          Geographical Congress, pp. 563-568.

J-315.   Kalesnik, S. V. 1973. "The Training of
          Geographers (on the Curriculum of a College
          Department of Physical Geography," Soviet
          Geography: Review and Translation, Vol. 14, pp.
          634-637.

J-316.   Keatinge, M. W. 1902. "Geography as a
          Correlating Subject," Geographical Teacher, Vol.
          1, pp. 145-149.

J-317.   Keely, Vivien. 1984. "Geography and
          Environmental Education in Schools," Geography,
          Vol. 69, pp. 138-140.

J-318.   Keith, John A. H. 1923. "Geography in the
          Normal School," Journal of Geography, Vol. 22,
          pp. 196-197.

J-319.   Kekoni, Karl. 1926. "Geography in the Schools
          of Finland," Journal of Geography, Vol. 25, pp.
          67-71.

J-320.   Keltie, J. Scott. 1885. "Geographical
          Education," Royal Geographical Society Supp.
          Paper, Vol. 1, pp. 439-594.

J-321.   Keltie, J. Scott. 1885. "Geographical
          Education," Scottish Geographical Magazine, Vol.
          1, pp. 497-505.

J-322.   Keltie, J. Scott. 1886. "Geographical Education
          on the Continent and the Appliances for Teaching
          the Subject," Journal of the Manchester
          Geographical Society, Vol. 2, pp. 241-258.

J-323.   Keltie, J. Scott. 1891. "Recent Progress of
          Geographical Education in England," Journal of
          the Manchester Geographical Society, Vol. 7, p.
          263.

J-324.   Kennamer, Lorrin G., Jr. 1953. "Beginnings in
         Geographic Education," Journal of Geography, Vol.
         52, pp. 72-77.

J-325.   Kent, W. A. 1980. "Geography and Environmental
         Education," Geographical Viewpoint, Vol. 9, pp.
         19-28.

J-326.   Khvalynskaya, M. S. 1984. "Economic Geography
         of Higher Education in the USSR," Soviet
         Geography: Review and Translation, Vol. 25, pp.
         381-389.

J-327.   Kirchwey, Clara B. 1916. "Geography in the
         Junior High School," Journal of Geography, Vol.
         14, pp. 291-294.

J-328.   Knowlton, Daniel C. 1921. "The Relation of
         Geography to the Social Studies in the
         Curriculum," Journal of Geography, Vol. 20, pp.
         225-234.

J-329.   Kochergin, P. G. 1961. "The Scientific
         Principles of the Content of a Geography Course
         of the Soviet Eight-Year School," Soviet
         Geography: Review and Translation, Vol. 2, No.
         8, pp. 46-51.

J-330.   Kohn, Clyde F. 1974. "Challenges to Graduate
         Education in Geography," Mississippi Geographer,
         Vol. 2, pp. 11-18.

J-331.   Kohn, Clyde F. 1982. "Looking Back, Working
         Ahead," Journal of Geography, Vol. 81, pp. 44-46.

J-332.   Kopf, Helen M. 1932. "One-Cycle or Two-Cycle
         Geography," Journal of Geography, Vol. 31, pp.
         193-198.

J-333.   Kostbade, J. Trenton. 1968. "The Regional
         Concept and Geographic Education," Journal of
         Geography, Vol. 67, pp. 6-12.

J-334.   Krapotkin, P. 1893. "On the Teaching of
         Physiography," Geographical Journal, Vol. 2, pp.
         350-359.

J-335.   Lanegran, David A. 1986. "Strengthening
         Geographic Education." [comment, Stultz]
         Professional Geographer, Vol. 38, p. 71.

J-336.   Laurie, Professor. 1886. "Method Applied to the
         Teaching of Geography in the School," Scottish
         Geographical Magazine, Vol. 2, pp. 449-460.

J-337.   Laws, K. J. 1983. "The Past as a Key to the
          Present: Historical Geography in the
          Curriculum," Geographical Education, Vol. 4, pp.
          93-106.

J-338.   Lawson, D. E. 1941. "Geography Then and Now,"
          Elementary School Journal, Vol. 41, pp. 597-604.

J-339.   LeHeron, R. B. and Williams, D. B. 1981.
          "Geography Is Not What Geographers Do, It's What
          They Learn," New Zealand Journal of Geography,
          Vol. 70, pp. 9-13.

J-340.   Lee, David R. 1974. "Existentialism in
          Geographic Education," Journal of Geography, Vol.
          73, pp. 13-19.

J-341.   Lee, Roger. 1983. "Teaching Geography: The
          Dialectic of Structure and Agency," Journal of
          Geography, Vol. 82, pp. 102-109.

J-342.   Lee, Roger. 1983. "Why Geography? The Choice
          of Geography in Higher Education," Philippine
          Geographical Journal, Vol. 27, pp. 1-36.

J-343.   Lenon, Barnaby. 1987. "Undergraduates in 1990,"
          Area, Vol. 19, pp. 265-266.

J-344.   Lewis, G. Malcolm. 1982. "The Milieu of
          Geography Within Higher Education in the United
          Kingdom in the 1980s," Journal of Geography in
          Higher Education, Vol. 6, pp. 141-150.

J-345.   Libee, Michael. 1984. "Geography in Higher
          Education: Way We're in Trouble and How to Get
          Out," Journal of Geography, Vol. 83, pp. 5-6.

J-346.   Limbird, A. 1986. "A Mission for Geographers in
          the Secondary Schools of Canada," Operational
          Geographer, No. 10, p. 5.

J-347.   Lineback, Neal G. 1986. "Physical Geography and
          the Core Curriculum: One Department's
          Experience," Professional Geographer, Vol. 38,
          pp. 274-278.

J-348.   Logan, Richard F. 1977. "The Potential Role of
          Geography in the Pre- Collegiate Curriculum,"
          California Geographer, Vol. 17, pp. 107-113.

J-349.   Lounsbury, John F. 1968. "College Geography in
          the United States," Journal of Geography, Vol.
          67, pp. 282-287.

J-350.   Lyde, L. W. 1908. "The Teaching of Geography as
          a Subject of Commercial Instruction,"
          Geographical Teacher, Vol. 4, pp. 163-168.

J-351. Mabogunje, A. L. 1962. "School Inspection in
        Geography," Nigerian Geographical Journal, Vol. 5,
        pp. 135-138.

J-352. MacDonald, William. 1961. "Geography in the
        English School," Journal of Geography, Vol. 60,
        pp. 310-312.

J-353. Mackie, G. B. 1917. "The Teaching of Geography,"
        Scottish Geographical Magazine, Vol. 33, pp.
        157-163.

J-354. Mackinder, H. J. 1890. "On the Necessity of
        Thorough Teaching in General Geography as a
        Preliminary to the Teaching of Commercial
        Geography," Journal of the Manchester Geographical
        Society, Vol. 6, pp. 1-6.

J-355. Mackinder, H. J. 1903. "Geographical Education,"
        Journal of Geography, Vol. 2, pp. 499-506.

J-356. Mackinder, H. J. 1903. "Geography in Education,"
        Geographical Teacher, Vol. 2, pp. 95-101.

J-357. Mackinder, H. J. 1904. "The Development of
        Geographical Teaching of Nature Study,"
        Geographical Teacher, Vol. 2, pp. 191-197.

J-358. Mackinder, Sir Halford. 1921. "Geography as a
        Pivotal Subject in Education," Geographical
        Journal, Vol. 57, pp. 376-384.

J-359. Macomber, Frank G. 1924. "Loose-Leaf Geography,
        Education, Vol. 45, pp. 47-56.

J-360. Maksakovskii, V. P. 1987.   "Raising the Level of
        Geography Teaching," Soviet Geography: Review and
        Translation, Vol. 29, pp. 87-99.

J-361. Marcus, Melvin G. 1979. "The Range of
        Opportunity in Applied Physical Geography,"
        Geographical Survey, Vol. 8, No. 4, pp. 3-4.

J-362. Marcus, Robert B. 1958. "The Status of Geography
        in the Teacher Education Institutions of the
        South," Journal of Geography, Vol. 57, pp.
        236-241.

J-363. Markov, K. K. 1968. "Methodological Principles
        of the Curriculum of a Geography Faculty," Soviet
        Geography: Review and Translation, Vol. 9, pp.
        358-367.

J-364. Marston, C. E. 1933. "The Elementary Principal
        as a Supervisor of Geography," Journal of
        Geography, Vol. 32, pp. 21-26.

J-365. Martin, H. C. 1905. "Geography in Schools,"
        Journal of the Manchester Geographical Society,
        Vol. 21, pp. 104-112.

J-366. Martin, Maude Cottingham. 1926. "Geography in
        the Junior High School," Journal of Geography,
        Vol. 25, pp. 250-257.

J-367. Martis, Kenneth C. 1979. "Don't Teach Your
        Students Geography," Geographical Survey, Vol. 8,
        No. 1, pp. 3-5.

J-368. Maze, W. H. 1946. "The Teaching of Geography in
        Australian and New Zealand Universities,"
        Australian Geographer, Vol. 5, pp. 77-83.

J-369. McBain, F. C. A. 1967. "Some Observations on
        Geography Courses in Nigerian Secondary Schools,
        Nigerian Geographical Journal, Vol. 10, pp. 56-64.

J-370. McCluer, Leon. 1960. "Some Observations on the
        Place and Growth of College Geography," Memorandum
        Folio, Vol. 12, pp. 73-77.

J-371. McCluer, Leon. 1961. "A Survey of the Emphasis
        on Geography in Our Public and High Schools,"
        Memorandum Folio, Vol. 13, pp. 94-98.

J-372. McConnell, W. R. 1924. "The Place of Geography
        in the Junior High School," Journal of Geography,
        Vol. 23, pp. 49-58.

J-373. McConnell, W. R. 1925. "Objectives of Geography
        Instruction," Journal of Geography, Vol. 24, pp.
        203-212.

J-374. McConnell, Wallace R. 1933. "Problems of
        Instruction in Geography," Journal of Geography,
        Vol. 32, pp. 149-151.

J-375. McDowell, Linda and Bowlby, Sophia. 1983.
        "Teaching Feminist Geography," Journal of
        Geography in Higher Education, Vol. 7, pp. 97-108.

J-376. McMillan, Eva M. 1911. "The Present Status of
        Geography Teaching," Journal of Geography, Vol.
        10, pp. 73-80.

J-377. McMurry, C. A. 1895. "Geography as a New School
        Subject: Propositions and Criticisms,"
        Educational Review, Vol. 9, pp. 448-463.

J-378. McMurry, Frank M. 1929. "The Selection of
        Subject Matter for Geography in the Elementary
        School," Journal of Geography, Vol. 28, pp.
        153-168.

J-379.   McNee, Robert B.   1971.   "The Organizational
         Philosophy for a Graduate Seminar in Geography:
         One Man's View," Journal of Geography, Vol. 70,
         pp. 519-524.

J-380.   Meles, I. J.   1941.   "Teaching of Geography,"
         Geographical Review of India, Vol. 3, No. 2, N.P.

J-381.   Meyer, Alfred H.   1946.   "College Geography and
         Its Relation to Teacher Training in Secondary
         Schools," Journal of Geography, Vol. 45, pp.
         45-79.

J-382.   Meyer, Carl S.   1942.   "Geography for the Junior
         Colleges," Journal of Geography, Vol. 41, pp.
         221-227.

J-383.   Miller, George J.   1920.   "The National Council of
         Geography Teachers," Journal of Geography, Vol.
         19, pp. 69-75.

J-384.   Miller, George J.   1925.   "Geography as a Social
         Science in the Junior High School," Journal of
         Geography, Vol. 24, pp. 241-349.

J-385.   Miller, George J.   1932.   "Geography in English
         and in American Schools: Some Contracts," Journal
         of Geography, Vol. 31, pp. 120-127.

J-386.   Miller, George J.   1933.   "The Training of
         Teachers of Geography," Journal of Geography, Vol.
         32, pp. 145-148.

J-387.   Miller, Jack W., et al.   1972.   "Research in
         Geographic Learning," Journal of Geography, Vol.
         71, pp. 197-240.

J-388.   Miller, Vincent.   1960.   "Observations on the
         Goals and Methods of Regional Courses," Journal of
         Geography, Vol. 59, pp. 371-377.

J-389.   Miller, William.   1910.   "Practical Geography in
         Schools," Scottish Geographical Magazine, Vol. 26,
         pp. 353-365.

J-390.   Miller, William T.   1929.   "The Balance Between
         Fact and Judgment Work in Geography," Journal of
         Geography, Vol. 28, pp. 298-304.

J-391.   Milojevic, Borivojez.   1956.   "The Teaching of
         Regional Geography at the Universities,"
         Proceedings - Eighteenth International
         Geographical Congress, pp. 583-588.

J-392.   Moles, Richard.   1983.   "A Structure for Geography
         as a Second Level Subject," Geographical
         Viewpoint, Vol. 12, pp. 32-45.

J-393.   Moles, Richard. 1984-85. "Planning Post-Primary
          Geography Teaching," Geographical Viewpoint, Vol.
          13, pp. 14-30.

J-394.   Monk, Janice. 1977. "Issues Confronting
          Geographic Educators in Europe and the U.S.S.R.,"
          Professional Geographer, Vol. 29, pp. 379-385.

J-395.   Monk, Janice. 1983. "Integrating Women into the
          Geography Curriculum," Journal of Geography, Vol.
          82, pp. 271-273.

J-396.   Moore, E. 1964-65. "Geography in Alberta
          Schools," Albertan Geographer, No. 1, pp. 26-28.

J-397.   Moore, William C. 1906. "What a Child Ought to
          Know at the End of His School Geography," Journal
          of Geography, Vol. 5, pp. 320-325.

J-398.   Morris, Gwyn. 1891. "The Teaching of Commercial
          Geography," Journal of the Manchester Geographical
          Society, Vol. 7, pp. 328-331.

J-399.   Morris, John W. 1959. "Geography vs. The School
          and You," Journal of Geography, Vol. 58, pp.
          59-71.

J-400.   Morris, John W. 1965. "Geography-Separate Course
          or Integrated?" Journal of Geography, Vol. 64, pp.
          202-205.

J-401.   Morris, Joseph Acton. 1938. "On the Teaching of
          Physical Geography," Proceedings - Fifteenth
          International Geographical Congress, pp. 84-88.

J-402.   Morrow-Jones, Hazel A. 1986. "The Colorado
          Experience [in High School Geography],"
          Professional Geographer, Vol. 38, pp. 74-75.

J-403.   Muir, T. S. 1912. "Geography in Scottish
          Schools," Scottish Geographical Magazine, Vol. 28,
          pp. 534-540.

J-404.   Mulliner, Beulah A. 1912. "The Development of
          Physiography in American Textbooks," Journal of
          Geography, Vol. 10, pp. 319-324.

J-405.   Murphy, E. A. C. 1933. "What Good is
          Physiography?" School Science and Mathematics,
          Vol. 33, pp. 767-772.

J-406.   Murray, L. 1985. "Fostering Student Research in
          Geography - a Practical Workshop for Teachers,"
          Geographical Education, "Vol. 5, pp. 34-36.

J-407.   Myers, John L. 1928. "Ancient Geography in
          Modern Education," Scottish Geographical Magazine,
          Vol. 44, p. 257.

J-408.   Nag, B. B. 1936. "Geography - The Sick Man of
         the School-Curriculum," Geographical Review of
         India, Vol. 1, No. 1, N.P.

J-409.   Natoli, Salvatore. 1984. "The Invisible
         Geography Teachers and the Profession,"
         Professional Geographer, Vol. 36, pp. 89-92.

J-410.   Nolan, M. Olive. 1928. "Correlation of
         Geography, History, Civics and Economics," Journal
         of Geography, Vol. 27, pp. 76-81.

J-411.   Nolan, Olive. 1925. "Motivating the Curriculum
         Thru Geography," Journal of Geography, Vol. 24,
         pp. 157-162.

J-412.   Nolan, Olive. 1927. "The Socialization of
         Geography," Education, Vol. 48, pp. 229-236.

J-413.   Nuttall, Sheila E. 1984. "New Courses in Further
         Education: The Geographer's Contribution,"
         Geography, Vol. 69, pp. 244-249.

J-414.   Oboli, H. O. N. 1957. "The Teaching of Local
         Geography in Secondary Schools," Nigerian
         Geographical Association, Vol. 1, pp. 14-16.

J-415.   Ocitti, J. P. 1971. "A Revolutionary School
         Geography Syllabus in East Africa," East African
         Geographical Review, No. 9, pp. 3-10.

J-416.   O'Flynn, G. 1982. "Towards an Understanding of
         Development Education," Geographical Viewpoint,
         Vol. 11, pp. 5-17.

J-417.   Ogilvie, Alan G. 1924. "Modern Geography as a
         Study and as an Aid," Scottish Geographical
         Magazine, Vol. 40, pp. 65-74.

J-418.   Ogilvie, F. G. 1913. "Geographical Studies in
         the Schools of England and Wales," Proceedings -
         Tenth International Geographical Congress, pp.
         1426-1430.

J-419.   Ojo, G. J. A. 1964. "The New West African School
         Certificate Geography Syllabus," Nigerian
         Geographical Journal, Vol. 7, pp. 47-53.

J-420.   Okunrotifa, P. O. 1969. "Towards a Curriculum
         Reform in High School Geography," Nigerian
         Geographical Journal, Vol. 12, pp. 155-161.

J-421.   Okunrotifa, P. O. 1971. "The Aims and Objectives
         of Geographic Education," Nigerian Geographical
         Journal, Vol. 14, pp. 221-230.

J-422.   Okunrotifa, P. O. 1974. "A Study of Geography
          Teaching in Some Welsh Secondary Schools,"
          Nigerian Geographical Journal, Vol. 17, pp.
          165-172.

J-423.   Oliveira, L. 1972. "Geography in Modern
          Education," Proceedings - Twenty- Second
          International Geographical Congress, pp.
          1057-1058.

J-424.   Olumide, A. O. 1958. "Geography in the Secondary
          School Curriculum," Nigerian Geographical Journal,
          Vol. 2, pp. 37-39.

J-425.   O'Malley, M. P. 1977. "Viewpoints on
          Geographical Education: A Decade of Change," New
          Zealand Journal of Geography, No. 63, pp. 1-8.

J-426.   Orchard, John E. 1930. "The Introductory Course
          in Economic Geography in the School of Business,"
          Journal of Geography, Vol. 29, pp. 187-198.

J-427.   Orford, E. J. 1938. "The Importance of
          Geographical Teaching for the Good Understanding
          Between the Peoples," Proceedings - Fifteenth
          International Geographical Congress, pp. 16-22.

J-428.   Oxford, E. J. 1918. "Geography: What Facts
          Shall We Teach," Journal of Geography, Vol. 17,
          pp. 114-118.

J-429.   Paddock, Miner H. 1904. "Physical Geography in
          Our Public Schools," Education, Vol. 25, pp.
          162-163.

J-430.   Parker, Edith P. 1933. "Principles Underlying
          the Construction of a Geography Curriculum,"
          Journal of Geography, Vol. 32, pp. 136-138.

J-431.   Parkins, A. E. 1926. "Some Tendencies in
          Elementary Education and Their Possible Effect on
          Geography," Journal of Geography, Vol. 25, pp.
          81-89.

J-432.   Pattison, William D. 1968. "Regional Geography
          in the American School: Clarification of an
          Opportunity," Journal of Geography, Vol. 67, pp.
          398-402.

J-433.   Peake, Linda. 1985. "Teaching Feminist
          Geography: Another Perspective," Journal of
          Geography in Higher Education, Vol. 9, pp.
          186-190.

J-434.   Peattie, Roderick. 1921. "Introductory Geography
          for Colleges," Journal of Geography, Vol. 20, pp.
          318-320.

J-435.   Pinkney, D. G.   1907.   "The Neglect of Geography
          in Our Schools,"   Geographical Teacher, Vol. 4,
          pp. 15-18.

J-436.   Podanchuk, V. D., Otalenko, M. A. and Tolcarskiy,
          N. K.   1962.   "The New Geography Programs for the
          Eight-Year and General Middle Schools of the
          Ukranian SSR," Soviet Geography: Review and
          Translation,   Vol. 3, pp. 3-13.

J-437.   Poiker, Thomas K.   1985.   "Geographic Information
          Systems in the Geographic Curriculums,"
          Operational Geographer, No. 8, pp. 38-41.

J-438.   Powell, J. M.   1984.   "Curriculum Reform and the
          'Constituency' Challenge: Recent Trends in Higher
          School Geography," Australian Geographical
          Studies, Vol. 20, pp. 275-295.

J-439.   Probald, F.   1981-82.   "The Status of Geographical
          Education in Hungary,"   Annales-Universitaties
          Scientiarum Budapestensis de Rolando Eotvos
          Nominatae, Sectio Geographica, Vols. 16-17, pp.
          89-97.

J-440.   Proctor, Nigel.   1984.   "Geography and the Common
          Curriculum," Geography, Vol. 69, pp. 38-47.

J-441.   Prunty, Merle C. Jr.   1966.   "What 'Concepts' and
          What 'Sequences'?" Journal of Geography, Vol. 65,
          pp. 300-301.

J-442.   Putnam, R. G.   1967.   "Geography in Canadian
          Secondary Schools," Canadian Geographer, Vol. 11,
          pp. 230-234.

J-443.   Ramsey, E. E.   1911-1912.   "Physical Geography in
          High Schools," School Science and Mathematics,
          Vol. 11, pp. 838-848; Vol. 12, pp. 45-54, 114-125.

J-444.   Ramsay, James A.   1913.   "The Use of Place-Names
          in the Teaching of Geography," Scottish
          Geographical Magazine, Vol. 29, pp. 429-432.

J-445.   Rechlin, Alice Merten.   1962.   "High School
          Geography and the College Admissions Officer,"
          Journal of Geography, Vol. 61, pp. 193-195.

J-446.   Reclus, M. Elisee.   1901.   "The Teaching of
          Geography," Scottish Geographical Magazine, Vol.
          17, pp. 393-399.

J-447.   Redway, Jacques W.   1904.   "Final Results in the
          Study of Geography," Journal of Geography, Vol. 3,
          pp. 447-450.

J-448.   Redway, Jacques.   1908.   "Getting at the
         Essentials in Geography Teaching," Education,
         Vol. 29, pp. 65-75.

J-449.   Relph, Edward, 1974. "Graduate Education in
         Geography: A Critique and a Proposal,"
         Professional Geographer, Vol. 26, pp. 4-8.

J-450.   Renner, G. T. 1930. "The Geography Curriculum,"
         Journal of Geography, Vol. 29, pp. 344-352.

J-451.   Renner, G. T. 1931. "The Introductory Geography
         Course in Science," Journal of Geography, Vol. 30,
         pp. 33-38.

J-452.   Renner, G. T. and Keith, J. W. 1953. "We are
         Overlooking Geography," National Education
         Association Journal, Vol. 42, pp. 436-437.

J-453.   Renner, Magme Pratt. 1926. "Geography as a Care
         Subject for the Curriculum," Journal of
         Geography, Vol. 25, pp. 72-75.

J-454.   Reynolds, Joan Berenice. 1904. "The Regional
         Method of Teaching Geography," Geographical
         Teacher, Vol. 2, pp. 224-228.

J-455.   Richason, Benjamin. 1951. "Geography in the
         Junior Colleges of the United States," Journal of
         Geography, Vol. 50, pp. 246-256.

J-456.   Ridgley, Douglas C. 1923. "Geography for Rural
         Schools," Journal of Geography, Vol. 22, pp.
         108-113.

J-457.   Ridgley, Douglas C. 1926. "The Necessity of
         Accurate Knowledge About Places," Journal of
         Geography, Vol. 25, pp. 169-175.

J-458.   Ridgley, Douglas C. 1929. "Two New Courses of
         Study in Geography," Journal of Geography, Vol.
         28, pp. 318-326.

J-459.   Ridgley, Douglas C. 1931. "Junior High School
         Geography," Journal of Geography, Vol. 30, pp.
         232-234.

J-460.   Ridgley, Douglas and James, Preston E. 1924.
         "Geographic Principles and Their Application to
         the Teaching of Geography," Journal of Geography,
         Vol. 23, pp. 136-141.

J-461.   Roberts, Raymond H. 1957. "How Textbooks
         Influence the Curriculum in Geography," Journal of
         Geography, Vol. 57, pp. 250-256.

J-462.   Robinson, J. Lewis. 1966. "The Need for Urban
          Geography in Our High Schools," Journal of
          Geography, Vol. 65, pp. 236-240.

J-463.   Robinson, J. Lewis. 1967. "Trends in Geography
          in Canadian Universities," B. C. Geographical
          Series, No. 8, pp. 47-56.

J-464.   Rooper, T. G. 1901. "Methods of Teaching
          Geography," Geographical Teacher, Vol. 1, pp.
          4-10.

J-465.   Rosen, Sydney. 1957. "A Short History of High
          School Geography, Journal of Geography, Vol. 56,
          pp. 405-413.

J-466.   Rumble, Heber Eliot. 1943. "Morse's School
          Geographies: An Eighteenth- Century Science
          Textbook Series Used at the Junior-High-School
          Level," Journal of Geography, Vol. 42, pp.
          174-180.

J-467.   Rusk, R. C. 1906. "Imagination in Teaching
          Geography," Geographical Teacher, Vol. 3, pp.
          239-243.

J-468.   Ryabchiicov, A. M. 1961. "The Can on Higher
          Education and the Problems of University
          Geography," Soviet Geography: Review and
          Translation, Vol. 2, No. 8, pp. 3-18.

J-469.   Salisbury, Rollin D. 1909. "The Teaching of
          Geography - A Criticism and Suggestion," Journal
          of Geography, Vol. 8, pp. 49-55.

J-470.   Salisbury, Rollin D. 1910. "Physiography in the
          High School," Journal of Geography, Vol. 9, pp.
          57-64.

J-471.   Salter, Christopher L. 1976. "Geography in the
          K-12 Curriculum: Where to Locate It and How to
          Get It There," California Geographer, Vol. 16, pp.
          63-84.

J-472.   Salter, Christopher L. 1977. "Learning Through
          Landscape," California Geographer, Vol. 17, pp.
          1-10.

J-473.   Salter, Christopher L. 1983. "What Geographers
          See," Journal of Geography, Vol. 82, pp. 50-53.

J-474.   Salter, Christopher L. 1986. "Geography and
          California's Educational Reform: One Approach to
          a Common Cause," Annals of the Association of
          American Geographers, Vol. 76, pp. 5-16.

J-475.   Salter, Christopher.   1986.   "Response to Stultz's
          Enhancing High School Geography," _Professional
          Geographer_, Vol. 38, p. 72.

J-476.   Salter, C.   1986.   "Geography and Curricular
          Reform," _Focus_, Vol. 36, pp. 32-33.

J-477.   Sauer, Carl O.   1918.   "The Condition of Geography
          in The High School and Its Opportunity," _Journal
          of Geography_, Vol. 16, pp. 143-147.

J-478.   Saveland, Robert N.   1958.   "How the Curriculum
          Influences Textbooks in Geography," _Journal of
          Geography_, Vol. 57, pp. 242-249.

J-479.   Scarfe, N. V.   1948.   "School Geography," _New
          Zealand Geographer_, Vol. 4, pp. 183-188.

J-480.   Scarfe, N. V.   1955.   "The Teaching of Geography
          in Canada," _Canadian Geographer_, No. 5, pp. 1-8.

J-481.   Scarfe, N. V.   1964.   "Geography as an Autonomous
          Discipline in the School Curriculum," _Canadian
          Geographer_, Vol. 8, pp. 45-50.

J-482.   Scarfe, N. V.   1965.   "Depth and Breadth in School
          Geography," _Journal of Geography_, Vol. 64, pp.
          153-158.

J-483.   Scarfe, Neville V.   1959.   "Geography Across the
          Curriculum," _Journal of Geography_, Vol. 58, pp.
          111-121.

J-484.   Scarfe, Neville V.   1964.   "Geography as an
          Autonomous Discipline in the School Curriculum,"
          Journal of Geography, Vol. 63, pp. 297-301.

J-485.   Schlesinger, A. M. et al.   1923.   "Tentative
          Formulations of (1) the Purpose of the Social
          Studies in the Schools and (2) the Distinctive
          Contribution of Each Field of Study," _Journal of
          Geography_, Vol. 22, pp. 75-79.

J-486.   Schmieder, Allen G.   1969.   "Some Trends and Their
          Implications for Geographic Education," _Journal of
          Geography_, Vol. 68, pp. 208-215.

J-487.   Scott, Ralph C.   1984.   "Trends in Introductory
          Physical Geography College Textbooks," _Journal of
          Geography_, Vol. 83, pp. 269-272.

J-488.   Sellors, Richard Pickering.   1913.   "Geography.
          The Courses of Instruction in the Schools of New
          South Wales," _Proceedings - Tenth International
          Geographical Congress_, pp. 1479-1498.

J-489.   Semple, Ellen Churchill.   1904.   "Emphasis Upon
          Anthropo-Geography in Schools," Journal of
          Geography, Vol. 3, pp. 366-374.

J-490.   Semple, Ellen Churchill.   1904.   "Emphasis Upon
          Anthropogeography in School," Proceedings - Eighth
          International Geographical Congress, pp. 657-663.

J-491.   Sewell, W. R. Derrick and Mitchell, Bruce.   1984.
          "Geographers, The Policy Process and Education,"
          Operational Geographer, No. 5, pp. 23-28.

J-492.   Shaw, Earl B.   1958.   "Forces Contributing to
          Changes in Geographic Education," Journal of
          Geography, Vol. 57, pp. 55-63.

J-493.   Shaw, Earl B.   1960.   "Changing Geography,"
          Professional Geographer, Vol. 12, No. 6, pp.
          11-13.

J-494.   Silberbach, J. H.   1889.   "On the Teaching of
          Elementary Commercial Geography in Primary and
          Secondary Schools, and in a Minor Degree of
          Elementary Technical Instruction," Journal of the
          Manchester Geographical Society, Vol. 5, pp.
          151-172.

J-495.   Simon, David.   1987.   "UGC, IBG and the Future of
          Geography in British Higher Education," Area, Vol.
          19, pp. 355-358.

J-496.   Slater, F.   1979.   "A Strategy for Determining
          Objectives in Curriculum Construction in
          Geography," Geographical Viewpoint, Vol. 8, pp.
          5-16.

J-497.   Slater, F. and Spicer, B.   1979.   "Towards an
          Expanded Model of Curriculum Development and
          Diffusion in Education," Geoforum, Vol. 10, pp.
          243-250.

J-498.   Slater, Francis.   1987.   "Optical Analysis:
          Prisms in Geographic Thought and the Geography
          Teacher," New Zealand Journal of Geography, No.
          83, pp. 8-11.

J-499.   Smart, Alice M.   1956.   "The Use of Geography in
          Educational Planning," Proceedings - Eighteenth
          International Geographical Congress, pp. 598-602.

J-500.   Smith, Guy-Harold.   1961.   "Geography Teaching
          Loads in American Universities," Professional
          Geographer, Vol. 13, No. 3, pp. 11-16.

J-501.   Smith, J. Russell.   1906.   "The Place of Economic
          Geography in Education," Bulletin of the American
          Geographical Society of New York, Vol. 38, pp.
          108-111.

J-502.   Smith, J. Russell. 1924. "Geography and the
         Higher Citizenship," Progressive Education, Vol.
         1, pp. 77-80.

J-503.   Smith, J. Russell. 1925. "Geographic Mythology
         as Evidenced by the Facts and Prevailing Teaching
         About Tropical Agriculture," Annals of the
         Association of American Geographers, Vol. 15, pp.
         43-44.

J-504.   Smith, James H. 1918. "Geography in the Junior
         High School," Journal of Geography, Vol. 16, pp.
         188-189.

J-505.   Smith, Keith. 1983. "Training in Physical
         Geography: the NERC Connection," Area, Vol. 15,
         pp. 289-293.

J-506.   Smith, Peter R. 1987. "Geographical Education in
         Schools: The Continuing Debate," Area, Vol. 19,
         pp. 255-256.

J-507.   Smith, S. 1981. "The School Numbers Debate - Are
         Geographers Losing the Numbers Game?" Geography
         Bulletin, Vol. 13, pp. 93-100.

J-508.   Smith, Susan J. 1984. "Practicing Humanistic
         Geography," Annals of the Association of American
         Geographers, Vol. 74, pp. 353-374.

J-509.   Smith, T. Alford. 1908. "Physical Geography as
         an Essential Part of School Geography,"
         Geographical Teacher, Vol. 4, pp. 221-229.

J-510.   Smith, Villa B. 1945. "High School Geography and
         Geographic Thinking," Journal of Geography, Vol.
         44, pp. 232-238.

J-511.   Smith, Warren D. 1917. "Some Aspects of the
         Study of Geography with Suggestions for Its
         Promotion," Journal of Geography, Vol. 16, pp.
         103-107.

J-512.   Snook, Ivan. 1987. "Shaping a Curriculum," New
         Zealand Journal of Geography, No. 84, pp. 11-15.

J-513.   Solomon, R. J. 1965. "Ourselves as Others See
         Us: An Antipodean View," Professional Geographer,
         Vol. 17, No. 1, pp. 7-10.

J-514.   Solov'yer, A. I. 1965. "The Present State and
         Tasks of Higher Geography Education," Soviet
         Geography: Review and Translation, Vol. 6, pp.
         28-46.

J-515.   Solov'yeva, M. G.   1961.   "The Training of Broadly
         Qualified [Geography-Biology] Teachers in
         Pedagogic Institutes," <u>Soviet</u> <u>Geography</u>:   <u>Review</u>
         <u>and</u> <u>Translation</u>, Vol. 2, No. 9, pp. 3-20.

J-516.   Soons, Jane M.   1987.   "Geography: Cultural or
         Physical?" <u>New</u> <u>Zealand</u> <u>Journal</u> <u>of</u> <u>Geography</u>, No.
         84, pp. 8-11.

J-517.   Sorensen, Clarence Woodrow.   1959.   "The Direction
         of High School Geography," <u>Journal</u> <u>of</u> <u>Geography</u>,
         Vol. 58, pp. 89-92.

J-518.   Soulsby, Eve M.   1976.   "Innovation in Scottish
         School Geography," <u>Geographical</u> <u>Viewpoint</u>, Vol. 5,
         pp. 48-59.

J-519.   Spetz, Dennis L.   1986.   "Strengthening Geography
         in Kentucky," <u>Professional</u> <u>Geographer</u>, Vol. 38,
         pp. 256-257.

J-520.   Stanescu, M. and Popescu, A.   1975.   "Geography in
         School," <u>Geoforum</u>, Vol. 6, pp. 74-76.

J-521.   Stanley, Raymond W.   1960.   "The Role of Geography
         in General Education," <u>California</u> <u>Geographer</u>, Vol.
         1, pp. 29-34.

J-522.   Stark, Mabel C.   1922.   "Some Suggestions for
         Needed Lines of Emphasis in Normal School
         Geography," <u>Journal</u> <u>of</u> <u>Geography</u>, Vol. 21, pp.
         245-253.

J-523.   Stark, Mabel C.   1923.   "Teaching Value of
         Geographic Regions," <u>Journal</u> <u>of</u> <u>Geography</u>, Vol.
         22, pp. 81-86.

J-524.   Stephenson, O. W.   1945.   "Still More Geography in
         the Schools," <u>Journal</u> <u>of</u> <u>Geography</u>, Vol. 44, pp.
         1-11.

J-525.   Stiles, D.   1943.   "Why Not Teach Geography?"
         <u>Harper's</u>, Vol. 186, pp. 626-632.

J-526.   Stoltman, Joseph P.   1986.   "The Michigan
         Experience in Geographical Education,"
         <u>Professional</u> <u>Geographer</u>, Vol. 38, pp. 73-74.

J-527.   Sturgeon, M. K.   1887.   "The Teaching of
         Elementary Geography - A Practical Lesson with
         Models," <u>Journal</u> <u>of</u> <u>the</u> <u>Manchester</u> <u>Geographical</u>
         <u>Society</u>, Vol. 3, pp. 85-91.

J-528.   Stutz, Frederick P.   1985.   "Enhancing High School
         Geography at the Local Level," <u>Professional</u>
         <u>Geographer</u>, Vol. 37, pp. 391-395.

J-529.   Sukhwal, Bheru. 1984. "Geography in Indian
         Secondary Schools," National Geographical Journal
         of India, Vol. 30, pp. 223-230.

J-530.   Surface, G. T. 1907. "Geography in the High
         School," Journal of Geography, Vol. 6, pp.
         348-354.

J-531.   Swain, George W. Jr. 1963. "The Role of College
         and University Geography Departments in Improving
         the Teaching and Course Content of High-School
         Geography," Journal of Geography, Vol. 62, pp.
         339-352.

J-532.   Swartz, David J. 1933. "Concerning the Revision
         of Courses of Study in Geography," Journal of
         Geography, Vol. 32, pp. 329-334.

J-533.   Symonds, Clare. 1925. "High School Geography,"
         Journal of Geography, Vol. 24, pp. 314-323.

J-534.   Symonds, Clare. 1929. "Geography in High
         Schools," Journal of Geography, Vol. 28, pp.
         25-29.

J-535.   Szekely, Beatrice Bench, ed. 1987. "The New
         Soviet Secondary School Geography Curriculum:
         Editor's Introduction," Soviet Geography: Review
         and Translation, Vol. 29, pp. 3-9 [entire volume
         pp. 3-99].

J-536.   Tang, Jianzhang, et al. 1983. "Geography in
         Higher Education in China," Journal of Geography
         in Higher Education, Vol. 7, pp. 77-84.

J-537.   Teggart, Frederick J. 1919. "Human Geography and
         the University, An Opportunity for the
         University," Journal of Geography, Vol. 18, pp.
         142-148.

J-538.   Thomas, Benjamin E. 1949. "College Geography in
         the Rocky Mountain States," Journal of Geography,
         Vol. 48, pp. 160-170.

J-539.   Thomas, Frank H. 1952. "Economically Distressed
         Areas and the Role of the Academic Geographer,"
         Professional Geographer, Vol. 14, No. 2, pp.
         12-16.

J-540.   Thomas, Oline J. 1917. "The Development and
         Present Organization of Elementary School
         Geography in the United States," Journal of
         Geography, Vol. 15, pp. 213-220.

J-541.   Thomas, Helen Goss. 1920. "How Shall We Teach
         Geography?" Journal of Geography, Vol. 19, pp.
         250-255.

J-542.   Thomas, Lewis F.   1950.   "An Appraisal of Teaching
          Geography at the   College, University and Graduate
          School Level," Journal of Geography, Vol. 49, pp.
          133-140.

J-543.   Thompson, Keith W.   1961.   "An Assessment of
          Graduate Schools of Geography in the United States
          of America," Australian Geographer, Vol. 8, pp.
          138-139.

J-544.   Thralls, Zoe A.   1929.   "Qualifications Requisite
          for Teaching Geography," Journal of Geography,
          Vol. 28, pp. 244-252.

J-545.   Thralls, Zoe A.   1932.   "Criteria for the
          Selection and Organization of Subject Matter in
          Geography," Journal of Geography, Vol. 31, pp.
          324-330.

J-546.   Thralls, Zoe A.   1933.   "The Program Proposed for
          the Elementary School," Journal of Geography, Vol.
          32, pp. 139-141.

J-547.   Tomkins, G. S. and Hardwick, F. C.   1963.
          "Current Trends in School Geography with Special
          Reference to the Responsibility of the
          Professional Geographer and Some Comments on the
          Training of Geography Teachers," Canadian
          Geographer, No. 4, pp. 89-103.

J-548.   Trimble, Stanley W.   1986.   "Declining Student
          Performance in College Geography and the
          Down-Writing of Texts," Professional Geographer,
          Vol. 38, pp. 270-273.

J-549.   Trudgill, Stephen T.   1977.   "Environmental
          Sciences/Studies: Depth and Breadth in the
          Curriculum," Area, Vol. 9, pp. 266-269.

J-550.   Uchida, Kan-ichi.   1952.   "Present-day Geography
          Education in Japan," Proceedings - Seventeenth
          International Geographical Congress," pp. 709-712.

J-551.   UNESCO.   1951.   The Teaching of Geography - and
          International Understanding, Australian
          Geographer, No. 9, pp. 250-253.

J-552.   Vaniria, Louis M.   1959.   "Geography Associations
          and the Teacher," Journal of Geography, Vol. 58,
          pp. 238-243.

J-553.   Vogeler, Ingolf.   1977.   "Dialectic Teaching in
          Geography," Journal of Geography, Vol. 76, pp.
          257-261.

J-554.   Vol'f, M. B. et al. 1976. "Geography Education
         in the U.S.S.R. and Ways of Improving It," Soviet
         Geography: Review and Translation, Vol. 17, pp.
         581-593.

J-555.   Von Engeln, O. D. 1912. "Emil Von Sydon and the
         Development of German School Cartography,"
         Bulletin of the American Geographical Society,
         Vol. 44, pp. 846-848.

J-556.   Wadley, David. 1983. "Postgraduate Education and
         Thesis Writing in Australian Geography: A
         Critique," Australian Geographical Studies, Vol.
         21, pp. 109-120.

J-557.   Wahlquist, Wayne L. 1986. "The Utah Success
         Story [in High School Geography]," Professional
         Geographer, Vol. 38, pp. 253-254.

J-558.   Walford, Rex. 1982. "British School Geography in
         the 1980s: An Easy Test?" Journal of Geography in
         Higher Education, Vol. 6, pp. 151-160.

J-559.   Walford, Rex. 1986. "Finding Grenada on the
         Map," Area, Vol. 18, pp. 56-57.

J-560.   Walford, Rex and Williams, Michael. 1985.
         "Geography and the School Curriculum: The Recent
         Role of the Geographical Association," Area, Vol.
         17, pp. 317-321.

J-561.   Walker, I. L. 1966. "Geography As Invention,"
         Senior Scholastic [teacher edition], Vol. 89, Sup.
         8, October 14.

J-562.   Wallis, B. C. 1915. "Geography in Schools: A
         Reply [to Chisholm]," Scottish Geographical
         Magazine, Vol. 31, pp. 542-546.

J-563.   Warman, Henry J. 1952. "A Survey of the Research
         in Geographic Education," Journal of Geography,
         Vol. 51, pp. 309-322.

J-564.   Warman, Henry J. 1958. "Changing Emphases in
         Geographic Education," Journal of Geography, Vol.
         57, pp. 219-228.

J-565.   Warman, Henry J. 1963. "The Care of Geography
         Education," Journal of Geography, Vol. 62, pp.
         289-296.

J-566.   Warman, Henry J. 1965. "Geography Teaching and
         the Structure of the Discipline," Journal of
         Geography, Vol. 64, pp. 197-201.

J-567.   Warman, Henry J. 1966. "Geographsheds," Journal
         of Geography, Vol. 65, pp. 408-409.

J-568.   Warman, Henry J.   1968.   "Geography in the
         Elementary Schools of the   United States," Journal
         of Geography, Vol. 67, pp. 262-273.

J-569.   Warman, Henry J.   1970.   "Perpetual
         Transformation: A Concept of Change and Choice,"
         Journal of Geography, Vol. 69, pp. 531-538.

J-570.   Warren, Col. Sir C.   1887.   "Address on
         Geographical Education," Journal of the Manchester
         Geographical Society, Vol. 3, pp. 259-273.

J-571.   Waterman, S.   1979.   "Developments in Geographic
         Education in Israel," Geographical Viewpoint,
         Vol. 8, pp. 60-66.

J-572.   Watson, C.   1969.   "This Geography is Something to
         Sing About," American Education, Vol. 5, pp.
         14-18.

J-573.   Watson, J. Wreford.   1962.   "Geography and History
         Versus 'Social   Studies,'" Journal of Geography,
         Vol. 61, pp. 125-129.

J-574.   Webb, Robert M.   1972.   "Place Location in
         Geographic Education: Anathema or Exigency,"
         Ecumene, Vol. 4, pp. 18-21.

J-575.   Webber, M. J.   1980.   "Literature for Teaching
         Quantitative Geography: Technique By, For, But Not
         of Geographers," Environment and Planning A, Vol.
         12, pp. 1083-1090.

J-576.   Wessinger, Esther.   1918.   "The Value of Place
         Geography in a Commercial Geography Course,"
         Journal of Geography, Vol. 17, pp. 162-163.

J-577.   Whipple, G.   1941.   "Human Geography: From Slogan
         to Actuality," Elementary School Journal, Vol. 41,
         pp. 337-346.

J-578.   Whitaker, J. R.   1943.   "The Place of Geography in
         the Social Stuides: From the Viewpoint of
         Conservation Education," Journal of Geography,
         Vol. 42, pp. 12-21.

J-579.   Whitaker, J. Russell.   1951.   "Conservation and
         the College Professor," Memorandum Folio of the
         Southeastern Association of American Geographers,
         Vol. 2, pp. 1-6.

J-580.   Whitbeck, R. H.   1910.   "Where Shall We Lay the
         Emphasis in Teaching Geography?" Education, Vol.
         31, pp. 108-116.

J-581.   Whitbeck, R. H.   1912.   "Suggested Modifications
         in High School   Geography," Journal of Geography,
         Vol. 10, pp. 184-189.

J-582.   Whitbeck, R. H.   1913.   "Commercial Geography as a
          Secondary School Study," Journal of Geography,
          Vol. 11, pp. 49-55.

J-583.   Whitbeck, R. H.   1914.   "Geography in City High
          Schools," Journal of Geography, Vol. 13, pp. 1-8.

J-584.   Whitbeck, R. H.   1914.   "What Shall School
          Geography Include?" Journal of Geography, Vol. 12,
          pp. 344-345.

J-585.   Whitbeck, R. H.   1915.   "An Important Movement in
          Geography," Journal of Geography, Vol. 13, pp.
          270-273.

J-586.   Whitbeck, R. H.   1915.   "Ideals and Aims in
          Elementary Geography," Journal of Geography, Vol.
          14, pp. 65-70.

J-587.   Whitbeck, R. H.   1916.   "One Urgent Need in the
          Field of Educational Geography," Annals of the
          Association of American Geographers, Vol. 6, pp.
          132.

J-588.   Whitbeck, R. H.   1922.   "The Journal in the Field
          of Education," Journal of Geography, Vol. 21, pp.
          7-11.

J-589.   Whitbeck, Ray Hughs.   1916.   "The Aims and Work of
          the National Council of Geography Teachers,"
          Journal of Geography, Vol. 15, pp. 53-57.

J-590.   Whitbeck, Ray Hughs.   1918.   "Geography Teachers,"
          Journal of Geography, Vol. 17, pp. 107-110.

J-591.   White, Andrew D.   1918.   "College Students'
          Ignorance of Geography in 1857," Journal of
          Geography, Vol. 16, pp. 355-356.

J-592.   White, C. Langdon and Williams, Joseph E.   1945.
          "Will Geography Be a Core Subject in the Post-War
          Secondary School Curriculum? Journal of
          Geography, Vol. 44, pp. 11-16.

J-593.   Whitehand, J. W. R.   1973.   "Radicalism and
          Conservatism in University Courses," Area, Vol.
          5, pp. 193-199.

J-594.   Whitehouse, Wallace E.   1918.   "Geographical
          Teaching Methods: Criticisms and Suggestions,"
          Scottish Geographical Magazine, Vol. 34, pp.
          321-330.

J-595.   Whitney, Rev. J. P.   1886.   "The Place of
          Historical Geography in Higher Education," Journal
          of the Manchester Geographical Society, Vol. 2,
          pp. 106-107.

J-596.   Whomsley, John P.   1984.   "Who Trains Teachers and
          For What?" Geography, Vol. 69, pp. 56-61.

J-597.   Wilhelm, E. J. Jr.   1968.   "The Role of
          Biogeography in Education," Journal of Geography,
          Vol. 67, pp. 526-529.

J-598.   Wilhelm, Eugene J., Jr.   1972.   "Geography and
          Enviromental Education in Virginia," Virginia
          Geographer, Vol. 7, pp. 17-19.

J-599.   Williams, Michael and Catling, Simon.   1985.
          "Geography in Primary Education," Geography, Vol.
          70, pp. 243-245.

J-600.   Willmer, J. E.   1962.   "Geography and Education in
          the Secondary School - Some Comments," Bulletin -
          Ghana Geographical Association, Vol. 7, No. 1-2,
          pp. 3-13.

J-601.   Willmer, J. E.   1966.   "A Plea for a New
          Interpretation of Geography in Education,"
          Nigerian Geographical Journal, Vol. 9, pp.
          155-162.

J-602.   Wilson, Leonard S.   1948.   "Geographic Training
          for the Postwar World: A Proposal," Geographical
          Review, Vol. 38, pp. 575-589.

J-603.   Wilson, Leonard S.   1948.   "The Position of
          Regional Geography in Current Liberal Arts
          Education," Journal of Geography, Vol. 47, pp.
          141-150.

J-604.   Wilson, Martha.   1925.   "Our Geographical
          Ignorance," Education, Vol. 45, pp. 547-549.

J-605.   Winslow, Isaac O.   1904.   "The Scope of Geography
          for Elementary Schools," Proceedings - Eighth
          International Geographical Congress, pp.
          1030-1033.

J-606.   Winslow, Isaac O.   1904.   "What Should Graduates
          from Elementary Schools Know About Geography,"
          Journal of Geography, Vol. 3, pp. 458-462.

J-607.   Winsted, Huldah L.   1912.   "Geography in American
          Universities," Journal of Geography, Vol. 10, pp.
          309-316.

J-608.   Wise, M. J.   1975.   "A University Teacher of
          Geography," Transactions - Institute of British
          Geographers, No. 66, pp. 1-16.

J-609.   Wise, M. J.   1986.   "The Scott Keltie Report,
          1885, and the Teaching of Geography in Great
          Britain," Geographical Journal, Vol. 152, pp.
          367-382.

J-610.   Wolforth, John. 1986. "School Geography - Alive
         and Well in Canada?" Annals of the Association of
         American Geographers, Vol. 76, pp. 17-24.

J-611.   Woodring, Paul. 1984. "Geography's Place in
         Basic Education," Journal of Geography, Vol. 83,
         pp. 143-144.

J-612.   Wooldridge, S. W. 1947. "Geographical Science in
         Education," Geographical Journal, Vol. 109, pp.
         198-207.

J-613.   Wooldridge, S. W. 1950. "Reflections on Regional
         Geography in Teaching and Research," Transactions
         and Papers - Institute of British Geographers, No.
         16, pp. 1-12.

J-614.   Worley, Lillian. 1950. "The Geographer's
         Contribution to Education for Resource
         Management," Annals of the Association of American
         Geographers, Vol. 40, pp. 131-132.

J-615.   Worth, C. 1982. "Cartography and Portsmouth
         Polytechnic," South Hampshire Geographer, Vol. 14,
         pp. 2-7.

J-616.   Young, Ann. 1983. "Post-Graduate Education,"
         Australian Geographical Studies, Vol. 21, pp.
         296-297.

J-617.   Yunns, M. 1952. "Post-Graduate Teaching in
         Indian Universities," Geographer, Vol. 5, No. 1,
         pp. 44-50, No. 2, pp. 48-52.

J-618.   Zobel, Herbert L. 1961. "High School Geography
         Textbooks (1918-1941) and Their Relationship to
         Classroom Instruction," Journal of Geography, Vol.
         60, pp. 416-420.

Author Index

Aay, H. F-1
Abbe, C. B-1, H-1
Abler, R. A-1, A-2
Abler, R. F. F-2, G-1
Abrahams, P. P. D-1
Achmatowicz-Otok, A. D-481
Ackerman, E. A. A-3, A-4,
  B-2, C-1, F-3, F-4, G-2
Adams, C. C. B-3, E-1, H-2,
  G-3, G-4
Adams, J. S. A-2, C-2, F-5,
  I-1
Adams, P. G. A-5
Adams-Reilly, A. A-373
Adejuyigbe, O. D-2, J-1
Adrian, C. D-3, H-3, H-4
Afable, P. G. G-5
Afolabi, O. D-4
Agafonov, N. T. C-3, C-4,
  D-5, D-6, H-5, H-6, H-7,
  H-527
Agnew, J. A. A-396, C-5,
  F-6, F-7
Ahmad, G. M. F-9
Ahmad, H. A. D-185
Ahmad, K. S. D-7, F-10,
  I-2
Ahmad, N. A-6, D-11
Ahmad, S. M. D-8, D-9
Ahmah, A. F-8
Ahmed, H. A. J-171

Ahnert, F. D-12, F-11, F-12
Ahsan, S. R. D-13, J-2
Aiken, C. S. B-4, B-5
Aitchinson, A. E. H-8
Aiyar, T. S. S. F-13
Akande, M. D. G-6
Akhtar, R. D-14
Al'Amiri, S. S. A. H-9
Al'Brut, M. I. E-2, H-13,
  H-14, H-15, H-16
Alpert, H. G-7
Al'tman, L. P. D-21, H-19
Alampiyev, P. M. D-16
Alan, J. A. H-17
Alao, N. D-17
Alampiyer, P. M. H-10,
  H-11, H-12
Alavi, S. M. Z. A-7
Alcaraz, A. P. D-18
Alcock, F. I. D-19, H-18
Alexander, J. W. C-6, E-3,
  F-14
Alexander, L. M. B-6
Alexandravskaya, O. A. B-7,
  B-8, B-9, B-10
Ali, S. M. D-20
Allan, D. A. B-11, B-12
Allan, J. A. E-4, E-5
Allen, A. M. J-3
Allen, L. R. C-7, F-15
Alley, J. H-266

Allix, A.   F-16
Alpert, H.   C-8
Alston, A. H. G.   B-13
Altengarten, J.   F-17
Altengarten, J. S.   A-8
Al-Amiri, S. S. A.   D-15
Amad, K. S.   F-18
Amadeo, D.   A-9, E-88, E-91,
   F-386
Amadev, N. S.   F-19
Anderson, A. G.   D-22
Anderson, A. W.   C-10
Anderson, E.   E-56, G-148
Anderson, E. W.   B-14
Anderson, J.   B-17, F-20,
   F-21, H-20
Anderson, J. H.   B-15, F-23
Anderson, J. R.   B-16, C-9,
   F-24, G-8, I-3
Anderson, James   F-22
Anderson, R. C.   J-4
Anderson, S. A.   H-21
Anderson, T. D.   A-325
Andrews, A. C.   G-9, G-10
Andrews, D. J.   G-11
Andrews, H. F.   B-18, B-19,
   D-23, D-24, F-25, J-5
Angel, S.   E-6, F-26
Annenkov, V. V.   D-25, G-12
Annette, M.   D-26
Anokhin, A. A.   G-13, H-22,
Anonymous C-11, B-20, B-21,
   B-22, B-23, B-24, B-25,
   B-26, B-27, B-28, B-29,
   B-30, B-31, B-33, B-34,
   B-35, B-36, B-37, B-38,
   B-39, B-40, B-41, B-42,
   B-43, B-44, B-45, B-46,
   B-47, B-48, B-49, B-50,
   B-51, B-52, B-53, B-54,
   B-55, B-56, B-57, B-58,
   B-59, D-27, D-28, D-29,
   D-30, D-31, D-32, D-33,
   D-34, D-35, D-36, D-37,
   D-38, D-39, D-40, D-41,
   D-42, D-43, D-44, D-45,
   D-46, D-47, D-48, D-49,
   D-50, D-51, E-7, E-8, E-9,
   F-27, F-28, F-29, F-30,
   F-31, F-32, F-33, F-34,
   F-35, F-36, F-37, F-38,
   F-39, F-40, F-41, F-42,

   G-14, G-15, G-16, G-17,
   G-18, G-19, G-20, G-21,
   G-22, G-23, G-24, G-25,
   G-26, G-27, G-28, G-29,
   G-30, G-31, G-32, G-33,
   G-34, G-35, G-36, G-37,
   G-38, G-39, G-40, G-41,
   G-42, I-4, I-5, J-6, J-7,
   J-8, J-9, J-10, J-11,
   J-12, J-13, J-14, J-15,
   J-16, J-17, J-18, J-19,
   J-20, J-21, J-22, J-23,
   J-24, J-25, J-26, J-27,
   J-28, J-29
Anrick, C. J.   G-43
Anstey, R. L.   B-60
Antonini, G.   D-52
Antonora, I. F.   D-53, D-54,
   H-35
Anuchin, V. A.   A-11, E-10,
   F-43, F-44, F-45, F-46,
   F-47, F-48, G-44
Applebaum, W.   E-11, I-6,
   I-7, I-8
Appleton, J.   A-12, C-12,
   H-36
Appleton, J. B.   I-9, I-10
Archer, J. C.   E-12, H-37
Armand, A. D.   E-13
Armand, D. L.   F-49
Armitage, E.   H-38, J-30,
   J-31, J-32
Armstrong, P.   B-61
Armstrong, T. H.   J-33
Aschmann, H.   C-13, J-34,
   J-35
Asheim, B. T.   D-55, F-50,
   H-39
Ashworth, G. J.   H-40
Asley, W. B.   G-45
Atkinson, E.   J-36
Atwood, R. S.   J-37
Atwood, W. W.   B-62, F-52,
   G-46, G-47, G-48, G-49,
   H-41, J-38, J-39, J-40,
   J-41
Auakumovic, I.   A-443
Auble, P.   B-63
Augelli, J. P.   F-53, G-50,
   H-42
Aujac, G.   B-64
Aurousseau, M.   B-65, H-43

Avosyuk, G. A.   C-14
Babcock, W. H.   A-13
Baber, Z.   F-54, F-55, J-42
Babicz, J.   B-66, B-67, B-68
Bachelet, C. E.   B-87
Back, C. D. J.   F-56
Bacon, P.   A-14
Bacon, H. P.   J-43
Badcock, B.   B-69
Bagchi, I.   G-51
Bagchi, K.   D-56, F-57,
   F-58, J-44
Bagchi, K. G.   I-11
Bagdasaryan, A. B.   D-57
Bagley, W. C.   J-45
Bagrow, L.   A-15, A-16
Bahrin, T. S.   B-70
Bailey, P.   G-52, J-47, J-48
Bailly, A. S.   D-58, F-59,
   G-53, H-44
Baker, A. R. H.   A-17, A-18,
   D-59, F-60, F-61, H-45,
   H-46, H-47, H-48
Baker, A. R. W.   B-71
Baker, D.   F-62
Baker, E. V.   I-12
Baker, J.   B-72, B-73, D-60
Baker, J. N. L.   A-19, B-74,
   B-75, B-76, D-61, F-63
Baker, M.   D-62, D-63
Baker, P. R.   H-49
Baker, O. E.   B-77
Baker, S. J. K.   B-78
Baker, V. R.   H-50, H-51
Bakis, H.   H-52
Bako, E.   D-64, H-53
Balbour, K. M.   H-54
Balchin, W.   A-20
Balchin, W. G. V.   B-79,
   F-64, G-54
Bale, J.   A-21
Bale, J. R.   F-65, H-55
Balfour, H.   F-66, F-67
Ball, J.   A-22
Ball, J. M.   J-49
Ballas, D. J.   H-56, H-57
Baranskiy, N. N.   F-68, J-50
Barber, D.   F-346
Barbier, B.   H-58
Barbour, G. B.   B-80, F-69
Barbour, K. M.   D-65, D-66
Barker, D.   G-55

Barker, S. M.   A-410
Barker, W. H.   D-67, H-59,
   J-51
Barnes, A. E.   A-23
Barnes, C. C.   J-52
Barnes, C. P.   B-81, B-82
Barnes, H. E.   F-71
Barnes, T.   F-72, H-60
Barns, B. A.   F-70
Baron, P.   D-312, H-451
Barr, B. M.   B-83, D-68
Barr, W.   G-56
Barrows, H. H.   A-24, F-73,
   J-53, J-54
Bartholomew, J.   B-85, D-69,
   E-14
Bartholomew, J. G.   B-84,
   G-57
Bartlett, R. A.   A-25
Barton, B.   F-74
Barton, T. F.   B-86, G-58,
   I-13, J-55
Bascom, J.   H-61
Bassin, M.   D-70
Basu, A. N.   D-71, J-56
Baugh, R. E.   D-72
Baulig, H.   B-88
Baumann, D. D.   C-152
Bayer, J. M.   D-489
Beaner, S. H.   G-59
Beard, D. P.   G-60
Beasley, C. R.   F-75
Beaujeu-Garnier, J.   A-26
Beaumont, J.   E-15, G-61
Beaver, S. H.   G-62, G-63
Beavon, K. S. O.   D-73
Beazly, C. R.   A-27, A-28
Beck, A. D.   G-64
Beck, C. W.   F-76
Beck, H.   A-29, B-89
Beck, R. C.   I-14
Becker, B. K.   D-74
Becker, C.   D-75
Beckinsale, R. P.   A-92,
   B-90, B-91, H-145
Beckman, Martin   A-30
Bederman, S. H.   B-92
Beel, M.   F-27
Beesley, K.   H-62
Beguin, H.   E-16
Begvin, H.   F-78
Bein, F. L.   G-65

Beishlag, G.   G-66
Bell, A. M.   J-57
Bell, W. S.   J-58
Bellotti, H.   J-59
Belov, M. I.   H-63
Bengston, N. A.   G-67, J-60,
    J-61
Bennett, C. F. Jr.   H-64,
    H-65
Bennett, D.   H-66
Bennett, R.   G-68
Bennett, R. J.   A-31, A-449,
    D-76, E-17
Bennetts, T.   J-62
Bentham, G.   G-69
Benthien, B.   H-67
Berdoulag, V.   A-32, B-93,
    B-94, F-79
Berg, L. L.   A-33
Bergen, J. V.   G-70, J-63
Bergsten, K. E.   B-95, B-96
Bergstrom, R. C.   C-15
Berkner, L. V.   F-80
Berman, M.   B-97, B-98,
    G-71, G-72
Bernard, F. E.   F-1053
Berry, B. J. L.   A-34, A-35,
    A-36, A-37, A-38, B-99,
    E-18, E-19, E-20, E-21,
    G-73, G-74, H-69, H-70,
    I-15, I-16
Berry, W. J.   F-86
Beukema, H.   D-77
Beyer, R.   B-100
Beyers, W. B.   E-22
Bhattacharyya, A.   F-87
Biddle, D. S.   J-64
Billinge, M.   H-71
Billings, M.   A-17, A-39,
    F-88
Binatarto, R.   H-72
Bingham, E.   J-65
Binney, M.   A-279
Birch, W.   G-75
Bird, C.   J-66
Bird, J.   E-23, E-24, F-89,
    F-90, F-92, G-76, J-67
Bird, J. H.   B-101, B-102,
    F-93, F-94
Birkenhauer, J. A. C.   B-103
Birtles, T. G.   G-77
Bishop, A.   F-95

Bishop, A. L.   D-78, G-78
Bishop, G.   G-79, G-80
Bisson, J.   B-104
Black, L. D.   B-105, D-79,
    D-581
Black, R. B.   B-106
Bladen, W. H.   A-41
Blades, M.   C-158
Blakemore, M.   E-25
Blakemore, M. J.   H-73
Bland, F. A.   F-97
Blant, J. M.   E-26, E-27,
    F-98, F-99, F-100, F-101,
    F-102, F-103, F-104, F-105
Blaut, J. M.   G-81, H-75
Bleasdale, S.   G-82
Block, R. H.   B-107, B-108
Blomfield, C. J.   J-68
Blouet, B. W.   A-42, A-43,
    A-44, B-109, B-110
Blowers, A. T.   F-106, G-83
Blunden, J. R.   B-111, C-16
Blyn, G.   H-76
Board, C.   A-45, H-77
Boardman, D.   A-46, J-69
Boardman, P.   A-47
Boardman, S. J.   A-48
Boas, F.   F-107
Boateng, E. A.   F-108
Boddy, M.   H-339
Bodman, A. R.   G-84
Boehm, R. G.   G-85, J-70
Boesch, H.   F-109
Boggs, S. W.   A-49, C-17,
    C-18, D-80, G-86
Bohland, J.   H-78, J-71
Bollinger, C. J.   B-112
Bolshakov, V. D.   D-81
Bombay Society   G-87
Bond, A. R.   A-321
Bone, R. M.   D-82
Bonwer, K.   C-20
Boots, B. N.   E-28
Borchert, J. G.   D-83, H-79
Borchert, J. R.   E-29,
    F-110, G-88, H-80, J-72
Bose, N. K.   C-19
Bosque-Sendra, J.   D-84,
    H-81
Bosse, D.   B-113
Botting, D.   A-50
Bowden, M. J.   A-277

Bowden, M. N. J.   B-114
Bowen, E. G.   B-115, B-116,
   D-85, F-112, G-89
Bowen, M.   A-51, C-21
Bowen, M. J.   B-117, E-30
Bowie, I. J. S.   D-86
Bowie, W.   E-31
Bowlby, S.   F-113, G-90,
   G-91, J-375
Bowler, I. R.   H-82
Bowman, I.   A-52, A-53,
   B-118, B-119, B-120,
   F-114, F-115, F-116,
   F-117, F-118, G-92, I-17
Boyce, R. R.   B-121, E-32
Brack, E. V.   G-367
Bradshaw, M.   H-83
Bradshaw, M. J.   G-93
Bramwell, A.   J-73
Branom, M. E.   C-22, F-119
Breitbart, M. M.   G-95
Bremer, H.   D-87
Brenchley, D. L.   C-165
Brereton, C.   J-74
Brewer, J. G.   A-54
Brian, J. L. B.   F-81, F-82,
   F-83, F-84, F-85
Bridges, R. C.   B-122,
   B-123, G-96
Briel, E. V.   J-75
Briggs, D. J.   E-33, H-84
Briggs, J.   D-88, G-97
Brigham, A. P.   A-55, B-124,
   B-125, B-126, D-89, G-98,
   G-99, G-100, G-101, J-76,
   J-77, J-78, J-79, J-80
Bringham, A. P.   F-120,
   F-121, F-122, F-123
Britton, R.   H-85
Britton, R. L.   G-102
Broc, N.   B-127, B-128,
   B-129
Brock, E. J.   B-130, H-86
Brock, J. O. M.   B-131
Broek, Jan O. M.   D-305
Broek, J. O. M.   A-56,
   F-503, G-103, H-87, H-88
Bronsky, A.   J-81
Brookfield, H. C.   D-90,
   F-124, F-125, H-89, H-90
Brooks, C. F.   B-132, B-133,
   B-134, C-33, F-127, H-91

Brooks, E.   I-18
Brooks, L.   J-82
Broude, H. W.   G-104
Browett, J.   E-34, F-128,
   F-129, H-92
Brown, E.   A-57
Brown, E. H.   A-58, D-91,
   H-93, H-94, H-95
Brown, L. A.   A-59, A-60,
   A-61, E-89, H-96, H-323
Brown, R. C.   H-97
Brown, R. H.   B-139, J-83
Brown, R. M.   B-136
Brown, R. N. R.   C-130,
   G-105
Brown, S.   H-98
Brown, S. E.   B-137, B-138
Brown, T. N. L.   A-62
Brown, W. G.   C-24
Branom, W. J.   C-25, F-131
Browne, W. R.   B-139
Browne, W. A.   F-132
Browne, J.   A-63
Browning, C. E.   A-64, F-133
Bruce, W. S.   B-141
Bruk, S. I.   D-92, H-99
Bruman, H.   B-142
Brunhes, J.   A-65, F-134,
   F-135
Brunn, S. D.   G-106
Brunsden, D.   A-152
Brunsolen, D.   F-136
Brusa, C.   A-107
Bryan, P. W.   F-137
Bryan, K.   B-143, B-144,
   H-100
Bryan, M. L.   E-35, H-101
Bryant, H. G.   B-145
Bryce, J.   J-84, J-85
Bryce, V.   G-107
Buchanan, R. O.   G-108,
   G-109, J-86
Buchanan, J. Y.   C-26
Bucher, W.   B-146
Budin, M.   H-102, I-56,
   J-273
Bunbury, E. H.   A-66, A-67
Bune, W.   B-147
Bunge, W.   G-110, G-111,
   G-112, G-113, G-114
Bunge, W. W.   A-68, A-69,
   E-36, E-37, F-140, F-141,

F-142, F-143, F-144,
F-145, F-146, F-147,
F-148, F-149, F-150,
F-151, F-152
Bunkse, E. V. B-148
Bunting, T. E. E-38, H-103
Buranelli, V. A-70
Burgess, R. F-153
Burgess, J. A-71, A-181,
C-27
Burghardt, A. H-104
Burghardt, A. F. G-115
Burgy, J. H. B-149
Burke, J. D. J-87
Burley, T. M. H-105
Burmeister, K. H. B-158,
B-159
Burnett, A. H-106
Burnett, A. D. A-72
Burnett, G. W. D-570
Burnett, P. H-107, H-108
Burrill, M. F. F-155,
F-156, F-157
Burrill, M. B-150, B-151
Burton, I. E-39, F-158,
F-159, H-109
Bushong, A. D. B-152,
B-153, B-154, G-116
Butler, G. G-117
Butler, R. W. H-110
Butler, Adam, J. F. H-111
Buttimer, A. A-73, A-74,
A-75, A-76, C-28, F-160,
F-161, F-162, F-163, H-112
Buttner, M. B-67, B-155,
B-156, B-157, B-158,
B-159, B-160, B-161,
F-164, H-113
Butzer, K. W. A-77, B-162,
H-114
Buursink, J. F-165
Byrd, D. V. F-166
Bywater, V. B-163
Cahnman, W. J. F-167
Cain, S. A-78
Calef, W. B-164, E-230
Calkins, R. D. H-115
Calvin, D. D. F-168
Cambis, M. A-79
Campbell, C. K. H-116
Campbell, E. M. J. B-165,
H-181

Campbell, F. D-93, G-118
Campbell, J. B. H-117
Campbell, M. R. F-169
Campbell, R. D. E-40
Campbell, T. B-166
Cantor, L. M. A-80, G-119
Capelle, R. B. F-170
Carchedi, G. F-171
Carey, E. P. C-29
Caris, S. F-172, G-120
Carlson, A. W. H-118,
H-119, H-120
Carlstein, T. A-81
Carney, F. C-30
Carol, H. B-167, D-94,
F-109, F-173
Carpenter, C. C. F-174
Carpenter, F. O. H-121,
H-122, J-88
Carpenter, N. A-82
Carre, F. B-168
Carrega, P. H-123
Carter, F. D-6, D-95
Carter, G. F. B-169, B-170,
F-175, H-124
Carter, R. L. H-125
Carthew, A. G-121, J-89
Casada, J. A. B-171, B-172
Casartelli, L. C. J-90
Caster, H. W. A-15
Castner, H. W. D-97, H-126
Catling, S. J-599
Chakkaborty, S. C. C-31
Chamberlain, J. F. F-176
Chamberlain, T. C. A-83
Chamberland, J. F. J-91,
J-92, J-93, J-94, J-95
Chambers, W. T. H-127
Chandler, T. J. C-32, J-96
Chang, S. D-100, E-239,
F-896, H-128
Chang, C. Y. D-98
Chang, K. D-99
Chao, L. A-96, B-173, D-101
Chapman, A. D. D-102
Chapman, G. G-122
Chapman, G. P. A-84, E-41
Chapman, J. G-123
Chapman, J. D. F-177,
F-178, F-179, H-129,
H-130, H-131
Chapman, R. L. B-94

Chapman, S.   B-174
Chappell, J.   A-85, B-175
Chappell, J. E.   D-101,
   D-104, E-42, F-180, F-181,
   H-132, H-133
Chardon, R. E.   F-182
Charlier, R. H.   D-105,
   D-106, D-107
Charlier, P. S.   D-107
Chatterjee, S. P.   A-86,
   A-87, D-108, F-183, F-184,
   F-185, F-186, H-134, J-97
Chatterjee, S. C.   D-109
Cheng-Siang, C.   H-135
Chernyayeva, F. A.   B-176
Cherry, G. E.   A-88
Chestang, E. L.   J-98
Chester, C. M.   B-177
Chetwoode, P.   B-178, B-179,
   B-180
Chief Directorate   J-99
Chief Directorate of Schools
   D-110
Chien, C. S.   D-111
Chih-hai, H.   G-124
Chisholm, G.   F-188, F-189,
   F-190, H-136, H-137
Chisholm, G. G.   B-181,
   D-112, D-113, D-114,
   D-115, J-100, J-101
Chisholm, M.   A-89, A-90,
   A-91, C-34, C-35, E-43,
   F-191, F-192, G-125,
   H-138, H-139, H-140
Cho, G. C. H.   B-182
Chojnicki, Z.   E-44, E-45,
   F-193, H-141, H-142
Chokor, B. A.   H-143
Chopman, C.   C-33
Chorley, R. J.   A-92, A-93,
   A-94, A-95, B-91, E-46,
   H-144, H-145
Chovinard, V.   F-194, F-195
Chow, C.   B-183
Christensen, K.   F-196
Christensen, D. E.   C-36
Christie, P.   F-197
Chu, K. Y.   D-116
Chu, D. K. Y.   D-575, D-576,
   D-577
Chuanjun, W.   A-96, D-117
Chung, C.   D-682

Chung, Y. P.   D-118
Church, R. J. H.   B-184,
   B-185, D-119, D-120, D-121
Churchill, W.   B-186
Cjang, S.   C-149
Claeson, C. F.   F-198
Clark, A.   F-199, F-200,
   F-201, G-126, J-102
Clark, A. H.   B-187, C-37,
   D-122, H-146
Clark, C.   G-127
Clark, C. G.   F-281
Clark, G.   H-147, H-148,
   H-149
Clark, G. L.   F-202, F-203,
   H-150
Clark, K. G. T.   F-204,
   F-205
Clark, M.   G-128
Clark, N.   D-367
Clark, R.   J-103, J-104
Clark, R. B.   A-98
Clark, W. A. V.   E-32
Clarke, J. I.   A-99, D-123,
   H-151, H-152
Clarke, M.   F-206
Clarkson, J. D.   C-38, E-47
Claval, J. C.   J-105
Claval, P.   A-247, D-124,
   D-125, D-126, E-48, F-207,
   F-208, F-209, F-210,
   F-211, G-129
Clayton, K.   D-127, F-214,
   H-153, H-154, H-155
Clayton, K. M.   F-212,
   F-213, G-130, I-19
Clenerly, P.   H-156
Clerk, G.   G-131, G-132,
   G-133
Cleverly, P.   J-106
Cliff, A. D.   A-100, E-49,
   E-50
Cloke, P. J.   H-158, H-159
Close, C. F.   F-215, F-216,
   F-217, F-218, G-135
Clout, H.   D-129
Coates, B.   G-136, J-107
Coates, D. R.   A-101
Coffey, W. J.   A-102
Cohen, S. B.   A-103, G-137
Colby, C. C.   F-219, G-138
Colby, C. G.   B-188, B-189,

B-190, B-191, B-192
Cole, J. P.   A-104
Coleman, G.   E-51
Colenutt, B.   F-900
Collins, M. F.   H-160
Collinson, A. S.   H-161
Colten, C. E.   H-162
Colter, C.   A-105
Comeaux, M. C.   B-193, B-194
Committee of Fifteen F-220,
  J-108
Committee on Training J-109
Common, R.   I-20, I-21, I-22
Conacher, A. J.   D-130,
  H-163
Conde, S. G.   D-131
Conkling, E. C.   H-164
Conn, H.   J-110
Connell, J.   G-139
Conrad, J.   D-132
Conroy, W. B.   J-111
Conzen, M. P.   H-165, H-166,
  H-167
Cook, E. K.   J-112
Cook, I.   F-374
Cook, J. P.   J-113
Cook, K. L.   B-195
Cooke, R. V.   A-106, D-133,
  F-222
Cooke, P.   F-221
Coones, P.   D-134
Cooper, A. D.   G-140
Cooper, C. E.   J-114
Cooper, S. H.   C-39, F-223,
  I-23
Coppens, L. M.   B-196
Coppock, J. T.   E-52, E-53,
  H-168, H-169, H-170
Corley, N. T.   B-197
Corna-Pellegrini   A-107
Corner, D. J.   D-135, H-171
Corpoz, O. D.   F-224
Cosgrove, D.   F-225, G-141,
  G-142, G-143, G-144
Cosgrove, D. E.   E-54,
  H-172, H-173, H-174, H-175
Costa, J. E.   A-108, H-176,
  H-334
Cotet, P.   B-198
Cottler, J.   A-109
Couclelis, H.   A-183, E-55,
  F-226, F-227, F-228, F-229

Coughlan, R.   B-199
Coull, J. R.   H-177
Coulson, M. R. C.   J-115
Coulter, J. W.   F-230,
  F-231, F-232, J-116
Coulton, R.   D-136
Council, The   B-200
Coves, E.   A-110
Cowen, J. B.   C-40, F-223,
  J-117
Cowie, P. M.   J-118
Cox, K.   C-41
Cox, K. R.   H-178
Cox, N.   E-56, G-148
Cox, P.   G-145, G-146, G-147
Coyne, J.   J-119
Cramer, R. E.   G-149
Crane, A. O.   A-111
Cranston, H. V.   J-120
Crary, D.   E-547
Creary, J. P.   G-150
Cressey, G. B.   A-112,
  B-201, F-234, G-151
Cribin, J. A.   H-179
Crisler, R. M.   B-202
Crist, R. E.   D-137, F-235
Critzner, C.   H-180
Crone, G.   B-203
Crone, G. R.   A-113, A-114,
  A-115, A-116, B-204,
  B-205, B-12, D-184, F-237,
  H-181
Cross, C. I.   G-152
Cross, W. K.   B-206, D-138
Crowe, P. R.   F-238
Crowley, J. M.   H-182
Crush, J.   D-139, H-183
Cuary, D.   H-184
Cucu, V.   D-542, D-543
Cullen, I. G.   H-185
Culling, W. E. H.   F-239
Cullum, G. W.   B-207
Cumberland, K. B.   B-208,
  D-140, F-240, F-241, F-242
Cundall, L. B.   H-186
Cunningham, F. F.   B-209,
  B-210, F-243, J-121
Currey, B.   G-153
Curry, L.   E-58, F-244,
  H-187
Curry, M.   F-72, F-245,
  F-246, F-247, F-248, H-188

Cutshall, A. G-154, I-24
Cutter, S. C. G-155
Cutter, S. L. F-249, I-25
Cuzzort, R. P. A-146
Czekenska, M. D-141
Dagenais, P. D-143
Dainelli, G. B-211
Daish, J. B. G-156
Dakin, W. S. J-122
Dalgleish, W. S. D-144
Dalton, K. G. D-145
Daly, C. P. H-189, H-190
Daly, Chief Justice D-146,
    D-147, D-148, D-149,
    D-150, D-151, D-152
Daniels, P. W. D-153, H-919
Dann, E. W. C-42, F-250,
    F-251, J-123, J-124
Darby, H. C. A-117, A-118,
    C-43, D-154, D-155, F-252,
    F-253, H-191, H-192, H-193
Darby, N. C. G-157
Darinskiy, A. V. J-50,
    J-125, J-126
Darkoh, M. B. K. D-156
Darrah, W. C. A-119
Darroch, A. J-127
Darton, N. H. B-212, B-213
Darwin, C. B-214
Darwin, L. F-254, F-255,
    F-256
Das, H. P. J-128
Das Gupta, S. P. B-215
Dastes, F. D. F-288
Daupaquier, J. A-120
Davey, C. J-174
Davgun, S. K. F-257
David, M. E. A-121
David, T. F-258
Davidson, A. D-157, J-129
Davies, D. H. G-158, H-194
Davies, G. L. H-197
Davies, G. L. H. A-122,
    A-123, B-216, H-195
Davies, J. L. D-314, H-196
Davies, R. J. F-259
Davies, W. K. D. F-260,
    F-736
Davies, W. K. E. A-124
Davis, B. E. G-159
Davis, C. L. D-158
Davis, D. F. G-160

Davis, D. H. E-59
Davis, G. L. D-159
Davis, N. G-227
Davis, R. M. D-160
Davis, W. H. B-217
Davis, W. M. A-125, B-218,
    B-219, B-220, D-161,
    F-261, F-262, F-263,
    F-264, F-265, F-266,
    F-267, F-268, F-269,
    F-270, F-271, F-272,
    G-161, G-162, G-163,
    H-198, J-130, J-131,
    J-132
Davitaya, F. F. D-330
Dawkins, W. B. H-199
Dawson, A. H. J-133
Dawson, G. M. D-162
Day, M. D. F-273, F-274
Daysch, G. H. J. C-44
Da-Dao, L. D-142
de Blij, H. J. F-276
De Bres, K. H-202
de Freetas, C. R. F-277
De Jong, G. A-129
De Souza, A. R. B-227,
    B-228, B-229, B-230, E-60,
    F-280, G-174, G-175
de Terra, H. A-134
De Vorsey, L. B-231, B-232
De Vos, A. H-210
Deacon, R. A-126
Dean, C. B. G-164
Dean, K. G. H-200
Dean, W. G. B-221, B-222,
    G-165
Dear, M. F-203, F-275
Dearden, P. H-201
Deasy, G. G. G-166, G-167,
    G-168
Debenham, F. A-127
Debord, J. A-128
DeBres, K. B-223
Demek, J. H-203
Dement'yev, V. A. D-163
Demko, G. J. B-224, D-25
Dendrinos, D. S. A-130
Denevan, W. M. H-204
Denis, J. A-131, B-225
Dennis, R. H-205, H-206,
    H-207
Derbyshire, E. H-208

Derruau, M.   B-226
Deselincourt, A.   A-132
Deshpande, C. D.   D-164,
   D-165, G-169, J-134
Deskins, D. R.   A-133,
   D-166, G-170, G-171,
   G-172, G-173, G-346, G-413
de Souza, A.   J-135
Dever, G. E. A.   H-209
Devonshire, B.   J-136
Dexter, L. A.   G-322
Dickinson, J. C.   I-26
Dickinson, J. P.   F-281,
   F-283
Dickinson, R. E.   A-135,
   A-136, A-137, A-138,
   A-139, A-140, F-282, H-211
Dicks, D.   A-141
Dickson, H. N.   H-212
Dickson, K. B.   H-213
Diettrich, S.   J-137
Dijkink, G. J. W.   J-138
Dikshit, K.   D-167, F-284
Dikshit, O.   D-168, F-468
Dikshit, R. D.   G-176,
   H-214, H-215
Diller, A.   A-142
Dillion, M. A.   J-139
Dima, N.   D-169, G-177
Dingelstedt, V.   D-170,
   J-140
Dixey, F.   H-216
Dmitrevskiy, Y. D.   F-631,
   H-528
Dobson, J. R.   I-27, I-28
Dodge, R. E.   F-285, J-141,
   J-142, J-13, J-144, J-145,
   J-146, J-147, J-148,
   J-149, J-150, J-151,
   J-152, J-153, J-154,
   J-155, J-156, J-157,
   J-158, J-159
Dodge, Richard E.   B-233,
   B-234
Dodge, Stanley D.   B-235
Dodoo, R.   F-287
Doerr, A. H.   C-46, D-171,
   H-217, H-691
Doherty, J.   D-172, J-160
Dohrs, F. E.   G-178
Dollfus, O.   F-288
Doornkamp, J. C.   D-173,

   H-218
Doran, M. T.   G-179
Dorflinger, J.   B-823
Dorigo, G.   E-61
Doughty, R. W.   F-289, H-219
Douglas, I.   F-290, I-29,
   H-220
Douglas, J. N.   H-221
Dow, M. W.   G-180
Downes, A.   B-236, B-237,
   D-174
Downs, R. M.   E-62, F-291,
   H-222
Doyle, A.   D-175, J-161
Doyle, F. J.   H-224
Drake, C.   D-176, G-181
Draper, D.   A-311, F-735
Drdos, J.   H-225
Driver, F.   F-292
Drummond, R. R.   D-177
Dryer, C. R.   D-178, F-293,
   F-294, G-182, J-163
Duboc, J. L.   J-164
Duff, M. E.   G-183
Duffield, B. S.   D-179,
   H-226
Dugdale, G. S.   B-238, G-184
Duke, B.   H-815
Duke of Argyll   D-47
Dukie, Dusan   B-239
Dumas, W.   D-180
Dunbar, G. S.   A-143, A-144,
   A-145, B-240, B-241,
   B-242, B-243, B-244, C-48,
   D-181, D-182, G-186,
   G-187, G-188, G-189,
   H-227, H-228, H-229,
   J-165
Duncan, S. S.   F-297, F-298,
   H-230, H-340
Duncan, O. D.   A-146, A-220
Duncan, B.   A-146
Duncan, J. S.   C-5, F-7,
   F-295, F-296, F-931
Dunn, A. J.   A-92
Durden, D.   I-30, H-231
Durrenberger, R. W.   A-147
Dury, G. H.   B-245, C-49,
   D-183,   G-190, H-232,
   H-233, H-234
Dwyer, D. J. H-235
Dyck, H.   D-506

Dziewonski, K. E-63, E-64,
  F-299, H-236
Dzik, A. K. H-237
Earl of Ronaldshay G-191,
  G-192, G-193
Earley, A. G-194
Earth Science Committee,
  H-238, J-166
East, W. G. A-148, A-444,
  B-246, G-195, H-239
Eckert, M. H-240
Eder, H. M. G-196
Edington, M. A. A-149
Edington, J. M. A-149
Edmonds, R. L. D-269, H-381
Edmonds, W. J. H-117
Education Committee J-167,
  J-168
Edwards, K. C. D-184
Edwards, K. J. H-241
Ehrenberg, R. B390
Ehrenberger, D. S. C-15
Eichenbaum, J. E-65, F-300
Eisen, E. E. J-169
Elan, W. W. J-170
El-Bushra, E. S. D-185,
  J-171
Elder, P. D. I-31
Eliot-Hurst, M. E. A-150,
  C-50, C-51, H-97, H-242
Elkins, T. H. D-186, D-187,
  H-243, J-172
Ellen, R. C-52
Elliott, H. M. A-151
Elliott, F. E. E-66
Embleton, C. A-152, D-188,
  H-244
Emerson, P. J-173
Emery, F. V. B-247, B-248
Emery, J. S. J-174
Enedy, J. G-197, I-32
Englebert, E. C-53
Entrikin, J. N. B-249,
  B-250, B-251, B-252,
  F-301, F-302, F-303
En-Yong, W. D-101
Epstein, B. J. I-33, H-245,
  J-175
Ericksen, N. J. H-246
Ernst, J. A. F-304, H-247
Erodi, B. D-189
Erskine, J. Y.   D-190,

J-176
Esakov, V. A. B-253, B-254
Estes, J. E. E-67, H-248
Ettema, W. A. H-249
Evans, A. D-371
Evans, I. M. A-153
Evenden, L. J. G-198, H-250
Eyles, J. A-154, A-155,
  A-156, E-68, E-138, F-305,
  F-306, F-307, F-308,
  G-199, H-251, H-252,
  H-253, H-254, H-255
Eyre, J. D. B-255
Fagles, R. A-157
Fahy, G. C-54, D-192,
  J-184, J-185
Fair, T. J. D. I-34, J-177
Fairbanks, H. W. F-309,
  H-256, J-178, J-179, J-180
Fairchild, W. B. B-256,
  B-257, B-258, B-259,
  B-260, G-200, G-201, J-181
Falconer, J. D. H-257
Falick, A. J. H-258
Faniran, A. D-194
Faris, J. T. A-158
Farley, A. L. H-259, I-35
Farmer, B. H. D-195, F-310
Farnham, A. W. J-182
Farrell, B. H. G-202, J-183
Farrell, W. C. E-131,
  F-547, H-260
Farrington, I. E-69
Fayed, Y. D-196
Fealman, J. D. G-203
Fedorovich, B. A. D-197
Fedosseyev, I. A. B-261,
  B-262
Fel, S. Y. D-198, H-261
Felland, N. B-263, B-264
Fellman, J. D. F-311, H-262
Fellmann, J. D. G-312,
  G-313, G-314, J-186
Fenneman, N. M. C-55, C-56,
  F-312, F-313, H-265
Ferguson, A. H-266
Ferrell, E. H. B-265
Feygin, Y. G. H-13
Field, R. T. H-600
Fifer, J. V. F-314, H-267
Finch, V. C. F-315, F-316,
  F-317, H-268, J-187

Fincher, R.   D-199, F-194, F-195, H-269, H-270
Findlay, H. J.   J-188
Fine, B.   J-189
Fink, L. D.   G-204, G-205, G-206, G-207, H-271, J-190, J-191, J-192, J-193
Finke, L. L.   H-272
Firth, C. H.   A-159
Fischer, C.   B-266
Fischer, E.   A-160, D-200, D-201
Fischer, H.   D-202
Fish, O. C.   J-194
Fisher, C. A.   F-318, G-208, H-273
Fisher, W. B.   J-195
Fitzgerald, W.   E-70, F-319
Fitzpatrick, S.   D-203, J-185, J-196, J-197, J-198
Fitzsimmons, M.   F-320
Fleisher, P. J.   A-108
Fletcher, C. R. L.   B-267
Fleure, H. J.   F-321, F-322, F-323, F-324, F-325, G-209
Flowerdew, R.   A-161, D-204, J-198
Flowers, R.   F-326
Floyd, B.   C-57, H-274, H-275, H-276
Floyd, B. N.   D-205, E-71, E-72, F-327, F-328, F-329, F-330, F-331, F-332, F-333, G-210, G-211
Fogelberg, P.   B-268
Fonaroff, L. S.   H-277, H-278
Fonseca, J. W.   G-274
Foord, J.   F-113, G-90, H-279, H-280
Foote, D. C.   H-281
Forbes, D.   D-3, H-5, H-282
Forbes, D. K.   G-212, G-213
Forbes, S. V.   B-269
Ford, D.   F-334
Ford, L.   F-335, F-336
Ford, L. R.   H-283, H-284
Forde, C. C.   G-214
Forde, C. D.   F-337
Forer, P. C.   F-338, G-215, G-216

Foresta, R.   F-339
Fosberg, F. R.   C-58, H-285
Foster, A.   I-36, J-199
Foster, H. D.   H-287, H-288
Foster, L.   G-218, H-286
Foster, L. T.   G-217, I-37, I-38, J-200
Foster, T. S.   J-201
Fotheringham, A. S.   D-206
Foust, B.   J-135
Fox, G. C.   F-340
Fradkin, N. G.   H-289
Francaviglia, R. V.   F-341
Fraser, J. K.   B-270
Frazer, W. J.   G-219
Frazier, J.   A-162
Frazier, J. W.   H-290, H-291, H-292, H-293, H-294, I-39, I-40, I-41
Freedman, T. W.   D-207, D-208, D-209, D-210, D-211
Freedom, G. S.   H-295
Freeman, D. B.   A-163
Freeman, O. W.   F-342, F-343
Freeman, T.   G-220
Freeman, T. W.   A-164, A-165, A-166, A-167, B-271, B-272, B-273, B-274, B-275, B-276, B-277, G-221, G-222, G-223, H-296, J-255
Freestone, R.   B-278
French, R. A.   B-279, D-212, D-213, G-224, H-297
Freshfield, D. W.   J-202, J-203, J-204, J-205, J-206
Frey, A. E.   A-91
Friberg, J. C.   E-73
Frick, M. L.   J-207
Friis, H.   F-334, G-225
Friis, H. R.   A-168, B-280
Frolov, Y. S.   E-74
Fuch, R. J.   H-299
Fuchs, R. J.   B-224, D-214
Fuchs, V.   J-208, J-209
Fuggle, R. F.   D-215
Fuller, G.   G-226, G-227
Fuller, G. D.   B-3, B-281
Fund, A. K.   A-421
Furguson, A.   F-346
Furman, A. V.   F-345
Fuson, R. H.   A-169, G-228,

J-210
Fussell, T. B-282
Fyson, A. G-229
Gabler, R. E. B-283
Gade, D. W. B-284, G-230
Gage, M. B-285
Gaile, G. L. F-346, G-231
Gaile, G. A-170
Gale, N. E-75, F-228, F-347
Gale, S. A-171, E-65, E-76,
E-77, F-300, F-348, F-349,
F-350, F-351, F-352,
F-765, H-300
Gallagher, J. W. B-286
Gallois, L. D-216, J-211
Gamble, C. D-59
Gananathan, V. S. F-353,
G-232, J-212
Gannett, H. F-354
Ganssen, R. H-301
Gardner, D. P. J-214
Gardner, J. F-355
Garfinkel, M. A. J-215
Garland, J. H. J-216
Garner, B. J. H-302, H-303
Garnett, A. D-217, J-217
Garnier, B. J. D-218,
F-356, G-234, I-42
Garofaco, D. G-235
Garrison, W. L. A-172,
A-173, E-78, E-79, F-357,
F-358, G-236
Garnett, A. G-233
Garrett, M. J. J-218,
J-219
Gartner, R. B-287
Gaspar, J. D-219
Gates, N. C. E-80
Gatrell, A. C. A-174, E-81,
E-82, F-359, F-360, F-361,
G-237
Gault, F. B. G-238
Geddes, A. B-288, C-60
Geddes, P. B-289, G-239,
G-240, J-220
Geiger, P. P. D-220
Geikie, J. H-304
Gelfond, L. B-290
Gelyakova, T. M. H-305
Genthe, M. K. B-291, D-221,
F-362, J-221, J-222,
J-223, J-224

Gentille, J. G-241, I-43
George, P. G-242
Georgiou, Z. D-222
Gerald, A. C. G-243
Gerasimov, I. P. A-175,
B-292, D-223, D-224,
D-225, D-226, D-227,
D-228, D-229, D-230,
D-231, D-232, D-233,
D-234, D-235, E-84, F-49,
F-363, F-364, F-365,
G-244, G-245, G-246,
G-247, G-248, G-383,
H-306, H-307, H-308, I-44
Gerenchuk, K. I. F-366,
F-367, G-249
Gerlach, J. G-250, G-251
Gerlack, J. D. D-236
Gersmerhl, P. J. H-309
Gertler, M. S. H-310
Gibbons, A. F. F-962
Gibbs, D. G-252
Giblin, B. B-293
Gibson, E. M. D-237, G-253,
I-45
Gibson, K. D. E-119
Gibson, L. E. F-368, G-254,
J-225
Gier, J. F-369
Giffard, E. O. F-370
Gilbert, A. D-238, F-371
Gilbert, A. H. B-294
Gilbert, E. B-295
Gilbert, E. W. A-176,
A-177, B-296, B-297,
B-298, B-299, F-372,
F-373, H-311, H-312
Gilg, A. W. C-61
Gill, D. F-374
Gill, O. E-85
Gillman, C. F-375, I-46
Gillman, D. C. G-256, G-257
Gillmore, D. G-255, J-185
Gillmore, D. A. D-239,
D-240, D-241, J-226, J-227
Ginkel, H. D-242, D-243
Ginsburg, N. F-376, G-258
Ginsburg, N. S. H-313
Glacken, C. H-314
Glacken, C. J. A-178
Gladkov, N. A. B-300, D-244
Glassner, M. I. C-62, I-47,

I-48

Glick, T. F.   F-377, F-378, F-379, H-315

Glover, T.   A-179

Glowacki, W.   F-380, J-228

Goddard, S.   A-180

Gokhman, V. M.   D-245, D-246, F-381, F-382, H-316

Gold, J. R.   A-71, A-181, B-301, B-302, G-259, H-317, H-318, H-319, H-328, H-329

Goldberg, M. A.   F-383

Goldberger, J.   B-303

Goldenberg, L. A.   H-320

Goldie, G. T.   F-384, G-260, G-261, G-262, G-263

Golledge, R.   F-229

Golledge, R. G.   A-9, A-182, A-183, E-75, E-86, E-87, E-88, E-89, E-90, E-91, F-347, F-385, F-386, F-387, F-388, F-389, F-390, G-264, G-265, H-321, H-322, H-323

Gomes, H.   I-49

Goodchild, M. F.   E-92, F-391, F-392, G-266, G-267, J-229

Goode, J. P.   D-247, E-93, G-268, G-269, H-324, H-325, H-326, J-230

Goode, N. J.   H-327

Goodenough, W.   F-393, G-270, G-271

Goodey, B.   G-272, H-318, H-319, H-328, H-329

Goodridge, J. C.   G-273, H-330

Gopsill, G. H.   A-184

Gorbatsevich, R. A.   H-331

Gordon, G.   J-231

Gordon, M. F.   G-274

Gore, C.   A-185

Gottmann, J.   A-186, B-304, D-248, D-249, H-332

Goudie, A.   A-187

Goudie, A. S.   B-305, B-306, B-307, B-308, F-394

Gould, P.   A-2, A-183, A-188, A-189, D-250, E-94, E-95, E-96, E-97, E-98,

F-395, F-396, F-397, F-398, F-399, G-275, G-276, J-232

Gould, W. T. S.   D-251, J-233

Gouldie, A. S.   D-453

Gourou, P.   B-309

Gourov, P.   G-400

Gouthier, H. L.   E-83

Gowing, D.   B-310

Grace, M.   J-185

Graf, W. L.   H-176, H-333, H-334

Graham, J.   F-402

Graham, E.   F-401

Grano, O.   B-311

Grant, C. J.   D-252

Granzenmuller, K.   J-213

Grassmuck, E.   J-234, J-235

Graves, B. G.   H-335

Graves, N.   A-21, F-403

Graves, N. J.   D-253, G-277, G-278, G-279, G-280, G-281, H-336, H-337, H-338, J-236, J-237, J-238

Gray, A.   D-88

Gray, F.   C-63, F-405, G-282, H-339, H-340, J-239

Gray, M.   H-341

Green, D. G.   G-406

Green, F. H. W.   F-407, G-283

Green, H. L.   H-342

Green, J. L.   J-240

Greene, F. B.   B-312

Greenberg, J.   H-343

Greenough, G. B.   G-284, G-285

Greensberg, D. A.   F-1049

Greenwood, D. R.   J-241

Greenwood, R. H.   H-344

Greer-Wooten, B.   D-58, H-44, H-281, J-242

Gregor, H. F.   D-254, H-345

Gregory, D.   A-18, A-39, D-255, E-99, G-286, H-346

Gregory, D. J.   A-190, A-191

Gregory, J. W.   B-313, D-256

Gregory, K. J.   A-192, H-347, I-50

Gregory, N.   G-287

Gregory, P.   B-314

Gregory, R. A.   J-243
Gregory, S.   A-193, D-257,
    E-100, F-408, G-288,
    G-289, G-290, G-291,
    H-348, H-349, J-244
Gregory, W. M.   J-245, J-246
Gregson, N.   F-409, H-280,
    H-350
Griffen, P.   A-194
Griffin, D. W.   C-64, H-351
Griffin, P. F.   J-247
Griffith, D. A.   A-195,
    E-17, E-101, F-410
Grigg, O.   E-102
Grigg, D.   F-411, H-352
Grigg, D. B.   B-315
Grigoryev, A. A.   E-103,
    F-412
Grimm, F. M.   B-316
Gritzner, C.   H-353, H-354,
    H-355, H-356
Gritzner, C. F.   G-149,
    J-248, J-249
Gross, H. H.   J-250, J-251
Grossman, L.   C-65
Grosvenor, G.   A-196
Grosvenor, G. H.   G-292
Grosvenor, G. M.   G-293,
    G-294, G-295
Grotewald, A.   B-317
Grounds, F. O.   J-252
Gudonyte, M.   D-258
Gueffroy, E. M.   B-318
Guelke, L.   E-38, E-104,
    E-105, F-414, F-415,
    F-416, F-417, F-418,
    F-419, F-420, F-421,
    F-422, F-423, G-296,
    H-103, H-357, H-358
Guelke, L. T.   A-197, A-198
Guerlack, H.   B-319
Guginman, I.   B-320
Guilcher, A.   B-321
Gulley, J. H. M.   H-359
Gulley, J. L. M.   B-322
Gulois, B.   B-323
Gumilev, L. N.   F-424
Gunn, A. M.   J-253
Gurevich, B. L.   E-106,
    F-381
Gustafson, G.   G-197, I-32
Gutierre de MacGregor, M. T.

B-324
Guyot, A.   A-199, A-200
Guzman, L. E.   H-360
Gvozdetskiy, N. A.   H-361
Gwynn, S.   A-201
Haas, W. H.   B-325, F-425,
    J-254
Haase, G.   H-362
Habibur-Ratiman, M.   A-202
Hadjimichalis, C.   F-926
Haegen, H.   D-259
Hagerstrand, T.   D-260,
    E-107, F-426, G-297
Haggett, P.   A-91, A-94,
    A-95, A-203, A-204, A-205,
    E-108, H-363
HaHari, M.   D-261, H-364
Haigh, M. J.   B-301, F-427,
    G-298, I-51, J-255
Haines-Young, R. H.   F-428,
    H-366
Haining, R. P.   E-17
Hajdu, Z.   D-263, H-365
Hajdu, J. B.   D-262
Haken, H.   F-429
Hakylut, R.   A-206
Hale, J. R.   A-207
Hall, A. R.   B-326
Hall, D. H.   A-208
Hall, E. F.   B-327
Hall, P.   G-299, G-300,
    H-367
Hall, R.   F-431, G-301,
    G-302, J-256
Hall, R. B.   A-209, B-328,
    F-430
Hallam, C. A.   I-3
Hallam, A.   A-210
Hallinan, M.   D-264, J-257,
    J-258, J-259
Halliwell, J. O.   A-211
Halperin, W. C.   F-389
Halverson, L. H.   J-260
Hamill, L.   G-303, H-368
Hamilton, J. W.   J-261
Hamilton, W. R.   G-304,
    G-305, G-306
Hammond, E. H.   H-369
Hampton, P.   H-370
Hance, W. A.   B-329
Handey, L. R.   H-371
Hanley, W. S.   B-330

Hans, W. H.   H-372
Hansen, W.   G-307
Hansis, R.   H-373
Hanson, E. P.   A-212
Hanson, R. M.   F-432
Hanson, S.   E-189, F-433,
  F-740, G-308, H-644
Hansson, S.   F-462
Hard, A.   B-331
Hard, G.   H-374
Hardest, D. L.   H-375
Hardwick, F. C.   J-547
Hardwick, W. G.   F-434
Hare, F. K.   D-265, D-266,
  D-267, F-435, F-436,
  F-437, H-376, H-377, I-52
Hare, R.   J-262
Harkema, R. C.   D-268, G-309
Harley, J. B.   B-332, E-109,
  H-73, H-74, H-378
Harnapp, V. R.   H-379
Harney, D.   B-333
Harper, R.   J-263, J-264,
  J-265, J-266, J-267
Harper, R. M.   B-334
Harries, K. D.   F-438
Harris, B.   E-110, F-439,
  F-440, H-380
Harris, C.   F-441
Harris, C. D.   A-213, B-99,
  B-335, B-336, B-337,
  B-338, B-339, D-269,
  D-270, G-310, G-311,
  G-312, G-313, G-314, H-381
Harris, F. D.   G-315
Harris, R. C.   B-340, D-271,
  H-382, H-383
Harris, W. T.   J-268
Harrison, C.   A-408
Harrison, C. M.   H-922
Harrison, J. D.   C-67, C-68,
  F-442, H-384, I-53, I-54
Harrison, I. G.   G-382
Harrison, R. T.   B-463,
  E-165, F-443, F-444,
  F-656, F-658
Harshbarger, R.   D-273
Harshbarger, H.   F-445
Hart, J. F.   A-214, E-111,
  F-446, G-316, G-317,
  G-318, G-319, G-320
Hartman, G. W.   H-385

Hartmann, R.   H-386
Hartshorne, R.   A-215,
  A-216, B-341, B-342,
  B-343, B-344, E-112,
  E-113, I-55, F-447, F-448,
  F-449, F-450, F-451,
  F-452, F-453, F-454,
  F-455, F-456, F-457,
  F-458, H-387, H-388, H-389
Harvey, D.   A-217, A-218,
  F-459, F-460, F-461, H-390
Harvey, M.   A-219
Hasegawa, N.   D-274
Hauer, J.   D-275, H-391
Haughton, S. H.   H-392
Hauser, P. M.   A-220
Hausladen, G.   D-276, G-321,
  H-393
Hawley, A.   A-221, H-394
Hawley, A. J.   B-346
Hawley, C. E.   G-322
Hay, A.   F-463
Hay, A. M.   G-323
Hay, I.   F-464
Hayden, R. S.   C-69
Hayes, E. S.   C-70
Hayward, D. F.   D-277
Healey, R. G.   F-465
Hearn, T. J.   H-483
Heathcote, G. E. A.   D-278
Heathcote, R. L.   D-278
Heawood, E.   E-114
Hecock, R. D.   J-219
Heenan, B.   H-395
Hegen, E. E.   B-347
Heiges, H. E.   G-324, G-325,
  H-844, I-130
Helburn, N.   D-279, F-466,
  G-326
Helgren, D. M.   J-269
Helleiner, F.   J-270
Helleiner, F. M.   G-327
Hellen, J. A.   D-385, F-467,
  H-396, H-554
Hellprin, A.   D-280
Henderson, B.   J-271
Henderson, H.   B-348
Henderson, H. C. K.   G-328
Henkel, W. C.   H-397, J-272
Henry, A. J.   B-349
Henry, N. F.   H-294, I-41,
  I-56, J-273

Henry, J. T.   F-468
Heppell, R. C.   J-274
Hepple, L. W.   H-398, J-275
Hepworth, M. E.   H-399
Herbert, F.   G-329
Herbertson, A. J.   D-281,
   F-469, H-400, I-57, J-276,
   J-277, J-278, J-279,
   J-280, J-281, J-282,
   J-283, J-284, J-285
Herick, C. A.   J-286
Herin, R.   D-282
Herman, T.   B-350, G-330
Herndon, G. M.   B-351
Herrick, C. A.   H-401, H-402
Herrmann, A. M.   B-352
Hescinga, M. W.   D-283
Heske, H.   B-353, D-284,
   H-403
Hewes, L.   B-354, G-331
Hewitt, K.   E-115, F-470
Hewland, J. L.   G-332
Hewlett, E. G.   J-287, J-288
Hey, R. D.   E-116, H-404
Hickox, D. H.   G-333
Hicks, D.   C-71
Higbee, E. C.   I-58
High, J.   J-289
Highsmith, R. M.   I-59
Hight, J.   D-285, H-405
Hill, A. D.   F-471
Hill, A. R.   H-406
Hill, W.   J-290
Hilling, D.   D-286, F-472
Hills, E. H.   G-334
Hills, T. L.   J-291
Hillyer, V. M.   A-222
Hiltner, J.   I-115
Hilton, T. E.   H-407, H-408
Hinderink, J.   F-473
Hines, H. H.   F-474, G-335
Hinks, A. R.   H-409
Hirst, P.   I-60
Hobbs, W. H.   B-355
Hodge, G.   I-61
Hodgkins, A. R.   H-410
Hodgson, H. B.   H-411
Hoekveld, G. A.   H-412
Hoffman, M.   D-385, H-554
Hoffman, P. P.   D-287, G-336
Hogarth, D. G.   F-475, I-62,
   I-63

Hoggart, K.   F-476, H-413
Hoheisel, K.   B-160, B-356,
   B-357, B-358, B-359
Hohnholz, J. H.   F-477
Holcomb, B.   F-478
Holdich, T. H.   F-479,
   G-337, G-338, G-339,
   G-340, H-414, H-415
Holland, P. G.   H-416
Holly, B. P.   A-219
Holmes, D. H.   B-360
Holmes, E. E.   G-341
Holmes, J.   G-342
Holmes, K. L.   B-361
Holtgrieve, D.   B-362
Holt-Jensen, A.   A-223
Hones, G. H.   G-343
Honeybone, R. C.   B-363
Hong, C.   D-288
Hong, Key, Y.   E-117, E-118,
   F-480
Hooson, D.   A-224, B-364,
   D-289, D-290, D-291,
   D-292, D-293, D-294
Hooson, D. J. M.   H-417
Hoover, E. M.   F-481
Hope, G.   H-418
Hornbeck, D.   F-482, H-419
Horne, W. R.   G-344
Horton, J.   D-176, G-181
Horton, F. E.   A-37
Horvath, R. J.   G-346
Hosgood, B.   G-453
Hotles, K.   B-365, I-64
Hotles, R.   B-365, B-366,
   E-120, I-64
House, J. W.   A-225, I-65,
   J-244
Howarth, O. J. R.   A-140,
   A-254, G-345
Howatts, R. J.   E-119
Howe, G. M.   D-295
Hoy, D. R.   D-72, D-296
Hoyle, B. S.   B-368, B-369
Hozayen, S. A. S.   D-297
Hsieh, C. M.   B-370, D-298
Hsu, G. T.   D-299
Hu, C. Y.   B-761, D-300
Hubbard, G. D.   F-483,
   F-484, H-420, J-292,
   J-293, J-294
Huckle, J.   C-73

Huckle, J. F.   J-295, J-296
Hudman, L. E.   F-485, G-347
Hudson, B. J.   B-371
Hudson, G. D.   E-121, G-348,
    H-421
Hudson, J. C.   E-122, F-486,
    F-487
Hudson, R.   F-488
Hufferd, J.   F-489
Huffert, J.   E-123
Huggett, R. J.   F-490
Hultquist, N. B.   E-124,
    G-349
Humphries, W. J.   B-372
Hung, F.   J-297
Hungrin, J. J.   D-52
Hunt, G.   B-373
Hunt, J.   C-74, H-422
Hunter, J. M.   F-491, H-423,
    I-66
Huntington, A. M.   B-374
Huntington, C. C.   F-492,
    F-493, H-424
Huntington, E.   A-226,
    B-375, B-376, B-377, C-75,
    C-76, E-125, F-494, F-495,
    F-496, F-497, F-498,
    F-499, F-500, F-501,
    H-425, J-298
Hutchinson, H. B.   G-350
Hutchinson, L.   H-426
Hutton, J. F.   G-351
Huziner, G. A.   D-302, H-427
Hyde, R.   B-378
Hyland, G.   G-352
Hyman, G. M.   E-6, F-26
Ibn-Batuta   A-227
Ikhavorai, I. A.   D-303,
    D-304
Il'yina, L. N.   H-428
Il'yina, R. P.   C-77
Ilie, I. D.   B-379
Ilyichev, L. F.   F-502
Inamullah, M.   H-429
Inglis, H. R. G.   B-380
Innis, H. A.   D-305, F-503
Inskeep, E. L.   C-78, H-430
Iofa, L. Y.   H-431
Ireland, R. P.   J-299
Ironside, R. G.   E-85
Irwing, H. W.   E-126
Isaac, E.   H-432

Isachenko, A. G.   B-381,
    D-306, D-307, F-504,
    F-505, F-506, F-507,
    H-433, H-434
Isard, W.   A-228, A-229,
    E-127, E-128, E-129,
    F-508, F-509
Ivan, A.   H-435
Iyer, S. S.   C-79, F-510
Jaatinen, S.   B-382
Jackman, A. H.   H-436
Jackowski, A.   H-924
Jackson, E. P.   J-300
Jackson, J. B.   F-511,
    F-512, F-513
Jackson, J. N.   C-80, D-308,
    H-437, H-438
Jackson, J. R.   F-514
Jackson, P.   A-231, E-130,
    F-515, F-516, G-353,
    H-175, H-177, H-439,
    H-440, H-441, H-442, H-443
Jackson, R. H.   H-444
Jackson, S. P.   B-383,
    G-354, G-355, H-445
Jackson, W. A. D.   D-309,
    D-310, F-517, H-446, J-301
Jacobsen, N. K.   B-384
Jacobson, D.   H-447, J-302
Jaffe, H.   A-109
Jahr, A.   D-311, J-303
Jain, D.   B-385
Jakel, R.   B-161, B-386
Jakle, J. A.   A-230, H-448,
    H-449
James, P. E.   A-233, A-234,
    A-235, A-236, A-237,
    B-387, B-388, B-389,
    B-390, F-518, F-519,
    F-520, F-521, F-522,
    F-523, F-524, F-525,
    F-526, F-527, F-528,
    F-529, G-356, G-357,
    G-358, H-450, J-304,
    J-305, J-460
Janu, M.   D-312, H-451
Janelle, D. G.   F-392
Janke, J.   B-391
Jansen, A. C. M.   F-530,
    H-452
Jay, L. J.   B-393, B-394
Jeans, D. N.   D-313, D-314,

F-531, F-532, H-453
Jeffries, E.   C-81, F-533
Jen, M. N.   D-315
Jenkins, A.   H-714
Jenkins, H.   G-359
Jenks, G. F.   H-454, J-306
Jennings, J. N.   F-534,
   G-366
Jensen, J. G.   J-307
Jensen, J. R.   H-455
Jewel, W.   G-361
Jinazali, M.   F-535
Joerg, W. L. G.   B-395,
   B-396, D-316, D-317,
   F-536, H-456
John, B. S.   F-537
Johnson, B. A.   G-362
Johnson, C.   F-538, F-539,
   F-540, F-541
Johnson, D.   B-397, F-542,
   F-543, F-544
Johnson, D. W.   A-238
Johnson, E. R.   H-457
Johnson, H.   A-239
Johnson, H. B.   F-545, F-546
Johnson, H. G.   G-363, G-364
Johnson, J. H.   A-106, D-18,
   E-53, E-131, F-547
Johnson, L.   F-548, F-549,
   G-366
Johnson, L. J.   G-365
Johnson, P. G.   H-458
Johnston, D. F.   A-240
Johnston, H. H.   B-399,
   B-400
Johnston, R. J.   A-241,
   A-242, A-243, A-244,
   A-245, A-246, A-247,
   B-398, C-82, C-83, C-84,
   D-319, D-320, E-132,
   E-133, E-134, E-135,
   E-136, E-137, F-550,
   F-551, F-552, F-553,
   F-554, F-555, F-556,
   F-557, F-558, F-559,
   F-560, F-561, F-562,
   F-563, G-367, G-368,
   G-369, G-370, G-371,
   G-372, H-459, H-460,
   H-461, H-462, H-463,
   H-464, H-465, H-466
Johnston, W. B.   B-401

Jones, C. F.   A-235, D-321,
   G-373
Jones, D. K. C.   A-152,
   H-467
Jones, E.   D-322, E-139,
   F-564, F-565, H-468
Jones, E. L.   G-374
Jones, G. W.   G-375
Jones, H.   A-248, C-85
Jones, J. A. C.   H-177
Jones, K.   G-218, H-286
Jones, K. G.   G-217, I-38,
   J-206
Jones, M.   G-376
Jones, R.   G-377, H-471
Jones, R. L.   H-469, H-470
Jones, S. B.   E-140, F-566,
   F-567, F-568, H-472,
   H-473, J-308
Jones, S. V.   F-569, F-570,
   F-571, F-572
Jones, W. D.   E-141
Jong, W. W.   B-402
Jopling, A.   D-323, H-474
Jordan, T. G.   H-475
Joseph, K.   J-309
Juillard, E.   G-378, J-310
Jumper, S. R.   G-379, G-380,
   G-381, G-382, J-311
Kaatz, M. R.   I-67, J-312
Kadar, L.   D-324
Kalapesi, A. S.   J-313
Kalesnik, S. V.   D-326,
   D-327, D-328, D-329,
   D-330, G-383, H-476, H-477
Kalesnitz, S. V.   J-314,
   J-315
Kalinin, F. P.   D-695
Kalinin, G. P.   G-384
Kalkstein, L. S.   H-600
Kamerling, D. S.   D-287,
   G-336
Karan, P. P.   A-41, B-403
Kariel, H. G.   F-573
Kariya, P.   F-574
Karpinski, L. C.   C-86,
   H-478
Karpov, L. N.   B-404
Kasai, Y.   B-405
Kasperson, R. E.   A-249
Kasperson, R.   F-575
Kataria, M. S.   I-68

Kates, R. W.   F-576, H-479, I-16

Kay, G.   A-250

Kay, J.   G-385, G-386

Keane, J.   A-251

Keane, T.   H-480

Kearns, G.   B-406, H-481, H-482

Kearsley, G. W.   H-483

Keasbey, L. M.   H-484, H-485

Keates, J. S.   H-486

Keatinge, M. W.   J-316

Kedleston, E. C.   G-387, G-388, G-389

Keeler, F. L.   H-487

Keelerman, A.   F-577, H-488

Keely, V.   J-317

Keith, J. A. H.   J-318

Keith, J. W.   J-452

Kekoni, K.   D-331, J-319

Kellner, L.   A-252

Keltie, J. S.   A-253, A-254, A-255, D-332, D-333, G-390, G-391, G-392, G-393, G-394, J-320, J-321, J-322, J-323

Kemp, H. S.   B-407

Kemp, R.   G-395

Kennamer, L. G.   G-396, J-324

Kennedy, B.   F-578

Kenning, H. J.   F-580

Kent, A.   A-256

Kent, R. B.   G-397

Kent, W. A.   H-489, J-325

Kenzer, M. S.   F-579

Kermea, T.   G-398

Kerr, D. P.   H-490

Kersten, E. W.   B-408

Kevning, H. J.   H-491, H-492

Khan, S.   F-582, G-399

Khan, M. A.   F-581

Khvalynskaya, M. S.   H-493, J-326

Kibria, K. F.   F-583

Kiewietdejonge, I. C. J.   B-409

Kilchenmann, A.   E-143, E-144

Kimble, G. H. T.   A-257, B-410, B-411, B-412, F-584, F-585, F-586,
F-587, F-588, F-589, G-400

Kincer, J. B.   D-334, H-494, H-495

Kindle, E. M.   B-413

King, C. A. M.   A-104, B-414

King, L. J.   A-258, E-145, E-146, E-147, E-148, F-590, F-591, F-592, F-593, F-594, H-496

King, Margaret J.   H-57

King, R.   A-259, E-149, F-595

Kinvig, R. H.   F-596

Kipnis, B.   D-335

Kirby, A.   E-150, F-597, H-497, H-498

Kirchwey, C. B.   J-327

Kirk, W.   F-598, F-599, H-499

Kirkby, R.   C-87, D-336

Kirkpatrick, J. B.   E-151, F-600

Kirwan, L. P.   C-88, F-601

Kish, G.   B-415, D-337, F-602, G-402

Kish, G. A.   A-260

Kiss, G.   D-338, H-500

Kissling, C. C.   G-403

Kitts, D. B.   B-416, F-603

Kiuchi, S.   A-262, D-339, H-501

Klee, G. A.   C-89

Klein, C.   G-378, J-310

Klimm, L.   F-604

Kliot, N.   H-502

Knadler, G.   A-263, B-417

Kniffen, F. B.   G-404, H-503

Knight, C. G.   E-152

Knight, D. B.   F-605, F-606

Knight, P.   F-607

Knight, P. G.   G-405, G-406

Knirk, C. F.   H-504

Knopp, L.   F-608, G-407

Knos, D. C.   G-408

Knowlton, D. C.   J-328

Knox, P.   H-505, I-69, I-70

Kochergin, P. G.   D-340, J-329

Koelsch, W. A.   A-264, B-418, B-419, B-420, B-421, B-422, G-409

Koerner, G. E.   F-609

Kohl, H. D-341
Kohn, C. F. A-295, E-153,
  J-330, J-331
Kohn, C. L. D-342
Kolb, A. B-423
Kolesnik, S. Y. E-142
Kollmorgan, W. M. F-610
Kollmorgen, W. M. B-424
Kolosovskiy, N. N. F-611
Komar, I. V. D-343
Kondracki, J. B-425
Kondrat'yev, K. Y. F-412
Konovalenko, V. G. B-426,
  D-344, F-612
Konstantinov, F. V. C-90
Konstantinov, O. A. C-91,
  D-345, D-346, D-347,
  D-348, D-349, F-613,
  F-614, G-410, G-411,
  H-506, H-507, H-508
Kopf, H. M. J-332
Koreshy, K. V. D-350, H-509
Koroscil, P. M. H-510
Kostbade, J. T. F-615,
  F-616, J-333
Kostrowicki, J. D-351,
  D-352, H-511
Koval'skaya, N. Y. C-170,
  D-655
Kovalev, S. A. H-512, H-513
Kovalevskiy, V. P. D-353
Kozolov, V. I. D-92, H-99
Krackover, S. A-388
Krackowizer, A. M. F-617
Kracht, J. B. J-70
Kramer, F. L. B-427, B-428
Krapotkin, P. H-514, H-515,
  J-334
Kraus, H. H-516
Kravath, F. F. A-265
Kriesel, K. M. B-429
Krivolutskiy, A. Y. H-517
Kroenig, L. H-518
Krolzik, U. D. F. B-430
Krone, P. F-618, H-519
Kropotkin, P. F-619
Kropotkin, P. A. F-620,
  F-621
Krout, I. V. B-431
Kruczala, J. F-622
Krumme, G. H-520
Krupenikov, I. A. D-354

Krzysztof, P. E-154
Kuchler, A. W. F-623, F-624
Kuchler, D. A. D-355
Kuhn, M. W. F-688
Kuhu, M. W. C-102
Kuklinski, A. B-432, D-356,
  D-357, D-358
Kumm, H. K. W. D-359
Kundig-Steiner, W. D-360
Kunze, D. B-433, D-361
Kupper, V. I. D-362
Kurath, H. A-266
Kuriyan, G. H-521
La Rocque, A. J. I-71
Laborde, E. D. F-625
Lackey, E. E. F-626
Lacoste, S. G-412
Ladylea, C. A. F-627
Lagarde, L. B-435
LaGory, M. A-267
Laitz, A. L. F-628
Lamey, R. B-436
Landgraf, J. L. C-92
Langdon, K. P. H-522
Lane, B. B-437, D-363
Lanegran, D. A. A-268,
  J-335
Langnas, I. A. A-269
Langton, J. F-629
Lankiewicz, D. F-630
Laponc, J. A. H-523
Lapworth, C. C-93
Larimore, A. E. G-346,
  G-413
Larkham, P. J. G-414
Larkin, R. G-415
Larsen, R. D. C-68, I-54
Latham, G. R. H-817
Latham, J. P. E-155
Lattimore, O. B-438, D-364
Lauria, M. F-608, G-407,
  H-466
Laurie, Prof. J-336
LaValle, P. E-156, G-416,
  H-524
Lavin, S. E-12
Lavrov, S. B. D-246, D-365,
  E-157, F-631, F-632, H-6,
  H-316, H-525, H-526,
  H-527, H-528
Law, B. C. D-366, G-417
Lawless, R. I. D-602

Lawrence, H.   A-153
Laws, K. J.   H-529, J-337
Lawson, D. E.   J-338
Lawton, R.   B-439, F-633,
    F-634, G-418, G-419
Lay, T. J.   H-334
Lazar, M.   B-440
Le Boutillier, T.   B-442
le Lannou, M.   F-638
Lea, D. A. M.   D-367
Leach, B.   F-635, G-420,
    H-530
Leacock, S.   G-421
Learmonth, A. T. A.   B-441,
    D-368, H-531, H-532, H-533
Learmonth, A.   A-270
Lee, A. G.   I-72
Lee, C.   H-534, H-535
Lee, C. F.   D-369, D-370
Lee, D.   D-371
Lee, D. R.   F-636, G-422,
    G-423, G-424, G-425,
    G-426, G-427, J-340
Lee, K. S.   D-372
Lee, R.   C-27, E-68, F-306,
    G-428, J-341, J-342
Lee, W. T.   A-271
Lee, Y.   H-536
Leeming, F.   D-373
LeHeron, R. B.   E-158,
    F-637, G-429, J-339
Leigh, M. D.   G-430
Leighly, J.   A-272, B-443,
    B-444, B-445, B-446,
    B-447, B-448, B-449,
    B-450, D-375, E-159,
    E-160, F-639, G-431,
    H-537, H-538
Leitner, H.   H-539
Lemon, J.   G-432
Lemons, H.   I-73
Leng, K.   D-374, G-433
Lennon, I.   F-640
Lenon, B.   J-343
Lentz, P.   G-434
Leont'yev, N. F.   D-376,
    H-540
Leszczycki, S.   B-451,
    B-453, D-377, F-641
Levin, M. G.   D-92, H-99
Levine, G. J.   H-541
Lewis, E. W.   D-378

Lewis, G. M.   D-379, J-344
Lewis, L. T.   G-435, H-542
Lewis, N. D.   G-226
Lewis, P. W.   F-642
Lewis, Peirce   G-436
Lewis, R. A.   B-453
Lewthwaite, G.   H-543
Lewthwaite, G. R.   F-643,
    F-644
Ley, D.   A-273, A-274,
    F-296, F-645, F-646,
    F-647, F-648, F-649,
    H-545, H-546, H-547
Leykina, K. S.   H-548
Liang, P.   D-380
Libbe, M.   G-437, G-438,
    G-439
Libbee, M.   J-71
Libbey, W. E.   B-454
Libby, W.   B-455
Libee, M.   J-345
Lichtenberger, E.   D-381,
    D-382, E-161, H-549
Lieber, S. R.   E-162
Lier, J.   G-440, G-441
Light, R. V.   B-456, F-650,
    G-442, H-550
Lillywhite, J.   C-94, H-551
Limbird, A.   B-457, D-383,
    F-651, J-346
Lincoln, D.   D-384, F-652
Lindsay, H.   F-653, F-654,
    G-443, G-444
Lineback, N. G.   H-552,
    J-347
Linge, G. J. R.   H-553
Lingstone, D. N.   F-443,
    F-444
Linke, M.   B-458, D-385,
    H-554
Linton, D. L.   B-85, B-459
Lipetz, G. Y.   E-163, H-555
Little, C.   B-460
Little, H. P.   G-445
Livingstone, D. N.   A-275,
    B-461, B-462, B-463, C-95,
    D-386, E-164, E-165,
    F-655, F-656, F-657,
    F-658, G-446
Lloyd, T.   G-447
Lobeck, A. K.   B-464
Lock, C.   C-96, F-660,

H-556, H-557
Lockhead, E. N.   D-387,
  F-659, G-448
Logan, M. I.   H-558
Logan, R. F.   J-348
Logsdon, J. W.   G-449
Lonaroff, L. S.   H-559
Longstaff, T. G.   B-465
Lornell, C.   H-560
Losberg, F. R.   H-561
Lounsbury, J.   G-450, H-562,
  I-75
Lounsbury, J. F.   I-74,
  J-349
Lovell, W. G.   H-563
Lowenthal, D.   A-276, A-277,
  A-278, A-279, B-466,
  B-467, B-468, B-469,
  E-166, F-661, F-662,
  F-663, F-664, G-452
Lowman, J.   H-564
Lowther, G. R.   H-565
Lu, W. B.   D-180
Luchs, R. J.   D-388
Ludermann, H.   D-389, I-76
Ludwig, G. S.   I-77
Luk, S. H.   D-390
Lukerman, F.   C-97, D-391,
  F-665, F-666, F-667,
  F-668, G-452, H-566
Lunden, T.   D-392, H-567
Lundgrew, J. O. J.   D-393,
  H-568
Lutwack, L.   A-280
Lutz, H. F.   D-394
Lyde, L. W.   G-453, J-350
Lydolph, P. E.   H-569
Lynam, E.   A-281, H-570
Lyons, E.   F-669
Lyons, H. G.   G-454
Ma, L. J. C.   D-395
Mabogunje, A. L.   D-396,
  D-397, H-571, J-351
MacAlister, D.   D-398
Macalla, R. J.   G-455
MacDonald, W.   D-399, J-352
MacDonald, J. R.   F-670
Maceachren, A. M.   E-167,
  H-572, H-573
MacGregor, D. R.   B-470
Mackay, J. R.   E-168, E-169,
  E-170, E-171, H-574,

H-575, H-576, H-577, H-578
MacKaye, B.   A-282
Mackenzie, L.   G-456
Mackenzie, S.   F-113, G-90
Mackie, G. B.   J-353
Mackinder, H. J.   D-400,
  D-401, F-671, F-672,
  F-673, F-674, F-675,
  F-676, F-677, G-457,
  G-458, G-459, J-354,
  J-355, J-356, J-357, J-358
MacKinnon, R. D.   E-172
MacLean, K.   B-471
Macomber, F. G.   J-359
Mag, J. A.   B-472
Maier, J.   D-75
Mair, A.   F-678
Makkreel, R.   A-283
Maksakovskii, V. P.   J-360
Makunina, A. A.   C-98, H-579
Malecki, E. J.   D-402,
  H-580, H-581
Malik, R. A.   H-892
Malley, I. M.   D-403
Mallory, W.   A-284
Malmberg, G.   H-582
Manheim, F. J.   B-473
Manion, T.   E-173, F-679
Manning, E. W.   I-78
Manshord, W.   I-79
Manson, G.   A-285, G-460
Manzie, A. A.   F-680
Marantz, H.   E-174, F-681
Marble, D.   A-38
Marble, D. F.   A-172, A-173
Marbut, C. F.   H-583, H-584,
  H-585
Marchand, B.   C-99, E-176,
  E-177, F-682
Marcus, M. G.   D-404, E-178,
  F-683, G-461, G-462,
  H-586, H-587, H-588, I-81,
  J-361
Marcus, R. B.   J-362
Mardin, O.   B-474, H-589
Marinick, A. M.   D-405
Marion, D.   B-475
Mariot, P.   D-406, H-590
Markham, A. H.   A-286
Markham, C. R.   A-287,
  C-100, G-463, G-464,
  G-465, G-466, G-467,

G-468, G-469, G-470,
G-471, G-472, G-473,
G-474, G-475, G-476,
G-477, G-478, G-479,
G-480, G-481
Markov, K. K. B-476, H-591,
H-592, H-593, J-363
Markovin, A. P. D-407,
H-594
Marotz, G. A. G-482, H-595,
I-82
Marschner, F. J. B-477,
E-179, H-596
Marsden, W. E. B-478, B-479
Marsh, A. A-288
Marsh, G. P. A-289
Marshall, A. B-480
Marshalla, S. K. D-408
Marshall-Cornwall, J.
B-481, B-482
Marston, C. E. J-364
Marston, S. A. G-483
Marti-Henneberg, J. B-483,
B-484
Martin, A. F. F-684, F-685
Martin, A. I. B-485
Martin, G. B-491
Martin, G. J. A-234, A-236,
A-237, A-290, A-291,
A-292, B-486, B-487,
B-488, B-489, B-490,
F-529, F-686, G-358,
H-597
Martin, H. C. J-365
Martin, J. E. F-687, H-598
Martin, L. B-492, B-493,
B-494
Martin, M. C. J-366
Martin, R. A-39
Martinson, T. L. G-485
Martis, K. C. J-367
Mason, C. H. C-101
Mason, P. F. C-102, F-688
Massam, B. H-599
Massam, B. H. I-83
Massey, D. A-293
Mather, D. B. F-689
Mather, J. R. H-600
Mather, P. M. H-601
Mathes, F. E. C-103, H-602
Mathes, P. M. E-181
Mathewson, K. B-495

Mathieson, R. S. D-409,
E-180
Matley, I. C-104, D-410
Matley, I. M. B-496, F-690,
F-691
Matore, G. F-692
Matsui, T. F-693
Matznetter, J. B-497
Maury, M. B-498
May, J. H-603, H-604, H-605
May, J. A. A-294, D-411
Mayer, J. D. H-608
Mayer, H. M. A-295, G-486,
H-606, H-607, I-84
Mayergoyz, J. M. H-609
Maze, W. H. D-412, D-413,
J-368
Mazur, E. F-694, H-610
McAdie, A. E-182, F-695
McArthur, J. L. H-611,
H-612
McBain, F. C. A. D-414,
J-369
McBoyle, G. A-296, G-487
McBride, J. J-112
McCarthy, J. J. D-677
McCarty, H. H. E-183,
F-696, F-697, F-698,
H-613, H-614
McCluer, L. J-370, J-371
McColl, R. W. H-615
McConnell, H. A-297
McConnell, J. E. H-616
McConnell, W. R. J-372,
J-373, J-374
McCorkle, B. B-499
McCourt, W. E. F-699
McCune, S. D-415, D-416,
D-417, F-700
McDaniel, R. I-85
McDermott, P. A-298
McDonald, J. R. D-418,
D-419, D-420
McDowell, L. J-375
McGee, T. G. D-421, E-184
McGee, E. R. A-299
McGlashan, N. D. H-617
McHugh, K. E. H-619
McIntire, E. G. D-420
McIntire, W. G. B-500
McIntyre, L. B-501
McKay, D. V. D-423

McKay, I. A. A-300

McKay, J. D-423, D-424

McKim, W. D-426

McKinney, W. M. B-502, C-105

McKnight, T. D-427

McLaughlin, J. F-701

McLellan, A. G. I-86

McLennon, M. H-620

McManis, D. R. B-503

McMillan, E. M. J-376

McMurray, K. C. H-621

McMurry, F. M. J-378

McNee, R. B. B-504, C-106, C-107, C-108, E-185, F-702, F-703, H-622, H-623, J-379

McQueen, A. E. F-704

Meacor, T. H-560

Mead, W. R. B-505, F-900

Meadows, M. E. D-428, H-624

Mears, E. H-625

Medvedkov, Y. V. F-705, H-626, H-627

Meinig, D. W. A-301, B-506, F-706

Meinzer, O. E. H-628

Meir, A. A-387, E-186, F-707, F-708, F-709

Melezin, A. D-429, H-629

Meles, I. J. J-380

Menens, H. F. F-304

Menk, E. J-59

Mensching, H. G. B-507, H-630

Mercer, D. A-302, C-109, F-710, F-711, H-632

Mercier, C. B-266

Meston, L. F-712

Meyen, E. B-508

Meyer, A. H. D-430

Meyer, C. S. J-382

Meyer, H. C. D-431, H-633

Meyer, W. B. B-509

Meynen, E. B-510

Middleton, C. F-713

Middleton, D. B-511

Miernyk, W. H. A-303

Mihailescu, V. B-512, D-432, F-714

Mikesell, M. B-513

Mikesell, M. W. A-304, C-110, C-111, H-634

Mikhaylov, Y. P. D-433, E-187, F-715

Mikos, M. J. B-514, D-434

Mil'kov, F. N. H-635

Mill, H. R. A-305, B-515, C-112, D-435, D-436, F-716, F-717, F-718, F-719, F-720, F-721, F-722

Miller, D. H. B-516, F-723, H-636

Miller, E. W. F-724, F-725

Miller, G. J. F-726, F-727, F-728, J-383, J-384, J-385, J-386

Miller, J. P. D-437, H-637

Miller, J. W. J-387

Miller, M. A-306

Miller, O. M. B-517

Miller, R. B-518, D-438

Miller, V. J-388

Miller, V. P. Jr. H-638

Miller, W. J-389

Miller, W. T. J-390

Mills, W. J. F-729, F-730, F-731, H-639

Mills, H. R. I-87

Milne, A. K. J-174

Milne, K. B-519

Milner I-88

Milojevic, B. D-439, J-391

Minamoto, S. B-520, B-521, D-440

Minghi, J. V. A-249

Mings, R. C. H-707

Minkel, C. W. D-441, D-442

Minshull, R. A-307, A-308

Mints, A. A. D-443, E-188

Mintz, A. A. F-732, F-733, H-640

Mirsky, J. A-309

Misra, H. N. B-522

Misra, R. P. A-310

Misra, A. B. F-734

Mitchel, B. F-735

Mitchell, B. A-296, A-311, J-491

Mitchell, J. B. F-736

Mitchell, J. K. F-737

Mitchell, L. C-113

Mitchell, L. S. F-738, H-641, H-642

H-641, H-642
Mitchell, R. B.   C-114
Mitra, S.   D-444
Mitzman, A.   A-312
Mizvoka, F.   D-445, F-789
Mock, D.   G-218, H-286,
   H-643
Mock, D. R.   I-89
Moles, R.   J-392, J-393
Molyneaux, G. A.   A-8
Momsen, J. H.   D-446, D-447
Momsen, R. P.   D-448
Monbeig, P.   B-523
Monk, J.   D-449, E-189,
   F-740, H-644, J-394, J-395
Monkhouse, F. J.   A-313,
   F-741
Monmonier, M. S.   H-645,
   I-90
Monroe, E.   A-314
Montefiore, A. C.   F-742
Mood, F.   A-315
Moodie, D. W.   H-646, H-647
Mookarjee, S.   F-743, F-744,
   H-648
Moolag, S.   I-91
Moore, E.   D-450, J-396
Moore, E. G.   H-96
Moore, R. K.   A-421
Moore, W. C.   J-397
Morgan, D.   J-192
Morgan, W. B.   C-115, E-190
Morison, S. E.   A-316, A-317
Morley, D.   I-92
Morrill, R.   H-649
Morrill, R. J.   B-524, B-525
Morrill, R. L.   E-191,
   E-192, F-745, F-746,
   F-747, F-748, F-749, I-93
Morris, G.   J-398
Morris, J. A.   H-651, J-401
Morris, J. W.   C-116, E-193,
   F-750, J-399, J-400
Morrison, A. J.   B-526
Morrison, J. L.   H-650
Morrow-Jones, H. A.   J-402
Moscheles, J.   H-652
Mosley, J. G.   C-117
Moss, R. P.   C-115, E-194,
   E-195, F-751, F-752
Mossman, J.   A-318
Moy, K.   G-10

Mowat, C. L.   B-527
Mozgalin, S. E.   H-7
Muehrcke, P. C.   H-653
Mugerauer, R.   F-753
Muir, R.   H-654, H-655
Muir, T. S.   D-451, J-403
Mukerjee, S.   B-528
Muller, J. C.   E-196, H-656
Muller, P. O.   H-657
Mulliner, B. A.   H-658,
   J-404
Mumford, J.   H-659
Munton, R. J.   D-453
Murphey, R.   A-319
Murphy, E. A. C.   H-660,
   J-405
Murphy, R. E.   D-454,
   E-197, F-754, F-755,
   H-661, H-662
Murray, L.   J-406
Murray, M. A.   D-455, H-663
Murray, N.   D-456
Murton, B.   G-226, G-227
Muschett, F. D.   H-666
Musk, L. F.   H-667, H-668,
   H-669, H-670, H-671
Mvrzayev, E. M.   B-529,
   B-530, D-457, D-458,
   H-664, H-665
Myklebost, H.   B-531
Nader, G. A.   H-672
Nag, B. B.   J-408
Nailiang, W.   A-96
Najdu, J. G.   D-508, H-738
Nakand, T.   F-756
Nardy, J. P.   B-532
Nash, P.   C-118
National   Academy   of
Sciences, A-320
Natoli, S.   J-409
Natoli, S. J.   A-321
Naughton, P. W.   I-94
Nedelco, E.   B-533
Neft, D. S.   A-322
Nesterov, A. I.   D-459
Newbigin, M. I.   D-460,
   F-757
Newcomb, R. M.   B-534, H-673
Newman, J. L.   E-198
Newman, O.   A-323
Newman, R. P.   B-535
Newson, L.   H-674

Neyfakh, A. M.   H-675
Neyfokh, A. M.   F-758
Nichols, D. A.   G-235
Nicholson, N. L.   D-461,
  D-462
Nickerson, M. G.   F-759
Nicod, J.   B-536
Nientied, P.   H-676
Nikishoov, M. I.   D-463,
  H-677
Nikitin, N. P.   D-464, H-678
Nilsson, P.   H-582
Nimigeanu, G.   B-537
Nishioba, H.   D-465
Nobis, H. M.   B-67
Noble, A. G.   D-395
Nogami, M.   D-479, H-695
Noh, T.   A-209, D-466
Nolan, E. J.   B-538
Nolan, M. O.   C-119, J-410,
  J-411, J-412
Noltze, R. H.   B-539
Nordstrom, K. F.   E-199,
  H-679, H-680
Norton, W.   A-324, F-760,
  H-681, H-682, H-683, H-684
Norton, W. H.   C-120
Norwine, J.   A-325
Nowak, W. S.   C-121, C-122
Nozawa, H.   A-326, F-970
Nunley, R. E.   D-467, E-200
Nunn, P.   B-541, H-685
Nunn, G. E.   B-540
Nuttall, S. E.   J-413
Nystuen, J. D.   E-201
O'Brien, D.   C-57, F-333,
  H-274
O'Dell, A. C.   C-44
O'Keefe, P.   E-246, F-763,
  F-919
O'Laughlin, J.   I-149
O'Loufhlin, J.   H-688,
  H-689, H-690, H-891
O'Riordan, T.   C-126
O'Sullivan, P.   A-329
Obenbrugge, J.   D-468, H-686
Oboli, H. O. N.   J-414
Ocitti, J. P.   D-469, J-415
O'Flynn, G.   J-416
Ogden, P. E.   C-123
Ogg, F. A.   F-761
Ogilvie, A. G.   B-542,

  C-124, F-761, H-687, J-417
Ogilvie, F. G.   D-470, J-418
Ogundana, B.   D-471
Ojo, G. J. A.   D-472, D-473,
  J-419
Okunrotifa, P. O.   D-474,
  D-475, D-476, J-420,
  J-421, J-422
Oldham, R. D.   F-764
Oliver, R.   A-327
Olivera, L.   J-423
Olson, J. A.   C-125
Olson, R. E.   D-477, H-691
Olsson, G.   A-171, A-189,
  F-765
Olumide, A. O.   J-424
Olwig, K.   B-543, B-544
Oman, C.   D-478, H-692
O'Malley, M. P.   J-425
Onokerhoraye, A. G.   A-328
Openshaw, S.   E-202
Orata, P. T.   F-766
Orchard, J. E.   J-426
Ord, J. K.   A-100
Ord, K.   E-50
Orford, E. J.   J-427, J-428
Orme, A. R.   F-767, H-693
Ormeling, F. J.   B-545,
  B-546
Orton, W.   H-694
Osterhard, H. J.   F-768
Ota, Y.   D-479, H-695
Otalenko, M. A.   D-500,
  J-436
Otok, S.   D-480, D-481,
  H-696
Ottens, H. F. L.   D-482,
  H-697
Oughton, M.   B-547
Overton, D. J. B.   F-769
Overton, J. D.   E-203, H-698
Owen, E. E.   F-770
Owens, I. F.   F-338, G-216
Paasi, A.   B-548, H-699
Pacione, M.   A-331
Paddock, M. H.   F-771,
  H-700, J-429
Padgett, H. R.   H-701
Page, R. W.   F-773
Page, J. L.   B-549
Paine, A. D. M.   H-702
Pal, S. K.   H-703

Pal'gov, N. N.   D-197
Pallot, J.   D-483
Palm, R.   A-268, F-774
Pansa, G.   B-55
Papageorgiou, G. J.   F-772
Papy, L.   B-551, B-552,
   D-484
Parker, A. J.   H-886
Parker, E. P.   J-430
Parker, F. W.   C-127
Parker, G.   A-332, D-485,
   H-704
Parker, I.   B-553
Parker, W. H.   A-333, B-299
Parkes, D.   A-81
Parkins, A. E.   J-431
Parks, G. B.   A-334, A-335
Parry, J. T.   D-486, H-705
Parson, R. L.   C-128
Parsons, J. J.   B-554,
   B-555, C-129, F-775
Parten, J.   B-614, H-763
Partsch, J.   D-487
Pastoureau, M.   B-556
Pasqualetli, M. J.   H-706
Paterson, J. L.   A-336
Paterson, J. H.   D-488,
   F-776
Patmore, J. A.   F-777
Patrick, A. L.   B-557
Pattanayak, D. P.   D-489
Patten, J. H. C.   F-778
Pattison, W.   E-204
Pattison, W. D.   B-558,
   F-780, J-432
Pattison, W. P.   B-559
Pattmore, J. A.   H-160
Patton, D. J.   B-560
Patton, O. C.   F-781, I-95
Peake, L.   J-433
Pearce, D. G.   H-58, H-707
Pearcy, G. E.   B-561, H-708
Peattie, R.   A-337, A-338,
   A-339, C-130, F-782, J-434
Pederson, L. R.   B-562
Pedrini, L.   D-490, H-709
Peel, R. F.   B-563
Peet, J. R.   A-340, F-783,
   F-784, F-785, F-786,
   F-787, F-788, H-710
Peet, R.   B-564, D-491,
   E-205, E-206, E-207, E-208

Pellegrini, G. C.   D-492,
   H-711
Peltier, L. C.   H-712
Penck, A.   H-713
Penrose, B.   A-341
Pepper, D.   H-714
Perkins, W. L.   F-789
Perpillion, A.   D-493
Perrett, M. E.   D-494
Perry, A.   F-790
Petch, J. R.   H-366
Peterman, W. A.   B-565
Pethybridge, R.   D-495
Peucker,   B-566
Pfeifer, G.   A-342, B-567
Philips, P. D.   F-791
Phillips, M.   D-496
Phillips, M. V.   B-568,
   H-715
Philo, C.   F-292
Phlipponnenau, M.   H-716
Pickles, J.   A-343
Pico, R.   I-96
Piersma, A.   F-1028
Piggott, C. A.   D-497, H-717
Pike, R. J.   E-209, F-792
Pinchemel, P.   F-793
Pinkerton, J.   A-344
Pinkney, D. G.   J-435
Pipkin, J.   A-267
Pipkin, J. S.   A-345
Pirie, G. H.   D-498
Pithawalla, M. B.   D-499,
   H-718
Pitte, J. R.   B-569
Pitts, F. R.   E-210, H-719
Pitty, A. F.   A-346
Piveteau, J. L.   F-794
Plakhotnik, A. F.   F-795
Platt, R. R.   H-720
Platt, R. S.   A-347, B-570,
   E-211, F-797, F-798,
   F-799, F-800, F-801
Pleat, H.   F-802
Pletnikov, Y. K.   F-796
Pleva, E. G.   B-571
Plewe, E.   B-572, B-573
Pocock, D.   F-803, F-804,
   F-805
Pocock, D. C. D.   A-348,
   C-131, E-212
Podanchuk, V. D.   D-500,

J-436
Podolyau, V. Y.   H-721
Poiiac Pollock, N. C.   H-722
Poiker, T. K.   H-723, H-724,
   J-437
Poikwe, R. K.   W-213
Pokshishevskiy, V. V.
   C-132, D-501, D-502,
   D-503, D-504, F-806,
   F-807, H-513, H-548,
   H-725, H-726, H-727,
   H-728, H-729, H-730, H-731
Polizzi, N. T.   D-505
Polo, M.   A-349
Polyan, P. M.   F-808, H-732
Poole, S. P.   I-97, I-98
Popescu, A.   J-520
Popovici, I.   B-574
Popp, N.   B-575, B-576
Porritt, J.   A-350
Porteous, D.   D-506
Porteous, J. D.   F-809
Porter, P. W.   B-577, E-214,
   F-810, F-811, H-733
Porter, R. S.   B-578
Portman, A.   F-812
Portugali, J.   C-133
Potter, S. R.   B-579
Pouliot, D. F.   F-760
Powell, J.   A-302, D-423,
   D-424
Powell, J. M.   B-580, B-581,
   B-582, B-583, B-584,
   B-585, B-586, B-587,
   B-588, B-589, B-590,
   D-507, F-813, J-438
Prasad, H.   F-814
Pratt, G.   F-648
Pratts, J. D.   H-298
Pravada, J.   H-734
Pred, A.   A-36, B-591,
   E-215, E-216, F-815,
   F-816, F-817, F-818,
   F-989, H-872
Preobrazhenskiy, V. S.
   E-157, E-188, F-49, F-632,
   F-732, F-819, H-735, H-736
Prescott, J. R. V.   D-508,
   H-737, H-738
Preston, D. A.   F-820
Preston, D. F.   D-509
Preston-Whyte, R. A.   F-821

Price, E. T.   F-822
Price, R. J.   H-739
Prince, H.   H-740
Prince, H. C.   F-823, F-824
Pringle, T. R.   H-298
Probald, F.   J-439
Probold, F.   D-510
Proctor, N.   B-592, J-440
Prudden, H.   B-593
Pruitt, A. M.   C-134
Pruitt, E. L.   B-594
Prunty, M. C.   D-511, J-441
Pryde, P. R.   F-825, H-741
Pulle, F. L.   D-512
Pulyarki, F. A.   F-826
Putnam, D. F.   B-595
Ptunam, R. G.   J-442
Pye, N.   E-217, F-827
Pyle, G. F.   H-742
Pyne, S.   H-51
Quaining, M.   A-351
Quill, H.   A-352
Quirk, B.   F-828
Racine, J. B.   F-59
Radeff, A.   B-484
Raffestin, C.   B-266
Rafiullah, S. M.   F-829
Rahman, S. M. H.   A-353
Raisz, E.   B-597, D-513,
   E-219, H-743, H-744
Raitviir, T.   H-745
Rakhilin, V. K.   B-598
Ramchandran, P. S.   B-599
Ramon, K.   F-830
Ramsay, J. A.   J-444
Ramsey, E. E.   H-746, J-443
Rasmussen, K.   E-220, F-831
Ratzel, F.   A-354
Raup, H. F.   B-602
Raup, H. M.   B-600, B-601,
   C-135, H-547
Ravenhill, W.   B-603
Rayner, J. N.   A-182
Reborahi, C. E.   D-514
Rechlin, A. M.   J-445
Reclus, E.   F-832
Reclus, M. E.   J-446
Redclift, M.   F-833
Redmond, R. L.   B-604
Redway, J. W.   J-447, J-448
Reed, H. H.   F-835
Reeder, E. H.   E-221

Reeds, L. G.   H-748
Reenberg, A.   E-220, F-831
Rees, R.   B-605, B-606
Reiner, T. A.   F-508, F-509
Reitsma, H. A.   F-836, F-837
Reitsma, H. J. A.   D-515
Relph, E.   A-355, A-356,
   J-449
Relph, E. C.   E-222, F-838,
   F-839
Remvick, H.   F-249
Renfrew, C.   C-136, C-137,
   E-223, F-840
Renner, G. T.   C-138, C-139,
   E-224, F-841, F-842,
   H-749, J-450, J-451, J-452
Renner, M. P.   J-453
Renwick, H.   G-155
Reynolds, J. B.   J-454
Reynolds, T. C.   H-750
Rhind, D.   E-225, E-226
Rich, J. L.   B-607, C-140,
   F-843
Richards, G.   C-141
Richards, P.   D-516, H-751
Richason, B.   J-455
Richling, A.   H-752
Richter, G.   H-753
Richter, H.   H-362
Ridd, M. K.   A-285
Riddell, J. B.   D-517, H-754
Ridgley, D. C.   F-844,
   J-456, J-457, J-458,
   J-459, J-460
Rigdon, V.   A-357
Rigdon, V. E.   B-608, H-755
Rikkinen, K.   B-609
Rimmer, P. J.   G-212, H-756,
   H-757
Riordan, T. O.   G-130
Ristow, W. W.   B-610
Ritchie, G. S.   B-611
Rizvi, A. I. H.   D-518,
   H-758
Rizvi, S. Q. A.   B-612,
   H-759
Roberts, N.   F-77
Roberts, R. H.   J-461
Roberts, S. H.   D-519
Robertson, C. J.   D-520
Robertson, D. L.   E-227
Robertson, J. M.   B-616

Robertson, S.   F-845
Robinson, A.   A-358
Robinson, A. H.   B-613,
   E-228, F-846, H-760
Robinson, E. V. D.   H-761
Robinson, G.   B-614, H-762,
   H-763
Robinson, G. W. S.   F-847
Robinson, J. L.   C-142,
   D-521, D-522, D-523,
   D-524, D-525, D-526,
   D-527, D-528, F-848,
   H-764, H-765, J-462, J-463
Robinson, M. E.   F-849
Robson, B. T.   D-133, H-766
Rodgers, A.   B-615, D-529
Rodriguez, V.   D-84, H-81
Roepke, H. G.   I-99
Rogers, G. F.   B-616, D-530,
   H-767
Rogerson, C.   D-139, H-183
Rogerson, C. M.   D-73
Roglic, J.   D-531, D-532,
   F-850
Rohman, F.   B-596
Rolfe, W. D. I.   A-359
Romanova, M. M.   B-617
Romanowski, J.   F-851, H-768
Rondinelli, D.   A-360
Rooper, T. G.   J-464
Roorbach, G. B.   F-852
Rorabacher, J. A.   C-143,
   F-853
Rose, H. M.   A-361
Rose, J. K.   B-618, B-619,
   I-100
Rosen, S.   J-465
Rosenkranz, E.   B-620
Roterus, V.   E-230
Rowntree, L.   F-854, H-769,
   H-770
Rowley, V. M.   A-362, A-363
Rowley, G.   C-144
Roxby, P. M.   F-855, F-856,
   F-857
Rrothero, R. M.   I-101
Rudra, K.   B-621
Ruiz-Gomez, M. M.   B-622
Rumble, H. E.   B-623, J-466
Rumley, D.   D-533
Ruppert, K.   D-75, H-771
Rusk, R. C.   J-467

Rushton, G. F-858, H-772
Russell, J. A. B-624,
B-625, I-102, I-103, I-104
Russell, R. J. H-773
Ryabchikov, A. M. B-626,
D-534
Ryabchiikov, A. M. J-468
Ryabchokov, A. M. C-145
Ryan, B. A-364, B-627,
F-859
Ryba, R. H. G-343
Rzepa, Z. B-628
Saarinen, T. F. H-774
Sack, R. D. A-365, F-860,
F-861, F-862, F-863,
F-864, F-865, F-866,
F-867, F-868
Sack, R. E-231, E-232
Sada, P. O. D-535, D-536
Saenz de Calzada, C. H-775
Sager, R. A. F-298
Saha, S. C-146
Sakamoto, M. H-776
Salan, A. T. D-538
Saleh, N. A. D-539
Salenz, C. D-537
Salikov, N. A. E-233
Salichtchev, K. A. H-777,
H-778
Salisbury, R. D. J-469,
J-470
Salishchev, K. A. D-540,
H-779, H-780
Salita, D. C. D-541
Salome, A. I. B-629
Salt, J. D-153
Salt, W. D-153
Salter, C. L. F-869, J-471,
J-472, J-473, J-474,
J-475, J-476
Samuels, M. A-274
Samuels, M. S. A-366
Sanderson, M. B-630, B-631,
H-781, I-150
Sandru, I. D-542, D-543
Sanguin, A. L. B-632, D-544
Santos, J. M. D-84, H-81
Sargent, R. H. B-633
Sarkar, R. M. B-634
Sauer, C. O. B-635, B-636,
B-637, B-638, E-141,
F-870, F-871, F-872,

F-873, F-874, F-875,
H-782, H-783, H-784,
J-477
Saulter, G. F-881
Saushkin, J. G. D-545
Saushkin, Y. G. A-367,
B-639, B-640, B-641,
B-642, D-546, D-547,
D-548, E-106, E-234,
F-382, F-876, F-877,
F-878, F-879, F-880,
F-1136, G-384, H-785,
H-786, H-787, I-106
Saveland, R. N. J-478
Savors, A. B-643
Saxena, H. M. H-788
Sayer, A. E-235, E-236,
F-882, F-883, H-789
Sayer, R. A. F-884
Scarfe, N. E. B-644
Scarfe, N. V. D-549, F-885,
J-479, J-480, J-481,
J-482, J-483, J-484
Scarfe, W. B-645
Scargill, D. I. D-550,
F-886
Schaefer, F. K. E-237,
F-887
Schick, M. F-888
Schlesinger, A. M. J-485
Schmenner, R. W. A-368
Schmieder, A. G. J-486
Schnore, L. F. C-148
Schoen, M. G. B-646
Schofer, J. P. H-790
Scholler, P. B-365, I-64
Scholten, A. B-647
Schoolmaster, F. A. I-107
Scott, R. C. J-487
Schoy, C. D-551
Schreuders, H. I-108
Schroder, F. A-369
Schroder, K. H. B-648
Schroder, P. H-791
Schroeder, K. D-552
Schultz, R. R. F-889
Schulz, J. B-649
Schwarz, G. B-650
Scott, D. D-553, F-890,
H-792
Scott, E. P. G-413
Sdasyvk, G. V. B-626,

D-246, E-157, F-632, H-316
Seager, J. H-793, I-109
Seamon, D. F-891, F-892,
  F-893, H-794
Seleg, J. E. F-894
Sell, J. L. H-774
Sellors, R. P. D-554, J-488
Semevskiy, B. N. D-555,
  D-556, D-557, D-558,
  D-559, E-238
Semple, E. C. A-370, F-895,
  J-489, J-490
Senda, H. D-560, H-795
Senger, L. W. C-149, E-239,
  F-896
Sereno, P. D-561, H-796
Sevrin, R. B-651
Sewell, W. R. I-110
Sewell, W. R. D. J-491
Seymour, W. A. A-371
Shabad, T. B-652, H-797,
  I-111
Shafer, R. J. A-372
Shafi, M. D-562
Shafti, M. B-653, I-112
Shairp, J. C. A-373
Shaler, N. S. A-374
Shalowitz, A. B-654
Shanklin, G. H-798
Shantz, H. L. B-655
Shaw, D. D-563
Shaw, E. B. J-492, J-493
Shchukin, I. S. H-799
Sheail, G. M. B-656
Sheail, J. C-150
Shearer, M. H. C-151
Shepherd, I. D. H. B-302
Sheppard, E. D-564, F-897,
  H-800
Sherwood, M. B-657
Shibanov, F. A. B-658,
  B-659, D-565, D-566,
  H-801, H-802
Shirley, R. W. A-375
Shitara, H. D-567, H-803
Shlemon, R. J. H-804
Shnitnikov, A. V. H-805
Showket, I. A-376
Shul'gin, A. M. H-806
Sibert, L. E. D-166, G-171
Siddall, W. R. A-377,
  D-568, F-898

Sidorenko, A. V. H-807
Sieve, K. C-46
Sigeriest, H. E. I-113
Silberbach, J. H. J-494
Silk, J. F-899
Silvernail, R. G. H-808
Simmons, I. F-900
Simmons, I. G. H-809, H-810
Simmons, J. W. D-569, H-811
Simon, D. J-495
Simon, W. A-378
Simons, M. F-403
Simpson-Housley, P. A-284,
  F-627
Sims, J. H. C-152
Sindiga, I. D-570
Singh, C. P. D-571
Singh, D. N. B-660, D-572,
  D-573, H-812
Singh, J. H-813
Singh, L. H-815
Singh, M. D-574, H-814
Singh, R. H-815
Singh, R. G. H-816
Singh, R. L. F-901, F-902,
  F-903
Singh, R. P. B. B-661,
  E-240, F-903, F-904
Sinnhuber, K. B-662, B-663
Siple, P. A. I-114
Sit, V. D-116, D-575,
  D-576, D-577
Sitwell, O. F. G. B-664,
  E-241, F-680, F-905, H-817
Skelton, R. A. A-379,
  A-380, H-181
Skinner, A. W. C-153, F-906
Slabczynski, W. B-68, B-665
Slater, D. D-491, E-208,
  F-787, F-907
Slater, F. E-242, F-908,
  J-496, J-497, J-498
Slaymaker, O. F-909
Smail, J. C. B-666
Small, R. J. H-818
Smart, A. M. J-499
de Smidt, M. H-819
Smidt, D. D-578
Smidt, M. D-243
Smith, G. H. J-500
Smith, J. H. J-504
Smith, J. R. J-501, J-502,

J-503
Smith, K.   J-505
Smith, P. R.   J-506
Smith, S.   J-507
Smith, S. J.   J-508
Smith, T. A.   J-509
Smith, V. B.   J-510
Smith, W. D.   J-511
Smirnov, A. M.   B-641,
    F-880, F-910
Smirnov, L. Y.   E-243, F-911
Smita, H. T.   H-820
Smith, A.   G-237
Smith, B. W.   H-821, I-115
Smith, C. H.   B-667
Smith, C. J.   F-912
Smith, D. M.   A-381, F-900,
    F-913, H-253, H-822,
    I-116, I-117
Smith, E. L.   B-668
Smith, G.   B-669
Smith, G. H.   B-670, B-671,
    B-672, E-244, H-823
Smith, J. P.   H-177, H-824
Smith, J. R.   A-382, B-673,
    C-154, D-579, D-580,
    F-914, F-915, F-916, H-825
Smith, K.   H-826
Smith, N.   B-674, B-675,
    E-245, E-246, F-917,
    F-918, F-919, H-827, I-118
Smith, P. J.   C-155
Smith, P. S.   B-676, B-677
Smith, R. V.   H-642
Smith, S. J.   A-231, E-247,
    F-920, F-921, H-828
Smith, T. A.   H-829
Smith, T. R.   B-676, B-677,
    F-922
Smole, W. J.   D-582
Smyth, W. J.   H-830
Snook, I.   J-512
Sochava, V. B.   C-156,
    D-583, E-249, F-923,
    F-924, H-831, I-119
Soja, E. W.   F-925, F-926
Solntsev, V. A.   F-927,
    F-928
Solomon, R. J.   J-513
Solot, M.   B-679
Solov'yer, A. I.   J-50,
    J-514

Solov'yeva, M. G.   J-515
Sommers, L. M.   D-584, F-929
Sommers, L. S.   I-120
Songqiao, Z.   A-96
Sonnenfeld, J.   E-250, F-930
Soons, J. M.   J-516
Sopher, D. E.   F-931
Sorenson, A. D.   F-1052
Sorenson, C. W.   J-517
Soulsby, E. M.   D-585, J-518
Sowerbutts, E.   I-121
Sparks, E. E.   C-157
Spate, O. H. K.   D-586,
    D-587, F-932, F-933,
    F-934, F-935, F-936, H-832
Specklin, R.   B-688
Speil, L. J.   G-172, G-173
Spencer, C.   C-158
Spencer, D. S.   H-833
Spencer, J. E.   B-689,
    F-937, H-834
Speth, W.   C-159
Speth, W. W.   B-690, B-691,
    B-692, F-938
Spetz, D.   J-519
Spilhaus, M. W.   A-383,
    F-939
Spinelli, J. G.   H-821,
    H-835
Spiridonov, A. I.   H-836
Spoehr, A.   F-940
Spote, A. P.   B-687
Spote, O. H. K.   B-680,
    B-681, B-682, B-683,
    B-684, B-685, B-686, B-687
Springett, J.   H-177
Srivastava, M. P.   E-251
Stablein, G.   B-693, H-837
Stafford, J. H.   C-160
Stager, J. K.   H-838
Stamp, J.   F-941
Stamp, L. D.   A-384, B-694,
    F-942, I-122, I-123
Stamp, R. M.   F-943
Stander, E.   D-588
Stanescu, M.   J-520
Stanislawski, D.   B-695
Stanley, C.   F-944
Stanley, H. M.   D-589
Stanley, R. W.   J-521
Stanley, S. D.   F-286
Stark, M. C.   J-522, J-523

Starkey, O. P. B-696, B-697
Stea, D. E-27
Steed, G. P. F. F-945
Steel, R. W. A-385, A-386,
    D-590, D-591, D-592,
    E-252, F-946, H-312
Steers, H. D-593
Steers, J. A. B-698, B-699
Steinbrink, J. A-22, H-125
Steiner, G. A-157
Steinhauser, F. R. F-947
Steinitz, M. H-793, I-109
Stepanova, Y. A. D-504
Stephens, N. B-700
Stephenson, D. P. F-948
Stephenson, O. W. J-524
Stermberg, H. D-594, D-595
Stern, E. A-387, A-388
Stevens, A. F-949
Stevenson, W. I. B-701
Stewart, J. Q. F-950
Stiles, D. J-525
Stoddart, D. R. A-389,
    B-702, B-703, B-704,
    B-705, B-706, D-596,
    F-951, F-952, F-953,
    F-954, F-955, F-956,
    F-957, H-839, H-840
Stolberg, I. C-161
Stolman, J. A-22
Stoltman, J. P. J-526
Stone, A. D-597
Stone, K. H. E-253, F-958
Storper, M. F-959, H-841,
    H-842
Storrie, M. C. B-707
Stout, C. L. A-391
Strabo,   A-392
Strahler, A. E-254, H-843
Straszewicz, L. I-125
Strate, J. B. C-162
Straw, T. F. I-124
Street, J. M. D-388
Strong, H. M. F-960, F-961,
    I-126, I-127, I-128, I-129
Student, A. B-85
Stupina, V. M. H-735
Sturgeon, M. K. J-527
Stutz, F. H-844, I-75,
    I-130
Stutz, F. P. J-528
Sugden, D. A-393

Sugden, D. E. C-163, H-845
Sugden, J. F. F-962
Suizu, I. D-598, F-963
Sukhaval, B. D-599, J-529
Sullivan, W. B-708
Sullivan, M. E. D-600,
    F-964
Sun, P. H-846
Sun, P. S. D-601
Sundaram, K. V. A-394
Surface, G. T. B-709, J-530
Sutherland, W. J. F-965,
    F-966
Sutton, K. B-710, D-602
Su-Fen, L. E-255
Swain, G. W. J-531
Swain, P. H. E-256
Swartz, D. J. J-532
Sweet, D. H-847
Sweet, D. C. C-164
Sweeting, M. M. D-603
Sykes, P. A-395
Symonds, C. J-533, J-534
Szava-Kovats, E. F-967
Szekely, B. B. D-604, J-535
Szymanski, R. A-396, C-184,
    E-277, F-1093
Taaffe, E. J. A-397, F-968,
    F-969
Tait, J. B. D-605, H-848
Tait, P. G. A-373
Takeuchi, K. D-606, D-607,
    F-970, H-849
Talarchek, G. M. F-971
Tamaskar, B. G. D-608,
    H-850
Tamsma, R. B-711
Tanabe, H. A-398
Tang, J. D-609, H-535,
    J-536
Tang, D-370
Tarqul'yan, V. O. E-13
Tata, R. J. F-972
Taylor, B. D-610
Taylor, D. R. F. A-399,
    D-611, D-612, H-851
Taylor, E. B-712
Taylor, E. G. R. A-400,
    A-401, A-402, B-713,
    B-714, B-715, B-716,
    B-717, F-973, F-974,
    F-975, F-976

Taylor, G. A-403, A-404,
  F-977, F-978, F-979,
  F-980, I-131
Taylor, J. A. A-405, E-257,
  H-852, H-853, H-854
Taylor, M. A-298
Taylor, P. J. A-72, D-613,
  D-614, D-615, E-258,
  E-259, F-981, F-982,
  H-855, H-856
Taylor, S. M. D-616
Taylor, T. G. A-406
Taylor, Z. D-617, H-857
Teggart, F. J. D-618,
  D-619, I-132, J-537
Teitz, M. B. A-407
Teller, J. T. B-718, D-620
Temple, P. B-719, D-621
ter Welle-Heethuis, J. C. P.
  D-482
Terekhov, N. M. D-463,
  H-677
Terjung, W. H. H-858
Tewari, A. K. D-622
Tharnes, J. B. C-137
Theakstone, W. H. A-408
Thirunaranan, B. M. D-623
Thisei, J. F. E-16
Thom, B. G. F-983, H-999
Thom, B. J. H-859
Thomale, E. D-624, H-860
Thoman, R. S. B-720, D-625,
  D-626, F-984, H-861,
  H-862, H-863
Thomas, B. E. D-627, D-628,
  F-985, H-864, J-538
Thomas, C. B-721, B-722,
  D-630
Thomas, D. B-723
Thomas, F. H. I-133, J-539
Thomas, H. G. J-541
Thomas, L. F. J-542
Thomas, M. J. H-865
Thomas, O. J. D-629, J-540
Thomas, W. L. A-409
Thompson, D. J. H-866
Thompson, I. D-124
Thompson, J. P. D-631,
  I-134
Thompson, K. F-986
Thompson, K. W. J-543
Thong, L. B. E-260

Thornes, J. B. H-867
Thornes, J. E. D-633,
  D-634, H-868, I-135, I-136
Thornthwaite, C. W. D-635,
  F-987
Thorpe, D. D-636, H-871,
  I-137
Thorpe, H. D-637
Thovez, J. P. B-724
Thrall, G. I. F-988
Thralls, Z. A. J-544,
  J-545, J-546
Thrower, N. B-725, B-726
Thrift, N. A-81, D-638,
  F-989, F-990, F-991,
  F-992, H-872, H-873
Thrift, N. J. G-213
Thrower, N. J. W. D-639
Tidswell, W. V. A-410
Tietz, W. F-993, H-874
Tiggesbaumker, G. B-727
Tilley, P. D. B-728, B-729
Timar, L. H-875
Tinkler, K. J. A-411,
  E-261, E-262, F-994
Tiwari, R. N. B-730
Tobin, G. A. F-995
Tobler, W. E-61
Tobler, W. R. H-876
Tolcarskiy, N. K. D-500,
  J-436
Tomkins, G. A. B-731, D-640
Tomkins, G. S. D-641,
  F-996, J-547
Tomlinson, R. F. E-263
Tooley, R. V. A-412, A-413
Torayah, A. S. A-414
Tornquist, G. F-997, F-998,
  H-877
Tout, D. G. H-667
Tower, W. S. F-999, F-1000,
  F-1001, F-1002
Towler, J. D-642
Towler, J. O. C-165
Tozer, H. F. A-415, A-416
Tremble, S. W. H-334
Trewartha, G. H-878
Treyvish, A. I. F-808
Trimble, S. W. J-548
Trindell, R. T. B-732
Tripathi, M. P. A-417
Tripathi, S. M. P. D-643

Trivers, J.   J-239
Trudgill, P.   H-879
Trudgill, S. T.   H-880,
    J-549
Trusov, Y. P.   D-644
Tsegmid, S.   D-645
Tsujita, U.   B-733, B-734
Tuan, Y.   A-418, A-419
Tuan, Y. F.   H-881
Tuan, Yi-Fu   C-166, E-264,
    E-265, F-1003, F-1004,
    F-1005, F-1006, F-1007,
    F-1008, F-1009, F-1010,
    F-1011, F-1012, F-1013,
    F-1014
Tufte, E. R.   A-420
Tung, T. H.   E-128, E-129
Turner, B. C.   B-735
Turner, F. J.   C-167
Turner, M. E.   H-179
Turnock, D.   B-736, B-737,
    D-466, D-467, H-882
Tweedie, A.   B-738
Twidace, C. R.   B-130, H-86
Tyrell, J. B.   B-739
Uchida, K.   D-648, J-550
Uhlig, H.   E-266, F-1015
Ulaby, F.   A-421
Ulack, R.   D-649, D-650
Ullman, E. L.   A-422, C-168,
    H-883
Ulrich, J.   B-740
UNESCO   D-651, J-551
Un Rii, H.   D-372
Unstead, J. F.   B-741,
    C-169, E-267, F-1016,
    F-1017, H-884
Unwin, D. J.   F-1018, F-1009
Unwin, J. W.   D-652, D-653,
    E-268, E-269
Unwin, T.   D-496, F-1020
Uren, P. C.   D-654, H-885
Urry, J.   A-191
Vale, T. R.
Valentey, D. I.   C-170,
    D-655
Vallance, T. G.   B-68
Vallaux, C.   B-742
Van Burkalow, A.   H-887
Van Cleef, E.   A-423, A-424,
    B-743, C-121, F-1021,
    F-1022, F-1023, F-1024,

F-1025, F-1026, F-1027,
    H-888, H-889, I-138
van den Berg, G. J.   H-68
Van Der Laan, L.   F-1028
Vaniria, L. M.   J-552
Van Paassen, C.   A-330,
    F-1029
Van Royen, W.   B-744, H-893
Van Valkenburg, S.   B-745,
    H-894
Van Weespe, J.   D-259
Vance, J. E.   H-890
Vance, R. B.   F-1030
Vander Velde, E.   D-456
Vander Wusten, H.   H-891
Vanderhill, B. G.   H-892
Varenius, B.   A-425
Varjo, U.   H-895
Varlas, V. Y.   F-1031
Vascovic, M.   B-746, D-656,
    H-896
Vasilevskiy, L. I.   D-657,
    H-897
Vaughn, J. E.   B-747
Vaughn, N.   F-1032
Vedenin, Y. A.   H-735
Veen, A. W. L.   D-658,
    F-1033
Veldman, J.   D-275, H-391
Vinge, C. L.   F-929, F-1034
Vining, J. W.   C-173
Vink, A. P. A.   D-659, H-898
Visher, S. S.   B-748, B-749,
    B-750, B-751, B-752,
    B-753, B-754, B-755,
    B-756, B-757, B-758,
    B-759, B-760, B-76,
    F-1035, F-1036, F-1037,
    H-899, H-900
Vitek, J. D.   A-101
Vogeler, I.   G-175, J-135,
    J-553
Vol'f, M. B.   D-660, J-554
Vol'skiy, V. V.   H-901
Von Engeln, O. D.   B-762,
    B-763, B-764, D-661,
    F-1038, H-902, J-555
Von Richthofen, B. F.
    F-1039
Voronov, A. G.   D-662, H-903
Vovil, R. J.   D-663, I-139
Vuicich, G.   G-399

Wadley, D. D-664, J-556
Wagner, P. D-665, D-666,
  D-667, D-668
Wagner, P. L. F-1040,
  F-1041, F-1042, H-904,
  H-905
Wagstaff, J. M. C-174,
  F-1044, F-1045
Wagstaff, J. W. C-137
Wahlquist, W. L. J-557
Waites, B. B-765, B-766
Wake, W. H. B-767
Walford, R. A-21, D-669,
  F-1046, J-558, J-559,
  J-560
Walker, D. F-1047
Walker, G. H-906
Walker, H. J. B-768
Walker, I. L. J-561
Walker, J. B-282
Walker, R. A. E-270,
  F-1048, F-1049
Wall, G. H-110
Wallis, B. C. E-271, H-907,
  J-562
Wallis, H. B-769, B-770,
  H-908
Walmsley, D. J. E-272,
  E-273, F-1050, F-1051,
  F-1052
Walsh, F. H-909
Walter, B. J. F-1053
Walters, R. B-771
Walton, J. F-369
Walton, K. B-772
Wanklyn, H. A-426
Wann, T. A-427
Ward, D. B-773, F-1054,
  H-910, H-911
Ward, H. B-325
Ward, R. D-670, H-916
Ward, R. D. B-776, B-777,
  H-912, H-913, H-914, H-915
Ward, R. G. B-774, B-775,
  D-367
Warf, B. F-1055, F-1056
Warkentin, J. B-778
Warman, H. J. A-428, B-779,
  F-1057, G-243, J-563,
  J-564, J-565, J-566,
  J-567, J-568, J-569
Warner, C. I-140

Warnes, A. A-429
Warnes, A. M. H-917, H-918,
  H-919
Warntz, W. A-430, A-431,
  C-175, F-1058, F-1059,
  F-1060, F-1061, H-920,
  H-921
Warren, A. E-174, F-681,
  H-922
Warren, C. J-570
Warren, K. D-173
Warszynska, J. D-671,
  H-923, H-924
Wartnz, W. F-950
Warwick, G. T. B-301
Wasserman, W. H-925
Waterman, S. D-335, D-672,
  D-673, H-926, J-571
Waters, R. C-176, D-674
Watson, C. F-1062, J-572
Watson, J. W. B-780, B-781,
  C-177, C-178, D-592,
  D-675, F-1063, F-1064,
  J-573
Watson, M. K. F-1065
Watts, D. H-927
Watts, Sheldon J. F-1066
Watts, Snsou J. F-1066
Weaver, C. F-1067
Weaver, D. C. B-782
Weaver, J. C. H-928
Webb, M. J. H-929
Webb, R. M. J-574
Webb, W. P. C-179
Webber, M. J. A-432, E-274,
  J-575
Weber, P. D-75
Weichhart, P. A-433
Weir, T. C-180
Weiss-Altaner, E. F-59
ter Welle-Heethuis, J. G. P.
  H-697
Wellings, P. D-676, H-30
Wellings, P. A. D-677
Welsted, J. D-678
Wescoat, J. C. Jr. H-931
Wessinger, E. H-932, I-141,
  J-576
West, H. G. F-1068
Wharton, W. J. L. F-1069
Whatman, N. H. B-783
Wheatley, P. F-1070

Wheeler, J. O.   F-1071,
   F-1072, H-933, H-934,
   H-935
Wheeler, K.   B-784
Whipple, G.   F-1073, J-577
Whitaker, J. R.   B-785,
   C-181, F-1074, H-936,
   J-578, J-579
Whitbeck, R. H.   B-786,
   F-1075, F-1076, F-1077,
   F-1078, F-1079, F-1080,
   F-1081, H-9937, H-938,
   I-142, J-580, J-581,
   J-582, J-583, J-584,
   J-585, J-586, J-587,
   J-588, J-589, J-590
White, A. D.   J-591
White, A. S.   D-679
White, C. L.   I-143, J-592
White, G. F.   B-192, B-787,
   C-182, C-183
White, P.   G-136, J-107
White, S.   F-1083, H-940
White, S. E.   F-1082, H-939
White, W. R.   F-1084
Whitehand, J. W. R.   F-1085,
   F-1086, F-1087, F-1088,
   H-941, H-942, H-943, J-593
Whitehouse, W. E.   J-594
Whitelegg, J.   E-173, F-679
Whitmore, F. C.   H-944
Whitney, J. P.   H-945, J-595
Whittlesey, D.   A-434,
   F-1089, F-1090, F-1091,
   H-946, H-947
Whittlesey, D. S.   B-788,
   E-275, I-144, I-145
Whomsley, J. P.   J-596
Widdis, R. W.   E-276, F-1092
Wilbanks, T.   G-439
Wilbanks, T. J.   C-184,
   C-185, E-277, F-1093,
   H-948
Wilcock, A. A.   B-789,
   B-790, B-791, F-1094,
   F-1095
Wileman, D.   B-792
Wilford, J. N.   A-435
Wilhelm, E. J.   C-186,
   D-680, H-949, H-950,
   J-597, J-598
Wilkinson, C.   A-436

Willatts, E. C.   C-187
Williams, D.   B-793
Williams, D. B.   E-158,
   F-637, G-429, J-339
Williams, F. E.   B-794,
   B-795, B-796, B-797
Williams, F. L.   A-437
Williams, J. E.   J-592
Williams, J. F.   D-681,
   D-682, H-951
Williams, L.   C-188, H-952
Williams, M.   B-798, B-799,
   B-800, F-1096, F-1097,
   H-953, H-954, H-955,
   J-560, J-599
Williams, P.   G-213
Williams, S. W.   E-278,
   F-1089, F-1090, H-956
Williams, T. G.   F-1100
Williams, W. M.   F-742
Williamson, F.   E-89, H-323
Willmer, J. E.   J-600, J-601
Willmont, C. J.   A-170,
   H-600
Wilson, A. G.   A-438, E-279,
   E-280, F-206, F-1101,
   F-1102, F-1103
Wilson, C. W.   H-957
Wilson, H.   F-1104, H-958
Wilson, H. E.   A-439
Wilson, L. S.   J-602, J-603
Wilson, M.   F-1105, J-603
Wilson, T. D.   F-1106
Wilson, T. P.   C-189
Winchester, S. W. C.   H-959
Winid, B.   D-683
Winkler, E.   C-190, F-1107
Winkler, K. J.   C-191
Winsberg, M. D.   B-801,
   C-192, F-1108
Winslow, I. O.   J-605, J-606
Winsted, H. L.   J-607
Winston, V. H.   B-806
Wirick, B. C.   J-59
Wirth, E.   F-1109
Wise, D. A.   I-146
Wise, M.   D-684
Wise, M. J.   B-802, B-803,
   B-804, B-805, F-1110,
   H-960, H-961, J-608, J-609
Wisner, B.   I-147, F-1111,
   F-1112, H-962

Witfogel, K.   F-1113
Witmer, R. E.   I-3
Wolf, K.   D-75
Wolf, L. G.   B-807
Wolfe, L. E.   F-1114
Wolfe, P.   A-431
Wolfe, R. I.   H-963
Wolforth, J.   D-685, E-281,
   F-1115, J-610
Wolley, P.   I-60
Wolport, J.   F-894
Wong, E. Y.   B-173
Wood, E.   A-441
Wood, H. A.   H-964
Wood, J. D.   A-442, D-686,
   H-965
Wood, L. J.   F-1116, H-966
Wood, P.   H-967, H-968,
   H-969
Wood, P. A.   E-282
Wood, T. F.   F-1117
Wood, W. A.   B-808
Woodcock, G.   A-443
Woods, K. J.   A-156
Woods, R.   H-970
Wooldridge, S. W.   A-384,
   A-444, J-612, J-613
Woolmington, E.   F-277
Woolstencraft, R. P.   H-971
Worley, L.   H-972, J-614
Worsley, P.   H-973
Worth, C.   D-687, H-974,
   J-615
Wright, J.   H-975, H-976,
   H-977, H-978, H-979
Wright, J. K.   A-445, A-446,
   A-447, A-448, B-809,
   B-810, B-811, C-193,
   C-194, D-689, D-690,
   D-691, D-692, F-1118,
   F-1119, F-1120, I-148
Wrigley, G. M.   B-812, B-813
Wrigley, N.   A-449, E-283,
   E-284, E-285, E-286, H-980
Wrofel, A.   F-1121
Wusten, H.   I-149
Wyckoff, W.   G-321
Wyckoff, W. L.   D-693
Wynn, G.   D-694, H-981
Yacher, L.   B-814
Yanitskiy, N. F.   D-698,
   F-1134

Yassen, D.   A-297
Yates, J.   F-1122
Yates, T.   H-982
Yeates, M. H.   A-450, A-451
Yeates, J.   H-983, I-150
Yefremov, Y. K.   D-695,
   F-1123, F-1124, H-984,
   H-985, H-986, H-987,
   H-988, I-151
Yeomans, E.   F-1125
Yermolayev, M. M.   F-1126
Young, A.   J-616
Young, B. J.   H-989
Young, R. W.   E-287, F-1127
Younghusband, F.   D-696
Yugai, R. L.   B-815, B-816,
   B-817, B-818
Yugay, R. L.   H-990
Yun'yev, I. S.   D-695
Yunns, M.   D-697, J-617
Zabelin, I. M.   B-819
Zabelin, I.   F-1128
Zaborski, J.   F-1129
Zaidi, I. H.   B-820
Zakharov, N. D.   F-1130
Zakrzewska, B.   H-991, H-992
Zdorkowski, G.   H-993
Zeben, L. J.   H-994
Zekkel, Y. D.   H-995
Zelinsky, W.   A-452, C-196,
   C-197, E-288, F-1131,
   F-1132, F-1133, G-436,
   H-996, H-997
Zerbi, M. C.   D-492
Zerki, M. C.   H-711
Zhekulin, V. S.   H-998
Zhirmunskiy, M. M.   D-698,
   F-1134
Zhongming, S.   B-821
Ziauddin, S. M.   A-453
Zimmerman, F.   B-822
Zimmerman, R. C.   H-999
Zimmerman, S.   B-823
Zinyama, L. M.   D-699
Zobel, H. L.   J-618
Zobler, L.   H-1000
Zodorkowski, G.   C-195
Zonn, L. E.   H-1001, I-152
Zonneveld, J. I. S.   F-1135,
   H-1002
Zubakov, V. A.   H-1003
Zuckerman, S. M.   E-69

Zvonkova, T. V.   F-1136,
   H-1004, H-1005
Zylack, S.   A-296

Subject Index

Aerial photography H-248
Agricultural geography
  H-82, H-128, H-168, H-275,
  H-352, H-390, H-928
American Indians H-372
Applied geography H-84,
  H-102, H-157, H-216,
  H-228, H-231, H-245,
  H-249, H-259, H-283,
  H-286, H-290, H-291,
  H-292, H-293, H-294,
  H-327, H-355, H-360,
  H-384, H-419, H-430,
  H-452, H-505, H-562,
  H-588, H-643, H-716,
  H-798, H-821, H-844
Architecture H-284
Behaviorial geography H-44,
  H-103, H-107, H-178,
  H-185, H-246, H-300,
  H-317, H-318, H-319,
  H-321, H-329, H-518,
  H-619, H-699, H-772,
  H-794, H-817
Bibliography H-167
Biogeography H-38, H-124,
  H-182, H-201, H-241,
  H-285, H-307, H-309,
  H-406, H-416, H-469,
  H-470, H-522, H-561,
  H-585, H-624, H-747,
  H-767, H-806, H-840,
  H-852, H-853, H-854,
  H-886, H-887, H-899,
  H-903, H-922, H-927,
  H-949, H-950, H-999
Cartography H-18, H-29,
  H-53, H-59, H-73, H-74,
  H-77, H-126, H-132, H-135,
  H-161, H-171, H-181,
  H-189, H-224, H-236,
  H-261, H-326, H-422,
  H-433, H-454, H-456,
  H-478, H-486, H-540,
  H-554, H-570, H-572,
  H-573, H-574, H-575,
  H-576, H-577, H-578,
  H-589, H-596, H-645,
  H-650, H-653, H-659,
  H-677, H-720, H-723,
  H-734, H-736, H-743,
  H-744, H-777, H-778,
  H-779, H-780, H-790,
  H-791, H-801, H-802,
  H-814, H-815, H-850,
  H-851, H-876, H-902,

H-908, H-925, H-974,
    H-976, H-978
China Institute of Geography
    H-313
Clark University H-662
Climatology   H-91, H-212,
    H-220, H-376, H-472,
    H-494, H-495, H-516,
    H-538, H-569, H-595,
    H-600, H-667, H-668,
    H-669, H-670, H-671,
    H-719, H-803, H-805,
    H-858, H-868, H-869,
    H-870, H-915, H-952
Colonial studies H-312
Communication H-52
Commercial geography H-8,
    H-115, H-121, H-122,
    H-240, H-371, H-401,
    H-402, H-520, H-761,
    H-932, H-937, H-957
Computers H-790
Conservation H-169, H-392,
    H-936
Crime, geography of H-536,
    H-564, H-959
Cultural determinism H-133
Cultural geography   H-28,
    H-56, H-57, H-64, H-65,
    H-75, H-87, H-118, H-119,
    H-133, H-173, H-175,
    H-177, H-180, H-203,
    H-204, H-225, H-281,
    H-314, H-354, H-356,
    H-373, H-375, H-432,
    H-439, H-475, H-523,
    H-544, H-546, H-547,
    H-560, H-634, H-638,
    H-683, H-684, H-679,
    H-770, H-783, H-817,
    H-824, H-834 H-881, H-904,
    H-905, H-906, H-940, H-958
Development studies H-49,
    H-72, H-92, H-249, H-282,
    H-423, H-930, H-964
Earth science H-238, H-477,
    H-611, H-612, H-682, H-888
Ecology   H-285, H-557,
    H-561, H-883
Economic geography H-5,
    H-10, H-11, H-12, H-13,
H-14, H-15, H-16, H-19,
    H-21, H-27, H-34, H-35,
    H-60, H-69, H-88, H-97,
    H-108, H-125, H-136,
    H-137, H-141, H-142,
    H-150, H-187, H-188,
    H-231, H-262, H-268,
    H-273, H-274, H-276,
    H-310, H-324, H-325,
    H-344, H-345, H-360,
    H-363, H-370, H-400,
    H-410, ·H-426, H-428,
    H-484, H-485, H-487,
    H-490, H-491, H-493,
    H-496, H-506, H-507,
    H-508, H-512, H-513,
    H-520, H-526, H-527,
    H-543, H-548, H-553,
    H-555, H-557, H-566,
    H-609, H-613, H-614,
    H-622, H-623, H-625,
    H-626, H-640, H-662,
    H-675, H-678, H-701,
    H-725, H-727, H-728,
    H-729, H-730, H-731,
    H-768, H-782, H-785,
    H-786, H-787, H-787,
    H-789, H-813, H-819,
    H-825, H-832, H-841,
    H-842, H-861, H-862,
    H-863, H-874, H-877,
    H-889, H-901, H-907,
    H-938, H-920, H-921,
    H-929, H-951, H-960,
    H-1000, H-1005
Education   H-89, H-293,
    H-336, H-337, H-338,
    H-353, H-444, H-534, H-535
Energy H-129, H-130, H-131,
    H-706, H-741, H-948
Environmental perception
    H-90, H-639, H-774
Environmental science
    H-109, H-153, H-155,
    H-163, H-219, H-330,
    H-445, H-489, H-666,
    H-880, H-949, H-961
Fieldwork H-195, H-679
Folk geography H-530, H-560
G.I.S. H-74, H-656, H-724
Geodness H-409

Geology H-33, H-199, H-263, H-304

Geographers H-271, H-823

Geography H-229, H-274, H-315, H-377, H-379, H-411, H-415, H-514, H-525, H-528, H-582, H-632, H-732, H-733, H-784, H-797, H-831, H-910, H-911, H-979

Geomorphology H-9, H-50, H-51, H-83, H-86, H-93, H-95, H-100, H-114, H-117, H-145, H-154, H-176, H-195, H-197, H-208, H-216, H-218, H-233, H-234, H-244, H-287, H-288, H-301, H-306, H-333, H-334, H-347, H-404, H-408, H-420, H-458, H-474, H-601, H-630, H-685, H-695, H-702, H-703, H-705, H-762, H-799, H-804, H-807, H-818, H-836, H-839, H-845, H-859, H-867, H-873, H-953, H-973, H-991, H-992, H-995

Gerontology H-917

Glaciology H-805

Historic preservation H-283

Historical geography H-45, H-47, H-48, H-63, H-71, H-95, H-134, H-146, H-162, H-165, H-166, H-167, H-172, H-174, H-179, H-183, H-190, H-191, H-192, H-193, H-205, H-206, H-207, H-213, H-229, H-239, H-247, H-296, H-297, H-298, H-311, H-320, H-346, H-357, H-359, H-364, H-378, H-382, H-383, H-397, H-411, H-431, H-434, H-447, H-448, H-449, H-453, H-481, H-482, H-499, H-510, H-519, H-529, H-563, H-565, H-620, H-646, H-647, H-673, H-674, H-681, H-692, H-694,

H-698, H-718, H-740, H-763, H-792, H-793, H-795, H-796, H-816, H-832, H-875, H-884, H-954, H-945, H-955, H-965, H-975, H-981, H-990, H-996, H-998, H-1000, H-1003

Housing H-230, H-503

Human H-4, H-99, H-185, H-194, H-269, H-308, H-322, H-323, H-328, H-350, H-370, H-386, H-441, H-461, H-479, H-492, H-542, H-644, H-939, H-917, H-956

Hydrology H-220, H-628, H-916

Industrial location H-256, H-427, H-504, H-581, H-968, H-968, H-969

Information H-399

International trade H-164, H-616

Landscape studies H-184, H-198, H-201, H-225, H-362, H-476, H-579, H-610, H-985

Linguistics H-879

Literary geography H-111

Location theory H-597

Marine geography H-591, H-593

Maritime geography H-258

Marketing geography H-125, H-245, H-342, H-368, H-661, H-788

Marxism H-459, H-530, H-710

Medical geography H-6, H-76, H-209, H-237, H-272, H-274, H-278, H-305, H-531, H-532, H-533, H-550, H-559, H-594, H-603, H-604, H-605, H-608, H-617, H-618, H-663, H-721, H-742, H-775, H-776, H-887, H-913, H-914

Meteorology H-480, H-494, H-820, H-912

Migration resarch, H-939

Military geography H-295,

H-335, H-436, H-712,
H-885, H-944
Oceanography   H-250, H-429,
H-593, H-848
Palynology   H-241
Perceptual geography H-103,
H-222, H-223, H-318,
H-319, H-328, H-329,
H-358, H-394, H-772,
H-966
Photogrammetrists   H-224
Physical geography   H-1,
H-8, H-14, H-17, H-33,
H-36, H-94, H-123, H-144,
H-156, H-186, H-190,
H-217, H-232, H-257,
H-289, H-303, H-307,
H-341, H-348, H-361,
H-366, H-369, H-374,
H-435, H-517, H-537,
H-552, H-586, H-587,
H-588, H-602, H-611,
H-612, H-635, H-636,
H-637, H-651, H-664,
H-680, H-691, H-693,
H-700, H-713, H-739,
H-746, H-773, H-781,
H-799, H-804, H-810,
H-826, H-829, H-837,
H-838, H-843, H-898,
H-984, H-986, H-987,
H-1002, H-1004, H-1005
Physiography   H-264, H-265,
H-515, H-583, H-584,
H-658, H-660
Planning   H-7, H-10, H-20,
H-68, H-143, H-201, H-421,
H-430, H-437, H-438,
H-505, H-509, H-511,
H-551, H-606, H-607,
H-621, H-764, H-865,
H-893, H-994
Policy, geography and
H-170, H-452, H-645, H-934
Political geography   H-23,
H-31, H-37, H-104, H-106,
H-140, H-202, H-214,
H-215, H-221, H-267,
H-331, H-332, H-365,
H-367, H-387, H-388,
H-389, H-398, H-403,

H-413, H-414, H-443,
H-446, H-457, H-457,
H-459, H-460, H-462,
H-463, H-464, H-466,
H-473, H-497, H-498,
H-500, H-567, H-597,
H-599, H-615, H-633,
H-648, H-649, H-654,
H-676, H-688, H-689,
H-690, H-696, H-704,
H-708, H-714, H-738,
H-827, H-833, H-855,
H-856, H-891, H-894,
H-909, H-926, H-946,
H-947, H-971, H-977,
H-989
Popular culture   H-57,
H-118, H-119
Population geography   H-7,
H-151, H-152, H-395,
H-407, H-417, H-418,
H-461, H-513, H-629,
H-726, H-835, H-878, H-970
Pragmatism   H-290
Psychogeography   H-343
Publications   H-313
Quality of life   H-78, H-993
Quanitative geography   H-81,
H-236, H-349, H-425,
H-524, H-555, H-601,
H-787, H-800, H-980
Radical geography   H-61,
H-75, H-173, H-655, H-822,
H-962
Recreational geography
H-40, H-67, H-116, H-160,
H-483, H-642, H-735,
H-808, H-896, H-963
Regional geography   H-115,
H-548
Regional science   H-185,
H-488
Religion geography of
H-113, H-219, H-521,
H-541, H-717
Remote sensing   H-17, H-80,
H-101, H-455
Resource geography   H-266,
H-358, H-809, H-931, H-972
Research   H-22, H-96, H-268
Retail geography   H-98,

Research H-22, H-96, H-268
Retail geography H-98,
  H-327, H-866, H-871, H-919
Rural geography H-147,
  H-148, H-149, H-157,
  H-158, H-159, H-391, H-892
Sea industries H-701
Settlement geography H-475
Social geography (see also
  Human geography) H-6,
  H-16, H-20, H-22, H-30,
  H-39, H-108, H-112, H-227,
  H-230, H-242, H-243,
  H-250, H-251, H-252,
  H-253, H-254, H-255,
  H-260, H-279, H-280,
  H-312, H-316, H-350,
  H-424, H-440, H-442,
  H-443, H-468, H-492,
  H-545, H-652, H-722,
  H-745, H-766, H-771,
  H-828, H-830, H-857,
  H-860, H-895, H-900,
  H-918, H-982, H-1001
Spatial analysis H-597,
  H-883
Sports geography H-55,
  H-105, H-905
Survey H-224
Teaching H-25
Technological change H-580
Transportation geography
  H-70, H-242, H-657, H-812,
  H-844, H-857, H-864,
  H-897, H-933, H-934, H-935
Tourism H-58, H-85, H-110,
  H-120, H-226, H-451,
  H-549, H-568, H-590,
  H-641, H-707, H-709,
  H-849, H-897, H-923,
  H-924, H-988
Urban geography H-3, H-4,
  H-43, H-62, H-79, H-111,
  H-127, H-139, H-211,
  H-235, H-270, H-299,
  H-302, H-328, H-339,
  H-340, H-351, H-380,
  H-381, H-385, H-412,
  H-450, H-465, H-471,
  H-501, H-539, H-558,
  H-571, H-627, H-672,
  H-697, H-711, H-765,
  H-811, H-846, H-847,
  H-882, H-890, H-941,
  H-942, H-943
Welfare H-66
Zoogeography H-2, H-24,
  H-64, H-96

Biographical Index

Abbe, C. B-349
Ackerman, E. A. B-560,
  B-787
Adams, C. C. B-601
Adams, J B-603
Ahmad, K. S. B-820
Allan, D. A. B-666
Al-Muqaddasi. B-647
Ancel, J. B-688
Anderson, J. R. B-801
Anuchin, D. N. B-253
Anuchin, V. A. B-300, B-640
Apianus, P. B-359
Applebaum, W. B-63
Arbos, P. B-226
Aristotle. B-319
Atwood, W. W. B-201
Aurousseau, M. B-278, B-590
Baer, K. B-792
Bagley, J. W. B-597
Baker, O. E. B-4, B-761
Bald, W. B-707
Baranskiy, N. N. B-652
Baransky, N. N. B-626
Barbari, J. de B-679
Barlon, R. B-715
Barnes, C. P. B-477
Barnett, R. L. B-486
Barrows, H. B-175
Barrows, H. H. B-192
Barrows, J. B-611

Bartholomew, J. G. B-11,
  B-12
Bates, H. W. B-13
Bause, E. B-100
Bengston, N. A. B-744
Behaim, M. B-498
Bennett, H. H. B-82, B-557
Berg, J. S. B-529, B-530
Berg, L. S. B-476
Bernard, A. B-710
Best, R. H. B-56
Bierce, A. B-113
Birdseye, C. H. B-633
Blanchard, W. O. B-549
Blanche, J. B-536
Blodget, L. B-241
Blumenstock, D. I. B-636
Boas, F. B-732
Boggs, S. W. B-6
Bose, N. K. B-215, B-634,
  B-646
Bourne, W. B-714
Bowen, E. G. B-51, B-722,
  B-723
Bowman, I. B-4, B-170,
  B-199, B-200, B-489,
  B-542, B-580, B-675, B-813
Boyd, L. A. B-808
Brandel, F. B-569
Bratescu, C. B-537
Brigham, A. P. B-34, B-35,

B-136, B-143, B-234,
B-493, B-677, B-786, B-794
Brigham, M. T.   B-98
Brigham, O. E.   B-77
Broek, J.   B-545
Brooks, A. H.   B-657, B-676
Brooks, C. F.   B-745
Brown, R. H.   B-196, B-235
Brown, R. N. R.   B-277,
B-459
Bryan, K.   B-788
Bryant, H. G.   B-795
Buchanan, R. O.   B-48
Buchanan, T. O.   B-803
Budel, J.   B-507
Busching, A. F.   B-161
Byrd, R. E.   B-106
Capot-Rey, R.   B-104
Carey, H. C.   B-509
Cassiver, E.   B-249
Cerceda, J. D.   B-622
Chardin, P. T   B-163
Charpentier, J. de   B-718
Chisholm, G. G.   B-36, B-471
Christaller, W.   B-99,
B-167, B-365, B-366
Clark, A. H.   B-340, B-503,
B-773
Colby, C. C.   B-164, B-337
Columbus, C.   B-540, B-716
Conrey, G. W.   B-670
Constable, J.   B-606
Cook, O. F.   B-284
Cooke,   B-775
Cooley, W. D.   B-122
Cope, E. D. C.   B-127
Copernicus   B-319
Copernicus, N.   B-67
Corley, N. T.   B-197
Cornish, V.   B-305, B-766
Cortambert, E.   B-128
Cotton, C. A.   B-285
Coulter, J. W.   B-807
Cowler, G. D.   B-3
Cowles, H. C.   B-281, B-616
Craft, F. A.   B-139
Cressey, G. B.   B-350
Curzon, G. N.   B-307
Cvijic, J.   B-746
d'Abbadie, A.   B-556
Darton, N. H.   B-751

Darwin, C.   B-61, B-214,
B-702, B-705
Darwin, L.   B-515
David, M.   B-320
Davidson, G.   B-243
Davis, W. M.   B-88, B-90,
B-91, B-118, B-126, B-144,
B-195, B-494, B-608, B-698
Davity, P.   B-294
De Brahm, J. G.   B-526,
B-527
De Brahm, W. G.   B-232
Dee, J.   B-713
del Villar, E. H.   B-483
De Voto, B.   B-669
De Witt, S.   B-610
Dickinson, R. E.   B-49,
B-562
Die, J.   B-496
Dimitresco-Aldern, A.   B-198
Dion, R.   B-322
Dodge, R. E.   B-756
Dokuchaer, V. V.   B-254
Drake, F.   B-361
Drapeyron, L.   B-129
Dryer, C. R.   B-188
Drygalski, E. von   B-727
Dubey, R. N.   B-730
Eckert, M.   B-645
Edwards, K. C.   B-47
Eiselen, E.   B-227
Emerson, F. V.   B-125
Eratosthenes,   B-64
Fairbanks, H. W.   B-558
Fairchild, W. B.   B-329
Fairgrieve, J.   B-363, B-644
Farrington, A.   B-700
Fawcett, C. B.   B-275
Fedchenko, A. P.   B-816
Fenneman, N. M.   B-146,
B-607, B-627, B-771
Fernald, M. L.   B-600
Finch, V. C.   B-190, B-342
Finley, J. H.   B-119
Fisher, C. A.   B-50
Fleure, H. J.   B-115, B-116
Fluer, H. J.   B-43
Forbes, J. D.   B-210
Formozos, A. N.   B-598
Forrest, J.   B-589
Foster, A.   B-335

Freeman, O. W.   B-17
Frere, B.   B-248
Freshfield, D.   B-465
Gannett, H.   B-213
Garrett, H.   B-108
Geaner, S. H.   B-57
Geddes, A.   B-596, B-599,
   B-780
Geddes, P.   B-701
Geikie, A.   B-478
Geikie, J.   B-29, B-33,
   B-479
Gerlach, A. C.   B-151
Gerlach, A. G.   B-16
Glareanus, H.   B-356
Gidden, A.   B-314
Gilbert, E. W.   B-273, B-614
Gilman, D. C.   B-810
Goode, J. P.   B-325, B-488
Gordon, R.   B-247
Gordon, R. J.   B-269
Gottmann, J.   B-364
Goyder, G. W.   B-586, B-798
Grano, J. G.   B-311
Granos, J. G.   B-548
Grant, J. A.   B-171
Green, F. H. W.   B-52
Gregory, H. E.   B-755
Gregory, J. W.   B-37
Grigoryev, A. A.   B-819
Gross, H. H.   B-282
Grosvenor, G. H.   B-2
Gullinee, F. P.   B-220
Gurevvich, B. L.   B-642
Guthrie, W.   B-246
Guyot, A.   B-60, B-454
Guyot, A. H.   B-265
Hagerstrand, T.   B-591
Hakluyt, R.   B-712
Hall, C. W.   B-492
Halley, E.   B-174, B-726
Hamilton, W. R.   B-238
Harris, C.   B-615
Hart, J. F.   B-228
Harvey, D.   B-69
Hassert, E. E. K.   B-550
Haushofer, K.   B-353
Hayes, I. L.   B-207
Heilprin.   B-145, B-312,
   B-442, B-538
Heilprin, A.   B-27, B-455

Heinrich, F. J.   B-583
Henderson, H. C. K.   B-52
Herbertson, A. J.   B-30,
   B-41, B-298
Hettner, A.   B-341, B-573
Hilgard, E. W.   B-334
Hillard, G. S.   B-473
Himly, L.   B-93
Hinder, J. G.   B-103
Hinks, A. R.   B-699
Hitchcock, C. B.   B-517
Ho, R.   B-70, B-182
Hobbs, W. H.   B-328
Hogarth, D. G.   B-267
Hohnel, L.   B-352
Holmes, J. M.   B-587
Holway, R. S.   B-635
Hoover, J. W.   B-194
Hora, S. L.   B-39
House, J. W.   B-24
Hughes, W.   B-747
Hult, R.   B-609
Humboldt, A.   B-341
Huntington, E.   B-580,
   B-678, B-680, B-686, B-750
Hutchings, G. E.   B-784
Hutton, J.   B-216, B-578
Huxley, A.   B-703
Innis, H. de   B-94
Innis, H.   B-244, B-553
Isachsen, F. E.   B-531
Jackson, J.   B-306
James, P. E.   B-490, B-661
Jefferson, M.   B-120, B-753
Jefferson, T.   B-709
Jennings, J. N.   B-687
Jobberns, G.   B-208, B-783
Joerg, W. L. G.   B-280
Johnson, D.   B-464, B-809
Johnston, H. H.   B-172
Johnston, R. J.   B-302
Jones, L. R.   B-805
Jones, W. D.   B-191
Judson, J. T.   B-130
Kant, E.   B-157, B-160,
   B-341, B-463
Keckermann, B.   B-155
Keith, A.   B-748
Keith, J. W.   B-767
Keltie, S.   B-804
Kelvin, L.   B-684

Kendall, O.D.   B-563
Ketchall, E.   B-469
Keuning, H. J.   B-711
Kimbley, G. H. T.   B-456
Kincer, J. B.   B-758
Kirchhoff, A.   B-510
Klimm, L. E.   B-453, B-625
Ko-Chen, C.   B-173
Kohl, J. G.   B-566
Kohn, C. F.   B-229
Krasnov, A. N.   B-7
Kropotkin, P.   B-323
Kropotkin, P. A.   B-10,
   B-579
Krummel, J. G. O.   B-740
Kubarg, J. S.   B-665
L'Almeida, P. C.   B-552
Larcom, T. A.   B-15
Lathrop, H. O.   B-318
Lattimore, O.   B-333, B-535
Lautensach, H.   B-728
Law, B. C.   B-528
Learnmouth, A.   B-111
Lefevre, M. A.   B-225
Leighly, J.   B-516
Leightly, J. B.   B-661,
   B-735
Leland, J.   B-206
Lelewel, J.   B-514, B-628
Lenin, V.   B-641
Levasseur, E.   B-532
Lewis.   B-288
Light, R. V.   B-604
Linton, D. L.   B-301
Linton, H. J.   B-43
Livingstone.   B-313
Livingstone, B.   B-84
Lobeck, A. K.   B-672
Loewe, F.   B-790
Lomonosov, M. V.   B-8
MacCarthy, O.   B-92
Mackinder, H.   B-110
Mackinder, H. J.   B-295,
   B-296, B-297, B-299,
   B-326, B-673, B-741
Maconochie, A.   B-774
Malthus.   B-310
Manley, G.   B-656
Market, C. F.   B-655
Markham, C.   B-31
Markham, C. R.   B-793

Marsh, G. P.   B-466, B-467,
   B-543
Martin, L.   B-797
Massip, S.   B-292
Matthes, F. E.   B-749
May, J. M.   B-259, B-724
Mayhew, H.   B-782
McCleelan, M. L.   B-602
McGee, W. J.   B-212, B-308
Mehedinti, S.   B-512, B-574
Meikle-John, J. M. D.   B-521
Melanchthon, P.   B-156
Melik, A.   B-721
Mercator.   B-654
Mercator, G.   B-327, B-717
Mihailescu, V.   B-736, B-737
Mill, H. R.   B-140, B-272,
   B-812
Milne, G.   B-519
Misra, R. N.   B-522
Mitchell, T. L.   B-584
Moir, D. G.   B-58
Moodie, A. E. F.   B-165
Morrill, K. L.   B-230
Morse, J.   B-135, B-623
Moses.   B-347
Munster, S.   B-158
Mushketov, I. V.   B-815
Myers, S. K.   B-539
Nelson, H.   B-96
Neustruev, S. S.   B-817
Nicholson, N. T.   B-571
Oberhummer, E.   B-823
Obruchev, V. A.   B-279
O'Deel, A. C.   B-772
Ogawa, T.   B-734
Orchard, J. E.   B-696
Orghidan, N.   B-533
Ormsby, H.   B-185
Park, M.   B-518
Park, R.   B-250
Parkins, A. E.   B-785
Partsch, J. F. M.   B-650
Pavlov, A. P.   B-617
Peary, R. E.   B-355
Peattie, R.   B-671
Peel, J. H. B   B-593
Peel, R. F.   B-59
Penck, A.   B-508
Penck, W.   B-764
Pinkerton, J.   B-664, B-789

Pitties, H. F. B-484
Platt, R. R. B-264
Platt, R. S. B-336, B-343, B-720
Poole, S. P. B-624
Popper, K. R. B-101, B-102
Post, L. C. B-193
Price, A. G. B-585
Primmer, G. H. B-149
Proudfoot, M. J. B-87
Prunty, M. C. B-5
Ptolemy. B-472, B-621
Raisz, E. J. B-613, B-814
Ratzel, F. B-316, B-513, B-637, B-691
Ravenstein, E. G. B-315
Reclus, E. B-240, B-242, B-543, B-704
Reclus, M. E. B-22, B-289, B-293
Reisch, G. B-358
Reis, P. B-474
Remezov, S. Y. B-658
Rennell, J. B-237
Renner, G. B-223, B-561
Rheticus, G. J. B-159
Rich, J. L. B-80
Richter, E. B-303
Richthofen, F. von B-1, B-25
Rilfer, C. B-572
Ritter, C. B-458, B-663
Robinson, J. L. B-83
Robinson, K. W. B-738
Rockhill, W. W. B-186
Romer, E. B-66
Rosier, W. B-266
Ross, C. R. B-643
Rotch, A. L. B-777
Roxby, P. M. B-274
Roy, W. B-332
Russell, R. J. B-500, B-768
Rychkov, P. I. B-818
Salichtchev, K. A. B-546
Salisbury, R. D. B-559, B-570, B-757
Sarwick, L. S. B-452
Sauer, C. B-142, B-495, B-679
Sauer, C. O. B-252, B-354, B-444, B-445, B-447, B-448, B-450, B-534, B-554, B-555, B-577, B-689, B-695, B-735, B-800
Saushkin, Y. G. B-224
Schafer, F. K. B-147
Schmitthenner, H. B-620
Schoun, J. F. B-543
Schrader, F. B-127
Schumacher, E. F. B-384
Schwerin, H. H. von B-95
Scoresby, W. B-765
Scott, R. F. B-141
Semple, E. C. B-62, B-97, B-152, B-153, B-154, B-181, B-189, B-290, B-346, B-811
Shabad, T. B-339, B-806
Shaler, N. S. B-26, B-233, B-461, B-462
Shantz, H. L. B-594
Shepard, F. P. B-321
Shiga, S. B-520
Sibbald, R. B-247
Siegfried, A. B-632
Sievers, W. B-491
Singh, R. L. B-660
Skelton, R. A. B-769
Smailes, A. E. B-55
Smeds, H. B-268
Smee, D. K. B-46
Smith, A. B-781
Smith, G. A. B-511
Smith, G. H. B-137
Smith, J. R. B-4, B-697
Smith, P. S. B-150
Smith, T., Jr. B-187
Smolenski, J. B-451
Snodgress, C. P. B-470
Solch, J. B-497
Somerville, M. B-72, B-74, B-547, B-630
Sonnenfeld, J. B-544
Sowerbutts, E. B-24
Stamp, D. B-184, B-803
Stamp, L. D. B-653
Steers, J. A. B-706
Stefansson, V. B-221, B-708
Stevens, I. B-506
Steward, J. H. B-690
Stoffler, J. B-357

Strabo. B-725
Strelbitsky, I. A. B-176
Strong, H. B-331
Strzelecki, P. E. B-68
Tamayo, J. L. B-324
Tarr, R. S. B-124, B-763
Tatham, G. B-778
Tatham, W. B-351
Tatishcher, V. N. B-9
Taylor, G. B-40, B-245,
  B-330, B-480, B-580,
  B-595, B-618, B-631,
  B-685, B-731
Taylor, T. G. B-65, B-581
Thomas, L. F. B-202
Thompson, D. B-739
Thorpe, H. B-719
Thorthwaite, C. W. B-443
Thralls, Z. A. B-568
Tillo, A. A. B-262
Tooley, R. V. B-166
Topelius, Z. B-505
Toulmin, G. H. B-578
Toynbee, A. B-680
Troll, C. B-162, B-729
Turner, F. J. B-362, B-107
Turner, J. M. W. B-606
Tzu, Mo B-183
Ullman, E. B-255, B-524,
  B-525
Uttley, M. E. B-668
Vallaux, C. B-168
Valsan, G. B-575, B-576
Van Cleef, E. B-138
Van Rogen, W. B-629
Van Valkenburg, S. B-779
Varenius, B. B-73, B-75
Verner, C. B-770
Vidal de la Blanche, J. M.
  B-742
Vidal de la Blanche, P.
  B-18, B-32, B-523
Virjevie, P. B-239
Visher, S. S. B-338, B-619
Volz, W. B-287
Von Humboldt, A. B-20,
  B-88, B-90, B-117, B-148,
  B-501, B-662
Von Sydon, E. B-762
Von Thuen B-317
Voyeikov, A. I. B-261

Waibel, L. H. B-131, B-567
Wallace, A. R. B-667
Ward, R. D. B-132, B-133,
  B-134, B-219, B-345
Watterson, A. W. B-286
Watts, F. B. B-222
Wegner, A. B-693
Weidman, S. B-112
Wellington, J. H. B-78
Weulersse, J. B-309
Wheatley, P. B-360
Whitbeck, R. H. B-796
Whitehead, A. N. B-565
Whittemore, K. T. B-86
Whittlesey, D. B-489
Williams, S. W. B-21
Willis, B. B-752
Wise, M. B-282
Wissler, C. B-169, B-692
Wittfgogel, K. B-564
Wooldridge, S. W. B-79,
  B-694, B-803
Wright, J. K. B-456
Wrigley, G. M. B-258, B-456
Xiake, X. B-821
Yamasaki, N. B-733
Yonge, E. L. B-263
Yung, W. B-475
Zelinsky, W. B-71

About the Compilers

CATHERINE L. BROWN, a resident of Portland, Maine, has been a planner for the Georgia Department of Defense, a program coordinator for the U.S.-Georgia China Council, and a library assistant. Her book, *The Urban South: A Bibliography,* was published by Greenwood Press in 1989.

JAMES O. WHEELER is the Merle Prunty, Jr., Professor of Geography at the University of Georgia, Athens. He is the author of *Economic Geography, The Urban Circulation Noose, American Metropolitan Systems, A Dictionary of Quotations in Geography,* and over 70 journal articles. He is coeditor of the bimonthly journal, *Urban Geography.*